International Dispute Resolution

Complex Dispute Resolution

Titles in the Series:

Foundations of Dispute Resolution
Volume I
Carrie Menkel-Meadow

Multi-Party Dispute Resolution, Democracy and Decision-Making
Volume II
Carrie Menkel-Meadow

International Dispute Resolution
Volume III
Carrie Menkel-Meadow

International Dispute Resolution
Volume III

Edited by

Carrie Menkel-Meadow

Georgetown University and University of California, USA.

Routledge
Taylor & Francis Group
LONDON AND NEW YORK

First published 2012 by Ashgate Publishing

2 Park Square, Milton Park, Abingdon, Oxfordshire OX14 4RN
711 Third Avenue, New York, NY 10017

Routledge is an imprint of the Taylor & Francis Group, an informa business

First issued in paperback 2018

British Library Cataloguing in Publication Data
International dispute resolution.
Volume III. – (Complex dispute resolution)
1. Pacific settlement of international disputes. 2. Dispute resolution (Law)
I. Series II. Menkel-Meadow, Carrie.
341.5'2-dc22

Library of Congress Control Number: 2011935177

ISBN 978-0-7546-2804-0 (hbk)
ISBN 978-1-138-37851-3 (pbk)

Contents

PART II NEW PROCESSES: INSTITUTIONS, INFORMAL AND HYBRID DISPUTE PROCESSES

PART III ISSUES IN NEW FORMS OF INTERNATIONAL AND TRANSNATIONAL DISPUTE RESOLUTION

PART IV CODA

Acknowledgements

The editor and publishers wish to thank the following for permission to use copyright material.

Robert B. Ahdieh (2004), 'Between Dialogue and Decree: International Review of National Courts', *New York University Law Review*, **79**, pp. 2029–36; 2045–62; 2161–63. Copyright © 2004 Robert B. Ahdieh.

Cambridge University Press for the essay: Jane Stromseth, David Wippman and Rosa Brooks (2006), 'Accountability for Atrocities: Moving Forward by Looking Backward?', in *Can Might Make Rights? Building the Rule of Law after Military Intervention*, Cambridge: Cambridge University Press, pp. 249–99. Copyright © 2006 Jane Stromseth, David Wippman and Rosa Brooks.

Copyright Clearance Center for the essays: Carrie Menkel-Meadow (2007), 'Restorative Justice: What is It and Does It Work?', *Annual Review of Law and Social Science*, **3**, pp. 161–87. Copyright © 2007 Annual Reviews, Inc.; John Hagan (2003), 'From Nuremberg', in *Justice in the Balkans: Prosecuting War Crimes in the Hague Tribunal*, Chicago, IL: University of Chicago Press, pp. 18–32. Copyright © 2003 University of Chicago Press – books; Carrie Menkel-Meadow (2009), 'Are There Systemic Ethics Issues in Dispute System Design? And What We Should [Not] Do About It: Lessons from International and Domestic Fronts', *Harvard Negotiation Law Review*, **14**, pp. 195–231. Copyright © 2009 Harvard University.

Hart Publishing for the essay: David Dyzenhaus (2003), 'Truth, Memory and the Rule of Law', in *Judging the Judges: Judging Ourselves: Truth, Reconciliation and Apartheid Legal Orders*, Oxford: Hart Publishing, pp. 1–6; 25–35, 178–83. Copyright © 1998, 2003 David Dyzanhaus.

John Wiley & Sons for the essays: Daniel Curran, James K. Sebenius and Michael Watkins (2004), 'Two Paths to Peace: Contrasting George Mitchell in Northern Ireland with Richard Holbrooke in Bosnia–Herzegovina', *Negotiation Journal*, **20**, pp. 513–37. Copyright © 2004 Blackwell Publishing; Laura Nader and Elisabetta Grande (2002), 'Current Illusions and Delusions about Conflict Management – In Africa and Elsewhere', *Law & Social Inquiry*, **27**, pp. 573–94. Copyright © 2002 American Bar Foundation.

John Wiley & Sons, Inc. for the essay: Andrea Kupfer Schneider (2005), 'Public and Private International Dispute Resolution', in M.L. Moffitt and R.C. Bordone (eds), *The Handbook of Dispute Resolution*, San Francisco: Jossey-Bass, pp. 438–54.

Journal of Dispute Resolution, University of Missouri for the essays: Carrie Menkel-Meadow (2003), 'Correspondences and Contradictions in International and Domestic Conflict Resolution: Lessons from General Theory and Varied Contexts', *Journal of Dispute*

Resolution, **2003**, pp. 319–52; Maya Goldstein Bolocan (2004), 'Rwandan Gacaca: An Experiment in Transitional Justice', *Journal of Dispute Resolution*, **2**, pp. 355–400.

Palgrave Macmillan for the essays: Jeswald W. Salacuse (2003), 'Special Barrier No. 2: Culture', in *The Global Negotiator: Making, Managing, and Mending Deals Around the World in the Twenty-First Century*, New York: Palgrave Macmillan, pp. 89–115; William Zartman (2003), 'The Timing of Peace Initiatives: Hurting Stalemates and Ripe Moments', in J. Darby and R. MacGinty (eds), *Contemporary Peacemaking: Conflict, Violence and Peace Processes*, New York: Palgrave Macmillan, pp. 19–29; John Paul Lederach (2003), 'Cultivating Peace: A Practitioner's View of Deadly Conflict and Negotiation', in J. Darby and R. MacGinty (eds), *Contemporary Peacemaking: Conflict, Violence and Peace Processes*, New York: Palgrave Macmillan, pp. 30–37.

Andrea Kupfer Schneider (1999), 'Getting Along: The Evolution of Dispute Resolution Regimes in International Trade Organizations', *Michigan Journal of International Law*, **20**, pp. 697–773. Copyright © 1999 Andrea Kupfer Schneider.

University of California Press for the essay: Robert D. Putnam (1993), 'Diplomacy and Domestic Politics: The Logic of Two-Level Games', in P.B. Evans, H.K. Jacobson and R.D. Putnam, *Double-Edged Diplomacy: International Bargaining and Domestic Politics*, Berkeley, CA: University of California Press, pp. 431–68. Copyright © 1993 The Regents of the University of California.

University of Chicago Press for the essay: Yves Dezalay and Bryant Garth (1996), 'Merchants of Law as Moral Entrepreneurs: Constructing International Justice out of the Competition for Transnational Business Disputes', in *Dealing in Virtue: International Commercial Arbitration and the Construction of a Transnational Legal Order*, Chicago, IL: University of Chicago Press, pp. 33–62.

Every effort has been made to trace all the copyright holders, but if any have been inadvertently overlooked the publishers will be pleased to make the necessary arrangement at the first opportunity.

Series Preface

The Complex Dispute Resolution series collects essays on the development of foundational dispute resolution theory and practice and its application to increasingly more complex settings of conflicts in the world, including multi-party and multi-issue decision-making, negotiations in political policy formation and governance, and international conflict resolution.

Each volume contains an introduction by the editor, which explores the key issues in the field. All three volumes feature essays which span an interdisciplinary range of fields – law, political science, game theory, decision science, economics, social and cognitive psychology, sociology and anthropology – and consider issues in the uses of informal and private as well as more formal and public processes. The essays also question whether the development of universal theoretical insights about conflict resolution is possible with variable numbers of parties and issues and in multicultural settings.

Taken together, the three volumes in this series present classic research essays on all aspects of complex dispute resolution and constitute an invaluable reference resource for libraries and academics in political decision-making, human rights, international relations and business and commercial law.

CARRIE MENKEL-MEADOW
Georgetown University and University of California, USA

Introduction

> 'There never was a good war or a bad peace.'
> *Benjamin Franklin*

Origins of Dispute Resolution

Many of the theories and practices of conflict resolution reviewed in the first two volumes in this series (*Foundations of Dispute Resolution* and *Multi-Party Dispute Resolution, Democracy and Decision-Making*) are in fact derived from the oldest practices of dispute resolution that originated in lands far away from Anglo-American-European legal and institutional developments. Whether dispute resolution began with King Solomon's choice about whether to 'split the baby' (was that arbitration or mediation?) or had its ancient origins in the practice of mediation in African moots or in Confucian China, human beings began resolving disputes long before any formal legal systems were developed (Roberts and Palmer, 2005). In that sense, dispute resolution is both older and more varied in form than formal legal systems and it is also, in its origins, a multicultural and multinational phenomenon.

Since disputes between people were taking place long before the existence of national boundaries, and since they now occur across so many national (and cultural, ethnic, religious) and other boundaries, conflict resolution processes are, and have always been, multicultural and transboundary: they draw upon a variety of both cultural and some 'uniform' practices, such as the use of third parties to either facilitate or decide in dispute matters (Shapiro, 1981), that existed long before there was any international 'rule of law'.

It is somewhat ironic that great efforts are now being made to transmit and 'export' modern developments in dispute resolution – especially game theory and strategic decision-making which really have their basis in attempts to understand and study 'foreign' or 'international' interactions during the Cold War – from hegemonic (primarily American) regimes to other places (see, for example, European Directive on Mediation, 2008; Woolf, 1996), including some of the places where 'alternative' dispute resolution first began – China (Lubman, 1967; Cohen, 1966; Palmer, 1989) and Africa (Nader and Grande, Chapter 16, this volume; Gulliver, 1979).

This volume, then, explores comparative, multicultural and transnational forms of dispute resolution – models, forms, and practices of conflict resolution that are not limited to national legal systems and formal courts. From their original location in small villages or homogeneous communities, dispute resolution processes have now moved into their own more formal institutions at local, national and international levels. At the same time, modern transnational life has also spawned new developments in the creation of many hybrid, multinational, international and informal, as well as formal, forms of dispute resolution, including both generalist and more specialized tribunals for various kinds of dispute resolution, such as the

Tribunal for the International Law of the Sea, ITLOS (Merrills, 2005) and the ad hoc criminal courts for crimes against humanity (Hagan, Chapter 14, this volume).

This volume also explores the creation of new forms of conflict resolution where 'resolution' may be conceived of in many different ways – apologies, forgiveness, restitution and reconciliation – and not only in more traditional forms of adjudication and decision, with monetary awards or injunctions or other judicial orders. Modern transnational dispute resolution is, in many ways, returning to some of its earliest roots (pun absolutely intended as, in some cultures, the eating or drinking of root-based substances forms the basis of reconciliation practices).

Different modes of dispute resolution in transnational and comparative settings have their origins in more varied, if simpler and older, forms than the movement towards 'A(lternative/ Appropriate)'DR in many legal systems. Especially in Anglo-American legal systems, the use of mediation, negotiated settlement and arbitration has recently increased as a reaction to overburdened and brittle (in terms of binary outcomes) court and litigation settings. In other systems and transnational settings, where courts and tribunals are largely a product of twentieth-century international law development, negotiation, mediation and some forms of arbitration have been part of both formal diplomacy and informal international relations for hundreds of years. In civil law systems, including both European and Asian court and legal systems, requirements to mediate or seek some alternative to commanded court-enforced judgment have been common for many years. Thus, in a sense, there has always been more choice about what forms of dispute resolution to use in transnational settings – for example, informal negotiation or mediation, diplomacy, political processes – and only more recently has some form of court or tribunal adjudication been available for some kinds of international or transnational disputes.

In the international arena some forms of dispute resolution are as old as commerce itself – from the earliest years of 'pre-national' trade, markets and traders needed dispute resolution for issues concerning price, quantity, quality and delivery of promised goods – thus was born private international dispute resolution, now more formalized in the many institutions which offer private international arbitration (for example, the International Chamber of Commerce (Paris), the London Court of International Arbitration (LCIA) and the China International Economic and Trade Arbitration Commission (CIETAC)) for disputes among private parties about commercial and trade issues.

Public international dispute resolution (addressing the more formal disputes between and among nation-states) is relatively new to the conflict resolution stage. A variety of developments, beginning with the first international recognition of the problem of piracy, to post-Peace of Westphalia (1648) state recognition, to the sad developments of modern wars in the nineteenth and twentieth centuries began to foster the creation of formal bodies for the adjudication, arbitration and negotiation of national boundary disputes, post-war treaties, maritime and admiralty issues, and, eventually, many modern treaties, on a wide variety of global issues of cooperation (nuclear disarmament, environment, health, human trafficking, human rights, commerce and trade, cultural matters and, now, anti-terrorism efforts).

Thus, the relationship of public and private dispute resolution to courts, governments, states and the rule of law, while complicated enough in more domestic settings, is even more complex in the international setting. On the one hand, there is less law and formal tribunal adjudication (there is no court of last resort with compulsory jurisdiction in international disputes); on the other hand, there is also greater risk of the use of force, violence and lawlessness to 'resolve' disputes in the international arena, as our sad human history has made clear. At the same time, incentives to resolve disputes without courts and formal tribunals and to use more and other methods of dispute resolution may be stronger – consider the need to resolve contract and other disputes in order to continue economic relations and the need to resolve diplomatic issues in order to continue to exist. As is now popularly, if still contestably, said, the globalization of trade, communication and all forms of human interaction (both positive in cultural exchanges and travel and negative in terrorism and war) has increased the need for new forms of 'globalized' (and accessible) dispute resolution across national boundaries and legal regimes, including both 'hard' and 'soft' law (Twining, 2009; Slaughter, 2004; Friedman, 2005).

International conflict resolution increasingly also offers the possibilities of multiple venues, processes and choices of law as parties may increasingly 'forum–shop' between national, regional and international courts, as well as between private or hybrid arbitral tribunals, such as the International Centre for Settlement of Investment Disputes (ICSID) depending on the location and subject-matter of the dispute (see Project on International Courts and Tribunals, 1997). Thus, in the international arena, *process pluralism* (Menkel-Meadow, 2011) is also *legal pluralism* (Berman, 2007) so that it is now possible for a single dispute (such as, for example, *Loewen Group* v. *United States*, 2003) to be heard in several different venues and the question of how different levels of dispute resolution bodies (sometimes across legal systems) respond, defer to or follow each other has become one of the major issues in modern legal globalization studies (see Ahdieh, Chapter 17, this volume).

With the development of new treaty obligations and new regional and international tribunals, particularly in new human rights undertakings and responsibilities – such as the European Court of Human Rights (Strasbourg) and the Inter-American Court of Human Rights (Costa Rica) – individuals and international organizations, in addition to state actors, may now have standing to make claims or be sued in a variety of dispute resolution venues. With the advent of new tribunals, old questions about the relationship of less formal processes (such as whether human rights claims should be negotiable and able to be settled outside of tribunals) to more formal, law-based rulings in courts have re-emerged along with issues about transparency and accountability for, or 'privatization' of, 'global justice' issues. As in any form of conflict resolution, questions of how power-and resource-based endowments differentially affect outcomes remain problematic – and are particularly well studied in some instances, such as private–state investor disputes (Franck, 2007) and trade disputes in the WTO (Ginsburg and Shaffer, 2010).

From Informalism to Formalism and Back Again

While anthropologists and historians may debate about what came first – command (adjudication and arbitration – remember King Solomon!) or consent (negotiation and mediation) – in human dispute processing, it is likely that informal forms of dispute resolution pre-date the development of more formal forms of third-party decision-making, with rules of procedure and evidence. In human communities the need to restore peace, coordinate action (hunting, farming, cooking, childrearing, protection and building) for human survival has required that somehow parties negotiate and resolve their differences, seeking some third-party assistance when they need to. In what are probably over-nostalgic appeals to such 'golden days' of community dispute resolution, we think of the advantages of informalism – speed of resolution, direct communication, easy enforcement and, yes, even transparency, publicity and precedent creation.

As communal life became more complex and humans ventured further than their own communities, disputes occurred between those with different values and cultural practices, and conflicts over resources and functions – not to mention the beginning of identity, control, colonization, domination, territorial and other forms of both interpersonal and intersystemic disputes (among the many causes of war) – resulted in the development of more complex forms of dispute resolution. We now regard it as human progress that we have moved from religious orders, trial by ordeal or battle, duels (Yarn, 2000) and Star Chambers to courts with rules of procedure, law and evidence (Langbein, 2003), which promise neutrality, fairness, equity and precedents (at least in the common-law world), even if they are also accompanied by complexity and formalism, delay, distance and 'limited remedial imaginations' (Menkel-Meadow, 2005).

While many legal and political science scholars still revere the formality of courts, rule of law and rules of procedure, dispute resolution scholars and practitioners (of whom I am one) see the modern developments of various forms of 'A'DR as a further elaboration in the evolutionary process of human decision-making. Courts and adjudication are one form of dispute resolution (formal, usually based on winner takes all, public, appealable in most systems, law-interpreting and law-making in common-law systems), but other forms of less formal dispute resolution have other attributes and potential advantages in some settings. One form of dispute resolution will not fit all, especially where we need contingency and flexibility, some ongoing accountability and, in some cases, privacy and often different kinds of outcomes than courts are authorized to award.

In legal history courts and formal and less formal tribunals developed simultaneously with many parallel forms of justice in secular and religious communities; they started at local levels and then proceeded to more centralized state institutions and to increasingly specialized units of dispute resolution – consider separate and specialized merchant courts and arbitration, religious mediation and arbitration, ethnic communities, workplaces and family forms of dispute resolution, all of which created their own dispute resolution, if not 'justice,' systems, separate from formal courts, in Asia, Europe and the United States (see for example, Roberts and Palmer, 2005; Bernstein, 1992; Auerbach, 1983; Greenhouse, 1986; Stone, 2001; Merry and Milner, 1993; Roberts, 1997; Saposnek, 1985). How formal institutions and courts influence bargaining endowments and negotiated outcomes and out-of-court behaviour has become as important a question in international dispute resolution as in general theory. This is evidenced by efforts to assess whether more human rights treaties and courts for crimes against humanity reduce certain forms of violence, (Kim and Sikkink, 2010), serve an educative function for the general population (Gibson, 2006) or create incentives to settle in international economic tribunals, just as in domestic (Busch and Reinhardt, 2000).

All of the basic processes of dispute resolution have been and are being used in international individual, private and public state settings. Private parties negotiate transnational business contracts (and then usually contract for private international arbitration to resolve any disputes). Diplomats, as public figures (and their delegates in private), conduct negotiations for political purposes (Fisher, Kopelman and Schneider, 1994), often having to rely on informal, but significant, political and economic endowments to achieve their goals. In hybrid variations of public and private processes, states negotiate treaties, often utilizing 'two-track' negotiations (Putnam, Chapter 3, this volume) with public and private faces; consider the Oslo peace accords for the Middle East which were essentially totally private negotiations with 'second-tier' negotiators. Treaty and other public negotiations track the categories of domestic conflict resolution with both dispute resolution (ending or pacifying wars and violent conflicts) and deal-making purposes (environmental, trade, economic and cultural treaty-making). The complexity of general negotiation theory is further complicated by issues about cultural differences in negotiation styles (see Salacuse, Chapter 4, this volume; Acuff, 2008). In public international negotiation, the question of whether negotiations should occur at all with truly evil regimes or individuals is even more important than the same question asked in non-public domestic settings (Margalit, 2010; Mnookin, 2010; Menkel-Meadow, 2010).

Theory development in international negotiation has been particularly rich, providing some of the canonical concepts now being tested in negotiation theory generally, including 'ripeness' and 'hurting stalemates' (Zartman, Chapter 6, this volume), multiple tracks of negotiation operating simultaneously, constituent and agent–principal issues, information-sharing strategies, and general trust and enforcement issues. There is also a growing richness in the dialogues between generalist or domestic theorists and international theorists as they test whether concepts developed in one sphere can inform another (Menkel-Meadow, Chapter 2, this volume; Watkins and Rosegrant, 2001; Graham and Requejo, 2008; Kremenyuk, 2002).

Adding a third party to both private and public international conflicts also replicates some of the foundational issues explored in Volume I: should the third party merely 'facilitate' communication between the parties, or should the 'muscle mediator' with its own power (consider the force and threats of US grants or refusals of aid when Henry Kissinger 'mediated' in the Middle East, Jimmy Carter 'mediated' in North Korea, or George Mitchell 'mediated' in Northern Ireland (Curran, Sebenius and Watkins, 2004, this volume)) use his clout to evaluate or even 'force' a settlement (consider Richard Holbrooke and the Dayton Accords for the Bosnia conflict (see Curran, Sebenius and Watkins, Chapter 5, this volume)? Should the mediator be 'neutral' or interested like a 'wise elder' in the community? As in domestic mediation, modern forms of private international mediation draw on expertise (intellectual property, technology and technical, as well as economic, expertise in international investment and construction disputes) and often use 'interested' or 'embedded' (in the relevant technical community) third-party neutrals. As explored in Volume II, questions of who should sit at the table of an international mediation – who are all the relevant stakeholders? – and whether the mediation should be conducted privately (and with caucuses) or publicly (through diplomatic efforts) are issues of great moment in international mediation.

Third-party neutrals who decide between states (public international arbitration) has long been part of the international dispute resolution repertoire, including important boundary decisions arbitrated by kings, presidents and other leaders from faraway continents. More recently, UN leaders (Kofi Annan and others) have used their public international office to both mediate and arbitrate significant international (and civil war) conflicts. Should decision-makers, such as arbitrators, be 'notables' with portfolios that include experience, reputation and 'clout'? Do parties need to know that their decision-makers have the authority to somehow enforce their judgments (say, by imposing sanctions of international organizations and through diplomatic tools) and 'awards' when there is no obvious or likely world court to enforce such decisions, in contrast to the legal effects of the UN New York Convention on the Recognition and Enforcement of Foreign Arbitral Awards (ratified by over 140 countries) which makes enforcement of private international arbitration awards relatively easy?

Formal adjudicative tribunals are relatively weak in the international sphere, with the so-called 'world court' (the International Court of Justice in The Hague) actually having only consensual, not compulsory, jurisdiction over disputes between states. In the formal arena the relationship of regional courts (the European Court of Justice, the European Court of Human Rights) to national courts (doctrines like 'margins of appreciation' (Hutchinson, 1999) and 'proportionality' allow for some national discretion in law-making) remains dialogic, complex and sometimes unclear. Comparative legal scholars now mine layers of legal regulations to debate whether the harmonization of laws and doctrine is desirable or even possible. Formality can have its costs when national sovereignty reasserts itself in some contested areas, now seen in migration, security, economic policy, trade restraints and human rights contexts in the European Union.

New international treaties and organizations have increasingly provided for 'tiers', layers and choices among and between both formal and informal processes of dispute resolution. Thus, the Law of the Sea Treaty permits choices of mediation, negotiation, arbitration and a specialized tribunal to resolve maritime and other disputes regarding water rights. The World Trade Organization has institutionalized a sort of hybridized arbitration system with experts that permits arguments, appeals and now *amicus curiae* briefs that are really closer to a litigation and adjudication system, while always preserving the option of negotiated settlements. The International Centre for Settlement of Investment Disputes, another hybrid arbitral system, now allows private investors to sue public states and to appeal in certain limited settings, creating a new international cadre of specialized professionals in dispute resolution – economists, lawyers, diplomats and arbiter-judges. Other international organizations, like the Bretton Woods organizations (the United Nations, World Bank, International Monetary Fund and now the World Trade Organization), which operate outside of any sovereign or international legal system, have created their own internal dispute resolution systems (usually mixtures and choices of informal mediation, settlement and Ombuds services, with more formal administrative court-like hearing processes) to promise justice to their own employees, clients and beneficiaries (see, for example, the World Bank's integrated dispute resolution processes for employees and Inspection Panel for investigations and dispute resolution of recipient–donor claims).

With the proliferation of new international tribunals and venues for dispute resolution, perhaps the greatest innovations have been new international processes and tribunals for human rights violations (principally new treaties and new courts, like the International Criminal Tribunal), post-conflict (both international and intrastate or civil wars) and democracy-generative processes and tribunals. Starting with post-military dictatorship transitions to democracy in Latin America, to the abolition of apartheid in South Africa, to post-genocide transition in Rwanda, and transitions from civil wars and newly independent nations (for example, East Timor) and reparations or other hearings on past atrocities (Cambodia), new forms of 'conflict resolution' have emerged, including truth and reconciliation commissions (Hayner, 2002) and hybrid institutions drawing on local and indigenous processes (for example, *gacaca* in Rwanda (Bolocan, Chapter 15, this volume), as well as combinations of international and domestic personnel and tribunals (Stromseth, Wippman and Brooks,

Chapter 13, this volume.) These processes, derivative of new 'alternative' processes in criminal law, 'victim–offender mediation' (Menkel-Meadow, Chapter 12, this volume) and deliberative democracy efforts (reviewed in Volume II), are truly innovative and varied, and combine elements of both more formal justice with the more direct forms of communication in informal 'meditative' processes. When these sometimes less formal processes are combined with public transparency (as with the publicly televised South African truth and reconciliation commissions, Gibson, 2006), ordinary citizens have been able to witness, if not participate in, new forms of conflict handling (if not resolution), including apologies, restitution and, in some cases, forgiveness. All of this has been accompanied by its own controversies and new canons of concerns:

- When should *amnesty* be permissible?
- Who decides who should be *forgiven?*
- What is the relation of less formal 'truth' commissions to formal *prosecutions* for crimes against humanity and redress for individual victims?
- How should informal institutions be *constituted?*
- What is the *authority* or legitimating source behind these new institutions?
- How *ad hoc* or *permanent* should these new institutions be?
- What is the relationship of temporary or ad hoc tribunals to *capacity-building* for the creation of *permanent* justice institutions in new regimes?
- What *remedies* should these new and hybrid processes provide?
- How do we know when a dispute or conflict has been truly *accounted* for?
- When does (or should) *transitional justice* be merged into more permanent governmental institutions, including both courts and other law-making bodies? (Consider whether *constitutive* bodies or transitional bodies should be permitted to 'morph' into more permanent bodies in new regimes).

Without resolution of these and other questions, international dispute resolution continues to provide new processes and venues for dealing with even more complex problems (online disputes, refugee border crossings, humanitarian aid, health, natural disasters and more gradual environmental degradation, new forms of atrocities, including human trafficking, viral wars and conflicts, transnational gangs, cyber warfare, terrorism and so on). While new forms of globalization increase human contact through travel and communication across borders, increased cross-border and cross-cultural contact also potentially increases the numbers, sources and sites of conflicts. As with all process pluralism, questions remain about the relation of informal conflict resolution to formal institutions and the rule of law. In international settings, this question is all the more difficult and poignant to deal with because of the relative absence of final and authoritative institutions; as several scholars in this volume argue, international adjudication may be adjudication in 'anarchy' (Ginsburg and McAdams, Chapter 11, this volume) or too much 'pluralism' (Berman, 2007). How do we determine how much process choice or process pluralism is 'optimal'? What is the proper relationship of informal to formal conflict resolution and justice?

Culture and Comparative Processes

As if all of these issues in dispute resolution generally were not difficult enough, international conflict resolution also presents the problems of negotiating, mediating, arbitrating and adjudicating among and between cultures (and races, ethnicities and classes as well). Legal systems, and their precursors and parallel processes in less formal institutions, are embedded in cultural systems of value, meaning and practices. Some nations deal with these issues as they attempt to deal with conflicts within increasingly multi-cultural societies, even within the same legal systems (consider immigrant-based nations like the United States, or the current populations of former colonial powers now 'reaping' what they have 'sown' as the formerly dominated colonized migrate to the colonizing powers (for example, United Kingdom, France, the Netherlands, Belgium, Italy, and Spain, to name but a few).

As supranational, religious and other legal systems, such as Shar'ia law, take hold in a variety of nation-states, conflicts of law proliferate as well. What decision rules should be used in subcultures within formal legal systems? Should separate religious or family law courts be recognized (Büchler, 2011)? Should religious practices (for example, the 'veil', female circumcision, 'honour' killings, polygamy) be formally recognized, permitted, prohibited or punished? (As this book goes to press, these issues are being decided in many national court systems, with different treatments of religious autonomy, tolerance or prohibition (though required secularism) in the United States, Canada, the UK, Australia, Germany, Turkey, Switzerland and France, just to name a few – see for example, *Begum (R)* v. *Headmaster of Denbigh High School*, 2006; Okin *et al.*, 1999). These are often questions to be considered by formal courts and are now receiving different treatment in many different venues, as scholars consider what should be the role of 'foreign' (or indigenous or religious or 'other') laws within any one sovereign legal system (Jackson, 2010). In some settings, informal courts or mediation or arbitration centres act in parallel to, or outside of, formal courts.

Consider how cultural differences can be handled, if not managed, in less formal dispute resolution venues. As scholars explore different ways of dealing with cultural differences in mediation, arbitration and negotiation (Kahane, 2003; LeBaron, 2003; Waldman, 2011), it is argued that less formal forms of dispute resolution, making use of more direct communication, translation or co-mediation, can better accommodate cultural differences with members of different cultures 'matching' the cultural, racial, ethnic or other identities of the parties, as it is termed in mediation (Gunning, 1995). Recently, the International Institute of Mediation in The Hague has developed criteria and credentialling for 'intercultural competence' in mediation (International Mediation Institute, 2011).

Other scholars criticize the treatment of 'culture' as a falsely reified dimension of conflict, where participants to disputes often belong to several cultural groups simultaneously (nationality, religion, professional or work culture, class and so on) and where culture itself is not a 'thing' but a constantly evolving context in any conflict situation (Avruch, 1998). Following the events of 11 September 2001, extreme claims of 'clash of civilizations' (Huntington, 1994) gained some ground whereas others in the conflict resolution field argued for more complex understandings of the interaction of demographic, political and economic issues in national, as well as individual, conflicts (Ignatieff, 1993; Lederach, 1995; Anderson, 1999), and still others suggested that, with education and practice in negotiation and other forms of dispute resolution, conflict resolution learning and practices might create their own form of 'cosmopolitan' practice and culture (Rubin and Sander, 1991).

Culture (in diversity) may also matter within dispute resolution processes as cultural, racial, gender, ethnic or class differences are deployed in conflicts differentially by both parties and third-party neutrals (Gadlin, 1994). Is 'neutrality' ever possible when people (both parties and neutrals) interact from different backgrounds (Gadlin and Pino, 1997)? And, as scholars Dezalay and Garth (Chapter 8, this volume) describe, conflict resolution professionals may themselves compete for hegemony as contesting cultures of dispute expertise, evidenced in the competition between the European 'grand old men', as founders of the field of international arbitration, and the newer litigation-oriented Anglo-American arbitration 'technocrats'. Yes, even conflict resolution has its own cultural disputes (Menkel-Meadow, 1997), even as it attempts to facilitate multicultural conflict resolution.

Finally, it is interesting to contemplate the 'culture' of international conflict resolution expertise. To the extent that the essays in this volume demonstrate rich and deep theoretical and practical expertise about the field itself, it remains a paradox to note how many professional diplomats, politicians and other conflict-handlers still proceed to create and attempt to resolve international conflicts without paying much heed to the academic and professional knowledge developed by those represented on these pages (and elsewhere in the literature). Just why this field remains so resistant to joining up theory and practice (and assessment) remains perplexing (Ginsburg and Shaffer, 2010). Are there generalizable principles and patterned empirical outcomes in international dispute resolution or are all international or intercultural disputes and conflicts *sui generis* or epiphenomenal, dependent on the characteristics of the conflicts, parties and would-be conflict resolvers? Only further work in this field will tell.

The Essays

This volume, which is divided into five Parts, provides descriptions, illustrations, and analyses of the great variety of forms of international dispute resolution from formal processes and institutions to newer informal processes, and hybrid tribunals, as it concludes with some provocative issues that confront the development of the field and its efficacy in the world.

Formal Dispute Resolution Processes: Negotiation, Mediation, Arbitration, Adjudication

Part I begins with a useful review essay by Andrea Kupfer Schneider (Chapter 1) describing the variations of dispute resolution forms of negotiation, mediation, arbitration and new hybrid tribunals in both private and public international law. In Chapter 2 Carrie Menkel-Meadow asks whether key canonical concepts developed in general or domestic dispute resolution theory also apply in international settings and vice versa – are deadlines or 'ripeness' in negotiations different, depending on context? Are the functions of third-party neutrals different in different settings?

Robert Putnam (Chapter 3) provides one of the classic descriptions of constituent–agent and secondary and secret processes in international processes in his description of 'two-track' negotiations in diplomacy settings. In Chapter 4 Jeswald Salacuse begins to explore the complex issues implicated in cultural differences as barriers to negotiation in international settings.

Applying different theories of third-party intervention and mediation, Daniel Curran, James Sebenius and Michael Watkins (Chapter 5) contrast the mediation styles of George Mitchell in Northern Ireland and Richard Holbrooke in Bosnia, demonstrating how personal qualities, context and type of dispute, as well as timing, can all affect whether disputes will be resolved collaboratively or with more command and 'muscle mediation' processes. This is a timely set of considerations as George Mitchell, an otherwise successful mediator, has, at the time of writing this Introduction, withdrawn from efforts at mediating the ongoing Middle East (Israel–Palestine) dispute.

William Zartman, one of the first contributors to international dispute resolution theory is represented here (Chapter 6) by his classic formulation of whether 'hurting stalemates' provide 'ripe moments' and incentives for third-party intervention to resolve disputes. Next, in contrast and in response to Zartman, long-time activist practitioner of peace John Paul Lederach (Chapter 7) suggests that there are no single 'ripe' moments in international dispute resolution – with good intentions and motivations, those engaged in disputes and conflicts can almost always accomplish something in dealing with their differences through engaged dialogue. Unlike 'fruits', disputes do not have a few 'good' (or bad) days. As we all know, they can linger and be 'dealt with' (or not) over much longer periods of time.

In Chapter 8 French sociologist Yves Dezalay and American legal scholar Bryant Garth provide a rich qualitative analysis of the development of international commercial arbitration. They describe the origins of the field in the work of European professors and practitioners in creating both a legal process and a new international *lex mercatoria* which is now being challenged by a younger group of 'legal technocrats' who seek to use Anglo-American litigation techniques to 'legalize' that which had been developed to provide more private and customized dispute resolution. This study is a model of how rigorous empirical study from both above and below (in-depth interviews with the major players) can reveal larger patterns and trends – in this case, the increasing competition for 'dispute resolution business' between conflict-resolution entrepreneurs offering different expertises and human, economic, professional and organizational capital.

To conclude Part I we return to the work of international dispute resolution scholar Andrea Kupfer Schneider (Chapter 9). Her summary and analysis of the evolution of a variety of old and new tribunals and legal regimes in the area of international economic trade is not only excellent in itself but is also useful and evocative in tracing the evolution of new international tribunals in various other areas of mixed competitive–cooperative strategic behaviour.

New Processes: Institutions, Informal and Hybrid Dispute Processes

Part II previews a variety of 'newer' processes and tribunals in international dispute resolution. In Chapter 10 Herbert Kelman describes the inventive 'problem-solving workshops' he and his group of colleagues pioneered to bring second-tier notables (not formal state officials and diplomats) to the table to discuss elements of difficult (and often intractable) international (and internal civil) conflicts, as in the Middle East and other highly conflict-ridden areas in the world.

Tom Ginsburg and Richard McAdams (Chapter 11) theorize another role for the multi-layered complexity and Babel-like quality of international dispute resolution tribunals and venues: even if the multiplicity of formal institutions cannot always clarify or enforce diverse international legal norms, the very existence of so many venues to elaborate, make and interpret international norms can result in 'expressive', if symbolic, norm creation which may, in fact, have an enforcement value of its own, even without a 'court of last resort' or a fully effective international legislature or army.

In Chapter 12 Carrie Menkel-Meadow describes the theories of restorative and restitutive justice, initially developed in domestic criminal and indigenous settings, which have inspired the formation of new kinds of transitional justice processes – truth and reconciliation processes at the national level and returns to, or revisions of, older local processes for 'reintegrating' torn societies after great violence and conflict, as in Rwandan *gacaca*, more fully described in Maya Goldstein Bolocan's essay (Chapter 15).

Jane Stromseth, David Wippman and Rosa Brooks (Chapter 13) describe a variety of new conflict resolution processes, intended to build legal, judicial, democratic and dispute resolution capacity in strife-torn or newly democratic societies. Some of these new tribunals (for example, in East Timor) draw on the now decades-old experience of ad hoc war crimes tribunals, but innovate and experiment with mixtures of international and local personnel and processes. Empirical assessment of these new hybrid processes continues apace, even as new forms are being developed (for example, prosecutions in the new court in Cambodia for the long ago, but still remembered, genocidal atrocities perpetrated by the Khmer Rouge regime). In Chapter 14 John Hagan reports on his studies of the prosecutions, for all too modern war crimes, in the specialized and ad hoc International Criminal Tribunal for the Former Yugoslavia, with in-depth interviews of prosecutors, judges and other participants, following adaptations made to the path-creating Nuremberg trials for crimes against humanity. How the learning of these institutions will affect developments in the now-permanent International Criminal Court remains to be seen (and studied) as the first prosecutions are now underway.

Issues in New Forms of International and Transnational Dispute Resolution

Part III surveys a variety of critical issues raised by both conventional and newer forms of international dispute resolution. Laura Nader and Elisabetta Grande (Chapter 16) argue strongly that the modern export of conflict management ideologies is just another form of imperialism or colonialism. Negotiated or mediated settlements in conflicts about resources (water, oil and land), especially when between developed and developing nations, tend to recapitulate power relations. Dispute resolution techniques become just another instrument in the hegemonic power of the rich over the poor, the North over the South, and the West over the East.

In Chapter 17 legal scholar Robert Ahdieh surveys the tensions created by the proliferation of so many new international tribunals. Do courts of different jurisdictions view each other as part of either horizontal or vertical lines of influence? Do regional courts 'determine' the outcomes for national courts (consider the relationship of the European Court of Human Rights to the national courts (and legislatures) of the members of the European community)? Can private international arbitration panels be in 'dialogue' with each other and with national and regional courts, or is the relationship more competitive and dialectic?

David Dyzenhaus (Chapter 18) criticizes the functioning of the South African Truth and Reconciliation Commission on the grounds that the judges and lawyers who facilitated and enforced the unjust apartheid regime did not appear before the commission and make full account of their especially significant 'guilty' complicity in that unjust regime. What is justice if the lawyers and judges responsible for unjust laws are not held to account? What are the limits of some of the newer and more 'forgiving' (through legal amnesty) forms of conflict resolution and reconciliation? In the next essay (Chapter 19) Carrie Menkel-Meadow suggests that these issues of reconciliation and mediated solutions must find some way to accommodate both justice for the past and peace for the future – there may be many processes and also great human variation in how individuals (and particular nation-states and cultures) seek to come to terms with past wrongs. Who has the power to forgive? Victims? The state? The community? Who should be punished for aggregate acts of inhumanity? The leaders? The implementers? What forms of restitution are possible? 'Rights of return' to land, to property (consider disputes over art seized by the Nazis and others), compensation for lost lives? These issues remain timelessly and sadly current as human conflicts continue to proliferate.

In a second essay Carrie Menkel-Meadow (Chapter 20) then explores how dispute system designers (those who create processes for conflict resolution in so many international and intranational, post-conflict settings) should consider the ethical dilemmas in their work. For whom are conflict processes created? Victims of great harms, new governments seeking stability, citizens seeking democracy or at least accountability of past regimes? To whom are system designers accountable? The users of conflict processes? The governments, international organizations or 'clients' who hire them? Others outside of the conflict? Their own profession? Similarly, Jean Sternlight, in the final essay of this volume (Chapter 21) asks the persistently relevant and difficult-to-resolve question of whether efforts to create new, less formal and more responsive processes of conflict resolution outside of courts is, or ought to be, consistent with the rule of law, assuming that we can establish what *the* rule of law is in our modern international, transnational and globalized existence.

Coda

While the efforts to develop more efficacious forms of international conflict resolution continue, seeking responsiveness and variability to more diverse and complex situations, it remains a concern of our field to assess how world peace and justice can best be achieved, especially where it is not really clear whether they can always be achieved together.

A final Coda at the end of this volume concludes with some final reflections on these questions.

References

Acuff, Frank L. (2008), *How to Negotiate Anything With Anyone Anywhere Around the World* (3rd edn), Chicago: AMACOM.

Anderson, Mary B. (1999), *Do No Harm: How Aid Can Support Peace – or War*, Boulder, CO: Lynne Rienner Publishers.

Auerbach, Jerold S. (1983), *Justice Without Law? Resolving Disputes Without Lawyers*, Oxford: Oxford University Press.

Avruch, Kevin (1998), *Culture and Conflict Resolution*, Washington, DC: United States Institute of Peace Press.

Begum (Application by R) v. *Headmaster of Denbigh School* (2006), United Kingdom House of Lords, 15.

Berman, Paul Schiff (2007), 'Global Legal Pluralism', *Southern California Law Review*, **80**, pp. 1155–237.

Bernstein, Lisa (1992), 'Opting Out of the Legal System: Extralegal Contractual Relations in the Diamond Industry', *Journal of Legal Studies*, **21**, pp. 115–57.

Büchler, Andrea (2011), *Islamic Law in Europe? Legal Pluralism and its Limits in European Family Laws*, Farnham: Ashgate Publishing.

Busch, M. and Reinhardt, E. (2000), 'Bargaining in the Shadow of the Law: Early Settlement in GATT/WTO Disputes', *Fordham International Law Journal*, **24**, pp. 158–72.

Cohen, Jerome Alan (1966), 'Chinese Mediation on the Eve of Modernization', *California Law Review*, 54, pp. 1201–26.

European Union (2008), 'Directive 2008/52/EC of the European Parliament and of the Council, May 21, 2008 on Certain Aspects of Mediation in Civil and Commercial Matters' *Official Journal of the European Union*, 24 May 2008. Available at: http://eur-lex.europa.eu/LexUriServ/LexUriServ.do?uri=OJ:L:2008:136:0003:0008:En:PDF.

Fisher, Roger, Kopelman, Elizabeth and Schneider, Andrea Kupfer (1994), *Beyond Machiavelli: Tools for Coping with Conflict*, Cambridge, MA: Harvard University Press.

Franck, Susan (2007), 'Empirically Evaluating Claims about Investment Arbitration', *North Carolina Law Review*, **86**, pp. 1–88.

Friedman, Thomas (2005), *The World is Flat: A Brief History of the 21st Century*, New York: Farrar, Straus & Giroux.

Gadlin, Howard (1994), 'Conflict Resolution, Cultural Differences and the Culture of Racism', *Negotiation Journal*, **10**, pp. 49–68.

Gadlin, Howard and Pino, Elizabeth Walsh (1997), 'Neutrality: A Guide for the Organizational Ombudsperson', *Negotiation Journal*, **13**, pp. 17–37.

Gibson, James (2006), *Overcoming Apartheid: Can Truth Reconcile a Divided Nation?*, New York: Russell Sage.

Ginsburg, Tom and Shaffer, Gregory (2010), 'How Does International Law Work?', in Peter Cane and Herbert M. Kritzer (eds), *The Oxford Handbook of Empirical Legal Research*, Oxford: Oxford University Press.

Graham, John L. and Requejo, William Hernandez (2008), *Global Negotiation: The New Rules*, New York: Palgrave Macmillan.

Greenhouse, Carol (1986), *Praying for Justice: Faith, Order and Community in an American Town*, Ithaca, NY: Cornell University Press.

Gulliver, P.H. (1979), *Disputes and Negotiations: A Cross Cultural Perspective*, New York: Academic Press.

Gunning, Isabelle (1995), 'Diversity Issues in Mediation: Controlling Negative Cultural Myths', *Journal of Dispute Resolution*, pp. 55–93.

Hayner, Priscilla (2002), *Unspeakable Truths: Transitional Justice and the Challenge of Truth Commissions*, New York and London: Routledge.

Huntington, Samuel (1994), 'The Clash of Civilizations?', in Armand Clesse, Richard Cooper and Yoshikazu Sakamoto (eds), *The International System after the Collapse of the East–West Order*, Dordrecht: Martinus Nijhoff Publishers.

Hutchinson, Michael R. (1999), 'The Margin of Appreciation in the European Court of Human Rights', *International and Comparative Law Quarterly*, **48**, pp. 638–50.

Ignatieff, Michael (1994), *Blood and Belonging: Journeys into the New Nationalism*, New York: Farrar, Straus & Giroux.

International Mediation Institute (2011), 'Draft Criteria for Approving Programs to Qualify Mediators for IMI Inter-Cultural Certification', at: http://www.imimediation.org/intercultural-certification-criteria.

Jackson, Vicki C. (2010), *Constitutional Engagement in a Transnational Era*, Oxford and New York: Oxford University Press.

Kahane, David (2003), 'Dispute Resolution and the Politics of Cultural Generalization', *Negotiation Journal*, **19**, pp. 5–27.

Kim, H. and Sikkink, K. (2010), 'Explaining the Deterrent Effect of Human Rights Prosecutions in Transitional Countries', *International Studies Quarterly*, **54**, pp. 939–63.

Kremenyuk, Victor (ed.) (2002), *International Negotiation: Analysis, Approaches, Issues* (2nd edn), San Francisco, CA: Jossey Bass.

Langbein, John (2003), *The Origins of Adversary Criminal Trial*, Oxford: Oxford University Press.

LeBaron, Michelle (2003), *Bridging Cultural Conflicts: A New Approach for a Changing World*, San Francisco, CA: Jossey Bass.

Lederach, John Paul (1995), *Preparing for Peace: Conflict Transformation Across Cultures*, Syracuse, NY: Syracuse Press.

Loewen Group v. *United States* (2003), *International Centre for the Settlement of Investment Disputes*, Case No. ARB (AF) 98/3, *International Legal Materials*, 42: 811 (26 June 2003).

Lubman, Stanley (1967), 'Mao and Mediation: Politics in Dispute Resolution in Communist China', *California Law Review*, **55**, pp. 1284–359.

Margalit, Avishai (2010), *On Compromises and Rotten Compromises*, Princeton, NJ: Princeton University Press.

Menkel-Meadow, Carrie (1997), 'When Dispute Resolution Begets Disputes of Its Own: Conflicts Among Dispute Professionals', *University of California Los Angeles Law Review*, **44**, pp. 1871–933.

Menkel-Meadow, Carrie (2005), 'Is the Adversary System Dead? Dilemmas of Legal Ethics as Legal Institutions and Roles Evolve', *Current Legal Problems*, **57**, pp. 85–115.

Menkel-Meadow, Carrie (2010), 'Compromise, Negotiation and Morality', *Negotiation Journal*, **26**, pp. 483–99.

Menkel-Meadow, Carrie (2011), 'Why and How to Study "Transnational" Law', *University of California Irvine Law Review*, **1**, pp. 97–129.

Merrills, J.G. (2005), *International Dispute Settlement* (4th edn), Cambridge: Cambridge University Press.

Merry, Sally Engle and Milner, Neal (1993), *The Possibility of Popular Justice: A Case Study of Community Mediation in the United States*, Ann Arbor, MI: University of Michigan Press.

Mnookin, Robert H. (2010), *Bargaining with the Devil: When to Negotiate, When to Fight*, New York: Simon & Schuster.

Okin, Susan Muller *et al.*, (1999), *Is Multi-Culturalism Bad for Women?*, ed. Joshua Cohen, Matthew Howard and Martha Nussbuam, Princeton, NJ: Princeton University Press.

Palmer, Michael (1989), 'The Revival of Mediation in the People's Republic of China: Extrajudicial Mediation in W.E. Butler (ed.), *Yearbook on Socialist Legal Systems*, Dobbs Ferry, NY: Transnational Books.

Project on International Courts and Tribunals (1997), at: http://www.pict-pcti.org.

Roberts, Marion (1997), *Mediation in Family Disputes: Principles of Practice* (2nd edn), Aldershot: Arena.

Roberts, Simon and Palmer, Michael (2005), *Dispute Processes: ADR and the Primary Forms of Decision Making*, Cambridge: Cambridge University Press.

Rubin, Jeffrey Z. and Sander, Frank E.A. (1991), 'Culture, Negotiation, and the Eye of the Beholder', *Negotiation Journal*, **7**, pp. 249–54.

Saposnek, Donald T. (1985), *Mediating Child Custody Disputes: A Systematic Guide for Family Therapists, Court Counselors, Attorneys and Judges*, San Francisco, CA: Jossey Bass.

Shapiro, Martin (1981), *Courts: A Comparative and Political Analysis*, Chicago, IL: University of Chicago Press.

Slaughter, Anne-Marie (2004), *A New World Order*, Princeton, NJ: Princeton University Press.

Stone, Katherine van Wezel (2001), 'Dispute Resolution in the Boundaryless Workplace', *Ohio State Journal of Dispute Resolution*, **16**, pp. 467–89.

Twining, William (2009), *General Jurisprudence: Understanding Law from a Global Perspective*, Cambridge: Cambridge University Press.

Waldman, Ellen (ed.) (2011), *Mediation Ethics: Cases and Commentaries*, San Francisco, CA: Jossey Bass.

Watkins, Michael and Rosegrant, Susan (2001), *Breakthrough International Negotiations: How Great Negotiators Transformed the World's Toughest Post-Cold War Conflicts*, San Francisco, CA: Jossey Bass.

Woolf, Lord Harry (1996), *Access to Justice: Final Report to the Lord Chancellor on the Civil Justice System of England and Wales*, London: HMSO.

Yarn, Douglas H. (2000), 'The Attorney as Duelist's Friend: Lessons from the Code Duello', *Case Western Reserve Law Review*, **51**, pp. 69–113.

Part I
Formal Dispute Resolution Processes: Negotiation, Mediation, Arbitration, Adjudication

[1]

Public and Private International Dispute Resolution

Andrea Kupfer Schneider

Conflict resolution is neither new nor uniquely American. People have been using forms of negotiation, mediation, and arbitration since they started living together in groups. As both domestic and international dispute resolution processes have evolved to meet changing needs, information exchange between the two disciplines can better inform practitioners and theorists in both areas. Each dispute resolution process operates differently among various countries, in diverse contexts. This chapter will highlight some of the developments in each of the international dispute resolution processes and identify interesting parallels between domestic and international controversies over where, how, and when to use dispute resolution.

Public international dispute resolution traditionally refers to disputes among countries, for example, between the United States and Iraq. Private international dispute resolution, in contrast, applies in the context of disputes among individuals or companies from different countries, for example, between U.S.-based Kodak and Japan-based Fuji over ownership of intellectual property. For the purpose of organization, this chapter divides disputes between those that are public and those that are private. As a descriptive matter, however, this simplistic division no longer captures fully the reality of modern disputes. Many disputes are neither wholly public nor wholly private. As companies invest in foreign countries at an increasing rate, there are now direct disputes between these companies and the governments of the countries. Nongovernmental organizations (NGOs), such as Amnesty International or the World Wildlife

Foundation, have entered the fray of international disputes and often negotiate directly with governments for policy changes. Finally, within intergovernmental organizations such as the European Union (EU) and the World Trade Organization (WTO), individuals, countries, and the organization itself can all be involved in a dispute. Traditional modes of dispute resolution have evolved to take note of these new parties involved in international disputes and to provide stimulating models for comparison with the evolution in domestic dispute resolution.

At the same time, some of the theories and models used in domestic dispute resolution offer useful insights into international negotiations. For example, much as labor negotiators in the United States must adopt strategies for dealing with their constituencies, so must diplomats concern themselves with domestic interest groups. Other theories drawn from domestic dispute resolution may need to be modified to take account of the international parties at the table. For example, some of our most cherished beliefs in domestic processes (such as the neutrality of the mediator) are either diluted or nonexistent in many international mediations.

INTERNATIONAL NEGOTIATION

The next section discusses both private and public international negotiation. In the private arena, globalization has had a great impact on standardizing certain terms of negotiation and facilitating private international negotiations. At the same time, globalization has required the consideration of a broader constituency in public negotiations.

Private International Negotiations: Individual to Individual

Cultural differences are perhaps the most salient issues raised in negotiations between individuals from different countries, even in diplomatic negotiations. U.S. Trade Representative Charlene Barshefsky's experiences negotiating with the Chinese Trade Minister turned as much on the cultural differences of negotiating with the Chinese as they did on the policy differences between the United States and China.[1]

Less experienced negotiators often make the mistake of focusing on those similarities and differences they can see between themselves and the negotiator on the other side. They focus, for example, on things such as race, gender, and culture, rather than on less visible characteristics such as education, negotiation style, experience, level of preparation, or negotiation authority and parameters.[2] Researchers have found that personality, negotiation style, or professional training could have just as much influence on negotiation behavior as does culture. While it is important to be aware of potential cultural differences (and avoid behavior that would be perceived as insulting), negotiators also need to be wary of assuming that every difference derives from culture.[3]

In addition to highlighting cultural differences, international negotiations raise heightened concerns about clear communication. Terms that mean one thing in one country may not mean the same thing in other countries. Governing law and enforcement in the event of a breach of contract are also more complicated in international negotiations than in domestic negotiations. Addressing a breach of contract is typically easier in a context involving only domestic parties than if one or more of the parties to the contract is located abroad. Negotiations within a single country benefit from having one set of laws that apply to contracts and a court system well-versed in contract interpretation according to that law. No single court system interprets private law at the international level.

As the world has become more interdependent, however, and these issues arise repeatedly, some of them have become much easier to manage. For example, international treaties now govern issues of contract interpretation and terms across many countries.[4] Furthermore, while enforcement of a contract in another country's court system would have been quite difficult years ago, the growth of international arbitration and treaties concerning judicial cooperation make both arbitration and litigation easier. In many other respects, private international negotiations and domestic negotiations operate similarly.[5]

Public International Negotiation: Country to Country

The studies of international diplomacy, international relations, and foreign affairs all primarily relate to the issue of how governments communicate with one another about a variety of issues. In the domestic realm, some theorists have divided negotiation into *dispute settlement negotiation* versus *deal-making negotiation*.[6] These theorists suggest that the negotiation might be conducted differently in one context versus the other. Similarly, in the international context, sometimes countries engage in deal-making negotiations—for example, to craft the terms of a treaty regarding trade practices such as the negotiation among Mexico, Canada, and the United States regarding the North American Free Trade Agreement (NAFTA). At other times, countries must deal with the aftermath of a dispute (dispute settlement negotiation)—for example, when one country arrests the citizen of another country.

This domestic division between disputes and deals, however, often is too simplistic for international negotiations for two reasons. First, as discussed earlier, domestic dispute settlement has the backdrop of a single court system and governing law. If the parties do not reach agreement, they can turn to the courts to resolve the issue. At the international level, one country does not usually have the ability to sue another in an international court because countries do not grant these courts jurisdiction. (Some famous exceptions exist—for example, Nicaragua brought a case in the International Court of Justice (ICJ) against the United States in the mid-1980s for violating Nicaraguan sovereignty with the U.S. naval blockade.[7] This, of course, raises the issue of enforcement, since the ICJ relies on voluntary compliance with its rulings.)

Second, many disputes that reach the U.S. court system are between parties that do not need to work with each other in the future unless they choose. In international relations, few countries can exist without engaging in relations with other countries on a regular basis. The future relationship is not optional for countries that expect to be involved in most important international issues. Even with those countries with whom the United States has no official relationship, such as Cuba, ongoing communication and negotiation continues through multiple unofficial channels.

Historically, the focus in international negotiations has been on the diplomat or leader who conducts the negotiation. The importance of diplomats and their ability to negotiate has long been recognized by international law. Some of the earliest treaties on record deal with diplomatic immunity and the freedom of messengers to travel even in wartime.[8] Perhaps one of the most famous political science treatises ever, *The Prince*, is primarily a book of negotiation advice to the Florentine leader on how he should deal with the populace and with other countries.[9] Much analysis of international negotiation continues to give diplomats advice on conducting negotiations.

Advice to international negotiators often resembles generalized negotiation advice, and, as with most forms of advice, different schools of thought have developed. Much like the difference between an adversarial and problem-solving approach in any negotiation, different political science schools—realist, regime theory, public choice, liberal international relations—provide different approaches on how a country should determine its interests and, by implication, how these interests should be pursued.[10] Much of the advice for individual diplomats, whose long-term relationships and reputation are a key measure of their worth, more clearly reflects what we would call a problem-solving approach.[11] A diplomat should be trustworthy (although not completely trusting), clear in communication (with extra attention paid to the potential for miscommunication through translation), flexible, and concerned with the interests of the other side.[12]

More recently, the focus on the individual leader or diplomat has been supplemented by the study of the interaction between the leader and his or her constituency. In nondemocratic forms of government, leaders might not take the interests and opinions of a broad citizenry into account when formulating policy and negotiating with other countries. In democracies, however, a leader can rarely ignore the public. A democratic leader who wants to be a statesman on the international scene is first and foremost an elected politician and, probably, a politician facing reelection at some point. This means that in

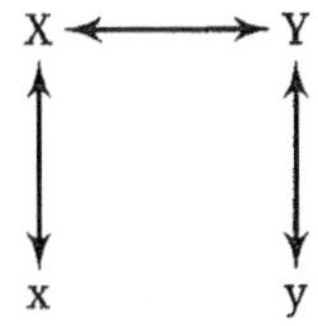

Figure 27.1. Two-Level Negotiation.

international negotiations there are actually two levels of negotiations happening at once (Figure 27.1). The first negotiation is between the two leaders, X and Y. Each of those leaders, however, must negotiate with their domestic constituencies (x and y) to back their international policy.

The discussion of such multiple negotiations is called "Two-Level Games."[13] The impact of multiple negotiations clearly complicates the original negotiation between leaders. A domestic constituency can tie the hands of a leader—for example by threatening to vote the leader out of office. This can make it difficult for the negotiators to reach and sustain agreement. Conversely, a belligerent constituency can help lend credence to the argument that it is the other side that must concede, implying to them that "your hands are tied." Just as we might use an analysis of a bargaining zone to see if two individuals can reach an agreement in a domestic negotiation, the impact of two-level diplomacy can either expand or narrow the range of agreements as well as help determine which party gets more of the surplus good.

A final issue in international negotiation is whether one should negotiate at all. Are there parties with whom we should not negotiate? The old saying is that if you are going to sup with the devil, use a long spoon. Sometimes, leaders believe that no spoon is long enough to make negotiating appropriate. Winston Churchill refused to negotiate with Hitler because Churchill felt it would give Hitler respect he did not deserve. Some U.S. leaders explain their refusal to negotiate with Cuba in similar terms. Many countries refuse to negotiate with terrorists out of fear of setting a precedent of negotiation or conferring legitimacy on the terrorists. Should the United States have negotiated with the Taliban rather than invading Afghanistan? Should the United States have negotiated with Saddam Hussein rather than invading Iraq? Are there any circumstances in which we should negotiate with terrorists?[14] Experts on terrorism argue that any negotiation strategy must take into account the type of terrorist. An "absolutist" terrorist is someone whose goal is complete anarchy and destruction of the political system.[15] Many people would put Osama bin Laden in this category and argue that negotiation with him would be fruitless and immoral. At the other end of the spectrum is the hostage-taker with an agenda (much like a domestic hostage-taker), looking for specific action or money. With this type of terrorist—for example, kidnappers in

Columbia—negotiation can be helpful.[16] In the vast middle, of course, falls the terrorist-or-freedom-fighter distinction in which some would label the actor as a terrorist and others would argue that the terrorist actions stem from a goal of political change. Examples of this type of terrorists would include the IRA, the PLO, and Chechen separatists. Negotiation with such groups may bring results, as in Northern Ireland, but many people would worry about the precedent set by negotiating, the morality of negotiating and, of course, whether any negotiation would actually bring peace.[17]

INTERNATIONAL MEDIATION

Adding a neutral party to the negotiation to facilitate the conversation among the disputants shifts the negotiation to a mediation. In this section on international mediation, I examine the increasing use of mediation in private international commercial disputes as well as the key issues of who, when, and how third party intervention should occur in public international disputes.

Private Mediation

Mediation between individuals or companies from different countries has increased dramatically in the past several years. While international arbitration has long historic roots, international mediation among private parties is a more recent development. This growth in international private mediation is primarily due to the popularity and growth of mediation within countries more generally. Companies that engage in domestic mediation to solve problems want the same options for dispute resolution with overseas customers or clients.

Many international disputes arise between private disputants who have important ongoing relationships. Suppliers and distributors, shippers and receivers, and many other international business partners face the same range and number of disputes as one would expect to see in domestic business relationships. Mediation offers an opportunity to resolve disputes without damaging the parties' long-term ability to work together. Other advantages of mediation, including speed, cost-efficiency, and party control of outcome, are often highlighted against the choice of litigation. In the international arena, litigation is an even less attractive alternative (at least for one party), since one party will have to litigate in the "home state" of the other disputant. The time, energy, expense, and expertise required for litigation is greater in a foreign country, giving companies in private international disputes even more reason to prefer mediation. Finally, foreign judgments sometimes pose enforcement challenges, risking yet another round of litigation.

International mediation raises important legal and procedural issues in addition to those already discussed regarding negotiation. How will the mediation agreement be enforced? Under what law should it be interpreted? Different countries may have different laws concerning the confidentiality of mediation and any privileges for the mediator. These legal issues should be clarified prior to the mediation. Procedural issues for the mediation process, such as choosing the mediator and location, are the same as in domestic mediations, though the concern with mediator neutrality and appearances of bias may be highlighted in a cross-cultural setting. Parties must decide whether the mediator should be from a country different from the participants or whether the location should be in a third country. Furthermore, the mediator may also need to handle communication or translation issues. Setting up an international mediation has become easier in recent years as mediation providers globalize their services and as international arbitration providers add mediation to their services.[18]

International Public Mediation: Intervening in Country-to-Country Disputes

International mediation, like international negotiation, has a long history in international relations. World leaders, such as the pope or the Holy Roman Emperor, tried to mediate disputes among other world leaders to end war and reach agreements. The Treaty of Westphalia in 1648, known for establishing the concept of sovereignty as we know it today, explicitly thanks the Ambassador of the Republic of Venice for his long efforts in mediating the end of the Thirty Years War. With the creation of international organizations such as the United Nations, mediation has become even more institutionalized and promoted as an alternative to warfare. This section will discuss three primary issues in international mediation: how to decide who acts as the mediator, how to determine when mediation might work, and how the mediation or intervention should actually occur.

Historically, mediators in international disputes were world leaders who brought the stature and power of their office or their country to the mediation table. For example, the mediator could be the pope or a representative of the pope's office, who would urge the two Catholic countries to end their dispute. One example of this was the pope's mediation in the late 1970s between Argentina and Chile over maritime rights near the Beagle Channel. The Beagle Channel was home to three barren islands near the southern tips of each country. Sovereignty over the islands could determine fishing and oil exploration rights. Both international arbitration and direct negotiation had failed, and the countries were preparing for military action when the Vatican intervened to mediate a peaceful end of the dispute. The United Nations today also serves as the secular equivalent of the pope's role in intervening in international conflicts.

The mediator can also come from a country with an interest in the dispute or in the parties, such as the United States trying to resolve a dispute between two U.S. allies. Alexander Haig's attempt to avert the Falklands War between Great Britain and Argentina is an example of an unsuccessful mediation; Jimmy Carter's mediation between Israel and Egypt at Camp David or, more recently, Richard Holbrooke's mediation to the end of the Bosnian conflict through the Dayton Accords are quintessential examples of success. Mediators have also come from neighboring countries who want to see the conflict on their borders ended and demonstrate regional leadership. Costa Rica's mediation of the El Salvadoran civil war (which involved Nicaragua and Honduras as well) is one example; South Africa's ongoing mediation effort toward resolving the wars in the Congo is another.

Unlike domestic mediators, international mediators cannot possibly be neutral, objective, or disinterested because the mediator has a distinct interest in the outcome of the mediation. This is particularly true when the alternative is violence. When a neighbor intervenes (as in El Salvador), the fear of violence spilling over, regional destabilization, and refugee issues are sufficient to make the dispute a national interest. Similarly, in many of the disputes in which the United States engages, it prefers to be involved and to receive credit for working out the dispute.[19] For example, even though bilateral negotiations between Egypt and Israel were progressing without U.S. involvement at the end of the 1973 Arab-Israeli war, Secretary of State Henry Kissinger forced an end to bilateral negotiations and insisted on mediating the dispute. One could also argue that the United States pushed the Bosnian Muslims to accept a settlement in the Dayton Accords, when a better offer might have been available at a later date, in order to be able to announce the resolution of the dispute. Furthermore, international country-to-country mediation is public, implicating the reputation of the mediating party even more clearly than in a domestic mediation context.

Another issue in international mediation is the determination of *when* it makes sense to intervene in a conflict. If the parties ask for help, then the answer is relatively straightforward. Other times, however, the mediator steps forward on behalf of the world community to try to end the conflict. Some theorists have argued that a situation needs to be "ripe"—having deteriorated sufficiently for the parties to view mediation as an attractive alternative.[20] For example, if one party is convinced that military force will prevail or that the conflict is not that painful, then that party will have little incentive to resolve the dispute through mediation. Some theorists argue that the parties will only participate in real mediation when military force is not successful or the situation has devolved into a "mutually hurting stalemate."[21] An example of a stalemate that was ready for mediation might be Northern Ireland and George Mitchell's successfully mediated Good Friday Accords. Other theorists disagree with this assessment and argue that international mediation is not like picking ripe apples but rather is more like cultivation, in which a mediator needs to work with the parties over time to develop both the relationship and the possible solution.[22] Long-term mediation efforts by both intergovernmental and nongovernmental organizations between Armenia and Azerbaijan over territorial disputes could be an example of relationship cultivation.

Finally, intervention in international disputes is also broader than just the mediation process. As more NGOs become involved in conflict resolution, interventions have become multifaceted. Years ago, intervention meant the traditional shuttle diplomacy among high-level diplomats, but today intervention can come in multiple forms, including community-building activities between disputing groups led by an NGO such as Search for Common Ground or Mercy Corps, humanitarian efforts led by Doctors Without Borders, and focused peacemaking efforts led by the United Nations or regional intergovernmental organizations. These efforts are known as multitrack diplomacy, involving citizens in different parts of society. Part of the ongoing task for those involved in international conflict is to coordinate these activities so that the mediation at the diplomatic level works in conjunction with the humanitarian efforts at the local level, building on existing peacemaking efforts.[23]

INTERNATIONAL ARBITRATION AND HYBRID PROCESSES

This section reviews the history of how international commercial arbitration became so widespread and then discusses the use of arbitration and hybrid processes to resolve disputes among countries.

Private International Arbitration

Arbitration has its roots in international commercial dispute resolution. Merchant guilds in Europe developed arbitration as a swift and fair method for dealing with commercial disputes across borders when domestic laws were varying and unclear. The popularity and ease of international commercial arbitration persists today. Much like domestic arbitration, international arbitration can offer the advantages of speed, cost-efficiency, finality, and subject-matter expertise of the arbitrator. In addition, avoiding litigation in foreign courts remains a significant advantage.

Countries have encouraged the use of arbitration to resolve commercial disputes by committing to enforce arbitration awards. As of this writing, 134 countries have signed the New York Convention on the Recognition and Enforcement of Foreign Arbitral Awards (1958).[24] This treaty provides that enforcement of arbitral awards among the signatory countries shall be virtually automatic—much faster than the process required to enforce a foreign court judgment. Under the New York Convention, there are very few reasons for a court to set aside an arbitration award. These limited grounds for setting aside or refusing recognition of an award include procedural defects such as improper notice of hearings, inappropriate composition of the arbitral panel under various rules and doctrines, or failure of the arbitration award to be within the contemplated agreement of parties. An award can also be set aside in some limited cases when recognition or enforcement of the award would be contrary to public policy of the enforcing country.

Responding to the proliferation of international arbitration, international arbitration centers worldwide have developed arbitral rules and procedures based on legal and cultural differences. These centers offer disputants a choice in location, rules, and underlying law, making international arbitration even more popular. Some of these arbitration centers include the London Court of International Arbitration, the American Arbitration Association, the Center for Public Resources in New York, and the International Chamber of Commerce in Paris, as well as centers in Stockholm, Hong Kong, and the Middle East. Centers such as these start by providing a basic set of procedures and can also help choose and appoint the arbitrators, organize the logistics of the arbitration, and coordinate the exchange of documents, reports, and experts.

Public International Arbitration and Mixed Processes

Arbitration between countries was rare historically. Countries usually want to resolve disputes among themselves and not have a third party impose a decision on them. For example, the Permanent Court of Arbitration, created in 1899 to voluntarily resolve disputes between countries, has heard only forty-seven cases. One famous arbitration in U.S. history was the *Alabama* arbitration case between the United States and Great Britain growing out of the U.S. Civil War. The United States accused Great Britain of helping the South in violation of its obligation as a neutral under international law; rather than negotiate the claims or resort to force, both countries agreed to arbitration. An arbitration panel agreed with the United States and awarded it over $15 million in damages.[25]

In the late twentieth century, more countries started to turn to arbitration for a number of reasons. First, the International Court of Justice (ICJ), created in 1945, has had great success in acting as an arbiter between countries over issues such as boundaries, territorial disputes, and fishing rights. Using the ICJ is most attractive for countries in contexts in which the dispute is law-based, the issue is politically sensitive enough that compromise would be difficult, and the stakes are low enough that the use of force would be absurd. For example, the United States and Canada could not reach a negotiated agreement over fishing rights in the Gulf of Maine. Compromising for either country would have been politically difficult with important domestic constituencies involved. The countries submitted the case to the ICJ and used a panel process by which the parties agreed to five judges with maritime expertise. This process, which looked much like arbitration, successfully resolved the case between the two neighbors.[26]

The second reason for the expansion of arbitration between countries is the creation of new forums to handle disputes. For example, the WTO was created in 1994 with a separate dispute settlement body to arbitrate trade cases between countries. The disputes are heard by rotating panels of arbitrators with expertise in trade law. More recently, the United Nations established a tribunal to hear disputes arising under the Law of the Sea Convention.[27]

A third reason that arbitration has expanded internationally is that countries are often involved in disputes with private parties rather than with another country. Neither the ICJ nor the WTO process is available to private parties to pursue their investment disputes with countries. Domestic courts are also not available because countries often have sovereign immunity both at home and in foreign courts. Therefore, the International Centre for the Settlement of Investment Disputes (ICSID), established under the World Bank, was created to handle disputes between countries and private parties to facilitate investment and development. Most of the United States's bilateral investment treaties around the world, as well as NAFTA, refer any dispute arising under the treaty to ICSID or ad hoc arbitration rules created by the United Nations Commission on International Trade Law (UNCITRAL). An example of this type of dispute would be one well-known case under NAFTA involving a Canadian company arbitrating against the United States for an unfair state jury trial outcome.[28] These public-private disputes have been growing dramatically as foreign investment grows.

The expansion of arbitration has also led to the development of mixed processes to deal with different types of disputes and parties. The development of international hybrid processes responds to the varying needs of the states for control over the outcome, level of enforcement desired, different parties involved, and underlying international law. For example, as discussed earlier, Chapter Eleven of NAFTA deals with disputes between private investors and the host country, using and enforcing arbitration under the New York Convention rules. Other provisions of NAFTA permit arbitration only between the member countries rather than arbitration with private companies.[29] Another variation is found at the WTO, where the panel process between states alone is supplemented by the right of appeal. WTO member countries wanted to ensure that the international trade law is applied consistently and narrowly across cases. Enforcement under the WTO, however, remains with each country's executive branch rather than its court system.

Table 27.1 outlines the different types of international regimes available for resolving disputes and examines different factors that make up these regimes. The first factor, "direct effect," refers to whether the settlement is immediately enforceable as a matter of domestic law, or whether a separate domestic proceeding must occur. Second, "standing" indicates whether only countries

Table 27.1. International Dispute Resolution Regimes and Their Different Factors.

Factors / *Regimes*	*Direct Effect*	*Standing for Private Actors*	*Supremacy*	*Transparency*	*Enforcement*
Negotiation	No	No	None	Optional	Negotiation
Investment arbitration	Yes	Yes	Only as to that award	Optional	Likely
International adjudication	No	No	Supreme, but not integrated into domestic law	Yes	Varying: None (NAFTA) to Retaliation (WTO)
Supranational Court	Yes	Yes, directly and indirectly	Supreme and integrated	Yes	Fines and damages; domestic remedies also

Source: "Getting Along: The Evolution of Dispute Resolution Regimes in International Trade Organizations," *Michigan Journal of International Law,* 1999, *20,* 697. Reprinted with permission of Andrea K. Schneider.

or also individuals can bring a case. The third column, "supremacy," shows whether a ruling is supreme and trumps domestic law. If the ruling is not supreme, then countries are not required to follow it. Transparency is the issue of how open and understandable the process is. Are the opinions published? Does the public have access to the oral arguments and briefs? If the process is transparent, more parties are likely to use the process as well as grant it legitimacy. The final factor is enforcement and punishment; whether there are ramifications for ignoring a ruling. For example, the European Court of Justice can award damages to an individual harmed by lack of action on the part of a country, and these awards are enforceable in the country's domestic courts.

International Regimes Available for Resolving Disputes

The challenge moving forward in international dispute resolution is to be creative and flexible in developing institutions to resolve disputes. The Internet Corporation for Assigned Names and Numbers (ICANN) is an example of such a creative institution. Any party who believes that a domain name should belong to him or her can lodge a complaint with ICANN under its dispute settlement procedures. For example, Harvard University could file a complaint with ICANN to settle a dispute over ownership of a Website at Harvard.com.[30] Serving both private and public parties, ICANN uses arbitration to resolve these disputes in a timely and fair fashion.[31]

PARALLEL ISSUES IN DOMESTIC AND INTERNATIONAL DISPUTE RESOLUTION

There are many interesting and evolving parallel questions in domestic and international dispute resolution. The most striking difference between the two is the question of mediator neutrality. In the domestic context, most scholars and commentators have argued that mediators ought to remain neutral.[32] In the international context, however, such a concern is virtually unheard of—perhaps because the concept of neutrality holds such a different meaning in the international arena.

There are also two intriguing parallels—the question of representing a constituency in a negotiation leading to "two-level" diplomacy and the evolution of arbitration and adjudication processes to meet the changing needs of the parties and disputes.

Three additional parallel debates are interesting to examine. First, both domestic and international mediation practitioners often debate the appropriateness of different approaches to mediation. For example, domestic mediators disagree over the primacy of the so-called "transformative" approach to mediation. This approach emphasizes how disputants deal with one another, with the particular resolution of a specific dispute a secondary purpose. While some mediators prefer this practice, others worry that the transformative approach is either unnecessary or harmful when the real point of the mediation is to resolve the dispute. This debate is mirrored in the ongoing debates about how to intervene in international disputes. Some theorists argue, much like transformative mediation practitioners, that long-term international dispute resolution is only possible with the transformation of the relationship between the factions. Other theorists argue that solving the problem and ending the violence must take priority over retraining the parties to think differently about the conflict and each other. These theorists might agree, for example, that rewriting textbooks in an effort to change underlying mind-sets may be a noble cause. In the face of costly, ongoing conflict, however, they would argue that an immediate goal of relationship-building and cultural change is too remote.

A second debate concerns which disputes should be settled by a court versus which should employ some other dispute resolution process. Domestically, this debate has continued with the growth of ADR as some theorists argue that settlement is bad for the justice system.[33] There has also been some debate about the merits of diplomacy versus the judicialization of international disputes.[34] Is it better for the United States and the European Union to negotiate disputes over tariffs that favor certain former European colonies, or is it better for the WTO to resolve the disputes?[35] Some international relations experts lament the loss of diplomatic flexibility that accompanies judicialization, while others laud the creation of international courts as the true sign of progress in relations between countries.

Finally, the use of mandatory arbitration for consumer disputes remains very controversial in the academic literature on arbitration (although quite settled in the courts at the moment).[36] Those who disfavor mandatory arbitration argue that arbitration is the wrong process for the uninformed and obligated public who buy a computer, apply for a credit card, or use the hospital emergency room. Similarly, there is some debate about what cases the WTO should hear. While the WTO may be a suitable process for trade disputes, critics argue that too many other disputes are being swept into WTO jurisdiction under the rubric of trade. These critics argue that environmental and human rights cases were not meant to be decided under trade law by a group of trade experts.[37] Others argue that the expansion of the WTO process is a positive development that allows more cases to be uniformly decided.

CONCLUSION

Understanding how international dispute resolution operates can help us understand where dispute resolution started, how it has developed, and what international and domestic dispute resolution contexts can take from each other in order to work best. It is important to recognize that much of mediation has its roots in native practices from around the world, while domestic arbitration's roots are a history of successful international commercial cases. As international interactions developed and changed, so have dispute resolution processes changed to meet these needs in a variety of ways that should inspire ongoing domestic experimentation. Finally, debates about with whom to negotiate, mediator neutrality, and appropriate subject matter for dispute resolution can provide interesting reflections and counterparts to evolving domestic discussions.

Notes

1. See E. Walsh, "The Negotiator," *The New Yorker,* March 18, 1996, pp. 86–97.
2. See J. Z. Rubin and F.E.A. Sander, "Culture, Negotiation, and the Eye of the Beholder," *Negotiation Journal,* 1991, *7,* 249–254.
3. See J. K. Sebenius, "Caveats for Cross-Border Negotiations," *Negotiation Journal,* 2002, *14,* pp. 121–134; and J. W. Salacuse, "Ten Ways That Culture Affects Negotiating Style: Some Survey Results," *Negotiation Journal,* 1998, *14,* 221–240.
4. See *United Nations Convention on Contracts for the International Sale of Goods,* April 10, 1980, S. Treaty Doc. No. 98–99.

5. See, for example, *Hague Convention on the Recognition and Enforcement of Foreign Judgments in Civil and Commercial* Matters, 144 United Nations Treaty Series 249, February 1, 1971.
6. See F.E.A. Sander and J. Rubin, "The Janus Quality of Negotiation: Dealmaking and Dispute Settlement," *Negotiation Journal,* 1988, *4,* 109–113.
7. See *Military and Paramilitary Activities in and Against Nicaragua (Nicaragua* v. *United States),* 1986 International Court of Justice 14 (June 27, 1986).
8. See, for example, Sir Ernest Mason Satow, *Satow's Guide to Diplomatic Practice,* ed. Lord Gore-Booth (London: Longman, 1979). An early example of a mutual defense is the treaty between the Jews and Romans, circa 160 B.C. See M. W. Janis and J. E. Noyes, *International Law Cases and Commentary* (St. Paul, Minn.: West Publishing Company, 2001).
9. See N. Machiavelli, *The Prince* (2nd ed.), trans. H. Mansfield (Chicago: University of Chicago Press, 1998).
10. See, for example, A. Slaughter, "International Law and International Relations Theory: A Dual Agenda," *American Journal of International Law,* 1993, *87,* 205–244.
11. See I. W. Zartman and M. R. Berman, *The Practical Negotiator* (New Haven, Conn.: Yale University Press, 1982).
12. See R. Fisher, E. Kopelman, and A. K. Schneider, *Beyond Machiavelli: Tools for Coping with Conflict* (Cambridge, Mass.: Harvard University Press, 1994).
13. See R. D. Putnam, "Diplomacy and Domestic Politics: The Logic of Two-Level Games," in P. Evans, H. Jacobson, and R. Putnam (eds.), *Double-Edge Diplomacy: International Bargaining and Domestic Politics* (Berkeley, Calif.: University of California Press, 1993), pp. 431–468.
14. See R. H. Mnookin, "When Not to Negotiate: A Negotiation Imperialist Reflects on Appropriate Limits," *University of Colorado Law Review,* 2003, *74,* pp. 1077–1097.
15. See R. E. Hayes, S. R. Kaminski, and S. M. Beres, "Negotiating the Non-Negotiable: Dealing with Absolutist Terrorists," *International Negotiation,* 2003, *8,* 451–467.
16. See G. O. Faure, "Negotiating with Terrorists: The Hostage Case," *International Negotiation,* 2003, *8,* 469–494.
17. See "Negotiating with Terrorists and Non-State Actors: The Journey to World Peace," Symposium 4, *The Cardozo Journal of Conflict Resolution,* 2003.
18. For example, the American Arbitration Association has both expanded overseas and expanded into offering mediation services (American Arbitration Association, "International Centre for Dispute Resolution"). [http://www.adr.org/index2.1.jsp?JSPssid=15732]; and [http://www.adr.org/index2.1.jsp?JSPssid=15732&JSPsrc=upload < \\ > LIVESITE < \\ > focusArea < \\ > international < \\ > AAA175 current.htm]. Last visited October 2004.
19. See M. A. Levitt, "Kilometer 101: Oasis or Mirage? An Analysis of Third-Party Self-Interest in International Mediation," *Mediation Quarterly,* 1997, *15,* 155–176.

20. See I. W. Zartman, "The Timing of Peace Initiatives: Hurting Stalemates and Ripe Moments," in J. Darby and R. M. Ginty (eds.), *Contemporary Peacemaking: Conflict, Violence and Peace Processes,* Vol. 19 (New York: Palgrave Macmillan, 2003).
21. Zartman, "The Timing of Peace Initiatives," 2003, p. 19.
22. See J. P. Lederach, "Cultivating Peace: A Practitioner's View of Deadly Conflict and Negotiation," in J. Darby and R. M. Ginty (eds.), *Contemporary Peacemaking: Conflict, Violence and Peace Processes,* Vol. 33 (New York: Palgrave Macmillan, 2003).
23. See R. Ricigliano, "Networks of Effective Action: Implementing an Integrated Approach to Peacebuilding," *Security Dialogue,* 2003, *34*(4), 445–462.
24. See United Nations, New York Convention on the Recognition and Enforcement of Foreign Arbitral Awards, New York, June 1958.
25. See M. W. Janis, *An Introduction to International Law* (New York: Aspen Publishers, 2003).
26. See *Case Concerning Delimitation of the Maritime Boundary in the Gulf of Maine Area,* 1984 International Court of Justice 246 (Oct. 12, 1984).
27. See http://www.un.org/Depts/los/index.htm for a description of the tribunal.
28. See *Loewen Group, Inc. and Loewen* v. *United States,* Case No. ARB (AF)/98/3 (2003).
29. See, for example, *Cross-border Trucking Services,* NAFTA Ch. 20 Arb. Trib., February 6, 2001. [http://www.worldtradelaw.net/nafta20/truckingservices.pdf]. Last visited October 2004.
30. See Internet Corporation for Assigned Names and Numbers (ICANN). [http://www.icann.org/dndr/udrp/policy.htm]. Last visited September 2004.
31. See E. Katsh, J. Rifkin, and A. Gaitenby, "E-Commerce, E-Disputes, and E-Dispute Resolution: In the Shadow of E-Bay Law," *Ohio State Journal on Dispute Resolution,* 2000, *15,* 705–727.
32. For a different view of mediator responsibility, see L. Susskind, "Environmental Mediation and the Accountability Problem," *Vermont Law Review,* 1981, *6,* 1–47.
33. See O. Fiss, "Against Settlement," *Yale Law Journal,* 1984, *93,* 1073–1090.
34. See, for example, E. Petersmann, "Constitutionalism and International Organizations," *Northwestern Journal of International Law & Business,* 1966–1967, *17,* 398–451.
35. See, for example, J. L. Dunoff, S. R. Ratner, and D. Wippman, *International Law Norms, Actors, Process* (New York: Aspen Law & Business, 2002), discussing the Banana Wars between the United States and the European Union at the World Trade Organization.
36. See J. R. Sternlight, "Rethinking the Constitutionality of the Supreme Court's Preference for Binding Arbitration: A Fresh Assessment of Jury Trial, Separation of Powers, and Due Process Concerns," *Tulane Law Review,* 1997, *72,* 1–99; and

J. R. Sternlight, "Panacea or Corporate Tool? Debunking the Supreme Court's Preference for Binding Arbitration," *Washington University Law Quarterly,* 1996, *74,* 1–11.

37. See G. C. Shaffer, "The World Trade Organization Under Challenge: Democracy and the Law and Politics of the WTO's Treatment of Trade and Environment Matters," *Harvard Environmental Law Review,* 2001, *25,* 1–92; and J. Atik, "Identifying Antidemocratic Outcomes: Authenticity, Self-Sacrifice, and International Trade," *University of Pennsylvania Journal of International Economic Law,* 1998, *19,* 229–253.

[2]

Correspondences and Contradictions in International and Domestic Conflict Resolution: Lessons from General Theory and Varied Contexts

*Carrie Menkel-Meadow**

I. Introduction: Is General Theory Possible?

Does the field of conflict resolution have any broadly applicable theories that "work" across the different domains of international and domestic conflict? Or, are contexts, participants, and resources so "domain" specific and variable that only "thick descriptions" of particular contexts will do? These are important questions which have been plaguing me in this depressing time for conflict resolution professionals, from September 11, 2001 (9/11), to the war against Iraq. Have we learned anything about conflict resolution that really does improve our ability to describe, predict, and act to reduce unnecessary and harmful conflict? These are the questions I want to explore in this essay, all the while knowing that I will ask more questions than I have answers to. My hope is to spark more rigorous

---

* Professor of Law, Georgetown University, and Director, Georgetown-Hewlett Program in Conflict Resolution and Legal Problem Solving. Thanks especially to my colleague and friend Jean Sternlight for her invitation, hospitality, and intellectual stimulation. Thanks to the remarkable program of Dispute Resolution at the University of Missouri-Columbia for its interest, faculty, students, and on-going production of new knowledge and practice. Some of these thoughts were sparked by my participation in the 2002 Hewlett Conference on "Practice to Theory" in New York in March 2002, which focused on conflict theory and practice in hostage settings, international disputes and conflicts, community and church conflicts and approaches to conflict resolution, and the events of September 11, 2001. For some of the thoughts that stimulated me there, see the special issue of NEGOTIATION JOURNAL devoted to the conference, vol. 18, No. 4 2002, edited by Sandra Cheldelin, Melanie Greenberg, Christopher Honeyman, and Maria R. Volpe. Thanks to my wonderful colleagues in the Culture and Conflict Resolution Group in Washington D.C. (Kevin Avruch, Carol Izumi, Melanie Greenberg, Howard Gadlin, Christopher Honeyman, Homer LaRue, Donna Stienstra, and Wally Warfield) whose conversations on these and other topics in the last few years has deeply enlightened and engaged me. And finally, thanks to a variety of my international and comparative law colleagues at Georgetown who have permitted my "transboundary" (and somewhat amateur) incursion into their field as I travel the actual globe with intellectual and practical exports, with, I hope, the right amount of wonder and humility.

attention to the possibility of "comparative dispute resolution" study and practice, using key concepts, theories, empirical studies, practical wisdom, and experiential insights to spark and encourage more "multi-level" and multi-unit analysis of some of our "shared" propositions.

I begin with some skepticism that our efforts to create a "general" theory of conflict resolution across widely different domains is in fact possible, although I have tried to define it and explain it myself.[1] Perhaps it is the condition of the world at the present moment, teetering at the edge of a fragility unknown to even the survivors of the Cold War and World War II, due to the unpredictable, non-nation state possibilities of "viral" conflicts and "wars." Or, perhaps it is my sociological bent to see the "varieties" in human behavior and the "conditions" of human situations, rather than the "grand meta-theories" of some forms of social theory and science, but I think that at present, our field of conflict resolution has little in the way of generalizable propositions that work (explain, describe, predict, and prescribe) across all domains.

I do not mean that we have no accumulated learning or "mid-level" theories or organizing frameworks to structure our knowledge bases and facilitate our "practical reasoning" (for those of us who are practitioners, as well as theorists, researchers, and teachers). I will review some of that "propositional knowledge" here (and others have also done creditable syntheses of what we know already),[2]

---

1. *See* Carrie Menkel-Meadow, *Alternative Dispute Resolution*, *in* ENCYCLOPEDIA OF THE BEHAVIORAL AND SOCIAL SCIENCES (2001); Carrie Menkel-Meadow, *Alternative Dispute Resolution*, *in* LEGAL SYSTEMS OF THE WORLD (Herbert Kritzer ed., 2002); Carrie Menkel-Meadow, *Alternative Dispute Resolution*, *in* OXFORD COMPANION TO AMERICAN LAW (Kermit Hall ed., 2002); Carrie Menkel-Meadow, *Conflict Resolution*, *in* ENCYCLOPEDIA OF COMMUNITY (2003); Carrie Menkel-Meadow, *Conflict Theory*, *in* ENCYCLOPEDIA OF COMMUNITY (2003).

2. *See* KEVIN AVRUCH, CULTURE AND CONFLICT RESOLUTION (1998) [hereinafter AVRUCH, CULTURE]; BARRIERS TO CONFLICT RESOLUTION (Kenneth Arrow et al. eds., 1995); Morton Deutsch, *Cooperation and Conflict: A Personal Perspective on the History of the Social Psychological Study of Conflict*, *in* INTERNATIONAL HANDBOOK OF ORGANIZATIONAL TEAMWORK AND COOPERATIVE THINKING (M.A. West et al. eds., 2003) [hereinafter Deutsch, *Cooperation and Conflict*]; THE HANDBOOK OF CONFLICT RESOLUTION: THEORY AND PRACTICE (Morton Deutsch & Peter T. Coleman eds. 2000) [hereinafter THE HANDBOOK]; MORTON DEUTSCH, THE RESOLUTION OF CONFLICT: CONSTRUCTIVE AND DESTRUCTIVE PROCESSES (1973); ROGER FISHER, ET AL., COPING WITH INTERNATIONAL CONFLICT: A SYSTEMATIC APPROACH TO INFLUENCE IN INTERNATIONAL NEGOTIATION (1997); FRED. C. IKLE, HOW NATIONS NEGOTIATE (1964); INTERNATIONAL NEGOTIATION: ANALYSIS, APPROACHES, ISSUES (Victor A. Kremnyuk ed., 2d ed. 2002) [hereinafter INTERNATIONAL NEGOTIATION]; LOUIS KRIESBERG, CONSTRUCTIVE CONFLICTS: FROM ESCALATION TO RESOLUTIONS, (2d ed. 2002); HUGH MIALL ET AL., CONTEMPORARY CONFLICT RESOLUTION: THE PREVENTION, MANAGEMENT AND TRANSFORMATION OF DEADLY CONFLICTS (1999); DEAN PRUITT ET AL., SOCIAL CONFLICT: ESCALATION, STALEMATE AND SETTLEMENT (1986); HOWARD RAIFFA ET AL., NEGOTIATION ANALYSIS: THE SCIENCE AND ART OF COLLABORATIVE DECISION MAKING (2002); JEFFREY Z. RUBIN & BERTRAM BROWN, THE SOCIAL PSYCHOLOGY OF BARGAINING AND NEGOTIATION (1975); STUDIES IN INTERNATIONAL MEDIATION: ESSAYS IN HONOR OF JEFFREY Z. RUBIN (Jacob Bercovitch ed., 2002) [hereinafter STUDIES IN INTERNATIONAL MEDIATION]; MICHAEL WATKINS & SUSAN ROSEGRANT, BREAKTHROUGH INTERNATIONAL NEGOTIATION: HOW GREAT NEGOTIATIONS TRANSFORMED THE WORLD'S TOUGHEST POST-COLD WAR CONFLICTS (2001); Kevin Avruch, *Type I and Type II Errors in Culturally Sensitive Conflict Resolution Practice*, 20 CONFLICT RESOL. Q. 351 (2003). This is a very partial bibliography of some of the scholarly works which have attempted field synthesis. Any reader will be struck with the relative lack of inter-penetration of fields, that is mutual citations from domestic (United States) negotiation and conflict resolution, and international relations treatments of conflict resolution. Some of this is changing with funding (Hewlett Foundation and other initiatives), practice (Search for Common Ground's new domestic initiatives, *at* http//:www. sfcg.org (last visited Nov. 20, 2003), and a newer generation of scholars who are working

but I want to explore some of the divergences of domestic conflict resolution from international conflict resolution studies and suggest that we might profitably learn by studying contrasts, exposing level or unit errors of generalization and analysis, rather than hoping we will uncover or describe "deep structures" that will inform our work at all levels of conflict. While there are some very interesting analogies, metaphors, classifications, taxonomies, and occasionally, even a "concept"[3] that work across levels and domains, I suggest here that those occasions may be rarer than we think and often may be misleading. I prefer the "thick description"[4] of sociology and anthropology that tells us that context may matter a great deal, as does the history, culture, personality, situations, geography, economics, and politics that construct those contexts.[5] While we in the field of conflict resolution have been pushing hard to learn lessons from our case studies so that we can ask "how is the Mideast crisis like Northern Ireland?" or "what do disputes between different ethnic and racial groups in the United States teach us about possible peaceful co-existence in other multi-ethnic nation-states?," I have come to think that we may be better off asking "how is Northern Ireland different from the Mideast crisis?" and "what makes each multi-ethnic nation-state different in its

in both fields. How many younger students of our field know that the book ROGER FISHER & WILLIAM URY, GETTING TO YES (Bruce Patton ed., 2d ed., Penguin Books 1991) (1981) was inspired by Fisher's earlier work in international conflict, ROGER FISHER, INTERNATIONAL CONFLICT FOR BEGINNERS (1969), not by domestic legal disputes? This failure to read, learn, and cite outside the boundaries of our limited fields has been lamented in the "theory-practice" divide, in the "legal" vs. "other professions" division in domestic conflict resolution (or "ADR") and in the division between trade (private) negotiations and diplomatic and human rights (public) negotiations in the international field.

3. As explored more fully in the text, notions of "ripeness," "deadlines," and "shape of the table" (participating parties), "dual-track negotiations" (public and private, caucus and no-caucus or "shuttle diplomacy"), and "relationship building" (from familial to international relations) have transcended domains and have served useful explanatory and prescriptive functions across domains.

4. *See* CLIFFORD GEERTZ, LOCAL KNOWLEDGE (1983).

5. There is a growing literature, both in anthologies and book-length treatments, of richly described case studies of conflict resolution "stories," told both to "thickly describe" those contexts and to attempt to elucidate "patterns" or teachings for generalizable descriptions, predictions, and prescriptions for the field. I like to call these "peace stories." *See* PETER ACKERMAN & JACK DUVALL, A FORCE MORE POWERFUL: A CENTURY OF NON-VIOLENT CONFLICT (2000); LAWRENCE BACOW & MICHAEL WHEELER, ENVIRONMENTAL DISPUTE RESOLUTION (1984); GAIL BINGHAM, RESOLVING ENVIRONMENTAL DISPUTES: A DECADE OF EXPERIENCE (1986); THE CONSENSUS BUILDING HANDBOOK: A COMPREHENSIVE GUIDE TO REACHING AGREEMENT (Lawrence Susskind et al. eds., 1999) [hereinafter THE CONSENSUS BUILDING HANDBOOK]; THE DISPUTING PROCESS: LAW IN TEN SOCIETIES (Laura Nader & Harry F. Todd. eds., 1978); FORGIVENESS AND RECONCILIATION: RELIGION, PUBLIC POLICY AND CONFLICT TRANSFORMATION (Raymond G. Helmick et al. eds., 2001); HERDING CATS: MULTIPARTY MEDIATION IN A COMPLEX WORLD (Chester Crocker et al. eds., 1999); MICHAEL IGNATIEFF, BLOOD AND BELONGING: JOURNEYS INTO THE NEW NATIONALISM (1993); SUSAN COLLIN MARKS, WATCHING THE WIND: CONFLICT RESOLUTION DURING SOUTH AFRICA'S TRANSITION TO DEMOCRACY (2000); MEDIATION IN INTERNATIONAL RELATIONS: MULTIPLE APPROACHES TO CONFLICT MANAGEMENT (Jacob Berkovitch & Jeffrey Z. Rubin eds., 1992); GEORGE J. MITCHELL, MAKING PEACE (1999); RESOLVING INTERNATIONAL CONFLICTS: THE THEORY AND PRACTICE OF MEDIATION (Jacob Bercovitch ed., 1996); CARMEN SIRIANI & LEWIS FRIEDLAND, CIVIC INNOVATION IN AMERICA: COMMUNITY EMPOWERMENT, PUBLIC POLICY AND THE MOVEMENT FOR CIVIC RENEWAL (2001); TURBULENT PEACE: THE CHALLENGES OF MANAGING INTERNATIONAL CONFLICT (Chester Crocker et al. eds., 2001) [hereinafter TURBULENT PEACE]; WORDS OVER WAR: MEDIATION AND ARBITRATION TO PREVENT DEADLY CONFLICT (Melanie Greenberg et al. eds., 2000) [hereinafter WORDS OVER WAR]; *see also* Robert Malley & Hussein Agha, *Camp David: The Tragedy of Errors*, 48 NEW YORK REV. BOOKS 59 (2001).

approaches to 'dealing with diversity?'" What is the significance of "difference" that may illuminate what we can know about conflict resolution across different domains? To explore that question in a reasonable time and space here, I will limit myself to a few propositional examples of conflict resolution "knowledge":

1. Structures of conflicts and conflict resolution;

2. Processes of conflicts and conflict resolution;

3. Concepts in conflict resolution (such as "deadlines," "ripeness," "needs and interests," and "relationships");

4. People in conflict (their motivations, choices, socialization, and variability); and finally,

5. Alternatives to conflict or conflict resolution.

My hope is to set an agenda for a richer exploration of "comparative dispute resolution." Like the questioning academic and practitioner that I am, I remain somewhat skeptical, or at least agnostic, about whether those of us who are "conflict resolution professionals" can ply our trades, whether theoretical, empirical, or practical, across all domains simultaneously.

I focus here on three aspects of conflict resolution across domains:

1. The development of a relatively well-developed, if contested, body of knowledge about the theory and practice of conflict resolution in the American "domestic" sphere, notably, negotiation,[6] mediation,[7] and other forms of "ADR" interventions in legal, community, environmental, commercial, family, public policy, and other kinds of disputes or conflicts;[8]

6. *See* MAX BAZERMAN & MARGARET NEALE, NEGOTIATING RATIONALLY (1992); FISHER & URY, *supra* note 2; DAVID LAX & JAMES SEBENIUS, THE MANAGER AS NEGOTIATOR (1986); ROBERT MNOOKIN ET AL., BEYOND WINNING: NEGOTIATING TO CREATE VALUE IN DEALS AND DISPUTES (2000); RAIFFA, *supra* note 2; WILLIAM ZARTMAN & MARGARET BERMAN, THE PRACTICAL NEGOTIATOR (1982); Carrie Menkel-Meadow, *Toward Another View of Legal Negotiation: The Structure of Problem Solving*, 31 UCLA L. REV. 754 (1984) [hereinafter Menkel-Meadow, *Toward Another View*].

7. *See* ROBERT BARUCH BUSH & JOSEPH FOLGER, THE PROMISE OF MEDIATION (1994); KIMBERLEE KOVACH, MEDIATION (2003); CHRISTOPHER MOORE, THE MEDIATION PROCESS (3d ed. 2003); Leonard Riskin, *Understanding Mediators' Orientations, Strategies and Techniques*, 1 HARV. NEG. REV. 7 (1996).

8. CARRIE MENKEL-MEADOW, LELA LOVE, ANDREA KUPFER SCHNEIDER & JEAN STERNLIGHT, APPROPRIATE DISPUTE RESOLUTION: BEYOND THE ADVERSARIAL MODEL FOR DISPUTE PROCESSING, LEGAL PROBLEM SOLVING AND CONFLICT RESOLUTION (forthcoming 2004); CARRIE MENKEL-MEADOW, DISPUTE PROCESSING AND CONFLICT RESOLUTION: THEORY, PRACTICE AND POLICY (2003); JACQUELINE NOLAN-HALEY, ALTERNATIVE DISPUTE RESOLUTION IN A NUTSHELL (2d ed. 2002).

2. The relationship of international relations theory[9] and conflict resolution theory, research and practice in diplomatic, nation-state, human rights, and other "public" conflicts,[10] and trade,[11] business, and "private" conflict resolution;[12] and,

3. The highly contested "exportation" of American-style dispute resolution to both the international arena and to national or "domestic" nations, systems, or cultures outside of the United States.[13]

II. THREE TRUE STORIES

A. Culture Matters

Like many dispute resolution professionals, I began to be asked in the mid-1980s to "go abroad" and teach "negotiation," "mediation," or "conflict resolution" in a wide variety of other countries, with widely different "needs and interests." In some cases the invitations came from lawyers who just wanted some of the new American "skills training" in negotiation in traditional legal matters; in other cases, innovative legal educators were interested in developing experiential learning and clinical programs; in other cases, the focus was on developing institutions alternative to governmental structures (because of corruption or distrust in the conventional institutions, or for desires to develop innovative and alternative

9. *See* BENEDICT ANDERSON, IMAGINED COMMUNITIES (1991); TED ROBERT GURR, PEOPLES VERSUS STATES: MINORITIES AT RISK IN THE NEW CENTURY (2000); DONALD HOROWITZ, ETHNIC GROUPS IN CONFLICT (1985); SAMUEL P. HUNTINGTON, POLITICAL ORDER IN CHANGING SOCIETIES (1969); INTERNATIONAL REGIMES (Stephen D. Krasner ed., 1983); NEOREALISM AND ITS CRITICS (Robert O. Keohane ed., 1986); STEPHEN M. WALT, THE ORIGINS OF ALLIANCES (1987); KENNETH N. WALTZ, THEORY OF INTERNATIONAL POLITICS (1979).

10. *See* ROGER FISHER ET AL., BEYOND MACHIAVELLI: TOOLS FOR COPING WITH CONFLICT (1994). *See also* Fen Osler Hampson, *Parent, Midwife or Accidental Executioner? The Role of Third Parties in Ending Violent Conflict*, *in* TURBULENT PEACE, *supra* note 5; Louis Kriesberg, "The Growth of the Conflict Resolution Field," *in* TURBULENT PEACE, *supra* note 5; Saadia Touval & I. William Zartman, "International Mediation in the Post-Cold War Era," *in* TURBULENT PEACE, *supra* note 5; *see* sources cited *supra* note 5.

11. *See* JOHN JACKSON, THE JURISPRUDENCE OF GATT AND WTO (2001); Andrea Kupfer Schneider, *Getting Along: The Evolution of Dispute Resolution Regimes in International Trade Organizations*, 20 MICH. J. INT'L L. 697 (1999).

12. *See* JEANNE M. BRETT, NEGOTIATING GLOBALLY (2001); DEAN ALLEN FOSTER, BARGAINING ACROSS BORDERS (1992); JESWALD SALACUSE, MAKING GLOBAL DEALS (1991).

13. *See* THOMAS CAROTHERS, AIDING DEMOCRACY ABROAD (1999); YVES DEZALAY & BRYANT G. GARTH, DEALING IN VIRTUE (1996); JOHN PAUL LEDERACH, PREPARING FOR PEACE (1995); Raymond Cohen, *Negotiating Across Cultures*, *in* TURBULENT PEACE, *supra* note 5; Laura Nader & Elisabetta Grande, *Current Illusions and Delusions about Conflict Management – In Africa and Elsewhere*, 27 LAW & SOC. INQUIRY 573 (2002) [hereinafter Nader, *Current Illusions and Delusions*]; Elizabeth Mertz, *Introduction* to *From the Trenches and Towers: Current Illusions and Delusions About Conflict Management in Africa and Elsewhere*, 27 LAW & SOC. INQUIRY 567 (2002). *See also* Staff Reporters, *State Department Seeks Proposals to Promote ADR Overseas*, ADRWORLD.COM, July 18, 2002, *at* http://adrworld.com (suggesting different uses of arbitration, mediation, and negotiation in different regions of the world, and requesting proposals for training and exchange programs); Symposium, *Export/Import: American Civil Justice in a Global Context*, 52 DEPAUL L. REV. 253-675 (2002); Department of State Notice 4064, 67 Fed. Reg. 46008 (July 11, 2002) (requesting grant proposals for "cooperative international projects to introduce American and Foreign participants to each other's social, economic, and political structures).

structures, even where there was no caseload delay problem); in yet other cases, the needs were more urgent, seeking effective ways to solve intractable problems (of human co-existence, of environmental harm, or scarce resource allocation). I resisted many of these invitations to interesting and exotic places, not because I don't like to travel (I do), but because as a sociologically trained lawyer, I was exquisitely sensitive to what I thought were the cultural determinants and variants of how and why particular processes might work in particular places and institutions and I was reluctant to assume that American-style "problem-solving negotiation" or the ethnocentric "mediative talking cure"[14] would work in other places. After some years of giving academic papers and talks, but not doing "trainings," I was persuaded to do some negotiation and mediation training in two places I thought "closest" to American culture, a Scandinavian country[15] and the United Kingdom. Training programs in negotiation and mediation are participatory, experiential, and call for role-playing and demonstrations of activities—in short, active and "public" learning. In the late 1980s and early 1990s, just before much of this material we study and the practices we use actually caught on, I found both sets of lawyers quite traditional, reticent, and fearful of American-style "informality." Everyone was very polite, and while both nations have, in fact, heartedly endorsed many of these processes,[16] there was a definite and formal chill in the air (different from the loud and brash hostility of American lawyers who would resist negotiation, mediation, and ADR training because they thought I wanted to "kill the lawyers").[17] European lawyers liked their formality, notarized documents, and expertise which hierarchically separated them from clients needing their help. As strange as our practices of formal discovery might be, openly "sharing," not only facts, but "feelings," "interests," and "needs" did not go over well in those earlier days in traditional legal settings.

Fast forward a decade or more, when after some forays into "informal" Australia, mediation-experienced Japan (in a different way, of course),[18] and our imitative sister up north (Canada),[19] all with greater success, I began to teach negotia-

14. *See* Carrie Menkel-Meadow, *The Many Ways of Mediation: The Transformation of Traditions, Ideologies, Practices and Paradigms*, 11 NEGOTIATION J. 217 (1995).

15. Which shall go nameless here–you should hear the nationalist jokes the Scans tell on each other . . . even Garrison Keillor might be offended. *See* GARRISON KEILLOR, A PRAIRIE HOME COMPANION PRETTY GOOD JOKE BOOK at 140-52 (2000). Do we need some conflict resolution jokes to get us through these trying times?

16. I was quite active in England during the drafting of the Woolf Report on Civil Justice Reform which requires some forms of dispute resolution and gives management control of cases to judges in a mixture of American and European styles of adjudication. *See* Lord Woolf, *Access to Justice-Interim Report to the Lord Chancellor on the Civil Justice System in England and Wales* (June 1995), *at* http://www.lcd.gov.uk/civil/interfr.htm; *see also* Carrie Menkel-Meadow, *The Future(s) of Civil Litigation: Dream or Nightmare: Lessons from the American Experience*, *in* SHAPING THE FUTURE: NEW DIRECTIONS IN LEGAL SERVICES (Roger Smith ed., 1995); Carrie Menkel-Meadow, *Will Managed Care Give Us Access to Justice?*, *in* ACHIEVING CIVIL JUSTICE (Roger Smith ed., 1996).

17. A complaint I actually received in a mediation training program for family lawyers in Los Angeles in the mid-1980s.

18. *See* Taimie L. Bryant, *Family Models, Family Dispute Resolution and Family Law in Japan*, 14 UCLA PAC. BASIN L.J. 1 (1995).

19. I have taught in Canada a great deal, at the University of Toronto, Osgoode Hall, University of British Columbia, Victoria, etc. I am formally on the faculty of Osgoode's LL.M. program in ADR, which actually pre-dated any formal graduate law programs in ADR in the United States. So, some-

tion, mediation, and ADR in South America (in among other places, the land where there are more psychiatrists per capita than here–Argentina!). Instead of reticence, I was met with great enthusiasm as lawyers, clients, government officials, diplomats, and others more willingly embraced both informality (even in highly bureaucratic cultures and legal systems) and the "talking cure." Indeed, everyone was talking so fast, my weak Spanish skills were soon left behind as the skilled simultaneous translators I worked with tried to find appropriate words for our American concepts.[20]

I don't want to be what I have come here to criticize, a cultural stereotyper who oversimplifies or homogenizes cultures, whether national, governmental, or professional, but some "cultures" do assimilate and use this "conflict resolution technology" better than others. Time, of course, had moved on, bringing with it, regional trading groups like NAFTA, the EU, and Mercosur (forcing some interpenetration of legal cultures just to do business), but my experience in South America was different from that in Europe and is quite different from that of the early pioneers who went to Russia and Eastern Europe after the fall of the Berlin Wall,[21] or to some other countries with totally corrupt legal systems (some places I won't name here, in our own hemisphere).

What lessons have we learned? Culture matters. "Talking" cultures like Argentina, Paraguay, and other Latin American cultures, closer to us culturally and demographically, as well as geographically and geologically, than our own so-called "motherland," the UK, may, in some circumstances, be more amenable to "exportation" and assimilation of our forms of dispute resolution than some other places, including those whose legal systems appear closer to our own (common law vs. civil law). Of course, different cultures and legal systems will adapt and use our structures and processes to meet their own needs, so there may be both adaptation and "deformation" of our exports, a subject I'll return to below. But, it is wrong, in my view, to say that we can easily export American-style ADR anywhere, and equally wrong to say that it is always wrong and imperialistic to do so.[22] Exportation of ADR techniques and theories must be culturally and politically sensitive to the host nations or cultures and recognize that ADR, like American-style democracy,[23] Constitutionalism, or litigation can be abused,[24] corrupted,

---

times we have to imitate too. There are now several LL.M. programs in the United States, including at the University of Missouri-Columbia and Georgetown University.

20. Nothing dramatizes "intercultural work" more than working with translators (in my case from several different Spanish-speaking countries) as they try to capture the nuances and colloquial expressions of concepts slightly different from or "alien" to their own varied cultures. For example, in translating some of the standard video tapes I use (CPR's business mediation tape, *Prosando vs. High Tech* or the Center for Mediation in Law's *Saving the Last Dance: Mediation through Understanding* (intellectual property and employment)), highly technical and "emotional" terms of art, like "caucusing," "looping," and "reframing" may be difficult to capture, even with (or perhaps especially with) translators who are certified "legal or diplomatic translators."

21. *See* Emily Stewart Haynes, *Mediation as an Alternative to Emerging Post-Socialist Legal Institutions in Central and Eastern Europe*, 14 OHIO ST. J. ON DISP. RESOL. 257 (1997); Kathryn Hendley, *The Spillover Effects of Privatization in Russian Legal Culture*, 5 TRANSNAT'L. L. & CONT. POLS. 39 (1995); Raymond Shonholtz, *Conflict Management Training: A Transformative Vehicle for Transitional Democracies*, 2 INT'L NEG. J. 21 (1997).

22. *See* Nader, *Current Illusions and Delusions*, *supra* note 13.

23. *See* CAROTHERS, *supra* note 13 (evaluating the success of our "democratization" projects abroad). *See also* Cynthia Alkon, "*The Cookie Cutter Syndrome: Legal Reform Assistance Under Post-Communist Democratization Programs*, 2002 J. DISP. RESOL. 327; Christopher Honeyman &

or transformed when it is "transplanted." On a more optimistic note, it may also be that totally new or unfamiliar systems, like some forms of American mediation or arbitration, may actually turn out to be the *lingua franca* or new "common denominator" in regional systems of trade or diplomacy when there is distrust or lack of knowledge of differing legal traditions, just as international arbitration has been used to avoid or transcend the complexities of international litigation.[25]

B. *"When Will They Ever Learn?": Does Theory Inform or Explain the Modern World?*

Now that I teach, practice, and study abroad, I have joined the international cadre of conflict resolution professionals teaching, training, and even mediating and arbitrating in many other locations. As the international scholar, teacher, and practitioner that I have somewhat reluctantly become, I have immersed myself in international relations theory and its own intellectual disputes as well as read countless case studies of the work of our brothers and sisters who have always been international conflict resolution professionals (whether by formal training or governmental authority, such as Henry Kissinger, Jimmy Carter, George Mitchell, and Dennis Ross—all skilled conflict resolution interveners with little or no formal training in the mediation and negotiation skills we rigorously teach our students). To read from recently published reports of the "successes" of Camp David, the Oslo channel, the Dayton Accords, and, most depressingly, the "successful" North Korean nuclear proliferation negotiations of 1993-1995,[26] is to realize how unstable and how resistant to generalizations these "successes" have been. Even with the full power and insights of academic and diplomatic "intelligence," as well as our decades of experience in complex bi-lateral and multilateral situations, so many of our "trouble spots" are ready to explode again–perhaps with far more deadly force or animosity than ever before. And of course, there is 9/11 and the "clash of civilizations"[27] that has replaced the schism of the Cold War with a more insidious and largely undefined polarity of the "axis of evil" versus an unidentified whom—us, the good Allies? And just who are our allies now anyway? Clearly, even with all of the teaching and learning of conflict resolution, negotiation theory, structural vs. "international society" schools, and

---

Sandra Cheldelin, "*Have Gavel, Will Travel: Dispute Resolution's Innocents Abroad*," CONVENOR NEWSLETTER, (Convenor Conflict Resolution, Madison, Wis.), *available at*, http://www.convenor.com/madison/gavel.htm (last visited Nov. 22, 2003); Symposium, *The Americanization of International Dispute Resolution*, OHIO ST. J. ON DISP. RESOL. (forthcoming 2003).

24. In systems where there are corrupt judicial systems, ADR, or the use of mediation or arbitration, is not likely to be a corrective. If judges can be bribed (or killed, as in Colombia), then private arbitrators or mediators are much easier to "control," both by those with power, whether legitimate or not, and money. *Cf.* Thomas J. Moyer & Emily Stewart Haynes, *Mediation As a Catalyst for Judicial Reform in Latin America*, 18 OHIO ST. J. ON DISP. RES. 619 (2003).

25. *See, e.g.*, ANDREAS F. LOWENFIELD, INTERNATIONAL LITIGATION AND ARBITRATION (2d ed. 2002).

26. *See* Rock Tang, "*The North Korea Nuclear Proliferation Crisis*," *in* WORDS OVER WAR, *supra* note 5; WATKINS & ROSEGRANT, *supra* note 2.

27. *See* AMY CHUA, WORLD ON FIRE (2003); CULTURE MATTERS: HOW HUMAN VALUES SHAPE HUMAN PROGRESS (Lawrence E. Harrison & Samuel P. Huntington eds., 2000); THOMAS L. FRIEDMAN, THE LEXUS AND THE OLIVE TREE: UNDERSTANDING GLOBALIZATION (1999); SAMUEL HUNTINGTON, THE CLASH OF CIVILIZATIONS (1996).

post-Cold War cosmopolitanism[28] or "the end of history,"[29] we are no closer to world peace than we ever were, and perhaps we are a good deal more distant from it. It is a depressing time to be in conflict resolution. How ephemeral are our "successes"; how quickly scuttled are decades worth of detente and understanding only to be undermined by "networks" of "crazies, crusaders, or criminals"[30] or more predictably, "regime changes," whether by election or by force!

What lessons have we learned? None, I fear. To quote from two of my favorite songs of the Sixties: "Yes, and how many deaths will it take/ till he knows/ that too many people have died?"[31] "When will they ever learn,/ when will they ever learn?"[32] I do wonder if we have "learned" anything in international diplomatic activity, derived from all of the "flowering" of theory and practice in conflict resolution in the last two or three decades. How do leaders, policy makers, and diplomats learn and use, if at all, the teachings of our field?[33] And, more depressingly and dramatically, what assumptions of rationality, world views, and desired ends—"peaceful co-existence," survival, democracy, and capitalism[34]—do our theories make? Can we have a theory to use when dealing with those who do not share the assumptions on which our theories are constructed?[35]

C. Context is Everything: We Cannot Over-Generalize

Last spring, I moderated a session at a conference on "'Practice to Theory' in Conflict Resolution"[36] involving several skilled law enforcement experts in negotiating with hostages, in primarily domestic-urban settings. The theory of the conference planners was that we would learn from the practitioners in extreme negotiation situations about what theory informed their practice and what lessons from negotiation "in extremis" might serve us in more "ordinary" settings (like simple and complex lawsuits). I learned several things from that interaction: first,

28. IGNATIEFF, *supra* note 5; MICHEAL WALZER, ON TOLERATION (1997).

29. Francis Fukuyama, "The End of History," THE NAT'L INT., 1989, *at* http://www.marxists.org/reference/subject/philosophy/works/us/fukuyama.htm (last visited Nov. 22, 2003).

30. *See* Jack Cambria et al., *Negotiation Under Extreme Pressure: The "Mouth Marines" and the Hostage Takers*, 18 NEGOTIATION J. 331 (2002).

31. BOB DYLAN, *Blowin in the Wind*, *on* THE FREEWHEELIN' BOB DYLAN (Columbia Records 1963).

32. PETER, PAUL & MARY, *Where Have All The Flowers Gone?*, *on* PETER, PAUL & MARY (Sanga Music Inc.-BMI 1962).

33. Like many of us, as a student of conflict resolution, I start each day by scanning the news for any evidence that our current lead "negotiators" and global strategists are demonstrating any knowledge of negotiation or conflict resolution theory. We may "win" the war, but in my view Saddam Hussein is the only one who has mastered the techniques of negotiation–holding his "concessions" to the end and embarrassing the bravura of our unilateral actions–let's see where we are when this is published. Military might might dominate over negotiation, but that is short-term victory, the longer term will certainly be more complicated.

34. We are not, alas, at "the end of history" with democratic capitalism regnant. *See* Fukuyama, *supra* note 29.

35. This is the global or "cross-cultural" version of what I used to call the $64,000 question (now $1 million?) in "domestic" legal negotiation. How can you be a problem-solver when the other side doesn't share your goals or ends, or want to play your game? *See*, FISHER & URY, *supra* note 2, at 107-43, 153-54.

36. The conference was sponsored by the Hewlett Foundation, George Mason University's Institute for Conflict Analysis and Resolution, and the City University of New York's Dispute Resolution Consortium, and it was held at John Jay College of Criminal Justice and at the United Nations.

there was little theory that was useful "in the moment" to these skilled negotiators. They developed that "je ne sais quoi" we call "judgment" from years of experience[37] and could make terrible mistakes if their "calls" were wrong (often based on rather primitive taxonomies like "crazies, crusaders, and criminals").[38] Second, their taxonomies or classifications were developed post hoc, because they needed to transmit their learning to new recruits, juniors in the field who were now "educated" in classrooms, as well as in the field of experience – a form of field "inductive" method of hypothesis generation.[39] It sounded pretty crude – three categories of hostage takers with appropriately adapted techniques and approaches for negotiation.[40] Where would the 9/11 terrorists be in that taxonomy? Third, and most interestingly, the experienced hostage negotiators articulated a very clear negotiation plan–"just keep them talking" (which is where they got their nickname, "the mouth marines"), keep people safe, and "end the interaction. We are not problem-solvers."[41]

So, this kind of negotiation is radically different from the kind of "deep problem-solving" that negotiators seeking Pareto-optimal,[42] pie expanding, or creative solutions would be engaged in. Context matters. Hostage negotiators are fascinating and necessary to our survival, but ultimately, may have very little to tell us about negotiations that are not about hostages. The ability to generalize both their theory and practice may, in fact, be quite limited. Negotiations with hostages may have their own goals and ends ("end it safely and as quickly as possible," don't take on solving the underlying problems), techniques (keep talking and "never say no"), and categories ("crazies, crusaders, and criminals"), which produce "stock" responses or scripts, and role divisions (separate the talkers-negotiators from the tactical forces who may have to shoot if negotiations fail).

Experienced hostage negotiators have now accumulated enough knowledge from hundreds of situations that they think they have developed structures, processes, techniques, and theories. And then there was Waco.[43] Even within similar "contexts," people who don't fit the categories, or changes in personnel or leadership or failure to coordinate action, or any number of things can make even the most context-specific theories fail. As hostage negotiators define their roles to act in relatively "short-term" settings (usually no more than twenty-four hours), when a "situation" goes longer, as in Waco, the structures, processes, and interventions may have to change. Just taking care of the "short-term" safety may not be enough.

37. *See* GARY KLEIN, SOURCES OF POWER: HOW PEOPLE MAKE DECISIONS (1998) (describing the "pattern recognition" form of learning that characterizes those who make decisions in emergent situations (such as firefighters)).

38. *See* Cambria, *supra* note 30.

39. *See* ROBERT EMERSON, CONTEMPORARY FIELD RESEARCH (1998); CAROL H. WEISS, EVALUATION (2d ed. 1997); SOCIAL SCIENCE RESEARCH AND DECISION–MAKING (1980).

40. One of these skilled negotiators has turned his "theory in use" (see DONALD SCHON, THE REFLECTIVE PRACTITIONER (1983)) into more "c's"–context, conversation, containment. Cambria, *supra* note 30, at 334.

41. *Id.* at 335.

42. *See* RAIFFA, *supra* note 2.

43. JAYNE SEMINARE DOCHERTY, LEARNING LESSONS FROM WACO: WHEN THE PARTIES BRING THEIR GODS TO THE NEGOTIATION TABLE (2001).

What lessons have we learned? Even seemingly tightly circumscribed contextual domains may be difficult to generalize about and certainly some contexts are so specific they do not lend themselves to any further generalization. Will 9/11 happen again? Waco? What can we or should we learn in this situation that is useful for other "similar" situations? What can we define as "similar"? Is hostage taking of ones' own community (Waco) the same as taking hostages in a 7-Eleven store, in a foreign embassy (Iran, Peru), on American property abroad, or of a part of one's own "nation" (Palestinians, Tutsis)? And how can we avoid the opposite bias, of seeing too much "similarity" when there is none—the distortions of recentness and vividness causing us to "over-generalize" from our most recent experience and see causal patterns from after the fact, otherwise known as the "hindsight bias."[44]

Let us explore what lessons we have, and can, learn more systematically from attempts to generalize conflict resolution theories across domains. My argument here is that I think we may actually learn more from exploring "differences" or "contradictions" in the application of general theories to more discrete conflict resolution domains, than attempting to build grand, general theories across dissimilar contexts. I will use a few illustrative examples here, from attempts to generalize theory about structure, process, common "concepts," personnel involved in and alternatives to conflict and conflict resolution.

III. STRUCTURES OF CONFLICT AND CONFLICT RESOLUTION

Negotiation and conflict resolution theory, like international relations theory in political science, have developed "models" or "structures" of explanatory frameworks. These are schemas (often with accompanying pictures, charts, and graphs) plotting the structure of conflict and cooperation that expand, deflate, escalate and then resolve, settle, or exhaust a dispute or conflict. There has been some convergence and coordination of theoretical structures in both domestic and international conflict.[45] From anthropologist P.H. Gulliver's mapping of alternating processes of conflict, contention, concession, and conciliation, derived from negotiations in African moots and other "foreign" locales[46] (or the alternation of "virtuous and vicious cycles" in negotiations), to the adaptation of such models to the stages and phases of negotiation in litigation (orientation-opening, agenda setting, demands-conflicts, bargaining-brainstorming, concessions-problem-

44. *See* BAZERMAN & NEALE, *supra* note 6; Leigh Thompson & Janice Nadler, *Judgmental Biases in Conflict Resolution and How to Overcome Them*, *in* THE HANDBOOK, *supra* note 2.

45. Of course each field has its own internal debates and disputes about which pictures, charts, and graphs are most accurate, even with widely disparate and contested approaches. In conflict resolution, we continue to debate whether disputes are more likely to be distributive (zero-sum), requiring competitive behaviors, or integrative (using problem-solving and coordination behaviors). *See* P. Terrence Hopmann, *Bargaining and Problem Solving: Two Perspectives on International Negotiation*, *in* TURBULENT PEACE, *supra* note 5, at 445; James J. White, *The Pros and Cons of Getting to Yes*, 34 J. LEGAL. EDUC. 115 (1984); Roger Fisher, *Comment to James J. White's article "The Pros and Cons of Getting to Yes,"* 34 J. LEGAL EDUC. 120 (1984). In international relations, theorists and empiricists argue about "realism" vs. "liberalism" and "power structural" vs. "international society" conceptions of inter-state conflicts and interventionism. *See, e.g.*, Jack S. Levy, *Theories of Interstate and Intrastate War: A Levels-of-Analysis Approach*, *in* TURBULENT PEACE, *supra* note 5, at 3.

46. P.H. GULLIVER, DISPUTES AND NEGOTIATIONS: A CROSS CULTURAL PERSPECTIVE (Sandra B. Burman & Barbara E. Harrell-Bond eds., 1979).

solving, agreement, execution)[47] and in mediation[48] (opening statements, ground rules, narratives-statement of issues, needs, interests, facilitated negotiation and problem solving, dealing with conflict, agreement, reality testing and execution)[49], conflict resolution has "structures."[50] These structures, or theoretical frameworks, organized in the minds of both theorists and empirical students of conflict resolution revolve around some seemingly "universal" or generalized patterns—the dilemmas of competition and cooperation,[51] the strategic sharing of information to either reveal or hide one's "true bottom line or reservation price," the dilemmas of trust and strategy, depending on whether goals are self-interest maximization or some form of joint problem solving,[52] the assumptions of tacit, but operational, social norms[53] such as reciprocity and fairness,[54] the difficulties of acting in situations of uncertainty[55] and when a host of identified social, cognitive, and other "biases" hinder accurate information processing,[56] and motivations and goal satisfaction are hard to measure. These identified patterns have in turn given shape to something that often looks like a football or soccer field: two polarized sides competing for "ground" on a scale, usually, of monetary values (but this easily becomes land and power in international settings).

In turn, we have identified a variety of transdisciplinary "concepts," such as the ZOPA or zone of possible agreement,[57] bottom lines or reservation prices, Pareto optimality-efficiency frontiers (when we move to a two axis, multi-issue negotiation that looks remarkably like a supply and demand curve from economics)[58] and now BATNAs[59] (best alternative to a negotiated agreement), WATNAs (worst alternative to a negotiated agreement), and ATNA's (all or any alternatives

---

47. *See* Carrie Menkel-Meadow, *The Stages and Phases of Negotiation*, *in* David Binder & Carrie Menkel-Meadow, ABA LAWYERING SKILLS PROGRAM, INSTRUCTORS' MANUAL (1983) [hereinafter Menkel-Meadow, *Stages*]; GERALD R. WILLIAMS, LEGAL NEGOTIATION AND SETTLEMENT (1983).

48. MOORE, *supra* note 7; KOVACH, *supra* note 7.

49. *See* Center for Mediation in Law, Mediation Training Materials, The Five Stages of Mediation, at 2 (2002).

50. I. William Zartman, *The Structure of Negotiation*, *in* INTERNATIONAL NEGOTIATION, *supra* note 2, at 71. Note this article is titled "the" structure of negotiation, not "a" structure of negotiation or "the structures" of negotiation.

51. See works of Morton Deutsch in social psychology, *supra* note 2.

52. Denominated the "creating and claiming" negotiation dilemma by two scholars who have worked in many domains. *See* LAX & SEBENIUS, *supra* note 6.

53. Legal scholar Mel Eisenberg argued long ago that negotiations, both within the litigation and transaction settings, were characterized by attention to "norms," including both behavioral norms and substantive or "legal norms." Melvin Eisenberg, *Private Ordering Through Negotiation: Dispute Settlement and Rulemaking*, 89 HARV. L. REV. 637 (1976). The newer version of this argument is Robert H. Mnookin & Lewis Kornhauser, *Bargaining in the Shadow of the Law: The Case of Divorce*, 88 YALE L.J. 950 (1979).

54. BAZERMAN & NEALE, *supra* note 6.

55. JUDGMENT UNDER UNCERTAINTY: HEURISTICS AND BIASES (Daniel Kahneman et al. eds., 1982); RICHARD NISBETT & LEE ROSS, HUMAN INFERENCES: STRATEGIES AND SHORTCOMINGS OF SOCIAL JUDGMENT (1980).

56. BARRIERS TO CONFLICT RESOLUTION, *supra* note 2; Chris Guthrie et al., *Inside the Judicial Mind*, 86 CORNELL L. REV. 777 (2001); Donald C. Langevoort, *Behavioral Theories of Judgment and Decision Making in Legal Scholarship: A Literature Review*, 51 VAND. L. REV. 1499 (1998); Robert H. Mnookin, *Why Negotiations Fail: An Exploration of Barriers to the Resolution of Conflict*, 8 OHIO ST. J. ON DISP. RESOL. 235 (1993).

57. RAIFFA, *supra* note 2, at 108.

58. *See id.* at 263.

59. FISHER & URY, *supra* note 2.

to a negotiated agreement)[60] for purposes of measuring and deciding accurately between and among "best, worst and most likely" scenarios in litigation decision trees[61] or strategic military or diplomatic negotiations.

We have also derived something close to a few "scientific propositions" such as:

> 1. High demands and aspirations generally do better in distributive negotiation games unless there is stalemate or walk-out because the high demand is so unreasonable it terminates the negotiation;[62]
>
> 2. The predicted outcome of a two-party, single issue (pricing) negotiation will very often be the mid-point between the first two demands (a "split the difference" outcome);[63]
>
> 3. Matters will often "settle" for values that are closer to the transaction costs ("nuisance value") than any rational economic or other merit value in the matter;[64] and,
>
> 4. Reciprocated cooperation may be more robust and gain-producing than competitive defection (in repeated or iterated interactions).[65]

Similarly, virtually all negotiation texts, treatises, and analyses develop some version of the three or four choices of "strategies," "styles," or "behavioral repertoires" that must be chosen: competition (contending, dominating, claiming), yielding (cooperating, compromising), problem-solving (collaborating, integrating, creating),[66] or "mixed"[67] strategies.

More formal international relations models of global negotiation and conflict resolution theory have the same ideational "base," even if more elaborately explained. "Structural" analysis focuses on the dynamics of bi-polar systems (the Cold War) versus more multi-lateral and "international systems" approaches to strategic conflict strategies and management. As in legal conflict resolution, there are issues of representation problems, such as agent-principal, constituency man-

---

60. These are my terms, in use for years, but many negotiation analysts have used their own versions of this recognition that many kinds of alternatives have to be weighed in making choices during a negotiation or other conflict resolution process.

61. *See* Marjorie Corman Aaron & David P. Hoffer, *Decision Analysis as a Method of Evaluating the Trial Alternative*, *in* DWIGHT GOLANN, MEDIATING LEGAL DISPUTES: EFFECTIVE STRATEGIES FOR LAWYERS AND MEDIATORS (1996).

62. RAIFFA, *supra* note 2, at 109-28. *See also* Russell Korobkin & Chris Guthrie, *Opening Offers and Out-of-Court Settlement: A Little Moderation May Not Go A Long Way*, 10 OHIO ST. J. ON DISP. RESOL. 1 (1994).

63. RAIFFA, *supra* note 2, at 109-28.

64. Janet Cooper Alexander, *Do the Merits Matter? A Study of Settlements in Securities Class Actions*, 43 STAN. L. REV. 497 (1991).

65. ROBERT AXELROD, THE COMPLEXITY OF COOPERATION (1997); ROBERT AXELROD, THE EVOLUTION OF COOPERATION (1984).

66. *See* I. WILLIAM ZARTMAN, RIPE FOR RESOLUTION: CONFLICT AND INTERVENTION IN AFRICA (updated ed. 1989); FISHER & URY, *supra* note 2; Menkel-Meadow, *Stages*, *supra* note 47; Mary Parker Follett, *Constructive Conflict*, *in* PROPHET OF MANAGEMENT (Pauline Graham ed., 1996).

67. LAX & SEBENIUS, *supra* note 6.

agement, and power analysis. But international relations must deal with multiple actors and focus on "unit" analysis, identifying the negotiators as states, leaders, individual diplomats, regional coalitions, or international bodies. The structure is made more complex and can't be played entirely on a bi-lateral soccer field.

It is no accident that there are seemingly many "correspondences" in structural analyses of conflict resolution across domestic and international domains. The theories of these structures emanate from essentially the same source–post World War II and Cold War "game theory,"[68] which elaborated a number of "games" or "hypothetical" strategic and mathematical simulations, most notably, but not exclusively, "the Prisoner's Dilemma"[69] game. This game in particular models how two parties, and then more than two parties, choose to act under conditions of variable communication rules and with variable pay-off schemes. Proliferating studies (in various laboratory and other "simulated" settings, including recently developed computer tournaments) were designed to elaborate "optimal strategies" for specified conditions, based on Cold War (and mostly bi-lateral) scenarios. The template which has emerged from this rich vein of research has been "mined" and applied to so many forms of negotiated and strategic interactions, it is often difficult to remember that they are still "games," and games with many assumptions built into the "rules."

Without denying the usefulness of game theoretic insights for elucidating structures and "moves" in elaborated hypothetical situations, it is also useful to consider the assumptions on which these maps and structures have been built. Until relatively recently, conflict resolution in law and related areas focused almost exclusively on two-party games, assuming plaintiffs and defendants in a litigation structure, with specified information rules (discovery in litigation, modified by more "disclosing" negotiation customs). More recently, work in domestic negotiation has recognized that in domestic legal disputes, as in the international arena, most conflicts and disputes are multi-party,[70] requiring new maps and theories. Coalition theory and group process theory,[71] long used in international relations, are making their way into domestic and legal conflict resolution theory, with borrowed learning from sociology and social psychology,[72] but the theoretical power may be limited in different contexts.

---

68. *See* AVINASH DIXIT & SUSAN SKEATH, GAMES OF STRATEGY (1999); R. DUNCAN LUCE & HOWARD RAIFFA, GAMES AND DECISIONS (1957); JOHN VON NEUMANN & OSKAR MORGENSTERN, THEORY OF GAMES AND ECONOMIC BEHAVIOR (1967).

69. *See* WILLIAM POUNDSTONE, PRISONER'S DILEMMA 11-64 (1992). *See also* DOUGLAS BAIRD ET AL., GAME THEORY AND THE LAW (1998).

70. *See* Carrie Menkel-Meadow, *The Trouble With the Adversary System in a Postmodern, Multicultural World*, 38 WM. & MARY L. REV. 5 (1996).

71. *See* LEIGH L. THOMPSON, MIND AND HEART OF THE NEGOTIATOR 188-219 (2d ed. 2000); Gary Goodpaster, *Coalitions and Representative Bargaining*, 9 OHIO ST. J. ON DISP. RESOL. 243 (1994); Cass R. Sunstein, *Deliberative Trouble? Why Groups Go to Extremes*, 110 YALE L. J. 71 (2000).

72. *See* Solomon Asch, *Effects of Group Pressure Upon the Modification and Distortion of Judgments*, *in* GROUP LEADERSHIP AND MEN (H. Guetzkow ed., 1951); ROBERT B. CALDINI, INFLUENCE: THE PSYCHOLOGY OF PERSUASION (1993); Deutsch, *Cooperation and Conflict*, *supra* note 2; IRVING L. JANIS, GROUPTHINK (1983); JOSEPH LUFT, GROUP PROCESSES (3d ed. Mayfield Publishing Co. 1984) (1963); STANLEY MILGRAM, OBEDIENCE TO AUTHORITY: EXPERIMENTAL VIEW (1983); Stanley Milgram, *Behavorial Study of Obedience*, 67 J. ABNORMAL PSYCHOL. & SOC. PSYCHOL. 371 (1963).

Game theory and strategy in conflict resolution all too often assume rationality, individual gain maximization, whether from an economic or power perspective and externally manipulated information endowments. This assumption of rational gain or rational choice has been increasingly questioned by anthropologists who challenge its "cultural" assumptions,[73] political scientists and social psychologists who question its empirical reality,[74] and feminist theorists who question its epistemological origins.[75] What if most disputes are not two-party? What if maximizing "gain," however measured, is not the only goal? What if communication is not binary (on or off), but a combination of revelations, guarded sharing, reciprocal messages, misleading statements, and outright deceptions, which are themselves "negotiated"? What if the players in the game are not all playing with the same pay-off structure (goals or ends) or resources with which to play the game? What if new games are introduced, such as "Truth and Reconciliation Commissions" which are neither punishment ("prisoner's dilemma") nor restorative (mediation) but some new mixture of confession, accountability, and forgiveness?[76] How do the new "games" get written into the canon that creates the structures and maps of our theory?[77]

In a provocative book, political scientist Benjamin Miller has recently argued that polarized opponents, such as in the Cold War, were actually able to engage in a variety of cooperative activities because of the "balance" produced by nuclear deterrence. This in turn introduced more predictability into world conflicts than the current unstable multi-national post-Cold War alignments.[78] Two hegemons, the Soviet Union and the United States, could restrain more "minor disputes" within their spheres of influence, as well as "contain" each other. With unilateral action (of one hegemon) or diffusion of power with many multiple actors, some forms of restraint and control of conflict are removed, and alliance and regional influence declines with an increase in local conflicts. How prescient Miller was—his work was written long before our recent failures to develop a "coalition" within our own NATO alignment on disarming and warring with Iraq. Diffusion of power may actually make some forms of cooperation less likely in international relations. Miller's structures, which divide intended and unintended conflicts and

73. *See* AVRUCH, CULTURE, *supra* note 2; Kevin Avruch, *Culture and Negotiation Pedagogy*, 16 NEGOTIATION J. 339 (2000).

74. *See* BEYOND SELF-INTEREST (Jane Mansbridge ed., 1990); DONALD P. GREEN & IAN SHAPIRO, PATHOLOGIES OF RATIONAL CHOICE THEORY (1994); JANE J. MANSBRIDGE, BEYOND ADVERSARY DEMOCRACY (1994).

75. *See* CONFLICT AND GENDER (Anita Taylor & Judi Beinstein Miller eds., 1994); GENDER, PEACE AND CONFLICT (Inger Skjelsboek & Dan Smith eds., 2001); Deborah M. Kolb, *More than Just a Footnote: Constructing a Theoretical Framework for Teaching about Gender in Negotiation*, 16 NEGOTIATION J. 347 (2000); Carrie Menkel-Meadow, *Negotiating with Lawyers, Men and Things: The Contextual Approach Still Matters*, 17 NEGOTIATION J. 257 (2001); Carrie Menkel-Meadow, *Teaching about Gender and Negotiation: Sex, Truths and Videotape*, 16 NEGOTIATION J. 357 (2000).

76. *See* MARTHA MINOW, BETWEEN VENGEANCE AND FORGIVENESS: FACING HISTORY AFTER GENOCIDE AND MASS VIOLENCE (1998).

77. In a classic example of sociological "labeling" theory, the very name of the game can alter behaviors in the game. *See* Lee Ross, *Reactive Devaluation in Negotiation and Conflict Resolution*, *in* BARRIERS TO CONFLICT RESOLUTION, *supra* note 2 (showing that the games, although identical in content, called "Wall Street" or "Social Work" produced different behaviors in the players). *See also* Robert H. Frank et al., *Do Economists Make Bad Citizens?*, 10 J. ECON. PERSP. 187 (1996); Robert H. Frank et al., *Does Studying Economics Inhibit Cooperation?*, 7 J. ECON. PERSP. 159 (1993).

78. BENJAMIN MILLER, WHEN OPPONENTS COOPERATE (2002).

cooperative acts among conflicting and cooperating nation-states and regional coalitions, is an example of the kind of rigorous and far more complex "modeling" we need to understand the varieties of contexts in which conflict resolution is practiced.[79] Note, however, that for all the criticism of bi-polarism in modern dispute resolution theory, Miller's thesis suggests that a powerful "two-party" game may actually have led to more stability or "equilibria" points, in game theoretic terms.

Miller suggests that with the demise of the two-party power "balance," new models might be necessary, such as a return to a nineteenth century notion of a "concert" of nations, which produced more "peace" in part of the nineteenth century than we had in the twentieth.[80] His models may turn out to be too rigid as well as too dependent, in my view, on the interesting results that come from aggregating data on world conflicts, a quantitative "game" that social scientists play to look for Durkheimian "social facts"[81] and patterns that may not be visible to the "naked eye." In my view, this fascinating effort at knowledge acquisition makes many errors of "unit analysis." It is virtually impossible to "code" all the variables that go into each global conflict (such as the measures of intra-national and international "incidents" of violence, economic factors, political party structures, ethnic-religious demographics, weapons, and other resource measures) though some have argued we should begin to develop such data bases for domestic, as well as international, conflicts and disputes.[82] Miller also demarcates "crisis management" (e.g. Cuban missile crisis) from more "normal" efforts at international conflict management and cooperation (resource sharing, war prevention, peaceful interventions, etc.), suggesting that, as with domestic hostage negotiations, we may need to have separate models and structures for "short-term" emergent situations and longer-term, iterated negotiations and conflict prevention interventions.

Sadly, however, Miller, like the reporters of "successes" in North Korea and the Mideast in the mid-1990s, cannot do much to explain a post-9/11 world. With multi-national loyalties (Al Qaeda and other militant and fundamentalist Arab organizations) and new technologies for communication and sabotage, some have

---

79. *Id.*

80. *Id.*

81. *See* EMILE DURKHEIM, SUICIDE (John A. Spaulding & George Simpson trans., reissue ed. 1997); Carrie Menkel-Meadow, *Durkheimian Epiphanies: The Importance of Engaged Social Science in Legal Studies*, 18 FLA. ST. L. REV. 91 (1990).

82. There has been a very active debate on the possibilities of developing metrics for measuring conflict and dispute resolution successes at the domestic level, well behind the work already conducted by quantitative international relations scholars. *See* Cary Coglianese, *Is Satisfaction Success? Evaluating Public Participation in Regulatory Policy Making*, *in* THE PROMISE AND PERFORMANCE OF ENVIRONMENTAL CONFLICT RESOLUTION (Rosemary O'Leary & Lisa A. Bingham eds., 2003); JAMES S. KAKALIK ET AL., JUST, SPEEDY AND INEXPENSIVE? (2000) (featuring the debate around the issuance of the RAND study of court management devices and ADR in federal courts); DONNA STIENSTRA ET AL., REPORT TO THE JUDICIAL CONFERENCE COMMITTEE ON COURT ADMINISTRATION AND CASE MANAGEMENT: A STUDY OF THE FIVE DEMONSTRATION PROGRAMS ESTABLISHED UNDER THE CIVIL JUSTICE REFORM ACT OF 1990, (The Federal Judicial Center 1997); LAWRENCE SUSSKIND ET AL., MEDIATING LAND DISPUTES: PROS AND CONS (Lincoln Land Institute April 2000); Cary Coglianese, *Empirical and Experimental Methods of Law: Empirical Analysis and Administrative Law*, 2002 ILL. L. REV. 1111 (2002); Craig A. McEwen & Elizabeth Plapinger, *Rand Report Points Way to Next Generation of ADR Research*, DISP. RESOL. MAG., Summer 1997, at 10; Carrie Menkel-Meadow, *When Dispute Resolution Begets Disputes of Its Own: Conflicts Among Dispute Professionals*, 44 UCLA L. REV. 1871 (1997).

called our current conditions a "viral war," where the stateless "enemies" move easily through porous boundaries of both physical and computer space, issuing decentralized, non-state, non-"party" orders or "authority" for actions to be taken, not "negotiated."

Other analysts have noted that not only *who* we have conflicts with, but *what* we have disputes about may further particularize and change our theoretical structures–whether we consider current international conflicts as driven by ideology (democracy vs. fundamentalism) or resources (oil, labor, water etc.). Fault lines of conflict and regional and global cooperation and competition may change the "neighborhoods" of disputing and alter both geographical lines of demarcation, as well as geo-political lines of negotiation, alignments, and potential zones of violence.[83] What happens when a neighborhood or community dispute escalates to a global dispute? Is there any useful analogy from our major urban conflagrations and search for national peace? Here, the structural component is a strong national government, with multiple layers of social control, whether by law enforcement or multiple political entities. The power and legitimacy of our "international government," while always contested, seems increasingly divided and weak, not to mention without its own legitimate legal enforcement mechanisms.[84] The structures and theories of conflict resolution must also take into account "maps" of the regime (or absences) of law and legal institutions standing as "back-ups" to the negotiation and mediative processes currently being described.

It is not clear what the ZOPAs, BATNAs, and "bottom lines" are in some of these modern international conflicts. It is quite clear, however, that we are not playing on a soccer field—our "turf" has been "invaded" and so we planned an unauthorized incursion onto a whole other field. The globe, by the way, is round, not flat, and it is time, I think, to have the pictures of our theories conform to spatial reality. Efforts to create multi-lateral coalitions are failing as I write (things will likely be different by the time this is published) and Miller's hopes for a conflict preventing "concert" of democratic nations to act as a sort of self-appointed third party neutral (more in the med-arb model than the "pure mediator") does not appear to be taking shape. Our opponents, whomever they currently are (Saddam Hussein, Kim Il Sung, Osama Bin Laden and Al Qaeda), may be playing a "prisoner's dilemma game," but maximizing their own well being does not appear to be a major goal. "Freedom's just another word for nothing left to lose," as Janis Joplin would say.[85]

The assumptions of the pictures and structures we have developed for domestic negotiation and conflict resolution models do not translate well when we are dealing with non-rational actors. Perhaps negotiating with hostage takers will have more relevance, but I doubt it, because we are likely to damage many innocent people when the tactical forces come in and we have not been very successful at the "keep them talking" strategy. Negotiation and conflict resolution models and structures assume that we want to keep playing games together (the great

83. Michael T. Klare, *The New Geography of Conflict*, 80 FOREIGN AFF. 49 (2001).

84. When the superpower refuses to acknowledge the international court, it is hard to know how enforcement will be achieved. Behind the pictures of football fields and prisoners' cells lies a court, a state, a referee, or some third party, with ultimate ability to "force" a solution if a consensual one is not reached.

85. JANIS JOPLIN, *Me and Bobby McGee*, *on* PEARL (Columbia 1971).

relief of the resolution of the Cuban missile crisis was that the Soviets did want to keep playing, not dying) and that we can "map" moves on a two-dimensional space. While expanding our models and pictures to include multi-lateralism (internationally) and multi-partyism (in American domestic disputes) has begun to change the structures slightly, I think we are prisoners of our own game. These structures (of two-party mini-max games) are so strongly imbedded in our learning, and our leaders' consciousnesses, that I know even I still process and analyze all negotiations through these lenses. Increasingly, I think there is something wrong with these pictures. While it would be nice to have the scientific rigor of a negotiation structure that worked across domains, I don't think we currently have one. It might behoove us to start imagining, creating, thinking about, and drawing some "structures" that more accurately describe the particularity of the situations, both internationally and domestically. How about photography with its specificity, rather than abstract graphs?

IV. PROCESSES OF CONFLICT AND CONFLICT RESOLUTION

In many ways the study and practice of conflict and conflict resolution originated in international dispute resolution. International relations, peace studies, and anthropological studies of disputing outside of the United States all predate the "modern" ADR movement.[86] Nevertheless, the techniques, technology, and apparatus of conflict resolution "processes" are much more professionalized and developed in domestic dispute resolution. From the proliferation of texts and training programs in negotiation, mediation, facilitation, consensus building, and now dialoging, the domestic dispute resolution field has professionalized, if not fully credentialed, its practical knowledge base. Techniques are offered for problem-solving, integrative and principled bargaining, interest-based bargaining in labor negotiations,[87] mediation as a general process, and mediation tailored to environmental, intellectual property, community, family, and commercial disputes. The technology of dispute resolution is a growing import-export business. Almost anyone who has been trained as a mediator can turn around and train others—a slavish adherence to the medical model of clinical education—"see one, do one, teach one." Some professionals in the field were trained domestically and now work internationally (I am one of those); others began working internationally (perhaps at high levels of diplomacy, with or without training) and now work domestically (many former politicians, Cabinet officers, and state department officials); others are experts in particular geographical areas of the world, or in particular subject matters of disputes, and a whole cadre of diplomats, retired judges, and other "elder statesmen" become mediators, arbitrators, and negotiators

86. For a well-told history of mediation, arbitration, and conciliation in the United States, see JEROLD S. AUERBACH, JUSTICE WITHOUT LAW? (1983). However, the modern dispute resolution movement, in law, is usually dated from the 1976 Pound Conference where Frank Sander delivered his "Varieties of Dispute Processing" paper, subsequently to be termed the "Multi-Door Courthouse." Frank E.A. Sander, *Varieties of Dispute Processing*, 70 F.R.D. 111 (1976).

87. *See* RICHARD E. WALTON ET AL., STRATEGIC NEGOTIATIONS: A THEORY OF CHANGE IN LABOR-MANAGEMENT RELATIONS (1994) (specifying propositions derived from a "strategic" approach to negotiations in the changed labor-management context, distinguishing the "social contract" (on-going goals) from the "substantive outcomes" (particularities in the final agreements)).

by virtue of their status or prior achievements in the world, without any formal training at all.

With the increased sensitivity to different process technologies and differentiation of processes, it is easy to see some of the correspondences of techniques and also some of the dangers of moving from one level to another. In mediation, for example, the separate "caucus" sessions at which parties reveal their real "underlying interests" can be likened to the "back channels" or "dual-track" negotiations of diplomatic disputes. The same tensions between public and transparent proceedings and more secretive and confidential meetings exist in both realms, though the role of the press, democratic government processes, and the sheer numbers of people involved may make disclosure slightly more likely in international settings. At the same time, the likely fact of multiple layers of negotiators makes it more possible to actually have totally secret negotiations take place (including the "fictionalized" "Walk in the Woods")[88] in the international arena.

There are also some correspondences in the role of representatives and the internal negotiations of constituencies, like clients with lawyers, union members with union negotiators, governments with diplomats, and the larger polity and the formal state, but these analogies should not be taken too far.[89] Internal negotiations in international matters are often as complex as any "across the table" negotiations and because international negotiations are often binding on a full polity with generational effects, ratification by those actually affected by a negotiation is quite different from other agent-led negotiations, if it exists at all.

The role of third parties varies in different contexts, though again, there has been some borrowing (mostly one-way in my view and mostly not for the better) from the international sphere to the domestic. The notion of the embedded and interested "wise elder" as mediator cum shuttle diplomat has been growing since Henry Kissinger's many efforts in the Mideast. Senior diplomats and government officials from the United States, with clear geo-political interests of their own, have been intervening in disputes as mediators, arbitrators, and "judges" for several decades now, and sadly, in my view, this idea of the enmeshed mediator (or mediator with "muscle" or "expertise") has now infiltrated public policy, legal, and even family disputes, returning to some of the ancient inspirations for the mediator in rural cultures where "wise elders" were the only acceptable authority.[90]

In the domestic context, mediators often prefer to think of themselves as "third party neutrals" engaged in a detached and unbiased "facilitative" process. Of course, in reality, all of these characteristics (neutrality, detachment and lack of bias,[91] as well as "facilitative"[92]) are contested. But, increasingly, retired judges,

88. LEE BLESSING, A WALK IN THE WOODS: A PLAY IN TWO ACTS (1988) (giving a fictionalized account of the private relations of two top-level diplomats, which is said to reflect the process by which the Gorbachev regime negotiated itself into a new world order).

89. For an effort to explore the issues in agent-principal negotiations across domains, see NEGOTIATING ON BEHALF OF OTHERS (Robert H. Mnookin & Lawrence E. Susskind eds., 1999).

90. MARTIN SHAPIRO, COURTS: A COMPARATIVE AND POLITICAL ANALYSIS 6 (1986).

91. *See* Howard Gadlin & Elizabeth Pino, *Neutrality: A Guide for the Organizational Ombudsperson*, 13 NEGOTIATION. J. 17 (1997). *See generally* Carrie Menkel-Meadow, *Introduction* to MEDIATION: THEORY, PRACTICE AND POLICY (Carrie Menkel-Meadow ed., 2001).

92. *See, e.g.*, Lela Love, *The Top 10 Reasons Why Mediators Should Not Evaluate*, 24 FLA. ST. U. L. REV. 937, 939 (1997).

elder statesmen, and other "notables" engage in shuttle diplomacy to settle major class action lawsuits, community disputes, and in the case of some politicians, like Jesse Jackson or Jimmy Carter, may intervene in international disputes without formal portfolio, authority, or training.

Often the dynamics of domestic and international conflicts might seem similar.[93] For example, when asked how the United States was attempting to get allies for its proposed resolution in the UN to authorize war against Iraq, one major senior official in Washington said, "this is just like lobbying for legislation in Congress—threats and promises, sticks and carrots, money for pet projects, threats to take aid away,"[94] a "standard" log-rolling negotiation process. On the other hand, even with all the turn-over in Congress, lobbying for legislation usually focuses around two relatively stable parties and "opponents." These days we appear to change our allies for international strategic reasons almost yearly. Consider the U.S. "friendships" with Iraq, Iran, Colombia, Pakistan, India, Russia, and others. Consider what this does to notions of trust building and reputation markets[95] as they are conceptualized in domestic negotiation theory.

Most significantly, some modern international conflicts, both interstate and intra-state (South Africa, Rwanda, Argentina, Israel and its Arab neighbors) can demonstrate some of the fallacy of blind application of domestic conflict resolution processes, such as mediation. Mediation's ideology as a problem solving device, asks people to focus on the future, contrasted to adjudication, arbitration, and litigation, which seeks to find the facts and judge the truth of what happened before, in order to provide some remedial relief in the present. This model of future orientation will not often be effective in inter-ethnic, race-based, or genocidal conflicts, or conflicts following or during mass violence or "unjust" regimes and wars. While the disadvantages of "ignoring" the past have also been noted domestically, primarily by feminists[96] and race theorists, who seek a focus on the past for accountability and "justice" in mediation, for the most part, mediation has kept its eye on the "on-going" or future relationship.[97] Attempts to avoid the conflicts and disagreeable arguments about "what happened" before in the standard forms of mediation will not work as peace seekers attempt to mediate long-standing ethnic conflicts, especially when marked by bloodshed, violence, long-standing economic inequalities, or other historical unfairness. So overuse or misappropriated use of domestic mediation models will not work to achieve "truth and reconciliation" in such climates. Fortunately, new processes have come out of

93. For one effort to describe "the" negotiation process, as a universalized set of issues, see Christopher Dupont & Guy-Olivier Faure, *The Negotiation Process*, *in* INTERNATIONAL NEGOTIATION, *supra* note 2.

94. National Public Radio, *All Things Considered*, Feb. 25, 2003 (notes on file with author).

95. *See* Eleanor Holmes Norton, *Bargaining and the Ethics of Process*, 64 N.Y.U. L. REV. 493 (1989).

96. *See, e.g.*, Trina Grillo, *The Mediation Alternative: Process Dangers for Women*, 100 YALE L.J. 1545 (1991).

97. Most descriptions of mediation quote Lon Fuller's famous sentence about the ability of mediation to "re-orient the parties to each other," assuming a continuing "future" relationship. *See* Lon Fuller, *Mediation–Its Forms and Its Functions*, 44 S. CAL. L. REV. 305 (1971).

such conflicts (such as Truth and Reconciliation Commissions)[98] and these might, in turn, have some influence in some of our domestic disputes.[99]

Similarly, feminists, race theorists, and other critics have focused on the recurring issues of power imbalances (whether economic, political, temporal, social, class, racial, ethnic, religious, or gendered)[100] in the assumptions that most conflict resolution processes make about party participation. This is one process issue that has actually lent itself to devising process strategies that have been effective or at least suggestive, across domains. Alliances with other "weak" parties, demands for representation, refusal to participate, funding of resources to participate, and strategic "irrationality" (think Saddam Hussein or North Korea), have enabled the less powerful in a number of contexts to enhance their power in various processes, whether through rational "game-playing" strategies or efforts to break or change the game. This is an area that clearly merits "comparative" and multiple-level study.

Wholesale or thoughtless transfer of Americanized "talking cures" of "talking it out" in mediation are less likely to work in reticent cultures or in cultures where social unequals cannot meet and discuss to consensually negotiate their problems. Negotiation and mediation processes, however staged or structured, involve strategies of communication and speech. With the wide variety of difficult communication issues in domestic mediation and negotiation (information sharing, trust, empowerment, problem solving, active listening, reframing,[101] etc.), adding the complexities of "culture," whether intercultural or mixed-cultural,[102] in other contexts, suggests that conflict resolution processes will be more variable than uniform, and therefore making export of American models likely to be somewhat problematic. Even with our own focus on "multi-cultural" mediation and increased sensitivity to the communication and teleological issues involved in such processes domestically, our commitments to equality, democracy, and "multiculturalism," however deeply held within our own nation, are deeply ideologically, culturally, and legally based in the U.S. political culture. Our "process imperialism" is one of the complaints of such critics as Laura Nader[103] who suggests, at the least, that these are acts of cultural imperialism and, at the worst, that international and U.S. bodies, like USAID, the State Department, the World Bank, and the International Monetary Fund are imposing U.S. styles of dispute resolution (in mediation and commercial and investment arbitration) in nations that have neither

---

98. *See* Kevin Avruch & Beatriz Vejarano, *Truth and Reconciliation Commissions: A Review Essay and Annotated Bibliography*, 2 SOC. JUSTICE: ANTHROPOLOGY, PEACE AND HUMAN RIGHTS 47 (2001).

99. There is some evidence of this in a recent settlement of the Cincinnati civil rights class action against the police department. *See* In re Cincinnati Policing, Collaborative Agreement, No. C-1-99-317, *at* http://www.ariagroup.com/FINAL_document.html (last visited Nov. 22, 2003); *see also* JAY ROTHMAN, RESOLVING IDENTITY-BASED CONFLICTS (1997).

100. *See* Richard Delgado et al., *Fairness and Formality: Minimizing the Risk of Prejudice in Alternative Dispute Resolution*, 1985 WIS. L. REV. 1359 (1985); Carrie Menkel-Meadow, *Do the Haves Come Out Ahead in Alternative Judicial Systems? Repeat Players in ADR*, 15 OHIO ST. J. ON DISP. RESOL. 19 (1999); Iris Marion Young, *Activist Challenges to Deliberative Democracy*, 29 POL. THEORY 670 (2001).

101. *See* DOUGLAS STONE ET AL., DIFFICULT CONVERSATIONS (1999).

102. THE CONFLICT AND CULTURE READER (Pat Chew ed., 2001).

103. *See* Nader, *Current Illusions and Delusions*, *supra* note 13.

the resources, nor the legal system, to support such "exogenously" created institutions.[104]

With increasing attempts to conceptualize the differences between bi-lateral and multi-lateral negotiation and dispute resolution processes, some have argued that bi-lateral negotiations permit greater informality and situation-specific "rules" or norms of procedure, where multi-lateral negotiations are more likely to lead to formalism and the need for formal "rules of process" and "rules of decision," such as those producing majority votes and compromise or lowest common denominator solutions.[105] While international negotiations may be characterized by greater formality, such as the need for translators, trans-system rules of procedure, customs of diplomacy, etc., domestic multi-party negotiations have, in fact, been the occasion for relatively great innovation, with Lawrence Susskind's "Rules of Consensus Building"[106] substituting for "Robert's Rules of Order"[107] and permitting "consensus" rules of process and decision that actually "improve" outcomes away from compromises and lowest common denominators to searches for "better outcomes" that attempt to hear and take account of multiple party needs and interests.[108] Here the interesting question is whether less formal Non-Governmental Organizations (NGOs) in the international arena will more successfully introduce less formal and different kinds of processes to the more "formal" and "official" channels of negotiation. Again, I suspect, context (which issues, which groups, which nations or other demarcations) will have greater effects on process innovation than any "universal" process intervention.

In the commercial realm, many commentators have noted that American litigation processes are transforming European and civil law traditions in international arbitrations, choking them with discovery, motions, and other adversarial practices, like cross-examination and other proceedings that are said to be displacing European actors (both lawyers and arbitrators) with Americans, in the competition for legal and occupational control of this process.[109] Similarly, although

---

104. *Id.* In the "import-export" business of ADR some argue that absence of a legitimate and trusted legal system prevents full assimilation and acceptance of a supplementary set of institutions to offer different forms of conflict resolution (I am one of these), while others suggest that ADR institutions may be developed to substitute for underdeveloped or corrupt legal systems. *See* Alkon, *supra* note 23.

105. Franz Cede, *The Legal Perspective on International Negotiations*, *in* INTERNATIONAL NEGOTIATION, *supra* note 2, at 151.

106. THE CONSENSUS BUILDING HANDBOOK, *supra* note 5, at 99-136. *See also* SUSAN CARPENTER & W.J.D. KENNEDY, MANAGING PUBLIC DISPUTES (2d. ed. 2001); E. FRANKLIN DUKES ET AL., REACHING FOR HIGHER GROUND (2000).

107. HENRY M. ROBERT, ROBERT'S RULES OF ORDER (10th ed. Perseus Pub. 2000) (1876).

108. I do not want to overdraw the domestic and international claims here. Consensus building processes have been used in many international disputes and policy settings, such as the Kyoto Accords, other environmental causes, human rights treaties, etc. Furthermore, the domestic use of such processes as consensus building and negotiated rule-making remain controversial. *See* Cary Coglianese, *Assessing Consensus: The Promise and Performance of Negotiated Rule-Making*, 46 DUKE L. J. 1255 (1997); Jody Freeman, *Collaborative Government in the Administrative State*, 45 UCLA L. REV. 1 (1997); Philip J. Harter, *Negotiating Regulations*, 71 GEO. L. J. 1 (1982).

109. *See* DEZALAY & GARTH, *supra* note 13; Bryant G. Garth & Yves Dezalay, *Fussing About the Forum: Categories and Definitions as Stakes in a Professional Competition*, 21 LAW & SOC. INQUIRY 285 (1996); *see also* Bryant G. Garth, *Privatization and the New Market for Disputes: A Framework for Analysis and a Preliminary Assessment*, 12 STUDIES L. POL. & SOC'Y 367 (1992) (focusing on the domestic side of "competitions" of different processes within the justice system).

intended to be "alternative" international bodies for dispute settlement, the ICSID and WTO are also said to be looking more and more like American-style adjudicative fora, rather than international arbitral or even mediative bodies. In the commercial arena, private business ventures, utilizing aspects of both bi-lateral and multi-lateral negotiations are probably more likely to develop process innovations and opportunities for flexible and informal conflict resolution possibilities, including the use of some mediation processes in transactional (joint venture capital) settings.[110]

So, does it matter that none of the processes of conflict resolution are "pure" anymore, or that they travel, either well or not, but get transformed in the process of trans-border movement? As I have noted elsewhere,[111] Lon Fuller, the "founding" jurisprude of ADR, warned us of the "moral integrity" of each process we might use to resolve disputes or create legislation or other social norms for human interaction.[112] While I am a firm believer that the primary forms can be combined to provide flexible hybrids and adaptation to particular settings, I worry that thoughtless transposition of different processes to different cultures is not good, either for the processes themselves or the people affected by them. U.S.-style ADR was a reaction to the rigidity, slowness, expense, and adversarial structure of U.S. courts, as well as a claim for increased participation in a highly developed democratic, if grid-locked, polity.[113] Transfer of our ADR processes to other places without those "back-up" traditional institutions may be doomed to fail, such as when arbitration is offered or "crammed down" by the State Department or World Bank as a condition of financial aid, where the arbitration system and administering agency is no less corrupt than the corrupt courts it was designed to replace or supplement.

Traditions of disputing, whether in private matters or public, may vary in terms of when only the main "parties" are brought in and when other "stakeholders," interested parties, or the larger community will be engaged. Thus, students of process will have to expand and broaden the theories derived from bilateral negotiations, adversarial litigation models, and even the triadic threesome of mediation or arbitration. More sophisticated theory development is proceeding in multi-party processes in such domestic settings as consensus building, multiparty and class-action litigation, as well as community and environmental disputes. International disputes have more often been multi-party and conceptualized as such (even with the binarism of Cold War analysis). Whether coalition formation, third party intervention, representative and constituent participation, ratification, process rules, and decision rules (the "conceptual tools" of multi-party dis-

110. *See* Christophe Dupont, *International Business Negotiations*, *in* INTERNATIONAL NEGOTIATION, *supra* note 2.

111. Carrie Menkel-Meadow, *Mothers and Fathers of Invention: The Intellectual Founders of ADR*, 16 OHIO ST. J. ON DISP. RESOL. 1, 13-22 (2000).

112. LON FULLER, THE PRINCIPLES OF SOCIAL ORDERING (Kenneth I. Winston ed., 2001).

113. Debates about whether the founding impulses for ADR were "quantitatively" based on caseload reduction and efficiency or "qualitatively" based on more party participation and better outcomes for the parties continue apace. *See, e.g.*, Carrie Menkel-Meadow, *Pursuing Settlement in an Adversary Culture: A Tale of Innovation Co-opted or the Law of ADR*, 19 FLA. ST. U. L. REV. 1 (1991).

pute resolution) can be generalized to many different contexts and levels of action remains an open research question.[114]

Though I am an avid student of general conflict resolution theories and am particularly interested in research questions about the role (and ethics) of third party intervention,[115] as well as dyadic and multi-party negotiations, even when not "facilitated," I think studies of the processes of direct, as well as facilitated, negotiation and the role of third party intervention need to be contextually sensitive. Intervention in family disputes, though also about relationships, is not the same as intervention in international disputes, where cultural "sensitivity," history, expertise, and other factors may distinguish the types of processes and interventions to be used.

V. CONCEPTS IN CONFLICT RESOLUTION

In addition to our "construction" of universalized models of structure and process, the field of conflict resolution has isolated a number of "concepts" of inquiry. As legal and social anthropologists like Laura Nader and Richard Abel attempted to redefine "disputes" as a more universal and capacious concept for comparative study, away from the legalized forms of "cases,"[116] we have identified a number of concepts in our field, with expectations of multi-level explanatory purchase. I will simply mention a few here, as illustrations of efforts we need to make to be careful while studying these concepts rigorously and critically across domains.

One of the most important contributions of modern conflict resolution theory has been the move from "positions," "offers," or "demands" to "underlying interests."[117] While this important conceptual and terminological "move" has assisted our ability to develop problem-solving processes in both domestic and international contexts,[118] by focusing on the underlying "causes" or larger context of the conflicts that cause "disputes," this terminology has itself been criticized for its instrumental, preference-seeking, and utility-based rationalistic or economic conception of what motivates people in conflict. In the international arena, John Burton made an early claim for a theory of "human needs,"[119] as I have done (with a feminist and social welfare impulse) in the domestic sphere.[120] These terms are important. The "needs" theory asks us to look "behind" the stated "interests," just as the re-conceptualization of "interests" asked us to look "behind" the stated demands or "positions." A focus on "needs" asks us to consider not just what

114. For some attempts to specify general principles here, see RAIFFA, *supra* note 2; James K. Sebenius, *Sequencing to Build Coalitions: With Whom Should I Talk First?*, *in* WISE CHOICES: DECISIONS, GAMES, AND NEGOTIATIONS (Richard J. Zeckhauser et al. eds., 1996).

115. *See* Carrie Menkel-Meadow, *The Lawyer as Consensus Builder: Ethics for A New Practice*, 70 TENN. L. REV. 63 (2002).

116. *See* Richard Abel, *A Comparative Study of Dispute Institutions in Society*, 8 LAW & SOC'Y REV. 217 (1973); Nader, *Current Illusions and Delusions*, *supra* note 13.

117. *See* FISHER & URY, *supra* note 2; Menkel-Meadow, *Toward Another* View, *supra* note 6.

118. JOHN W. BURTON, CONFLICT & COMMUNICATION (1969); JOHN W. BURTON, CONFLICT: RESOLUTION AND PREVENTION (1990); JOHN BURTON, RESOLVING DEEP-ROOTED CONFLICT: A HANDBOOK (1987).

119. JOHN W. BURTON, CONFLICT: HUMAN NEEDS THEORY (1990).

120. Menkel-Meadow, *Toward Another View*, *supra* note 6.

parties in negotiations or conflicts can demand or articulate for themselves, but asks us to focus on basic human needs, whether Maslovian[121] or some other framework, to go beyond what parties claim and to focus on social justice issues. "Needs" may include such intangibles as respect, dignity, care, sympathy, empathy, apology, and recognition, or such material items as economic aid, income stability, land, food, shelter or "ownership," and control. Asking questions about "needs" may help us develop models of conflict resolution and negotiation that go beyond the "rational" into what some, like Jon Elster[122] and I,[123] have called the emotional, passionate, or spiritual (or religious) realms, which are not captured in game theoretic pictures of conflict resolution, and which seem ever more relevant to current conflicts. At the same time that "needs" appear "underneath" interests and other expressions of what parties desire in a negotiation or conflict setting, there may be other, newer ways to describe these concerns, when contexts are more varied. Whether "needs" or "interests" operate similarly in domestic and international settings (whether in individual or collective settings) also requires more study. Those who facilitate multi-party or constituent based negotiations know how difficult it is to develop, articulate, and negotiate with group-negotiated "goals." Note that "goals" itself has an instrumental ending point; more astute negotiators and conflict professionals have long noted how party desires, needs, and interests are more dynamic than many "negotiation plans" would suggest. What we want and why we want it is not just a product of our own "utilities," but also a function of comparative assessments–the concept of "relative deprivation" should be as important to us conceptually as "reactive devaluation." When one party learns what another "has," "wants," or "needs," those stated desiderata may well change in the comparison dynamics that is the fuel of many conflict processes.

The focus on "relationships" in negotiation and conflict resolution has long been with us. Indeed, one of the most robust analytical concepts has been the consideration of whether those engaged in negotiation or conflict resolution are having a "one-shot" interaction or a "repeated" interaction. Much of negotiation and conflict resolution theory turns on these notions of "one-off" or "continuing relations." Recently, those in the international field have even come to adopt the full psychological terms of family therapy and mediation to note the importance of creating, sustaining, and working on "relationships."[124] It is important to note, however, that relationships come in many forms—the relationships of states to each other (mediated and affected by who are the leaders, diplomats, and official spokespeople of a state over time) are different than the relationships of citizens or inhabitants of different states (tourists, refugees, and abstracted "others"); litigants may be former partners, lovers, continuing business dealers, or total strangers. Just as in personal relationships, in the international realm, there are complex

121. ABRAHAM H. MASLOW, MOTIVATION AND PERSONALITY (2d ed. 1970).

122. JON ELSTER, ALCHEMIES OF THE MIND: RATIONALITY AND THE EMOTIONS (1999); JON ELSTER, SOLOMONIC JUDGMENTS: STUDIES IN THE LIMITATIONS OF RATIONALITY (1989).

123. Carrie Menkel-Meadow, *Introduction* to DISPUTE PROCESSING AND CONFLICT RESOLUTION: THEORY, PRACTICE AND POLICY (2003); Carrie Menkel-Meadow, *The Lawyers' Role(s) in Deliberative Democracy* (2000) (unpublished manuscript, on file with the author).

124. HAROLD H. SAUNDERS, A PUBLIC PEACE PROCESS: SUSTAINED DIALOGUE TO TRANSFORM RACIAL AND ETHNIC CONFLICTS 31-46 (1999).

blood and affinity ties. The point here is that while I truly welcome the "turn" toward the human element in all negotiations, we must develop more sophisticated theories about relationships. If the pop psychology market continues to sell endless copies of books on how to improve one's personal relationships, then certainly the kinds of relationships that exist in legal, community, national, and international disputes must be more variable than the bi-modal "one-shot vs. continuing." It is clear that some relationships are "coerced" when we share a family, living quarters, or geographic boundary; others are chosen—ties of love and marriage (in some cultures) and organizational participation; others are "strategic alliances" in business or global politics and most importantly, all of these relationships shift and change themselves over time, as conditions, including affective, economic, political, and strategic, change themselves. Consider the amazing transformation of relations in Europe from World War II to the present and our own relations with Japan, Germany, Russia, and China, just to mention a few that have changed radically in a matter of decades. Our relations with other "strategic partners" may be more "promiscuous." Our conceptualizations of relationships in conflict resolution and negotiation need more variability than they currently have to be of much use in description, prescription, and prediction.

Finally, as a third example, let me focus on the concepts of "ripeness" and "deadlines" or the temporal theories of conflict management. As my great negotiation mentor has said, "You gotta know when to hold 'em, know when to fold them."[125] Timing in conflict resolution is a matter of "judgment." In international relations, William Zartman developed the notion of "ripeness" for resolution or intervention when the parties are in a "hurting stalemate."[126] A version of this concept informs much legal dispute resolution as well, such as when judges intervene in settlement conferences or cases are settled on the courthouse steps. But, more recently, in both domestic litigation and international affairs, we have begun to think about creating more positive approaches to "ripeness" with interveners and others acting more actively to "prevent" conflict or to bring the parties together before they hurt each other so deeply that they are no longer able to communicate with each other. "Ripeness," in other words, can be created and manipulated by skilled negotiators or interveners. At the same time, we have also learned that intervention too early may not work, as in the case of court-annexed mediation programs that ask the parties to mediate or arbitrate without enough discovery to have information to know what is at stake or to make accurate assessments of the value or strength of the legal claims.[127] Just as with "fruit" from where the ripeness metaphor[128] is derived, conflicts may be "unripe" or "overripe." Unlike fruit, "ripeness" in dispute resolution can occur at many points along the way.[129]

125. KENNY ROGERS, *The Gambler*, *on* THE GAMBLER (United Artists 1978).

126. ZARTMAN, *supra* note 66.

127. *See* Elizabeth Plapinger & Donna Stienstra, *Eastern District of Pennsylvania Mediation Program*, *in* ADR AND SETTLEMENT IN THE FEDERAL DISTRICT COURTS 241-42 (1996).

128. Though I don't have time or space to pursue it here, it is interesting to explore the language and "metaphors" of conflict resolution across domains to track their sources and etymology, as well as their robustness across domains. *See, e.g.*, Victor M. Sergeev, *Metaphors for Understanding International Negotiation*, *in* INTERNATIONAL NEGOTIATION, *supra* note 2, (describing "bargaining," "joint choice," and "joint construction of the future" as metaphors that have informed modern international negotiations).

129. *See* WORDS OVER WAR, *supra* note 5, at 9-10.

Timing may be everything, but there may also be many entry points, and opportunities to "re-enter" after some failures. What can we learn about "ripeness," across domains, to determine when we can nudge the process along and "construct" opportunities for effective resolution and when do we have to wait for the parties to force themselves into "hurting stalemates?" Should we be allowed to be inactive and guilty bystanders as people kill or hurt each other? When should we intrude?[130]

At the other end of the temporal spectrum, the use of "deadlines" is often theorized or used descriptively to promote, force, or encourage conflict resolution. Whether in the setting of firm trial deadlines,[131] or in artificially created deadlines, such as George Mitchell's "Easter deadline" in the Northern Ireland peace talks,[132] critical deadlines or fixed end-dates are often considered a useful way to promote final "ripeness." Ironically, I find this one of the most interesting and contradictory concepts in conflict resolution studies. While George Mitchell credits the Easter deadline (agreed to by all the parties, he says, because they wanted agreement) as facilitating an end to a multi-year negotiation process, and a multi-decade (if not multi-century) dispute, President Clinton's efforts a few years later to create deadlines with the expiration of his own term in office (and the Israeli election that cost Barak his job) failed to bring a peace agreement to the Mideast, even though, allegedly both parties wanted to make an agreement there too.[133]

So, it is not that deadlines or ripeness always have predicted or desirable effects. The more interesting questions for study are under what conditions can deadlines or other limiting events produce agreements and under what conditions can speeding a process along actually hurt a negotiation process? Have we learned anything generalizable about the timing and life-course of disputes or is this one of those areas, as I suspect it is, that is deeply contextual and dependent on histories and personalities of the parties, as well as of the interveners. Unlike most lawsuits and most domestic disputes, international disputes, especially long ones, will have many changes of personnel, whether through elective processes, other succession processes, or changes of regimes and leadership. The issues of "timing" are not severable from the people involved. Unlike propositions of physical science, I doubt whether we will ever have generalizable principles about the timing of disputes. It is not "chaos theory" or "relativity," but neither is it "gravity." As I turn next to some issues of personnel in conflict resolution, you might pick your own favorite "concepts" of conflict resolution and ask how well the theory behind those "concepts" has been developed across domains.

---

130. This of course implicates both the domestic ethical problems explored in the aftermath of the Kitty Genovese killing and the study of "prosocial" psychology, as well as the now active field of humanitarian intervention in the international relations field. *See* ACCOUNTABILITY FOR ATROCITIES (Jane Stromseth ed., 2003); HUMANITARIAN INTERVENTION (J.L. Holzgrefe & Robert O. Keohane eds., 2003).

131. *See* MAURICE ROSENBERG, THE PRETRIAL CONFERENCE AND EFFECTIVE JUSTICE (1964).

132. *See* MITCHELL, *supra* note 5, at 143-46.

133. Of course, insiders in that negotiation now say both parties were not really serious about reaching agreement, with blame being placed on both sides. *See* Malley & Agha, *supra* note 5; DENNIS ROSS, THE MIDDLE EAST PEACE (forthcoming).

VI. PEOPLE IN CONFLICTS

Whatever one thinks about the conceptual maps elaborated above to describe conflict resolution processes, dispute resolution and negotiation are enacted by people who execute behaviors, whether systematically "framed" by schemas or models or not.[134] Actors in negotiation and conflict resolution activities can be individuals, agents, or representatives for others, groups, organizations, diplomats, leaders, or "ad hoc" negotiators (e.g. hostage takers and terrorists). For those of us who study conflict resolution, we are likely to at least try to employ one model or other. Others, particularly those not exposed to conflict resolution theory, may act from "default" perspectives set by role (assumptions of competition for lawyers and economists; helping or altruistic behavior for social workers, nurses, or clergy) or "culture"[135] (the set of rules, expectations, and solutions to problems so deeply ingrained, it may feel like water to a fish, or air to humans). The people who enact conflict resolution are the ones who "mess up" the theory, failing to conform to the structures and pictures of our "rational" selves, or selves needing categories. Thus, in addition to considering how the actors differ in different contexts, such as direct negotiations, bilateral dispute resolution, representative or multi-lateral negotiations, family disputes, complex international diplomatic disputes, or international business investment or ventures, we must consider whether the great variety of human behavior can in fact be boxed in by theories of behavior that may be "culturally" specific. By "cultural" I do not mean only the crass and "monolithic" descriptions of national, ethnic, or religious culture ("do as the Romans, Chinese, Japanese, Americans, Arabs, or Israelis do," though the studies of such "national character" variations continue to proliferate, in business schools, as well as in practical "how to negotiate" guides), but the "professional cultures" that develop as well ("cosmopolitan," "international diplomatic," "legal professional," and even "negotiation" culture).[136] How do the people in conflict processes affect what is possible?

---

134. Remember that so much of the work of modern cognitive and social psychology is to demonstrate departures from "rational" behavior. I have always thought that with most people who act, from many different motives, the more interesting question to explain is when people conform to "rational" modeling behavior. I prefer the question which asks, "How do people behave?" (descriptively), rather than assuming deviation from some social scientist's assumption of "rationality."

135. For a more useful exposition of "post-modern" understandings of culture, see AVRUCH, CULTURE, *supra* note 2. For a more stilted and somewhat discredited view of "cultural" determinants of negotiation behavior, see BRETT, *supra* note 12; Stephen E. Weiss, *Negotiating with "Romans" - Part 1*, SLOAN MGM'T REV., Winter 1994, at 51; Stephen E. Weiss, *Negotiating with "Romans" - Part 2*, SLOAN MGM'T REV., Spring 1994, at 85. *See also* Jeswald W. Salacuse, *Intercultural Negotiation in International Business*, 8 GROUP DECISION & NEGOTIATION 217 (1999).

136. With the growing numbers of foreign students in American business, law, and public policy schools, exposed to "our" modern negotiation theory, an international class of "problem-solving negotiators" is being created. Thus, Jeff Rubin, among others, who has trained such students has suggested that when we ask about the cultural inputs into conflict resolution behaviors we need to ask, "what culture" is affecting behavior and "under what conditions does what culture become salient?". *See* GUY-OLIVIER FAURE & JEFFREY Z. RUBIN, CULTURE AND NEGOTIATION (1993); Jeffrey Z. Rubin & Frank E.A. Sander, *Culture, Negotiation and the Eye of the Beholder*, 7 NEGOTIATION J. 249 (1991). *See also* Guy-Olivier Faure, *International Negotiation: The Cultural Dimension*, *in* INTERNATIONAL NEGOTIATION, *supra* note 2, at 392. Contrast this work to efforts to describe issues of "culture" and "diversity" or "racism" in more domestic treatments of conflict resolution. *See, e.g.*, Howard Gadlin, *Conflict Resolution, Cultural Differences and the Culture of Racism*, 10 NEGOTIATION J. 33 (1994);

As indicated above, although focus on third party interventions in disputes began in international relations (consider our study of all the great diplomatic treaties and the roles of Machiavelli, Metternich, Talleyrand, Nicolson, Chamberlain, Kissinger, Carter, George Mitchell, Kofi Annen, Ralph Bunch as international interveners), study of and classifications of third party activity seems far more advanced in domestic conflict resolution theory. With the sophisticated debates about "evaluative" vs. "facilitative" mediation[137] and whether "neutrality," "embedded expertise," or legal training is required of third party neutrals (whether mediators, arbitrators, facilitators or leaders of public policy consensus processes), the "professionalization" of the role of the third party has led to a robust set of issues for consideration in the practice of third party intervention. In the international arena, by contrast, although there are many sophisticated practitioners with diplomatic portfolios, other qualifications such as education, training on issues of neutrality, practice protocols, and ethics, seem relatively newer and underdeveloped.[138]

Indeed, for all of the successes or "failures" of modern international diplomatic negotiation (peace, trade agreements, the European Union, NAFTA, Mercosur, the Mideast, South and Latin America), the action appears to be with the NGOs, or creative academic theorists or practitioners, developing new approaches to conflict resolution, outside the formal models of international relations and diplomacy, such as "problem solving workshops," "public peace processes," and reconciliation conferences, etc. (consider Harold Saunders, John Paul Lederach,[139] John Burton, Kenneth and Elise Boulding, and Johan Galtung, just to name a few).[140]

Thus, systematic study of successful conflict resolution processes requires us to examine the individual sources of innovation, which for a newly developing field, may occur outside of the formal channels of both theory building (universities) and practice (formal state institutions in both the international and national contexts). In my view, we have yet to capture useful and generalizable principles

---

THE CONFLICT AND CULTURE READER, *supra* note 102; Isabelle Gunning, *Diversity Issues in Mediation: Controlling Negative Cultural Myths*, 1995 J. DISP. RESOL. 55.

137. Leonard L. Riskin, *Understanding Mediators' Orientations, Strategies and Techniques: A Grid for the Perplexed*, 1 HARV. NEGOT. L. REV. 7, 24-50 (1996).

138. I do not mean to minimize the work of Jimmy Carter in Haiti, Camp David, or North Korea, or George Mitchell in Northern Ireland or any of the other distinguished "helpers" in the Mideast, but whenever I read reports or memoirs of these events (including the now emerging reports of the Clinton administration efforts in the Mideast), I am always startled by how little attention is paid or thought given to all of the theories, models, structures, and concepts of conflict resolution discussed above. Just what are they studying in the State Department? International relations and diplomatic schools, like Tufts University, have been teaching these principles, but the era of the "amateur" diplomat (*see* KAZUO ISHIGURO, THE REMAINS OF THE DAY 123 (1989)) seems far from being over. I have been struck by listening to reports of the "Great Negotiators" (an award now given by the Harvard Program on Negotiation each year) how devoid of references to "our" theory their reports are. Good academic synthesizers, like James Sebenius, Howard Raiffa, Roger Fisher, or Robert Mnookin, can draw out theoretical generalizations, but often practitioners do not speak the language of theory. Gatherings of domestic mediators, on the other hand, are noted for their debates about models, theories, frameworks, and competing techniques. Is there a difference in domestic and international conceptualization of the third party role? And if so, why?

139. JOHN PAUL LEDERACH, BUILDING PEACE (1997).

140. *See* Louis Kriesberg, *Varieties of Mediating Activities and Mediators in International Relations*, *in* STUDIES IN INTERNATIONAL MEDIATION, *supra* note 2, at 219-34.

from the "peace stories" told in the case studies and memoirs of participants, whether as negotiators, activists, victims, participants, or third party interveners.[141]

Useful points of comparison here are the obvious differences in the use of "interested" neutrals with "muscle" or power in international matters and the ideology, and in some cases, requirements of "neutrality" in domestic settings.[142]

VII. ALTERNATIVES TO CONFLICT AND CONFLICT RESOLUTION?

Perhaps the most salient factor distinguishing domestic from international conflict resolution is the backdrop of the "rule of law" or "violence" as "alternatives" to consensual settlements of disputes. As negotiation theory now asks us to map BATNAs, WATNAs, and ATNAs, it is particularly important to explore how the influence of courts and enforcement institutions—or the lack thereof—affect the conduct of consensual bargaining and conflict resolution. While legal enforcement is not available to all domestic disputants because of economics or access to justice and lawyers, the question of the importance of the "role of law" as a measure of fairness in litigation disputes, policy formation, resource allocation, and transactional matters is now raised in a variety of both practice and theory contexts.[143]

International relations scholars, both political scientists and lawyers, have focused on the growing diversity of enforcement mechanisms in the international arena such as trade sanctions, economic sanctions, broadening standing for private enforcement of both trade and human rights violations, censorship, peacekeeping forces, humanitarian interventions, and all-out war.[144] Whether this growing menu of sanctioning possibilities has further "legalized" the international order without a global court or effective enforcement mechanism (especially in light of recent "non-state" and "unsanctioned" U.S. unilateral actions) remains to be seen, but here some important studies of comparison to domestic settings might be appropriate. Who participates in conflicts? Those given formal "standing" by a legal authority, stakeholders, or those who threaten physical or economic security

141. In my view the most elaborated field is that of domestic consensus building in public policy and environmental disputes. *See* BACOW & WHEELER, *supra* note 5; BINGHAM, *supra* note 5; THE CONSENSUS BUILDING HANDBOOK, *supra* note 5. We are just beginning to have some reports of mediation and settlements of major litigation class actions. *See also* STUART EIZENSTAT, IMPERFECT JUSTICE (2003) (discussing Holocaust litigation against Swiss and German banks and companies); PETER SCHUCK, AGENT ORANGE ON TRIAL (1986).

142. *See* Carrie Menkel-Meadow, *Ethics Issues in Arbitration and Related Dispute Resolution Processes: What's Happening and What's Not*, 56 U. MIAMI L. REV. 949 (2002) (reviewing increasing regulation of neutrality and conflicts of interests issues in domestic and international arbitration); *see also* MODEL RULE FOR THE LAWYER AS THIRD PARTY NEUTRAL (developed by CPR-Georgetown Commission on Ethics and Standards in ADR 2002), *available at* http://www.cpradr.org (last visited Nov. 22, 2003).

143. *See* Robert J. Condlin, *Bargaining in the Dark: The Normative Incoherence of Lawyer Dispute Bargaining Role*, 51 MD. L. REV. 1 (1992); Robert Condlin, *Cases on Both Sides: Patterns of Argument in Legal Dispute Negotiation*, 44 MD. L. REV. 65 (1985); Owen M. Fiss, *Against Settlement*, 93 YALE L. J. 1073 (1984); Judith L. Maute, *Public Values and Private Justice: A Case for Mediator Accountability*, 4 GEO. J. LEGAL ETHICS 503 (1991); Jacqueline M. Nolan-Haley, *Court Mediation and the Search for Justice Through Law*, 74 WASH. U.L.Q. 47 (1996); Lawrence Susskind, *Environmental Mediation and the Accountability Problem*, 6 VT. L. REV. 1 (1981).

144. *See* ACCOUNTABILITY FOR ATROCITIES, *supra* note 130; HUMANITARIAN INTERVENTION, *supra* note 130; Schneider, *supra* note 11.

or well-being from inside or from outside? Who intervenes? Self-appointed mediators, formally authorized actors (e.g. UN mediators, peacekeeping forces, weapons inspectors, court-appointed mediators or arbitrators, privately chosen third party neutrals)? What are the criteria used to intervene to try to settle or resolve disputes? What is the role of formal law? Is it custom? Is it power (military, economic, or political)? On what basis are agreements crafted (partial, comprehensive, contingent, permanent, trades, compromises)? What monitoring, enforcement is established?[145] Who is affected by outcomes or agreements reached (or not)? How do third parties affect the consequent or resulting situation (e.g. refugees, "ethnic cleansing," minorities, etc.)? How are non-formal enforcement mechanisms created (e.g. coalitions, multi-lateral actions, reconciliation or redistributive proceedings)? How do changing actors (new leaders, whether elected or otherwise) change the environment? How "interdependent" are parties on each other? How do multiple issues impact particular negotiations? What "linkages" are made or forced, (e.g., what "trades" occur on such issues as nuclear proliferation, economic aid, democratization)? While there are many problems of unit and level analysis here, it seems particularly useful to examine how different kinds of "alternatives" to conflict resolution mechanisms operate in different spheres.

Does the ultimate sanction of "the rule of law" or court decision affect domestic dispute resolution differently than "violence" or economic sanctions affect international disputes? What role does compliance or reputation play in both domains? Has the relative increase of formal international organizations (the International Criminal Court, the War Crimes Courts, or the WTO) affected compliance with both formal rules, norms, and less formal customs? Does a proliferation of dispute resolution mechanisms help bring order, peace, and justice, or, does it permit more strategic "gaming" or movement from one forum to another?

VIII. Some Concluding Thoughts: Are There More Correspondences or More Contradictions?

I am an optimistic person, committed to both justice and peace, to equality and democracy, and most importantly to human survival and flourishing.[146] The last few decades of the development of the field of conflict resolution, in law, business, policy, and other schools, in its interdisciplinary nature and in its practice, have been particularly exciting for all of us who have contributed ideas and hard work. I am a great admirer of grand theory and the hopes for "systematic"[147] approaches to conflict study which aim for some universal "acontextuality" across a variety of domains. Yet, I know that even from the beginning of my own work in legal negotiations, I saw the differences in litigation and transactional negotiations. I even suggested a list of "contextual" factors early on that I thought would affect how negotiations were conducted and which of several negotiation "orient-

145. *See* Arild Underdal, *The Outcomes of Negotiation*, *in* INTERNATIONAL NEGOTIATION, *supra* note 2, at 110.

146. *See* Carrie Menkel-Meadow, *Practicing "In the Interests of Justice" in the Twenty-First Century: Pursuing Peace as Justice*, 70 FORDHAM L. REV. 1761 (2002).

147. *See* Howard Raiffa, *Contributions of Applied Systems Analysis to International Negotiation*, *in* INTERNATIONAL NEGOTIATION, *supra* note 2, at 5.

ing frameworks" would have to be chosen in those different contexts.[148] Perhaps I am a product of my mid-to-late twentieth century education, influenced by sociology, feminism, epistemology, post-modernism (and modernism before it), and common law legal reasoning, but to me facts matter, conditions differ, and very few "grand" and "meta-theories" in the social sciences and law have fully stood the test of time,[149] especially as we have come to ask who are the creators of theory and what are their purposes?[150] While I continue to admire those who attempt to create "acontextual" theory in our field (now focused on elaborating the differences between bi-lateral and multi-lateral negotiation),[151] applying economic, mathematical, or even psychological models to human decision making, I can't help but think, especially in light of current events (and many actors, including terrorists committed to fundamentally different belief systems, as well as our own leaders, who seem equally insensitive to global well-being), that human conflict makers and conflict resolvers will not easily be "contained" in universal boxes or categories. Because I think these things, I offer the following suggestions for future "contextualized" studies for moving our field productively along, in theory and in practice, with the hope that even without universal theories we can learn more about how to prevent deadly and dangerous conflict and violence:

1. Under what social, political, cultural, and economic conditions do particular forms of conflict resolution (adversarial, competitive, violent or collaborative, cooperative, and problem solving) emerge?

2. What kinds of interventions/actors/circumstances change the course, scope, or method of conflict resolution?

3. What kinds of circumstances require different forms of conflict resolution activities? (e.g., how does "short-term" violence prevention or amelioration differ from longer term reconciliation and relationship-developing action)?

4. What roles can "insiders" (stakeholder participants) to a conflict play?

5. What roles can "outsiders" ("interested parties," "affected parties," or "neutral parties") to a conflict play?

6. How does the locus (familial, local, national, cultural, intercultural, international) of the conflict affect the possible processes and outcomes that are available (a form of "level" or unit of analysis "reality testing")?

---

148. *See* Carrie Menkel-Meadow, *Legal Negotiation: A Study of Strategies in Search of a Theory*, 1983 AM. B. FOUND. RES. J. 905-37.

149. Indeed, our Constitution, flawed from the beginning with its toleration of slavery, has "lasted" only because of a Civil War (violence), many amendments (legislative and constitutional "dispute resolution and negotiation") and always changing interpretation ("post-modernism" and hermeneutics).

150. *See* SANDRA HARDING, WHOSE SCIENCE? WHOSE KNOWLEDGE? (1991).

151. *See* Howard Raiffa, LECTURES ON NEGOTIATION ANALYSIS (1997).

7. How much commitment to similar goals, "world views," values, or processes,[152] is required to create a "conflict resolution" process?

8. How can we develop structures, concepts, and languages that are protean enough to have explanatory purchase across domains, but "open" enough to be studied and examined across levels of disputing and conflicts?

9. What varieties of interventions and dispute processing are possible and how are they related to each other (sequencing, series, continuing, multiple or parallel tracks)? [153]

10. How can dispute processes be "elicited" from those in dispute[154] (rather than "laid down" by those outside or "on top" of a dispute)?

11. What kinds of dispute or conflict resolution processes can be "institutionalized"? Which work better when maintained in "ad hoc," flexible forms?

12. What is the relation of formal "international relations" or "civil or criminal litigation" (state-based processes) theory and practices to more informal, flexible, and ad hoc processes or institutions (NGOs, "problem-solving workshops," etc.)? How much multiple level action is beneficial/tolerable and how much leads to difficulties of coordination?

I want to end by suggesting that although I am skeptical that we will develop a fully universal theory of conflict resolution, I am optimistic to think that we will actually learn something useful by examining our concepts across levels, and accumulating more "incremental knowledge,"[155] perhaps by rigorously exploring differences in contexts, rather than assumptions of sameness, uniformity, homogeneity of, or translatability across units of analysis.

If "third party intervention" and "deadline" setting or "ripeness" look different in different contexts we will have learned something. Lawsuits, even the

152. *Compare* STUART HAMPSHIRE, JUSTICE IS CONFLICT (2000) (opining that since we will never have agreement on substantive human goods and goals, the most we can hope for is some agreement on procedural fairness for resolving conflict) *with* Carrie Menkel-Meadow, *When Litigation is Not the Only Way: Consensus Building and Mediation as Public Interest Lawyering*, 10 WASH. U. J. L. & POL'Y 37 (2002) (giving author's commentary on JUSTICE IS CONFLICT). I am no longer sure whether we are any more likely to agree to procedural goals than substantive ones. Even Hampshire, whose work I admire, "universalizes" a belief in Anglo-American "adversary argument" (audi alteram partem–"hear the other side") as the best procedure by which to resolve human conflicts.

153. *See* Harold H. Saunders, *Prenegoiation and Circum-negotiation: Arenas of the Multilevel Peace Process*, *in* TURBULENT PEACE, *supra* note 5, at 483.

154. *See* LEDERACH, *supra* note 13.

155. From my own experience, I can attest that my mediation retainer agreement has expanded over the years to more than fifteen single-spaced pages because I learn something from each new case I take and add refinements to the explanations, promises, representations, and covenants I make with parties in mediation. My resistance to a single "form" retainer agreement is similar to my distaste for grand theory, boilerplate clauses, and "off the shelf" training programs. Like my retainer agreements, every training in dispute resolution I do is tailor-made for the clients in each particular setting.

longest ones, usually settle more quickly than centuries of inter-racial or inter-ethnic conflict. The threat of an authoritative decision maker may hasten voluntary settlement over situations where there is no enforcing authority, but agreements reached consensually when there is no outside threat of decision may be longer-lasting and more easily complied with. Learning to live with differences within national boundaries or regional trade zones may provide a variety of "exemplars" for different modes of co-existence. If we are truly looking for "solutions" to domestic and international conflicts, disputes, and problems, than we should be open to as many different and contextually specific ideas as it will take. Though I doubt that there is a single theory to fit all human problems for decision, I think we can get better at it by "comparing and contrasting" specifics, rather than assuming uniformity or generality. I urge you to find your favorite conflict resolution idea, model, or concept and try it out in a few different places. Our theory and our practice will be all the richer and deeper for it.

[3]

Diplomacy and Domestic Politics

The Logic of Two-Level Games

Robert D. Putnam

INTRODUCTION: THE ENTANGLEMENTS OF DOMESTIC AND INTERNATIONAL POLITICS

Domestic politics and international relations are often somehow entangled, but our theories have not yet sorted out the puzzling tangle. It is fruitless to debate whether domestic politics really determine international relations, or the reverse. The answer to that question is clearly "Both, sometimes." The more interesting questions are "When?" and "How?" This paper offers a theoretical approach to this issue, but I begin with a story that illustrates the puzzle.

One illuminating example of how diplomacy and domestic politics can become entangled culminated at the Bonn Summit Conference of 1978.[1] In the mid-1970s, a coordinated program of global reflation, led by the "locomotive" economies of the United States, Germany, and Japan, had been proposed to foster Western recovery from the first oil shock.[2] This proposal had received a powerful boost from the incoming Carter Administration and was warmly supported by the weaker countries, as well as the Organization for Economic Cooperation and Development and many private economists, who argued that it would overcome international payments imbalances and speed growth all around. On the other hand, the Germans and the Japanese protested that prudent and successful economic managers should not be asked to bail out spendthrifts. Meanwhile, Jimmy Carter's ambitious National Energy Program remained deadlocked in Congress, while Helmut Schmidt led a chorus of complaints about the Americans' uncontrolled appetite for imported oil and their apparent unconcern about the falling dollar. All sides conceded that the world economy was in serious trouble, but it was not clear which was more to blame—tight-fisted German and Japanese fiscal policies, or slack-jawed U.S. energy and monetary policies.

At the Bonn Summit, however, a comprehensive package deal was approved, the clearest case yet of a summit that left all participants happier than when they arrived. Helmut Schmidt agreed to additional fiscal stimulus, amounting to 1 percent of GNP; Jimmy Carter committed himself to decontrol domestic oil prices by the end of 1980; and Takeo Fukuda pledged new efforts to reach a 7-percent growth rate. Secondary elements in the Bonn accord included French and British acquiescence in the Tokyo Round trade negotiations; Japanese undertakings to foster import growth and restrain exports; and a generic American promise to fight inflation. All in all, the Bonn Summit produced a balanced agreement of unparalleled breadth and specificity. More remarkably, virtually all parts of the package were actually implemented.

Most observers at the time welcomed the policies agreed to at Bonn, although in retrospect there has been much debate about the economic wisdom of this package deal. However, my concern here is not whether the deal was wise economically, but how it became possible politically. My research suggests, first, that the key governments at Bonn adopted policies different from those that they would have pursued in the absence of international negotiations—but second, that agreement was possible only because a powerful minority within each government actually favored on domestic grounds the policy being demanded internationally.

Within Germany, a political process catalyzed by foreign pressures was surreptitiously orchestrated by expansionists inside the Schmidt government. Contrary to the public mythology, the Bonn deal was not forced on a reluctant or "altruistic" Germany. In fact, officials in the Chancellor's Office and the Economics Ministry, as well as in the Social Democratic Party and the trade unions, had argued privately in early 1978 that further stimulus was domestically desirable, particularly in view of the approaching 1980 elections. However, they had little hope of overcoming the opposition of the Finance Ministry, the Free Democratic Party (part of the government coalition), and the business and banking community, especially the leadership of the Bundesbank. Publicly, Helmut Schmidt posed as reluctant to the end. Only his closest advisors suspected the truth: that the Chancellor "let himself be pushed" into a policy that he privately favored, but would have found costly and perhaps impossible to enact without the summit's package deal.

Analogously, in Japan a coalition of business interests, the Ministry of International Trade and Industry (MITI), the Economic Planning Agency, and some expansion-minded politicians within the Liberal Democratic Party pushed for additional domestic stimulus, using U.S. pressure as one of their prime arguments against the stubborn resistance of the Ministry of Finance (MOF). Without internal divisions in Tokyo, it is unlikely that the foreign demands would have been met; but without the external pressure, it is even more unlikely that the expansionists could have overridden the powerful MOF: "Seventy percent foreign pressure, 30 percent internal politics," was the disgruntled judgment of one MOF insider; "Fifty-fifty," guessed an official from MITI.[3]

In the American case, too, internal politicking reinforced, and was reinforced by, the international pressure. During the summit preparations, American negotiators occasionally invited their foreign counterparts to put more pressure on the Americans to reduce oil imports. Key economic officials within the administration favored a tougher energy policy, but they were opposed by the President's closest political aides, even after the summit. Moreover, Congressional opponents continued to stymie oil price decontrol, as they had under both Nixon and Ford. Finally, in April 1979, the President decided on gradual administrative decontrol, bringing U.S. prices up to world levels by October 1981. His domestic advisors thus won a postponement of this politically costly move until after the 1980 presidential election, but in the end, virtually every one of the pledges made at Bonn was fulfilled. Both proponents and opponents of decontrol agree that the summit commitment was at the center of the administration's heated intramural debate during the winter of 1978–79, and instrumental in the final decision.[4]

In short, the Bonn accord represented genuine international policy coordination. Significant policy changes were pledged and implemented by the key participants. Moreover—although this counterfactual claim is necessarily harder to establish—those policy changes would very probably not have been pursued (certainly not on the same scale and within the same time frame) in the absence of the international agreement. Within each country, one faction supported the policy shift being demanded of its country internationally, but that faction was initially outnumbered. Thus, international pressure was a necessary condition for these policy shifts. On the other hand, without domestic resonance, international forces would not have sufficed to produce the accord, no matter how balanced and intellectually persuasive the overall package. In the end, each leader believed that what he was doing was in his nation's interest—and probably in his own political interest, too, even though not all his aides agreed.[5] Yet without the summit accord, he probably would not (or could not) have changed policies so easily. In that sense, the Bonn deal successfully meshed domestic and international pressures.

Neither a purely domestic nor a purely international analysis could account for this episode. Interpretations cast in terms either of domestic causes and international effects ("second-image")[6] or of international causes and domestic effects ("second-image-reversed")[7] would represent merely "partial equilibrium" analyses and would miss an important part of the story, namely, how the domestic politics of several countries became entangled via an international negotiation. The events of 1978 illustrate that we must aim instead for "general equilibrium" theories that account simultaneously for the interaction of domestic and international factors. This paper suggests a conceptual framework for understanding how diplomacy and domestic politics interact.

DOMESTIC-INTERNATIONAL ENTANGLEMENTS: THE STATE OF THE ART

Much of the existing literature on relations between domestic and international affairs consists either of ad hoc lists of countless "domestic influences" on foreign policy or of generic observations that national and international affairs are somehow "linked."[8] James Rosenau was one of the first scholars to call attention to this area, but his elaborate taxonomy of "linkage politics" generated little cumulative research, except for a flurry of work correlating domestic and international "conflict behavior."[9]

A second stream of relevant theorizing began with the work by Karl Deutsch and Ernst Haas on regional integration.[10] Haas, in particular, emphasized the impact of parties and interest groups on the process of European integration, and his notion of "spillover" recognized the feedback between domestic and international developments. However, the central dependent variable in this work was the hypothesized evolution of new supranational institutions, rather than specific policy developments, and when European integration stalled, so did this literature. The intellectual heirs of this tradition, such as Joseph Nye and Robert Keohane, emphasized interdependence and transnationalism, but the role of domestic factors slipped more and more out of focus, particularly as the concept of international regimes came to dominate the subfield.[11]

The "bureaucratic politics" school of foreign-policy analysis initiated another promising attack on the problem of domestic-international interaction. As Graham Allison noted, "Applied to relations between nations, the bureaucratic politics model directs attention to intra-national games, the overlap of which constitutes international relations."[12] Nevertheless, the nature of this "overlap" remained unclarified, and the theoretical contribution of this literature did not evolve much beyond the principle that bureaucratic interests matter in foreign-policy-making.

More recently, the most sophisticated work on the domestic determinants of foreign policy has focused on "structural" factors, particularly "state strength." The landmark works of Peter Katzenstein and Stephen Krasner, for example, showed the importance of domestic factors in foreign economic policy. Katzenstein captured the essence of the problem: "The main purpose of all strategies of foreign economic policy is to make domestic policies compatible with the international political economy."[13] Both authors stressed the crucial point that central decision-makers ("the state") must be concerned simultaneously with domestic and international pressures.

More debatable, however, is their identification of "state strength" as the key variable of interest. Given the difficulties of measuring "state strength," this approach courts tautology,[14] and efforts to locate individual countries on this ambiguous continuum have proved problematic.[15] "State strength," if reinterpreted as merely the opposite of governmental fragmentation, is no doubt of some interest in the comparative study of foreign policy. However, Gourevitch is quite correct to complain that "the strong state-weak state argument suggests that . . . the identity of the governing coalition does not matter. This is a very apolitical argument."[16] Moreover, because "state structures" (as conceived in this literature) vary little from issue to issue or from year to year, such explanations are ill-suited for explaining differences across issues or across time (unless "time" is measured in decades or centuries). A more adequate account of the domestic determinants of foreign policy and international relations must stress *politics*: parties, social classes, interest groups (both economic and non-economic), legislators, and even public opinion and elections, not simply executive officials and institutional arrangements.[17]

Some work in the "state-centric" genre represents a unitary-actor model run amok. "The central proposition of this paper," notes one recent study, "is that the state derives its interests from and advocates policies consistent with the international system at all times and under all circumstances."[18] In fact, on nearly all important issues "central decision-makers" disagree about what the national interest and the international context demand. Even if we arbitrarily exclude the legislature from "the state" (as much of this literature does), it is wrong to assume that the executive is unified in its views. Certainly this was true in *none* of the states involved in the 1978 negotiations. What was "the" position of the German or Japanese state on macroeconomic policy in 1978, or of the American state on energy policy? If the term "state" is to be used to mean "central decision-makers," we should treat it as a plural noun: not "the state, it . . ." but "the state, they. . . ." Central executives have a special role in mediating domestic and international pressures precisely because they are directly exposed to both spheres, not because they are united on all issues nor because they are insulated from domestic politics.

Thus the state-centric literature is an uncertain foundation for theorizing about how domestic and international politics interact. More interesting are recent works about the impact of the international economy on domestic politics and domestic economic policy, such as those by Alt, Evans, Gourevitch, and Katzenstein.[19] These case studies, representing diverse methodological approaches, display a theoretical sophistication on the international-to-domestic causal connection far greater than is characteristic of comparable studies on the domestic-to-international half of the loop. Nevertheless, these works do not purport to account for instances of reciprocal causation, nor do they examine cases in which the domestic politics of several countries became entangled internationally.

In short, we need to move beyond the mere observation that domestic factors influence international affairs and vice versa, and beyond simple catalogs of instances of such influence, to seek theories that integrate both spheres, accounting for the areas of entanglement between them.

TWO-LEVEL GAMES: A METAPHOR FOR DOMESTIC-INTERNATIONAL INTERACTIONS

Over two decades ago, Richard Walton and Robert McKersie offered a "behavioral theory" of social negotiations that is strikingly applicable to international conflict and cooperation.[20] They pointed out, as all experienced negotiators know, that the unitary-actor assumption is often radically misleading. As Robert Strauss said of the Tokyo Round trade negotiations: "During my tenure as Special Trade Representative, I spent as much time negotiating with domestic constituents (both industry and labor) and members of the U.S. Congress as I did negotiating with our foreign trading partners."[21]

The politics of many international negotiations can usefully be conceived as a two-level game. At the national level, domestic groups pursue their interests by pressuring the government to adopt favorable policies, and politicians seek power by constructing coalitions among those groups. At the international level, national governments seek to maximize their own ability to satisfy domestic pressures, while minimizing the adverse consequences of foreign developments. Neither of the two games can be ignored by central decision-makers, so long as their countries remain interdependent, yet sovereign.

Each national political leader appears at both game boards. Across the international table sit his foreign counterparts, and at his elbows sit diplomats and other international advisors. Around the domestic table behind him sit party and parliamentary figures, spokesmen for domestic agencies, representatives of key interest groups, and the leader's own political advisors. The unusual complexity of this two-level game is that moves that are rational for a player at one board (such as raising energy prices, conceding territory, or limiting auto imports) may be impolitic for that same player at the other board. Nevertheless, there are powerful incentives for consistency between the two games. Players (and kibitzers) will tolerate some differences in rhetoric between the two games, but in the end either energy prices rise or they don't.

The political complexities for the players in this two-level game are staggering. Any key player at the international table who is dissatisfied with the outcome may upset the game board; and conversely, any leader who fails to satisfy his fellow players at the domestic table risks being evicted from his seat. On occasion, however, clever players will spot a move on one board that will trigger realignments on other boards, enabling them to achieve otherwise unattainable objectives. This "two-table" metaphor captures the dynamics of the 1978 negotiations better than any model based on unitary national actors.

Other scholars have noted the multiple-game nature of international relations. Like Walton and McKersie, Daniel Druckman has observed that a negotiator "attempts to build a package that will be acceptable both to the other side and to his bureaucracy." However, Druckman models the domestic and international processes separately and concludes that "the interaction between the processes . . . remains a topic for investigation."[22] Robert Axelrod has proposed a "Gamma paradigm," in which the U.S. president pursues policies vis-à-vis the Soviet Union with an eye toward maximizing his popularity at home. However, this model disregards domestic cleavages, and it postulates that one of the international actors—the Soviet leadership—cares only about international gains and faces no domestic constraint, while the other—the U.S. president—cares only about domestic gains, except insofar as his public evaluates the international competition.[23] Probably the most interesting empirically based theorizing about the connection between domestic and international bargaining is that of Glenn Snyder and Paul Diesing. Though working in the neo-realist tradition with its conventional assumption of unitary actors, they found that, in fully half of the crises they studied, top decision-makers were *not* unified. They concluded that prediction of international outcomes is significantly improved by understanding internal bargaining, especially with respect to minimally acceptable compromises.[24]

Metaphors are not theories, but I am comforted by Max Black's observation that "perhaps every science must start with metaphor and end with algebra; and perhaps without the metaphor there would never have been any algebra."[25] Formal analysis of any game requires well-defined rules, choices, payoffs, players, and information—and even then, many simple two-person, mixed-motive games have no determinate solution. Deriving analytic solutions for two-level games will be a difficult challenge. In what follows I hope to motivate further work on that problem.

TOWARD A THEORY OF RATIFICATION: THE IMPORTANCE OF "WIN-SETS"

Consider the following stylized scenario that might apply to any two-level game. Negotiators representing two organizations meet to reach an agreement between them, subject to the constraint that any tentative agreement must be ratified by their respective organizations. The negotiators might be heads of government representing nations, for example, or labor and management representatives, or party leaders in a multi-party coalition, or a finance minister negotiating with an IMF team, or leaders of a House-Senate conference committee, or ethnic-group leaders in a consociational democracy. For the moment, we shall presume that each side is represented by a single leader or "chief negotiator," and that this individual has no independent policy preferences, but seeks simply to achieve an agreement that will be attractive to his constituents.[26]

It is convenient analytically to decompose the process into two stages:

1. Bargaining between the negotiators, leading to a tentative agreement; call that Level I.
2. Separate discussions within each group of constituents about whether to ratify the agreement; call that Level II.

This sequential decomposition into a negotiation phase and a ratification phase is useful for purposes of exposition, although it is not descriptively accurate. In practice, expectational effects will be quite important. There are likely to be prior consultations and bargaining at Level II to hammer out an initial position for the Level I negotiations. Conversely, the need for Level II ratification is certain to affect the Level I bargaining. In fact, expectations of rejection at Level II may abort negotiations at Level I without any formal action at Level II. For example, even though both the American and Iranian governments seem to have favored an arms-for-hostages deal, negotiations collapsed as soon as they became public and thus liable to de facto "ratification." In many negotiations, the two-level process may be iterative, as the negotiators try out possible agreements and probe their constituents' views. In more complicated cases, as we shall see later, the constituents' views may themselves evolve in the course of the negotiations. Nevertheless, the requirement that any Level I agreement must, in the end, be ratified at Level II imposes a crucial theoretical link between the two levels.

"Ratification" may entail a formal voting procedure at Level II, such as the constitutionally required two-thirds vote of the U.S. Senate for ratifying treaties, but I use the term generically to refer to any decision-process at Level II that is required to endorse or implement a Level I agreement, whether formally or informally. It is sometimes convenient to think of ratification as a parliamentary function, but that is not essential. The actors at Level II may represent bureaucratic agencies, interest groups, social classes, or even "public opinion." For example, if labor unions in a debtor country withhold necessary cooperation from an austerity program that the government has negotiated with the IMF, Level II ratification of the agreement may be said to have failed; ex ante expectations about that prospect will surely influence the Level I negotiations between the government and the IMF.

Domestic ratification of international agreements might seem peculiar to democracies. As the German Finance Minister recently observed, "The limit of expanded cooperation lies in the fact that we are democracies, and we need to secure electoral majorities at home."[27] However, ratification need not be "democratic" in any normal sense. For example, in 1930 the Meiji Constitution was interpreted as giving a special role to the Japanese military in the ratification of the London Naval Treaty;[28] and during the ratification of any agreement between Catholics and Protestants in Northern Ireland, presumably the IRA would throw its power onto the scales. We need only stipulate that, for purposes of counting "votes" in the ratification process, different forms of political power can be reduced to some common denominator.

The only formal constraint on the ratification process is that since the identical agreement must be ratified by both sides, a preliminary Level I agreement cannot be amended at Level II without reopening the Level I negotiations. In other words, final ratification must be simply "voted" up or down; any modification to the Level I agreement counts as a rejection, unless that modification is approved by all other parties to the agreement.[29] Congresswoman Lynn Martin captured the logic of ratification when explaining her support for the 1986 tax-reform bill as it emerged from the conference committee: "As worried as I am about what this bill does, I am even more worried about the current code. The choice today is not between this bill and a perfect bill; the choice is between this bill and the death of tax reform."[30]

Given this set of arrangements, we may define the "win-set" for a given Level II constituency as the set of all possible Level I agreements that would "win"—that is, gain the necessary majority among the constituents—when simply voted up or down.[31] For two quite different reasons, the contours of the Level II win-sets are very important for understanding Level I agreements.

First, *larger win-sets make Level I agreement more likely,* ceteris paribus.[32] By definition, any successful agreement must fall within the Level II win-sets of each of the parties to the accord. Thus, agreement is possible only if those win-sets overlap; and the larger each win-set, the more likely they are to overlap. Conversely, the smaller the win-sets, the greater the risk that the negotiations will break down. For example, during the prolonged prewar Anglo-Argentine negotiations over the Falklands/Malvinas, several tentative agreements were rejected in one capital or the other for domestic political reasons; when it became clear that the initial British and Argentine win-sets did not overlap at all, war became virtually inevitable.[33]

A brief, but important, digression: *The possibility of failed ratification suggests that game-theoretical analyses should distinguish between* voluntary *and* involuntary defection. Voluntary defection refers to reneging by a rational egoist in the absence of enforceable contracts—the much-analyzed problem posed, for example, in the prisoner's dilemma and other dilemmas of collective action. Involuntary defection instead reflects the behavior of an agent who is unable to deliver on a promise because of failed ratification. Even though these two types of behavior may be difficult to disentangle in some instances, the underlying logic is quite different.

The prospects for international cooperation in an anarchic, "self-help" world are often said to be poor because "unfortunately, policy-makers generally have an incentive to cheat."[34] However, as Axelrod, Keohane, and others have pointed out, the temptation to defect can be dramatically reduced among players who expect to meet again.[35] If policy-makers in an anarchic world were in fact constantly tempted to cheat, certain features of the 1978 story would be very anomalous. For example, even though the Bonn agreement was negotiated with exquisite care, it contained no provisions for temporal balance, sequencing, or partial conditionality that might have protected the parties from unexpected defection. Moreover, the Germans and the Japanese irretrievably enacted their parts of the bargain more than six months before the President's action on oil price decontrol and nearly two years before that decision was implemented. Once they had done so, the temptation to the President to renege should have been overpowering, but in fact virtually no one on either side of the decontrol debate within the administration dismissed the Bonn pledge as irrelevant. In short, the Bonn "promise" had political weight, because reneging would have had high political and diplomatic costs.

However, in any two-level game, the credibility of an official commitment may be low, even if the reputational costs of reneging are high, for the negotiator may be unable to guarantee ratification. The failure of Congress to ratify abolition of the "American Selling Price" as previously agreed during the Kennedy Round of trade negotiations is one classic instance; another is the inability of Japanese Prime Minister Sato to deliver on a promise made to President Nixon during the "Textile Wrangle."[36] A key obstacle to Western economic coordination in 1985–87 was the Germans' fear that the Reagan Administration would be politically unable to carry out any commitment it might make to cut the U.S. budget deficit, no matter how well-intentioned the President.

Unlike concerns about voluntary defection, concern about "deliverability" was a prominent element in the Bonn negotiations. In the post-summit press conference, President Carter stressed that "Each of us has been careful not to promise more than he can deliver." A major issue throughout the negotiations was Carter's own ability to deliver on his energy commitments. The Americans worked hard to convince the others, first, that the President was under severe domestic political constraints on energy issues, which limited what he could promise; but second, that he could deliver what he was prepared to promise. The negotiators in 1978 seemed to follow this presumption about one another: "He will do what he has promised, so long as what he has promised is clear and within his power."

Involuntary defection, and the fear of it, can be just as fatal to prospects for cooperation as voluntary defection. Moreover, in some cases, it may be difficult, both for the other side and for outside analysts, to distinguish voluntary and involuntary defection, particularly since a strategic negotiator might seek to misrepresent a voluntary defection as involuntary. Such behavior is itself presumably subject to some reputational constraints, although it is an important empirical question how far reputations generalize from collectivities to negotiators, and vice versa. Credibility (and thus the ability to strike deals) at Level I is enhanced by a negotiator's (demonstrated) ability to "deliver" at Level II; this was a major strength of Robert Strauss in the Tokyo Round negotiations.[37]

Involuntary defection can only be understood within the framework of a two-level game. Thus, to return to the issue of win-sets, the smaller the win-sets, the greater the risk of involuntary defection, and hence the more applicable the literature about dilemmas of collective action.[38]

The second reason why win-set size is important is that *the relative size of the respective Level II win-sets will affect the distribution of the joint gains from the international bargain.* The larger the perceived win-set of a negotiator, the more he can be "pushed around" by the other Level I negotiators. Conversely, a small domestic win-set can be a bargaining advantage: "I'd like to accept your proposal, but I could never get it accepted at home." Lamenting the domestic constraints under which one must operate is (in the words of one experienced British diplomat) "the natural thing to say at the beginning of a tough negotiation."[39]

This general principle was, of course, first noted by Thomas Schelling nearly thirty years ago:

> The power of a negotiator often rests on a manifest inability to make concessions and meet demands. . . . When the United States Government negotiates with other governments . . . if the executive branch negotiates under legislative authority, with its position constrained by law, . . . then the executive branch has a firm position that is visible to its negotiating partners. . . . [Of course, strategies such as this] run the risk of establishing an immovable position that goes beyond the ability of the other to concede, and thereby provoke the likelihood of stalemate or breakdown.[40]

Writing from a strategist's point of view, Schelling stressed ways in which win-sets may be manipulated; but even when the win-set itself is beyond the negotiator's control, he may exploit its leverage. A Third World leader whose domestic position is relatively weak (Argentina's Alfonsin?) should be able to drive a better bargain with his international creditors, other things being equal, than one whose domestic standing is more solid (Mexico's de la Madrid?).[41] The difficulties of winning Congressional ratification are often exploited by American negotiators. During the negotiation of the Panama Canal Treaty, for example, "the Secretary of State warned the Panamanians several times . . . that the new treaty would have to be acceptable to at least sixty-seven senators," and "Carter, in a personal letter to Torrijos, warned that further concessions by the United States would seriously threaten chances for Senate ratification."[42] Precisely to forestall such tactics, opponents may demand that a negotiator ensure himself "negotiating room" at Level II before opening the Level I negotiations.

The "sweet-and-sour" implications of win-set size are summarized in Figure 1, representing a simple zero-sum game between X and Y. X_M and Y_M represent the maximum outcomes for X and Y, respectively, while X_1 and Y_1 represent the minimal outcomes that could be ratified. At this stage, any agreement in the range between X_1 and Y_1 could be ratified by both parties. If the win-set of Y were contracted to, say, Y_2 (perhaps by requiring a larger majority for ratification), outcomes between Y_1 and Y_2 would no longer be feasible, and the range of feasible agreements would thus be truncated in Y's favor. However, if Y, emboldened by this success, were to reduce its win-set still further to Y_3 (perhaps

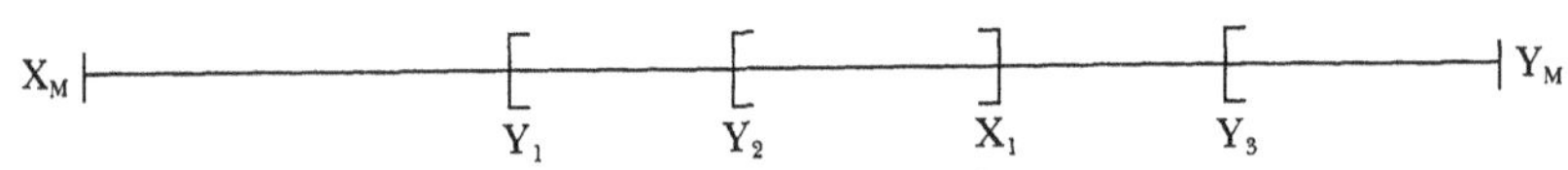

Figure 1. Effects of reducing win-set size

by requiring unanimity for ratification), the negotiators would suddenly find themselves deadlocked, for the win-sets no longer overlap at all.[43]

DETERMINANTS OF THE WIN-SET

It is important to understand what circumstances affect win-set size. Three sets of factors are especially important:

Level II preferences and coalitions
Level II institutions
Level I negotiators' strategies

Let us consider each in turn.

1. The Size of the Win-set Depends on the Distribution of Power, Preferences, and Possible Coalitions among Level II Constituents

Any testable two-level theory of international negotiation must be rooted in a theory of domestic politics, that is, a theory about the power and preferences of the major actors at Level II. This is not the occasion for even a cursory evaluation of the relevant alternatives, except to note that the two-level conceptual framework could in principle be married to such diverse perspectives as Marxism, interest-group pluralism, bureaucratic politics, and neo-corporatism. For example, arms negotiations might be interpreted in terms of a bureaucratic politics model of Level II politicking, while class analysis or neo-corporation might be appropriate for analyzing international macroeconomic coordination.

Abstracting from the details of Level II politics, however, it is possible to sketch certain principles that govern the size of the win-sets. For example, the lower cost of "no-agreement" to constituents, the smaller the win-set.[44] Recall that ratification pits the proposed agreement, *not* against an array of other (possibly attractive) alternatives, but only against "no-agreement."[45] No-agreement often represents the status quo, although in some cases no-agreement may in fact lead to a worsening situation; that might be a reasonable description of the failed ratification of the Versailles Treaty.

Some constituents may face low costs from no-agreement, and others high costs, and the former will be more skeptical of Level I agreements than the latter. Members of two-wage-earner families should be readier to strike, for example, than sole breadwinners, and small-town barbers should be more isolationist than international bankers. In this sense, some constituents may offer either generic opposition to, or generic support for, Level I agreements, more or less independently of the specific content of the agreement, although naturally other constituents' decisions about ratification will be closely conditioned on the specifics. The size of the win-set (and thus the negotiating room of the Level I negotiator) depends on the relative size of the "isolationist" forces (who oppose international cooperation in general) and the "internationalists" (who offer "all-purpose" support). All-purpose support for international agreements is probably greater in smaller, more dependent countries with more open economies, as compared to more self-sufficient countries, like the United States, for most of whose citizens the costs of no-agreement are generally lower. Ceteris paribus, more self-sufficient states with smaller win-sets should make fewer international agreements and drive harder bargains in those that they do make.

In some cases, evaluation of no-agreement may be the *only* significant disagreement among the Level II constituents, because their interests are relatively homogeneous. For example, if oil imports are to be limited by an agreement among the consuming nations—the sort of accord sought at the Tokyo summit of 1979, for example—then presumably every constituent would prefer to maximize his nation's share of the available supply, although some constituents may be more reluctant than others to push too hard, for fear of losing the agreement entirely. Similarly, in most wage negotiations, the interests of constituents (either workers or shareholders) are relatively homogeneous, and the most significant cleavage within the Level II constituencies is likely to be between "hawks" and "doves," depending on their willingness to risk a strike. (Walton and McKersie refer to these as "boundary" conflicts, in which the negotiator is caught between his constituency and the external organization.) Other international examples in which domestic interests are relatively homogeneous except for the evaluation of no-agreement might include the SALT talks, the Panama Canal Treaty negotiations, and the Arab-Israeli conflict. A negotiator is unlikely to face criticism at home that a proposed agreement reduces the opponents' arms too much, offers too little compensation for foreign concessions, or contains too few security guarantees for the other side, although in each case opinions may differ on how much to risk a negotiating deadlock in order to achieve these objectives.

The distinctive nature of such "homogeneous" issues is thrown into sharp relief by contrasting them to cases in which constituents' preferences are more heterogeneous, so that any Level I agreement bears unevenly on them. Thus, an internationally coordinated reflation may encounter domestic opposition *both* from those who think it goes too far (bankers, for example) *and* from those who think it does not go far enough (unions, for example). In 1919, some Americans opposed the Versailles Treaty because it was too harsh on the defeated powers, and others because it was too lenient.[46] Such patterns are even more common, as we shall shortly see, where the negotiation involves multiple issues, such as an arms agreement that involves tradeoffs between seaborne and airborne weapons, or a labor agreement that involves tradeoffs between take-home pay and pensions. (Walton and McKersie term these "factional" conflicts, because the negotiator is caught between contending factions within his own organization.)

The problems facing Level I negotiators dealing with a *homogeneous* (or "boundary") conflict are quite different from those facing negotiators dealing with a *heterogeneous* (or "factional") conflict. In the former case, the more the negotiator can win at Level I—the higher his national oil allocation, the deeper the cuts in Soviet throw-weight, the lower the rent he promises for the Canal, and so on—the better his odds of winning ratification. In such cases, the negotiator may use the implicit threat from his own hawks to maximize his gains (or minimize his losses) at Level I, as Carter and Vance did in dealing with the Panamanians. Glancing over his shoulder at Level II, the negotiator's main problem in a homogeneous conflict is to manage the discrepancy between his constituents' expectations and the negotiable outcome. Neither negotiator is likely to find much sympathy for the enemy's demands among his own constituents, or much support for his constituents' positions in the enemy camp. The effect of domestic division, embodied in hard-line opposition from hawks, is to raise the risk of involuntary defection and thus to impede agreement at Level I. The common belief that domestic politics is inimical to international cooperation no doubt derives from such cases.

The task of a negotiator grappling instead with a *heterogeneous* conflict is more complicated, but potentially more interesting. Seeking to maximize the chances of ratification, he cannot follow a simple "the more, the better" rule of thumb; imposing more severe reparations on the Germans in 1919 would have gained some votes at Level II, but lost others, as would hastening the decontrol of domestic oil prices in 1978. In some cases, these lines of cleavage within the Level II constituencies will cut across the Level I division, and the Level I negotiator may find silent allies at his opponent's domestic table. German labor unions might welcome foreign pressure on their own government to adopt a more expansive fiscal policy, and Italian bankers might welcome international demands for a more austere Italian monetary policy. Thus transnational alignments may emerge, tacit or explicit, in which domestic interests pressure their respective governments to adopt mutually supportive policies. This is, of course, my interpretation of the 1978 Bonn Summit accord.

In such cases, domestic divisions may actually improve the prospects for international cooperation. For example, consider two different distributions of constituents' preferences as between three alternatives: A, B, and no-agreement. If 45 percent of the constituents rank these A > no-agreement > B, 45 percent rank them B > no-agreement > A, and 10 percent rank them B > A > no-agreement, then both A and B are in the win-set, even though B would win in a simple Level-II-only game. On the other hand, if 90 percent rank the alternatives A > no-agreement > B, while 10 percent still rank them B > A > no-agreement, then only A is in the win-set. In this sense, a government that is internally divided is more likely to be able to strike a deal internationally than one that is firmly committed to a single policy.[47] Conversely, to impose binding *ex ante* instructions on the negotiators in such a case might exclude some Level I outcomes that would, in fact, be ratifiable in both nations.[48]

Thus far we have implicitly assumed that all eligible constituents will participate in the ratification process. In fact, however, participation rates vary across groups and across issues, and this variation often has implications for the size of the win-set. For example, when the costs and/or benefits of a proposed agreement are relatively concentrated, it is reasonable to expect that those constituents whose interests are most affected will exert special influence on the ratification process.[49] One reason why Level II games are more important for trade negotiations than in monetary matters is that the "abstention rate" is higher on international monetary issues than on trade issues.[50]

The composition of the active Level II constituency (and hence the character of the win-set) also varies with the politicization of the issue. Politicization often activates groups who are less worried about the costs of no-agreement, thus reducing the effective win-set. For example, politicization of the Panama Canal issue seems to have reduced the negotiating flexibility on both sides of the diplomatic table.[51] This is one reason why most professional diplomats emphasize the value of secrecy to successful negotiations. However, Woodrow Wilson's transcontinental tour in 1919 reflected the opposite calculation, namely, that by expanding the active constituency he could ensure ratification of the Versailles Treaty, although in the end this strategy proved fruitless.[52]

Another important restriction of our discussion thus far has been the assumption that the negotiations involve only one issue. Relaxing this assumption has powerful consequences for the play at both levels.[53] Various groups at Level II are likely to have quite different preferences on the several issues involved in a multi-issue negotiation. As a general rule, the group with the greatest interest in a specific issue is also likely to hold the most extreme position on that issue. In the Law of the Sea negotiations, for example, the Defense Department felt most strongly about sea-lanes, the Department of the Interior about sea-bed mining rights, and so on.[54] If each group is allowed to fix the Level I negotiating position for "its" issue, the resulting package is almost sure to be "non-negotiable" (that is, non-ratifiable in opposing capitals).[55]

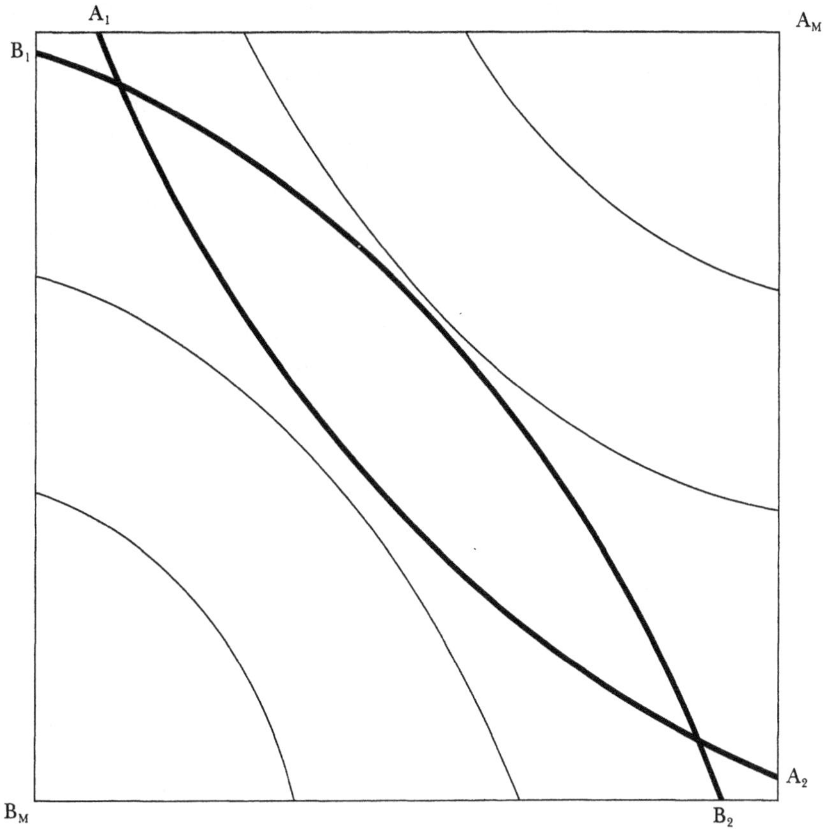

Figure 2. Political indifference curves for two-issue negotiation

Thus, the chief negotiator is faced with tradeoffs across different issues: how much to yield on mining rights in order to get sea-lane protection, how much to yield on citrus exports to get a better deal on beef, and so on. The implication of these tradeoffs for the respective win-sets can be analyzed in terms of iso-vote or "political indifference" curves. This technique is analogous to conventional indifference-curve analysis, except that the operational measure is vote loss, not utility loss. Figure 2 provides an illustrative Edgeworth box analysis.[56] The most-preferred outcome for A (the outcome which wins unanimous approval from both the beef industry and the citrus industry) is the upper right-hand corner (A_M), and each curve concave to point A_M represents the locus of all possible tradeoffs between the interests of ranchers and farmers, such that the net vote in favor of ratification at A's Level II is constant. The bold contour A_1–A_2 represents the minimal vote necessary for ratification by A, and the wedge-shaped area northeast of A_1–A_2 represents A's win-set. Similarly, B_1–B_2 represents the outcomes that are minimally ratifiable by B, and the lens-shaped area between A_1–A_2 and B_1–B_2 represents the set of feasible agreements. Although additional subtleties (such as the nature of the "contract curve") might be extracted from this sort of analysis, the central point is simple: the possibility of package deals open up a rich array of strategic alternatives for negotiators in a two-level game.

One kind of issue linkage is absolutely crucial to understanding how domestic and international politics can become entangled.[57] Suppose that a majority of constituents at Level II oppose a given policy (say, oil price decontrol), but that some members of that majority would be willing to switch their vote on that issue in return for more jobs (say, in export industries). If bargaining is limited to Level II, that tradeoff is not technically feasible, but if the chief negotiator can broker an international deal that delivers more jobs (say, via faster growth abroad), he can, in effect, overturn the initial outcome at the domestic table. Such a transnational issue linkage was a crucial element in the 1978 Bonn accord.

Note that this strategy works not by changing the preferences of any domestic constituents, but rather by creating a policy option (such as faster export growth) that was previously beyond domestic control. Hence, I refer to this type of issue linkage at Level I that alters the feasible outcomes at Level II as *synergistic linkage*. For example, "In the Tokyo Round, . . . nations used negotiation to achieve internal reform in situations where constituency pressures would otherwise prevent action without the pressure (and tradeoff benefits) that an external partner could provide."[58] Economic interdependence multiplies the opportunities for altering domestic coalitions (and thus policy outcomes) by expanding the set of feasible alternatives in this way—in effect, creating political entanglements across national boundaries. Thus, we should expect synergistic linkage (which is, by definition, explicable only in terms of two-level analysis) to become more frequent as interdependence grows.

2. *The Size of the Win-set Depends on the Level II Political Institutions*

Ratification procedures clearly affect the size of the win-set. For example, if a two-thirds vote is required for ratification, the win-set will almost certainly be smaller than if only a simple majority is required. As one experienced observer has written: "Under the Constitution, thirty-four of the one hundred senators can block ratification of any treaty. This is an unhappy and unique feature of our democracy. Because of the effective veto power of a small group, many worthy agreements have been rejected, and many treaties are never considered for ratification."[59] As noted earlier, the U.S. separation of powers imposes a tighter constraint on the American win-set than is true in many other countries. This increases the bargaining power of American negotiators, but it also reduces the scope for international cooperation. It raises the odds for involuntary defection and makes potential partners warier about dealing with the Americans.

The Trade Expansion Act of 1974 modified U.S. ratification procedures in an effort to reduce the likelihood of Congressional tampering with the final deal and hence to reassure America's negotiating partners. After the American Selling Price fiasco, it was widely recognized that piecemeal Congressional ratification of any new agreement would inhibit international negotiation. Hence, the 1974 act guaranteed a straight up-or-down vote in Congress. However, to satisfy Congressional sensitivities, an elaborate system of private-sector committees was established to improve communication between the Level I negotiators and their Level II constituents, in effect coopting the interest groups by exposing them directly to the implications of their demands.[60] Precisely this tactic is described in the labor-management case by Walton and McKersie: "Instead of taking responsibility for directly persuading the principals [Level II constituents] to reduce their expectations, [the Level I negotiator] structures the situation so that they (or their more immediate representatives) will persuade themselves."[61]

Not all significant ratification practices are formalized; for example, the Japanese propensity for seeking the broadest possible domestic consensus before acting constricts the Japanese win-set, as contrasted with majoritarian political cultures. Other domestic political practices, too, can affect the size of the win-set. Strong discipline within the governing party, for example, increases the win-set by widening the range of agreements for which the Level I negotiator can expect to receive backing. For example, in the 1986 House-Senate conference committee on tax reform, the final bill was closer to the Senate version, despite (or rather, *because of*) Congressman Rostenkowski's greater control of his delegation, which increased the House win-set. Conversely, a weakening of party discipline across the major Western nations would, ceteris paribus, reduce the scope for international cooperation.

The recent discussion of "state strength" and "state autonomy" is relevant here. The greater the autonomy of central decision-makers from their Level II constituents, the larger their win-set and thus the greater the likelihood of achieving international agreement. For example, central bank insulation from domestic political pressures in effect increases the win-set and thus the odds for international monetary cooperation; recent proposals for an enhanced role for central bankers in international policy coordination rest on this point.[62] However, two-level analysis also implies that, ceteris paribus, the stronger a state is in terms of autonomy from domestic pressures, the *weaker* its relative bargaining position internationally. For example, diplomats representing an entrenched dictatorship are less able than representatives of a democracy to claim credibly that domestic pressures preclude some disadvantageous deal.[63] This is yet another facet of the disconcerting ambiguity of the notion of "state strength."

For simplicity of exposition, my argument is phrased throughout in terms of only two levels. However, many institutional arrangements require several levels of ratification, thus multiplying the complexity (but perhaps also the importance) of win-set analysis. Consider, for example, negotiations between the United States and the European Community over agricultural trade. According to the Treaty of Rome, modifications of the Common Agricultural Policy require unanimous ratification by the Council of Ministers, representing each of the member states. In turn, each of those governments must, in effect, win ratification for its decision within its own national arena; and in coalition governments, that process might also require ratification within each of the parties. Similarly, on the American side, ratification would (informally, at least) necessitate support from most, if not all, of the major agricultural organizations; and within those organizations, further ratification by key interests and regions might be required. At each stage, cleavage patterns, issue linkages, ratification procedures, side-payments, negotiator strategies, and so on, would need to be considered. At some point in this analytic regress the complexity of further decomposition would outweigh the advantages, but the example illustrates the need for careful thought about the logic of multiple-level games.

3. The Size of the Win-set Depends on the Strategies of the Level I Negotiators

Each Level I negotiator has an unequivocal interest in maximizing the other side's win-set, but with respect to his own win-set, his motives are mixed. The larger his win-set, the more easily he can conclude an agreement, but also the weaker his bargaining position vis-à-vis the other negotiator. This fact often poses a tactical dilemma. For example, one effective way to demonstrate commitment to a given position in Level I bargaining is to rally support from one's constituents (for example, holding a strike vote, talking about a "missile gap," or denouncing "unfair trading practices" abroad). On the other hand, such tactics may have irreversible effects on constituents' attitudes, hampering subsequent ratification of a compromise agreement.[64] Conversely, preliminary consultations at home, aimed at "softening up" one's constituents in anticipation of a ratification struggle, can undercut a negotiator's ability to project an implacable image abroad.

Nevertheless, disregarding these dilemmas for the moment, and assuming that a negotiator wishes to expand his win-set in order to encourage ratification of an agreement, he may exploit both conventional side-payments and generic "good will." The use of side-payments to attract marginal supporters is, of course, quite familiar in game theory, as well as in practical politics. For example, the Carter White House offered many inducements (such as public works projects) to help persuade wavering senators to ratify the Panama Canal Treaty.[65] In a two-level game, the side-payments may come from unrelated domestic sources, as in this case, or they may be received as part of the international negotiation.

The role of side-payments in international negotiations is well known. However, the two-level approach emphasizes that the value of an international side-payment should be calculated in terms of its marginal contribution to the likelihood of ratification rather than in terms of its overall value to the recipient nation. What counts at Level II is not total national costs and benefits, but their incidence, relative to existing coalitions and proto-coalitions. An across-the-board trade concession (or still worse, a concession on a product of interest to a committed free-trade congressman) is less effective than a concession (even one of lesser intrinsic value) that tips the balance with a swing-voter. Conversely, trade retaliation should be targeted neither at free-traders nor at confirmed protectionists, but at the uncommitted.

An experienced negotiator familiar with the respective domestic tables should be able to maximize the cost-effectiveness (to him and his constituents) of the concessions that he must make to ensure ratification abroad, as well as the cost-effectiveness of his own demands and threats, by targeting his initiatives with an eye to their Level II incidence, both at home and abroad. In this endeavor Level I negotiators are often in collusion, since each has an interest in helping the other to get the final deal ratified. In effect, they are moving jointly toward points of tangency between their respective political indifference curves. The empirical frequency of such targeting in trade negotiations and trade wars, as well as in other international negotiations, would be a crucial test of the relative merits of conventional unitary-actor analysis and the two-level approach proposed here.[66]

In addition to the use of specific side-payments, a chief negotiator whose political standing at home is high can more easily win ratification of his foreign initiatives. Although generic good will cannot guarantee ratification, as Woodrow Wilson discovered, it is useful in expanding the win-set and thus fostering Level I agreement, for it constitutes a kind of "all-purpose glue" for his supporting coalition. Walton and McKersie cite members of the United Auto Workers who, speaking of their revered leader, Walter Reuther, said, "I don't understand or agree with this profit-sharing idea, but if the Red Head wants it, I will go along."[67] The Yugoslav negotiator in the Trieste dispute later discounted the difficulty of persuading irredentist Slovenes to accept the agreement, since "the government [i.e., Tito] can always influence public opinion if it wants to."[68]

Note that each Level I negotiator has a strong interest in the popularity of his opposite number, since Party A's popularity increases the size of his win-set, and thus increases both the odds of success and the relative bargaining leverage of Party B. Thus, negotiators should normally be expected to try to reinforce one another's standing with their respective constituents.

Partly for this reason, and partly because of media attention, participation on the world stage normally gives a head of government a special advantage vis-à-vis his or her domestic opposition. Thus, although international policy coordination is hampered by high transaction costs, heads of government may also reap what we might term "transaction benefits." Indeed, the recent evolution of Western summitry, which has placed greater emphasis on publicity than on substance, seems designed to appropriate these "transaction benefits" without actually seeking the sort of agreements that might entail transaction costs.[69]

Higher-status negotiators are likely to dispose of more side-payments and more "good will" at home, and hence foreigners prefer to negotiate with a head of government rather than with a lower official. In purely distributive terms, a nation might have a bargaining advantage if its chief negotiator were a mere clerk. Diplomats are acting rationally, not merely symbolically, when they refuse to negotiate with a counterpart of inferior rank. America's negotiating partners have reason for concern whenever the American president is domestically weakened.

UNCERTAINTY AND BARGAINING TACTICS

Level I negotiators are often badly misinformed about Level II politics, particularly on the opposing side. In 1978 the Bonn negotiators were usually wrong in their assessments of domestic politics abroad; for example, most American officials did not appreciate the complex domestic game that Chancellor Schmidt was playing over the issue of German reflation. Similarly, Snyder and Diesing report that "decision-makers in our cases only occasionally attempted such assessments, and when they tried they did pretty miserably. . . . Governments generally do not do well in analyzing each other's internal politics in crises [and, I would add, in normal times], and indeed it is inherently difficult."[70] Relaxing the assumption of perfect information to allow for uncertainty has many implications for our understanding of two-level games. Let me illustrate a few of these implications.

Uncertainty about the size of a win-set can be both a bargaining device and a stumbling block in two-level negotiation. In purely distributive Level I bargaining, negotiators have an incentive to understate their own win-sets. Since each negotiator is likely to know more about his own Level II table than his opponent does, the claim has some plausibility. This is akin to a tactic that Snyder and Diesing describe, when negotiators seek to exploit divisions within their own government by saying, in effect, "You'd better make a deal with me, because the alternative to me is even worse."[71]

On the other hand, uncertainty about the opponent's win-set increases one's concern about the risk of involuntary defection. Deals can only be struck if each negotiator is convinced that the proposed deal lies within his opposite number's win-set, and thus will be ratified. Uncertainty about Party A's ratification lowers the expected value of the agreement to Party B, and thus Party B will demand more generous side-payments from Party A than would be needed under conditions of certainty. In fact, Party B has an incentive to feign doubt about Party A's ability to deliver, precisely in order to extract a more generous offer.[72]

Thus, a utility-maximizing negotiator must seek to convince his opposite number that his own win-set is "kinky," that is, that the proposed deal is certain to be ratified, but that a deal slightly more favorable to the opponent is unlikely to be ratified. For example, on the energy issue in 1978, by sending Senator Byrd on a personal mission to Bonn before the summit, and then by discussing his political problems in a lengthy tete-à-tete with the Chancellor, Carter sought successfully to convince Schmidt that immediate decontrol was politically impossible, but that decontrol by 1981 was politically do-able. Kinky win-sets may be more credible if they pivot on what Schelling calls a "prominent" solution, such as a 50-50 split, for such outcomes may be distinctly more "salable" at home. Another relevant tactic is for the negotiator actually to submit a trial agreement for ratification, in order to demonstrate that it is not in his win-set.

Uncertainty about the contours of the respective "political indifference curves" thus has strategic uses. On the other hand, when the negotiators are seeking novel packages that might improve both sides' positions, misrepresentation of one's win-set can be counterproductive. Creative solutions that expand the scope for joint gain and improve the odds of ratification are likely to require fairly accurate information about constituents' preferences and points of specific neuralgia. The analysis of two-level games offers many illustrations of Zartman's observation that all negotiation involves "the controlled exchange of partial information."[73]

RESTRUCTURING AND REVERBERATION

Formally speaking, game-theoretic analysis requires that the structure of issues and payoffs be specified in advance. In reality, however, much of what happens in any bargaining situation involves attempts by the players to restructure the game and to alter one another's perceptions of the costs of no-agreement and the benefits of proposed agreements. Such tactics are more difficult in two-level games than in conventional negotiations, because it is harder to reach constituents on the other side with persuasive messages. Nevertheless, governments do seek to expand one another's win-sets. Much ambassadorial activity—wooing opinion leaders, establishing contact with opposition parties, offering foreign aid to a friendly, but unstable, government, and so on—has precisely this function. When Japanese officials visit Capitol Hill, or British diplomats lobby Irish-American leaders, they are seeking to relax domestic constraints that might otherwise prevent the administration from cooperating with their governments.

Another illuminating example of actions by a negotiator at the opposing Level II to improve the odds of ratification occurred during the 1977 negotiations between the International Monetary Fund and the Italian government. Initial IMF demands for austerity triggered strong opposition from the unions and left-wing parties. Although the IMF's bargaining position at Level I appeared strong, the Fund's negotiator sought to achieve a broader consensus within Italy in support of an agreement, in order to forestall involuntary defection. Accordingly, after direct consultations with the unions and leftist leaders, the IMF restructured its proposal to focus on long-term investment and economic recovery (incidentally, an interesting example of targeting), without backing off from its short-term demands. Ironically, the initial Communist support for this revised agreement subsequently collapsed because of conflicts between moderate and doctrinaire factions within the party, illustrating the importance of multilevel analysis.[74]

In some instances, perhaps even unintendedly, international pressures "reverberate" within domestic politics, tipping the domestic balance and thus influencing the international negotiations. Exactly this kind of reverberation characterized the 1978 Summit negotiations. Dieter Hiss, the German sherpa and one of those who believed that a stimulus program was in Germany's own interest, later wrote that summits change national policy

> only insofar as they mobilize and/or change public opinion and the attitude of political groups. . . . Often that is enough, if the balance of opinion is shifted, providing a bare majority for the previously stymied actions of a strong minority. . . . No country violates its own interests, but certainly the definition of its interests can change through a summit with its possible tradeoffs and give-and-take.[75]

From the point of view of orthodox social-choice theory, reverberation is problematic, for it implies a certain interconnectedness among the utility functions of independent actors, albeit across different levels of the game. Two rationales may be offered to explain reverberation among utility-maximizing egoists. First, in a complex, interdependent, but often unfriendly world, offending foreigners may be costly in the long run. "To get along, go along" may be a rational maxim. This rationale is likely to be more common the more dependent (or interdependent) a nation, and it is likely to be more persuasive to Level II actors who are more exposed internationally, such as multinational corporations and international banks.

A second rationale takes into account cognitive factors and uncertainty. It would be a mistake for political scientists to mimic most economists' disregard for the suasive element in negotiations.[76] Given the pervasive uncertainty that surrounds many international issues, messages from abroad can change minds, move the undecided, and hearten those in the domestic minority. As one reluctant late-comer to the "locomotive" cause in 1978 explained his conversion, "In the end, even the Bank for International Settlements [the cautious Basel organization of central bankers] supported the idea of coordinated reflation." Similarly, an enthusiastic advocate of the program welcomed the international pressure as providing a useful "tailwind" in German domestic politics.

Suasive reverberation is more likely among countries with close relations, and is probably more frequent in economic than in political-military negotiations. Communiqués from the Western summits are often cited by participants to domestic audiences as a way of legitimizing their policies. After one such statement by Chancellor Schmidt, one of his aides privately characterized the argument as "not intellectually valid, but politically useful." Conversely, it is widely believed by summit participants that a declaration contrary to a government's current policy could be used profitably by its opponents. Recent Congressional proposals to ensure greater domestic publicity for international commentary on national economic policies (including hitherto confidential IMF recommendations) turn on the idea that reverberation might increase international cooperation.[77]

Reverberation as discussed thus far implies that international pressure expands the domestic win-set and facilitates agreement. However, reverberation can also be negative, in the sense that foreign pressure may create a domestic backlash. Negative reverberation is probably less common empirically than positive reverberation, simply because foreigners are likely to forgo public pressure if it is recognized to be counterproductive. Cognitive balance theory suggests that international pressure is more likely to reverberate negatively if its source is generally viewed by domestic audiences as an adversary rather than an ally. Nevertheless, predicting the precise effect of foreign pressure is admittedly difficult, although empirically, reverberation seems to occur frequently in two-level games.

The phenomenon of reverberation (along with synergistic issue linkage of the sort described earlier) precludes one attractive short-cut to modeling two-level games. If national preferences were exogenous from the point of view of international relations, then the domestic political game could be modeled separately, and the "outputs" from that game could be used as the "inputs" to the international game.[78] The division of labor between comparative politics and international relations could continue, though a few curious observers might wish to keep track of the play on both tables. But if international pressures reverberate within domestic politics, or if issues can be linked synergistically, then domestic outcomes are not exogenous, and the two levels cannot be modeled independently.

THE ROLE OF THE CHIEF NEGOTIATOR

In the stylized model of two-level negotiations outlined here, the chief negotiator is the only formal link between Level I and Level II. Thus far, I have assumed that the chief negotiator has no independent policy views, but acts merely as an honest broker, or rather as an agent on behalf of his constituents. That assumption powerfully simplifies the analysis of two-level games. However, as principal-agent theory reminds us, this assumption is unrealistic.[79] Empirically, the preferences of the chief negotiator may well diverge from those of his constituents. Two-level negotiations are costly and risky for the chief negotiator, and they often interfere with his other priorities, so it is reasonable to ask what is in it for him.

The motives of the chief negotiator include:

1. Enhancing his standing in the Level II game by increasing his political resources or by minimizing potential losses. For example, a head of government may seek the popularity that he expects to

accrue to him if he concludes a successful international agreement, or he may anticipate that the results of the agreement (for example, faster growth or lower defense spending) will be politically rewarding.

2. Shifting the balance of power at Level II in favor of domestic policies that he prefers for exogenous reasons. International negotiations sometimes enable government leaders to do what they privately wish to do, but are powerless to do domestically. Beyond the now-familiar 1978 case, this pattern characterizes many stabilization programs that are (misleadingly) said to be "imposed" by the IMF. For example, in the 1974 and 1977 negotiations between Italy and the IMF, domestic conservative forces exploited IMF pressure to facilitate policy moves that were otherwise infeasible internally.[80]
3. To pursue his own conception of the national interest in the international context. This seems the best explanation of Jimmy Carter's prodigious efforts on behalf of the Panama Canal Treaty, as well as of Woodrow Wilson's ultimately fatal commitment to the Versailles Treaty.

It is reasonable to presume, at least in the international case of two-level bargaining, that the chief negotiator will normally give primacy to his domestic calculus, if a choice must be made, not least because his own incumbency often depends on his standing at Level II. Hence, he is more likely to present an international agreement for ratification, the less of his own political capital he expects to have to invest to win approval, and the greater the likely political returns from a ratified agreement.

This expanded conception of the role of the chief negotiator implies that he has, in effect, a veto over possible agreements. Even if a proposed deal lies within his Level II win-set, that deal is unlikely to be struck if he opposes it.[81] Since this proviso applies on both sides of the Level I table, the actual international bargaining set may be narrower—perhaps much narrower—than the overlap between the Level II win-sets. Empirically, this additional constraint is often crucial to the outcome of two-level games. One momentous example is the fate of the Versailles Treaty. The best evidence suggests, first, that perhaps 80 percent of the American public *and* of the Senate in 1919 favored ratification of the treaty, if certain reservations were attached; and second, that those reservations were acceptable to the other key signatories, especially Britain and France. In effect, it was Wilson himself who vetoed this otherwise ratifiable package, telling the dismayed French Ambassador, "I shall consent to nothing."[82]

Yet another constraint on successful two-level negotiation derives from the leader's existing domestic coalition. Any political entrepreneur has a fixed investment in a particular pattern of policy positions and a particular supporting coalition. If a proposed international deal threatens that investment, or if ratification would require him to construct a different coalition, the chief negotiator will be reluctant to endorse it, even if (judged abstractly) it could be ratified. Politicians may be willing to risk a few of their normal supporters in the cause of ratifying an international agreement, but the greater the potential loss, the greater their reluctance.

In effect, the fixed costs of coalition-building thus imply this constraint on the win-set: How great a realignment of prevailing coalitions at Level II would be required to ratify a particular proposal? For example, a trade deal may expand export opportunities for Silicon Valley, but harm Aliquippa. This is fine for a chief negotiator (for example, Reagan?) who can easily add Northern California yuppies to his support coalition and who has no hope of winning Aliquippa steelworkers anyhow. But a different chief negotiator with a different support coalition (for example, Mondale?) might find it costly or even impossible to convert the gains from the same agreement into politically usable form. Similarly, in the 1978 "neutron bomb" negotiations between Bonn and Washington, "asking the United States to deploy [these weapons] in West Germany might have been possible for a Christian Democratic government; for a Social Democratic government, it was nearly impossible."[83] Under such circumstances, simple "median-voter" models of domestic influences on foreign policy may be quite misleading.

Relaxing the assumption that the chief negotiator is merely an honest broker, negotiating on behalf of his constituents, opens the possibility that the constituents may be more eager for an agreement (or more worried about "no-agreement") than he is. Empirical instances are not hard to find: in early 1987, European publics were readier to accept Gorbachev's "double-zero" arms-control proposal than European leaders, just as in the early 1970s the American public (or at least the politically active public) was more eager for a negotiated end to the Vietnam War than was the Nixon Administration. As a rule, the negotiator retains a veto over any proposed agreement in such cases. However, if the negotiator's own domestic standing (or indeed, his incumbency) would be threatened if he were to reject an agreement that falls within his Level II win-set, and if this is known to all parties, then the other side at Level I gains considerable leverage. Domestic U.S. discontent about the Vietnam War clearly affected the agreement reached at the Paris talks.[84] Conversely, if the constituents are (believed to be) hard-line, then a leader's domestic weakness becomes a diplomatic asset. In 1977, for example, the Americans calculated that "a delay in negotiating a treaty . . . endangered [Panamanian President Omar] Torrijos' position; and Panama without Torrijos most likely would have been an impossible negotiating partner."[85] Similarly, in the 1954 Trieste negotiations, the weak Italian government claimed that "'Unless something is done in our favor in Trieste, we can lose the election.' That card was played two or three times [reported the British negotiator later], and it almost always took a trick."[86]

My emphasis on the special responsibility of central executives is a point of affinity between the two-level game model and the "state-centric" literature, even though the underlying logic is different. In this "Janus" model of domestic-international interactions, transnational politics are less prominent than in some theories of interdependence.[87] However, to disregard "cross-table" alliances at Level II is a considerable simplification, and it is more misleading the lower the political visibility of the issue, and the more frequent the negotiations between the governments involved.[88] Empirically, for example, two-level games in the European Community are influenced by many direct ties among Level II participants, such as national agricultural spokesmen. In some cases, the same multinational actor may actually appear at more than one Level II table. In negotiations over mining concessions in some less developed countries, for example, the same multinational corporation may be consulted privately by both the home and host governments. In subsequent work on the two-level model, the strategic implications of direct communication between Level II players should be explored.

CONCLUSION

The most portentous development in the fields of comparative politics and international relations in recent years is the dawning recognition among practitioners in each field of the need to take into account entanglements between the two. Empirical illustrations of reciprocal influence between domestic and international affairs abound. What we need now are concepts and theories that will help us organize and extend our empirical observations.

Analysis in terms of two-level games offers a promising response to this challenge. Unlike state-centric theories, the two-level approach recognizes the inevitability of domestic conflict about what the "national interest" requires. Unlike the "second-image" or the "second-image-reversed," the two-level approach recognizes that central decision-makers strive to reconcile domestic and international imperatives simultaneously. As we have seen, statesmen in this predicament face distinctive strategic opportunities and strategic dilemmas.

This theoretical approach highlights several significant features of the links between diplomacy and domestic politics, including:

the important distinction between voluntary and involuntary defection from international agreements;

the contrast between issues on which domestic interests are homogeneous, simply pitting hawks against doves, and issues on which domestic interests are more heterogeneous, so that domestic cleavage may actually foster international cooperation;

the possibility of synergistic issue linkage, in which strategic moves at one game-table facilitate unexpected coalitions at the second table;

the paradoxical fact that institutional arrangements which strengthen decision-makers at home may weaken their international bargaining position, and vice versa;

the importance of targeting international threats, offers, and side-payments with an eye toward their domestic incidence at home and abroad;

the strategic uses of uncertainty about domestic politics, and the special utility of "kinky win-sets";

the potential reverberation of international pressures within the domestic arena;

the divergences of interest between a national leader and those on whose behalf he is negotiating—and in particular, the international implications of his fixed investments in domestic politics.

Two level games seem a ubiquitous feature of social life, from Western economic summitry to diplomacy in the Balkans, and from coalition politics in Sri Lanka to legislative maneuvering on Capitol Hill. Far-ranging empirical research is needed now to test and deepen our understanding of how such games are played.

This essay was first published in *International Organization* 42 (Summer 1988): 427–460. An earlier version was delivered at the 1986 Annual Meeting of the American Political Science Association. For criticisms and suggestions, I am indebted to Robert Axelrod, Nicholas Bayne, Henry Brady, James A. Caporaso, Barbara Crane, Ernst B. Haas, Stephan Haggard, C. Randall Henning, Peter B. Kenen, Robert O. Keohane, Stephen D. Krasner, Jacek Kugler, Lisa Martin, John Odell, Robert Powell, Kenneth A. Shepsle, Steven Stedman, Peter Yu, members of research seminars at the Universities of Iowa, Michigan, and Harvard, and two anonymous reviewers. I am grateful to the Rockefeller Foundation for enabling me to complete this research.

NOTES

1. The following account is drawn from Robert D. Putnam and C. Randall Henning, "The Bonn Summit of 1978: A Case Study in Coordination" in

Richard N. Cooper et al., *Can Nations Agree? Issues in International Economic Cooperation* (Washington, D.C.: The Brookings Institution, October 1989), pp. 12–140; and Robert D. Putnam and Nicholas Bayne, *Hanging Together: Cooperation and Conflict in the Seven-Power Summits*, rev. ed. (Cambridge, Mass.: Harvard University Press, 1987), pp. 62–94.

2. Among interdependent economies, most economists believe, policies can often be more effective if they are internationally coordinated. For relevant citations, see Putnam and Bayne, *Hanging Together*, p. 24.

3. For a comprehensive account of the Japanese story, see I. M. Destler and Hisao Mitsuyù, "Locomotives on Different Tracks: Macroeconomic Diplomacy, 1977–1979," in I. M. Destler and Hideo Sato, eds., *Coping with U.S.-Japanese Economic Conflicts* (Lexington, Mass.: D. C. Heath, 1982).

4. For an excellent account of U.S. energy policy during this period, see G. John Ikenberry, "Market Solutions for State Problems: The International and Domestic Politics of American Oil Decontrol," *International Organization* 42 (Winter 1988): 151–177.

5. It is not clear whether Jimmy Carter fully understood the domestic implications of his Bonn pledge at the time. See Putnam and Henning, "The Bonn Summit," and Ikenberry, "Market Solutions."

6. Kenneth N. Waltz, *Man, the State, and War: A Theoretical Analysis* (New York: Columbia University Press, 1959).

7. Peter Gourevitch, "The Second Image Reversed: The International Sources of Domestic Politics," *International Organization* 32 (Autumn 1978): 881–911.

8. I am indebted to Stephan Haggard for enlightening discussions about domestic influences on international relations.

9. James Rosenau, "Toward the Study of National-International Linkages," in his *Linkage Politics: Essays on the Convergence of National and International Systems* (New York: Free Press, 1969); as well as his "Theorizing Across Systems: Linkage Politics Revisited," in Jonathan Wilkenfeld, ed., *Conflict Behavior and Linkage Politics* (New York: David McKay, 1973), esp. p. 49.

10. Karl W. Deutsch et al., *Political Community in the North Atlantic Area: International Organization in the Light of Historical Experience* (Princeton, N.J.: Princeton University Press, 1957); and Ernst B. Haas, *The Uniting of Europe: Political, Social, and Economic Forces, 1950–1957* (Stanford, Calif.: Stanford University Press, 1958).

11. Robert O. Keohane and Joseph S. Nye, *Power and Interdependence* (Boston: Little, Brown, 1977). On the regime literature, including its neglect of domestic factors, see Stephan Haggard and Beth Simmons, "Theories of International Regimes," *International Organization* 41 (Summer 1987): 491–517.

12. Graham T. Allison, *Essence of Decision: Explaining the Cuban Missile Crisis* (Boston: Little, Brown, 1971), p. 149.

13. Peter J. Katzenstein, ed., *Between Power and Plenty: Foreign Economic Policies of Advanced Industrial States* (Madison: University of Wisconsin Press, 1978), p. 4. See also Katzenstein, "International Relations and Domestic Structures: Foreign Economic Policies of Advanced Industrial States," *International Organization* 30

(Winter 1976): 1–45; Stephen D. Krasner, "United States Commercial and Monetary Policy: Unravelling the Paradox of External Strength and Internal Weakness," in Katzenstein, *Between Power and Plenty*, pp. 51–87; and Krasner, *Defending the National Interest: Raw Materials Investments and U.S. Foreign Policy* (Princeton, N.J.: Princeton University Press, 1978).

14. For example, see Krasner in Katzenstein, p. 55: "The central analytic characteristic that determines the ability of a state to overcome domestic resistance is its strength in relation to its own society."

15. Helen Milner, "Resisting the Protectionist Temptation: Industry and the Making of Trade Policy in France and the United States during the 1970s," *International Organization* 41 (Autumn 1987): 639–665.

16. Gourevitch, "The Second Image Reversed," p. 903.

17. In their more descriptive work, "state-centric" scholars are often sensitive to the impact of social and political conflicts, such as those between industry and finance, labor and business, and export-oriented versus import-competing sectors. See Katzenstein, *Between Power and Plenty*, pp. 333–336, for example.

18. David A. Lake, "The State as Conduit: The International Sources of National Political Action," paper delivered at the 1984 Annual Meeting of the American Political Science Association, p. 13.

19. James E. Alt, "Crude Politics: Oil and the Political Economy of Unemployment in Britain and Norway, 1970–1985," *British Journal of Political Science* 17 (April 1987): 149–199; Peter B. Evans, *Dependent Development: The Alliance of Multinational, State, and Local Capital in Brazil* (Princeton, N.J.: Princeton University Press, 1979); Peter Gourevitch, *Politics in Hard Times: Comparative Responses to International Economic Crises* (Ithaca, N.Y.: Cornell University Press, 1986); Peter J. Katzenstein, *Small States in World Markets: Industrial Policy in Europe* (Ithaca, N.Y.: Cornell University Press, 1985).

20. Richard E. Walton and Robert B. McKersie, *A Behavioral Theory of Labor Negotiations: An Analysis of a Social Interaction System* (New York: McGraw-Hill, 1965).

21. Robert S. Strauss, "Foreword," in Joan E. Twiggs, *The Tokyo Round of Multilateral Trade Negotiations: A Case Study in Building Domestic Support for Diplomacy* (Washington, D.C.: Georgetown University Institute for the Study of Diplomacy, 1987), p. vii. Former Secretary of Labor John Dunlop is said to have remarked that "Bilateral negotiations usually require three agreements—one across the table and one on each side of the table," as cited in Howard Raiffa, *The Art and Science of Negotiation* (Cambridge, Mass.: Harvard University Press, 1982), p. 166.

22. Daniel Druckman, "Boundary Role Conflict: Negotiation as Dual Responsiveness," in I. William Zartman, ed., *The Negotiation Process: Theories and Applications* (Beverly Hills, Calif.: Sage, 1978), vol. 1, pp. 100–101, 109. For a review of the social-psychological literature on bargainers as representatives, see Dean G. Pruitt, *Negotiation Behavior* (New York: Academic Press, 1981), pp. 41–43.

23. Robert Axelrod, "The Gamma Paradigm for Studying the Domestic Influence on Foreign Policy," paper delivered at the 1987 Annual Meeting of the International Studies Association.

24. Glenn H. Snyder and Paul Diesing, *Conflict Among Nations: Bargaining, Decision Making, and System Structure in International Crises* (Princeton, N.J.: Princeton University Press, 1977), pp. 510–525.

25. Max Black, *Models and Metaphors* (Ithaca, N.Y.: Cornell University Press, 1962), p. 242, as cited in Duncan Snidal, "The Game *Theory* of International Politics," *World Politics* 38 (October 1985): 36n.

26. To avoid unnecessary complexity, my argument throughout is phrased in terms of a single chief negotiator, although in many cases some of his responsibilities may be delegated to aides. Later in this paper I relax the assumption that the negotiator has no independent preferences.

27. Gerhardt Stoltenberg, *Wall Street Journal Europe*, Oct. 2, 1986, as cited in C. Randall Henning, *Macroeconomic Diplomacy in the 1980s: Domestic Politics and International Conflict Among the United States, Japan, and Europe*, Atlantic Paper no. 65 (New York: Croom Helm, for the Atlantic Institute for International Affairs, 1987), p. 1.

28. Ito Takashi, "Conflicts and Coalition in Japan, 1930: Political Groups and the London Naval Disarmament Conference," in Sven Groennings et al., eds., *The Study of Coalition Behavior* (New York: Holt, Rinehart, and Winston, 1970); Kobayashi Tatsuo, "The London Naval Treaty, 1930," in James W. Morley, ed., *Japan Erupts: The London Naval Conference and the Manchurian Incident, 1928–1932* (New York: Columbia University Press, 1984), pp. 11–117. I am indebted to William Jarosz for this example.

29. This stipulation is, in fact, characteristic of most real-world ratification procedures, such as House and Senate action on conference committee reports, although it is somewhat violated by the occasional practice of appending "reservations" to the ratification of treaties.

30. *New York Times*, Sept. 26, 1986.

31. For the conception of "win-set," see Kenneth A. Shepsle and Barry R. Weingast, "The Institutional Foundations of Committee Power," *American Political Science Review* 81 (March 1987): 85–104. I am indebted to Professor Shepsle for much help on this topic.

32. To avoid tedium, I do not repeat the "other things being equal" proviso in each of the propositions that follow. Under some circumstances, an expanded win-set might actually make practicable some outcome that could trigger a dilemma of collective action. See Vincent P. Crawford, "A Theory of Disagreement in Bargaining," *Econometrica* 50 (May 1982): 607–637.

33. The Sunday Times Insight Team, *The Falklands War* (London: Sphere, 1982); Max Hastings and Simon Jenkins, *The Battle for the Falklands* (New York: Norton, 1984); Alejandro Dabat and Luis Lorenzano, *Argentina: The Malvinas and the End of Military Rule* (London: Verso, 1984). I am indebted to Louise Richardson for these citations.

34. Matthew E. Canzoneri and Jo Anna Gray, "Two Essays on Monetary Policy in an Interdependent World," International Finance Discussion Paper no. 219 (Board of Governors of the Federal Reserve System, February 1983).

35. Robert Axelrod, *The Evolution of Cooperation* (New York: Basic Books, 1984); Robert O. Keohane, *After Hegemony: Cooperation and Discord in the World*

Political Economy (Princeton, N.J.: Princeton University Press, 1984), esp. p. 116; and the special issue of *World Politics,* "Cooperation Under Anarchy" (Kenneth A. Oye, ed.), 38 (October 1985): 1–254.

36. I. M. Destler, Haruhiro Fukui, and Hideo Sato, *The Textile Wrangle: Conflict in Japanese-American Relations, 1969–1971* (Ithaca, N.Y.: Cornell University Press, 1979), pp. 121–157.

37. Gilbert R. Winham, "Robert Strauss, the MTN, and the Control of Faction," *Journal of World Trade Law* 14 (September/October 1980): 377–397; and Winham, *International Trade and the Tokyo Round* (Princeton, N.J.: Princeton University Press, 1986).

38. This discussion implicitly assumes uncertainty about the contours of the win-sets on the part of the Level I negotiators—for if the win-sets were known with certainty, the negotiators would never propose for ratification an agreement that would be rejected.

39. Geoffrey W. Harrison, in John C. Campbell, ed., *Successful Negotiation: Trieste 1954* ((Princeton, N.J.: Princeton University Press, 1976), p. 62.

40. Thomas C. Schelling, *The Strategy of Conflict* (Cambridge, Mass.: Harvard University Press, 1960), pp. 19–28.

41. I am grateful to Lara Putnam for this example. For supporting evidence, see Robert R. Kaufman, "Democratic and Authoritarian Responses to the Debt Issue: Argentina, Brazil, Mexico," *International Organization* 39 (Summer 1985): 473–503.

42. William Mark Habeeb and I. William Zartman, *The Panama Canal Negotiations* (Washington, D.C.: Johns Hopkins Foreign Policy Institute, 1986), pp. 40, 42.

43. Several investigators in other fields have recently proposed models of linked games akin to this "two-level" game. Kenneth A. Shepsle and his colleagues have used the notion of "interconnected games" to analyze, for example, the strategy of a legislator simultaneously embedded in two games, one in the legislative arena and the other in the electoral arena. In this model, a given action is simultaneously a move in two different games, and one player maximizes the sum of his payoffs from the two games. See Arthur Denzau, William Riker, and Kenneth Shepsle, "Farquharson and Fenno: Sophisticated Voting and Home Style," *American Political Science Review* 79 (December 1985): 1117–1134; and Kenneth Shepsle, "Cooperation and Institutional Arrangements," paper delivered the Harvard–M.I.T. Conference on Institutional Change (Dedham, Mass., February 1986). This approach is similar to models recently developed by economists working in the "rational expectations" genre. In these models, a government contends simultaneously against other governments and against domestic trade unions over monetary policy. See, for example, Kenneth Rogoff, "Can International Monetary Policy Cooperation be Counterproductive?" *Journal of International Economics* 18 (May 1985): 199–217; and Roland Vaubel, "A Public Choice Approach to International Organization," *Public Choice* 51 (1986): 39–57. George Tsebelis ("Nested Games: The Cohesion of French Coalitions," *British Journal of Political Science* 18 [April 1988]: 145–170) has developed a theory of "nested games" in which two alliances play a competitive game to determine

total payoffs, while the individual players within each alliance contend over their shares. Fritz Sharpf ("A Game-Theoretical Interpretation of Inflation and Unemployment in Western Europe," *Journal of Public Policy* 7 [1988]: 227–257) interprets macroeconomic policy as the joint outcome of two simultaneous games; in one, the government plays against the unions, while in the other it responds to the anticipated reactions of the electorate. James E. Alt and Barry Eichengreen ("Parallel and Overlapping Games: Theory and an Application to the European Gas Trade," *Economics and Politics* 1 [1989]: 119–144) offer a broader typology of linked games, distinguishing between "parallel" games, in which "the same opponents play against one another at the same time in more than one arena," and "overlapping" games, which arise "when a particular player is engaged at the same time in games against distinct opponents, and when the strategy pursued in one game limits the strategies available in the other." Detailed comparison of these various linked-game models is a task for the future.

44. Thomas Romer and Howard Rosenthal, "Political Resource Allocation, Controlled Agendas, and the Status Quo," *Public Choice* 33 (1978): 27–44.

45. In more formal treatments, the no-agreement outcome is called the "reversion point." A given constituent's evaluation of no-agreement corresponds to what Raiffa, in *Negotiation,* terms a seller's "walk-away price," that is, the price below which he would prefer "no-deal." No-agreement is equivalent to what Snyder and Diesing, in *Conflict Among Nations,* term "breakdown," or the expected cost of war.

46. Thomas A. Bailey, *Woodrow Wilson and the Great Betrayal* (New York: Macmillan, 1945), pp. 16–37.

47. Raiffa, (*Negotiation,* p. 12) notes that "the more diffuse the positions are within each side, the easier it might be to achieve external agreement." For the conventional view, by contrast, that domestic unity is generally a precondition for international agreement, see Michael Artis and Sylvia Ostry, *International Economic Policy Coordination* (Chatham House Papers no. 30; London: Routledge and Kegan Paul, 1986), pp. 75–76.

48. "Meaningful consultation with other nations becomes very difficult when the internal process of decision-making already has some of the characteristics of compacts between quasi-sovereign entities. There is an increasing reluctance to hazard a hard-won domestic consensus in an international forum." Henry A. Kissinger, "Domestic Structure and Foreign Policy," in James N. Rosenau, ed., *International Politics and Foreign Policy* (New York: Free Press, 1969), p. 266.

49. See James Q. Wilson, *Political Organization* (New York: Basic Books, 1975), on how the politics of an issue are affected by whether the costs and the benefits are concentrated or diffuse.

50. Another factor fostering abstention is the greater complexity and opacity of monetary issues; as Gilbert R. Winham ("Complexity in International Negotiation," in Daniel Druckman, ed., *Negotiations: A Social-Psychological Perspective* [Beverly Hills, Calif.: Sage, 1977], p. 363) observes, "Complexity can strengthen the hand of a negotiator vis-à-vis the organization he represents."

51. Habeeb and Zartman, *The Panama Canal Negotiations.*

52. Bailey, *Woodrow Wilson.*

53. I am grateful to Ernst B. Haas and Robert O. Keohane for helpful advice on this point.

54. Ann L. Hollick, *U.S. Foreign Policy and the Law of the Sea* (Princeton, N.J.: Princeton University Press, 1981), esp. pp. 208–237; and James K. Sebenius, *Negotiating the Law of the Sea* (Cambridge, Mass.: Harvard University Press, 1984), esp. pp. 74–78.

55. Raiffa, *Negotiation,* p. 175.

56. I am indebted to Lisa Martin and Kenneth Shepsle for suggesting this approach, although they are not responsible for my application of it. Note that this construction assumes that each issue, taken individually, is a "homogeneous" type, not a "heterogeneous" type. Constructing iso-vote curves for heterogeneous-type issues is more complicated.

57. I am grateful to Henry Brady for clarifying this point for me.

58. Gilbert R. Winham, "The Relevance of Clausewitz to a Theory of International Negotiation," delivered at the 1987 annual meeting of the American Political Science Association.

59. Jimmy Carter, *Keeping Faith: Memoirs of a President* (New York: Bantam Books, 1982), p. 225.

60. Winham, "Robert Strauss" and *International Trade;* and Twiggs, *The Tokyo Round.*

61. Walton and McKersie, *A Behavioral Theory,* p. 321.

62. Artis and Ostry, *International . . . Coordination.* Of course, whether this is desirable in terms of democratic values is quite another matter.

63. Schelling, *Strategy,* p. 28.

64. Walton and McKersie, *A Behavioral Theory,* p. 345.

65. Carter, *Keeping Faith,* p. 172. See also Raiffa, *Negotiation,* p. 183.

66. The strategic significance of targeting at Level II is illustrated in John Conybeare, "Trade Wars: A Comparative Study of Anglo-Hanse, Franco-Italian, and Hawley-Smoot Conflicts," *World Politics* 38 (October 1985): 157: retaliation in the Anglo-Hanse trade wars did not have the intended deterrent effect, because it was not (and perhaps could not have been) targeted at the crucial members of the opposing Level II coalition. Compare Snyder and Diesing, *Conflict Among Nations,* p. 552: "If one faces a coercive opponent, but the opponent's majority coalition includes a few wavering members inclined to compromise, a compromise proposal that suits their views may cause their defection and the formation of a different majority coalition. Or if the opponent's strategy is accommodative, based on a tenuous soft-line coalition, one knows that care is required in implementing one's own coercive strategy to avoid the opposite kind of shift in the other state."

67. Walton and McKersie, *A Behavioral Theory,* p. 319.

68. Vladimir Velebit, in Campbell, *Successful Negotiation,* p. 97. As noted earlier, our discussion here assumes that the Level I negotiator wishes to reach a ratifiable agreement; in cases (alluded to later) when the negotiator's own preferences are more hard-line than his constituents', his domestic popularity might allow him to resist Level I agreements.

69. Transaction benefits may be enhanced if a substantive agreement is

reached, although sometimes leaders can benefit domestically by loudly rejecting a proffered international deal.

70. Snyder and Diesing, *Conflict,* pp. 516, 522–523. Analogous misperceptions in Anglo-American diplomacy are the focus of Richard E. Neustadt, *Alliance Politics* (New York: Columbia University Press, 1970).

71. Snyder and Diesing, *Conflict,* p. 517.

72. I am grateful to Robert O. Keohane for pointing out the impact of uncertainty on the expected value of proposals.

73. I. William Zartman, *The Fifty-Percent Solution* (Garden City, N.Y.: Anchor Books, 1976), p. 14. The present analysis assumes that constituents are myopic about the other side's Level II, an assumption that is not unrealistic empirically. However, a fully informed constituent would consider the preferences of key players on the other side—for if the current proposal lies well within the other side's win-set, then it would be rational for the constituent to vote against it, hoping for a second-round proposal that was more favorable to him and still ratifiable abroad; this might be a reasonable interpretation of Senator Lodge's position in 1919 (see Bailey, *Woodrow Wilson*). Consideration of such strategic voting at Level II is beyond the scope of this paper.

74. John R. Hillman, "The Mutual Influence of Italian Domestic Politics and the International Monetary Fund," *The Fletcher Forum* 4 (Winter 1980): 1–22. Luigi Spaventa (in "Two Letters of Intent: External Crises and Stabilization Policy, Italy, 1973–77," in John Williamson, ed., *IMF Conditionality,* [Washington, D.C.: Institute for International Economics, 1983], pp. 441–473) argues that the unions and the Communists actually favored the austerity measures, but found the IMF demands helpful in dealing with their own internal Level II constituents.

75. Dieter Hiss, "Weltwirtschaftsgipfel: Betrachtungen eines Insiders" [World Economic Summit: Observations of an Insider], in Joachim Frohn and Reiner Staeglin, eds., *Empirische Wirtschaftsforschung* (Berlin: Duncker and Humblot, 1980), pp. 286–287.

76. On cognitive and communications explanations of international cooperation, see, for example, Ernst B. Haas, "Why Collaborate? Issue-Linkage and International Regimes," *World Politics* 32 (April 1980): 357–405; Richard N. Cooper, "International Cooperation in Public Health as a Prologue to Macroeconomic Cooperation," in Cooper et al., *Can Nations Agree?*, pp. 178–254; and Zartman, *The Fifty-Percent Solution,* esp. part 4.

77. Henning, *Macroeconomic Diplomacy,* pp. 62–63.

78. This is the approach used to analyze the Anglo–Chinese negotiations over Hong Kong in Bruce Bueno de Mesquita, David Newman, and Alvin Rabushka, *Forecasting Political Events: The Future of Hong Kong* (New Haven, Conn.: Yale University Press, 1985).

79. For overviews of this literature, see Terry M. Moe, "The New Economics of Organization," *American Journal of Political Science* 28 (November 1984): 739–777; John W. Pratt and Richard J. Zeckhauser, eds., *Principals and Agents: The Structure of Business* (Boston: Harvard Business School Press, 1985); and Barry M. Mitnick, "The Theory of Agency and Organizational Analysis," paper delivered at the 1986 Annual Meeting of the American Political Science Associa-

tion. This literature is only indirectly relevant to our concerns here, for it has not yet adequately addressed the problems posed by multiple principals (or constituents, in our terms). For one highly formal approach to the problem of multiple principals, see R. Douglas Bernheim and Michael D. Whinston, "Common Agency," *Econometrica* 54 (July 1986): 923–942.

80. Hillman, "Mutual Influence," and Spaventa, "Two Letters."

81. This power of the chief negotiator is analogous to what Shepsle and Weingast, "Institutional Foundations," term the "penultimate" or "ex post veto" power of the members of a Senate-House conference committee.

82. Bailey, *Woodrow Wilson,* quotation at p. 15.

83. Robert A. Strong and Marshal Zeringue, "The Neutron Bomb and the Atlantic Alliance," paper delivered at the 1986 Annual Meeting of the American Political Science Association, p. 9.

84. I. William Zartman, "Reality, Image, and Detail: The Paris Negotiations, 1969–1973," in Zartman, *The Fifty-Percent Solution,* pp. 372–398.

85. Zbigniew Brzezinski, *Power and Principle* (New York: Farrar, Strauss, and Giroux, 1983), p. 136, as quoted in Habeeb and Zartman, *Panama Canal Negotiations,* pp. 39–40.

86. Harrison, in Campbell, *Successful Negotiation,* p. 67.

87. Samuel P. Huntington, "Transnational Organizations in World Politics," *World Politics* 25 (April 1973): 333–368; Keohane and Nye, *Power and Interdependence;* Neustadt, *Alliance Politics.*

88. Barbara Crane, "Policy Coordination by Major Western Powers in Bargaining with the Third World: Debt Relief and the Common Fund," *International Organization* 38 (Summer 1984): 399–428.

[4]

SPECIAL BARRIER NO. 2: CULTURE

Jeswald W. Salacuse

Although negotiating a purely domestic business deal and negotiating an international transaction have much in common, the factor that is almost always present in an international negotiation and generally absent from a domestic negotiation is a difference in culture among the parties. International business transactions cross cultures as well as borders. Culture profoundly influences how people think, communicate, and behave. It also affects the kinds of deals they make and the way they make them. Differences in culture between business executives—for example, between a Chinese public sector plant manager in Shanghai and an American division head of a family company in Cleveland—may therefore create barriers that impede or completely stymie the negotiating process.

THE MEANING OF CULTURE

What do we mean by culture? Culture consists of the socially transmitted behavior patterns, attitudes, norms, and values of a given community. Persons from that community use the elements of their culture to interpret their surroundings and guide their interactions with other persons. When executives from Houston Glue Company and Dallas Adhesive Co. negotiate their deal, they rely on their common culture to interpret each other's statements and actions. But when persons from two different cultures—for example, executives from Houston Glue and Budapest Adhesive—meet for the first time, they do not share a common pool of information and assumptions to interpret each other's statements, actions, and intentions. When a Hollywood film producer and a New York agent for a movie star agree to "do lunch and talk contract," they both know that they will be discussing a detailed document covering not only salary, but billing, advertising, rehearsal time, dressing room facilities, and a host of other matters peculiar to the U.S. entertainment industry. If, after the first martini, the agent says, "We want a gross deal," the producer understands immediately that the film star is seeking a portion of the film's gross revenues before deduction of expenses. And when the producer replies, "Nicholson he's not!" the agent knows that he has to convince the producer that his client is indeed in the category of performers like Jack Nicholson whose reputations command a percentage of gross revenues. Without adequate background knowledge, a person from another country—perhaps a bilingual French executive or an Argentinean rancher with excellent English—would find it difficult to understand the exchange between the producer and the agent because words like "gross deal" and even "contract" gain full meaning only when interpreted in light of the business culture of the U.S. entertainment industry. In many cases, words are just a code that you cannot understand unless you know the context and the background. Culture is an important part of the background and context of any deal.

Culture can therefore be seen as a kind of language, a "silent language" that the parties need in addition to the language they are speaking if they are to arrive at a genuine understanding.[1] Culture serves as a type of social adhesive that binds a group of people together and gives them a distinct identity as a community. It may also give them a sense that they are a community different from other communities.

Culture and nationality are not always the same thing. Within Nigeria, for example, the culture of the Ibos of the largely Christian southeastern part of the country and that of the Hausas of the mainly Muslim north are different and distinct. Similarly, individual corporations and professions may have their own organizational or professional cultures whose norms and behavior patterns may predominate in certain respects over the ethnic or national cultures of their members. For example, a continuing concern in both domestic and cross-border mergers is the problem of blending the cultures of two companies after the deal has been signed, a difficult challenge even for firms from the same culture. While cultural values, attitudes, and behavior patterns may appear permanently embedded in a group, particularly in the context of an encounter between two different cultures, culture is in fact dynamic. It is constantly changing.

And finally, in considering culture's role in international negotiations and relationships, it is important to remember that the world has a staggering diversity of cultures. While executives sometimes speak of Asian culture as if it were homogeneous, in reality, Asia has many different and distinct cultures, from India to Laos, from Korea to Indonesia. Each has its own values and practices that may differ markedly from those prevailing in another Asian country—or indeed, in another part of the same country. The negotiating style of Koreans, for example, is not the same as that of the Lao. And even within countries that from outward appearances seem to have a fairly uniform cultural identity, significant regional differences may exist, such as in France between the business communities of Paris and of the *Midi.*

THE ELEMENTS OF CULTURE

One may conceive of the four cultural elements mentioned in the definition above—behavior, attitudes, norms, and values—as forming a series of concentric circles, like the layers of an onion.

Figure 7.1

Culture as an Onion

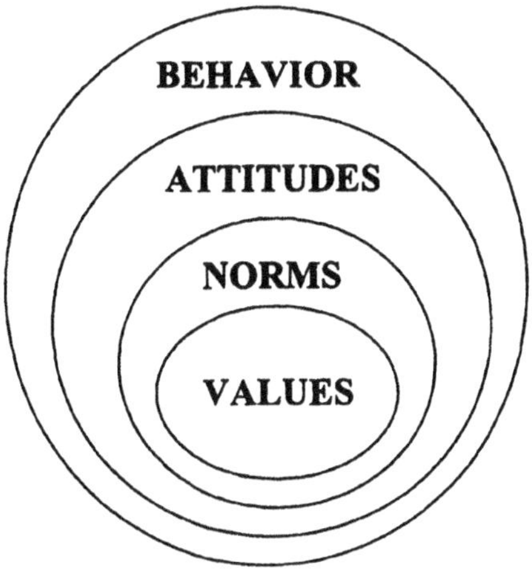

The process of understanding the culture of a counterpart in a negotiation is similar to peeling an onion. The outermost layer is behavior, the words and actions of one's counterpart. This is the layer that a deal maker first perceives in an intercultural negotiation. A second, inner layer consists of the attitudes of persons from that culture toward specific events and phenomena—for example, attitudes about beginning meetings punctually or the appropriate format of presentations. Attitudes may become evident to a counterpart in an intercultural negotiation only after protracted discussions. Next are norms, the rules to be followed in specific situations. Here, a negotiator may come to realize that a counterpart's seemingly rigid insistence on punctuality is not merely a personal idiosyncrasy but is based on a firm rule derived from that person's culture.

The innermost layer—the core—consists of values. One of the essential characteristics of a value is the belief by an individual or a group that a specific conduct is personally or socially preferable to an opposite conduct.[2] The way meetings are conducted, representatives chosen, and persons rewarded are usually based on certain values that are important to the culture of the individuals involved. Differences in values are often difficult for negotiators to detect and understand. Indeed, the parties to an international negotiation may discover their value differences only after they have signed the contract and have begun to work together. Once discovered, differences in cultural values between partners in an international joint venture may lead to severe conflict and ultimately the failure of their enterprise, a factor that may explain why many international ventures have a short life.

In their valuable book *The Seven Cultures of Capitalism*, Charles Hampden-Turner and Alfons Trompenaars report on the results of an extensive survey among 15,000 executives and employees from all over the world concerning their attitudes toward such basic management tasks as group decision making, hiring, rewarding employees, and making and applying rules. The authors found sharp differences that could only be explained by the respondents' differing cultural values. For example, with respect to group decision making, a wide variation among cultures existed as to whether they preferred to choose a person to represent a group by *consensus* (i.e., members of the group should meet and discuss candidates until almost everybody agrees on the same person) or by *adversarial democracy* (i.e., the group members should meet, nominate persons, vote and choose the person with a majority of votes, even if there is strong minority opposition). While 84.4 percent of the Japanese opted for consensus, only 37.7 percent of the Americans did so. One can imagine that this difference in cultural values about decision making, if not managed properly, might lead to conflict between Japanese and American joint-venture partners. The differences on this issue ought not to be viewed as a matter of East versus West. The Germans, who place a high value on social solidarity, favored consensus by 69 percent, as did a strong majority of the Dutch, Belgian, and French executives surveyed. On the other hand, only 35 percent the Italians, whose fractious political culture has resulted in fifty governments in fifty years, preferred consensus.[3]

Other kinds of value conflicts may arise in making, managing and mending global deals—for example, between individualism prized by Americans and communitarianism embodied in many Asian cultures, about whether it is more important to consider individual talent or the ability to fit into the organization when hiring an employee, about whether to reward persons on the basis of group performance or individual achievement only, and about whether an organization should favor or frown on the hiring of relatives of its executives. Differences in cultural values present themselves in international business transactions and relationships time after time and day after day, and they may ultimately turn what appeared to be a harmonious negotiation or business relationship into a continuing source of conflict between the parties.

Once the conflict surfaces, it may be exacerbated by the way the parties try to cope with it. One unfortunate tendency is for each side to extol its own cultural values and to denigrate those of the other side. For example, Americans, with their high store on individualism, will tend to see their value system positively. They would see themselves as supporting individual rights and human freedom, as putting the individual above the tyranny of the group, as knowing that a group prospers only when individuals prosper, and as efficient. Persons coming from cultures where communitarian values are prized will see themselves as unselfish, humane, for group interests and rights, and as knowing that the individual prospers only when the group prospers. Yet Americans, when confronted with a communitarian culture, may tend to ascribe to it only negative characteristics. So Americans, reacting to Japanese values in a decision to retain a fifteen-year employee whose performance has declined, might consider their Japanese counterparts as tolerant of freeloaders, giving in to the tyranny of the group, weak, and inefficient. On the other hand, the Japanese would probably characterize the Americans as ignoring the contributions and needs of the group, lacking loyalty, inhumane, and selfish. This kind of confrontational approach to negotiating cultural differences will only lead to increased conflict between the parties, conflict that can damage both the transaction and their relationship. In any negotiation, it is therefore important for negotiators to understand the values inherent in the culture of their counterparts and not to characterize those values in a negative way.

CULTURE'S IMPACT ON DEAL MAKING

Differences in culture between deal makers can obstruct negotiations in many ways. First, they can create misunderstandings in communication. If one American executive responds to another American's proposal by saying, "That's difficult," the response, interpreted against American culture and business practice, probably means that the door is still open for further discussion, that perhaps the other side should sweeten its offer. In some other cultures, for example, many in Asia, people may be reluctant to say a direct and emphatic "no," even when that is their intention. So when a Japanese negotiator in response to a proposal says, "That is difficult," he is clearly indicating that the proposal is unacceptable. "It is difficult," means "no" to the Japanese, but "maybe" to the American.

Second, cultural differences create difficulties not only in understanding words but also in interpreting actions. While Americans and Canadians may find it perfectly appropriate to conduct business discussions at lunch, Brazilian and Mexican executives may consider serious business negotiations to be totally out of place in that setting. Thus, there can be sharp cultural differences as to when and where deal making is appropriate.

Most Westerners expect a prompt answer when they make a statement or ask a question. The Japanese, on the other hand, tend to take longer to respond. As a result, negotiations with Japanese representatives are sometimes punctuated with periods of silence that seem excruciating to an American. For the Japanese, the period of silence is normal, an appropriate time to reflect on what has been said. The fact that they may not be speaking in their native language lengthens even more the time needed to respond.

From their own cultural perspective, Americans may interpret the Japanese silence as rudeness, lack of understanding, or a cunning tactic to get the Americans to reveal themselves. Rather than wait for a response, the American tendency is to fill the void with words by asking questions, offering further explanations, or merely repeating what they have already said. This response to silence may confuse the Japanese, who are made to feel that they are being bombarded by questions and proposals without being given adequate time to respond to any of them.

On the other hand, Latin Americans, who place a high value on verbal agility, have a tendency to respond quickly. Indeed, they may answer a point once they have understood it even though the other side has not finished speaking. While inexperienced American negotiators are sometimes confused by Japanese delays in responding, they can become equally agitated in negotiations with Brazilians by what Americans consider constant interruptions.

Third, cultural considerations also influence the form and substance of the deal you are trying to make. For example, when McDonald's began to franchise its operations in Asia, it considered itself to be selling not only hamburgers but, as one of its senior executives told the author, "an American experience." It was therefore reluctant to change its traditional American menu. Its franchisee in Thailand pressed hard for permission to sell noodles, a dish traditionally served on auspicious occasions like birthdays. McDonald's finally relented, and sales increased at its Thai restaurants as a result.

More substantively, differences in culture will invariably require changes in products, management systems, and personnel practices. For example, in Thailand, the relationship between manager and employee is more hierarchical than it is in the United States. Workers are motivated by a desire to please the manager, but they, in turn, expect their managers to sense their personal problems and be ready to help with them. Elsewhere, for example in Australia, employees neither expect nor want managers to become involved with their personal problems. Thus an Australian project in Thailand would need to change its concept of employee relations because of the local culture.

And finally, culture can influence negotiating style—the way persons from different cultures conduct themselves in a negotiation and make deals. Research indicates fairly clearly that negotiation practices differ from culture to culture.[4] Indeed, culture may influence how persons conceive of the very nature and function of negotiation. Studies of negotiating styles are abundant;[5] some focus on describing and analyzing the negotiating styles of particular groups. The practitioner's fascination with cultural negotiating styles seems to have spawned a distinct literary genre: the "Negotiating with . . ." literature. Numerous books and articles bearing such titles as "Negotiating with the Japanese," "Negotiating with the Arabs," and "Negotiating with the

Chinese" seek to lead the novice through the intricacies of negotiating in specified cultures. (For a bibliography of some of this work, see the appendix in this book.) Another approach to studying negotiating styles is cross-cultural and comparative, seeking to identify certain basic elements in negotiating styles and to determine how they are reflected in various cultures. The remainder of this chapter adopts this approach.

TEN WAYS THAT CULTURE AFFECTS DEAL MAKING

The great diversity of the world's cultures makes it impossible for any negotiator, no matter how skilled and experienced, to understand fully all the cultures that may be encountered. How then should an executive prepare to cope with culture in making deals in Singapore this week and Seoul the next? The following checklist identifies ten crucial areas where cultural differences may arise during the negotiation process. Knowledge of these ten factors may enable you to understand your counterpart and to anticipate possible misunderstandings.

1. Negotiating Goal: Contract or Relationship?

As we saw in chapter 2, negotiators from different cultures may tend to view the very purpose of a negotiation differently. For deal makers from some cultures, the goal of a business negotiation, first and foremost, is usually to arrive at a signed contract between the parties. American lawyers tend to represent this approach. For them, a signed contract is a definitive set of rights and duties that strictly binds the two sides, an attitude succinctly summed up in the statement "a deal is a deal."

Other cultures tend to consider that the goal of a negotiation is not a signed contract but the creation of a relationship between the two sides. Although the written contract expresses the relationship, the essence of the deal is the relationship itself. The difference in approach may explain why certain Asian negotiators, whose negotiating goal is often the creation of a relationship, tend to give more time and effort to prenegotiation, while Americans usually want to rush through this first phase in deal making. The activities of prenegotiation, whereby the parties seek to get to know one another thoroughly, are a crucial foundation for a good business relationship. They may seem less important when the goal is merely a contract.

It is therefore important to determine how your counterparts view the purpose of your negotiation. If relationship negotiators sit on the other side of the table, you need to be aware that merely convincing them of your ability to deliver on a low-cost contract may not be enough to land you the deal. You may also have to convince them, from the very first meeting, that your two organizations have the potential to build a rewarding relationship over the long term. On the other hand, if the other side is basically a contract deal maker, trying to build a relationship may be a waste of time and energy.

2. Negotiating Attitude: Win-Lose or Win-Win?

Chapter 2 also showed that because of differences in culture or personality, or both, business persons appear to approach deal making with one of two basic attitudes: that a negotiation is either a process in which both can gain (win-win) or a struggle in which, of necessity, one side wins and the other side loses (win-lose). Win-win negotiators see deal making as a collaborative and problem-solving process; win-lose negotiators see it as confrontational. In the latter situation, the parties see their goals as incompatible; in the former they consider themselves to have compatible goals. As you enter negotiations, it is important to know which type of negotiator is sitting across the table from you.

The presence of a win-lose negotiator on the other side of the table can impede deal making. Searching constantly for the negative implications of every proposal while failing to evaluate the positive side, this type of negotiator may simply take a position and refuse to budge. How should you negotiate with a win-lose deal maker?

First, without appearing to condescend, explain fully the nature of the proposed transaction. Do not assume that the other side has the same degree of business and financial knowledge as you do. Part of the intransigence may stem from a lack of understanding of the deal and an unwillingness to show ignorance. For example, in Asia the range of business acumen varies dramatically from the highly sophisticated negotiators of Hong Kong to the much less experienced business people in Laos.

Second, try to discover the other side's real interests. What do they really want out of the deal? Negotiators who encourage the other side to provide information about themselves, their interests, and their preferences generally achieve better results in understanding interests than those who do not. Earlier chapters have stressed the importance of understanding interests in order to reach agreement. In an international negotiation, cultural attitudes toward business secrecy complicate the process. Many foreign companies attach a much greater importance to the secrecy of a broad range of business information than do American corporations, which have to contend daily with the disclosure requirements of U.S. law and business practices. For example, although the salary of the CEO of a U.S. publicly traded corporation is a matter of public record, the salary of the president of a French corporation is a tightly kept secret. Although cultural differences among negotiators on what is and what is not considered secret can complicate information exchange, one principle that all cultures seem to respect is reciprocity. If you are open and provide information easily, the other side will be led to provide you with information. Your own openness may be the best way to get persons across the table to open up.

Third, to understand the other side's interests, you need to know something about its history and culture. China's troubled history of relations with the West and its justified pride in its own culture and accomplishments may cause joint-venture negotiations that place the Chinese party in a visible, second-class position to fail.

And finally, once you have identified the other side's interests, you have to develop proposals directed at satisfying those interests. Here, creativity and innovation are essential. In one negotiation between Bechtel, an international construction firm, and a foreign manufacturing corporation for the construction of an electrical cogeneration plant, the foreign negotiators insisted that if the plant did not operate at a specified standard, Bechtel would have to dismantle the entire plant and take it away. Bechtel was unwilling to make that guarantee. As the negotiations appeared to disintegrate, Bechtel negotiators understood that the real interest of the foreign corporation was not in having a cogeneration plant, but in having a reliable supply of electricity. They therefore proposed that, if the plant were defective, Bechtel would take it over and run it, provided that the purchaser agreed to buy all the electricity it produced. Ultimately, the two sides struck a deal on this basis.[6]

3. Personal Style: Informal or Formal?

Personal style concerns the way a negotiator talks to others, uses titles, dresses, speaks, and interacts with other persons. Culture strongly influences the personal style of negotiators. It has been observed, for example, that Germans have a more formal style than Americans.[7] A negotiator with a formal style insists on addressing counterparts by their titles, avoids personal anecdotes, and refrains from questions touching on the private or family life of members of the other negotiating team. An informal style negotiator tries to start the discussion on a first-name basis, quickly seeks to develop a personal, friendly relationship with the other team, and may take off his jacket and roll up his sleeves when deal making begins in earnest. Each culture has its own formalities that have special meanings within that culture. They are another means of communication among the persons sharing that culture, another form of adhesive that binds them together as a community. For an American or a Spaniard, calling someone by the first name is an act of friendship and therefore a good thing. For a Japanese or an Egyptian, the use of the first name at a first meeting is an act of disrespect and therefore a bad thing.

In the author's survey of negotiating styles among 310 professionals of twelve nationalities, a majority of the respondents within each cultural group, except for the Nigerians, claimed to have an informal negotiating style; however, the strength of this view varied considerably. While nearly 83 percent of the Americans considered themselves to have an informal negotiating style, only 54 percent of the Chinese, 53 percent of the Spanish, and 58 percent of the Mexicans took a similar view. Among the four European cultures represented in the survey, the French were the strongest in claiming an informal style (80 percent). Although both the Germans and the Japanese have a reputation for formality, only slightly more than one-quarter of the respondents in these two groups believed they had a formal negotiating style. Differences in cultures with respect to interpreting the meaning of the terms "formal" and "informal" may have influenced this result.

Figure 7.2

Personal Style: Formal or Informal?

	Nigeria	Spain	China	Mexico	U.K.	Argentina	Germany	Japan	India	Brazil	France	U.S.A.
Formal (%):	53	47	46	42	35	35	27	27	22	22	20	17

Negotiators in foreign cultures must respect appropriate formalities. As a general rule, it is always safer to adopt a formal posture and move to an informal stance, if the situation warrants it, than to assume an informal style too quickly.

4. Communication: Direct or Indirect?

Methods of communication vary among cultures. Some emphasize direct and simple methods of communication; others rely heavily on indirect and complex methods. The latter may use circumlocutions, figurative forms of speech, facial expressions, gestures, and other kinds of body language. In a culture that values directness, such as the American or the Israeli, you can expect to receive a clear and definite response to your proposals and questions. In cultures that rely on indirect communication, such as the Japanese, reaction to your proposals may be gained by interpreting seemingly vague comments, gestures, and other signs. What you will not receive at a first meeting is a definite commitment or rejection.

The confrontation of these styles of communication in the same negotiation can lead to friction. For example, the indirect ways Japanese negotiators express disapproval have often led foreign business executives to believe that their proposals were still under consideration when in fact the Japanese side had rejected them. In the Camp David negotiations that led to a peace treaty between Egypt and Israel, the Israeli preference for direct forms of communication and the Egyptian tendency to favor indirect forms sometimes exacerbated relations between the two sides. The Egyptians interpreted Israeli directness as aggressiveness and, therefore, an insult. The Israelis viewed Egyptian indirectness with impatience and suspected them of insincerity, of not saying what they meant.

In the author's survey, respondents in all the cultural groups by a high margin claimed to have a direct form of communication. Their organizational culture, their international experience, and their interpretation of the words "direct" and "indirect" may have strongly influenced their responses to the questionnaire. It is worth noting, however, that the two cultural groups with the largest percentage of persons claiming an indirect style were the Japanese and the French. The following table summarizes survey results on this question.

Figure 7.3

Communication Style: Direct or Indirect?

	Japan	France	China	U.K.	Brazil	India	Germany	U.S.A.	Argentina	Spain	Mexico	Nigeria
Indirect (%):	27	20	18	12	11	11	9	5	4	0	0	0

5. Sensitivity to Time: High or Low?

Discussions of national negotiating styles invariably treat a particular culture's attitudes toward time. It is said that Germans are always punctual, Latinos are habitually late, Japanese negotiate slowly, and Americans are quick to make a deal. Commentators sometimes claim that some cultures value time more than others, but this observation may not be an accurate characterization of the situation. Rather, negotiators may value differently the amount of time devoted to and measured against the goal pursued. For Americans, the deal is a signed contract and time is money, so they want to make a deal quickly. Americans therefore try to reduce formalities to a minimum and get down to business quickly. The Japanese and other Asians, whose goal is to create a relationship rather than simply sign a contract, need to invest time in the negotiating process so that the parties can get to know one another well and determine whether they wish to embark on a long-term relationship. They may view with suspicion aggressive attempts to shorten the negotiating time as efforts to hide something. For example, in one case that received significant media attention in the mid-1990s, a long-term electricity supply contract between an Enron subsidiary, the Dabhol Power Company, and the Maharashtra state government in India was subject to significant challenge and was ultimately cancelled on the grounds that it was concluded in "unseemly haste" and had been subject to "fast track procedures" that circumvented established practice for developing such projects in the past. Important segments of the Indian public automatically assumed that the government had failed to protect the public interest because the negotiations were so quick. In the company's defense, Rebecca Mark, chairman and CEO of Enron International, pointed out to the press: "We were extremely concerned with time, because time is money for us."[8]

This difference between the Indian and U.S. attitudes toward time was clearly revealed in the author's survey that asked 310 professionals whether they had a low or high sensitivity to time. Among all nationalities, the Indians had the largest percentage of persons who considered themselves to have a low sensitivity to time, as table 7.4 shows.

Although a majority of the respondents from all the cultural groups surveyed claimed to have a high sensitivity to time, the strength of the minority view on this question varied considerably among the groups. In addition to the Indians, the French, the Germans, and the Mexicans included a substantial percentage of respondents asserting a low sensitivity to time.

Figure 7.4

Time Sensitivity: High or Low?

	India	France	Germany	Mexico	Spain	Argentina	U.S.A.	Japan	China	Nigeria	U.K.	Brazil
Low (%):	44	40	36	33	21	15	15	9	9	7	6	0

6. Emotionalism: High or Low?

Accounts of negotiating behavior in other cultures almost always point to a particular group's tendency to act emotionally. According to the stereotype, Latin Americans show their emotions at the negotiating table, while the Japanese and many other Asians hide their feelings. Obviously, individual personality plays a role here. There are passive Latinos and hot-headed Japanese. Nonetheless, various cultures have different rules as to the appropriateness and form of displaying emotions, and these rules are brought to the negotiating table as well. Deal makers should seek to learn them.

In the author's survey, Latin Americans and the Spanish were the cultural groups that ranked themselves highest with respect to emotionalism in a clearly statistically significant fashion. Among Europeans, the Germans and English ranked as least emotional, while among Asians the Japanese held that position, but to a lesser degree. The following table summarizes the results with regard to emotionalism.

Figure 7.5

Emotionalism: High or Low?

	Brazil	Argentina	Mexico	Spain	China	U.S.A.	Nigeria	France	India	Japan	U.K.	Germany
High (%):	89	85	83	79	73	74	60	60	56	55	47	36

7. Form of Agreement: General or Specific?

Whether a negotiator's goal is a contract or a relationship, the negotiated transactions in almost all cases will be embodied in some sort of written agreement. Cultural factors influence the form of the written agreement that the parties make. Generally, Americans prefer very detailed contracts that attempt to anticipate all possible circumstances and eventualities, no matter how unlikely. Why? Because the deal is the contract itself, and one must refer to the contract to handle new situations that may arise. Other cultures, such as the Chinese, prefer a contract in the form of general principles rather than detailed rules. Why? Because it is claimed that the essence of the deal is the relationship between the parties. If unexpected circumstances arise, the parties should look to their relationship, not the contract, to solve the problem. So, in some cases, a Chinese negotiator may interpret the American drive to stipulate all contingencies as evidence of lack of confidence in the stability of the underlying relationship.

Among all respondents in the author's survey, 78 percent preferred specific agreements while only 22 percent preferred general agreements. Male and female participants responded in roughly the same proportions. The survey found that a majority of respondents in each cultural group preferred specific agreements to general agreements. This result may be attributed in part to the relatively large number of lawyers among the respondents, as well as to the fact that multinational corporate practice favors specific agreements and many of the respondents, regardless of nationality, had experience with such firms. The survey responses on this point may have been a case in which professional or organizational culture dominated national cultural traits. On the other hand, the degree of intensity of responses on the question varied considerably among cultural groups. While only 11 percent of the English favored general agreements, 45.5 percent of the Japanese and of the Germans claimed to do so.

Figure 7.6

Agreement Form: General or Specific?

	Japan	Germany	India	France	China	Argentina	Brazil	U.S.A.	Nigeria	Mexico	Spain	U.K.
General (%):	46	45	44	30	27	27	22	22	20	17	16	11

Occupational groups demonstrated wider variations, a finding that supports the notion that professional culture may dominate national culture on this question. For example, while 100 percent of the respondents with military backgrounds preferred specific agreements, only 64 percent of management and marketing persons and of diplomats and civil servants had a similar inclination,[9] as table 7.7 indicates:

Figure 7.7

Occupations and Agreement Form: General or Specific?

	Military	Students	Accounting/ Finance	Law	Engineering	Teaching	Diplomacy/ Public Sector	Management/ Marketing
Specific (%):	100	92	86	84	74	71	64	64

Some experienced executives argue that differences over the form of an agreement are caused more by unequal bargaining power between the parties than by culture. In a situation of unequal bargaining power, the stronger party always seeks a detailed agreement to "lock up the deal" in all its possible dimensions, while the weaker party prefers a general agreement to give it room to "wiggle out" of adverse circumstances that are bound to occur. A Chinese commune, as the weaker party in a negotiation with a multinational corporation, will seek a general agreement as a way of protecting itself against an uncertain future. According to this view, it is context, not culture, that determines this negotiating trait.

8. Building an Agreement: Bottom Up or Top Down?

Related to the form of the agreement is the question of whether negotiating a business deal is an *inductive* or a *deductive* process. Does it start from an agreement on general principles and proceed to specific items, or does it begin with an agreement on specifics, such as price, delivery date, and product quality, the sum total of which becomes the contract? Different cultures tend to emphasize one approach over the other. Some observers believe that the French prefer to begin with agreement on general principles, while Americans tend to seek agreement first on specifics. For Americans, negotiating a deal is basically making a series of compromises and trade-offs on a long list of particulars. For the French, the essence is to agree on basic principles that will guide and indeed determine the negotiation process afterward. The general principles become the framework upon which the contract is built.

A further difference in negotiating style is seen in the dichotomy between the building-down approach and the building-up approach. In the building down approach, the negotiator begins by presenting the maximum deal if the other side accepts all the stated conditions. In the building-up approach, one side begins by proposing a minimum deal that can be broadened and increased as the other party accepts additional conditions. According to many observers, Americans tend to favor the building-down approach, while the Japanese tend to prefer the building-up style.

The survey of negotiating styles found that the French, the Argentineans, and the Indians tended to view deal making as a top-down (deductive process); while the Japanese, the Mexicans and the Brazilians tended to see it as a bottom-up (inductive) process. The results among the twelve groups were as follows.

Figure 7.8

Style of Building Agreement: Top-Down or Bottom-Up

Top-Down	India	Argentina	France	U.K.	China	Germany	U.S.A.	Nigeria	Spain	Japan	Brazil	Mexico
(%):	74	70	67	54	54	54	47	47	46	45	42	33

9. Team Organization: One Leader or Group Consensus?

In any negotiation, it is important to know how the other side is organized, who has the authority to make commitments, and how decisions are made. Culture is one important factor that affects how executives organize themselves to negotiate a deal. Some cultures emphasize the individual while others stress the group. These values may influence the organization of each side in a negotiation.

One extreme is the negotiating team with a supreme leader who has complete authority to decide all matters. Many American teams tend to follow this approach. Other cultures, notably the Japanese and the Chinese, stress team negotiation and consensus decision making. When you negotiate with such a team, it may not be apparent who is the leader and who has the authority to commit the side. In the first type, the negotiating team is usually small; in the second it is often large. For example, in negotiations in China on a major deal, it would not be uncommon for the Americans to arrive at the table with three people and for the Chinese to show up with ten. Similarly, the one-leader team is usually prepared to make commitments more quickly than a negotiating team organized on the basis of consensus. As a result, the consensus type of organization usually takes more time to negotiate a deal.

Among all respondents in the author's survey, 59 percent tended to prefer one leader while 41 percent preferred a more consensus form of organization. Male and female respondents tended to follow this same distribution. On the other hand, the various cultural groups showed a wide variety of preferences on the question of team organization. The group with the strongest preference for consensus organization was the French. Many studies have noted French individualism.[10] Perhaps a consensus arrangement in the individual French person's eyes is the best way to protect that individualism. Despite the Japanese reputation for consensus arrangements, only 45 percent of the Japanese respondents claimed to prefer a negotiating team based on consensus. The Brazilians, the Chinese, and the Mexicans to a far greater degree than any other groups preferred one-person leadership, a reflection perhaps of the political traditions of those countries. The results of the survey on this point are summarized in table 7.9.

Occupational groups also revealed significant differences. For example, while 100 percent of the military respondents preferred a single leader for a negotiating team, only 43 percent of the accountants expressed a similar view, as is indicated in figure 7.10.

Within cultures, male and female respondents to this question demonstrated significant differences. Thus, 78 percent of American male respondents preferred a one-leader team organization, but only 35 percent of the female respondents expressed a similar preference. On the other hand, the small sample indicated that among Nigerians, 80 percent of the men preferred consensus arrangements while 80 percent of the women opted for one leader. In addition, a majority of the Japanese, Chinese, French, Spanish, Argentineans, and Brazilian women all preferred a one-leader approach to team organization.

Figure 7.9

Team Organization: One Leader or Consensus?

One Leader	Brazil	China	Mexico	U.K.	U.S.A.	Spain	Argentina	Germany	Japan	India	Nigeria	France
(%):	100	91	91	65	63	58	58	55	55	44	40	40

Figure 7.10

Occupations and Team Organization: One Leader or Consensus?

One Leader	Military	Engineering	Teaching	Students	Management/ Marketing	Law	Diplomacy/ Public Sector	Accounting/ Finance
(%):	100	68	62	62	61	56	50	43

10. Risk Taking: High or Low?

Research supports the conclusion that certain cultures are more risk averse than others.[11] In deal making, the negotiators' cultures can affect the willingness of one side to take risks—to divulge information, to try new approaches, and to tolerate uncertainties in a proposed course of action. The Japanese, with their emphasis on requiring large amounts of information and their intricate group decision-making process, tend to be risk averse. Americans, by comparison, are risk takers.

Among all respondents in the author's survey, approximately 70 percent claimed a tendency toward risk taking while only 30 percent characterized themselves as low risk takers. Here too, the distribution among men and women was similar and tended to follow that of all respondents as a group. Among cultures, the responses to this question showed significant variations. The Japanese are said to be highly risk averse in negotiations, and this tendency was affirmed by the survey which found Japanese respondents to be the most risk averse of the twelve cultures. Americans in the survey, by comparison, considered themselves to be risk takers, but an even higher percentage of the French, the British, and the Indians claimed to be risk takers. Figure 7.11 summarizes the survey results with respect to risk.

The survey also found significant differences among professional groups. For example, although 100 percent of the military respondents considered themselves to be high risk takers in negotiations, only 36 percent of the diplomats and civil servants characterized themselves similarly (see figure 7.12).

Generally, a large majority of males within each cultural group considered themselves high risk takers, with the exception of the Japanese (12.5 percent), the Spanish (39 percent) and the Mexicans (44 percent). Female re-

Figure 7.11

Risk Taking: High or Low?

	France	India	U.K.	China	U.S.A.	Nigeria	Argentina	Germany	Brazil	Mexico	Spain	Japan
High (%):	90	89	88	82	78	73	73	72	56	50	47	18

Figure 7.12

Occupations and Risk Taking: High or Low?

	Military	Accounting/ Finance	Engineering	Management/ Marketing	Students	Teaching	Law	Diplomacy/ Public Sector
High (%):	100	81	77	75	72	67	66	36

spondents who registered a higher percentage of risking taking than males from the same culture were U.S. women (86 percent), Spanish women (67 percent), and Mexican women (67 percent).

Faced with a risk-averse counterpart, how should a deal maker proceed? The following are a few steps to consider:

1. Don't rush the negotiating process. A negotiation that is moving too fast for one of the parties only heightens that person's perception of the risks in the proposed deal.
2. Devote attention to proposing rules and mechanisms that will reduce the apparent risks in the deal for the other side.
3. Make sure that your counterpart has sufficient information about you, your company, and the proposed deal.
4. Focus your efforts on building a relationship and fostering trust between the parties.
5. Consider restructuring the deal so that the deal proceeds step by step in a series of increments rather than all at once.

NEGOTIATING STYLES: A FRAMEWORK

Negotiating styles, like personalities, have a wide range of variation. The ten negotiating traits discussed above can be placed on a spectrum or continuum, as illustrated in the following chart. Its purpose is to identify specific negotiating traits affected by culture and to show the possible variation that each trait or factor may take. With this knowledge, a deal maker may be better able to understand the negotiating styles and approaches of counterparts from other cultures. Equally important, it may help negotiators determine how their own styles appear to those same counterparts.

Figure 7.13

The Impact of Culture on Negotiation

Negotiation Factors	Range of Cultural Responses		
Goal	Contract	←→	Relationship
Attitudes	Win-Lose	←→	Win-Win
Personal Styles	Informal	←→	Formal
Communications	Direct	←→	Indirect
Time Sensitivity	High	←→	Low
Emotionalism	High	←→	Low
Agreement Form	Specific	←→	General
Agreement Building	Bottom Up	←→	Top Down
Team Organization	One Leader	←→	Consensus
Risk Taking	High	←→	Low

OVERCOMING CULTURAL DIFFERENCES IN DEAL MAKING

In view of the importance of cultural differences in international negotiations and transactions, how should negotiators cope with them? The following are a few simple rules.

Rule No. 1: Learn the Other Side's Culture

In any negotiation, it is important to learn something about the other side's culture. Ideally, learning a culture other than your own requires several years of study, mastery of the local language, and prolonged residence in the country of that culture. An American faced with the task of negotiating a strategic alliance with a Thai company in Bangkok in two weeks' time cannot, of course, master Thai culture that fast. At best, the negotiator can learn enough to cope with some of the principal effects that Thai culture may have on making the deal.

History is an important window on a country's culture. So at the very least, the American should read a history of modern Thailand. If time permits, an executive might consult anthropological studies, reports on the current political situation, and accounts, if any, on negotiating with the Thais.

Consultation with persons who have had significant business experience in Thailand can also be helpful. International banks and transnational corporations may be excellent sources of advice on the impact of Thai culture on business. The U.S. Department of State and the American Embassy or consulate may also advise you on negotiating business deals in Thailand. Another source of advice may be a university with a Southeast Asian studies program. Finally, if you have hired a Thai lawyer, business consultant or interpreter to work on the deal with you, that person can also explain how the local culture affects the negotiating process, communications between the parties, the structure of the transaction, and the execution of the deal itself.

Rule No. 2: Don't Stereotype

If rule number one in an international negotiation is know the other side's culture, rule number two is avoid over-reliance on that knowledge. Not all Japanese evade giving a direct negative answer. Not all Germans tell you specifically what they think of a proposal. In short, negotiators who enter foreign cultures should be careful not to allow cultural stereotypes to determine their relations with local business people. Foreign business executives and lawyers will be offended if they feel you are not treating them as individuals but rather as cultural robots of a particular ethnic group. In addition to giving offense, cultural stereotypes can be misleading. Many times the other side simply does not run true to the negotiating form suggested by books, articles, and consultants. The reason, of course, is that other forces besides culture may influence a person's negotiating behavior. Specifically, these forces may include the negotiator's personality and experience, the organization represented, and the context of the particular negotiation in question.

Rule No. 3: Be Aware of Your Own Culture and How Others May Perceive It

Using the negotiating style framework and other guides, you should become aware of the basic elements of your own negotiating style and how your cultural values influence your approach to deal making, deal managing, and deal mending. For example, if you are highly sensitive to time during a negotiation and consider that time is money, you should be aware of that tendency and of the fact that it may cause friction with negotiators from cultures in which time does not have the same importance.

Rule No. 4: Find Ways to Bridge the Culture Gap

Generally, executives and lawyers who confront a culture different from their own tend to view it in one of three ways: an obstacle, a weapon, or a fortress. At the operational level, cultural differences are hardly ever seen as positive.

The conventional view among most American executives is that cultural differences are an obstacle to agreement and effective joint action. They therefore search for ways to overcome the obstacle. But a different culture in a business setting can become more than an obstacle; it can be seen as a weapon, particularly when a dominant party tries to impose its culture on the other side. For example, foreign counterparts may consider American lawyers' insistence on structuring a transaction "the way we do it in the United States" as the use of American culture as a weapon.

Faced with a culture that it perceives as a weapon, a party to a business deal may become defensive and try to use its own culture as a fortress to protect itself from what it perceives as a cultural onslaught. The Japanese have often adopted this approach when confronted with American demands to open their markets. France's drive to limit the use of English in advertising is a defensive response to what it considered to be the weapon of Anglo-Saxon culture. Groups fearful of globalization often raise their culture as a fortress to prevent incursion of foreign businesses whose practices are culturally threatening.

It may be helpful to try to think of cultural differences in yet another way. Differences in cultures tend to isolate individuals and groups from each other. In short, cultural differences create a gap between persons and organizations. The effective negotiators should seek to find ways to bridge that gap. Negotiators need to think of themselves as bridge builders. Often the action that people take when confronted with cultural differences serves only to widen the gap. In China, for example, an expatriate manager whose company was having problems with the Customs Department sent a middle-level employee to handle the matter, as he would have done if he had faced the same problem in the United States. In China, however, this approach failed. For reasons of saving face, high-level Chinese officials in the Customs Department refused to meet with the company representative and instead delegated an officer at a correspondingly low level to meet with him. As a result, the problem became the subject of interminable meetings but was never solved.

Bridges are often vital links between countries. Accordingly, effective joint action among persons and organizations of differing cultures requires a bridge over the culture gulf. One way to build that bridge is by using culture itself. If culture is indeed the glue that binds together a particular group of people, the creative use of culture between persons of different backgrounds is often a way to link those on opposite sides of the gap. The essence of the technique is to create community with the other side. Basically, there are four types of cultural bridge building that a deal maker should consider when confronted with a culture gap in a negotiation or transaction.

Bridge the gap using the other side's culture. One technique for bridging the gap is for a negotiator or manager to use elements of the other side's culture in their communications with that side. In international business, negotiators often try to use or identify with the other side's culture in order to build a relationship. For example, when President Anwar Sadat of Egypt negotiated with Sudanese officials, he always made a point of telling them that his mother had been born in the Sudan. He was thus using a common cultural thread to build a relationship with his counterparts. In effect, he was saying: "Like you, I am Sudanese, so we have common cultural ties. I understand you and I value your culture. Therefore you can trust me." Similarly, an African American managing a joint venture in Nigeria stressed his African heritage to build relationships with Nigerian counterparts. And an Italian American negotiating a sales contract in Rome emphasized his Italian background as a way of bridging the cultural gap that he perceived.

In his memoir, *Turmoil and Triumph*, former U.S. Secretary of State George Shultz gives a graphic example of how a Russian counterpart used American culture to build a bridge to the Americans during the Reykjavik summit. In an early meeting with Shultz, Marshal Sergei Akhromeyev, then deputy minister of defense, remarked that he was "one of the last of the Mohicans," meaning that he was the last of the Soviet World War II commanders still in service. When Shultz asked Akhromeyev where he learned the expression "last of the Mohicans," Akhromeyev replied that he had been raised on the tales of the American writer James Fenimore Cooper. The answer had an immediate impact of Shultz. It led him to conclude that

Akhromeyev was more open and ready for conversation than previous Soviet negotiators, that he was a man with a sense of history and an awareness of the American way, and that he was a person the Americans could deal with. "Literature can build bridges," Shultz wrote.[12]

Bridge the gap using your own culture. A second general approach to bridging the culture gap is to persuade or induce the other side to adopt elements of your culture. Successful implementation of this approach requires time and education. For example, in order to give a common culture to a joint venture, an American partner incurred significant costs by sending its foreign partner's executives to schools and training programs in the United States and then assigning them for short periods to the U.S. partner's own operations. The danger in this technique is that your foreign counterpart will view your culture as a weapon and therefore use its own culture as a fortress, creating the potential for heightened conflict.

Bridge with a combination of both cultures. A third approach to dealing with the culture gap is to build a bridge using elements from the cultures of both sides. In effect, culture bridging takes place on both sides of the gap and hopefully results in the construction of a solid integrated structure. The challenge in this approach is to identify the most important elements of each culture and to find ways of blending them into a consistent, harmonious whole that will allow business to be done effectively.

Bridge with a third culture. A final method of dealing with the culture gap is to build a bridge relying on a third culture that belongs to neither of the parties. Thus, for example, in a difficult negotiation between an American executive and a Chinese manager, both discovered that they had a great appreciation of French culture since they had both studied in France in their youth. They began to converse in French, and their common love of France enabled them to build a strong personal relationship. They used a third culture to bridge the gap between China and America.

A variation of this approach is to use a common professional culture to overcome national cultural differences. As the survey results indicated, sometimes the professional cultures of negotiators on certain issues appear stronger than their national cultures. This finding suggests that when companies from two different cultures face strong cultural differences at the negotiating table, they should seek to find a common culture in the professional backgrounds of the negotiators on both sides of the table. Thus, lawyers may be able to build relationships with lawyers and engineers with engineers. If an engineer on the other team seems to be creating an obstacle and is resistant to an agreement, it may be wise to select one of your own engineers, rather than one of your lawyers, to deal with him and to build a bridge over the cultural divide between the two companies.

Notes

1. Edward T. Hall, *The Silent Language* (Garden City, NY: Doubleday, 1959).
2. William C. Frederick, *Values, Nature and Culture in the American Corporation* (New York: Oxford University Press, 1995) 88.
3. Charles Hampden-Turner and Alfons Trompenaars, *The Seven Cultures of Capitalism: Value Systems for Creating Wealth in the United States, Japan, Germany, France, Britain, Sweden and the Netherlands* (New York: Doubleday, 1993).
4. S. E. Weiss, "Negotiating With the Romans," *Sloan Management Review* 35 (1994): 51, 85.
5. See, for example, Hans Binnendijk (ed.), *National Negotiating Styles* (Washington, D.C.: U.S. Department of State, 1987); N. C. G. Campbell et al., "Marketing Negotiations in France, Germany, the United Kingdom and the United States," *Journal of Marketing* 52 (1993): 49–62; and J. L. Graham et al., "Buyer-Seller Negotiations Around the Pacific Rim: Differences in Fundamental Exchange Processes," *Journal of Consumer Research* 15 (1988): 48–54.
6. Author's interview with Cordell Hull, Executive Vice President, Bechtel Group Inc., March 3, 1990, San Francisco, California.
7. Edward T. Hall and M. Reed Hall, *Understanding Cultural Differences* (Yarmouth, ME: Intercultural Press, 1990) 48.
8. "Enron's Rebecca Mark: 'You Have to be Pushy and Aggressive'" *Business Week*, February 24, 1997, at http://www.businessweek.com/1997/08/b351586.htm.
9. The students in the survey were graduate students, primarily in law and business, with considerably less work experience than the other professional groups surveyed. The student responses may be treated as representing persons without significant occupational experience.
10. Hall and Hall, *Understanding Cultural Differences*, 152.
11. Geert Hofstede, *Culture's Consequences: International Differences in Work-related Values* (Newbury Park, CA: Sage Publications, 1980), 152.
12. George Shultz, *Turmoil and Triumph: My Years as Secretary of State* (New York: Charles Scribner's Sons, 1993), 763.

[5]

Two Paths to Peace: Contrasting George Mitchell in Northern Ireland with Richard Holbrooke in Bosnia–Herzegovina

Daniel Curran, James K. Sebenius, and Michael Watkins

At first glance, one might expect great similarities between the approaches of two U.S. third parties, both white male Democrats, who acted during the 1990s to resolve two ethnic and religious-based conflicts in Europe. Yet, although each man achieved a substantial measure of success, at least in the short to medium term, a closer comparison of their approaches along a number of strategic dimensions serves to illustrate dramatic differences in the ways and means of third party actions. This article details such a comparison, and in the process sharpens the existing literature on international mediation and calls into question easy generalizations about the determinants of success by third parties in these kinds of conflicts.

While the Balkans have suffered hundreds of years of recurring bloodshed, the most recent war in Bosnia had its roots in the breakup of

Daniel Curran is director of the Humanitarian Leadership Program at Harvard Business School. His e-mail address is dcurran@hbs.edu.

James K. Sebenius is Gordon Donaldson Professor of Business Administration at Harvard Business School. His e-mail address is jsebenius@hbs.edu.

Michael Watkins is associate professor at Harvard Business School. His e-mail address is mwatkins@genesisadvisers.com.

Yugoslavia after the death of its communist leader Marshal Tito in the 1980s. The declarations of independence by many of the Yugoslav republics and the rise of nationalist leaders like Slobodan Milosevic in Serbia and Franjo Tudjman in Croatia with designs on each other's territory rapidly spiraled into full-scale, ugly warfare between Serbs and Croats, Croats and Bosnia's Muslim population, and Bosnia's Serbs and Muslims. The international community seemed unprepared to take decisive action to stop the conflict until brazen assaults by Bosnian Serbs on Muslim safe areas and revelations of concentration camps, massacres, and systematic rape exposed the ineffectual efforts of Europe and the United States.

In August 1995, Richard Holbrooke stepped in to lead a new, aggressive attempt to negotiate peace, ultimately backed up by North Atlantic Treaty Organization (NATO) air assaults and economic sanctions. After three months of frenetic shuttle diplomacy, Holbrooke and his team were able to negotiate a series of agreements on basic principles and a ceasefire that ultimately led to the Dayton Accords, ending the bloodiest European conflict since World War II; in total, the Balkan wars caused more than 100,000 deaths.

At roughly the same time, George Mitchell was agreeing to chair a British–Irish effort to break the deadlock on the issue, which had become the most significant roadblock to peace in Northern Ireland — the decommissioning of weapons by both sides in the conflict. In 1995, Mitchell was about to step into a three-hundred-year-old feud between a largely Catholic nationalist minority, which wanted the province to become part of Ireland, and the mainly Protestant unionist majority, which wanted the province to remain part of the United Kingdom. Paramilitary groups on both sides had been conducting terrorist attacks since the late 1960s in this slow-burning conflict that had cost more than three thousand Catholic and Protestant lives. Ten parties and two governments were involved in the peace process. Many of these parties refused to talk with each other, in some cases, those on the same side attacked each other, and a virtual chasm yawned between the negotiating positions on major issues.

As Mitchell moved on to chair the all-party talks that grew out of the decommissioning effort, he presided over the elections to the forum that chose delegates to the talks. An excruciating two-year process to define the rules and agenda for the talks ensued while the participants slowly disentangled the contentious issues. Finally, the parties made a two-week sprint to a final agreement by the self-imposed deadline of Easter 1998.

At least superficially, the efforts of George Mitchell in Northern Ireland and Richard Holbrooke in Bosnia offer strong similarities. Two white, male, Democratic, U.S. citizens assumed third-party roles in ethnic and religious conflicts in Europe in the latter half of the 1990s. Each man took actions leading to what most observers would regard as a provisional success — at least over the short to medium term, and certainly relative to violent alternatives. (For more detailed summaries of the relevant events in Bosnia and Northern Ireland, see Appendices One and Two.) Yet, the personalities of these two men could hardly be more different nor could they have taken more divergent approaches to their roles.

Closer examination reveals two very different people facing very different challenges and following very different strategies to help resolve bitter and protracted disputes. This article contrasts their approaches across a number of dimensions to help build an understanding of a range of third-party actions that may be appropriate and effective under certain circumstances.[1] The differences between the settlements obtained and questions about their long-term sustainability are large and, while relevant, beyond the scope of our comparison. The present article is not a structured focused comparison of the two situations but, rather, a presentation of contrasts between very different situations. As such, each case nicely highlights key aspects of the other and, by extension, a broader class of similar cases.[2]

Theoretical Approach

Ideally, insights from this effort will inform both explanatory and prescriptive theories, especially the emerging methodology of "negotiation analysis."[3] The standard negotiation analytic approach involves a carefully structured enumeration of the parties, the full set of their interests, the no-agreement alternatives, the process of their interaction, and, in particular, the interaction between cooperative moves to create value jointly and to claim it individually. Without presuming full game-theoretic rationality, barriers to and opportunities for negotiated agreement are typically assessed. The analysis is robust both to a "fixed" or fully specified "game" as well as conscious moves by the parties to change the game itself. While we will not go through a full-blown negotiation analysis in this article, our approach will be primarily informed by the negotiation analytic perspective.

The mediation process has been the subject of a number of specifically negotiation analytic accounts, more generally, by scholars of conflict resolution.[4] Sensibly, these accounts argue for an assessment of context (which we will provide) and characterize the kinds of approaches taken by mediators. For example, in a widely cited typology, Saadia Touval and William Zartman categorize three broad classes of mediator action: (1) communication-oriented and facilitative, getting the parties to hear and understand each other better; (2) formulation, oriented toward structuring elements of the process; and (3) manipulative or directive, aimed at the substantive elements of the dispute, both objective and perceptual.[5] Jacob Bercovitch et al. (1991) find that directive strategies — such as that employed by Richard Holbrooke in Bosnia — tend to be the most successful in general, even though facilitative approaches are employed most commonly. Later, refining the analysis to control for dispute type, Bercovitch and Paul Diehl (1997) concluded that the communication-facilitative approach — such as that used by George Mitchell — tends to be most productive for so-called intractable conflicts, such as those in Northern Ireland.

Yet our analysis seeks to go well beyond matching broad and general mediator approaches to context and dispute type. One of our prime objectives is to offer a much more specific set of categories into which the particular actions of third parties can be characterized. These categories are embedded in an evolving analytic framework that we have constructed to analyze the major choices made by Holbrooke and Mitchell (and, by extension, other third parties). This framework quickly moves past the standard negotiation analytic assessment — parties, interests, no-agreement options, cooperative and competitive moves, and the like — to several classes of third-party action in multiparty conflict situations.

This framework highlights the basic choices for those involved in third-party roles (as well as, more broadly, in negotiations). Third parties face three fundamental and early decisions: First, they have to determine their *basic objectives*. At first blush, seeking to foster an agreement among the warring parties might appear to be the obvious basic objective, but more subtle goals are possible: transforming relationships, modeling a more constructive process, delaying the conflict, and others. Second, they have to choose their *fundamental role* (e.g., neutral, advocate for one party or outside player, etc.). Third, they have to consider their best *means of influence* on the situation (e.g., forceful, persuasive, facilitative, and so forth). Along with these three key choices, the third party must, at least implicitly, formulate a strategy to form a "winning coalition" on behalf of the chosen objective. Supporting this *coalition strategy* are three concurrent and overlapping strands: (1) An *issues strategy* with respect to the substantive aspects of the agreements sought, (2) a *process strategy* with respect to the choices of process for the mediation, and (3) a *timing strategy* with respect to the timing of their efforts. These are neither independent from each other nor always equal in their influence on the negotiations. While many other formulations are possible, these dimensions at least capture major elements of the choices made by third parties. We will use this framework to compare the approaches of Mitchell and Holbrooke.

Comparisons of Fundamental Choices

Basic Objectives

Richard Holbrooke's evident objective was to stop the violent and bloody war in Bosnia — and he needed to do it quickly. He wanted an immediate and comprehensive deal that would end the killing and create a new Bosnia. His approach was deal-oriented, focused on the substantive issues at stake, and transactional. "What the U.S. wanted the most was a settlement, and what precisely that settlement consisted of was of secondary importance," wrote authors Michael Watkins and Susan Rosegrant in the Harvard Business School case "Getting to Dayton: Negotiating an End to the War in Bosnia" (Watkins and Rosegrant 1999: 24). Holbrooke was less focused on its long-term sustainability, and more interested in "getting the deal done." It took a scant three months from the time he became centrally involved in the conflict until the signing of the Dayton Accords.

George Mitchell's objective in Northern Ireland was also to end the conflict. He found party leaders from both sides who were articulate in their understanding that unemployment and violence were inextricably linked and that a durable peace rested on a foundation of trust and prosperity. Yet, their hatred for one another remained and they were unable to act to realize shared interests. Mitchell was amazed to find that, although the party leaders had lived together in the same community all of their lives, many of them literally did not talk with each other.

By contrast with Holbrooke, Mitchell's approach had the apparent objective of helping the political leadership of the warring factions of Northern Ireland to begin to cooperate in a rudimentary way in creating an institutional and constitutional framework in which the parties could govern Northern Ireland for the future. From the start of the all-party talks, he took almost two years in a highly process-oriented, relationship-focused effort at transforming the working and political relationships among key players.

Fundamental Role

The roles of Mitchell and Holbrooke were well aligned with their objectives. Holbrooke assumed the role of an advocate with substantial potential clout from both the U.S. and NATO. He had an unambiguous mandate and could claim strong powers to punish and reward. He and his team became "active engineers" in the process to meet a clear national interest of the U.S. to stop the violence as expeditiously as possible. The U.S. was already practicing maneuvers for a possible UN withdrawal from Bosnia involving 25,000 U.S. troops.

> Now officials said, U.S. policy had come down to two choices: Either send in troops to help with a humiliating and dangerous UN retreat, a move that could have crushing political consequences for the Clinton administration, or put U.S. leadership fully behind a negotiated solution so that the U.S. troops sent over would be implementing peace not backing away from failure. (Watkins and Rosegrant 1999: 9)

Ivo Daalder, a senior member of the U.S. National Security Council (NSC) recalled, "We were going to go with peace and we were going to do it at the highest level. The President was going to be involved, the Secretary of State would be involved, and we would put all of the resources of the U.S. government on this" (Watkins and Rosegrant 1999: 10). But they also faced a high cost of failure. Their plan for reaching a comprehensive settlement based on assertive diplomacy put U.S. credibility on the line.

Thus, their actions could be interpreted both as "solving" problems and tactical "manipulation." Throughout Holbrooke's shuttle diplomacy, for example, Serbian President Slobodan Milosevic would press Holbrooke for economic sanctions relief. But Holbrooke planned to save that incentive for an eventual peace conference. "I would tell him that it wasn't in my authority, that's Washington's. But I was always playing a game," Holbrooke recalled. Likewise, Holbrooke viewed the Balkan leaders as the most difficult he had ever dealt with. "They're thugs, they're murderers, they're entrenched," he declared. "They represent very small countries and movements that are beleaguered" (Watkins and Rosegrant 1999: 27).

By contrast, George Mitchell assumed the role of a neutral mediator on behalf of an agreement among the parties. The situation in Northern Ireland was of relatively peripheral concern to U.S. policy makers, although it had entangled a key ally (Britain) and served as something of a test bed for U.S. influence on post-Cold War ethnic conflicts. Mitchell first became involved in Northern Ireland in early 1995 when President Clinton announced his intention to sponsor a White House Conference on Trade and Investment in Northern Ireland and asked Mitchell to help organize the conference.

"The task seemed interesting and undemanding and would be over in a few months, so I said I would take it," wrote Mitchell (1999: 29). He stayed on for over a year, developing a commitment to the people and society.

Although the British government had long been reluctant to involve outsiders in what it saw as a domestic political matter, its leaders came to the conclusion that a peace settlement in Northern Ireland could benefit from a detached third-party role. Mitchell arrived without a strong interest in the final substance of the negotiated deal but with a desire that the needs of parties be met. He had an unclear mandate and no powers to tangibly reward or punish.

Over time, he blamed the problems of the province on the situation rather than the people. Mitchell viewed the leaders of Northern Ireland differently than Holbrooke viewed the Balkan leaders. "I was impressed by the energy and intelligence of the people. They are productive, literate, and articulate," he said. "But for all their modernity and literacy, [the leaders] of Northern Ireland have been divided by a deep and ancient hatred into two hostile communities; their enmity burnished by centuries of conflict" (Sebenius 2001a: 2).

Means of Influence

In Bosnia, Holbrooke arguably adopted an approach of "whatever it takes to force a deal." In the language of negotiation, it was a best alternative to a negotiated agreement (BATNA)-focused approach of lowering the value of no-agreement alternatives and influencing the dynamics to impose ever-higher costs on the various parties who refused to play. Holbrooke had the might of the U.S. and NATO to back up his mediation. He could greatly shape and manipulate the situation through bombing and promised aid and sanctions.

In August 1995, on the eve of his involvement, Holbrooke told the press, "If this peace initiative does not get dramatically moving in the next week or two, the consequences will be very adverse to the Serbian goals. One way or another, NATO will be heavily involved, and the Serbs don't want that" (Watkins and Rosegrant 1999: 12). He later followed up his threat with several weeks of sustained NATO bombing on Serbian targets.

By contrast to this BATNA-lowering approach, George Mitchell followed a strategy that focused on joint gains, continually alluding to the political and economic value of a deal. Mitchell had no formal power and only had a few carrots and sticks with which to influence negotiators and their constituents.

"I felt, throughout the discussion, that ultimately my ability to be effective would depend more upon gaining the participants' trust and confidence than on the formal description of my authority," Mitchell said. "I learned this in the Senate, where the position of majority leader was not created by the Constitution or by law." He would later tell a reporter, "I had no real power. All I had was the power of persuasion" (Germond and Witcover 1998: 888).

Mitchell sought to model constructive future dealings among the parties to show that, in living together in the future, they would be more productive and secure. Arguably, by analogy, Holbrooke was affecting a workable divorce while Mitchell was engaged in relationship therapy.

Comparisons of Strategies: Coalitional, Process, Issue, and Timing

Coalition Strategy: Minimum Necessary versus Maximum Feasible

Holbrooke's strategy in Bosnia, with respect to the various parties, consisted of four basic steps. First, he sought to simplify the overall decision making within the U.S., NATO, and the European Union (EU). He took steps to disentangle the U.S.-NATO-EU process from that of the UN with his efforts to do away with the infamous "dual key" arrangement requiring the approval of both UN and NATO officials to authorize air strikes.

Second, Holbrooke acted to take advantage of, and foster, the simplification of the hitherto fragmented Balkan parties. This was accomplished, in part, through exploiting the fortuitous actions of Milosevic in obtaining the "Patriarch Paper," which ensured that, in all negotiations, the interests of the Bosnian Serbs would be represented by Milosevic himself. Holbrooke's support of the strengthened Muslim–Croat Federation furthered the simplification process.

Third, he sought to apply considerable pressure on the Serbs to weaken their thus-far dominant position. He accomplished this in a number of ways. By acquiescing in Croat control of the Krajina (formerly under Serbian control), he solidified the Croatian role in an anti-Serbian coalition. He encouraged and took advantage of Croat and Muslim advances on the battlefield, by supporting their efforts, and further elevating Milosevic with a powerful NATO bombing campaign directed at the Bosnian Serbs.[6] Moreover, he argued for a continued economic embargo against Serbia. With the Serbs acting as a unit, and the Croatians and Bosnian Croats acting in concert with the Bosnian Muslims against the Serbs, the tide turned. Finally, when Bosnian Muslims began to press their newfound advantage on the battlefield, Holbrooke took steps to isolate the Bosnian Muslims, to block further battlefield progress by this group, and effectively to force a settlement.

In seeking an agreement, Holbrooke wanted the narrow participation of the minimum necessary number of parties, hardly a broad-based stakeholder effort (as was the case, for example, with the ten political parties who played roles in the all-party Northern Irish talks). His tightly defined mediation team then discouraged direct communication between the parties in favor of themselves acting as the conduit of information. Holbrooke had co-opted potential spoilers to the agreement, such as Serbian President Slobodan Milosevic, through enticements and later pushed them to make concessions.

This structural simplification mirrored some of the characteristics of generic eighteenth- and nineteenth-century balance of power and military and diplomatic strategies (Gulick 1955). When Holbrooke finally got the leaders together in Dayton, they were edgy, angry, and distrustful. But, drawing on his careful nurtured reputation as a wielder of great power, he kept them there by threatening that the alternative to agreement would be dire, and convincing them that he and his team provided the best opportunity for success.[7]

By contrast with Holbrooke's sequential, divide-conquer-and-force approach and desire to limit participation, George Mitchell carefully built an outwardly rippling, relatively inclusive, coalition of the center against the extremes. By seeking to bridge the Ulster Unionist Party and the Social Democratic Labor Party, as well as increasing nationalist involvement while retaining centrist unionist participation, Mitchell fostered the creation of a center and helped to give it voice in a manner that significantly displaced the prior political influence of the extremes.

He sought a wide participation of parties by first recommending the election to a negotiating forum and later allowing all parties to remain involved as long as they adhered to the "Mitchell Principles" of democracy and nonviolence. Throughout the negotiations, Mitchell and his loosely organized team encouraged the parties to communicate among themselves. During the early discussions on Strand One and Strand Two, he fostered a strategy that "marked some sort of graduation in the negotiation process with parties starting to get a sense of how serious others were about given issues. The importance of effective listening was now more apparent and relevant — at least to some" (Durkan 1999).

Mitchell effectively reduced the influence of potential spoilers to the agreement by allowing extremists from both sides to leave of their own accord. As for the parties still "inside" the talks, "signs of [positive] chemistry became evident as parties and personalities got back to each other's points or ideas in other than negative tones" (Durkan 1999). They seemed to identify with the process, which was only more defined by increased violence outside of the talks. The parties even shared their constituency sensitivities, giving reasons behind their positions. Some exchanged thoughts on how the negotiations could be advanced toward an agreement.

Outside the talks, the excluded parties' public relations were in high gear. Asked about it, Social Democratic and Labor Party (SDLP) member, Seamus Mallon responded, "Let others draft press releases, we have to draft an agreement" (Durkan 1999). The ultimate agreement emerged from this organic centrist coalition, which had grown at least somewhat more inclined to trust and respect one another.

Process Strategy: Control versus Consensus

Holbrooke essentially imposed a negotiation process by fiat. He engineered and manipulated representation in the talks and undertook his shuttles and summits to meet what he saw as the requirements of rapid closure. He apparently worried very little about explicitly defining a clear strategy for the negotiation process and disliked sharing his thoughts with others outside of his team. One of his team members stated, "Don't expect to find a piece of paper with a plan on it, it was not there. It was very much 'make it up as you go along'" (Watkins and Rosegrant 1999: 17). Another recalled, "Dick operated on a heuristic basis. It was purely intuitive and pragmatic" (Watkins and Rosegrant 1999: 17).

Holbrooke was a master at artfully concealing and revealing information in his actions. He frequently kept the international Contact Group in the dark, claiming that it was necessary to exclude the Europeans until the last moment due to their internal divisions. Having to accommodate extraneous demands was something Holbrooke was anxious to avoid (Watkins and Rosegrant 1999: 21). He paid close attention, however, to the details of the process by dictating the precise dimensions of negotiation tables at the summits and carefully arranging the accommodations at Dayton.

Holbrooke later characterized his own approach by saying, "It's a situation where you know what your long-term objective is, but you don't know what route you are going to take to get there. You have to be very flexible on tactics, but firm on goals" (Watkins and Rosegrant 1999: 17).

As part of the process, Holbrooke used the press to further the idea of an "abyss" in the event of no-deal and he consistently sought to lower expectations for the results he sought at each stage. Although the "Patriarch Paper" presented a phenomenal opportunity in the negotiations, Holbrooke downplayed it as a "procedural breakthrough." Once, after securing a commitment to continue NATO bombing, Holbrooke painted a gloomy picture for an interviewer, declaring, "Nothing is agreed upon until everything is agreed upon" (Sciolino 1995).

"He always painted a more negative picture than what was reality. Holbrooke never put himself in a position of having to backpedal from appearing to deliver more than he could actually deliver," according to one team member (Watkins and Rosegrant 1999: 20). Yet, when progress was made, Holbrooke trumpeted the publicity to lock in gains.

Holbrooke also used the press and the process as tools to build perceptions in the minds of the players of his personal credibility and power. In the midst of shuttle diplomacy for Bosnia, Holbrooke and his team visibly defused a long-standing — and possibly explosive — dispute between Macedonia and Greece over one long weekend. "It was an important action because it built up this aura of a negotiating team that in its spare time is able to rush off and resolve something that had been festering for six months," said one official (Watkins and Rosegrant 1999: 23).

By contrast, Mitchell acted as the steward of a deliberate process of principled inclusion. The delegates were formally elected to a comprehensive forum and had to endorse the "Mitchell Principles" of democracy and nonviolence in order to enter the talks and continue participating.

At first, Mitchell's chairmanship was not even accepted by the unionist parties. Mitchell recalled the first day of the talks. "When I entered the room and walked toward my seat, my attention was drawn to the DUP [Democratic Unionist Party] section by a noisy commotion. There, Dr. Paisley was standing and yelling in a loud voice, 'No. No. No. No.' He repeated it over and over again until I was in my seat. Before I could say or do anything, Paisley launched a blistering attack on the governments for 'imposing' me as chairman. He then led his delegates in a walkout" (Mitchell 1999: 49–50).

To gain acceptance, Mitchell agreed to dispense with the process and agenda created in advance by the Irish and British government. Instead, he agreed to negotiate his role, the rules, the agenda, and the procedures of the talks; including the principle of "sufficient consensus," which gave veto power to all of the largest players and ensured the reality of power sharing. For months, he and his team sought proposals from parties, provided comparative tables to guide discussion, and used bilateral meetings to ease things forward. One participant reflected, "The arguments revolved around the role and remit of the independent chairs; how comprehensive the agenda could be; whether or not parties had the right to raise issues free from veto; the principle of inclusion of parties 'related' to paramilitary groups on ceasefire; and the construction of a mechanism to secure agreed decisions where consensus proved impossible" (Durkan 1999).

Throughout the talks, Mitchell kept the process going at all costs — however threadbare it seemed at any given time. He and the other chairmen were routinely called upon to speak to the press. Mitchell used the press to hold out a "pot of gold" waiting at the end of a negotiated settlement. He felt a need to optimistically assess the state of the talks. But it grew difficult.

"We had settled into a grim routine," Mitchell said. "What little progress was made came very slowly. Then, at each break, when there inevitably would be assessments by the press, we were called on to give a positive 'spin'" (Mitchell 1999: 98).

Mitchell's process was highly transparent and, even in despairing moments, he found positive ways to interpret the talks' future potential to the parties and the press. Unlike Holbrooke, whose process actions built perceptions of personal credibility and power, which could be deployed to force a deal, Mitchell used the process to build perceptions of fairness, respect, dedication, and credibility.

When Mitchell decided to set a deadline for the talks, he negotiated it with the two governments and met with representatives of each of the parties several times, refining his proposal at each meeting. The proposal included a process for the preparation of two drafts that would allow all parties to object and make proposals for the final version so that there would be no last minute surprises. He effectively modeled the means of debate and governance that would be required by the institutions established under the Good Friday Agreement.

Issue Strategy: Substance versus Procedure

Richard Holbrooke placed more emphasis on substance than procedure in the Bosnian negotiations. His agenda for discussion changed frequently and always revolved around substantive issues. It was highly sequential, using shuttles and late-night diplomatic pressure to explore concessions and then hold summits to lock in gains and build momentum towards a larger package. At these summits, Holbrooke consistently sought a series of agreed-upon *principles* followed by *specifics on the issues*. His seven-member team artfully concealed and revealed information in order to benefit the process.

The first summit was "a tense affair with hostile officials clustered tightly around the custom-built table" (Watkins and Rosegrant 1999: 16), but Holbrooke emerged with a list of agreed basic principles that recognized Bosnia's existing borders, created two entities within Bosnia, and allowed each entity the right to establish ties with neighboring countries. The second summit, three weeks later, resulted in another contentious list of principles defining the structures of government such as a parliament, a presidency, a constitutional court, and a commitment to elections.

Holbrooke deferred for a later time toxic issues such as the map with boundaries and delimitations of the postconflict country, which he deemed to be "too hard." "We knew the map was going to be a horror when we got to it, and we didn't think we could make much progress on the map until we had other things straightened out, so we worked on these basic principles first," one of his team members explained (Watkins and Rosegrant 1999: 16). Still, Holbrooke sought to leave no issues that could be negotiated untouched. By the time the leaders arrived in Dayton, the U.S. State Department presented them with a comprehensive Framework Peace Agreement complete with annexes covering military issues, elections, the constitution, human rights, and an international police task force. The idea was to present them with a complete package and ram it through by way of an intensive negotiations process to be completed as rapidly as humanly possible.

By contrast, George Mitchell deferred the difficult substantive issues until the very end of his involvement in favor of focusing on negotiations over the procedures and agenda themselves. His early discussions slogged through arcane debates about rules. He not only negotiated the process and procedures for the all-party talks, but he negotiated a preliminary agenda, then a more detailed agenda with the parties — all of which took more than a year. This extreme procedural focus was a mirror image of Holbrooke's extreme substantive focus.

When Mitchell did deal with substantive issues, he methodically separated them into three strands for the parties to discuss the nuances of each issue. His team shared information widely in an effort to avoid surprises or misunderstandings. The parties canvassed their various proposals, concepts, and models but, more importantly, they explored each other's ideas, seeking further explanations or offering explanations for their own reservations or objections. The SDLP and Ulster Unionist Party (UUP) eventually had language-proofing sessions where they could identify and explain for each other their sensitivities about the sort of terms they were respectively using or likely to use (Durkan 1999).

Mitchell later repackaged the issues in the final agreement for mutual gain. Mitchell progressively isolated and deferred the hardest issue, decommissioning of IRA weapons, in the hope that enough of a relationship would be built up among the parties to tackle it later in a more productive way.

Timing Strategy: Forcing versus Fostering

Holbrooke's timing strategy called for building momentum by gaining early wins through agreements on principles. He then accelerated the pace with a series of partial agreements and forcible actions to prevent backsliding on promises. He used several imposed deadlines — backed with the threat of bombing — to forge agreements. He also made well-timed persuasive arguments — backed by intelligence data — to force parties to back down. He made what he called, "an arguable decision and close call" on October 4, 1995 to sit with Bosnian President Alija Izetbegovic and, using U.S. military estimates, convince him to cease the Muslim military offensive.

"It was a powerful presentation when we said 'it is time to stop the war and go to an international peace conference,'" said Holbrooke. "They knew that we were not visceral, knee-jerk, stop-the-war-immediately people, because we had gone now for close to two months letting the war proceed. So we had a lot of credibility when we finally said, 'Look, this is the first time we've suggested a cease-fire. We're worried. We think it's time'" (Watkins and Rosegrant 1999: 22). This ceasefire led to the negotiations at Dayton, which resulted in the final agreement.

By contrast, Mitchell's patient strategy used time, not only to begin to foster a more constructive relationship among the parties, but to increase their sense of respect, obligation, liking, and credibility toward him. Mitchell, in turn, used this credibility — and only his credibility — to create a culminating event in December 1997 when he felt further interaction was pointless.

> Much has been said about my patience. I have a lot of it, but I felt I had just about used it up. Rarely in my life have I felt as frustrated and angry. We have been meeting for a year and a half. For hundreds and hundreds of hours I had listened to the same arguments. Very little had been accomplished. It had taken two months to get an understanding on the rules to be followed once the negotiations began. Then it took another two months to get agreement on a preliminary agenda. Then we had tried for fourteen more months to get an accord on a detailed final agenda. We couldn't even get that, and we were about to adjourn for the Christmas break. Our failure . . . would be crushing . . . I began to think about a deadline. (Mitchell 1999: 126)

Mitchell deployed his hard-earned credibility on the final deadline, which he carefully negotiated with the parties and governments at the talks. To emphasize that this would be the parties' last clear chance for agreement, and that his participation was at an end, he stated at the outset of the final talks, "I am Humpty Dumpty. I can only jump once."

Table One
Differences between Holbrooke and Mitchell Approach

	Holbrooke Bosnia–Herzegovina	Mitchell Northern Ireland
Fundamental objectives	Deal-oriented Substantive Transactional	Process-oriented Relationship Transformational
Fundamental interest/ role	Mediator/advocate (with clout)	Mediator/neutral
Fundamental influence strategy	BATNA-focused "Whatever it takes"	Joint gains-focused Model-future dealings

The remarkable differences between Holbrooke and Mitchell are summarized in Table One, which outlines their fundamental choices and Table Two, which compares the strategies they each chose to employ. While suggestive, these categories of choice are neither mutually exclusive nor collectively exhaustive. In many respects, these two superficially similar third-party episodes could scarcely be more different, once critically examined.

Table Two
Strategies Employed by Holbrooke and Mitchell

Strategic Element	Holbrooke Bosnia–Herzegovina	Mitchell Northern Ireland
Coalition strategy	Simplify structure Equalize core parties Sequence	Coalition of center against extremes
Issue strategy	Process by fiat	Process an issue for negotiation
	Principles, then specifics	Procedure, then substance
	Sequential, then lock in gains	Separate into three strands, then package
	Defer deal-breakers	Decouple decommissioning
Process strategy	Engineer/manipulate representation	Principled inclusion (Mitchell Principles, "sufficient consensus")

Table Two
Continued

Strategic Element	Holbrooke Bosnia–Herzegovina	Mitchell Northern Ireland
	Sequence shuttles and summits	Keep going at all costs ("variable geometry")
	Conceal/reveal information	Highly transparent
	Use press to paint abyss/lower expectations, yet lock in gains	Relentlessly positive press spin
	Use process to build perceptions of personal credibility and power	Use process to build perceptions of fairness, dedication, and respect
Timing strategy	As fast as possible	As long as it takes
	Build "momentum" by early wins, accelerating series of partial agreements, forcible actions, and process choices	Use time to bootstrap sense of respect, obligation, liking, and credibility
		Expend personal credibility on final deadline

Yet a perusal of these tables immediately suggests a number of research questions. Apart from those in these two cases, how many distinct, "generic choices" are there in each of these categories? Is there a kind of "fit" among the situations, fundamental choices, and strategies with respect to parties, issues, process, and timing? How could a contingency theory be developed to guide action in these tough situations? Ideally, this comparison will stimulate more systematic work on negotiating strategy and architecture in multiparty conflicts.

The Men and Their Mission: Were Their Personalities, Experience, and Approaches a "Fit?"

The relatively bloodless comparisons of strategies and approaches in Tables One and Two largely sidestep the question of the specific individuals involved along with the "fit" between the person and the situation. Indeed, arguably as a function of the actors themselves, these twin cases — at least in their central tendencies — contrast force with tact, acting with listening, and manipulation with process stewardship. While Holbrooke turned to coercive means to forge a peace, Mitchell first created and then presided over a "Senate" in Northern Ireland.

Richard Holbrooke possessed one of the most assertive personalities in Washington. He could be bombastic and brash. Some considered him a "showman" and he had a reputation for being unpredictable and often difficult. He had served on the U.S. delegation to the Paris peace talks with the Vietcong in 1968 and, as Assistant Secretary of State for East Asian and Pacific Affairs, he had conducted difficult negotiations with the Chinese and with former Filipino President Ferdinand Marcos. "Holbrooke was probably the most forceful personality we could possibly find for this kind of negotiating effort," stated one top NSC official. "He's both brilliant and has a bullying personality, but that was seen as the combination we needed" (Watkins and Rosegrant 1999: 12). With Holbrooke as the negotiator, one State Department official added wryly, the new diplomatic initiative was assured high visibility.

Holbrooke was not only blunt and impatient, but he also used all the means at his disposal to force agreements. During the shuttle diplomacy in Bosnia, Holbrooke told Tudjman and Izetbegovic that he did not want them to take the strategic town of Banja Luka. Having already established formidable credibility and a reputation for the capacity to exert military power, he offered no concrete incentives for backing off but made it clear that further fighting would be against U.S. wishes. After a good deal of yelling, mostly at each other, the two leaders asked Holbrooke to announce the decision on their behalf.

"The parties didn't dare get in the way of Holbrooke," said U.S. Ambassador to Macedonia Christopher Hill. "He'd run them over." Another staff member stated, "He can be very tough on people, but he's a spectacular character to watch in action" (Watkins and Rosegrant 1999: 19, 22).

Both critics and supporters agreed that Holbrooke operated with an unusual degree of freedom for a government negotiator. Free rein was particularly important at the negotiating table. "When you're trying to bring this thing to a halt, this terrible war," Hill asserted, "you had to be empowered to make decisions on the spot, to move very quickly, and to assess the mood of people and the feel for the situation." Holbrooke vehemently agreed. "You cannot run a negotiation long-distance," he declared. "Tactical considerations for negotiation must be left to the negotiator" (Watkins and Rosegrant 1999: 22).

Holbrooke had scant willingness to let events unfold. At the Dayton Accords, he constantly harassed the delegations, arguing that it was their last chance to end the war with the help of the U.S. and the international community. "He browbeat people," said one NSC official. "He talks until they're tired. Everything was geared to getting this agreement, and he was working twenty-one, twenty-two hours a day on this stuff" (Watkins and Rosegrant 1999: 25).

"Senior staff knew that this was really make-or-break for the Administration," Hill said. "They felt very comfortable with the idea that Holbrooke was there trying to negotiate the best deal he could. Anything the parties will agree to is fine with us . . . What was critical was to persuade the parties that they had to close this deal."

That was precisely what Holbrooke was good at. Another official noted, "He was prepared to be . . . seductive when it was appropriate to be seductive, and . . . brutal when it was appropriate to be as brutal as it took. He is an operator . . . a deal maker" (Watkins and Rosegrant 1999: 16).

George Mitchell, on the other hand, had a reputation for being diligent, cautious, and levelheaded. He had served for fourteen years in the U.S. Senate, seven of those years as Democratic Majority Leader. Throughout his political career, he displayed a fairness and calm temperament that made him a natural intermediary between senators, administration officials, and staff. As a legislator, Mitchell was quiet and judicious. He massaged details and soothed tempers, always seeking consensus over mundane issues. He cared deeply about many liberal causes and understood the minutiae of his bills.

From his early days, Mitchell had a passionate commitment to the environment and immediately began the process of overhauling the *Clean Air Act*. It took him nine years to develop the legislation only to see his bill exposed to a filibuster on the Senate floor. After a rigorous month of two hundred and fifty hours of negotiations and endless arguments about minute details, he was finally able to pass the bill. "The negotiations involved over fifty senators, hundreds of staffers, and dozens of administration officials. Rarely does a bill consume a month of active consideration on the Senate floor. That is how long the clean air bill took" (Mitchell 1999: 12).

Similarly, a health care reform plan — about which Mitchell cared deeply but that ultimately failed — took him thirteen years of concerted effort. Political consultant and friend, Bob Shrum observed, "George Mitchell understands that the immediate pursuit of the instant success often yields neither success nor satisfaction" (Clymer 1994: 5).

In late 1992, Mitchell remarked about his steady ways, "Sometimes in the heat of battle people lose sight of the ultimate objectives and tactics become ends in themselves. That is a mistake" (Romano 1990: b3).

Mitchell developed a sense of patience and timing in the U.S. Senate where passion was more effective in opposition than when in the majority. Yet a restrained style did not imply an unwillingness to exert power; indeed, Mitchell could be fiercely partisan. In his early career, he learned when to use this passion. "It is a grave mistake," one Mitchell supporter warned, "to confuse fairness with weakness, to read tentativeness into his actions, rather than calculation" (Romano 1990: b3). Mitchell played a leading role in almost every major piece of legislation that passed through the Senate in those years. He frequently allowed room for events to unfold.

Part of his mandate as majority leader was to help prevent a second term for former President George H. W. Bush. Political writer Sidney Blumenthal described Mitchell's strategy, "With exquisite politesse and delicacy, through the protracted budget summit in 1990, Mitchell coaxed

Bush to abandon his iron-clad campaign pledge: 'no new taxes,' an act that repudiated the Reaganite theology and proved devastating to Bush politically" (Marantz 1994: 3). Mitchell's style allowed the breathing room for Bush to reverse himself — falling into what proved a lethal political trap.

It would be too easy to caricature and exaggerate the extent of the personality differences between Holbrooke and Mitchell, when in fact, observers have also remarked on Mitchell's toughness and Holbrooke's empathy and charm. Yet the contrasting central personality attributes and prior experiences of the two men were strongly consistent with the nature of the approaches they chose to the two conflicts. Perhaps ironically, the character of the two negotiated outcomes also seemed to differ along similar lines.

Representatives of the Republic of Bosnia and Herzegovina, the Republic of Croatia, and the Federal Republic of Yugoslavia hastily initialed Holbrooke's General Framework Agreement for Peace in Bosnia and Herzegovina. Even at the signing ceremony, however, Izetbegovic and the rest of his delegation described it as "a bitter and unjust peace" and called it a "brutal process" (Watkins and Rosegrant 1999: 26). Maintenance of the peace hinged on the on-going presence of outside military forces with many participants asserting that "if they were removed, the parties would be back killing each other the next day."

By contrast, the representatives of eight political parties, including the largest Catholic party, SDLP; and the largest Protestant party, UUP; and representatives of the Irish and British Governments, signed Mitchell's Belfast Agreement. At the signing ceremony, UUP leader David Trimble and John Hume of SDLP called it a "principled compromise" forged in "learning and understanding" (Mitchell 1999: 175).

It is hardly surprising that the personalities and experiences of Mitchell and Holbrooke seem to "fit" the elements of the third party strategies that each man employed as well as the kind of outcomes achieved. And a good case can be made that the two different approaches were appropriate to very different situations.

Concluding Thoughts

To sharpen the contrasts between these two men and the episodes in which they played central roles, consider the following thought experiment: Imagine the likely process and outcome in each case if Holbrooke had been assigned to Northern Ireland and Mitchell to Bosnia. While each man might have flexibly adapted to radically different situations, it is clear that simply juxtaposing the two approaches would sharply lower the chances of success in each case.

In seeking to draw conclusions and make generalizations from this discussion, we are, of course, up against the sharp limits of our data: two specific individuals with two distinct personalities and histories, two radically different mediation approaches, and two different conflict situations. Broader arguments of "fit" between individual, strategy, and situation cannot legitimately be advanced on the strength of this evidence. It is comforting that these results are consistent with the findings, cited earlier, of Zartman, Touval, Bercovitch, Anagnoson, and others. By relying on a negotiation analytic framework, however, this comparison permits a finer grained strategic and tactical exploration — coalitional, party, issue, process, timing — than the more general characterizations by other researchers of the mediation process (e.g., "directive," "communicative-facilitative," and so forth).

Perhaps the most important contribution of this comparison of the sharply divergent approaches taken in Northern Ireland and Bosnia is the challenge it poses to easy generalizations about effective mediation. Holbrooke's results may confound those who see the essence of successful mediation as scrupulous neutrality buttressed by patient, interest-based, empathetic joint problem solving to find mutually beneficial solutions. For others who may see the coercive diplomacy of Holbrooke as the essential ingredient to cutting though intractable and violent situations, the success of Mitchell's low-key, even-handed, endlessly persistent style may seem almost magical. Yet, in the course of their respective efforts, both men helped forge peace agreements in two immensely challenging situations that had defeated many prior attempts. While two data points do not a theory make, these twin cases highlight the range of tactical and strategic dimensions required of any candidate theory of third party action.

NOTES

We thank Hannah Riley Bowles for her insights on this article, and Kristen Schneeman for her research and writing assistance. We acknowledge the useful frameworks developed by Michael Watkins and Susan Rosegrant (2001) in their book, *Breakthrough International Negotiations: How Great Negotiators Transformed the World's Toughest Post-Cold War Conflicts*.

1. The accounts of Mitchell and Holbrooke in this article draw heavily on two detailed case studies, "'To Hell with the Future, Let's Get on with the Past': George Mitchell in Northern Ireland," Harvard Business School Case 9-801-393 (Sebenius 2001b) and "Getting to Dayton: Negotiating an End to the War in Bosnia," Harvard Business School Case 1-800-134 (Watkins and Rosegrant 1999), which can be obtained through http://www.hbsp.harvard.edu. The much fuller set of sources and citations contained in these underlying cases are incorporated in the present article by reference.

2. See George Alexander (1979: 43–68). The present comparison is more in the spirit of Faure's "most different systems design;" for an elaboration, see Andrew Faure Murray (1994).

3. See Lax and Sebenius (1986); Neale and Bazerman (1991); Raiffa (1982). For recent surveys, see Sebenius (1992, 2001a, 2002: 229–252). For a practitioner-oriented survey, see Sebenius (2000).

4. For negotiation analytic accounts of mediation, see, for example, Raiffa (1982), Lax and Sebenius (1986), as well as Antrim and Sebenius (1991). "Multilateral Conference Mediation: Tommy Koh and the Law of the Sea," in *Mediation in International Relations: Multilateral Approaches to Conflict Management*, edited by J. Bercovitch and J. Z. Rubin, London: Macmillan. More generally, scholars of conflict resolution have analyzed the mediation process; see Bercovitch, J. (1984). *Social Conflicts and Third Parties: Strategies of Conflict Resolution*, Boulder, CO: Westview; Bercovitch and Rubin; Kolb, D. (1983). *The Mediators*, Cambridge: MIT Press; Princen, T. (1992). *Intermediaries in International Conflict*, Princeton: Princeton University Press; Rubin, J. (1981). *The Dynamics of Third Party Intervention*, New York: Praeger; Touval, S. and I. W. Zartman

(1985). *International Mediation in Theory and Practice*, Boulder, CO: Westview; and Zartman, I. W. and S. Touval (1996). *International Mediation After the Cold War.*

5. Touval and Zartman (1985); see also the discussion by Bercovitch and Rubin (1983: 14–21).

6. Holbrooke stated, "Our view was that the negotiation was beginning to take place on the battlefield in a very advantageous way." In fact, the team members agree that the Federation advances were like a present being handed to them. Any land won back in battle that brought the map closer to the envisioned 51–49 percent split was land that would not have to be painfully exchanged at the table. From Watkins and Rosegrant (1999: 20).

7. If no middle ground could be found, Holbrooke warned, the consequences would be dire. "Let me just say that if Dayton and the peace process do not succeed, the country will slip back into war because the issues that led to war are unresolved," he declared. (Watkins and Rosegrant 1999: 27).

REFERENCES

Alexander, G. 1979. Case studies and theory development: The method of structured focused comparison. In *Diplomacy: New approaches in history, theory, and policy*, edited by P. Lauren. New York: Free Press.

Bercovitch, J. and P. Diehl. 1997. Conflict management of enduring rivalries. *International Interactions* 22: 299–320.

Bercovitch, J., T. Anagnoson, S. Touval, I. W. Zartman, and P. F. Diehl. 1991. Some contextual issues and empirical trends in the study of successful mediation. *Journal of Peace Research* 28: 7–17.

Clymer, A. 1994. The High Court is not everybody's dream. *The New York Times*, 17 April: 5.

Durkan, M. 1999. The negotiations in practice. In *Accord: Striking a balance: The Northern Ireland peace process*, edited by Clem McCartney. London: Conciliation Resources. Available from http://www.c-r.org/ireland/accord8/index.shtml.

Germond, J. W. and J. Witcover. 1998. The road to Northern Ireland. *The National Journal* 30(16): 888.

Gulick, E. V. 1955. *Europe's classical balance of power*. New York: Norton.

Lax, D. A. and J. K. Sebenius. 1986. *The manager as negotiator: Bargaining for cooperation and competitive gain.* New York: The Free Press.

Marantz, S. 1994. Mitchell has held interest in sports for half a century. *The Sporting News*, 12 June: 1.

Mitchell, G. 1999. *Making peace.* New York: Alfred A. Knopf.

Murray, A. F. 1994. Some methodological problems in comparative politics. *Journal of Theoretical Politics* 6(3): 307–322.

Neale, M. A. and M. H. Bazerman. 1991. *Cognition and rationality in negotiation.* New York: The Free Press.

Raiffa, H. 1982. *The art and science of negotiation.* Cambridge, MA: Harvard University Press, Belknap Press.

Romano, L. 1990. George Mitchell, the civil senator: The noncombative — and controversial — style of the majority leader. *The Washington Post*, 27 June: B2.

Sciolino, E. 1995. U.S. envoy highlights fine print on Bosnia. *The New York Times*, September 13, 1995.

Sebenius, J. K. 1992. Negotiation analysis: A characterization and review. *Management Science* 38(2): 18–38.

— — —. 2000. *Dealmaking essentials: Creating and claiming value for the long term, Item No. 2-800-443.* Boston, MA: Harvard Business School Publishing.

— — —. 2001a. *Negotiation analysis. International encyclopedia of the social and behavioral sciences*, edited by N. J. Smelser and P. B. Baltes. New York: Elsevier Science (Pergamon).

— — —. 2001b. "To hell with the future, let's get on with the past": George Mitchell in Northern Ireland. Harvard Business School Case 9-801-393. Boston: Harvard Business School Publishing. Available from http://www.hbsp.harvard.edu.

— — —. 2002. International negotiation analysis. In *International negotiation: Analysis, approaches, issues*, edited by V. Kremenyuk. San Francisco: Jossey-Bass.

Watkins, M. and S. Rosegrant. 1999. Getting to Dayton: Negotiating an end to the war in Bosnia. Harvard Business School Case 1-800-134. Boston: Harvard Business School Publishing.

— — —. 2001. *Breakthrough international negotiations: How great negotiators transformed the world's toughest post-Cold War conflicts.* San Francisco: Jossey-Bass.

Appendix One
Summary of Events in Bosnia

The Balkans had a history of hundreds of years of bloodshed. Fundamentally, however, the war in Bosnia had its roots in the breakup of Yugoslavia — a gradual process of disintegration that began in the late 1980s after the death of communist leader Marshal Tito — and in the rise of ethnic nationalism that had hastened Yugoslavia's end.

By 1989 Slobodan Milosevic, former leader of the Serbian Communist Party, had maneuvered himself into the presidency of Serbia. His increasingly overt nationalism, growing power base, and tightening grip on the Federal Army alarmed and intimidated Yugoslavia's smaller republics. Their fears were not unfounded; Milosevic's ambition was to create a Greater Serbia by annexing areas with large Serb populations.

In June 1991, the republic of Croatia, led by Franjo Tudjman — its first democratically-elected president and a nationalist as well — declared its independence. Both Milosevic and Tudjman had designs on the republic of Bosnia, which was home to substantial Serb and Croat communities. But Milosevic was also eyeing the Serb enclave of the Krajina in Croatia, and full-scale war erupted between Serbs and Croats in that region over the summer.

When the European Community conferred recognition on Croatia and Slovenia as independent nations, the Bosnian president, Alija Izetbegovic, concluded he must seek independence as well. The decision provoked a revolt by Serbs in Bosnia. Their leader, Radovan Karadzic, declared himself president of an independent Bosnian Serb republic and laid siege to the capital city of Sarajevo.

By late 1992 the Serbs had captured 70 percent of Bosnia, forcing some 750,000 Muslims from their homes. Reports emerged of Serb-run concentration camps, torture, and the systematic rape of Muslim women. The term "ethnic cleansing" came into use to describe efforts to create regions that were ethnically "pure." In early 1993, Bosnian Croats began seizing Bosnian territory and attacking Muslim civilians, creating yet another front in an increasingly ugly war.

Despite repeated appeals for help by Bosnian President Izetbegovic, the international community seemed unprepared to take decisive action to stop the conflict. From the start, the European Community (EC) wanted to take charge in the regional dispute, and the U.S. was all too eager to let it do so. In late 1991, the UN Security Council imposed an arms embargo on the entire former Yugoslavia, which disproportionately impacted the Muslims. The EC imposed trade sanctions, including an oil embargo, which were soon scaled back to apply only to Serbia. A UN Protection Force, UNPROFOR, was established for Bosnia, but its mission was poorly defined, and the U.S. decided not to contribute troops to the effort.

As a presidential candidate, Bill Clinton had faulted George Bush's hands-off policy in the Balkans. Shortly after taking office in early 1993, the Clinton Administration searched for ways to help the Bosnian Muslims without committing troops to the region. While the Europeans rejected its initial proposal to lift the arms embargo against Bosnia and employ strategic NATO air strikes against Bosnian Serb targets, the U.S. was able to pressure the UN and NATO to set new policies that would afford some protection for the Muslims. The Hague International War Crimes Tribunal was established, and the UN Security Council created six so-called "safe areas;" Muslim towns where UN peacekeepers provided a measure of safety from Serb and Croat assaults. In August 1993, NATO for the first time threatened air strikes against the Bosnian Serbs if they did not ease the siege of Sarajevo. The European allies, however, diluted the threat of retaliation by insisting on a "dual key" arrangement, which required approval from both the UN's conservative leadership and NATO before any action was taken.

By late 1993, the Europeans had tried and failed to negotiate three different peace plans for Bosnia. Then, in early 1994, a mortar fell on a busy Sarajevo marketplace, killing 68 and wounding more than 200. The U.S. insisted on NATO intervention, and NATO shot down four Bosnian Serb planes that were violating the no-fly zone, the alliance's first offensive operation.

Some limited progress was being made on the diplomatic front as well. U.S. officials were able to negotiate an alliance between the warring Muslims and Croats, stopping the fighting on one front, and creating a nascent coalition of parties against the Serbs. A new entity called the Contact Group, which included representatives from the U.S., France, Britain, Germany, and Russia, was formed to address the Balkan crisis. It proposed a series of constitutional principles and a new territorial split, which became the basis of future negotiations, giving 51 percent of Bosnia to the Muslim-Croat Federation and 49 percent to the Bosnian Serbs. Meanwhile, Bosnian Serb attacks on Sarajevo and other safe areas continued, as they quickly realized that NATO's retaliation amounted to little more than a slap on the wrist.

Finally, in July 1995, Bosnian Serbs took the safe area of Srebrenica as 400 Dutch peacekeepers looked on helplessly. As many as 7,000 Muslim men and boys were massacred. European credibility was in tatters, the British and French were considering canceling the UN mission altogether, and the whole thing was beginning to look like a foreign-policy disaster for President Clinton. U.S. policy makers became determined to launch a new diplomatic initiative to try to rescue victory from the jaws of defeat.

Among the first orders of business was to change the dual-key arrangement. The UN key was delegated to military representatives on the ground instead of the more cautious civilian leadership. NATO agreed to conduct preemptive air strikes if safe areas were seriously threatened.

After making it clear that the U.S. would press forward with or without a European endorsement, National Security Adviser Anthony Lake handed off the negotiating effort to Richard Holbrooke, the Assistant Secretary of State for Canadian and European Affairs. Holbrooke saw this challenge as not only ending the war, but also cobbling together the structure, incentives, and international support to allow a new, multiethnic Bosnia to emerge.

Bosnian Serbs quickly tested the resolve of the new initiative by lobbing a mortar into a Sarajevo marketplace, killing 37 and wounding more than 80. At the recommendation of Holbrooke's team, NATO immediately began massive bombing in retaliation.

In the midst of the air strikes, Holbrooke's team met with Milosevic. They were stunned when he presented them with a letter, dubbed the "Patriarch Paper," which answered what had been a key question for sixteen months: Who spoke for the Bosnian Serbs? The answer was Milosevic who, according to the document, would hold the tie-breaking vote on a six-person negotiating team of Serbs and Bosnian Serbs, half of whom would be chosen by Milosevic. "As soon as he produced that paper, I knew we were started," Holbrooke said.

Holbrooke felt it was time for the foreign ministers to meet. Convening such a meeting while NATO bombs were falling would project a strong message about U.S. leadership and control. He felt strongly that locking a few principles in place and announcing them to the world was critical to building momentum behind the process.

For the meeting of foreign ministers in Geneva, Holbrooke's team drafted a single page of relatively uncontroversial principles. It was important that the document represent real progress, yet not be so bold that the ministers would refuse to sign. The principles proposed included the creation of two entities within Bosnia, the Federation of Bosnia and Herzegovina and a Bosnian Serb region to be known as the Republika Srpska, following the Contact Group's 51-49 split. While the meeting was tense, the ministers ultimately signed the agreement.

NATO's bombing was proving to be surprisingly effective at wearing down the resolve of the Serbs in Belgrade and in Bosnia. But many NATO and UN officials were becoming anxious to end the air campaign, as they were running out of targets that posed limited risk to civilians. Holbrooke had to act fast to preserve the advantage that the military action gave him.

Holbrooke and his team met Milosevic at a hunting lodge outside of Belgrade. Milosevic pleaded for the bombing to be stopped and then sprang another surprise on the Americans: he asked whether they would be willing to meet with the Bosnian Serb leaders, who were waiting in a villa about two hundred meters away. Although the Americans' official position had been that they would not negotiate directly with the Bosnian Serbs, they decided to seize this critical opportunity. After hours of painful negotiation, a withdrawal agreement was signed, ending the siege of Sarajevo.

Meanwhile, the Muslim-Croat Federation was making unexpected advances on the battlefield. Although many in Washington disagreed, Holbrooke viewed this development favorably. Any land won back in battle that brought the map closer to the envisioned 51-49 split would not have to be painfully exchanged at the table. However, as Muslim forces closed in on Banja Luka, the largest Serb city in Bosnia, the U.S. considered the specter of 250,000 new refugees, intervention by Serbia, or the destabilization of Milosevic at a critical moment in the negotiating process. Further fighting also threatened to destroy the shaky Muslim-Croat Federation as it became increasingly evident that the Croats were the dominant partners in that alliance. Under pressure from Holbrooke, Tudjman and Izetbegovic agreed not to take the city.

Holbrooke scheduled a second meeting of the Balkan foreign ministers in New York, where he managed to get an agreement on a second set of basic principles defining a governmental superstructure to bind the two entities within Bosnia together, including a parliament, a presidency, courts, and democratic elections monitored by the international community.

The Balkan presidents consented to attend a peace conference at Wright-Patterson Air Force Base in Dayton, Ohio and agreed to stay as long as it took to reach a settlement. All were deeply war-weary, and each had an incentive to settle. Milosevic, in particular, had become a virtual champion for peace, since the U.S. had promised to suspend sanctions against Serbia once an agreement was signed.

The State Department worked furiously to prepare a comprehensive draft agreement, covering all the issues. Holbrooke busied himself with creating the right setting for the talks, down to the size of the table and the décor of the presidents' rooms. Meanwhile, revelations of massacres of Muslims in Bosnia, threats by Croatia of renewed military action, and tensions between Congress and the Clinton Administration over the role of U.S. troops in an implementation force threatened to derail the approaching talks.

For most of the participants, the Dayton negotiations were a grim process. Territorial disputes over Bosnia remained central, with the most emotional battle erupting over the possible partitioning of Sarajevo. Holbrooke continued to hammer at the delegations, sometimes working twenty-two hours a day. The General Framework Agreement for Peace in Bosnia, initialed by all the parties on November 21, 1995, ended the bloodiest European conflict since World War II.

Appendix Two
Summary of Events in Northern Ireland

By late 1995, George Mitchell — recently retired after fourteen years in the U.S. Senate — had undertaken several trade missions to Northern Ireland on behalf of President Clinton. He was becoming well acquainted with the leaders of the political parties as well as the representatives of the British and Irish governments. Moreover, he had gained their trust. In November, when President Clinton visited Belfast, the British asked him if Mitchell would chair a new International Body on Decommissioning of Weapons, created to separate from the political negotiations the issue that had become the most significant roadblock to peace. Mitchell agreed to chair the body, along with former Finnish Prime Minister Harri Holkeri and former Chief of the Canadian Defense Forces General John de Chastelain.

In broad relief, the troubles in Northern Ireland emerged because two groups of people, the nationalists and the unionists, want opposing political futures for the same territory: Northern Ireland, also known as Ulster Province. The nationalists are overwhelmingly Catholic and want the province to become part of Ireland. They form a minority in Ulster (about 40 percent). Extreme and uncompromising nationalists willing to use violence to achieve the goal of a united Ireland are known as "republicans." The unionists are overwhelmingly Protestant and want the province to remain part of the United Kingdom, in union with England. They form the majority in Ulster (about 60 percent). Extreme and uncompromising unionists are known as "loyalists."

Over the course of more than three hundred years, people from both communities gradually developed a keen sense of grievance and strong feelings of victimization. The unionists feel that they are a threatened minority on the larger island of Ireland. The nationalists feel that they are a threatened minority within Ulster.

Frustrations among Northern Ireland's Catholics eventually led to what was euphemistically called the "Troubles." Inspired in part by the civil rights movement in the United States, the Catholics mounted civil rights protests in Northern Ireland in 1968. Although the demonstrations were initially peaceful in character, the police began to react violently, which greatly increased the tension between Catholics and Protestants.

Out of this environment emerged the paramilitary Irish Republican Army (IRA), a radical group of Catholics committed to driving the British from Northern Ireland through a concerted campaign of terror. In response to the IRA, a number of radical Protestant groups sprang to life, merged into the Ulster Defense Association (UDA), and began revenge killings of Catholics. Over the next twenty-five years, more than three thousand people in Northern Ireland were killed in terrorist attacks launched by the IRA and opposing unionist paramilitary groups. Shouted at a rally in 1973, the chilling slogan, "To hell with the future, let's get on with the past!" underscored the acute and ever-present sense of historical grievance.

By the mid-1990s, there were ten parties that had a stake in the peace process. The largest (and, relatively speaking, the more moderate) on the nationalist side were Sinn Fein, led by Gerry Adams and widely described as the "political wing of the IRA;" and the Social Democratic and Labor Party (SDLP), led by John Hume. On the unionist side, the Ulster Unionist Party led by David Trimble, was the most prominent. Among the more extreme elements were the

Democratic Unionist Party (DUP), led by the fiery minister Ian Paisley, who frequently attacked moderate unionists such as Trimble for "selling out" the cause of the Protestant majority; the Ulster Democratic Party (UDP), linked with the UDA; the Progressive Unionist Party (PUP), linked to the Ulster Volunteer Force (UVF), another paramilitary group; the United Kingdom Unionist Party (UKUP); and the IRA.

This was the complex, conflict-laden environment into which Mitchell stepped in late 1995 as the International Body began its work. As a general rule, the parties absolutely refused to talk with each other. Sustained violence had become a way of life. Extremist voices dominated the society and the debate. This broader polarization was reflected in a virtual chasm between negotiating positions over major issues — most notably the one he was tasked with resolving, that of the decommissioning of weapons.

The report the chairmen released in January 1996 artfully deflected attention from what they knew would be a controversial position on decommissioning. They rejected the position insisted upon by the British government and the unionists that paramilitary groups would have to give up their arms prior to the entry into peace negotiations. Instead, they recommended that the decommissioning happen in parallel with the negotiations Stepping outside their mandate, they also recommended a process for all-party talks that would create a foundation of trust among the parties and build public confidence in the process. They recommended that participants in the talks subscribe to a specific set of principles of democracy, dialogue and nonviolence, which became known as the "Mitchell Principles." And they proposed that a popular election of delegates to a debate forum be held, from which each party would nominate representatives to attend the talks (a proposal viewed favorably by unionists).

Despite renewed violence by the paramilitaries, the forum election took place in May 1996. And adherence to the Mitchell Principles became the criteria by which parties were included in or excluded from the talks until their conclusion.

Mitchell, Holkeri, and de Chastelain were persuaded by the British and Irish governments to stay on and chair the all-party talks. They encountered immediate controversy when unionists refused to allow Mitchell to be seated as Chairman, feeling that the governments were imposing him on the talks, along with a set of ground rules and procedural guidelines. The DUP and the UKUP staged a walk-out. Mitchell felt it was important at this early stage to keep all the players in the fold, and so he abandoned the process and agenda created by the governments and instead began what would become three months of debate over the ground rules for the talks.

The rules that were eventually adopted in August 1996 included a complex voting structure called "sufficient consensus," intended to guarantee that any measures adopted by the parties at the talks had genuine broad support. In order to be adopted, any proposal had to meet four tests: (1) support from parties representing a majority of the voting population; (2) support from parties representing a majority of both Catholic and Protestant communities; (3) support from a majority of the parties present at the talks; and (4) support from both governments.

A debate began on an agenda for the talks, but it quickly became a rancorous argument over specific substantive issues and simple procedural issues. After fourteen months, the participants agreed to divide the substantive issues into three strands and to conduct a parallel dialogue on each. The first strand related to internal relations within Northern Ireland: the Protestant parties demanded continued sole rule by Britain or a strong Northern Ireland Assembly based on majority elections; the Catholic parties were not in favor of an Assembly unless it was carefully constructed to share power equally. The second strand had to do with relations between Northern Ireland and the Irish Republic: the nationalists demanded a political system that ensured cross-border bodies with executive powers established by the two governments; the unionists feared that close relations with the Republic were a step towards eventual re-union with Ireland. The final strand addressed relations between the British and Irish governments: The Republic of Ireland's constitution had enshrined within it a territorial claim to Northern Ireland; Britain maintained an officially declared strategic interest in Ulster despite any consent of its people, minority or majority.

The talks foundered repeatedly over the details of the decommissioning issue. By July 1997, Mitchell and the governments proposed that the debate over decommissioning be moved from the all-party talks to an International Commission on Decommissioning. Mitchell then insisted that substantive negotiations must begin in September. These would be the first talks on issues, other than rules and agendas, since he became chairman over a year before. The nationalist party Sinn Fein would be allowed into the talks in September if the IRA would declare a new cease-fire.

The prospect of Sinn Fein entering the talks — after a wave of IRA violence earlier in the year — created a serious problem for unionists. The DUP and the UKUP stormed out of the talks for the last time. When the IRA did announce a cease-fire, the UUP voted against every proposal to admit Sinn Fein to the talks, but Trimble remained at the table. Ironically, the actions of the hard-line unionist parties had opened the way for other unionists to participate more fully in the talks. As Mitchell wrote later, "Reaching agreement without their presence was extremely difficult; it would have been impossible with them in the room. [They had] made life miserable for Trimble and the UUP."

This was one example of the way Mitchell was able to use "variable geometry" or changing the format of the negotiations and their participants — whether intentional or accidental — to move the talks forward. In the fall of 1997, Mitchell held meetings in smaller rooms with limited numbers of participants in order to facilitate a more candid exchange of views and some hard bargaining. At first, the intimate setting improved the quality of the discussion. But by the end of the year, the debate began to deteriorate again. Discussions were well under way on most of the relevant issues, but few compromises were being made. Mitchell decided it was time to set a deadline.

The charter for the all-party talks was set to expire in June 1998. Working backwards from that date, Mitchell decided that an agreement by Easter would be symbolically meaningful and practical, allowing for a referendum in late May and an assembly election in late June, before the height of the Protestants' traditional and provocative "marching season." After meeting with representatives of each of the parties, he presented a timetable proposing two weeks of continuous discussion and negotiation from March 30 to April 9. The proposal included a process for the preparation of two drafts that would allow all parties to object and make proposals for the final version so that there would be no last-minute surprises.

Mitchell and his team did yeoman's work in order to produce a first draft that they believed might be acceptable to everyone. The parties still had sharply different objectives. The unionists wanted a continuation of the Union and a strong majority-run Northern Ireland Assembly. The nationalists wanted a united Ireland or an assembly in Northern Ireland in which the Protestant majority and the Catholic minority shared power. The make-up of the police force and criminal justice system, the strength of the north–south institutions, and the prevalent question of decommissioning all required careful wording.

At the eleventh hour, the British and Irish governments jeopardized the success of the talks by making an agreement on "strand two" outside the context of the talks. But they were convinced to compromise and make the north–south institutions (wanted by the nationalists) and the Northern Ireland Assembly (the priority for unionists) mutually interdependent and unable to function without one another. British Prime Minister Tony Blair contributed a last-minute letter offering the unionists his assurance that he would hold the IRA's feet to the fire on decommissioning. Trimble agreed on behalf of the unionists, and the Good Friday Accords were adopted on April 10, 1998.

Mitchell had succeeded in bringing to a spectacular photo finish a historic negotiation that had, in effect, consisted of more than a year-and-a-half of discussion of process and two weeks of active debate over substance.

[6]

The Timing of Peace Initiatives: Hurting Stalemates and Ripe Moments

William Zartman

While most studies on peaceful settlement of disputes see the substance of the proposals for a solution as the key to a successful resolution of conflict, a growing focus of attention shows that a second and equally necessary key lies in the timing of efforts for resolution.[1] Parties resolve their conflict only when they are ready to do so – when alternative, usually unilateral, means of achieving a satisfactory result are blocked and the parties feel that they are in an uncomfortable and costly predicament. At that ripe moment, they grab onto proposals that usually have been in the air for a long time and that only now appear attractive.

The idea of a ripe moment lies at the fingertips of diplomats. 'Ripeness of time is one of the absolute essences of diplomacy', wrote John Campbell.[2] 'You have to do the right thing at the right time', without indicating specific causes. Henry Kissinger did better, recognizing that 'stalemate is the most propitious condition for settlement'.[3] Conversely, practitioners are often heard to say that certain mediation initiatives are not advisable because the conflict just is not yet ripe. In mid-1992, in the midst of ongoing conflict, the Iranian Deputy Foreign Minister noted, 'The situation in Azerbaijan is not ripe for such moves for mediation.'[4]

The concept of a ripe moment centres on the parties' perception of a mutually hurting stalemate (MHS), optimally associated with an impending, past or recently avoided catastrophe.[5] The concept is based on the notion that when the parties find themselves locked in a conflict from which they cannot escalate to victory and this deadlock is painful to both of them (although not necessarily in equal degree or for the same reasons), they seek an alternative policy or way out. The catastrophe provides a deadline or a lesson indicating that pain can be sharply increased if something is not done about it now; catastrophe is a useful extension of MHS but is not necessary either to its definition or to its existence. Using different images, the stalemate has been termed the plateau, a flat and unending terrain without relief, and the catastrophe the precipice, the point where things suddenly and predictably get worse. If the notion of mutual blockage is too static to be realistic, the concept may be stated dynamically as a moment when the upper hand slips and the lower hand rises, both parties moving towards equality, with both movements carrying pain for the parties.[6]

The MHS is grounded in cost–benefit analysis, fully consistent with public choice notions of rationality[7] and public choice studies of war termination and negotiation,[8] which assume that a party will pick the alternative which it prefers, and that a decision to change is induced by increasing pain associated with the present (conflictual) course.[9] In game theoretic terms, it marks the transformation of the situation in the parties' perception from a prisoners' dilemma (PDG) into a chicken dilemma game (CDG),[10] or, in other terms, the realization that the status quo or no negotiation (DD, the south-east corner) is a negative-sum situation, and that to avoid the zero-sum outcomes now considered impossible (CD and DC, the north-east and south-west corners) the positive-sum outcome (CC, the north-west corner) must be explored.

Ripeness is necessarily a perceptual event, and as with any subjective perception, there are likely to be objective referents to be perceived. These can be highlighted by a mediator or an opposing party when they are not immediately recognized by the party itself, and resisted so long as the conflicting party refuses or is otherwise able to block out their perception. But it is the perception of the objective condition, not the condition itself, that makes for an MHS. If the parties do not recognize 'clear evidence' (in someone else's view) that they are in an impasse, an MHS has not (yet) occurred, and if they do perceive themselves to be in such a situation, no matter how flimsy the 'evidence', the MHS is present.

The other element necessary for a ripe moment is less complex and also perceptional: a way out. Parties do not have to be able to identify a specific solution, only a sense that a negotiated solution is possible and that the other party shares that sense and the willingness to search too. Without a sense of a way out, the push associated with the MHS would leave the parties with nowhere to go. Spokespersons often indicate whether they do or do not feel that a deal can be made with the other side and that requitement – i.e. the sense that concessions will be reciprocated, not just banked – exists, particularly when there is a change in that judgement.[11]

Ripeness is only a condition, necessary but not sufficient for the initiation of negotiations. It is not self-fulfilling or self-implementing. It must be seized, either directly by the parties or, if not, through the persuasion of a mediator. Thus, it is not identical to its results, which are not part of its definition, and is therefore not tautological. Not all ripe moments are so seized and turned into negotiations, hence the importance of specifying the meaning and evidence of ripeness so as to indicate when conflicting or third parties can fruitfully initiate negotiations.[12] Although ripeness theory is not predictive in the sense that it can tell when a given situation will become ripe, it is predictive in the sense of identifying the elements necessary (even if not sufficient) for the productive inauguration of negotiations. This type of analytical prediction is the best that can be obtained in social science, where stronger predictions could only be ventured by eliminating free choice (including the human possibility of blindness and mistakes). As such it is of great prescriptive value to policy-makers seeking to know when and how to begin a peace process.

Finding a ripe moment requires research and intelligence studies to identify the objective and subjective elements. Subjective expressions of pain, impasse and inability to bear the cost of further escalation, related to objective evidence of stalemate, data on numbers and nature of casualties and material costs, and/or other such indicators of MHS, along with expressions of a sense of a way out, can be researched on a regular basis in a conflict to establish whether ripeness exists. Researchers would look for evidence, for example, whether the fluid military balance in conflict – such as mountainous Karabagh, or the Burundian or Sri Lankan civil war, for example – has given rise at any time to a perception of MHS by the parties, and to a sense by authoritative spokespersons for each side that the other is ready to seek a solution to the conflict, or, to the contrary, whether it has reinforced the conclusion that any mediation is bound to fail because one or both parties believes in the possibility or necessity of escalating out of the current impasse to achieve a decisive military victory. Research and intelligence would seek to learn why Bosnia in the war-torn summer of 1994 was not ripe for a negotiated settlement and mediation would fail, and why it was in November 1995 and mediation could use that condition to achieve agreement.[13] Similarly, research would indicate that there was no chance of mediating a settlement in the Ethiopia–Eritrean conflict in the early 1980s and the early 1990s, or in the southern Sudan conflict in the 1990s, the skills of President Carter notwithstanding, because the components of ripeness were not present.[14]

While ripeness has not always been seized upon to open negotiations, there have been occasions when it has come into play, as identified by both analysts and practitioners. A number of studies beyond the original examination[15] have used and tested the notion of ripeness in regard to negotiations in Zimbabwe, Namibia and Angola, Eritrea, South Africa, the Philippines, Cyprus, Iran–Iraq, Israel, Mozambique, among others.[16] Touval's work on the Middle East[17] was particularly important in launching the idea. In general, these studies have found the concept applicable and useful as an explanation for the successful initiation of negotiations or their failure, while in some cases proposing refinements to the concept.

The most important refinements carry the theory onto a second level of questions about the effects of each side's pluralized politics on both the perceptions and uses of ripeness. What kinds of internal political conditions are helpful both for perceiving ripeness and for turning that perception into the initiation of promising negotiations? The careful case study by Stephen J. Stedman of the Rhodesian negotiations for independence as Zimbabwe takes the concept beyond a single perception into the complexities of internal dynamics. Stedman[18] specifies that some but not all parties must perceive the hurting stalemate, that patrons rather than parties may be the agents of perception, that the military element in each party is the crucial element in perceiving the stalemate, and that the way out is as important an ingredient as the stalemate in that all parties may well see victory in the alternative outcome prepared by negotiation (although some parties will be proven wrong in that perception). He also highlights the potential of leadership change for the subjective perception of an MHS where it had not been seen previously in the same objective circumstances, and of the threat of domestic rivals – rather than threats from the enemy – to incumbent leadership as the source of impending catastrophe, points also applied by Lieberfield[19] in his more recent comparison of the Middle East and South Africa.

The original formulation of the theory added a third element to the definition of ripeness, the presence of a valid spokesman for each side. As a structural element it is of a different order than the other two defining perceptual elements. Nonetheless, it remains of second-level importance, as Stedman and Lieberfield have pointed out. The presence of strong leadership recognized as representative of each party and that can deliver that party's compliance to the agreement is a necessary (while alone insufficient) condition for productive negotiations to begin, or indeed to end successfully.

Diplomatic memoirs have explicitly referred to ripeness by its MHS component. Chester A. Crocker, US Assistant Secretary of State for Africa between 1981 and 1989, patiently mediated an agreement for the withdrawal of Cuban troops from Angola and of South African troops from Namibia, then to become independent. For years an MHS, and hence productive negotiations, had eluded the parties. 'The second half of 1987 was ... the moment when the situation "ripened".'[20] Military escalations on both sides and bloody confrontations in south-eastern Angola beginning in November 1987 and in south-western Angola in May 1988 ended in a draw.

> By late June 1988, the ... Techipa–Calueque clashes in southwestern Angola confirmed a precarious military stalemate. That stalemate was both the reflection and the cause of underlying political decisions. By early May, my colleagues and I convened representatives of Angola, Cuba, and South Africa in London for face-to-face, tripartite talks. The political decisions leading to the London meeting formed a distinct sequence, paralleling military events on the ground, like planets moving one by one into a certain alignment.[21]

In his conclusion, Crocker identifies specific signs of ripeness, while qualifying that 'correct timing is a matter of feel and instinct'.[22] The American mediation involved building diplomatic moves that paralleled the growing awareness of the parties, observed by the mediator, of the hurting stalemate in which they found themselves.[23]

Alvaro de Soto, Assistant Secretary-General for Political Affairs at the United Nations, also endorsed the necessity of ripeness in his mission to mediate a peace in El Salvador. After chronicling a series of failed initiatives, he points to the importance of the Farabundo Marti National Liberation Front's (FMLN) November 1989 offensive, the largest of the war, which penetrated the main cities including the capital but failed to dislodge the government.

> The silver lining was that it was, almost literally, a defining moment – the point at which it became possible to seriously envisage a negotiation. The offensive showed the FMLN that they could not spark a popular uprising.... The offensive also showed the rightist elements in government, and elites in general, that the armed forces could not defend them, let alone crush the insurgents.... However inchoate at first, the elements of a military deadlock began to appear. Neither side could defeat the other. As the dust settled, the notion that the conflict could not be solved by military means, and that its persistence was causing

pain that could no longer be endured, began to take shape. The offensive codified the existence of a mutually hurting stalemate. The conflict was ripe for a negotiated solution.[24]

In Yugoslavia, Secretary of State James Baker looked for a ripe moment during his quick trip to Belgrade in June 1991 and reported the same day to President George Bush that he did not find it: 'My gut feeling is that we won't produce a serious dialogue on the future of Yugoslavia until all the parties have a greater sense of urgency and danger.'[25] Richard Holbrooke calls this 'a crucial misreading', as he did the later moment created by the Croatian Krajina offensive in August 1995.[26] Holbrooke[27] had his own image of the MHS (or the upper hand slipping and the underdog rising): 'The best time to hit a serve is when the ball is suspended in the air, neither rising nor falling. We felt this equilibrium had arrived, or was about to, on the battlefield [in October 1995]', and he tried to instil a perception of the ripe moment in the mind of Bosnian President Izetbegovic. It took the Croatian offensive, coupled with NATO bombing, to create an MHS composed of a temporary Serb setback and a temporary Croat advance that could not be sustained. A State Department official stated, 'Events on the ground have made it propitious to try again to get the negotiations started. The Serbs are on the run a bit. That won't last forever. So we are taking the obvious major step....'[28]

In his parting report as Under-Secretary-General of the United Nations, Marrack Goulding[29] specifically cited the literature on ripeness in discussing the selection of conflicts to be handled by an overburdened UN.

> Not all conflicts are 'ripe' for action by the United Nations (or any other third party)....It therefore behoves the Secretary-General to be selective and to recommend action only in situations where he judges that the investment of scarce resources is likely to produce a good return (in terms of preventing, managing and resolving conflict).

Some practitioners have given a more nuanced endorsement of the concept, although not all have read the conceptual fine print carefully. Itamar Rabinovich,[30] the careful historian and skilful ambassador in the failed negotiations between Israel and Syria, terms the concept 'a very useful analytical tool ... but ... less valuable as an operational tool', but he expects that 'ripeness will account for the success of negotiations' rather than simply provide a necessary but insufficient condition for their initiation.

Resistant reactions

There are intriguing problems raised by ripeness theory. One complication with the notion of a hurting stalemate arises when increased pain increases resistance rather than reducing it (it must be remembered that while ripeness is a necessary precondition for negotiation, not all ripeness leads to negotiation). Although this may be considered 'bad', irrational or even adolescent behaviour, it is a common reaction and one that may be natural and functional. Reinforcement is the normal response to opposition: 'don't give up without a fight', 'no gain without pain', 'hold the course, whatever the cost', 'when the going gets tough, the tough get going', and 'if at first you don't succeed, try, try again'. The imposition of pain to a present course in conflict is not likely to lead to a search for alternative measures without first being tested. The theory itself takes this into account by referring to the parties' perception that they cannot escalate an exit from their stalemate, implying efforts to break out before giving in (without being able to predict when the shift will take place).

Second, while escalation is commonly used in reference only to means of conducting the conflict, it also refers to other aspects of conflict behaviour, including ends and agents.[31] Pressure on a party in conflict often leads to the psychological reaction of worsening the image of the opponent, a natural tendency which is often decried as lessening chances of reconciliation but which has the functional advantage of justifying resistance. Particular types of adversaries such as 'true believers', 'warriors' or 'hardliners' are unlikely to be led to compromise by increased pain; instead, pain is likely to justify renewed struggle.[32] Justified struggles call for greater sacrifices, which absorb increased pain and strengthen determination. The cycle is functional and self-protecting. To this type of reaction, it is the release of pain or an admission of pain on the other side which justifies relaxation; when the opponent admits the error of its ways, the true believer can claim the vindication of its efforts which permits a management of the conflict.[33]

Implications

Inescapable as it may be, the most unfortunate implications of the notion of a hurting stalemate lie in its dependence on conflict. In itself, the concept explains the difficulty of achieving pre-emptive conflict resolution and preventive diplomacy, even though nothing in the definition of the MHS requires it to take place at the height of the conflict or at a high level of violence. The internal (and unmediated) negotiations in South Africa between 1990 and 1994 stand out as a striking case of negotiations opened (and pursued) on the basis of an MHS perceived by both sides on the basis of impending catastrophe, not of present casualties.[34] However, the greater the objective evidence, the greater the subjective perception of the stalemate and its pain is likely to be, and this evidence is more likely to come late, when all other courses of action and possibilities of escalation have been exhausted. In notable cases, a long period of conflict is required before the MHS sinks in.[35] Yet given the infinite number of potential conflicts which have not reached 'the heights', evidence would suggest that perception of an MHS occurs either (and optimally) at a low level of conflict, where it is relatively easy to begin problem-solving in most cases, or, in salient cases, at rather high levels of conflict. Thus, conflicts not treated 'early' appear to require a high level of intensity for an MHS perception to kick in and negotiations towards a solution to begin. To ripen for resolution at least those conflicts that have not been managed early, one must raise the level of conflict until a stalemate is reached, and then further until it begins to hurt, and then still more, to ensure the perception of pain, and then still more yet, to create the perception of an impending catastrophe as well. The ripe moment becomes the godchild of brinkmanship.

As the notion of ripeness implies, MHS can be a very fleeting opportunity, a moment to be seized lest it pass, or it can be of a long duration, waiting to be noticed and acted upon by mediators. The moment was brief in Bosnia but longer in Angola. In fact, failure to seize the moment often hastens its passing, as parties lose faith in the possibility of a negotiated way out or regain hope in the possibility of unilateral escalation. Worse yet, when a moment of joint perception of a hurting stalemate passes without producing any results, parties frequently fall back on their previous perceptions that the other side will never be ready and the only course left is to hope and fight for a total realization of one's goals, no matter how long it takes: 'Nothing is acceptable but a Palestinian/Israeli state with Jerusalem as its capital.' By the same token, the possibility of long duration often dulls the urgency of rapid seizure.

Another set of implications comes from the fact that the theory only addresses the opening of negotiations, as noted at the outset and often missed by the critics. Now that the initiation of negotiation is theoretically explained, people would like to see a theory that explains the successful conclusion of negotiations once opened. Can ripeness be extended in some way to cover the entire process, or does successful conclusion of negotiations require a different explanatory logic?

Practitioners and students of conflict management would also like to think that there could be a more positive prelude to negotiation, through the pull of an attractive outcome without the push of an MHS. Although examples are rare, as explained by prospect theory,[36] one case is the opening of the Madrid peace process on the Middle East in 1992[37] and another is the negotiation of the Jordan–Israel peace treaty of October 1994; still another may be boundary disputes which are overcome by the prospects of mutual development in the region.[38] But the mechanisms are still unclear, in part because the cases are so few. As in other ripe moments, these occasions provided an opportunity for improvement, but from a tiring rather than a painful deadlock.[39] In some views, the attraction lies in a possibility of winning more cheaply than by conflict (paradoxically, a shared perception), or else a possibility of sharing power that did not exist before.[40] In other views, enticement comes in the form of a new ingredient, the chance for improved relations with the mediating third party.[41] In other instances, the opportunity for a settlement grows more attractive because the issue of the conflict becomes dépassé, no longer justifying the bad relations with the other party or the mediator that it imposed. Such openings might be termed a mutually enticing opportunities (MEO), admittedly a title not as catchy as MHS and a concept not as well researched (or practised). Few examples have been found in reality.

But MEO is important in the broader negotiation process and has its place in extending ripeness theory. At most, ripeness theory can reach beyond the decision to negotiate into the negotiations themselves by indicating that the perception of ripeness has to continue during the negotiations if the parties are not to re-evaluate their positions and drop out, in the revived hopes of being able to find a unilateral solution through escalation. But negotiations completed under the shadow – or the push – of an MHS alone are likely to be unstable and unlikely to lead to a more enduring settlement. As Ohlson[42] and Pruitt[43] have pointed out, that is the function of the MEO. The negotiators must provide or be provided prospects for a more attractive future to pull them out of their conflict, once an MHS has pushed them into negotiations. The seeds of the pull factor begin with the way out that the parties vaguely perceive as part of the initial ripeness, but that general sense of possibility needs to be developed and fleshed out into the vehicle for an agreement, a formula for settlement and a prospect of reconciliation that the negotiating parties design during negotiations. When an MEO is not developed in the negotiations, they remain truncated and unstable, even if they reach a conflict management agreement to suspend violence, as in the 1984 and 1999 Lusaka agreements or the 1994 Karabakh ceasefire.[44]

The third set of implications have to do with the absence of ripeness. Unripeness should not constitute an excuse for second or third parties' inaction, even if one or both of the conflicting parties are mired in their hopes of escalation and victory. Crocker states very forcefully (in boldface in the original) that 'the absence of "ripeness" does not tell us to walk away and do nothing. Rather, it helps us to identify obstacles and suggests ways of handling them and managing the problem until resolution becomes possible'.[45] Crocker's own experience indicates, before and above all, the importance of being present and available to the contestants while waiting for the moment to ripen, so as to be able to seize it when it occurs. In the absence of a promising situation, either the 'second' party that is alone in feeling the hurt and perceiving the stalemate or the third party has a choice: either to ripen or to position.

Crocker lists a number of important insights for positioning:[46]

- give the parties some fresh ideas to shake them up;
- keep new ideas flexible to avoid getting bogged down in details;
- establish basic principles to form building blocks of a settlement;
- become an indispensable channel for negotiation; and
- establish an acceptable mechanism for negotiation and for registering an agreement.

Other strategies include preliminary explorations of items identified with pre-negotiations:[47]

- identify the parties necessary to a settlement;
- identify the issues to be resolved, and separate out issues not resolvable in the conflict;
- air alternatives to the current conflict course;
- establish contacts and bridges between the parties;
- clarify costs and risks involved in seeking settlement;
- establish requitement; and
- assure support for a settlement policy within each party's domestic constituency.

Since ripeness results from a combination of objective and subjective elements, both need attention. If some objective elements are present, persuasion is the obvious diplomatic challenge. Such was the message of Kissinger in the Sinai withdrawal negotiations[48] and Crocker in the Angolan negotiations,[49] among many others, emphasizing the absence of real alternatives (stalemate) and the high cost of the current conflict course (pain). If there is no objective indicator to which to refer, ripening may involve a much more active engagement of the mediator, moving that role from communication and formulation to manipulation.[50] As a manipulator, the mediator either increases the size of the stakes, attracting the parties to share in a pot that otherwise would have been too small, or limits the actions of the parties in conflict, providing objective elements for the stalemate. Such actions are delicate and dangerous, but on occasion necessary. US massive aid incentives to Israel and Egypt to negotiate a second Sinai withdrawal in 1975, NATO bombing of Serb positions in Bosnia in 1995 to create a hurting stalemate, or American arming of Israel during the October war in 1973 or of Morocco (after two years of moratorium) in 1981 to keep those parties in the conflict, respectively, among many others, are typical examples of the mediator acting as a manipulator to bring about a stalemate.

Practitioners need to employ all their skills and apply all the concepts of negotiation and mediation to take advantage of the necessary but insufficient condition in order to turn it into a successful peacemaking process when it exists, or to help produce it or stand ready to act on it when it does not as yet.

Notes

1. I. W. Zartman, 'Ripeness: the Hurting Stalemate and Beyond', in P. Stern & D. Druckman (eds), *International Conflict Resolution after the Cold War* (Washington, DC: National Academy Press, 2000).
2. J. Campbell, *Successful Negotiation: Trieste* (Princeton: Princeton University Press, 1976), p. 73.
3. H. Kissinger, *New York Times*, 12 October 1974.
4. AFP, 17 May 1992.
5. See I. W. Zartman & M. Berman, *The Practical Negotiator* (New Haven: Yale University Press, 1982); I. W. Zartman, 'The Strategy of Preventive Diplomacy in Third World Conflicts', in A. George (ed.), *Managing US–Soviet Rivalry* (Boulder, Colo.: Westview, 1983); S. Touval & I. W. Zartman (eds), *International Mediation in Theory and Practice* (Boulder, Colo.: Westview, 1985), pp. 11, 258–60, and I. W. Zartman, *Ripe for Resolution* (New York: Oxford University Press, 1985/1989).
6. The same logic has been identified in regard to domestic elite settlements, produced by costly and inconclusive conflict; 'Precisely because no single faction has been a clear winner and all factions have more nearly been losers, elites are disposed to compromise if at all possible.' M. Burton & J. Higley, 'Elite Settlements', *American Sociological Review*, LII, 2 (1994), 295–307 at 298.
7. See A. Sen, *Collective Choice and Social Welfare* (San Francisco: Holden-Day, 1970); K. Arrow, *Social Change and Individual Values* (Yale: Yale University Press, 1963), and M. Olson, *The Logical of Collective Action* (Schocken, 1965).
8. S. Brams, *Negotiation Games* (New York: Routledge, 1990) and *Theory of Moves* (Cambridge: Cambridge University Press, 1994); and Q. Wright, 'The Escalation of Conflicts', *Journal of Conflict Resolution*, IX, 4 (1965), 434–49.
9. Timing can refer to many things other than costs and benefits, including domestic political schedules, generational socialization and attitudinal maturation, among others.

For an excellent analysis based on the first, see W. Quandt, *Camp David* (Washington: Brookings, 1986). On the second, see R. Samuels et al., *Political Generations and Political Development* (Boston: Lexington, 1977). These are perfectly valid approaches, but ultimately they can be reduced to cost/benefits, calculated or affected by different referents. To note this is not to deny their separate value, but simply to justify the conceptual focus used here.

10. See J. Goldstein, 'The Game of Chicken in International Relations: an Underappreciated Model', MS, Washington School of International Service, American University (1998).
11. I. W. Zartman & J. Aurik, 'Power Strategies in De-escalation', in L. Kriesberg & J. Thornson (eds), *Timing the De-escalation of International Conflicts* (Syracuse: Syracuse University Press, 1991).
12. At the outset, confusion may arise from the fact that not all 'negotiations' appear to be the result of a ripe moment. Negotiation may be a tactical interlude, a breather for rest and rearmament, a sop to external pressure, without any intent of opening a sincere search for a joint outcome. Thus the need for quotation marks, or for some elusive modifier such as 'serious' or 'sincere' negotiations. It is difficult at the outset to determine whether negotiations are indeed serious or sincere, and indeed 'true' and 'false' motives may be indistinguishably mixed in the minds of the actors themselves at the beginning. Yet it is the outset which is the subject of the theory. The best that can be done is to note that many theories contain a reference to a 'false' event or an event in appearance only, to distinguish it from an event that has a defined purpose. Indeed, a sense of ripeness may be required to turn negotiations for side effects (F. Ikle, *How Nations Negotiate* (Harper & Row, 1964)) into negotiations to resolve conflict. In any case, unless the moment is ripe, as defined below, the search for an agreed outcome cannot begin.
13. S. Touval, 'Coercive Mediation on the Road to Geneva', *International Negotiation*, 3 (1996), 547–70; J. Goodby, 'When War Won out: Bosnian Peace Plans before Dayton', *International Negotiation*, 3 (1996), 501–23 and R. Holbrooke, *To End a War* (New York: Random House, 1998).
14. M. Ottaway, 'Eritrea and Ethiopia: Negotiations in a Transnational Conflict' and F. Deng, 'Negotiating a Hidden Agenda: Sudan's Conflict of Identities', both in I. W. Zartman (ed.), *Elusive Peace: Negotiating an End to Civil Wars* (Washington: Brookings, 1995).
15. Zartman & Berman, op. cit.; Zartman, 'Strategy'; Touval & Zartman, op. cit.; Zartman, *Ripe for Resolution*; I. W. Zartman, 'Ripening Conflict, Ripe Moment, Formula and Mediation', in D. BenDahmane & J. McDonald (eds), *Perspectives on Negotiation* (Washington, DC: Government Printing Office, 1986) and Zartman & Aurik, op. cit.
16. Touval & Zartman, op. cit.; R. Haas, *Conflicts Unending* (Yale: Yale University Press, 1990); S. Stedman, *Peacemaking in Civil War* (Lynne Rienner, 1991); Kriesberg & Thornson, op. cit.; T. Sisk, *Democratization in South Africa: the Elusive Social Contract* (Princeton: Princeton University Press, 1995); T. Norlen, *A Study of the Ripe Moment for Conflict Resolution and Its Applicability to Two Periods in the Israeli–Palestinian Conflict* (Uppsala: Uppsala University Conflict Resolution Program, 1995); F. Olser Hampson, *Nurturing Peace* (Washington, DC: USIP, 1996); Goodby, op. cit; M. Sala, 'Creating the "Ripe Moment" in the East Timor Conflict', *Journal of Peace Research*, XXXIV, 4 (1997), 449–66; K. Aggestram & C. Jönson, '(Un)ending Conflict', *Millennium*, XXXVI, 3 (1997), 771–94; M. Mooradian & D. Druckman, 'Hurting Stalemate or Mediation? The Conflict over Nagorno-Karabakh, 1990–95', *Journal of Peace Research*, XXXVI, 6 (1999), 709–27; N. Sambanis, 'Conflict Resolution Ripeness and Spoiler Problems in Cyprus', *Journal of Peace Research*, pending; and J. Stein & L. Pauly (eds), *Choosing to Cooperate: How States Avoid Loss* (Baltimore: The Johns Hopkins University Press, 1992).
17. S. Touval, *The Peace Brokers* (Princeton: Princeton University Press, 1982), pp. 228–32 and 328.
18. Stedman, op. cit., pp. 238 and 241–2.
19. D. Lieberfield, 'Conflict "Ripeness" Revisited: South African and Israeli/Palestinian Cases', *Negotiation Journal*, XV, 1 (1999), 63–82 and *Talking with the Enemy: Negotiation and Threat Perception in South Africa and Israel/Palestine* (New York: Praeger, 1999).

20. C. Crocker, *High Noon in Southern Africa* (Norton, 1992), p. 363.
21. Ibid., p. 373.
22. Ibid., p. 481.
23. Ibid., chapter 16.
24. A. DeSoto, 'Multiparty Mediation: El Salvador', in C. Crocker et al. (eds), *Herding Cats: the Management of Complex International Mediation* (Washington, DC: USIP, 1999), pp. 7–8.
25. J. Baker & T. deFrank, *The Politics of Diplomacy* (New York: Putnam, 1995).
26. Holbrooke, op. cit., pp. 27 and 73.
27. Ibid., p. 193.
28. *New York Times*, 19 August 1995, A7.
29. M. Goulding, *Enhancing the United Nations' Effectiveness in Peace and Security* (United Nations: Report to the Secretary-General, 30 June 1997), p. 20.
30. I. Rabinovich, *The Brink of Peace: the Israeli–Syrian Negotiations* (Princeton: Princeton University Press, 1998), p. 251.
31. J. Rubin, Z., Pruitt, G. Dean & S. H. Kim, *Social Conflict* (New York: McGraw-Hill, 1994).
32. E. Hoffer, *The True Believer* (New York: Harper Bros., 1951); H. Nicolson, *Diplomacy* (Oxford: Oxford University Press, 1960) and G. Snyder & P. Diesing, *Conflict among Nations* (Princeton: Princeton University Press, 1977).
33. R. L. Moses, *Freeing the Hostages* (Pittsburgh: University of Pittsburgh Press, 1996).
34. T. Ohlson & S. Stedman, *The New Is Not Yet Born* (Washington: Brookings, 1994); Sisk, op. cit., and Liberfield, op. cit.
35. Steiner & Pauly, op. cit.
36. D. Kahnerman & A. Tversky, 'Prospect Theory: an Analysis of Decisions under Risk', *Econometrica*, IIIL, 3 (1979), 263–91.
37. Baker & deFrank, op. cit.
38. K. J. Nordquist, 'Boundary Disputes: Drawing the Line', in I. W. Zartman (ed.), *Preventive Diplomacy: Avoiding Conflict Escalation* (Lanham: Rowman & Littlefield, 2000).
39. C. Mitchell, 'Cutting Losses', Working paper 9, Institute for Conflict Analysis and Resolution, George Mason University, appearing in a shorter version in *Paradigms: Kent Journal of International Relations*, IX, 2 (1995), 3.
40. Ibid., p. 7.
41. Touval & Zartman, op. cit., and H. Saunders, 'Guidelines B', unpublished manuscript (1991).
42. T. Ohlson, *Power Politics and Peace Politics* (Uppsala: University of Uppsala, Department of Peace and Conflict Research), Report 50.
43. D. Pruitt & P. Olczak, 'Approaching to Resolving Seemingly Intractable Conflict', in B. Bunker & J. Rubin (eds), *Conflict, Cooperation and Justice* (New York: Jossey-Bass, 1995).
44. Zartman, *Ripe for Resolution,* and Mooradian & Druckman, op. cit.
45. Crocker, op. cit., p. 471.
46. Ibid., pp. 471–2. See also Haas, op. cit. and Goulding, op. cit.
47. Stein & Pauly, op. cit.
48. M. Gatti, *The Secret Conversations of Henry Kissinger* (New York: Bantham, 1976).
49. Crocker, op. cit., pp. 381–2.
50. Touval & Zartman, op. cit. and D. Rothchild, *Managing Ethnic Conflict in Africa* (Washington: Brookings, 1997).

[7]

Cultivating Peace: a Practitioner's View of Deadly Conflict and Negotiation

John Paul Lederach

Introduction

'So do you think it may be possible to move towards dialogue, maybe initial, off record contacts to see what obstacles or possibilities exist for a negotiated process to end the conflict?' The question posed by our peace research team to the representatives of the Basque separatist movement was genuine though intuitively we knew the response. The heads shook slowly and the inevitable short answer emerged, 'No. It is going to be a hard two years', followed by a much more detailed justification and rationale.

The year of this conversation could have been 1991 prior to the Barcelona Olympic Games, or 1994 following the Olympics. Or it could have been January 2001, for the answer was much the same. The counterpart could just as well have been representatives of the Spanish government rather than the separatists. For that matter, the conversation could have taken place in Northern Ireland, Somalia or Colombia. In protracted conflict, the horizon of expectation is not the rise of peaceful change. The horizon is the regeneration of violence, steady and sure as the rising sun.

The conversation, much repeated in my experience as a conciliator, poses a dilemma that I often hear framed as a significant doubt and question from students in seminars and journalists in interviews. Is it possible to negotiate while the fighting is still raging, and when, for all practical purposes, neither side is expecting or even preparing for any significant change in the cycle of deadly conflict?

In this chapter I will formulate some initial responses to that question from the standpoint and perspective of a practitioner. Theoretically, the field abounds with suggestions. Most well known is the idea of 'ripeness' first articulated by Zartman in his important book *Ripe for Resolution*.[1] Over the past decade research and writing have focused on lessons gained from peace processes and the question of timing.[2] The arguments have suggested that negotiations, and in particular mediation and conciliation, need to read a situation with a capacity to determine whether the timing is right for nudging the conflict from violence to dialogue, and more specifically to agreements that end the open violence. Conditions, patterns and criteria have emerged to further develop this capacity, but in the end the metaphor created by 'ripeness' points towards a single important premise: change from cycles of deadly violence to negotiation is possible only when the conflict and its perpetrating actors have reached a certain maturation point, then conciliation and negotiation efforts can be introduced with greater effectiveness and success.

This chapter is not aimed at refuting the important research gained from the studies of peace processes in reference to criteria and patterns for successful intervention and negotiation in deadly conflict. I will provide a critique of the guiding metaphor – ripeness – and propose a reorientation of the practice of developing negotiated peace processes with particular reference to time periods prior to and following the opening of formal talks. These are reflections that emerge from my own direct experiences and I believe that while they provide an alternative view to the metaphor of ripeness they are complementary to the existing body of literature.

A critique of ripeness

I start with three observations as to why I have found ripeness a limited metaphor for practice and then suggest several alternative metaphors or guiding perspectives in reference to how practitioners might align their work when faced with the question of whether it is possible to work for peace and negotiations when fighting is still raging. Let me start with what I consider to be a few of the practical limitations of ripeness.

Ripeness is a rearview mirror

From the standpoint of practice ripeness theory and approaches present an awkward challenge and paradox. On the one hand, much of this theoretical emphasis has been pursued in order to create a 'predictive' capacity useful to conciliators and mediators as they engage with people involved in negotiation processes. Such a capacity offers the promise that if, as practitioners, we can recognize factors, conditions and characteristics of negotiation situations in settings of violent conflict we can effectively increase our capacity to achieve a settlement, or inversely, to know when it is not effective to proceed with the effort. In other words, ripeness proposes to provide a predictive capacity. This is a forward-looking skill orientation, one that assumes linearity of process capable of foretelling outcomes from conditions. To draw the metaphor, ripeness should serve as a large windscreen in a car providing a clear and expansive view of what is coming on the horizon such that the driver can adjust the manoeuvres to match the challenges of the approaching road.

However on the other side of the paradox, as I look back across my practical experience, unlike the metaphor suggests, peacebuilding generally, and negotiations in particular, have not entailed a 'ripeness' process where I have watched the process develop, like the seasonal maturation of an apple moving from blossom to red, juicy and ready-to-eat fruit. In fact, more often than not the opposite has been true. I have only recognized the keys to transformative change in retrospect and in differing ways in each context. For example, on several occasions in the Miskito/Sandinista negotiations, the times when all the conditions pointed to successfully opening the talks were precisely the moments when all our efforts as conciliations failed. They were, in fact, called off at least three times, and once within a day of starting. On the other hand, when they finally opened, what appeared to be a long-drawn-out entry in the airport where nearly everything fell apart again and seemed to point to a complete lack of ripeness, the talks that followed lasted about a week and were highly successful. 'Who would have known?' we commented time and again to ourselves.

To draw out the metaphor, 'ripeness' (as in recognizing that potential for change happened) was more like a rearview mirror than a windscreen. The roadway of protracted conflict, it seems, may be more akin to dynamic, nearly ameoba-like spaces than the linear and predictable development of fruit. And herein lies the limitation. Ripeness may be most useful in retrospect (as we look back we can account for things in our interpretation of the history), but is extremely weak in its predictive capacity from the standpoint of a practitioner and in fact may provide us with a lens that is not helpful for adapting constructively to the pathways of peacebuilding.

Time and again, in situations as varied as Northern Ireland, the Basque Country or the negotiations between the Philippine government and the communist insurgency, the moments when I thought there was the greatest potential for a significant move forward have been stagnant and even counterproductive. For a practitioner these time periods create an emotional roller coaster. The predictive view suggests significant change is near. Then just when hopes are high everything collapses, leading to a deep sense of despair and often urgent, at times inappropriate, responses to save the moment. Other times, exactly when all the predictive characteristics pointed to complete stagnation and even highly escalated cycles of violence, turned out to be the period when by way of some unexpected suggestion or event, a significant move forward was created.

These experiences have led me towards an attitude not driven by a predictive lens of visible factors but rather towards the development of a lens that does not focus excessively on what appear at any given moment to be the limitations of temporal conditions. In protracted conflict temporal conditions are ephemeral and non-linear, requiring paradoxical intentionality: a set of mediative attitudes that keep your feet on the ground (a realist view of the situation) and your head in the clouds (a hope-driven idealist view of the possible). Therefore, rather than orienting my action around predictive ripeness, I find the opposite is increasingly true in my work. I am carefully cautious when all appears ripe for settlement and innoculatingly naive when all appears hopelessly lost in the grip of calamity.

Ripeness is in the eye of the beholder

Among the many things I have learned in the school of hard knocks of protracted conflict is a simple idea with wide-ranging implications: the prevailing system is set up to create a permanently emerging crisis. This essentially has to do with time and response. I find that in situations with a long history of social division and violence the focus of attention is on the immediate situation and the crisis, event or impending disaster that just happened. This is accompanied by the common view that once this 'crisis' is dealt with we can move onto the deeper and longer-range concerns and needs. The tendency across the board is to be driven by the crisis. This I have found particularly true of people who are directly involved on one side or the other of the conflict, and as such there is a prevailing attitude that the situation is not ripe. In other words, ripeness is more often than not something perceived by outsiders with the luxury of dispassionate facts and factors. In the midst of week-to-week and month-to-month emergencies people rarely see their situations as 'ripe' for peace. Ripeness is in the eye of the beholder and few who live in the settings have the luxury of such vision.

This leads to practical and attitudinal dilemmas for the peacebuilder. The most critical shift required is to understand the process not as linear but *circular and linear*. Ripeness, however, depends exclusively on a linear metaphor of time and change. Circular and linear can be visualized as a horizontal spiral where there is circular movement creating at any given moment forward, upward, backward and downward movement *and* the whole of the circles is moving forward across time. These are actually the temporal experiences from within the situation that I have commonly experienced: things feel like they may be moving forward, then a crisis comes and it feels like everything has come to a standstill. At other times it can easily feel like it is moving backwards, or even collapsing. This is the immediate time circle, and it is continuous, a permanent feature of the system. The challenge is how to visualize the possibility of sustaining an overall forward movement over time visible in the lens of decades not months. This requires a capacity to envision a longer-term process and recognize opportunities for constructive change in the midst of crisis. In other words, it is a shift towards being crisis-responsive rather than crisis-driven. The key attitude and skill shift is that of adaptation of process that assumes and takes account of constant crisis rather than a linear view of maturation that assumes stepwise progression to resolution.

Ripeness sees mediator action as cherry picking

When I played basketball many years ago our coach had a phrase with which he provoked us whenever we missed an easy shot, 'I can't believe you missed that cherry picker.' Essentially it meant that a lot of work had gone into place and then just when everything was right and a giveaway opportunity was presented, the basket was missed.

There are times when I have the impression that the metaphor of ripeness leads towards an emphasis on mediator action as if it were 'cherry picking'. The impression emerges from two understandings about mediation that I believe have significant limitations and implications.

The first commonly held belief is that mediation lies primarily in the person, and often the personality of the mediator-as-the-actor rather than mediation-as-process with multiple roles, functions and activities carried out by a wide array of people.[3] Particularly critical to our discussion here is the idea that the mediator comes from outside the setting and outside the relationships in conflict, or what I have referred to as the 'outside–neutral' view of mediator role.[4] When the mediator provides an outside and neutral role in many cases they are 'in' and 'out' of the setting in terms of their actual physical presence. Ripeness is oriented towards providing terms of reference for this kind of action such that the mediator can gauge when it is most effective to push for agreement or renewed negotiation. What the ripeness metaphor does not provide is a sense of the long-term nature of the process, the building and sustaining of the relationships, nor the multiplicity of roles, activities and functions that may be necessary to make a sustained dialogue and change in the relationships possible.

The second commonly held belief is that the success of mediation is primarily judged by whether it produced an agreement rather than whether it helped create a space for constructive change in people, perceptions and relationships that are not always captured in the confines of a written negotiated document. Ripeness suggests the cherry is the agreement and that picking the cherry is like a mediation harvest. In my practical experience in conciliation work this tends to promote a measuring stick of success based on what is often the least important element for gauging the sustainability of the change process necessary to actually create the transformation from deadly conflict to respect, cooperation and increased peaceful interdependence. It is not a metaphor that provides a vision of cultivating the soil, planting the seeds or nourishing the seedling in the face of winds, burning sun or icy storms, all of which speak to process, relationship and sustainability rather than a momentary action.

Alternative metaphors to ripeness

What I just outlined suggests that from the standpoint of practice the ripeness metaphor has some limitations when applied to contexts of protracted deadly conflict. The metaphor suggests a focus on content and agreement making rather than being relationship and change-oriented. It places emphasis on the mediator's action and perception rather than on the mediation-as-process with multiple sets of action and people. It tends to have a shorter-term view of action in mind aimed at intense action in specific time frames (harvest) but not necessarily the slower and painstaking process of preparing and sustaining process. This suggests a need for additional and complementary metaphors emerging from and oriented towards the experience of practice. As I reflect on my own experience several come to mind.

Cultivation: the building of long-term authentic relationships

Over the past two decades my efforts at peacebuilding and conciliation have led me to the metaphor of cultivator more than harvester, towards nourishment of soil and plant more than picking the fruit. The images that accompany this complementary metaphor suggest an organic connection to context, the building of relationships, and a commitment to process over time. Each of the images provides an avenue towards answering the question posed at the beginning of the chapter: is it possible to pursue negotiations while deadly conflict is raging?

The cultivation metaphor suggests that a deep respect for, and connection to, the context is critical for sustaining a change process that is moving from deadly expressions of conflict to increased justice and peace in relationships. The context of protracted deadly conflict, like soil, is the people, commonly shared geographies but often sharply differing views of history, rights and responsibilities, and the formation of perception and understandings based on cultural meaning structures. Cultivation is recognizing that ultimately the change process must be taken up, embraced and sustained by people in these contexts. The cultivator, as a connected but outside element in the system, approaches this soil with a great deal of respect, the suspension of quick judgement in favour of the wisdom of adaptation, and an orientation towards supporting the change process through highs and lows, ebbs and flows of violence and thawing of tensions, whether or not the situation appears ripe. The cultivator gives attention to the well-being of the ecosystem, not just the quick production of a given fruit.

A relationship-centric orientation naturally emerges from the metaphor. This is built on a genuine concern for relationships, not an instrumentalist approach to people in order to achieve an external goal. This suggests a criterion of authenticity, which cannot be overstated from the perspective of cultivation. A relationship-centric orientation keeps the focus on people, realities of histories and perceptions as the source that generates and regenerates cycles of deadly conflict. The contentious content of specific agreements are often symbolic of this deeper level. In essence, you can resolve an issue but you till the soils of relationships if you are interested in sustained transformation and systemic health.

Both of the above images require a long-term commitment. I think this may be the single most important lesson learned over the years, a shift from thinking about negotiations as a 'ripe' moment in time towards understanding the preparation and support for a change process over a much longer period.[5] It requires you to shift from thinking in weeks and months to thinking in decades. If you have ever talked with farmers about their land you will hear them talking about years – decades and even a lifetime of relationship to the soil and the climate.

Accompaniment: the pace of presence

To understand accompaniment as a metaphor of peacebuilding and conciliation it is useful to break it down to its Latin origins. The word is built on two primary concepts *com* or with and *pani* or bread. A literal translation would be 'with bread'. In other words, this is a table metaphor. To accompany is to sit and share bread with another. In my mind there are a number of important images this metaphor places before us as practical guidelines.

First, sharing a table provides a sense of intimacy, of being inside a shared space of humanity with another. This takes us back to our earlier idea of relationship. But it goes further because the image suggests presence with another, a quality of what I once called 'alongsideness'.[6] This of course is very much a part of the image that the word 'accompany' creates: we walk alongside the journey of another. The image it suggests is a respect for the journey of others. It represents presence with others as they travel on their way.

The second intriguing aspect of this image is the idea of pace. When it is the journey of the other the pace is not forced or prescribed from outside, but must, if it is to be authentic, be directed from sources of leading that come from within.

In reference to peacebuilding this poses numerous difficult dilemmas, for more often than not the pace of moving from deadly cycles of conflict to more constructive, mutually beneficial and respectful cycles is extremely slow. And much of peacebuilding from outside is oriented towards getting that movement to happen more rapidly. However, if movement or compromise happens because one is obligated or forced, then the change is rarely authentic and sustainable, and plants the seeds of renewed destructive conflict that sprout at a later date. This becomes all the more complex when the accompaniment is with people across the lines of division, and when slowness towards change means a great deal of suffering for a lot of people.

Ripeness seems to answer this dilemma by suggesting that if we read the situation correctly we can determine when the greatest potential for change could happen and can then push for this change to take place. Accompaniment suggests an ongoing presence motivated by an interest in supporting a sustainable change process built on making opportunity available for genuine change motivated from within but not under obligation or external time frames. If we were to put this in more concrete detail it would suggest that conciliation work is not about moving in and out of a situation according to a measure of the potential for success. Rather, the activities of conciliation are about ongoing presence, a constancy of availability and a regularity of connection.

Naivety: the art of the possible

Naivety in the world of realpolitik is generally seen as foolishness, gullibility and weakness of understanding about the true character of politics, power relationships and even basic human nature. Those who are naive are those who with a Pollyannaish attitude make things worse and are usually taken advantage of and eaten up in the process. Applied to peacebuilding, this is a common critique of those who pursue peace, particularly at times when things appear to be falling apart and getting worse.

When I look back at my own experiences I should like to suggest the inverse may be true, that the key to significant change came not when I was capable of producing a hard, factual, objective view of a situation and the predictable outcomes. Rather it seemed to come from a kind of naivety that suspended the lens of presented reality, and with a commonsensical approach asked questions and pursued ideas that seemed out of line with reality as presented.

Paradoxically, naivety cuts both ways. It is equally naive for the little boy alongside the parade to point a finger and say out loud, 'the emperor has no clothes' (which is exactly what I felt when the Dayton Peace Accords were hatched), or the sustaining of hope and pursuing of a 'couple of ideas' as I heard from Irish colleagues when on numerous occasions the bombs in the ceasefire period seemed to bring everything to a halt.

For my own edification as a peacebuilder I have come to embrace the utility of naivety as the art of the possible. Naivety does not take what is presented on the surface and generally accepted as final truth as the primary measuring stick of how things work, are held together or fall apart. Naivety is unafraid of being perceived as stupid and has the courage the raise basic-questions, both of optimism when all seems impossible and of common-sense realism when everybody expects peace to happen because a paper was signed. In both instances, the art is in seeking a way to reach towards a deeper source of what is possible and needed to keep a constructive change process alive and healthy.

Epilogue

So what do I say when the journalist asks, 'And do you really believe it is possible to talk about negotiation and peace when war is raging?' I say hope is not negotiated. It is kept alive by people who understand the depth of suffering and know the cost of keeping a horizon of change as a possibility for their children and grandchildren. Quick fixes to long-standing violent conflict are like growing a garden with no understanding of seeds, soils and sweat. This conflict traces back across decades, even generations. It will take that long to sort out.

Journalists generally do not quote me in their papers. Sound bites about ripeness, people coming to their senses, and the need for realism and pressure seem to find their way into print more often. But I believe in cultivation. Cultivation as a metaphor suggests that the core of the peacebuilding work – fostering and sustaining committed, authentic relationships across the lines of conflict over time – does not rise and fall with the temporal ups and downs of the conflict cycles. It answers the question – is it possible to pursue peace when things are bad – with a resounding 'Yes!' Just as it also suggests that when things are suddenly headed towards an agreement the work is hardly over. It has only begun.

Notes

1. I. W. Zartman, *Ripe for Resolution: Conflict and Intervention in Africa* (New York: Oxford University Press, 1989).
2. See, for example, L. Kriesberg & S. J. Thorson, *Timing and De-escalation of International Conflicts* (Syracuse: Syracuse University Press, 1991).
3. C. Mitchell, 'External Peace-making Initiatives and Intranational Conflict', in M. I. Midlarsky (ed.), *The Internationalization of Communal Strife* (New York: Routledge, 1992).
4. P. Wehr & J. P. Lederach, 'Mediating in Central America', *Journal of Peace Research*, 28, 1 (February 1991), 86–98.
5. J. P. Lederach, *Building Peace: Sustainable Reconciliation in Divided Societies* (Washington, DC: United States Institute of Peace, 1997).
6. J. P. Lederach, 'Qualities of Practice for Reconciliation', in R. Helmick (ed.), *Reconciliation* (New York: Templeton Press, 2001).

[8]

Merchants of Law as Moral Entrepreneurs: Constructing International Justice out of the Competition for Transnational Business Disputes

Yves Dezalay and Bryant Garth

A central theme in sociolegal research is how the legitimacy of law is maintained so that it can provide a basis to govern matters that involve powerful economic and political entities (Hunt 1993).[1] The study of international commercial arbitration allows us to see how international private justice—lacking the legitimacy of the state court system—has become established and recognized almost universally as legitimate for business disputes. Competition among key actors and groups, as we shall see in this chapter, serves to construct legal legitimacy and at the same time promote law in the service of merchants. The competition, however, is not simply a matter of striving for business by offering better services. International commercial arbitration is a symbolic field, and therefore the competitive battles that take place within it are fought in symbolic terms among moral entrepreneurs. Battles fought in terms of legitimacy and credibility then serve a double role. They build careers and markets for those who are successful in this competition, and they build the legitimacy and credibility of international legal practices and international institutions (cf. the "schizophrenia" of the legal profession as described by Gordon 1984).

This is not to say that the construction of this global justice for transnational business disputes was "caused" only through some dynamic within the field of international commercial arbitration. The relationship is much more complex. The relative positions and indeed even the entry onto the field of many key players, as will be seen below and in chapter 4, relate to other factors of considerable importance—in particular, decolonization, the growth of international trade, and the power of Anglo-American law firms (in turn bolstered by their clientele). Our ambition, however, is not to confirm the simple promotional story of the inevitable growth of international commercial arbitration in response to the growth of international trade and commerce. It

1. Our study of legitimacy is mainly of arbitration entrepreneurs who promote the legitimacy of particular conceptions of arbitration. For empirical support for the proposition that the subjects of legal regulation also act in part out of beliefs in legitimacy, see Tyler and Mitchell (1994).

is to explain why the phenomenon termed international commercial arbitration has become more institutionalized and has a particular set of characteristics that, we submit, are not mere details but rather are important aspects of the emerging global economy.

Oppositions and Complementarities in the Field of International Commercial Arbitration

The field of international commercial arbitration is given its structure and its logic of transformation through oppositions and complementarities that we shall now begin to map. The key source of conflict, and also of transformation, is that between two generations—"grand old men" versus "technocrats." We therefore begin this section by showing what this conflict and the symbolic battles around it reveal about international commercial arbitration. We shall then focus on a related conflict, between academics and practitioners. After these oppositional relationships have been described, we shall turn in the next sections to the way that the conflicts have been managed in the case of one key institution, the International Chamber of Commerce in Paris, and to the role of large Anglo-American law firms in the transformation of relatively informal arbitration into "offshore litigation." The conflicts, the management, and the power of the large law firms are key ingredients in the success and current status of international commercial arbitration.

Grand Old Men and Technocrats

The starting point of the generational warfare is diverging ideas of arbitral competence—the characteristics that qualify one to be an arbitrator. For the pioneers of arbitration, exemplified especially, but not only, by very senior European professors imbued with the traditional values of the European legal elites,[2] the dominant opinion has been that arbitration should not be a profession: "Arbitration is a duty, not a career" (int. 173, 3). For true independence of judgment, in the words of another senior insider, "The person who goes into this business as an arbitrator to make a living should not be encouraged" (int. 37, 2). Arbitrators, they insist, should render an occasional service, provided on the basis of long experience and wisdom acquired in law, business,

2. A good discussion of the European aristocratic values is in Osiel (1989, 2033–39). This is not to say that the values do not echo in the United States, only that in the United States there has been, as Osiel notes, "a relatively unqualified embrace of the modern world of commerce and corporations" (2046). Compare Kronman 1993, which seeks to reassert the aristocratic values.

or public service.[3] Those who hold this opinion are, indeed, individuals who have risen to the top of their national legal professions and gained financial independence before being asked to serve as arbitrators.

The specific criteria for these "grand notable" arbitrators allow for numerous variations. Different countries and legal systems have different hierarchies in their legal professions. The great professors and a few high judges have for a long time controlled the arbitration terrain of Continental Europe,[4] while the comparable role is assumed in the Anglo-American system by the most respected of the practitioners, senior barristers or Queen's Counsel (QCs), or senior partners in firms of solicitors or U.S. law firms. Retired judges such as Lord Wilberforce have been important as well to England. The arbitration market has selected those at the top of their domestic professions to become senior arbitrators: "high profile, high visibility . . . national aura behind them" (int. 51, 18).

These relatively few grand old men,[5] as they are often referred to (there were no women), have played a central role in the emergence and the recognition of arbitration,[6] and they continue to have a quasi monopoly for very large matters. As a U.S. litigator stated, "There are some categories of disputes where you're going to need the grand old men who are known to each other" (int. 38, 18). Stated another longtime observer of the field, "In these big, big

3. Jean Robert, one of the respected founding fathers of international commercial arbitration, reportedly stated that "arbitrators are the well-paid unemployed." One leading member of the pioneering generation noted that to be "really independent," one had to be over seventy-five years of age and not dependent on further arbitration business (int. 158, 8).

4. This generation in Europe could also be defined as somewhat marginal in the sense that they were not content to simply work their way up national hierarchies through their patience and technical skill. They used their personal qualities and social characteristics to redefine the traditional careers and maintain an openness to new opportunities and approaches that were not strictly "legal," but rather at the crossroads of law, politics, and business.

5. Figure 1 gives numbers of the individuals we interviewed according to general characteristics, but we would define ten to fifteen of the senior individuals we interviewed as the most perfect embodiment of the characteristics of the pioneering generation.

6. More generally, it is typically the case that when a new symbolic field is being constructed it requires the personal legitimacy of "grand old men" or their equivalent to provide it with sufficient legitimacy to survive. Almost by definition, this process will apply to a specific time in the history of the legal field. Our preliminary research suggests that we can find precisely the same phenomenon in the early development of the field of international human rights.

cases, you go for people who have already years of experience" (int. 10, 12).[7] But these "divas"—sometimes defined also as dinosaurs—are increasingly criticized by a new generation of practitioners who came to arbitration because of the rapid growth of this market in the 1980s.

To the aura or the charisma of their elders, these new arrivals oppose their specialization and technical competence. In the words of a Swiss member of the new generation, "Arbitration was characterized by a limited, small group of impeccable, outstanding professionals—characters known around the world. . . . Today I have difficulty in seeing the outstanding personality [among] a big crowd of people" (int. 166, 33).[8] Put in more aggressive terms by a member of the same cohort, an arbitrator cannot now just step in "with all . . . [the] glorious past" and provide the "great old man's opinion" (int. 184, 6). Indeed, charisma is said even to be a source of error. In the words of an ICC insider, "Some of the biggest problems that we see are probably with some of the big names" (int. 134, 14). Why? "They're probably just more full of themselves than other people" (id., 14). Furthermore, "Sometimes an eminent arbitrator feels he doesn't have to explain things" (id., 25). A leading figure of the younger generation thus describes his generation as "technically better equipped in procedure and substance" (int. 148, 6).

They present themselves in this new generation as international arbitration professionals,[9] and also as entrepreneurs selling their services to business practitioners, contrasting their qualities[10] to the "amateurism" or "idealism" of

7. "I have two lists . . . two ways of thinking. I have what I call the big hitter . . . a grand monsieur . . . a man of sixty-five or seventy—a professor. . . the French- or German-style professor, or the ex-judge—retired judge" (int. 82, 14). The grand old man is for "a case that has political ramifications. . . . You need him for his eminence and respect" (id., 17).

8. Virtually all of the thirty-three arbitration specialists that we interviewed and noted graphically in figure 1, as well as many of the "arbitration bureaucrats," are major players in this generation.

9. The international characteristics of this generation are also captured in the following quotation: "[W]e had recently an arbitration and we did it in English. Place of arbitration was Vienna. And the way we conducted it was very much influenced by our common background of time in the United States. That was the one thing we had in common. Next thing we had in common was that we all knew some Latin. And some knowledge of Roman law. Third thing that we had in common was the German legal theory, which in Turkey, Switzerland, and Germany was also a common thing. And the fourth thing was that we all watched CNN and read the *Financial Times,* and you know" (int. 108, 45).

10. Several young Swiss arbitrators highlighted the difference between generations, in their opinion, by stating that, while they would stay awake all night to finish an

their predecessors.[11] This idea of change is well captured in an article by Jan Paulsson, a leading member of the new generation (also described in chapter 2):

> the age of innocence has come to an end . . . [and] the subject has inevitably lost some of its charm. Once the delightful discipline of a handful of academic *aficionados* on the fringe of international law, it has become a matter of serious concern for great numbers of professionals determined to master a process because it is essential to their business. They labor, but not for love. (Paulsson 1985, 2)

Indeed, now that arbitration has become accepted in commercial international mores, they assert, even citing Max Weber in one instance, that the time has come for the "routinization of charisma" essential to the transition from the stage of artisans to that of mass production (int. 104). This transition requires the "rationalization" of arbitration know-how.

These technocrats play key roles now in institutions like the International Chamber of Commerce, which they not only have come to direct but also have used for their education in arbitration. The quick route to arbitration expertise is through the major institutions, which hire young lawyers to administer the arbitrations.[12] These organizations, which the pioneers used for evangelical purposes to promote arbitration, now have added a more technical involvement in the administration of the arbitrations themselves.

The large Anglo-American law firms, which dominate the international market of business law, are also central to this conflict between grand old men and technocrats. With the growth of trade and the success of the pioneers in building international arbitration, they now consider it important to include this speciality in the gamut of services that they put at the disposition of their

arbitration and produce an award, the senior Swiss arbitrators would terminate the hearing at 5:00 P.M. for dinner and an evening at the opera.

11. We find this same opposition elsewhere, for example in economics. Engineers and also lawyers at a certain moment began to define themselves as economists to align themselves with the new expertise, but they were later dismissed by a new generation trained in the more technical aspects of economics (see Wade 1990).

12. The method is not only quick, but also one of the only ways to resolve the catch-22 of arbitration: It is necessary to have a reputation in international arbitration to gain access to arbitration. The new generation can through these institutions gain a control over the production of producers—arbitrators and arbitration lawyers. There are other ways to enter, but they are difficult. For example, the large law firms offer possibilities to younger lawyers, but they tend still to treat arbitration as only part of general litigation. It is hard to become a recognized expert.

multinational clients. The attitude of the large law firms has been to favor overtly this "banalization" and rationalization of arbitration, which permits them to introduce themselves into the closed "club" and to introduce the legal techniques that are at the basis of their preeminence. As a U.S. lawyer stated about the Swiss, "It's the younger generation that I like, because all of them have gone to school in the United States. They all speak fluent English. They know how to deal with Americans and English, and they move cases along" (int. 37, 34). Another U.S. expert, describing a particular individual of the new generation, is quite revealing:

> He'll make a fortune in this work if he keeps growing. And one of the reasons is he's not in the sense that you use that word, a "star," because he's never going to act like that. What you see is what you get. He'll do his work, he'll do it well, and people will keep coming back to him. But he won't be a pontificating presence. (Int. 7, 26)[13]

This opposition between grand old men and young technocrats—supported by Anglo-American firms—is one of the keys that permits decoding a great number of the debates and the fights—in scholarship as well as in institutions—that affect this field of practice. One controversy, discussed further below, is whether the major institutions, the ICC notably, are now too involved in the actual work of the arbitrators. A second is whether arbitration is becoming too much like litigation. The perspective of the senior generation is highly critical of both of these trends. A leading senior arbitrator thus reported that procedural infighting was "suicidal" to arbitration and that he was likewise "absolutely opposed to drowning arbitration in paperwork" (int. 173, 6). With respect to the ICC, the same individual noted that the weakness of the ICC was that its arbitration was "overly regulated" by the secretariat[14] who had "never seen arbitration from the inside" (id., 6).[15]

13. The new president of the Swiss Arbitration Association, succeeding one of the great stars of the senior generation, Pierre Lalive, makes the same point in his description of what he aspires to in arbitration: "a continuing challenge to overcome obstacles and to grow—not to grow to a 'super arbitrator,' but to an arbitrator with dignity, an open heart and mind and, above all: modesty" ("Profile of Arbitrator, Marc Blessing" 1991, 253).

14. A published article by Gillis Wetter (1990) of Sweden is unique for articulating these concerns in strong language. For example, he states that the "ICC Court . . . is an administrative institution that engages in rather far-reaching involvement in arbitration proceedings, yet offers relatively little administrative or intellectual support to arbitration tribunals" (1990, 95). Stephen Bond, then secretary-general of the ICC and a member of the new generation, wrote an equally strong response, published in the same journal (1990).

15. A criticism that can also be made of our work. An older, but fascinating, account of arbitration, which supports our attention to symbolic capital and the role of authority and expertise within the arbitral tribunal, is Mentschikoff and Haggard 1977.

This cleavage about the conduct of arbitration is also present in debates that appear much more academic. The best known of such debates concerns the so-called *lex mercatoria,* conceived by many as a return to an international law of business—a new "law merchant" independent from national laws (see generally Carbonneau 1990; de Ly 1992). Avoiding open criticism of the powerful grand old professors from France and Switzerland who, as discussed in chapter 4, reinvented this theory and applied it to commercial arbitration, the new generation prefers to focus on how it is applied by "other" arbitrators. A U.S. arbitration expert in a large law firm in Paris thus stated about the *lex mercatoria,*

> It's something that can be subject to abuse where an arbitrator doesn't feel like going through a difficult choice of law . . . or simply decides that something is *lex mercatoria* because that's an answer he feels is right. . . . The question is . . . whether commercial parties feel that it provides sufficient security and predictability—and how well arbitrators who don't have the abilities of [Berthold] Goldman [a senior French professor and the "father" of the *lex mercatoria*] are able to apply the theory and come up with suitable answers that are perceived as fair and reasonable by both parties. (Int. 104, 23; see also Paulsson 1990, 68; int. 10, 14)

It is as if only a few arbitrators with incontestable authority have the right to invoke the notion of *lex mercatoria.* All others must restrain themselves and carefully explicate the legal reasoning that prevents their decision from being condemned as arbitrary. As the quotation also indicates, Anglo-American practitioners tend not to support the Continental, academic *lex mercatoria* (see the lineup in Carbonneau 1990; Mustill 1987).

But beyond the contest between generations about what and whose characteristics should be at the center of international commercial arbitration, this fight for power contains the true transformation that is taking place—the passage from one mode to another for the production of arbitration and the legitimation of arbitrators. As is the case for the entire field of business law, the Anglo-American model of the business enterprise and merchant competition is tending to substitute itself for the Continental model of legal artisans and corporatist control over the profession (Dezalay 1992). In the same way, international commercial arbitration is moving from a small, closed group of self-regulating artisans to a more open and competitive business.

The arrival of new generations and greater competition, beginning in the late 1970s, can be seen as part of this process. We must be careful, however, not to overlook the personal dimension in this story. The break between the small group of artisans and today's arbitration professionals is not as pronounced as it might appear. A good number of these "angry young men" of arbitration are "new" arrivals only in the strict sense of the term. They are also the inheritors—or more precisely the disciples—of the grand old men.[16] They have been able to avoid waiting patiently for the retirement of their mentors in order to succeed them, which was the tradition in the artisanal model (and also in the classic Continental academic model). They have sought to jump these stages and profit from a boom in arbitration that created a demand that exceeded the capacity of the grand masters and the artisanal mode of production. The desire to promote their own technical competencies has led them to a position that devalues the wisdom and generalist experience of their notable mentors, whom they now characterize as dinosaurs. Since they are for the most part too young to compete with the charisma of grand old men, they must emphasize their technical sophistication.

The positions in these contests, however, are more tactical than permanent. It is not at all clear that these young technocrats are ready to renounce completely the attractions of charismatic arbitration, which present advantages both for the arbitrators and for the parties in conflict. Not surprisingly, a certain number of these technicians are seeking to take the prominence gained as international arbitration specialists and reinvest it in a more generalist professional profile.[17] The strategy of diversification may permit them to

16. It will suffice to note that many of the leaders of the new generation were closely connected to the most well known senior arbitrators. Among other examples, we may point to the close connections between Albert Jan van den Berg and Pieter Sanders in the Netherlands; the connection of numerous Swiss arbitrators to Pierre Lalive and the Lalive firm; the numerous disciples of the great French professor, René David, including Yves Derain, Julian Lew, and van den Berg; prominent French disciples to Pierre Bellet and Berthold Goldman. Indeed, the observation can be generalized. Even within U.S. law firms, we found that leading arbitration notables of the new generation, such as James Carter and David Rivkin, were promoted by notable mentors—Jack Stevenson and Robert von Mehren. The systems of patronage may no longer be as extreme as the European legal dynasties of the past, but there are artificial recreations of the same phenomenon. Because of the small size of the groups we investigated and the early stage of the development of the field, our project has noted connections that we are certain would be revealed in similarly detailed studies of other areas of legal practice.

17. A formerly quite active Swiss arbitrator, now involved in electoral politics, thus noted,

> I used to be fairly legalistic as an arbitrator. Give me the facts. Give me the law. And I'll decide it, okay. . . . I was impressed . . . when I was . . . secretary at several panels, for several arbitration panels where Pierre Lalive was the chairman. He . . . hardly ever decided a case. They would all be settled at some point. And that takes a lot of skill . . . from the chairman—skills which

come back into arbitration (or go elsewhere) as new versions of a senior arbitration elite, combining the qualities of expert and the social capital and experience of the charismatic notables.[18]

While it is useful to decode the contests through which the field and the markets of arbitration are constituted, the opposition between notables and technocrats may lead to confusion. The risk is that an objective content will be given to notions that exist only in their opposition. The notables and the technocrats are defined only in a relative manner, the one by relation to the other and also in a quite specific context. The same caution applies to the other major cleavage, which opposes practitioners and academic jurists.

Academics and Practitioners

The polarization between academics and practitioners has elements in common with that between notables and technocrats, but the practice-versus-academia conflict exists also on its own. It provides another key principle for understanding the positions and fights for influence in a field of practice in great measure conceived by and for (mainly Continental) academics but dominated increasingly by (mainly Anglo-American) practitioners. The controversy around the *lex mercatoria* is indicative also in this respect. The Anglo-American practitioners are nearly unanimous in their denunciation of a doctrinal construction that, according to them, allows academics to avoid the rigorous analysis of the facts, the formal law, and even the terms of the contract.[19]

In this controversy as well, it is clear that each side seeks to promote the value of the know-how or the competence that it has mastered the best. Academics—with a competitive advantage in theory—emphasize the *lex mercatoria* elaborated in countless academic books and articles. Practitioners promote the virtues of solid case law and thorough analysis of the facts. But this opposition is also only a relative one. The practitioners of arbitration even in

I clearly didn't have some years ago. And I think maybe I'm developing them a little more now. Probably a matter of aging. (Int. 178, 5)

18. An ambitious U.S. arbitration expert we asked about "future grand old men" replied, "The people my age who are clearly extremely good lawyers and who've devoted a good chunk of their career to international arbitration and so as a matter of course enter in the public eye" (int. 38, 22).

19. A well-known English QC from the commercial bar captures the feeling: "These people are just deciding by the seat of their pants. There's no such thing as the *lex mercatoria*" (int. 87, 34). An American lawyer in Paris makes the same point: "And we don't want *lex mercatoria.* We want to know what law it is. In fact we want to know which procedural law it is. We don't want to leave it up to the arbitrator" (int. 100, 12).

the Anglo-American countries carefully cultivate an intellectual image through publication and university affiliations. Lord Michael Mustill, for example, one of the leading English commercial judges, took the time to master the subtleties of the *lex mercatoria* in order to criticize it at a suitably high level (Mustill 1987). On the other side, the academics who are in the arbitration world—including the Continental ones—are often described as far from the pure academic model. One French academic imbued with the values of the academy thus looked down on academic arbitrators: "abundance of arbitrations" is not "abundance of intelligence" (int. 209, 1).

As a result of the contests for preeminence in the field, each of the competing groups seeks to gain a diversified portfolio of arbitration capital. That is to say, professors must show they can master business practicalities, and practicing lawyers must seek to show competence in sophisticated academic theories. Each group, in short, is in fact closer to the other than appears in the first place, and they complement each other admirably. The academic theorization of arbitration—"developed by the French and Swiss professors largely" (int. 85, 28)—gave the field its *lettres de noblesse* as a sophisticated legal expertise suitable for high-level practitioners. This academic pedigree has helped promote the acceptance and recognition of arbitration throughout much of the world.

In the same way, this rapprochement (or homologation) between professors and practitioners has served to open a market of arbitration well beyond what could have been created by a small group of learned jurists more preoccupied with doctrinal advances than with marketing. Transformations promoted by practitioners, similarly, have overcome the professors' resistance to basic Anglo-American conceptions of litigation—especially more attention to questions of fact and more openness to procedural tactics. Accordingly, the large Anglo-American law firms have become more willing to invest in this process. Anglo-American arbitrators have also changed through some rapprochement, becoming more open to Continental practices such as active judicial questioning and limits on pretrial discovery (Lowenfeld 1985).

The opposition and the complementarity between these different poles structures the field of arbitration, creating a dynamic that, we can see in retrospect, has allowed this field of practice to change and renovate itself over the past two decades. At the same time, the diversity of resources and competencies among the available—and competing—"private judges" has allowed different kinds of conflicts—great or small, exceptional or routine—to call on different types of arbitrators. As a result, international arbitration can reap the symbolic benefits and material prosperity of its generally accepted legitimacy in international business transactions.

The Management of Antagonisms and the Production of Universals: The International Chamber of Commerce

We can pursue these themes and hopefully avoid the problems of a simplistic or objectifying schematization by focusing in more detail on the emergence of modern arbitration around international commercial arbitration's preeminent institution—the International Chamber of Commerce in Paris (Ridgeway 1938). The success of the missionary enterprise of the founders[20] led to the diffusion of the ICC arbitration clause into business transactions around the world. With a rapid growth of international trade and commercial conflict, the resultant case boom challenged the ICC's structure. According to one of the key figures in this period of the ICC,

> in the late seventies [the ICC] started having problems because the number of cases increased quite dramatically. And the ICC, I think, at the time still only had five or six people in the secretariat. And that's when, I guess in 1980 or '81, there was this very significant effort by the ICC to organize itself administratively, to hire more people. (Int. 104, 2)

The ICC, as we shall see, necessarily became a more bureaucratic institution.

New Arrivals and the Expansion of the Market

The ICC had to administer the influx of new cases and, more importantly, to respond to the new problems posed by the arrival of a new clientele and, to a lesser degree, new arbitrators. The new arrivals were unfamiliar with the usages of an international arbitration coterie that was at the same time learned, militant, and a little marginal because of its shared hobby. The expansion of the market of Eurodollars, then the manna of petrodollars thanks to the oil crises in the 1970s, both enlarged and *reoriented* international trade. North-south conflicts became more important as the ICC became the focal point for the major arbitrations tied to the very large construction projects located especially in the Arab countries.

This opening to north-south conflicts coincided, somewhat paradoxically, with an accelerated American involvement in the practice of arbitration. One

20. Among countless examples of the role of the ICC in universalizing arbitration, we can point to the travels by ICC leaders around the world to sell the concept of arbitration, the role of the ICC in the 1958 New York Convention, which set the stage for the easy enforcement of arbitral awards in all signatory countries, and the relationship of the ICC to the International Council for Commercial Arbitration (ICCA), which sponsors the most important conferences and uses them to gain new terrain for arbitration.

reason is that, since the North American exporters were confronted with problems in the execution of their contracts, their law firms invested in the forum already accepted for these contracts—international arbitration, typically in Paris or Switzerland (and later through the Iran–United States Claims Tribunal operating in The Hague).[21]

Another reason for increased American (and English) involvement is that the multinationals of law arrived on the arbitration scene with technical facilities that were unique in the market. Serving both multinational enterprises and not infrequently third-world countries, they were well equipped for the mass of facts characteristic of these megalitigations with gigantic sums in controversy. As a result, the ICC saw both new parties from the south and new law practices from the north. And the market expanded considerably.

Competition in the Field

This rapid expansion of the market of arbitration naturally awakened new appetites (Clow and Stewart 1990). The ICC thus found itself more and more in competition with new arbitral institutions aiming at such or such segment of this very diverse market. One segment of the market could be defined in geographical terms, like East-West or Euro-Arab relations. Stockholm, for example, made its reputation with Soviet-U.S. disputes in particular and East-West in general (see chap. 9). Another segment might involve a type of specific case, like those concerning intellectual property. There are also efforts to promote alternative technologies for the administration of business disputes.[22]

The multiplication and diversification of places and institutions of arbitration promotes further competition. The ICC, for example, has been forced to adjust its general fee schedule downward to attract business clients, and some institutions seek to gain the favor of arbitrators by emphasizing that they allow the arbitrators to negotiate any fee arrangement they can obtain. Multinational law firms accelerate this competition by their ability to forum shop—both in contractual negotiations and after disputes arise—among institutions, sets of rules, laws, and arbitrators (Purcell 1992).

21. According to a British lawyer with a multinational law firm, referring to ICC arbitrations, "In the Middle East with the oil explosion and the huge contracts that were let in the late sixties and seventies, they gave rise to a good number of disputes. And there were a number of us in Western Europe who made a lot of money resolving them" (int. 85, 17).

22. Ironically, the promoters of alternative dispute resolution represent an echo, now from a new place, of precisely the arguments that the arbitration community once used to challenge the hegemony of the formal state justice systems (see chap. 8).

The ICC and the Universality of Arbitration

Even if the ICC has lost its position of quasi monopoly, it remains the central institution. A longtime British observer thus points out, "But the ICC is a great institution. I mean it's the leading arbitral, international arbitral institution in the world by a long way" (int. 85, 18; see also int. 91, 16; int. 66, 26; int. 52, 12; int. 95; int. 69). Potential clients see the ICC as trustworthy and respectable because of its senior status, and because it has preserved the missionary idealism of its origins. An American critic of the ICC agrees: "The ICC has of course the great advantage that they were in it from the beginning. And they have created this aura that if you have an ICC arbitration that the award is good and it will be enforced everywhere" (int. 57, 6).

As the status of the ICC indicates, history is a key legitimator in the legal field. No one can compete with tradition without ending up underscoring that one group is a new arrival and another the established elite, akin to the aristocracy. The passage of time also tends to obscure the politics that created an institution, thereby giving it an aura of naturalness. And this kind of legitimacy is probably especially important in a field where it is important to be able to claim a distance from business and politics.[23]

The ICC is the most universal of the arbitration institutions, able to brag even about having become a sort of United Nations (int. 106, 4) of commerce and of international arbitration. With members from some one hundred nations and national committees in sixty, it offers a powerful image of neutrality and legitimacy. In addition, ICC arbitration benefits from a double sponsorship—that of the world of business, since the parent organization remains a major business group, and that of the world of learned jurists, to which belong the founding fathers and an important fraction of arbitrators today. Finally, we can also note that the ICC has benefited from a close relationship with the state, evident in both the support it obtained from the French government and the "public-private" career profiles of key figures in the arbitration community (e.g., the retired French judge, Pierre Bellet).

The ICC has therefore become one of the principal places where the "politics" of arbitration is elaborated and expressed. There are innumerable committees and multiple networks of influence that gravitate around this institution. The court, for example, which is really an oversight committee that reviews arbitration appointments and decisions, appears to be particularly sensitive to the business clientele; the Institute of International Business Law

23. It is similarly interesting that one feature of the *lex mercatoria* is that it builds links to medieval times, suggesting that it is quite normal to have a special merchant law.

and Practice focuses on the academic side; and the secretariat guides the court and seeks to manage growth and change. Through exchanges and contests expressed in these and other ICC forums and networks, the ICC is able to make policy to regulate the relations of arbitration with the worlds of national law (essentially the new legislation and jurisprudence in matters of arbitration) and politics.[24]

The emergence of institutional networks around the ICC can also be seen as a true microcosm of the legal field. Between the first generation of charismatic pioneers and the experts of the ascending generations, one finds a sort of striking abridgment of the principal stages in the grand Weberian canvas (Weber 1978, 246–54, 784–816). We see first the legal *honoratiores*, embodying the wisdom of law and the social legitimacy necessary to the management of social conflicts. We then find institutionalization and the creation of a division of labor, which permits the development of a collective legitimacy dependent not on individual notables but rather on "the ICC" or even "law" or "international commercial arbitration."[25]

It is clear, however, that this project of routinization—even judicialization—of arbitration, supported strongly by the ICC bureaucracy while denounced as treason by the founding fathers, cannot be completely accomplished. Despite the changes, there remains a vital element of personal relations in this field. The system of selection and self-regulation of arbitrators created by the pioneers and resembling a club has remained quite essential to the prosperity of international commercial arbitration.

Despite the conflicts and differing positions taken with respect to the conduct of arbitration, the participants in the debates are still in key respects members of a common community. This community, like all organizations where professional relations are reproduced through an extraordinary network of personal ties, has a tendency to fix itself by ensuring that social interests are organized to make themselves heard better. The main organs of the ICC, by allowing this more personal debate and interchange, contribute crucially to the management of conflicts toward the success of international arbitration.

24. One recent example was the question of the appropriate attitude to adopt with respect to contracts and arbitration threatened by sociopolitical disturbances, such as was the case recently with the destruction of the Soviet bloc. Another is the difficult problem of what to do with the bribes, or baksheesh, that surface in accounts of much of international trade and investment. The ICC provides committees and forums to debate and resolve such issues.

25. An insider of the secretariat during the time of change thus noted, "When I started then it was more or less a group of friends, for the club. . . . And then with the expansion of the number of cases [it] was not any longer possible just to deal on a personal basis" (int. 108, 18).

Between the Club and the Market

The secretariat of the Court of Arbitration of the ICC makes no secret of its desire to open the market of arbitration beyond the narrow circle of the grand old men.[26] Certainly these efforts can be justified by the growth in the number of cases submitted to the ICC, as well as by their great geographical diversity (see Bond 1990). The arrival into arbitration of the third world and of the Anglo-Americans rendered necessary the recruitment of new arbitrators who did not fit the profile of the Continental academic or the other pioneers (Bond 1990, 120). Many new users are bound to nominate arbitrators—and a fortiori lawyers—from their own legal settings. According to Stephen Bond, then the secretary-general of the ICC, "In such instances, given the importance of party autonomy and consensus as basic principles of international commercial arbitration, the ICC has not refused confirmation of such persons, even when they are unknown to the Court itself" (Bond 1990, 121).

These newcomers, however, are by definition not the progeny of the club. Their entry into the practices and norms of the club cannot be ensured by a long apprenticeship or by an informal process controlled by a small group of senior men. The institutionalization of these tasks of enlisting new arbitrators and observing their performance, in fact, justifies the growth and transformation of the ICC bureaucracy (the secretariat) and also the Court of Arbitration. This "bureaucratization" of the ICC, and also the retention of two of the most controversial aspects of the ICC procedure—the terms of reference and the review of the arbitrators' opinions by the court—can therefore be seen as part of the effort to bring in newcomers, accommodate their situation, and preserve the universality of the ICC and arbitration.[27]

26. As one key representative of the secretariat mentioned, "There was an effort to broaden the pool." And new nationalities were also brought in partly because "it's important for the perception of the ICC as being international. And it's important in the perception of international arbitration as an institution, it's being universal" (int. 104, 7).

27. The terms of reference are a document that the parties must develop at the outset of the arbitration. Even those generally critical of the terms of reference, which includes most American and British lawyers, state that the terms of reference are "helpful if you've got inexperienced arbitrators or unprofessional arbitrators or those who might be likely to misbehave in some way" (int. 53, 8). Similarly, an English barrister notes that the English "hate the terms of reference. Now that is because they've never been exposed to an arbitration where there is some deficiency or some imbalance between the parties or their legal representative whether it's cultural or legal" (int. 93, 7). We suggest that this kind of process, which serves to produce belief in the rules of the game at the outset and build a common language, is quite common in places where the system has not yet been routinized.

The ICC court reviews decisions and has the power to ask arbitrators to rewrite.

This set of events helps to explain better the current ambivalence of the founding fathers with respect to the ICC—seen in their attitude toward "bureaucratization." It is an organization that they helped to build, and that celebrates them at all conferences and ceremonial occasions. But, at the same time, it is now dispossessing them from what constitutes a large part of their power. They are losing the informal control they could assert on a community of disciples, where loyalty could be rewarded by suggesting names for arbitration or for the activities of legal representation. We have here the classical scenario of an institution that is devouring its founding fathers in order to better follow their work.

The ICC and the Recentering of the Field of International Commercial Arbitration: The Arrival and Role of the Anglo-American Law Firms

The tensions implicated by these transformations are not explained only by a crisis of growth. They are also the corollary of displacement from the center of gravity of arbitration. The recentering favors the world of Anglo-American law firms, who have used their power in the international business world to impose their conception of arbitration and more largely of the practice of law.[28] It is thus no accident that, within the ICC itself, the politics of rationalization has been conducted since the beginning of the eighties by young Anglo-American lawyers recruited from outside of the club, and whose key words have been transparency, rationalization, and competition.[29] The Anglo-Americans, including the two most recent secretaries-general of the ICC (from the United States), have clashed with leading members of the senior arbitration club over a number of issues, including the necessity of bureaucratization. A recent example, which provides a good illustration of the conflict and the trend in management, has been the effort of the ICC to expand the requirements of ICC arbitrators to disclose relationships with counsel and other arbitrators.

Conflicts of Interest, Independence, and Transparency

According to an observer sympathetic to the controversial approach taken by the ICC secretariat,

---

According to an ICC insider, the ICC court returns to the arbitrators for revision about 15–20 percent of the awards rendered.

28. Arbitration is only one example of a recentering in favor of the Anglo-Americans that we find more generally through the internationalization of legal practice (Dezalay 1992; Garth 1980, 130–42).

29. As stated from the more recent perspective, "That frustration from the American community has to some degree gotten soft. And I think it's been helped a lot because . . . [of an] American secretary-general of the ICC" (int. 100, 8).

> The court took the view that the "declaration of independence" which is required to be signed by all proposed arbitrators should include a mention of any significant relationship between arbitrators proposed and counsel for parties in the arbitration. And there, what the Swiss [and many Europeans] objected to . . . is that the relationships that may exist between counsel and arbitrators are irrelevant, because they cannot possibly call into question the independence of the arbitrator. It's only the relationships with parties that arise. (Int. 134, 6)

The senior generation wants no disclosure of relationships between counsel and arbitrators. The ICC, supported by U.S. lawyers, has opted to support greater disclosure (compare Lowenfeld 1991; see Lalive 1991).

Conforming to the liberal logic that the new Anglo-American generation embodies, it is partly a matter of introducing competition in a market that was strongly cartelized. This objective can be pursued by multiplying the number of producers, and the large Anglo-American firms have had a role in increasing the number of arbitration suppliers (e.g., London, Sweden, Vienna) competing with the ICC. But it is even more essential and also more difficult to introduce a minimum of transparency in a community of specialists characterized by personal relations so complex and so entangled that they interdict access to this market by nonspecialists.[30] Broad disclosure can provide that kind of transparency.

Because of a mixing of roles, the same individuals who belong to the networks around the central institutions of arbitration are found in the roles of lawyers, coarbitrators, or chairs of the arbitral tribunal. The principal players therefore acquire a great familiarity with each other, and they develop also, we suspect, a certain connivance with respect to the role held by the adversary of the moment. The extraordinary flexibility of this rotation of roles contributes greatly to the smooth running of these mechanisms of arbitration.[31] It promotes the reaching of acceptable awards under a regime where the players do not speak of contradictions and antagonisms that, if formulated explicitly and disclosed, would create some difficulties of legitimation. "Adversaries" can protect the processes that provide their legitimacy and prosperity.

30. We do not mean that outsiders do not participate in ICC arbitrations, only that the repeat work and most effective representation will be within the club.

31. These kinds of relationships, discussed also in chapter 4, contribute to the smooth functioning generally of legal means of resolving disputes, since the advocates can both represent their clients forcefully and avoid dramatic clashes through their personal relations with opposing counsel (e.g., Eisenberg 1976; Mnookin and Kornhauser 1979). Certainly the English system of barristers who know each other well arguing before judges who come also from barristers' chambers is another example.

The potential problem confronted by outsiders and invoked by the ICC secretariat is evident in the words of a leading arbitrator of the new generation:

> This is a mafia. There are about, I suppose, forty to fifty people in Western Europe who could claim that they make their living doing this. I'm one of them. It took me, oh, probably close to fifteen years to get to the point that when I go as I do regularly to the Swiss Arbitration Association meeting twice a year, or I go to an ICC gathering, or an ICCA gathering that I will know and be recognized, and know and talk to a number, you know, the leading figures. And if you . . . that's how you just get into it. Now why is it a mafia? It's a mafia because people appoint one another. You always appoint your friends—people you know. It's a mafia because policymaking is done at these gatherings. (Int. 85, 27)

A self-identified U.S. "associate member" of the club stated, "They nominate one another. And sometimes you're counsel and sometimes you're arbitrator" (int. 50, 9).[32]

At the same time, it is clear that this somewhat mysterious accumulation and confusion of roles represents a formidable handicap for the occasional players. In order to risk playing on the field of international arbitration, it is necessary to be one of the initiated or to draw on the services of one of the initiated. In fact, the majority of specialists of arbitration earn much more from their activity as lawyers than from their activity as arbitrators. Service as arbitrator helps above all to build and to keep up prominence in the arbitration world.[33] By contrast, the activity of lawyer represents a quite profitable activ-

32. A U.S. litigator stated, "I've appeared in Scandinavia, in the U.K., in France, in Switzerland, and in Italy, and I run into the same lawyers everywhere it's the same names. . . . And so there are people who are almost always involved in some fashion or other if there's an arbitration involving a national event of their country. . . . [O]nce you go offshore, . . . it is a very fungible group and it's the same people over and over [as lawyers and arbitrators]" (int. 51, 11). A senior English arbitrator noted the dilemma: "You're often appointed a party arbitrator by someone with whom you have worked before," and "You know you're going to work with him again. Does that unconsciously bias one? I think that's a difficult one." But "not everybody is 100 percent honest and you know it's a very great advantage to find someone whose character you really do know and can depend on" (int. 97, 13–14).

33. This division between arbitrators and counsel, where the counsel is compensated more materially and the arbitrator more symbolically, is a general phenomenon of the legal world. For example, British QCs, when they are named to the bench, gain the prestige of becoming judges, lose some of their income, and fulfill the function of judging that is necessary for the survival of the system. And those who will take the cut in pay are typically those who are more interested in promoting the universals and

ity for the almost obligatory specialists who serve outsiders confronted with the procedure of arbitration. The approach of the ICC secretariat to some extent challenges this subtle mixing of roles, but clearly personal relations and membership in the "club" remain quite important to success in this field. The ICC is working on behalf of its view of legitimacy to give outsiders a little more access to the otherwise hidden connections between the arbitration players.[34]

Anglo-American Law Firms and Arbitration Insiders

This problem for outsiders highlighted by the ICC secretariat can apply not only to individuals from areas new to international commercial arbitration, but also to the large international law firms themselves. As noted above, the insiders' club of arbitration, while expanded since the days of the pioneers, still enjoys a quasi monopoly on the functions of arbitrator. This monopoly is difficult for multinational law firms to support. When large multinational law firms decided to intervene on the scene of arbitration, they could not be content with folding chairs around a table dominated by others. It is not simply a matter of gaining access to and learning the rules of the game; they insist—and have the power to insist—also on being able to play according to their own terms. That is to say, they insist on utilizing their language and the legal technology that assures their preeminence in the international market of business law. It has therefore been necessary for them not only to enter the closed club of ICC arbitration, but also to impose a redefinition of the rules of the game.[35]

While this strategy is perfectly rational from a strict economic and professional point of view, we believe there is also a more subjective dimension to the contests. The Anglo-American practitioners seek revenge with respect to

---

legitimacy of the system. From a more economic perspective, Richard Posner makes precisely the same point about U.S. judges (1995, 133).

34. This handicap, according to the ICC insiders of the current generation, causes distrust as well. "Appearance is very important. . . . I think one can assume in many international cases the level of mistrust, suspicion of the other party is greater than in a domestic situation." The mandatory disclosure of relationships between counsel and arbitrators could thus have real impacts: "If there is a party who, if there is disclosure of something and the court is more or less uncertain as to whether or not there is really a problem of independence. . . , the court, I think, is more willing to say let's replace the person. . . . Because what we want in the end is for parties to comply with the awards that are rendered" (int. 134, 7).

35. The terminology fits the perceptions of participants: for example, according to a senior observer, "The [U.S.] lawyers are changing the rules of the game" (int. 10, 7).

the intellectual Parisian salons. To understand the importance of the sociocultural shock that promotes this desire, it is necessary to consider the context of the 1970s, the time of the first great arbitrations tied to the construction of large factories in the oil-producing countries. On both sides of the arbitration world the level of incomprehension was total (see case study in chap. 5). The professional groups in effect could not recognize each other, nourishing solid prejudices with respect to each other.

The litigators debarked at Paris (or later The Hague for the Iran–United States Claims Tribunal) with a certain condescension about the procedure of arbitration—in their eyes nothing but a bastard form of process, a sloppy litigation. They were confronted by a community of learned patricians who, while they considered themselves to be cosmopolitans, were more familiar with the theory than with the legal practice of the Anglo-American world (int. 136, 4). They knew little of a recent evolution under the influence of a young generation of litigators, whose aggressive tactics, a "vulgar justice," were gaining ground in what was a gentlemen's world on Wall Street (see Caplan 1993, 121–75)

The divide was therefore not only between two cultures, but also between two generations—even two social classes. A sophisticated U.S. lawyer long active in international arenas put it this way:

> You take the sort of dyed-in-the-wool, hard-edge, brass knuckles American litigators whose style varies from region to region and, you know, put them into a sort of conventional, somewhat European, international arbitration and that's like inviting that thing off the street into a grand salon—makes about the same impression sometimes. (Int. 7, 6)

These pretentious litigators sought to impose the barbarian manners of the far West and the marginal East in the salons of old Europe. They were received as completely ignorant of the proper European ways of combining business disputes with the lofty production of jurisprudence, doctrine, and legal theory. They also tended to misjudge the Europeans because arbitration, in the opinion of the Americans, was associated with the relatively low status and perceived intellectual content of U.S. domestic arbitration (the less formal, compromise-oriented arbitration largely practiced in labor and smaller commercial conflicts under the auspices of the American Arbitration Association).

Arbitration, we could say, was mistranslated. The misunderstanding was total between these litigators, on one side, who wanted to fight on their own terrain of facts with their usual arms of adversary procedure, discovery, cross-examination; and the arbitrators on the other, for whom the noble terrain was that of law (see int. 49). Certainly after the first misunderstanding each side sought to bridge the gap. But in this private justice in the service of merchants, the relation of the forces was such that one made more inroads than the other.

The European arbitrators, including some of the most notable, were converted to the English language and to the usages of Anglo-Americans. Berthold Goldman, for example, one of the most famous pioneers, learned English at forty years of age; and his flexibility was noted as follows: "Cross-examination is not accepted in France . . . barbaric . . . primitive. And except for people like Goldman, . . . he's been cross-examining" (int. 136, 8). An American litigator with considerable arbitration experience noted that the senior arbitration experts "began to realize that clients seemed to like this [cross-examination and expert testimony,] and it was clearly affecting their business, and so I mean there were only two things they could do. . . . And I found again in my experience they embraced it" (int. 51, 32). Leading arbitrators allowed the tactical maneuvers that permitted winning or losing through contested searches for facts.

The multinational law firms recognized on their side that the arbitration game in the European context was rather more sophisticated than the domestic variant that they looked down upon in the United States, and they chose to invest in this new legal terrain. They attached themselves to the services of the initiated in order to avoid faux pas and to dress up their arguments in the distinguished language of *lex mercatoria.* But one can understand the resentment of these litigators, who were forced to pay the fees of the initiated under the pretext that one must have the required expertise in the learned language that was then de rigueur in the Parisian club of arbitration. From this perspective we can see the vigor of the offensive brought by the American lobby to enlarge the club and to rationalize the practice of arbitration such that it could become offshore—U.S.-style—litigation.

This warlike terminology may promote confusion. The fact that it does not appear as aggression is critical in this operation of redefinition and of recentering. Even if the attacks and the relations of force were quite real, the violence would remain symbolic in this symbolic field. The exportation of legal technologies involves less gunboat politics than the strategy of the fifth column. This operation began in the interior of the club and with the support—at least the connivance of the founding fathers. The fifth column in this process has been the Parisian offices of the American firms. For a small number of expatriate lawyers, often married to Europeans, the practice of international arbitration represented an excellent opportunity. It permitted them to profit from their double expertise and to serve as *courtiers* between two cultures.

Interest in arbitration helped to recruit top local talent, contributing to the local implantation of these large Anglo-American firms and favoring the constitution of a nucleus of Eurolawyers. In the 1970s, this establishment in Paris did not provoke the local barriers that tend to result from such efforts today. The bar did not then feel at all concerned by the quite limited international market. A few modernists—even visionaries—saw there an opportunity and incitement to reform legal practice and to develop Paris as an offshore legal market. They welcomed the chance to help reshape the domestic legal field.[36]

On their side, the founding fathers of arbitration could only enjoy these efforts of the *courtiers* who, by opening arbitration to all the North American markets, enlarged considerably the demand for an expertise that they had mastered better than anyone. The Americanization of arbitration thus occurred with much less reticence than has been perceived, since, at least in the beginning, it appeared to the pioneers as a recognition of the merits of arbitration and an investment in the practical field (see ICC 1984). The new consumers permitted the pioneers (finally) to receive very handsome dividends on their arbitration capital—a savoir faire and an experience accumulated for decades.

Arbitration as Litigation

But the reality of the relation of forces between this small club of learned artisans and these great conglomerates of legal experts was that, rather quickly, those who had opened the doors of their club to the Anglo-American practitioners became bothered by the transformation of approaches to arbitration under the influence of the "American lobby." Perhaps the trees had initially hidden the forest. The "Americans in Paris" may actually have fallen for the charm of arbitration in the Continental manner. But behind them was lined up an army of great law firms who, by the simple fact of their mode of organization, could only throw into profound disorder a game of arbitration conceived essentially by and for the civilian academic. As a British solicitor long active in arbitration observed, "If you ever want a bunch of lawyers who are completely inflexible about international arbitration and how to conduct it, it's the Americans" (int. 85, 21). Electing arbitration, says an American close to the new generation, "doesn't mean that I necessarily want to give up

36. The first efforts to reform the French legal profession, which culminated only in some higher status of the *conseils juridiques* and a merger of *avocats* and *avoués,* took place at this time. The image of a grand unified profession had to wait until the end of the eighties.

all the trappings of full-scale litigation and what might come with it" (int. 134, 16). And indeed, the Americans have imposed many of those trappings.

As a result, noted a prominent U.S. arbitrator, "American style practice has taken off. . . . A lawyer comes with a team—more attention to fact, motions, objections, delays. Beginning to look more like litigation" (int. 50, 3). A French leader of the older generation made the same point: "The role of the U.S. firms is growing," and they "utilize more and more Anglo-American devices" (int. 115, 4). It is no surprise that the leading arbitrators of the new generation emphasize their skills of case management. The most common statement about a very popular arbitrator today, Karl-Heinz Bockstiegel, is that he is "great in procedural management" (int. 148, 9).

The artisan and the factory cohabit with difficulty. As with respect to the general-practitioner physician and the modern hospital, the model of specialization and differentiation found in the great corporate structures inevitably puts into question the traditional Continental approach. With respect to the arbitration club, there has been pressure on the more or less cooperative mixing of roles that characterized the specialists of arbitration. We have seen the impact in the issue of conflicts of interest, but it goes deeper. The new protagonists have made the problem even more serious by refusing to consider the practice of international commercial arbitration as a specialty into itself. Only a handful of law firms installed for a long time in Paris, and for that reason rather marginal in the hierarchy of U.S. litigating firms, have chosen to invest in arbitration in the more traditional manner by constituting small teams of specialists.

The large American law firms continue to consider international arbitration as but one kind of "litigation" (or, more recently, "dispute resolution") among others. As a partner in a leading New York law firm observed, "Arbitration is considered by us to be an adjunct to litigation—litigation in the courts. It's simply a different forum" (int. 47, 3). In reaffirming their competence to treat this type of matter (at least after the litigators gained ascendancy), these large law firms reject the specificity of the terrain of arbitration. They repeat that it is but one in a menu of competences and solutions that they can propose to their clients in a case of difficulty. That at least is the approach of the litigators, who have acceded in the past several years to a dominant position in the large law firms (Nelson 1988). This territorial demand is easily understood. One does not renounce voluntarily, when in full vigor, a rather prestigious and lucrative practice, especially if this form of competence appears indispensable to success in the market of international transactions. But their insistence on their own approach and their refusal to make international arbitration a specialty make it necessary for the law firms to translate arbitration to fit the knowledge and self-conception of the litigator.

This category of practitioners has been constituted by borrowing but also by opposition between the two great groups that had dominated the field of legal practice in the United States: the corporate lawyers, who held the upper hand in the large firms of Wall Street thanks to their competence as negotiators in the creation of contracts; and the trial lawyers, whose talent was exercised essentially in conducting jury trials. Since enterprises began to change the legal scene through mergers and acquisitions, and also as a result of antitrust and other litigation, a new knowledge has been developed, that of specialist in taking charge of conflict situations (e.g., Caplan 1993). The art consists precisely in knowing how to combine judicial attacks and negotiation behind the scenes in order to lead to an optimal solution from the point of view of the interest of the client. These experts in the tactical administration of disputes consider judicial recourse not as an end in itself, but only as an argument and a means of pressure (cf. Margolick 1993). The negotiators consider judicial recourse as one of the weapons that can be deployed in a conflict that will almost surely end prior to a trial (e.g., Galanter 1985).

The specialists of this parajudicial negotiation are then at the antipode of the traditional Continental model found, not surprisingly, within the club of international commercial arbitration. That model is of an "auxiliary justice," where the duty of counsel is to clarify and aid the judge in rendering good justice. The conflict specialists from the United States (or elsewhere) do not feel any responsibilities except to their client. Furthermore, they offer their clients the ability to operate for tactical reasons in many jurisdictions or types of proceedings at once. This "legal superarmament" of multiple attacks and forum shopping escalates the warfare considerably on behalf of clients able to afford it. And for various reasons, it is a service that was successful in building the power and success of U.S.-style litigation for corporate clients in the 1980s.[37]

The large law firms have tended to practice the very same strategy when handling international disputes. Yet this pragmatic and tactical approach is opposed to the tacit usages of the arbitration club. In the community of the initiated, the proximity and interchangeability of roles makes the advocates comport themselves in a very subtle manner as auxiliaries of the arbitral tribunal. Defending the interests of their clients does not in a case push them to actions that jeopardize their own credibility or, worse still, the social legiti-

37. It is now somewhat under attack by proponents of a truce to the "arms race," such as the Center for Public Resources.

macy of arbitration.[38] Such an attitude would have been equivalent to professional suicide in building the practice of international commercial arbitration.

But it is not the same for the litigators. Their reference group and their criteria for success are different. While the career of arbitrators is in large part dependent on the goodwill of the grand old men who control access to and prominence in the field of arbitration, litigators depend only on their capacity to satisfy important clients. That is what determines their position in the hierarchy of the law firm (Nelson 1988). In short, where one group is obliged to be quasi-referential with respect to the dogmas and the customs upon which is reposed the collective faith in arbitration, the others have but one ambition—that is, winning a good result. To get that result, they are ready to exploit any procedural tactics and forums available to them. They are willing to create difficulties for their colleagues and the arbitral tribunal and even to damage the image of this justice—which had pretended to be rapid and less costly because informal.[39] One understands the irritation of the founding fathers confronted by these newcomers who permit themselves to transform the nature of arbitration by multiplying the incidents of procedure and technical appeals.

The litigators respond matter-of-factly that it is only a matter of fulfilling their duty as lawyers and protecting, by all legal means at their disposal, their clients' interest. Even to win some time, after all, is not of negligible value economically. At the same time, this general strategy, which conforms so perfectly to their mission as defenders of the interests of their clients, permits them also to promote their own conception of arbitration. If arbitration is no longer a last resort but rather one tactical recourse among others, it is no longer correct to make of it a protected preserve for a group of initiated. On the contrary, specialists or law firms that can play simultaneously in many places are in the position of strength.

The International Field Transformed: Toward a Delocalized Market for the Management of International Commercial Disputes

Competition and rationalization, especially as promoted by U.S. litigators, leads to the judicialization of international commercial arbitration. Some commentators, especially from the senior generation, see in this evolution toward the judicialization of arbitration the preview—and the cause—of its decline.

38. Examples of this role abound. Recent documentations of this kind of practice in the civil-law world include Olgiati 1995.

39. A lawyer for a large U.S. firm in Paris says simply: "You know the first advice you give to a defendant in an ICC case is take your time. When they ask for the deposit, don't pay it" (int. 129, 10). The skill is "to spin out the dispute for years" (id., 9).

What good, they say, is it to opt for arbitration when this alternative is at the same time slower and more costly, but also more uncertain, than recourse to the courts? This pessimistic vision, which is in fact a plea for a return to the sources, appears overstated. It is true that the system has been transformed, and the qualities that made arbitration successful for the pioneers seem to be little in evidence. But arbitration is far from withering away. It is in full vigor.[40]

Far from dissolving itself, it seems the community of arbitration specialists has moved a long way toward forming the nucleus of a sort of offshore justice. This expression, which alludes to fiscal paradises exploited by the operators of the great financial centers, is rather far from the unified international private system of justice—organized perhaps around one great *lex mercatoria*—that might have been imagined by some of the pioneering idealists of law. The current model can be understood much better as simply a delocalized and decentralized market for the administration of international commercial disputes, connected by more or less powerful institutions and individuals who are both competitive and complementary.

Conclusion

In this chapter we have mapped the relative positions of groups and individuals in the field of international commercial arbitration. We have been able to see both oppositions and complementarities. The players on the field compete vigorously, but in terms of the universals accepted—as a ticket to admission[41]—by all the players. Examples have included the grand old men and the technocrats, the Continental professors and the U.S. litigators, each promoting

40. Not surprisingly, the current state is celebrated by U.S. litigators in part because arbitration has been "judicialized." A recent U.S. volume "designed as an intellectual pause for reflection" on the state of international commercial arbitration and entitled *Towards "Judicialization" and Uniformity* brought one of the editors, a prominent member of the arbitration community, to the following conclusion: "International arbitration thus is in large measure a substitute for national court litigation," necessary only because the parties from different nationalities do not wish their "rights and obligations to be determined by the courts of the other party's state of nationality" (Brower 1993, x). From this perspective, the closer arbitration is to the general model of courts, the better.

41. The moral tenor of the debates comes in part from the fact that potential arbitrators must invest over a long period of time, promoting a kind of cult of disinterestedness, and because the potential arbitrators must demonstrate a distance from the parochial and particular aspects of their national portfolios. Persons with strong moral beliefs and an interest in universals are attracted. At the same time, the tendency of those in the field to try to diversify their portfolios to accommodate new positions and entrants allows the field to enlarge its coverage to become more universal in another sense.

its own mix of symbolic capital—for example, age and experience, technical know-how, theoretical sophistication, ability to represent clients vigorously, prestige in a particular national legal culture. What each group represents tends also to be what they contend is best suited for the legitimation of arbitrators and therefore for the long-term success of international commercial arbitration. The competition among these different actors in the field of international commercial arbitration—and, we submit, in law generally—thus simultaneously builds the market for particular legal services and the legitimacy of the resultant law.

This intense competition among merchants of law acting as moral entrepreneurs, in addition, requires some institutional management. Our research suggests that the International Chamber of Commerce, once the preserve of a small group of arbitration aficionados, was able to play that role and help to facilitate the transformation of the field in the 1980s. International commercial arbitration has to a great extent now been institutionalized as the generally accepted private legal process applicable to transnational business disputes.[42]

The transformation of the field, represented in figure 1, can be examined in both a general and a particular sense. First, there is a general story of rationalization and institutionalization, and second, an equally important story of details of the transformation. Those details are bound to exert a powerful influence on the conduct of international dispute resolution and on competition in the market for legal services.

The boom in the market for international commercial arbitration, the arrival of new players, and the competition and power of the large multinational law firms contributed to break the traditions of the small, learned, cosmopoli-

42. This account of the phenomenon of institutionalization, while based on Bourdieu, obviously has similarities to certain aspects of the "new institutionalism" in American sociology. There are many similarities, for example, between our approach and that taken by Paul DiMaggio to the process of "constructing an organizational field as a professional project" with respect to art museums in the United States (DiMaggio 1991). We share an emphasis on the complex interactions between professionalism and institutionalism, and on the transformation and institutionalization that takes place with its growth. The most notable differences between his study and our approach are first, since his research was based on archival records, it did not examine the importance of social capital despite its obvious relevance to the story; second, the effort to document the development of an institution in the DiMaggio account tends to avoid probing connections to the larger world around the processes he studies, for example, the changes in municipal politics or in the role of foundations; and third, while our approach fits reasonably well with the one he describes, our focus is on conflict found in the discourses and strategies of the relevant actors rather than specifically on institutions.

tan group that built the International Chamber of Commerce and the basic institutions of international commercial arbitration. The growth and accelerated competition, we have seen, were reflected in an accelerated Weberian transformation—the routinization of charisma and the ascendancy of legal rationality.

The general or Weberian line of this story, we suggest, will be repeated elsewhere in the successful development of an international or other legal field. The social capital and charisma (and even idealism) of elite lawyers respected for their careers and accomplishments helps to legitimate the legal institutions and approaches that they favor.[43] International businesses and national commercial entities, for example, have been more likely to accept the idea of arbitration by lawyers if the chosen lawyers are recognized members of an elite with credibility in the worlds of business and politics. Once the idea of arbitration is sufficiently established, however, it can become more rationalized and generalized as it gains further economic and numerical success.

It must be remembered, however, that even when successful over a long period of time, such a Weberian transformation is only a matter of degree. The conflicts that produce the transformation continue to have an impact on the field. The grand notable arbitrators are still influential, for example, and their services are called upon when disputes are outside the routine, requiring more political sensitivity and indeed more of the authority and clout that comes with their status.

Further, as noted before, the retrospective logic of the successful Weberian scenario should not be invoked to imply that the specific characteristics of this international legal field were natural or inevitable—the product of a slogan like globalism. The particular features cannot be understood if we limit ourselves to a retrospective account suggesting the inevitability of today's "more rational" version of international commercial arbitration. The fact that international commercial arbitration currently combines a certain amount of Continental legal theory, a major Parisian institution at the core of the field, and a practice that resembles offshore litigation as promoted by U.S. litigators—rather than, for example, a less adversarial Continental style of litigation or a central focus on London or New York's institutions for arbitration—comes from the specifics of the international legal field as it was first constituted and later transformed.

While international commercial arbitration has become more formal and expensive, more like U.S. litigation, it does not make sense to describe arbitra-

43. The social capital and charisma, especially in Europe, was also necessary to overcome the resistance to the involvement of lawyers in practices closely connected to business.

tion as a given process inevitably like U.S. litigation (or otherwise, as in the pioneer days of a less formal, more "gentlemanly" international arbitration). Arbitration has evolved in response to particular social factors, and the competition we have seen *continues* about the meaning and legitimacy of particular aspects of international commercial arbitration. Any resolution of the debates about arbitration—as with respect to law—is bound to be provisional.

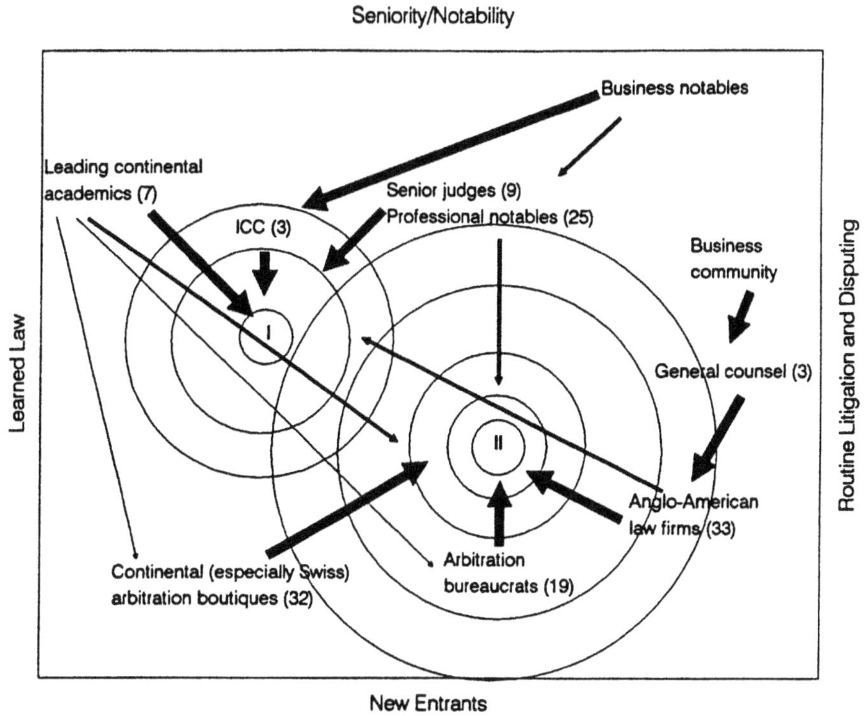

Figure 1. International Commercial Arbitration as a Field of Structured Opposition

NOTES: The shift toward new entrants, routine arbitration, and Anglo-American conceptions is represented by a move from I to II (roughly 1970–1990) in the "center of gravity" in the field of international commercial arbitration. This figure is limited to one period of transformation and largely to the central actors within the arbitration field. It seeks to show how the different actors are positioned with respect to the core of international commercial arbitration around 1970 and around 1990. The arrows show the direction of influence. The thin arrows show the more or less "disciple" relationship between two generations. The two thicknesses of other arrows show the relative strength of the influence. The numbers in parentheses are the number of people we interviewed who can be placed in these positions.

Phase I.

1. This phase is characterized by the reinvention, promotion, and institutionalization of international commercial arbitration out of the contributions of leading Continental academics, the International Chamber of Commerce, senior judges, and professional notables. We call this pioneering generation the "grand old men."

2. The leading academics contributed the "technology," especially the *lex mercatoria.*

3. The International Chamber of Commerce provided the institutional support and legitimacy in the world of business.

4. Senior judges brought the acceptance and recognition of the official justice system.

5. Professional notables brought connections and legitimacy with the domestic legal professions.

6. The Anglo-American law firms played a relatively small role.

Phase II.

1. This phase is characterized by the routinization and general acceptance of international commercial arbitration for business transactions, and its conduct as a form of "offshore litigation." The new center of gravity is farther from academic law and hostile to the *lex mercatoria.* A more precise division of labor can be seen in the new phase.

2. The Continental boutiques, containing many disciples of the earlier generations, provide the core of arbitrators for most cases.

3. The arbitration bureaucrats (including the ICC today), many of whom are also disciples of the earlier generation, contribute specific arbitration know-how and management.

4. The senior academics, senior judges, and professional notables continue to provide credibility and stature for the very high-stakes and politically sensitive cases. (Notables from areas new to arbitration also help to establish arbitration in new areas.)

5. The Anglo-American law firms provide much of the resources, clients, emphasis on fact-finding, and adversarial lawyering, and they also provide the major connections to general counsel and the business community.

References

Caplan, Lincoln. 1993. *Skadden: Power, Money, and the Rise of a Legal Empire.* New York: Farrar, Straus and Giroux.

Carbonneau, Thomas. 1989. *Alternative Dispute Resolution: Melting the Lances and Dismounting the Steeds.* Champaign: University of Illinois Press.

Clow, Robert, and Patricia Stewart. 1990. "International Arbitration: Storming the Citadels." *International Financial Law Review,* March, 1.

de Ly, Filip. 1992. *International Business Law and Lex Mercatoria.* North Holland, Netherlands: Elsevier.

Gordon, Robert. 1984. "The Ideal and the Actual in the Law: Fantasies and Practices of New York City Lawyers, 1870–1910." In Gerard Gawalt, ed., *The New High Priests: Lawyers in Post-Civil War America.* Westport, Conn.: Greenwood Press.

Hunt, Alan. 1993. *Explorations in Law and Society: Toward a Constitutive Theory of Law.* New York: Routledge.

Lalive, Pierre. 1991. "L'independence des arbitres dans le systeme CCL" 9, no. 1 *Bulletin of the Swiss Arbitration Association 46–48.*

Lowenfeld, Andreas. 1985. "The Two-Way Mirror: International Arbitration as Comparative Procedure." *Michigan Yearbook of International Legal Studies, 163–85.*

Margolick, David. 1993. *Undue Influence: The Epic Battle for the Johnson and Johnson Fortune.* New York: William Morrow.

Nelson, Robert L. 1988. *Partners with Power: Social Transformation of the Large Law Firm.* Berkeley and Los Angeles: University of California Press.

Ridgeway, G. 1938. *Merchants of Peace.* Boston: Little, Brown.

[9]

GETTING ALONG: THE EVOLUTION OF DISPUTE RESOLUTION REGIMES IN INTERNATIONAL TRADE ORGANIZATIONS

*Andrea Kupfer Schneider**

* Assistant Professor of Law, Marquette University Law School. J.D. Harvard Law School 1992, A.B. Princeton University. I am grateful to Jeffrey Atik, Frank Garcia, and Cherie O'Neal Taylor for their very helpful comments.

In the face of the remarkable growth of international organizations in the last fifty years, scholars in multiple disciplines have sought to explain why and how states cooperate. Dispute resolution is one of the most crucial components of international cooperation. Examining the dispute resolution regimes of international organizations in light of these theories can inform and help reform these evolving regimes.[1]

1. With this article, I hope to answer the continuing call to integrate law with other disciplines, including political science, international relations theory, and economics. *See, e.g.*, Kenneth W. Abbott, *Modern International Relations Theory: A Prospectus for International Lawyers*, 14 Yale J. Int'l L. 335 (1989); Anne-Marie Slaughter Burley, *International Law and International Relations Theory: A Dual Agenda*, 87 Am. J. Int'l L. 205 (1993) [hereinafter *A Dual Agenda*]; Anne-Marie Slaughter et al., *International Law and International Relations Theory: A New Generation of Interdisciplinary Scholarship*, 92 Am.

I. Importance of Studying International Dispute Resolution Regimes

The creation of the North American Free Trade Agreement ("NAFTA")[2] and the World Trade Organization ("WTO")[3] in this decade has clearly shifted the focus on international trade from bilateral agreements to multilateral and global agreements. This historic trend towards the growth of international trade organizations was accelerated by the apparent success of the European Union's efforts in the 1990's to revitalize the European economy and create the internal market of 1992.[4] The drive to mimic the European Union ("EU")[5] (and combat its strength) was then seen in the proliferation of regional organizations such as NAFTA, MERCOSUR,[6] Association of Southeast Asian Nations ("ASEAN"),[7] and the proposed Free Trade of the Americas.[8]

J. Int'l L. 367 (1998) (noting the increasing number of times that international lawyers and political scientists have drawn on each other's work).

2. North American Free Trade Agreement, Dec. 17, 1992, 32 I.L.M. 289 [hereinafter NAFTA].

3. Agreement Embodying the Results of the Uruguay Round of Trade Negotiations, Apr. 15, 1994, 33 I.L.M. 1125 (1994) [hereinafter WTO].

4. There is no question that trying to imitate the European Community ("EC") during the 1970s or 80s hardly seemed attractive. The paralysis of the European Commission and the member states is well-documented and the lack of progress in breaking down barriers led to accusations of "Euroscleroris." *See, e.g.*, John McCormick, The European Union 183–84 (1996). The focus on Europe 1992 and renewed agenda coming from the Single European Act in 1986 finally broke the EC from this pattern. *See* George A. Bermann, *The Single European Act: A New Constitution for the Community?*, 27 Colum. J. Transnat'l L. 529 (1989); Andrew Moravscik, *Negotiating the Single European Act: National Interests and Conventional Statecraft in the European Community*, 45 Int'l Org. 19 (1991) [hereinafter *Negotiating the Single European Act*].

5. Treaty on European Union, Feb. 7, 1992, 1992 O.J. (C224) 1. The EU was built on the original European Economic Community. Treaty Establishing the European Economic Community Mar. 25, 1957, 298 U.N.T.S. 11, [hereinafter Treaty of Rome].

6. MERCOSUR stands for Common Market of the South. It entered into force in 1992 following the adoption of the Treaty of Asunción in 1991. Treaty Establishing a Common Market, Mar. 26, 1991, Arg.–Braz.–Para.–Uru., 30 I.L.M. 1041 [hereinafter Treaty of Asuncion]. The common market envisioned by MERCOSUR has not yet been established. *See* Cherie O'Neal Taylor, *Dispute Resolution as a Catalyst for Economic Integration and an Agent for Deepening Integration: NAFTA and MERCOSUR?*, 17 Nw. J. Int'l L. & Bus. 850 (1996–97) [hereinafter *Dispute Resolution as a Catalyst*].

7. *See* Chad Bowman, *Southeast Asia Leaders Adopt 'Hanoi Plan' That Speeds Trade, Investment Liberalization*, 15 Int'l Trade Rep. 2122 (1998); Jason Gutierrez, *ASEAN Members Decide to Keep Free-Trade Target Despite Crisis*, 15 Int'l Trade Rep. 1299 (1998); *see also* Nobuo Kiriyama, *Institutional Evolution In Economic Integration: A Contribution To Comparative Institutional Analysis For International Economic Organization*, 19 U. Pa. J. Int'l Econ. L. 53 (1998) (applying economic analysis to ASEAN).

8. *See* Rossella Brevetti, *FTAA Negotiating Groups Converge on Miami for Official Talks*, 15 Int'l Trade Rep. 1510 (1998); Frank J. Garcia, *"Americas Agreement"—An Interim Stage in Building the Free Trade Area of the Americas*, 35 Colum. J. Transnat'l L. 63 (1996); Frank J. Garcia, *Decisionmaking and Dispute Resolution in the Free Trade Area*

At the same time, and no doubt in conjunction with the growth of trade organizations, international trade has become increasingly important both economically and politically. With each year, states find that an increasing part of their economy is dependent upon international trade, and the ripple effect of economic troubles has become more and more apparent even in the last year.[9] With the growing importance of international trade and investment, these issues have taken a front row seat in domestic politics. The debate over Fast Track authority in the United States,[10] the battle over International Monetary Fund ("IMF") programs in Asia,[11] the French agricultural strikes,[12] the uproar over mad cow disease,[13] and domestic support for defiance vis-a-vis the international economic community[14] are but a few examples of the passion international trade can evoke on the domestic political scene.

---

of the Americas: An Essay in Trade Governance, 18 MICH J. INT'L L. 357 (1997) [hereinafter *Essay in Trade Governance*].

9. *See* David Barboza, *Dow Up 23.17 As Late Rally Salvages Prices*, N.Y. TIMES, June 13, 1998, at D1; Federal News Service, *Hearing of the House Banking and Financial Services Committee Subject: Global Economic Problems Chaired By Representative Jim Leach*, September 14, 1998; Nicholas D. Kristof, *World Ills Are Obvious, the Cures Much Less So*, N.Y. TIMES, Feb. 18, 1999, at A1 (discussing how economic problems in the Far East impact the U.S. economy); Seth Mydans, *Crisis Aside, What Pains Indonesia is the Humiliation*, N.Y. TIMES, Mar. 10, 1998, at A9; Seth Mydans, *The Thai Gamble: Devaluing Currency to Revive Economy*, N.Y. TIMES, July 3, 1997, at D1; Alessandra Stanley, *In Dark Times, Russia's Economic Chief Looks on Bright Side*, N.Y. TIMES, Dec. 3, 1997, at A13; *The World Economy: Could It Happen Again?*, ECONOMIST, Feb. 20, 1999, at 19.

10. Fast Track authority grants the President the ability to negotiate trade agreements without any amendments by the Senate during ratification. On the Fast Track battle see Michael Carrier, *All Aboard the Congressional Fast Track: From Trade to Beyond*, 29 GEO. WASH. J. INT'L. L. & ECON. 687 (1996); Cherie O'Neal Taylor, *Fast Track, Trade Policy, and Free Trade Agreements: Why the NAFTA Turned Into a Battle*, 28 GEO. WASH. J. INTL. L. & ECON. 1 (1994); Charles Tiefer, *"Alongside" the Fast Track: Environmental and Labor Issues in FTAA*, 7 MINN. J. GLOBAL TRADE 329 (1998); Jill Abramson with Steven Greenhouse, *Labor Victory on Trade Bill Reveals Power*, N.Y. TIMES, Nov. 12, 1997, at A1; Peter Baker & Paul Blustein, *Clinton Searches for Middle on 'Fast Track'*, WASH. POST, Sept. 11, 1997, at A8; *'Fast Track' is Derailed*, N.Y. TIMES, Nov. 11, 1997, at A26; and *The Fast-Track Fight*, WASH. POST, Sept. 12, 1997, at A24.

11. *See* Nicholas D. Kristof, *Has the I.M.F. Cured or Harmed Asia? Dispute Rages After Months of Crisis*, N.Y. TIMES, Apr. 23, 1998, at D3; John W. Head, *Lessons From the Asian Financial Crisis: The Role of the IMF and the United States*, 7 KAN. J.L. & PUB. POL'Y., Spring 1998, at 70; *see generally* Rumu Sarkar, *The Legal Implications of Financial Sector Reform in Emerging Capital Markets*, 13 AM. U. INT'L. L. REV. 705 (1998).

12. *See* Maggie Urry, *Farmers Hope for a Richer Harvest*, FIN. TIMES (LONDON), Apr. 30, 1998, at 7; Craig A. Whitney, *World Briefing: France: Farmers Protest in Paris*, N.Y. TIMES, Feb. 9, 1999, at A8; *World News Briefs: Belgium: Farmers Protest*, N.Y. TIMES, Feb. 23, 1999, at A6.

13. *See* John Darnton, *Europe Orders Ban on Exports of British Beef*, N.Y. TIMES, Mar. 28, 1996, at A1; Alan Cowell, *Disease Tests European Cooperation*, N.Y. TIMES, Mar. 28, 1996, at A8.

14. *See* Mark Landler, *Malaysia Says Its Much-Criticized Finance Strategy Has Worked*, N.Y. TIMES, Feb. 14, 1999, at A10.

These events have spurred and accompanied the evolution of a variety of different dispute resolution regimes. These regimes evolved from differences in the international organizations themselves, their members and their goals. As the number of international organizations continues to grow, it has become increasingly important to categorize and analyze these dispute resolution regimes. While it sometimes appears as if each new international organization is reinventing the wheel in trying to figure out the balance between negotiation and adjudication, between supremacy over domestic laws and sovereignty of member states, some guidelines and general rules can be detected. Systematizing the regimes of dispute resolution and understanding their differences and unique balances will assist in both advising new organizations in setting up their dispute resolution systems and advising existing organizations on improving their dispute resolution mechanisms.

Furthermore, as more international trade organizations establish dispute resolution regimes that move away from negotiation, international law is being created in a way wholly different from the traditional model of international law. International treaties and customary law[15] are the two primary sources of international law.[16] Yet today, decisions handed down by international courts such as the European Court of Justice ("ECJ"), or other adjudicatory bodies, such as the WTO, are increasingly prominent on the international landscape and in relations between countries. These decisions, however, are ranked as the fourth source in international law[17] and have not been traditionally considered as binding as treaties or customary law.[18] One could argue that decisions issued by organizations created by treaties (i.e., the EU, WTO, NAFTA) are law under the original treaty, but the scope and breadth of these decisions seem to stretch this argument to the limit. We are faced with a pattern of extensive judicial lawmaking, yet an international consensus on the force of this law is lacking.

It is crucial that we examine the methods used to make these international decisions. While much focus has been given to the legislative processes in international organizations,[19] much more attention is

15. Customary law is created by state practice and *opinio juris*, the legal belief that such state action is legally required. Prior to their codification in treaties, laws concerning such diverse subjects as maritime boundaries, diplomatic immunities and actions for treaty breach were all customary laws.

16. U.N. Charter, Statute of the International Court of Justice, Chapter II, Article 38.

17. *Id.*

18. MARK W. JANIS, AN INTRODUCTION TO INTERNATIONAL LAW 141 (1993).

19. *See, e.g., Negotiating the Single European Act, supra* note 4, at 7 (focusing on how states negotiated qualified majority voting rules of the Single European Act); Joel Trachtman, *The Theory of the Firm and the Theory of the International Economic Organization: Toward Comparative Institutional Analysis*, 17 NW. J.INT'L L. & BUS. 470, 543–549 (1996–

needed at this stage of lawmaking. Increasingly, treaties have left their interpretation to some form of adjudicatory body rather than resorting to amending the treaty or creating new law legislatively. Thus, studying dispute resolution regimes and the variations that exist is a necessary first step in assessing how this new type of international law is being created.[20]

This article first explores five legal factors that differentiate between the types of dispute resolution regimes. These five factors—direct effect, standing, supremacy, transparency and enforcement—are not exhaustive. However, it is the differences in each of these factors and the combination of these factors that have dictated the form and function of the four current dispute resolution regimes currently in use by international trade organizations. Direct effect, standing, and supremacy are derived from legal theories of integration. When legal scholars have examined the development of international organizations, these factors have been isolated as determining the level of "constitutionalization" of the organization[21] and the extent to which dispute resolution is integrated into the domestic legal fabric. Direct effect measures the scope of rights granted to private actors. Standing, the opposite side of the same coin, determines whether rights under the agreement can be asserted by private actors. Supremacy reflects member states' willingness to relinquish sovereignty. Transparency refers to the clarity of procedures and decisions, and the extent to which they are made public. It has become an important factor in assessing the legitimacy of international organizations and clearly contributes independently to a regime's effectiveness.[22] Finally, enforcement measures the effectiveness of any international organization by focusing upon its compliance record.

Next, this article introduces a four-part clarification of dispute resolution regimes. I call these four regimes "Negotiation," "Investment Arbitration," "International Court," and "Supranational Adjudication." The Negotiation Regime is the place to start in analyzing dispute resolution. On the continuum of each of the legal factors outlined, it is

---

97) [hereinafter *Theory of the Firm*] (discussing the economic impact of voting rules changes in the Single European Act); Stephen Zamora, *Voting in International Economic Organizations*, 74 AM. J. INT'L L. 566 (1980).

20. For additional literature on judicial versus legislative lawmaking, *see* GUIDO CALABRESI, A COMMON LAW FOR THE AGE OF STATUTES (1982).

21. *See Dispute Resolution as a Catalyst*, *supra* note 6; Joseph H.H. Weiler, *The Transformation of Europe*, 100 YALE L.J. 2403 (1991) [hereinafter *The Transformation of Europe*]. For a slightly different approach to constitutionalization, *see* Ernst-Ulrich Petersmann, *Constitutionalism and International Organizations*, 17 NW. J. INT'L L. & BUS. 398 (1996–97).

22. *See, e.g.*, Juliet Lodge, *Transparency and Democratic Legitimacy*, 32 J. COMM. MKT. STUD. 343 (1994).

clearly the weakest in all of the factors.[23] Other regimes have evolved depending on how the organization has moved along the range on each of these variables. In the Investment Arbitration Regime, direct effect and standing for private actors is provided. In addition, enforcement is through domestic courts and remains relatively easy compared to other adjudication options. In Investment Arbitration, however, supremacy is limited to a single decision, transparency is optional, and remedies are limited. In the International Adjudication Regime, there is supremacy under international law, transparency of decisions, and, increasingly, a wider range of remedies. Again, however, this regime provides no direct effect, no standing for private actors, and enforcement that is limited to international law. The Supranational Court Regime moves along the continuum in all of these factors, providing direct effect, standing for private actors, supremacy, transparency, and enforcement with strong remedies. The choice of regimes could look like this:

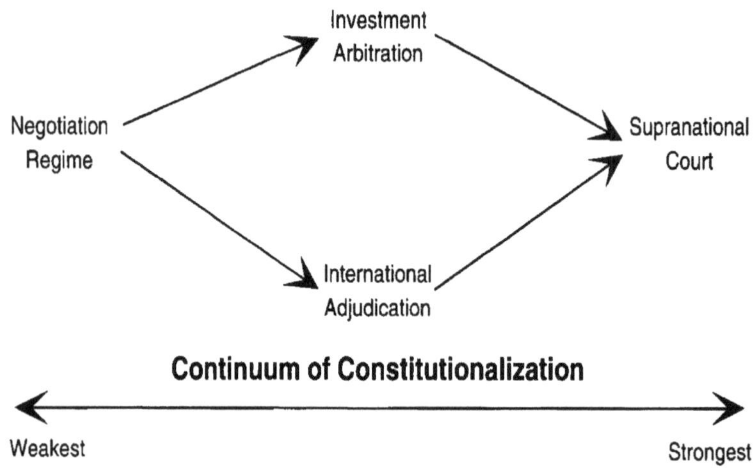

After reviewing the types of regimes, the next two sections in the article attempt to assess the effectiveness of current dispute settlement regimes. These sections turn first to variables from several disciplines, including law, political science and economics. After these theories and the variables that are most important to them have been identified, section four of this article then takes the dispute resolution regimes and studies them in light of the theoretical variables. This examination pro-

23. Many would argue that negotiation is the most effective way to resolve disputes because it relies on the relative power of states. The legal factors discussed in this article, however, measure the level of constitutionalization or judicialization of the regime. By this measure, the Negotiation Regime is the weakest.

vides an assessment of which regimes will be more effective given certain combinations of these variables and offers an analysis of which theory seems to best explain the current combination of dispute resolution regimes.

In section five of the article, I look at directions for future work in this area. I first look at problems and weaknesses with this regime analysis. For one, this study uses only one type of organization, which may make the lessons less applicable to other international organizations. Second, some of these regimes are based on emerging organizations so that there are very few cases available for testing and assessing. Third, this study assumes that the legal factors of each dispute resolution regime are each of equal value and also does not distinguish in importance between the theoretical variables listed in part three. Finally, this study assumes that the legal factors by which each regime is established are in fact the product of rational negotiation. In fact, as the EU demonstrates, the dispute resolution system could evolve differently and beyond the point where the original drafters of the organization intended.

The final component of section five suggests additional areas of research and study that would be useful in further developing this regime analysis. The lessons from having performed the regime analysis, even with its weaknesses, ultimately lead to questions about where we go from here. What can we learn about the evolution of dispute resolution systems? What advice can we provide to emerging international trade organizations? What further research should be done in order to draw lessons across legal disciplines from human rights, the environment, and other areas?

II. Differentiating Between Dispute Resolution Regimes

After reaching an understanding as to why the study of dispute resolution regimes is necessary and timely, we now turn to an examination of the legal factors that differentiate between these regimes. I have previously used these legal factors in an analysis of private involvement in international trade dispute resolution.[24] Here we use these factors in order to categorize existing dispute resolution regimes.[25]

---

24. *See* Andrea K. Schneider, *Democracy in Dispute Resolution: Individual Rights in International Trade Organizations*, 19 U. Pa. J. Int'l. Econ. L. 587 (1998).

25. The factors listed in this section are no doubt incomplete. Other factors of inquiry could include whether the decisions have precedential value, whether the decision is subject to review or appeal, and whether the panel is rotating or standing. *See e.g.*, Laurence R.

A. *Legal Factors Differentiating Between Dispute Resolution Regimes*

1. Direct Effect of Rights

In looking at the four dispute resolution regimes, one of the legal factors that differs among the regimes is whether or not private actors have rights under the treaty establishing the trade agreement. The phrases "self-executing" and "direct effect" are used synonymously and indicate those dispute resolution regimes where private actors do have rights granted under the treaty.[26] When private actors are granted direct effect of rights under the dispute resolution regimes, these actors can then protect their trade rights in their own domestic courts or in multinational fora.[27]

Most current trade agreements do not provide for direct effect of rights. Historically, Friendship, Commerce and Navigation Treaties ("FCN Treaties") were considered self-executing in the United States.[28] Ironically, although trade agreements have become more important—covering and affecting more sectors of the economy—recent trade agreements have not provided for direct effect.[29] As discussed below,

---

Helfer and Anne-Marie Slaughter, *Toward a Theory of Effective Supranational Adjudication*, 107 YALE L.J. 273 (1997).

26. *See* Schneider, *supra* note 24, at 595–96; *see also* T.C. HARTLEY, THE FOUNDATIONS OF EUROPEAN COMMUNITY LAW, 183–218 (1988); Ronald A Brand, *Direct Effects of International Economic Law in the United States and the European Union*, 17 NW. J. INT'L L. & BUS. 556 (1996–97); Pierre Pescatore, *The Doctrine of "Direct Effect": An Infant Disease of Community Law*, 8 EUR. L. REV. 155 (1983).

27. *See, e.g.*, Matt Schaefer, *Are Private Remedies in Domestic Courts Essential for International Trade Agreements to Perform Constitutional Functions with Respect to Sub-Federal Governments?*, 17 NW. J. INT'L L. & BUS. 609 (1996–97).

28. Asakura v. City of Seattle, 265 U.S. 332, 44 S.Ct. 515 (1924) (Japanese national sued the City of Seattle for the ability to open a pawn shop). The Court, quoting language from the treaty: "[t]he citizens. . . of each of the High Contracting Parties shall have the liberty to . . . reside in the territories of the other to carry on trade. . .[,]" held in favor of the Japanese national. For more on self-executing treaties, see Jordan J. Paust, *Self-Executing Treaties*, 82 AM. J. INT'L L. 760 (1988); Carlos Manuel Vázquez, *The Four Doctrines of Self-Executing Treaties*, 89 AM. J. INT'L L. 695 (1995); and Charles D. Siegal, *Individual Rights Under Self-Executing Extradition Treaties—Dr. Alvarez-Machain's Case*, 13 LOY. L.A. INT'L & COMP. L.J. 765 (1991).

29. In fact, these treaties have explicitly stated that there is no direct effect. *See* Uruguay Round Agreements Act, Pub. L. No. 103-465, 108 Stat. 4809 (1994). "No provision of any of the Uruguay Round Agreements, nor the application of any such provision to any person or circumstance, that is inconsistent with any law of the United States shall have effect." *Id.* at § 102(a)(1). See JOHN H. JACKSON, THE WORLD TRADING SYSTEM: LAW AND POLICY OF INTERNATIONAL ECONOMIC RELATIONS 79–105 (2nd ed. 1997) (discussing broadly U.S. law and the application of international trade treaties); John H. Jackson, *U.S. Constitutional Law Principles and Foreign Trade Law and Policy*, *in* NATIONAL CONSTITUTIONS AND INTERNATIONAL ECONOMIC LAW 65 (Meinhard Hilf & Ernst-Ulrich Petersmann eds., 1993) (reviewing the history of the application of trade treaties in U.S. law). *See also* Martin A. Rogoff, *Interpretation of International Agreements by Domestic Courts and the*

the Negotiation Regime and International Adjudication Regime have no direct effect. The Investor Arbitration Regime provides direct effect for only a narrow range of trade rights typically under bilateral investment treaties ("BIT's"). Only in the Supranational Court Regime do private actors have direct effect of a broad array of trade rights.

What we have witnessed in the last fifty years is an increased number of trade agreements with increased importance to domestic economies. These trade treaties have been designed to influence private actors—to invest, to import, and to export—and to encourage this behavior by promising governmental restraint from inequitable treatment. Nonetheless, although private actors make decisions based on the rights provided in these treaties, trade treaties have moved away from providing direct effect of rights.[30]

2. Standing before the Dispute Resolution Body

Closely linked to direct effect of rights are the fora available for private actors to protect these rights. Dispute resolution regimes differ in the identity of the parties entitled to bring cases and complaints to any dispute resolution body. Traditionally, under international law, only recognized states participated in dispute resolution, either through negotiations or in international courts.[31] Both the Negotiation Regime and the International Adjudication Regime reflect this traditional approach to standing. In the last fifty years, however, regimes have evolved that also provide standing to other entities. For example, in the Investor Arbitration Regime, private actors have standing to bring limited actions against states. In the Supranational Court Regime, private actors also have standing. In addition, an oversight body has standing to bring a case in the Supranational Court Regime.

Much has been written about the importance of standing because it affects the ability of parties to enforce a trade agreement. The advantages of private actor standing seem to fall into two major categories. First, when a private actor or an oversight body has the ability to

Politics of International Treaty Relations: Reflections on Some Recent Decisions of the United States Supreme Court, 11 AM. U.J. INT'L L. & POL'Y 559 (1996).

30. I am grateful to Steve Charnovitz for an interesting discussion on the anomaly of increasing importance of trade treaties and decreasing rights from these treaties, particularly when compared with human rights treaties that have moved more consistently to provide increased rights and direct effect of these rights. *See* Schneider, *supra* note 24, at 598–600. *See also* Thomas Cottier and Krista Nadakavukaren Schefer, *The Relationship Between World Trade Organization Law, National and Regional Law*, 1 J. INT'L ECON. L. 83 (1998) (outlining the advantages and disadvantages of direct effect of WTO law).

31. *See* Schneider, *supra* note 24, at 627.

enforce a trade agreement, more cases will be brought.[32] While states (and oversight bodies) face political obstacles to bringing cases against other states, private actors do not share this concern. Therefore, more suits are apt to be brought. Further, private actors are better able to police the agreement because they are directly affected by any violation and make an economic assessment based on that injury.

The second advantage of private actor standing is that citizens police their own government's compliance with the agreement.[33] If that task were left to states alone, no state would bring a case against itself. The best evidence of the significance of standing in terms of an international organization's development is the number of important EU cases brought by a private actor.[34]

3. Supremacy over Domestic Law

The third legal factor differentiating between dispute resolution regimes is whether the dispute resolution regimes create binding law for their member states. Under international law, any international agreement appropriately created is supreme to domestic law. (Of course, the supremacy of international law in the domestic arena is left to each state to determine.) However, states vary widely in terms of how and when

32. "By refusing to permit private parties to appear before the Court, the founders of the International Court foreclosed, as it turns out, the most fertile source of international litigation." JANIS, *supra* note 18, at 122; *see also* Schneider, *supra* note 24, at 629–30 & nn. 126–30.

33. *See* Robert Cover, *The Uses of Jurisdictional Redundancy: Interest, Ideology, and Innovation, in* NARRATIVE, VIOLENCE AND THE LAW: THE ESSAYS OF ROBERT COVER 51–93 (Martha Minow et al. eds., 1992) (arguing that jurisdictional redundancy, as exists between the federal and state system in the U.S. and also between the domestic systems and the EU, can effectively deal with the problems of the elite in a political system and is an appropriate method of dealing with conflicting values in a society). *But see* Kenneth W. Dam, *Extraterritoriality in an Age of Globalization: The Hartford Fire Case*, 1993 SUP. CT. REV. 289, 320–22 (1994) (arguing that, in the application of extraterritorial securities laws, the existence of private plaintiffs improperly moves the locus of foreign policy decision-making from the executive branch to the judicial branch).

34. *See* Case 26/62, N.V. Algemene Transport-en Expeditie Onderneming Van Gend en Loos v. Nederlandse Administratie der Belastingen 1963 E.C.R. 1 [hereinafter Van Gend en Loos] (establishing direct effect of the Treaty of Rome); Case 6/64, Costa v. Ente Nazionale per L'Energia Elettrica 1964 E.C.R. 585 [hereinafter Costa v. ENEL] (establishing supremacy of the Treaty of Rome); Case 41/75, Van Duyn v. Home Office 1974 E.C.R. 1337 [hereinafter Van Duyn] (establishing direct effect of directives); Case 43/75, Defrenne v. Societe Anonyme Belge De Navigation Aerienna Sabena 1976 E.C.R. 455 [hereinafter Defrenne] (recognizing horizontal direct effect [direct effect vis-à-vis private actors] from the Treaty of Rome); Case 106/89, Marleasing SA v. La Commercial International De Alimentacion SA 1990 E.C.R. I-4135 [hereinafter Marleasing] (finding no horizontal direct effect in the case of directives); Cases 6/90 and 9/90, Francovich and Others v. Italian Republic 1991 E.C.R. 5357 [hereinafter Francovich] (awarding damages stemming from non-implementation of a directive).

international law is incorporated into domestic law. [35] Furthermore, while many states are clear on the role of international treaties in their domestic legal system[36] few states have clearly set forth how international decisions arising from dispute resolution regimes should be treated. Therefore, we must look to each dispute resolution regime to see how decisions affect the member states and whether those decisions are considered supreme to domestic law.

The importance of supremacy in international organizations cannot be doubted. In the end, it is up to each state to comply with and enforce international law. If a domestic dispute resolution empowers the domestic judiciary to enforce an international decision, it is wholly different in scope and effectiveness than a dispute resolution regime in which doubt exists whether there is supremacy over domestic law.[37]

4. Transparency

The transparency of a dispute resolution regimes directly affects how it is used and perceived by the member states involved in each of the dispute resolution regimes. In examining the transparency of a dispute resolution regimes, we should examine both the rules of the dispute resolution regimes as well as the decisions resulting from the dispute resolution regimes. The procedures for the dispute resolution regimes set forth below vary from ad hoc and informal to published, clear and strict procedures. Similarly, results of using the dispute resolution regimes vary from confidential negotiated agreements or arbitration awards to regularly published tribunal decisions.

The level of transparency of the dispute resolution regimes is important in three ways that I have set forth previously:[38] publicity, precedent, and predictability. Publicity describes the level of public knowledge about the dispute resolution regimes. For example, when

35. Schneider, *supra* note 24, at 609–13. *See also* Symposium, *The Interaction Between National Courts and International Tribunals*, 28 N.Y.U. J. INT'L L. & POL'Y (1995–96).

36. *See, e.g.*, U.S. CONST. art. VI, cl. 2. ("This Constitution, and the Laws of the United States which shall be made in Pursuance thereof; and all Treaties made, or which shall be made, under the Authority of the United States, shall be the supreme Law of the Land. . . .") This interpretation of treaties is similar to the one in the United Kingdom and other Commonwealth states in which courts have found international treaties to be equal to national law. In these latter states, however, separate implementing legislation beyond ratification is needed to provide direct effect under these treaties. This has also been the case in the United States in more recent treaty implementation where treaties are not given direct effect unless expressly provided for in separate implementation legislation.

37. See for example Gabriel Albarracín et al., *The Relationship Between the Laws Derived From the Organs of MERCOSUR and the Legal Systems of the Countries That Comprise MERCOSUR*, 4 J. INT'L & COMP. L., 897 (1998) for a discussion on the confusion within the MERCOSUR as to how MERCOSUR laws should be applied.

38. *See* Schneider, *supra* note 24, at 613–14.

results are published, the process is clear, and decisions are explained, member states are more likely to comply with those rulings.[39] Precedent refers to the ability of dispute resolution regimes to provide persuasive or binding authority. While the doctrine of stare decisis is not used in international tribunals, these tribunals clearly cite previous decisions as persuasive.[40] Likewise, predictability of a dispute resolution regime is very important to its users because it creates confidence in the system.[41] Transparent rules and clear decisions are more likely to encourage states or private actors to become involved in a dispute resolution regime. Overall, transparency increases the legitimacy of the regime.[42]

5. Enforcement & Punishment

The final factor differentiating between dispute resolution regimes is the type of enforcement each regime provides. Unfortunately, the lack of compliance with international law and global enforcement mecha-

39. *See generally*, ABRAM CHAYES & ANTONIA HANDLER CHAYES, THE NEW SOVEREIGNTY: COMPLIANCE WITH INTERNATIONAL REGULATORY AGREEMENTS 22 (1995).

40. See for example, the WTO Shrimp-Turtle case, which makes reference to earlier GATT and WTO decisions. United States-Import Prohibition of Certain Shrimp and Shrimp Products, WT/DS58/AB/R (Oct. 12, 1998). For a critique of the current analysis on precedent, see Raj Bhala, *The Myth About Stare Decisis and International Trade Law* (Part One of a Trilogy), 14 AM. U. INT'L L. REV. 845 (1999).

41. The argument has also been made that permanent tribunals versus ad hoc panels add to predictability of a regime. *See, e.g., Dispute Resolution as a Catalyst, supra* note 6, at 890–899. Lack of regular use can also hurt predictability. *See, e.g.*, Helfer & Slaughter, *supra* note 25 at 301–03. For example, the lack of case law precedent as well as the review process make the arbitral facility under the International Centre for the Settlement of Investment Disputes (ICSID) less appealing to investors. Difficulty with interference by national courts has made ICSID even more unreliable. *See* Maritimes Int'l Nominees Establishment v. Republic of Guinea, 693 F.2d 1094 (D.C. Cir. 1982) (ICSID, Case No. ARB/84/4) (refusing to enforce the ICSID arbitral award); Monroe Leigh, *Judicial Decisions*, 81 AM. J. INT'L L. 206, 222–25 (1987) (detailing AMCO Asia Corp. v. Republic of Indonesia, ICSID Case No. ARB/81/1, 25 I.L.M. 1439 (1986), where the Indonesian government annulled the ICSID decision on the grounds that ICSID "manifestly exceeded its powers.")

42. *See* Pub. Citizen v. Office of the U.S. Trade Rep., 804 F. Supp. 385 (D.D.C. 1992); *see, e.g.*, Patti Goldman, *The Democratization of the Development of United States Trade Policy*, 27 CORNELL INT'L L. J. 631 (1994) (arguing that the secrecy and lack of public input in U.S. trade policy results in a policy that is biased toward trade liberalization at the expense of other values); Robert F. Housman, *Democratizing International Trade Decision-making*, 27 CORNELL INT'L L.J. 699 (1994) (discussing the undemocratic nature of international trade decision-making); Paul B. Stephan, *Accountability and International Lawmaking: Rules, Rents and Legitimacy*, 17 NW. J. INT'L L. & BUS. 681 (1996–97). There has even been litigation over this subject. In response to complaints about lack of transparency, a U.S. District Court ordered the United States Trade Representative to grant public access to submissions to GATT dispute resolution panels. *See* 804 F. Supp. 385 *supra*. The U.S. government is currently trying to increase transparency in the WTO. *See, e.g.*, Peter Menyasz, *U.S. Transparency Goals Seen Unlikely Focus of 1998 Review*, 15 INT'L TRADE REP. 1609 (1998).

nisms is a typical and somewhat tired critique of the field.[43] If one stops there, it would cripple further analysis of why international law is actually followed most of the time. That is why a focus on improving compliance with international law is necessary as we continue to create new institutions and new rules that provide us with the opportunity to increase enforcement and compliance.[44] Furthermore, particularly in the area of trade, it has been long argued that having a system of enforcement is important to promote trade.[45]

The existing dispute resolution regimes discussed below provide opportunities for enforcement at three different levels. The first level is when the trade agreement includes no formal adjudicatory procedure to remedy non-compliance. Any dispute about compliance would require additional negotiations or a new trade agreement. The second level is when the trade agreement has created some body to hear disputes over non-compliance. Depending on standing, states or private actors may have the ability to bring cases under the trade agreement in order to enforce the agreement. A third level of enforcement is when states or private actors can bring a case for non-compliance with a *decision* of the dispute resolution body. My prior analogy to traffic laws provides a helpful example here.[46] Creating a speed limit with no police enforcement is the first level of enforcement. The second level is where a police officer is able to write a traffic ticket in order to enforce the speed limit. The third level of enforcement is when an arrest warrant is issued in order to enforce payment of the ticket. Each of the dispute resolution regimes discussed in the article operate at different levels of enforcement.

Dispute resolution regimes also differ in the type of punishment provided to enforce the trade agreement. As dispute resolution regimes have evolved to provide for better enforcement, the punishment options have also improved. Under the Vienna Convention on Treaties, breach of a treaty meant that the non-breaching party may suspend the treaty.[47]

43. *See, e.g.*, Abbott, *Modern International Relations Theory, supra* note 1, at 336–8; G. Richard Shell, *Trade Legalism and Internationa l Relations Theory: An Analysis of the World Trade Organization*, 44 DUKE L.J. 829, 855–56 (1995).

44. *See* CHAYES & CHAYES, *supra* note 39.

45. Private actors will be more likely to trade if they know the rules will be enforced. *See, e.g.* Paul R. Milgrom et al., *The Role Of Institutions in the Revival of Trade: The Law Merchant, Private Judges, and the Champagne Fairs*, 2 ECON. & POL. 1 (1990). Institutions are able to deal with the problem of defection and improve the likelihood of governmental compliance as well. *See* George W. Downs, *Enforcement and the Evolution of Cooperation*, 19 MICH. J. INT'L L. 319 (1998).

46. *See* Schneider, *supra* note 24, at 620.

47. *See* Vienna Convention on the Law of Treaties, *opened for signature* May 23, 1969, art. 60, U.N. Doc. A/Conf. 39/27 (1969) [hereinafter Vienna Convention]. As a last resort, a

Dispute resolution regimes today provide for retaliation under the treaty, fines, and damages to harmed parties. This latter punishment is particularly noteworthy in that it mimics a domestic court's ability to remedy harm and is also narrowly tailored to punish each particular violation. The threat of real economic punishment judicially imposed is a relatively new one for international trade organizations. And although treaty-sanctified retaliation remains a blunt instrument of policy, it is definitely an improvement.[48] The shift in the relative seriousness of these remedies is already evident.[49]

The factors discussed in the previous section outline the variable ranges that dispute resolution systems can take. The following table sets forth the factors above as applied to the four regimes discussed more fully below.

Regimes/ Factors	Negotiation	Investment Arbitration	International Adjudication	Supranational Court
Direct Effect	No	Yes	No	Yes
Standing for Private Actors	No	Yes	No	Yes, directly and indirectly
Supremacy	None	Only as to that award	Supreme, but not integrated into domestic law	Supreme and Integrated
Transparency	Optional	Optional	Yes	Yes
Enforcement	Negotiation	Likely	Varying—None (NAFTA) to Retaliation (WTO)	Fines & Damages; Domestic Remedies also

party to a treaty may terminate its obligation by breach but must confront the consequences addressed by Article 60.

48. *See* Kishore Gawande & Wendy L. Hansen, *Retaliation, Bargaining, and the Pursuit of "Free and Fair" Trade*, 53 INT'L ORG. 117 (1999). Based on empirical work, the authors argue that retaliation and the threat of retaliation can be very effective. They also argue that the WTO will make threats even more powerful.

49. The U.S.-E.U. disputes over beef hormones and bananas demonstrate the gravity and impact of the new punishments provided under the WTO. *See, e.g., U.S. Threatens Europe With Duties in Beef Dispute*, N.Y. TIMES, May 15, 1999, at C2; Elizabeth Olson, *Latest Banana Squabble: Retroactivity of Sanctions*, N.Y. TIMES, Apr. 20, 1999, at C5; David E. Sanger, *Ruling Allows Tariffs by U.S. Over Bananas*, N.Y. TIMES, Apr. 7, 1999, at C1; Elizabeth Olson, *New Flare-Up in U.S.-European Banana Fight*, N.Y. TIMES, Mar. 3, 1999, at A4

B. *Negotiation Regime*

1. Individual Rights & Standing[50]

The first type of regime of an international dispute resolution system is the Negotiation Regime. The Negotiation Regime is exemplified by the dispute settlement system of the General Agreement on Trade and Tariffs ("GATT")[51] as it existed prior to the creation of the WTO as well as the current form of Chapter 20 of the NAFTA.[52] In this regime, most of the factors we have discussed are on the lower end of the range. Typically, individuals are not granted rights under the organizations that use negotiation as their regime nor are individuals involved in the negotiation process. Disputes under this system are resolved informally using diplomacy between states. For example, in a disagreement over alleged dumping, two states might make an ad hoc agreement to change the particular system discussed.[53] Historically, most disputes regarding trade, or anything else, have been resolved in this way.

2. Supremacy

Disputes under this regime are resolved by a negotiated agreement between states. This dispute resolution may result in changes to some law or practice in one or both states. More often, however, this type of dispute resolution agreement will not result in an amendment to an existing treaty or a new treaty itself, but rather will be a lesser type of commitment from the governments. Therefore, this dispute resolution will not be granted supremacy over domestic laws unless it, too, is considered international law under the respective domestic systems.[54]

3. Transparency

In terms of transparency, a negotiated agreement may be publicized, particularly when governments are trying to please a domestic constituency.[55] It may also provide an example for other negotiations over

50. For the purposes of this article, I use individuals and private actors interchangeably.

51. General Agreement on Trade and Tariffs, *opened for signature* Oct. 30, 1947, 61 Stat. A3, 55 U.N.T.S. 187 [hereinafter GATT].

52. NAFTA, *supra* note 2, Chapter 20.

53. *See, e.g., Japan to Extend Voluntary Export Restraints on Automobiles at Current 2.3 Million Units*, 7 INT'L TRADE REP. 115 (1990).

54. Unless this agreement resulted in a new treaty or executive agreement, this agreement would not be considered supreme to U.S. law. *See* Dames & Moore v. Regan, 453 U.S. 654 (1981).

55. For example, U.S. Ambassador to Japan Mike Mansfield announced the voluntary export restraint on Japanese cars in advance of the agreement. *See* Mike Tharp, *Car Pledge by Japanese is Predicted*, N.Y. TIMES, Mar. 26, 1981, at D5. *See also* Clyde H. Farnsworth

similar disputes, although this type of dispute resolution is clearly not precedent for any court.[56] Nor do negotiated agreements create predictability for individuals or other states. Unlike a court case, where previous cases can be analyzed and decisions examined, an upcoming negotiation cannot be easily predicted based on previously negotiated agreements.

4. Enforcement

Enforcement under a negotiation regime of dispute resolution is left to the respective states. There is no oversight institution. Any noncompliance with the underlying trade agreement would put the parties back at the negotiation table in order to work out the dispute. In other words, a negotiation regime relies on "first-order" compliance at all times.[57] States either follow the agreement or renegotiate a new agreement.[58]

C. *Investor Arbitration Regime*

The Investor Arbitration Regime was specifically created to give private actors both rights and remedies under the relevant international treaty. The move toward investment arbitration began with the creation of the International Centre for the Settlement of Investment Disputes ("ICSID") under the aegis of the World Bank.[59] A decade later, the UN Commission for International Trade Law ("UNCITRAL") drafted rules

& Daniel F. Cuff, *"Voluntary" Import Restraint*, N.Y. TIMES, Sept. 20, 1984, at D1. Publication of a draft agreement can also help move the negotiation process along. For example, the Dunkel Draft in the negotiating of the WTO and the White Paper prior to the Single European Act were both publicized. *See* ROBERT E. HUDEC, ENFORCING INTERNATIONAL TRADE LAW 233–39 (1993) [hereinafter ENFORCING INTERNATIONAL TRADE LAW] (discussing the Dunkel Draft of the WTO); Bermann, *supra* note 4, at 530–35 (discussing the political background and negotiating history up to the SEA). There is also the issue of strategic leaks where the information is leaked although not officially made public.

56. *But see*, Paul Lewis, *Europeans Welcome Auto Pact*, N.Y. TIMES, May 4, 1981, at D1 (noting that the Europeans would be requesting a voluntary export restraint similar to the one agreed to between Japan and the United States).

57. Schneider, *supra* note 24, at 617. First order compliance means that there is no enforcement power beyond the establishment of the rule itself.

58. For example, Japan and the U.S. have had to renegotiate their agreement on the auto parts market several times. *See, e.g., High Level Talks Slated With Japan on Auto Agreement*, 14 INT'L TRADE REP. 1714 (1997); *U.S. Frustrated by Japan's Progress on Car Sales, Dealerships in Auto Talks*, 14 INT'L TRADE REP. 1759 (1997); David Sanger, *Bottom Line: Business Over Politics*, N.Y. TIMES, July 30, 1995, at D5.

59. Convention on the Settlement of Investment Disputes Between States and Nationals of Other States, *opened for signature* Mar. 18, 1965, art. 5, 17 U.S.T. 1270, 575 U.N.T.S. 159, 4 I.L.M. 532 (1965) [hereinafter ICSID Convention]. *See also* Thomas L. Brewer, *International Investment Dispute Settlement Procedures: The Regime for Foreign Direct Investment*, 26 LAW & POL'Y INT'L BUS. 633, 655–56 (1995).

for adhoc arbitration.[60] This concept of permitting individuals to bring cases against states has since been copied in bilateral investment treaties[61] in order to encourage foreign direct investment[62] and outlined in NAFTA for investor disputes under Chapter 11B.[63]

1. Individual Rights

Under the treaties that establish investment arbitration, private actors are granted such rights as national treatment[64] or a minimum standard of treatment[65] in the host state. These rights are directly effective. In other

---

60. UNCITRAL Arbitration Rules, U.N. Doc. A/31/17, para. 57, 15 I.L.M. 701 (1976). *See also* ISAAK I. DORE, THE UNCITRAL FRAMEWORK FOR ARBITRATION IN CONTEMPORARY PERSPECTIVE (1993).

61. *See, e.g.*, Argentina-United States: Treaty Concerning the Reciprocal Encouragement and Protection of Investment, Nov. 14, 1991, art. IV, 31 I.L.M. 124, 131 (1992) [hereinafter Argentina-U.S. BIT].

62. *See* Kenneth Vandevelde, *Investment Liberalization and Economic Development: The Role of Bilateral Investment Treaties*, 36 COLUM. J. TRANSNAT'L. L. 501 (1998). The author notes that more than 160 countries have concluded at least one BIT and more than 1300 BIT's have been signed. *Id.* at 503. More than two-thirds of these have been signed since 1990. *Id.* at 503 n.8. *See also* Andrew T. Guzman, *Why LDCs Sign Treaties That Hurt Them: Explaining the Popularity of Bilateral Investment Treaties*, 38 VA. J. INT'L. L. 563 (1998).

63. NAFTA, *supra* note 2, Chapter 11B, at 642–646. A regime similar to investor arbitration is also established in the Environmental Side Accord to NAFTA. North American Agreement on Environmental Cooperation, art. 14(1) *supra* note 2. *See* Rex J. Zedalis, *Claims by Individuals in International Economic Law: NAFTA Developments*, 7 AM. REV. INT'L ARB. 115 (1996); Kal Raustiala, *International "Enforcement of Enforcement" Under the North American Agreement on Environmental Cooperation*, 36 VA. J. INT'L L. 721 (1996); David Lopez, *Dispute Resolution under NAFTA: Lessons from the Early Experience*, 32 TEX. INT'L L. J. 163, 184–192 (1997). A quasi-arbitral system is established under Chapter 19 of NAFTA for antidumping and countervailing duties cases. I do not discuss that process in this article because the panels under Chapter 19 apply national law rather than international law. For more information, see David A. Gantz, *Resolution of Trade Disputes Under NAFTA's Chapter 19: The Lessons of Extending the Binational Panel Process to Mexico*, 29 LAW & POL'Y INT'L BUS. 297 (1998).

64. Individuals granted rights under national treatment will receive the same treatment as the state's nationals. This is also referred to as the Equality of Treatment Doctrine. *See, e.g.*, Treaty of Friendship, Commerce and Navigation, Apr. 2, 1953, U.S.-Japan, art. IV (1), 4 U.S.T. 2063, 2067.

> Nationals and companies of either Party shall be accorded national treatment and most-favored-nation treatment with respect to access to the courts of justice and to administrative tribunals and agencies within the territories of the other Party, in all degrees of jurisdiction, both in pursuit and in defense of their rights.

Id.

65. According to the Minimum Standard of International Justice, a state must grant an alien at least a minimum standard of treatment, even if this means an alien would receive better treatment than the state's own nationals. Interestingly, more recent U.S. treaties combine both the national treatment and minimum standard. *See, e.g.*, Argentina-U.S. BIT, *supra* note 61.

cases, domestic implementing legislation will provide for the rights to become directly effective.[66] This makes sense because these types of treaties are specifically designed to encourage individual investment.

While an Investment Arbitration regime provides rights against the host government, none of these underlying treaties provide direct effect of rights against another individual. In other words, a private actor has no recourse against another private actor under this regime. Investment arbitration is established solely as a right and remedy between a private investor and the host state.[67] Further, because investment arbitration is only available against a host state, nationals have no recourse against their own government. Finally, rights under this regime have limited scope. Investment Arbitration is provided for only the narrow right of national treatment in most regimes. Any state action falling outside those parameters is unreachable.[68]

2. Individual Standing

In investment arbitration, private actors have the ability to bring cases directly against a state. This is quite an historic development in this century. First, individuals were historically seen as nationals of their state and, on the international plane, could only be represented by their government. Second, private suits against a government in domestic courts were also foreclosed due to laws that limited the grounds upon which states could be sued. This meant that foreign investors had little recourse to the host domestic legal system.[69] Third, even if a private ac-

> Each Party shall permit and treat investment, and activities associated therewith, on a basis no less favorable than that accorded in like situations to investment or associated activities of its own nationals or companies .... Investment shall at all times be accorded fair and equitable treatment, shall enjoy full protection and security and shall in no case be accorded treatment less than that required by international law.

Id., at art. II, at 129–30.

66. *See, e.g.*, North American Free Trade Agreement Implementation Act of 1993, Pub. L. No. 103–182, §§ 101–109, 107 Stat. 2057, 2061–68 (codified as amended at 19 U.S.C. § 3311 (1998)).

67. *See* Vandevelde, *supra* note 62, at 510.

68. Compare this to the rights of action under the EU. *See infra* note 98 and accompanying discussion.

69. In fact, in most states the government has full sovereign immunity both in law and in practice. *See* Louis L. Jaffe, *Suits Against Government and Officers: Sovereign Immunity*, 77 HARV. L. REV. 1 (1963). *See also* United States v. Lee, 106 U.S. 196, 204–223 (1882) (stating that the United States may only be sued by its own consent except where Congress has provided).

tor wanted to bring a suit in his own home court against the foreign state, most states had laws that provided foreign sovereign immunity.[70]

In the meantime, international commercial arbitration had become a popular method for resolving commercial disputes between private disputants because it provided a more neutral, fairer, and potentially faster way of resolving disputes.[71] This regime appealed to investors who were concerned with the potential bias, inefficiency, or unfamiliarity of foreign courts. By creating an international arbitration option between individuals and states, creators of this regime hoped that investors would be more willing to bring their business to these states because disputes could be resolved through this international neutral body.

ICSID has jurisdiction over any legal dispute arising out of an investment between a Contracting State and a national of any other Contracting State.[72] For a national of a Contracting State or a Contracting State to initiate proceeding under the ICSID, that party must submit a written request to the Secretary-General of ICSID detailing the issues in dispute, the parties, and consent to arbitration. After the dispute is certified by the Secretary-General of ICSID, an individual can have the case heard by an arbitral panel established by ICSID.[73]

3. Supremacy & Transparency

Arbitration decisions generally provide for damages and not a change in domestic laws.[74] Therefore, the issue of supremacy does not

70. *See, e.g.*, Foreign Sovereign Immunities Act of 1976, 28 U.S.C. § 1604 (1994) ("Subject to existing international agreements to which the United States is a party at the time of enactment of this Act a foreign state shall be immune from the jurisdiction of the courts of the United States. . ."); State Immunity Act, 1978, ch.33, part I (U.K.) (granting foreign sovereign immunity in the United Kingdom).

71. The International Chambers of Commerce (ICC), created in 1923, has been frequently used as a means for arbitration. In 1998, parties from over one hundred states filed a record 466 new requests for arbitration. *See* ICC World Business Organization (last visited Sep. 9, 1999) <http://www.iccwbo.org/court/front_topics/stat.asp>. For a very user-friendly guide to commercial arbitration, see MARTIN HUNTER ET AL., THE FRESHFIELDS GUIDE TO ARBITRATION AND ADR (1993).

72. ICSID Convention, *supra* note 59, art. 25. The parties must, however, consent to the use of the arbitration facility. *See id.* The use of ICSID has not been initiated by a Contracting State in complaint of an individual of another Contracting State even though the potential exists under the Convention provisions. *See generally* David A. Soley, *ICSID Implementation: An Effective Alternative to International Conflict*, 19 INT'L L. 521 (1985) (discussing the ICSID framework for dispute resolution).

73. ICSID Convention, *supra* note 59, art. 36. Unless the Secretary-General finds that the dispute falls outside the jurisdiction of the Centre, he will register the request and notify the parties. *See id.* at art. 36(3).

74. Neither the ICSID or UNCITRAL rules explicitly deny the panel the ability to proscribe a change in the law. However, arbitral panels have thus far only issued monetary awards. See *American Manufacturing & Trading Inc. v. Republic of Zaire*, ICSID ABR/93/1

really arise because there is no new law created. An arbitration decision can also be kept confidential if requested by the parties.[75] This means that the decision cannot provide precedent or predictability in the system because outside lawyers cannot analyze the panel's thinking.

4. Enforcement

In terms of enforcement, an investment arbitration system does provide for relatively effective enforcement. The Convention on the Recognition and Enforcement of Arbitral Awards ("New York Convention") provides that all signatory states shall enforce arbitral awards in their domestic courts.[76] As a result, if a state refuses to pay the arbitral award, the investor can go to the domestic court in that state or in any state where there are commercial assets[77] in order to enforce the judgment. Although the investor still must go to the domestic court, the New York Convention provides for straightforward enforcement.[78] In fact, many states that once ignored court orders from other states now will-

(1997) and *The Southern Pacific Properties Limited v. Arab Republic of Egypt*, ICSID ABR/84/3 (1992) for examples of monetary awards.

75. The ICSID Convention explicitly prohibits the publishing of awards without the consent of the parties. ICSID Convention, *supra* note 59, art. 48(5). Thus, the transparency of such a system remains questionable. *See* John B. Attanasio, *Rapporteur's Overview and Conclusions: Of Sovereignty, Globalization, and Courts*, 28 N.Y.U. J. INT'L L. & POL. 1 (1995–96) (addressing the factors that make the ICSID less credible than ICJ judgments). *But see*, J.A. Freedberg, *The Role of the International Council for Commercial Arbitration in Providing Source Material in International Commercial Arbitration*, 23 INT'L J. LEGAL INFO. 272, 279 (1995) (stating that even though the Convention requires consent to publish, many awards do get published).

76. Article III of the New York Convention states that "[e]ach Contracting State shall recognize arbitral awards as binding and enforce them in accordance with the rules of procedure of the territory where the award is relied upon, under the conditions laid down in the following articles." Convention on the Recognition and Enforcement of Foreign Arbitral Awards, June 10, 1958, art. 3, 21 U.S.T. 2517 [hereinafter New York Convention].

77. Any non-commercial asset would not be available for attachment pursuant to foreign sovereign immunities legislation. *See, e.g.*, Foreign Sovereign Immunities Act of 1976, 28 U.S.C. § 1604–06 (1994).

78. A party seeking enforcement must merely present an authenticated original award or certified copy of an award to the domestic court in which state recognition is sought with the original agreement to which the dispute has arisen. If requested, the documents must be translated in the official language in which the domestic court is situated by the party seeking enforcement. The domestic court can only refuse recognition for seven reasons: (1) incapacity of the parties or invalidity of the agreement to which the parties have subjected themselves, (2) lack of proper notice given to the defending party, (3) the award is outside the jurisdiction of the arbitration, (4) the arbitral authority was outside its jurisdiction, (5) the award is not binding on the parties, (6) the matter is unlawfully arbitrated under the domestic court's laws, or (7) the enforcement of the award would be against public policy. *See* Ramona Martinez, *Recognition and Enforcement of International Arbitral Awards Under the United Nations Convention of 1958: The "Refusal" Provisions*, 24 INT'L LAW. 487 (1990).

ingly comply with arbitral awards.[79] This method of enforcement, however, is limited to those states that have signed the New York Convention. While most developed states have signed it, there are a significant number of developing states that have not.[80]

D. *International Adjudication Regime*

The regime of international adjudication is the one that we are most familiar with under international law as the structure for resolving disputes between states. Evolving from the Permanent Court of Arbitration,[81] and the Permanent Court of International Justice,[82] the International Court of Justice ("ICJ") is the most recognized international court. In the trade arena, the WTO Dispute Settlement Understanding is closest to international adjudication.[83]

1. Individual Rights & Standing

Under the International Adjudication Regime, private actors are neither granted rights directly by the treaty establishing the international

79. Judgment of Oct. 21, 1987, Corte Superior de Justicia, *translated in* XVI YEARBOOK COM. ARB. 594 (1991); Judgment of Feb. 24, 1997, Tribunal Superior de Justicia, *translated in* IV YEARBOOK COM. ARB. 301 (1979); and Judgment of Aug. 1, 1977, Tribunal Superior de Justicia, *translated in* IV YEARBOOK COM. ARB. 302 (1979). *See also* Carl A. Valenstein et al., *Investor Dispute Resolution Under NAFTA*, 2 LATIN AMERICA LAW AND BUSINESS REPORT 15, 16 (March 1994); *Carl A. Valenstein & Andrea Kupfer Schneider, NAFTA's Arbitration Provisions Facilitate Resolution of Investor-Government Disputes*, US-MEX. FREE TRADE REP. (Feb. 18, 1994); Lisa C. Thompson, *International Dispute Resolution in the United States and Mexico: A Practical Guide to Terms, Arbitration Clauses, and the Enforcement of Judgment and Arbitral Awards*, 24 SYRACUSE J. INT'L L. AND COM. 1, 17–28 (1997).

80. Approximately 110 states have signed the New York Convention. Significant absentees include Brazil, Nicaragua, Honduras, Pakistan and many of the Central Asian former Soviet states. The membership of ICSID is larger with current membership at 131. *Membership*, NEWS FROM ICSID (ICSID, Washington, D.C.), Sum. 1998, at 1.

81. On July 29, 1899, the Permanent Court of Arbitration was established at the first Hague Peace Conference. The Convention for the Pacific Settlement of International Disputes detailed the PCA, which was to become the first dispute settlement mechanism between sovereign states. *See generally* Bette E. Shifman, *The Revitalization of the Permanent Court of Arbitration*, 23 INT'L J. LEGAL INFO. 284 (1995).

82. The Permanent Court of International Justice was established in 1921 by the League of Nations. The Court, as the first world's court, heard thirty-one cases and issued twenty-seven advisory opinions to international organizations. At the end of World War II, the establishment of the United Nations sparked the need for a new world court in consideration of concerns by the parties who were not signatories to the League of Nations. The International Court of Justice was formed in 1945. JANIS, *supra* note 18, at 118–21.

83. Final Act Embodying the Results of the Uruguay Round of Multinational Trade Negotiations, Annex 2: Understanding on Rules and Procedures Governing the Settlement of Disputes, Apr. 15, 1994, app. 1, *in The Results of the Uruguay Round of Multilateral Trade Negotiations*, 33 I.L.M. 1226, 1244 [hereinafter WTO Dispute Settlement Understanding].

court nor have any right of standing to bring cases before the court.[84] This regime exists to resolve disputes between states—inter-national disputes—and therefore individuals have not had recourse to this regime.[85] In some states, private actors may have the ability to petition their government to take action on their behalf.[86] In the United States, the US Trade Representative makes the final decision whether or not to bring the case and there is no judicial review of this action.[87]

84. Historically, individuals could request their government espouse their claims before the ICJ or other international court. *See* Lotus Case, P.C.I.J., Ser. A, No. 9 (1927). *See also* David M. Reilly and Sarita Ordonez, *Effect of the Jurisprudence of the International Court of Justice on National Courts*, 28 N.Y.U. J. INT'L L. & POL. 435 (1995–96) (analyzing *U.S. Citizens Living in Nicaragua v. Reagan* and the denial of individuals to bring a case in front of the ICJ).

85. There is already a debate as to whether private parties should be given standing in the WTO. *See, e.g.*, Daniel C. Esty, *Non-Governmental Organizations at the World Trade Organization: Cooperation, Competition, or Exclusion*, 1 J. INT'L ECON. L. 123 (1998). *But see* Jeffrey L. Dunoff, *The Misguided Debate Over NGO Participation at the WTO*, 1 J. INT'L ECON. L. 433 (1998) (arguing that private actors are already involved significantly).

86. Section 301 allows an individual to petition the United States government to initiate trade dispute resolutions. 19 U.S.C. § 2411 (1994). Under section 302 a party can petition the United States Trade Representative (USTR) to investigate a foreign government's policies or practices that are suspected to be hindering trade. *See id.* at § 2412. The USTR, under section 304, must investigate and determine if the foreign government has violated a trade agreement, benefits of any trade agreement are unreasonably being denied to the individual, or the foreign government is unjustifiably burdening or restricting U.S. commerce. *Id.* at § 2414. If the dispute involves a trade agreement, the USTR is obligated under section 303(a)(2) to first use the dispute settlement procedures provided under that agreement. *Id.* § 2413. For example, if a dispute involves infringements based on one of the Uruguay Round Agreements, the USTR must utilize the dispute resolution system of the WTO. If the USTR finds that a trade infringement is occurring and is convinced that the dispute should involve action by the United States it will pursue resolution of the dispute. *See* A. Lynne Puckett & William L. Reynolds, *Rules, Sanctions and Enforcement under Section 301: At Odds with the WTO?*, 90 AM. J. INT'L L. 675 (1996) (detailing conflicts between Section 301 and WTO policy); Jared R. Silverman, *Multilateral Resolution Over Unilateral Retaliation: Adjudicating the Use of Section 301 Before the WTO*, 17 U. PA. J. INT'L ECON. L. 233 (1996). The EU also has a procedure whereby private actors can request the EU take action against those governments violating free trade agreements. *See* Council Regulation 3286/94, 1994 O.J. (L 349) 71 [the Trade Barriers Regulation] (laying down EU procedures in the field of common commercial policy); Petros C. Mavroidis and Werner Zdouc, *Legal Means to Protect Private Parties' Interests in the WTO: The Case of the EC New Trade Barriers Regulation*, 1 J. INT'L ECON. L. 407 (1998).

87. The USTR has discretion in determining whether to initiate investigations from the petitions filed by interested individuals. *See* 19 U.S.C. § 2412(a)(2) (1994). If the USTR decides not to investigate, notice of such a determination with an explanation of reasons must be published in the Federal Register. *See id.* § 2412(a)(3); Erwin Eichman & Gary N. Horlick, *Political Questions in International Trade: Judicial Review of Section 301?*, 10 MICH. J. INT'L L. 735 (1989) (arguing that a denial by the USTR to pursue investigations of an individual's petition should be reviewed by the judiciary).

2. Supremacy & Transparency

Under international law, the decisions of the international court are supreme to the domestic law and the relevant state must change its behavior or laws to comply.[88] But the court's decision is not integrated into domestic law.

The decision is published and, thus, can provide persuasive precedent for similar disputes.[89] The procedure of an international court is usually transparent and well understood by international lawyers in the field as well as by national governments. The transparency of the system provides the opportunity for both practitioners and academics to analyze, improve, and comprehend this particular international dispute resolution system.[90]

3. Enforcement

Perhaps the most controversial part of international adjudication is the question of compliance and enforcement. Because international courts have not thus far had armies to forcibly carry out their decisions, many critics of the international system focus on those cases where states have chosen to ignore the international court. Similarly under GATT, states could delay the appointments of panels, effectively block adoption of panel reports and, on occasion, ignore panel decisions. For instance, after the U.S. asserted a complaint in 1981 under GATT against the European Community ("EC") concerning pasta export subsidies, the EC effectively blocked adoption of the panel report in favor of the United States. The United States resorted to indirect retaliation efforts that sparked countermeasures by the EC.[91] Without arguing as to

88. Of course, whether a state will follow that international decision is the subject of domestic law. In a monist system of international law, the decision would automatically become part of the domestic legal fabric. Under a dualist system, the international law must be incorporated into the domestic law according to the procedures established under domestic law. *See* JANIS, *supra* note 18, at 83–84.

89. *See* North Seas Continental Shelf Cases (F.R.G. v. Den.; F.R.G. v. Neth.), 1969 I.C.J. 3; Fisheries Case (U.K. v. Nor.), 1951 I.C.J. 116. For a further discussion on precedent in the ICJ, *see* MOHAMED SHAHABUDDEEN, PRECEDENT IN THE WORLD COURT (1996).

90. For example, in the past five years, there have been well over 2000 law review articles written on the International Court of Justice. Likewise, there have been over 1500 articles published about the World Trade Organization since its creation in 1994.

91. *See* ENFORCING INTERNATIONAL TRADE LAW, *supra* note 55, at 151–54 (citing Subsidies on Exports of Pasta Products, SCM/43, May 19, 1983, an unadopted decision, and other cases detailing GATT's ineffectiveness); *see also* Ernst-Ulrich Petersmann, *The Dispute Settlement System of the World Trade Organization and the Evolution of the GATT Dispute Settlement System Since 1948*, 31 COMMON MKT. L. REV. 1157, 1203–04 (1994) (enumerating some further problem areas of the GATT dispute settlement system).

whether an international court can ever truly "work," it is important to assess the level of enforcement a court can have.

Both GATT and the ICJ are examples of court systems that provide for no enforcement beyond censure of the international community.[92] These systems stop at second-order compliance—states should obey the law and, if held to be violating the law, should pay the fine (or change their law). The WTO outlines more stringent enforcement measures by providing a menu of enforcement options.[93] First, a state has the opportunity to follow the ruling and, usually, change the offending practice. Second, the state can continue the practice and pay damages to the harmed state.[94] If neither of these options are taken, the harmed state can retaliate.[95] The WTO provides that the harmed state must first retaliate

92. However, the enforcement of decisions in international law through voluntary compliance should not be underestimated. States regularly abide by unfavorable rulings in order to remain a law abiding member of the international community. Many penalties for noncompliance exist outside the agreement. *See* Downs, *supra* note 45, at 321. Furthermore, direct foreign aid, foreign investment, and World Bank projects are often linked to compliance under international law. For example, the World Bank has played a major role in the compliance of environmental laws in Mexico. *See Mexico's Environmental Controls for New Companies*, 2 No. 9 MEX. TRADE & L. REP. 15 (1992); David Barrans, Note, *Promoting International Environmental Protections Through Foreign Debt Exchange Transactions*, 24 CORNELL INT'L L.J. 65 (1991). *But see* Stephanie Guyett, Note, *Environment and Lending: Lessons of the World Bank, Hope for the European Bank for Reconstruction and Development*, 24 N.Y.U. J. INT'L L. & POL. 889 (1992) (for a criticism of the shortcomings of such an enforcement mechanism).

93. *See* Thomas J. Dillon, Jr., *The World Trade Organization: A New Legal Order for World Trade*, 16 MICH. J. INT'L L. 349 (1995) (discussing the effectiveness of the WTO with a comparison of the lack of enforcement under compliance mechanisms of the IMF or the World Bank). *See also* Matthew Schaefer, *National Review of WTO Dispute Settlement Report's: In the Name of Sovereignty or Enhanced WTO Rule Compliance*, 11 ST. JOHN'S J. LEGAL COMMENT. 307 (1996).

94. Under Article 21 and 22 of the WTO Dispute Settlement Understanding, if the party does not, within thirty days, state intentions for implementing recommendations of the adopted panel report and set a time period for compliance, the parties must commence negotiations for mutually accepted compensation. WTO Dispute Settlement Understanding, *supra* note 83, art. 21, at 1238–39. An economist might explain this provision as permitting "efficient breaches" of the WTO. Jeffrey L. Dunoff & Joel P. Trachtman, *Economic Analysis of International Law*, 24 YALE J. INT'L L. 1, 33 (1999). Compensation is regarded as a temporary stop gap measure until compliance in most cases. Only in cases of non-violation is compensation a long-term solution. *See* C. O'Neal Taylor, *The Limits of Economic Power: Section 301 and The World Trade Organization Dispute Settlement System*, 30 VAND. J. TRANSNAT'L L. 209, 287 [hereinafter *The Limits of Economic Power*] ("The DSU expressly states that in response to a non-violation finding by a panel, there is no obligation incurred by the offending party to withdraw the measure. Instead, the panel or Appellate Body can only recommend that the offending Member State make a 'mutually satisfactory adjustment.'"). *See also* Japan—Measures Affecting Consumer Photographic Film and Paper, WT/DS44/R at 27 (March 31, 1998).

95. Article 22 of the WTO Dispute Settlement Understanding allows the complaining party to request authorization from the Dispute Settlement Body (DSB) to retaliate. The DSB must grant authorization within thirty days unless there is a consensus against such

in the same sector of trade. However, if this is not effective, the WTO provides that cross-sector retaliation is permitted.[96] This newer evolution of the international adjudication regime has more teeth than its predecessors and attempts to correct some of the problems of the past.[97]

E. *Supranational Court Regime*

1. Individual Rights & Standing

A Supranational Court Regime of international dispute resolution is different from the International Adjudication Regime in a number of ways. First, private actors are granted rights under the constituent treaty and have the ability to bring their complaints to the supranational court. The clearest example of this type of individual involvement occurs in the European Union. Under the Treaty of Rome and pursuant to caselaw from the European Court of Justice, citizens of member states of the EU are granted rights directly from the treaty and

---

retaliation. Of course retaliation is only as strong as the state that is retaliating. WTO Dispute Settlement Understanding, *supra* note 83, art. 22. In the 50 years of GATT, retaliation has only been authorized once. The Netherlands retaliated against the United States for dairy quotas in 1953. ROBERT E. HUDEC, THE GATT LEGAL SYSTEM AND WORLD TRADE DIPLOMACY 181–200 (1990) [hereinafter THE GATT LEGAL SYSTEM] (covering the entire history of the "dairy quotas" case).

96. Article 22 of the WTO Dispute Settlement Understanding permits cross-sector retaliation if the previous retaliation, within the sector, is not deemed practical or effective. The determination of whether retaliation is "practical" or "effective" will be made by the complaining party, rather than the WTO Dispute Settlement Understanding. However, paragraph 4 limits the retaliation a government can impose to the equivalent of benefits that the defending state was impairing. WTO Dispute Settlement Understanding, *supra* note 83, art. 21. *See also* 19 U.S.C. 2411(a)(3) (imposing the same limitations).

97. *See* Mary E. Footer, *The Role of Consensus in GATT/WTO Decision-Making*, 17 NW. J. INT'L L. & BUS. 653 (1996–97); Curtis Reitz, *Enforcement of the General Agreement on Tariffs and Trade*, 17 U. PA. J. INT'L ECON. L. 555, 580 (1996); Paul Demaret, *The Metamorphoses of the GATT: From the Havana Charter to the World Trade Organization*, 34 COLUM. J. TRANSNAT'L L. 123 (1995).

legislation passed thereunder.[98] This direct effect under the EU is already quite revolutionary in comparison to most international treaties.[99]

The EU also provides private actors the opportunity to bring cases before the ECJ—directly to the ECJ or indirectly through their domestic courts. The impact of individual involvement in international dispute resolution cannot be underestimated.[100] Individuals play the important function of private enforcement agents.[101] As such, individuals can themselves ensure that the law is being followed rather than relying on states or an oversight body (such as the Commission in the case of the EU) to bring a case. States may feel reluctant to bring cases against other states for somewhat minor infractions. Furthermore, it may be in many states interests not to follow the letter of the law exactly or delay compliance with the numerous laws set out under the EU. If states permit this behavior between themselves, it becomes collusion to ignore the law at the expense of their citizens.[102]

While the oversight body is more likely to bring cases than a state, it, too, has the problem of a vast number of potential cases while maintaining its political agenda. The oversight body rarely has sufficient resources to check compliance with all laws or to bring all cases of noncompliance to the court. Individuals do not have the political baggage of

---

98. The ECJ has interpreted the language of Article 189 as conferring rights upon the nationals of Member States in certain circumstances. The Court has distinguished vertical direct effect, the rights of an individual to sue a governmental entity, from horizontal direct effect, the right of an individual to sue another individual. The Court has acknowledged vertical direct effect involving disputes arising from treaty articles, regulations, and directives. *See* Van Gend en Loos, *supra* note 34; Costa v. ENEL, *supra* note 34; Van Duyn v. Home Office, *supra* note 34; Case 152/84, Marshall v. Southampton and South-West Hampshire Area Health Authority, 1986 E.C.R. 723 [hereinafter Marshall]. However, the Court has not been so lenient on the rights of individuals established by horizontal direct effect. Although the Courts have recognized horizontal direct effect in disputes arising from treaty articles and regulations, the Court refuses to acknowledge horizontal direct effect in disputes arising from directives. *See* Defrenne *supra* note 34; Marleasing, *supra* note 34.

99. *See* Brand, *supra* note 26; David O'Keefe, *Judicial Protection of the Individual by the European Court of Justice*, 19 FORDHAM INT'L L.J. 901 (1996); Louis F. De Duca, *Teaching of the European Community Experience for Developing Regional Organizations*, 11 DICK. J. INT'L L. 485 (1993). In fact, the EU does not provide direct effect for other international treaties including the GATT. *See* Brand, *supra* note 26, at 572–79.

100. *See* Schneider, *supra* note 24.

101. *See The Transformation of Europe*, *supra* note 21, at 2421 (noting the importance of citizens to the EU judicial system); P.P. Craig, *Once upon a Time in the West: Direct Effect and the Federalization of EEC Law*, 12 OXFORD J. LEG. STUD. 453 (1992) (arguing that private enforcement agents are critical to the success of the EU system of direct effect). *See generally* Dinah Shelton, *The Participation of Nongovernmental Organizations in International Judicial Proceedings*, 88 AM. J. INT'L. L. 611 (1994) (arguing that nongovernmental organizations should be able to act as amici curiae in international courts).

102. *See generally* Carlos A. Ball, *The Making of a Transnational Capitalist Society: The Court of Justice, Social Policy, and Individual Rights Under the European Communities Legal Order*, 37 HARV. INT'L L.J. 307 (1996).

bringing a case against another state. Further, individuals can make a direct economic assessment about whether it is worth it to them to spend the time and money on litigation. For these reasons, where individuals are granted rights and where the benefits of the treaty are supposed to accrue directly to individuals, it makes sense to give individuals a remedy for violation of those rights.[103]

2. Supremacy

The name "supranational" in this regime comes from the fact that the court and its rulings are clearly supreme in all ways to domestic law. The rulings from the supranational court must be followed by domestic courts, legislatures, and the executive branch. That is in contrast, for example, to rulings under the International Adjudication Regime above, which are usually only directed to the executive branch.

Supremacy of a supranational court is also promoted when the decisions themselves are integrated into the domestic legal fabric as has been done with the referral system under the ECJ.[104] Because the ECJ makes the ruling on the law alone, the domestic court then renders the final decision applying the EU law to the facts at hand. In this way, the decision is one from a domestic court. As many commentators have noted, states are far less likely to ignore the decisions of their own court than they are of an international court.[105] One final element of supremacy is that domestic judges, under a supranational regime, are given the power of judicial review. Judges at any level may strike down domestic law as incompatible with EU law.[106]

103. In fact, this avenue to the court provided some of the most important cases in the judicial history of the ECJ. *See, supra* note 34. Furthermore, the ECJ hears more cases as preliminary references under Article 177 than directly. In the early years of the EEC, from 1958–1973, nearly two-third of all cases in front of the ECJ came through preliminary rulings. See the Commission's annual General Report on the Activities of the Communities *cited in* Stefan A. Riesènfeld, *Legal Systems of Regional Economic Integration*, 22 AM. J. COMP. L. 415, 426 (1974). This use of Article 177 references continues to increase. In 1993, the ECJ received 203 references which more than doubled the number of cases in 1980. *See* Sarah E. Strasser, *Evolution & Effort: The Development of a Strategy of Docket Control for the European Court of Justice & the Question of Preliminary References*, JEAN MONNET PAPERS (Harvard Law School, 1995). For a review of the most recent literature assessing the impact of individual litigants and EU law, see Walter Mattli & Anne-Marie Slaughter, *Revisiting the European Court of Justice*, 52 INT'L ORG. 177 (1998). The push to give private actors rights in the World Trade Organization is based on the strengths of the European Union. *See, e.g.* Schneider, *supra* note 24; Shell *supra* note 43, at 917–25.

104. *See* Attanasio, *supra* note 75, at 10–14; Lenore Jones, *Opinions of the Court of the European Union in National Courts*, 28 N.Y.U. J. INT'L L. & POL. 275 (1996).

105. *See* J.H.H. Weiler & Ulrich Haltern, *The Autonomy of the Community Legal Order—Through the Looking Glass*, 37 HARV. INT'L L. J. 411 (1996) (commenting on the well-established supremacy doctrine of the ECJ and its limitations).

106. *See, e.g.*, Mattli & Slaughter, *supra* note 103, at 200–04.

3. Transparency

Under this regime, the supranational court works hard at maintaining its transparency to its users. The procedures and membership of the court are well-known. The decisions are published rapidly (and in the ECJ's situation, also include the Advocate-General's opinion) in order to provide clear reasoning of the outcome. This helps ensure the predictability of the court and continually increases the comfort level of private attorneys practicing before the court.

4. Enforcement

The supranational court has a strong enforcement mechanism. First, cases can be brought for noncompliance with earlier court decisions—yet another level of enforcement in this system.[107] Second, the supranational court acts more like a domestic court in that it ensures damages are directly awarded to aggrieved individuals.[108] This power makes the national government more likely to comply with an international law in that it puts a price tag on noncompliance. Indeed, the costs of noncompliance can be severe and direct.[109] And in some ways, it makes

107. For example, see Case 169/87, Commission v. France, 1988 E.C.R. 4093 (in which the Commission was forced to bring France in front of the ECJ for the second time for noncompliance with an earlier court ruling on tobacco pricing) and Case 69/86, Commission v. Italy, 1987 E.C.R. 773 (enforcing a previous judgement against Italy for the quality control of produce).

108. *See* Case 14/83, Von Colson v. Land Nordrhein-Westfalen, 1984 E.C.R. 1891 (allowing individual workers to enforce their rights under a Community Directive on equal employment); Case 33/76, Rewe-Zentralfinanz eG v. Landwirtschafts-Kammer Für Das Saarland, 1976 E.C.R. 1989 (forcing Germany officials to refund illegal money charged to individuals for the inspection of imported apples even though the German statute of frauds had run on the claim). *See generally* O'Keefe, *supra* note 99; April Philippa Tash, Note, *Remedies for European Community Law Claims in Member State Courts: Toward a European Standard*, 31 COLUM. J. TRANSNAT'L L. 377 (1993).

109. *See* Francovich, *supra* note 34 (forcing Italy to compensate workers for damages suffered by non-implementation of a Community Directive dealing with workers' protection against bankrupt employers); Marshall, *supra* note 98 (imposing damages that exceeded the United Kingdom's statutory limitations); Case 70/72 Commission v. Germany, 1973 E.C.R. 813 (forcing Germany to not only cease the illegal payments of state aid but also to recover any aid already granted to its nationals). Remarkably, the ECJ has not imposed any fine thus far in a case brought by the Commission. Article 171 specifically states that the ECJ may, by the request of the Commission, impose a lump sum or penalty payments upon a Member State that refuses compliance. This Article was added to the Treaty on European Union by the request of Parliament concerned with the enforcement of Community law. *See* Treaty on European Union, *supra* note 5, Article 171(1) (stating that necessary measures shall be taken for enforcement of compliance, has been used by the ECJ); Lisa Borgfeld White, Comment, *The Enforcement of European Union Law: The Role of the European Court of Justice and the Courts Latest Challenge*, 18 HOUS. J. INT'L L. 833, 857 n.207 (1996) (listing the fifteen cases in violation of Article 171). However, the imposition of a fine, under Article 171(2), has yet to be employed. *See* Kenneth M. Lord, Note, *Bootstrapping an Environmental Policy*

compliance in the first place easier since a government can demonstrate how noncompliance will directly hurt the national treasury. Moreover, the enforcement power of the court helps the governments protect themselves against strong domestic lobbies.

These remedies are in addition to a requirement to change the law (as opposed to the choice granted in the WTO).[110] Furthermore, by replacing the traditional international law remedy of retaliation, the system is closer to a domestic court system. Violations of international law are treated like any other violation of the law. By eliminating retaliation, the supranational court system avoids escalation between states retaliating and cross-retaliating. It also avoids linkage between different trade issues: each problem is treated separately and judged on its own merits.

III. Political & Economic Variables for Deciding Which Regime is Appropriate

Now that we have outlined the four regimes of international dispute resolution, the next step is to outline the variables that help us determine the most appropriate regime for any given trade organization. These variables differ from the factors outlined in the previous section in that these variables are the political and economic factors behind the creation of international organizations. The first set of variables outlined the legal structures (or lack thereof) in the international dispute resolution system. This second set of variables applies a series of multidisciplinary integration theories to the dispute resolution regimes.

Several of these variables derive from responses to the realist theory of political science. Realism argued that states act only in their best interests in a system of anarchy. Yet realist theory was not able to explain why states would then form international organizations.[111] Regime theory, created as a response to realist theory, argued that states are rational

from an Economic Convent: The Teleogical Approach of the European Court of Justice, 29 Cornell Int'l L.J. 571, 604 n.325 (1996) (commenting on the lack of enforcement through use of fines); *see also* Michael J. McGuinness, *Recent Development*, 30 Stan. J. Int'l L. 579, 594 n.81 (1994) (reasoning the lack of enforcement by use of Article 171).

110. *See supra* note 94 and accompanying discussion.

111. *See* Abbott, *supra* note 1 at 336–38; *see also A Dual Agenda*, *supra* note 1 at 214–18 (discussing realism theory). For more on applying realism to international trade, see generally Robert Gilpin, U.S. Power and the Multinational Corporation: The Political Economy of Foreign Direct Investment (1975) and Hans J. Morgenthau, Politics Among Nations: The Struggle for Power and Peace (5th ed. 1973).

actors and would cooperate when it was in their best interests.[112] From regime theory came a theory of "mesoinstitutions"—a theory by Kenneth Abbott and Duncan Snidal that attempts to explain the presence of formal international organizations.[113] Moving away from both realist and regime theory, liberal international relations theory explains state cooperation by examining the impact of private actors on state choices and arguing that states will act based on the preferences of their populations.[114]

From economics, we have several different theories that have been identified as applying to international organizations and how they operate. The first is the theory of economic integration outlined by Bela Balassa explaining organizations that are created in order to facilitate economic cooperation.[115] The second is Ronald Coase's theory of the firm and a cost-benefit analysis as applied by Joel Trachtman to international organizations.[116] Finally, Joseph Weiler has applied Albert Hirschman's political and economic theory of exit, voice and loyalty to the EU to explain the EU's historical development.[117] Each of these

112. *See, e.g.*, INTERNATIONAL REGIMES (1983) (Stephen D. Krasner ed., 1983); Friedrich Kratochwil & John G. Ruggie, *International Organization: A State of the Art on an Art of the State*, 40 INT'L ORG. 753 (1986).

113. Kenneth W. Abbott and Duncan Snidal, Mesoinstitutions: The Role of Formal Organizations in International Politics, (1995) [hereinafter Mesoinstitutions] (unpublished manuscript on file with the author). Abbott and Snidal have published a revised version of this paper in the J. OF CONFLICT RESOLUTION. See *infra* note 155. Where possible, I have cited to the published article, however, the concept of Mesoinstitutions is only used in the unpublished manuscript. Additionally, the original concepts of facilitating versus producing organizations have been eliminated from the published article. The published article uses the concepts of centralization and independence to outline the range of potential activities. *See also Essay in Trade Governance, supra* note 8 (applying mesoinstitutional theory to the FTAA).

114. *See* Andrew Moravscik, *Taking Preferences Seriously: A Liberal Theory of International Politics*, 51 INT'L ORG. 513 (1997); *see also* Shell, supra note 43 (applying regime theory and liberal theory to propose reforms for the WTO).

115. BELA BALASSA, THE THEORY OF ECONOMIC INTEGRATION (1961). Balassa's theory has been widely applied by legal scholars in analyzing organizations. *See, e.g.*, Paul A. O'Hop, Jr., *Hemispheric Integration and the Elimination of Legal Obstacles Under a NAFTA-Based System*, 36 HARV. INT'L L.J. 127 (1995) (discussing importance of NAFTA to the establishment of the free trade zone in the Western Hemisphere); *Essay in Trade Governance, supra* note 8; *Dispute Resolution as a Catalyst, supra* note 6.

116. *The Theory of the Firm, supra* note 19. Also, see Dunoff & Trachtman, *supra* note 94 for an exhortation to apply law and economics to international law and Ronald S. Cass, *Economics and International Law*, 29 N.Y.U. INT'L L. & POL. 473 (1997) for encouragement of the application of economic theory of international law.

117. *The Transformation of Europe, supra* note 21, at 2411, citing A. HIRSCHMAN, EXIT, VOICE AND LOYALTY—RESPONSES TO DECLINE IN FIRMS, ORGANIZATIONS AND STATES (1970).

theories offer compelling explanations as to why states cooperate and what forms this cooperation can take.[118]

Albert Hirschman's political economic theory of exit, voice, and loyalty when applied to international organizations turns on the issue of sovereignty.[119] Therefore, this article examines the potential levels of retained sovereignty under international organizations. The next part turns to variables derived from the theory of mesoinsitutions—the potential functions of the international organization. These functions have been divided into facilitating international organizations and producing international organizations. Facilitating international organizations have decentralized cooperation through normative, consultative, supportive, and initiative functions. Producing international organizations, on the other hand, rely on centralized cooperation and a cession of some sovereignty in order to produce rules, assistance, and information.[120] Levels of economic integration are examined next derived from Balassa's theory of economic integration.[121] These first three sets of variables—concerns over sovereignty and goals and functions of the organization—reflect each state's national and political interests in joining international organizations.[122]

Analysis of the remaining variables—number of member states, level of economic, social and legal development, and type of government—are an attempt to look inside each state for how the state can function within each type of dispute resolution regime. These variables are suggested by a number of theories. First, economic analysis of international organizations focuses on the costs and benefits of such organizations. These costs can neatly be summarized as sovereignty costs—loss of autonomy, loss of future flexibility, potential loss of office—versus economic gains from liberalization, stability, and security.[123] This calculus is easy to understand and useful to apply at the outset for understanding states' motivations in signing trade

118. For an earlier examination of the variables leading to integration, *see* Ernst B. Haas, *The Study of Regional Integration: Reflections On the Joy and Anguish of Pretheorizing*, 24 INT'L ORG. 607 (1970).

119. HIRSCHMAN, *supra* note 117.

120. *See* Mesoinstitutions, *supra* note 113.

121. BALASSA, *supra* note 115, at 2.

122. *See also* Shell, *supra* note 43, at 834–39. Shell uses a variety of international relations theories to categorize models of dispute resolution. His Regime Management Model is based on regime theory where states balance free trade interests with autonomy interests. The Efficient Market Model is based on free trade theory and liberalism. Finally, the Trade Stakeholders Model is based on theories of liberalism and civic republicanism.

123. For more on balancing sovereignty and economic integration, see Joel P. Trachtman, *L'Etat, C'est Nous: Sovereignty, Economic Integration and Subsidiarity*, 33 HARV. INT'L L. J. 459 (1992) and Susan Hainsworth, *Sovereignty, Economic Integration, and the World Trade Organization*, 33 OSGOODE HALL L. J. 583 (1995).

agreements.[124] Economic variables should also matter in the choice of dispute resolution regime. Trachtman's adoption of the theory of the firm relies on power differentials and cost-benefit analysis to explain cooperation.[125] This cost-benefit analysis must examine the economic and social levels of each state and is also affected by the number of states participating in the international organization. Second, liberal international relations theory, coming from the Kantian tradition, would argue that the type of government and legal culture is important in terms of recognizing which private actors are actually represented by the government.[126] Finally, political bargaining theories also examine the number of states and the type of government of these states involved in international negotiations. Clearly, some of these variables are dependent on one another and perhaps repetitive. All of these variables cannot be equal in terms of determining state action. However, I believe for clarity, it is preferable to look first at each set of variables independently and then to evaluate their relative impact. This next section reviews each theory briefly and identifies the political or economic variable coming from the theory.

A. *Concerns Over Sovereignty—Exit, Voice & Loyalty*

When any state joins an international organization, there is, by definition, some relinquishment of sovereign power to the organization.[127] Some restriction is placed on the state (i.e., limits on tariff changes[128]), some procedure for grievances is designated (i.e., use of the ICJ for territorial disputes versus use of force[129]), or some organization is created for monitoring and coordinating state behavior (i.e., the Organization of American States[130]). In all of these cases, the sovereignty of a state, as it is classically defined,[131] is limited. Thus, the issue for a state joining any

124. *See* Jay Smith, Policing International Trade (1998) (unpublished Ph.D. dissertation, Stanford University) (on file with author); *see also* Guzman, *supra* note 62 (explaining why the economic gains from treaties cause less developed countries to sign investment treaties that overly limit their sovereignty).

125. *Theory of the Firm*, *supra* note 19, at 543–49.

126. *See* Moravscik *supra* note 114, at 513.

127. "To varying extents, organizations have developed legislative or quasi-legislative powers and dispute-settlement mechanisms raising common problems relating to relinquishment of sovereign prerogatives by members. . . ." FREDERIC L. KIRGIS, JR., INTERNATIONAL ORGANIZATIONS IN THEIR LEGAL SETTING v-vi (1993).

128. *See* GATT, *supra* note 51.

129. *See* UN Charter, Statute of the International Court of Justice, *supra* note 16.

130. Charter of the Organization of American States, Apr. 30, 1948, 2 U.S.T. 2394, 119 U.N.T.S. 3.

131. "Sovereignty is supreme authority, an authority which is independent of any other earthly authority." LASSA OPPENHEIM, 1 INTERNATIONAL LAW: A TREATISE 101 (1st ed. 1905). Sovereignty is defined in Black's Law Dictionary as "the supreme, absolute, and

international organization is to what extent it is willing to limit its sovereignty. More collectively, the issue is what type of structure are member states willing to create in order to assuage their concerns about sovereignty.

Joseph Weiler answered these questions with regard to the creation of the European Union[132] by using the Exit and Voice regime established by Albert Hirschman in *Exit, Voice and Loyalty.*[133] Hirschman originally applied these concepts in the framework of political economy to study the behavior of individuals in companies, organizations and, at the broadest level, states. He used the idea of voice to determine the ability of the individual to have influence on the behavior of the organization and to 'voice' their opinion.[134] Exit is the concept of leaving the organization, switching brands, or changing political parties when an individual is not happy with the behavior of the larger entity.[135] Loyalty, as used by Hirschman, is the dynamic by which individuals stay in organizations longer than they would otherwise and turn to the voice mechanism to effect change rather than exit.[136]

In his article, Weiler applied this construct to the history of the European Union, examining the trade-off between political representation in decision-making and the ability of member states to selectively exit, or ignore certain laws. He argued that as exit declines, the need for voice increases. In the case of the European Union, as the European Court of Justice ruled that EU rules have direct effect[137] and have supremacy[138] in the early 1960's, member states felt that more political representation was necessary. This need for voice precipitated the Empty Chair Crisis in 1965 and the Luxembourg Compromise in 1966 which permitted member states to veto any legislation directly affecting their national security. These actions delayed the intent of the Treaty of Rome to move to majority voting and kept the veto until the Single European Act of 1986. This analysis of the trade-off between voice and exit is an important one for any international organization and can be directly applied to dispute resolution mechanisms.

---

uncontrollable power by which any independent state is governed; supreme political authority. . ." BLACK'S LAW DICTIONARY 971 (6th ed. 1991). *See also* Louis W. Goodman, *Democracy, Sovereignty, and Intervention*, 9 AM. INT'L L. & POL'Y 27, 27–29 (1993) (giving historical analysis of sovereignty).

132. *The Transformation of Europe, supra* note 21.

133. HIRSCHMAN, *supra* note 117.

134. *Id.* at 4.

135. *Id.* at 4.

136. *Id.* at 77.

137. Van Gend en Loos, *supra* note 34.

138. Costa v. ENEL, *supra* note 34.

1. The Need for Exit

The evolution of the European Union has severely limited the ability of member states to ignore both legislation passed and court decisions. Court decisions have required timely implementation of legislation,[139] action in the face of non-implementation,[140] compliance with previous court decisions,[141] and, more recently, damages to individuals harmed by non-implementation.[142] Unless a member is totally going to exit the European Union, blatant violation of the dispute resolution mechanism is minimal.[143]

To carry Hirschman's theory into other trade agreements, the ability to selectively exit—to ignore particular rulings—is a distinct possibility. For example, one of the primary reasons that GATT was finally reformed into the WTO was because of the increasing use of selective exit by certain powerful member states (the United States, Canada, and Europe included.)[144] Clearly, one of the factors for any state to consider in deciding which type of dispute resolution regime it would like to join is the ability to selectively ignore decisions under the regime. That determination is made by the agreement establishing the regime, which will set forth whether decisions are binding and have supremacy.

A type of exit is the ability of states to prevent the regime from making decisions about certain issues. Again, GATT provides a helpful

---

139. *See, e.g.*, Joined Cases C-178/94, C-179/94, C-188/94, C-189/94, and C-190/94, Dillenkofer and Others v. Federal Republic of Germany, 1996 E.C.R. I-4845, [1996] 3 C.M.L.R. 469 (holding that Member State is responsible for damage suffered as result of failure to transpose directive in good time).

140. *See*, Frankovich, *supra* note 34; Case 70/72 Commission v. Germany, *supra* note 109.

141. *See, supra* note 107 and accompanying discussion.

142. In 1991, the ECJ instituted remarkable advancement for the enforcement of community law through the preliminary reference ruling in Francovich, *supra* note 34. *See* Rene Valladares, *Francovich: Light at the End of the Marshall Tunnel*, 3 U. MIAMI Y. B. INT'L L. 1 (1995). The ruling conferred liability upon a Member-State to an individual for damages incurred by nonimplementation of a directive. Thus, because Italy failed to implement a directive concerning the coverage of employees under insolvent employers, Italy was liable for the damages the employees suffered.

143. Of course, there are many violations still not brought to court and members have been able to find ways to avoid complete implementation. In addition, the idea that no member would ever exit the EU has been proven to be false as the EU evolves. For example, selective exit from the Maastricht Treaty was used by Denmark and the United Kingdom regarding the monetary union. *See* Christos Hadjiemmanuil, *European Monetary Union, the European System of Central Banks, and Banking Supervision: A Neglected Aspect of the Maastricht Treaty*, 5 TUL. J. INT'L & COMP. L. 105, 107–110 (1997).

144. *See* ENFORCING INTERNATIONAL TRADE LAW, *supra* note 55, at 352–355 (summarizing the increasing legal failures of the GATT in the 1980's and noting that GATT was clearly more responsive to the powerful states). This type of selective exit could also be considered voice because states had used selective exit to express their displeasure with GATT.

example. While some states ignored GATT panel rulings,[145] other states used the tactic of preventing a neutral GATT panel from even hearing the dispute.[146]

A final type of selective exit from a dispute resolution regime is to limit the neutrality of the decisionmakers. In dispute resolution regimes, the decisionmakers could range from a standing court,[147] to rotating panels appointed from experts,[148] to ad hoc appointees from the government.[149] The ability of member states to influence the decision politically is another way of permitting selective exit from those decisions which would be too controversial domestically.

2. The Need for Voice

Weiler showed that as the ability to exit decreases, the need for voice increases.[150] In an international organization, this can be reflected in a number of ways. First, member states might choose to narrowly limit the ability of the dispute resolution regime to hear disputes. For example, states might be able to claim national security exceptions, as in NAFTA,[151]

---

145. *See* ENFORCING INTERNATIONAL TRADE LAW, *supra* note 55 at 151–54 (discussing on the US-EC Pasta Subsidies case).

146. *See* ENFORCING INTERNATIONAL TRADE LAW, *supra* note 55, at 33–34, 54, and 68–69.

147. For example, the ECJ is a standing court. *See* L. NEVILLE BROWN & FRANCIS G. JACOBS, THE COURT OF JUSTICE OF THE EUROPEAN COMMUNITIES 1-2 (3rd ed. 1989).

148. The WTO and ICSID arbitral panels are appointed as needed from a list of approved experts. ICSID Convention, *supra* note 59; WTO Dispute Settlement Understanding, *supra* note 83, at art. 8.

149. *See* NAFTA, *supra* note 2, art. 2001(3)(a), at 693.

150. *The Transformation of Europe*, *supra* note 21, at 2410–2412.

151. *See, e.g.,* NAFTA Article 2102 on exceptions for national security:

> . . . [N]othing in this Agreement shall be construed:
>
> (a) to require any Party to furnish or allow access to any information the disclosure of which it determines to be contrary to its essential interests;
>
> (b) to prevent any Party from taking any actions that it considers necessary for the protection of its essential security interests
>
> (i) relating to the traffic in arms, ammunition and implements of war and to such traffic and transactions in other goods, materials, services and technology undertaken directly or indirectly for the purpose of supplying a military or other security establishment,
>
> (ii) taken in time of war or other emergency in international relations, or
>
> (iii) relating to the implementation of national policies or international agreements respecting the non-proliferation of nuclear weapons or other nuclear explosive devices; or
>
> (c) to prevent any Party from taking action in pursuance of its obligations under the United Nations Charter for the maintenance of international peace and security.

or structure the dispute so that only certain questions are raised in front of the regime, as in arbitration.[152]

The second way to increase voice is in the scope and content of the rules that are created under the treaty.[153] At the outset of the treaty, the entire organization can be limited as to the rules it covers. For example, concerns about giving up sovereignty can be met by restricting the treaty to the more narrow aim of free trade rather than pursuing a goal of broader integration. The question of voice continues to be relevant during the implementation of the treaty. If some organization exists it will, at a minimum, monitor and report the behavior of its members.[154] At a maximum, the organization will create rules to carry out the goals of the organization.[155] States concerned with maintaining voice will limit the types of cases permitted under the dispute resolution regime, limit standing to states, and create voting procedures that ensure continued voice in rule creation, such as vetoes or qualified majority voting.

3. The Existence of Loyalty

The concept of loyalty to international organizations is an interesting one and deserves more than the brief examination given here. The theory of loyalty, as Hirchmann uses it, suggests that members will choose to utilize their "voice" to change an organization, rather than "exit." The war between voice and exit is one that is continually fought on the battleground of the EU[156] and can also be found on a smaller scale

NAFTA, *supra* note 2, at art. 2102 at 669–700.

152. This is similar to the point discussed *supra* notes 161–63 and accompanying text about the limited scope of arbitrations under the Investment Arbitration Regime.

153. The Luxembourg Compromise is an example of maintaining voice as exit decreases by maintaining a veto over the rules created under the Treaty of Rome. *See The Transformation of Europe*, *supra* note 21, at 2423.

154. *See, e.g.*, Final Act Embodying the Results of the Uruguay Round of Multilateral Trade Negotiations, Apr. 15, 1994, Annex 3, (1994) WTO website, (last visited Oct. 16, 1999) <www.wto.org/wto/legal/finalact.htm> [hereinafter Trade Policy Review Mechanism]; *see also* NAFTA *supra* note 2, art. 513 at 363; *see also* John P. Fitzpatrick, *The Future of The North American Free Trade Agreement: A Comparative Analysis of the Role of Regional Economic Institutions and the Harmonization of Law in North American and Western Europe*, 19 HOUS. J. INT'L L. 1, 60–61 (1996).

155. *See* Kenneth W. Abbott & Duncan Snidal, *Why States Act Through Formal International Organizations*, 42 J. CONF. RES. 3, 15 (1998) [hereinafter *Why States Act*].

156. For example, the Luxembourg Compromise discussed *supra* note 153 is an example of maintaining loyalty and voice. Only the Single European Act, passed 10 years later, resolved this conflict between voice and exit by providing for qualified majority voting. Similarly, the decision by Denmark and the United Kingdom to stay out of the monetary union demonstrates loyalty and exit. The United Kingdom continues to debate the advantages of joining. *See* Alan Cowell, *Britain Gets Rough Agenda For Euro*, N.Y. TIMES, Feb. 24, 1999, at C1.

in other organizations.[157] What is interesting is that the balance between voice and exit is more clear when member states feel loyal to the international organization. This loyalty can stem from a variety of sources including a political belief in the overall goals of the organization or the conviction that the organization will benefit the domestic economy.

B. *Function of the Organization—Mesoinstitution Theory*

The second variable is the function of the organization stemming from mesoinstitutional theory. Kenneth Abbott and Duncan Snidal created the theories of mesoinstitutions in order to better understand formal international organizations.[158] They argue that regime theory[159] is incomplete without a more detailed understanding of why states cooperate. The term "meso" stems from the concept that international organizations are somewhere between the centralized state and decentralized anarchy written about so frequently in international relations theory.[160] Furthermore, international organizations exist in order to perform functions for states. Mesoinstitutional theory divides these functions primarily into two categories—facilitating and producing. Abbott and Snidal recognize, however, that many organizations lie somewhere along a spectrum of cooperation.[161] For the purposes of this article, I will briefly describe each category and then discuss how each would structure its dispute resolution regime.

1. Facilitating Organizations

Facilitating organizations operate by promoting state cooperation through four separate functions. By setting forth principles, norms or rules, the facilitating organization has a normative function. This function can be performed without any structure at all.[162] The second function—the consultative function—also requires very little structure in that organizations can provide for state interaction through meetings, conferences, and similar gatherings. The supportive function is the third function of a facilitating organization. Through this function, the inter-

157. For example, the US withdrew from UNESCO in protest over its policies and funding. *See U.S. Parts Ways with UNESCO*, N.Y. TIMES, Dec. 23, 1984, at A1. The US has also withheld funding from the United Nations in an effort to promote reform. *See* DAVID P. FORSYTHE, THE POLITICS OF INTERNATIONAL LAW: U.S. FOREIGN POLICY, 117–140 (1990) (explaining the battle over UN assessments during the Reagan administration).

158. Mesoinstitutions, *supra* note 113.

159. *See supra* note 112 and accompanying text.

160. *See, e.g.*, COOPERATION UNDER ANARCHY (Kenneth A. Oye ed., Princeton University Press 1986).

161. Mesoinsitutions, *supra* note 113.

162. *See id.* at 13.

national organization provides research, information, tracking, and possibly agendas for future meetings.[163] Abbott and Snidal note that the WTO Secretariat would be an example of an international organization performing this type of supportive function in two ways. First the WTO Secretariat researches state practices under the existing rules. Second, it assists with dispute settlement by helping to form ad hoc panels under the WTO Dispute Settlement Understanding and by assisting the panel itself.

A possible fourth function for the facilitating organization is the initiative function. The secretariat of an international organization may call members together on its own initiative and draft an agenda. Again, Abbott and Snidal use the WTO as an example of this, citing a negotiating text put forth by GATT Director-General Dunkel, the Dunkel draft, as a catalyst in moving the Uruguay Round negotiations forward. The Trade Policy Review Mechanism, under which member state trade policies are monitored, is also given as an example of the initiative function.[164] It is clear that even without more formal dispute resolution structures, the facilitating organization can encourage compliance with the underlying trade norms.

2. Producing Organizations

Producing organizations are considered the more classic international organizations with substantial bureaucracies and budgets and concurrent losses in state independence. Abbott and Snidal analogize these organizations to corporations where states are the owners but not the managers.[165] In exchange for both the monetary and sovereignty costs, these producing organizations produce various benefits: rules, technical assistance, information, legitimacy, and financial support. These benefits can be grouped under two categories—efficiency and legitimacy. Producing organizations provide gains in efficiency by pooling risks or assets, managing joint production between member states, and reducing transaction costs through the creation of coordination points—rules, standards and specifications. These organizations also enhance legitimacy through their perceived neutrality and independence. For example, actions that a state might not undertake independently are laundered when these actions occur through an or-

163. *See id.* at 13–17; *Why States Act*, *supra* note 155, at 12.

164. Mesoinsitutions, *supra* note 113, at 17–18. *See* Trade Policy Review Mechanism, *supra* note 154.

165. Mesoinsitutions, *supra* note 113, at 20–21.

ganization.[166] Other functions performed by a neutral international organization include trustee,[167] allocator,[168] information source,[169] or community representative.[170] Also, under the heading of legitimacy is the concept that an international organization can act as a neutral arbiter when disputes arise.

Abbott and Snidal analyze this neutral function in terms of dispute resolution by dividing the potential roles between facilitative intervention versus binding intervention. Facilitative intervention—through good offices, mediation, inquiry, or fact-finding—reduces the transaction costs of diplomacy by helping states overcome bargaining deadlocks and generating possible solutions.[171] Binding intervention can clarify rights and duties and interpret the underlying treaty.[172] The threat of binding intervention is also, in and of itself, an important promoter of compliance.[173]

Thus, the variable coming from mesoinstitution theory is the function of the international organization. In terms of looking at the dispute

---

166. This function is called laundering. *See id.* at 28–30. One example would be the reallocation of EU dues to certain sectors of the economy. The traditional underwriting of agriculture would probably not be acceptable in a state-to-state form but are laundered through the EU. Similarly, support to less economically developed regions—southern Italy, Greece, etc—would probably not be as effective state-to-state. *See also Why States Act, supra* note 155, at 18–19.

167. *See* Mesoinstitutions, *supra* note 113, at 31–34. Abbott and Snidal use the example of the UN Compensation Fund after the Gulf War as one example. *Why States Act, supra* note 155, at 20–21.

168. *See* Mesoinstitutions, *supra* note 113, at 34–35. The international organization is relied upon to allocate scarce resources such as radio frequencies or financial resources. *See Why States Act, supra* note 155, at 21–22.

169. *See* Mesoinstitutions, *supra* note 113, at 35–36. The international organization can create data directly, collect national data, and create standards for reporting. Even when information is reported nationally, a neutral agency provides more legitimacy for this information.

170. *See* Mesoinstitutions, *supra* note 113, at 40–43. The international organization can act as the representative of the community be it global like the UN or regional. *See Why States Act, supra* note 155, at 24–26.

171. Mesoinstitutions, *supra* note 113, at 37. *See also* ROGER FISHER ET AL., BEYOND MACHIAVELLI 123–32 (outlining how third party roles could be designed to better facilitate international negotiations).

172. *See* Mesoinstitutions, *supra* note 113, at 37.

173. *See* Mesoinstitutions, *supra* note 113, at 37; Geoffrey Garrett, *International Cooperation and Institutional Choice: The European Community's Internal Market*, 46 INT'L ORG 533, 555 (1992) (discussing the case where the threat of Commission action against Denmark caused the Danish government to pay damages without any case being brought). Denmark awarded a contract to build the Great Belt Eastern Bridge to a domestic company after receiving foreign bids. A British-French consortium threatened to bring a complaint to the Commission. The Commission threatened to bring a case against Denmark and the Danish government paid damages to the consortium rather than proceed with the case. *See id.*; *see also* Robert H. Mnookin & Lewis Kornhauser, *Bargaining in the Shadow of the Law: The Case of Divorce*, 88 YALE L. J. 950 (1979) (describing this negotiating phenomenon).

resolution regime outlined in this article, it is clear that the Negotiation Regime fits under a facilitative organization and the concept of facilitative intervention. Binding intervention—through arbitration or a court—is used in producing organizations and under the latter three dispute resolution regimes. Therefore, if states prefer to utilize a facilitative organization, a Negotiation Regime is logical. However, if states plan to create a producing organization—with the costs and benefits outlined above—some binding intervention is part of that system.

C. *Level of Economic Integration*

The third variable is the level of economic integration planned for the member states. The goals of economic integration clearly impact the type of organization desired and the best regime for dispute resolution. In the field of international trade, the goals of the organization can be neatly divided into the level of integration desired by the member states.[174] While the level of economic integration desired depends on a variety of factors, the primary factor is clearly the desire for economic growth and stability.[175]

1. General Tariff Reduction

A significant proportion of trade agreements avoids economic integration of any kind and focuses primarily on tariff reduction. The GATT is a global example of an agreement to further tariff reduction without promoting economic integration.[176] The purpose of these agreements is

---

174. *See* BALASSA, *supra* note 115. Balassa categorizes the levels of economic integration as follows: free trade area, customs union, common market, economic union and complete economic integration. Each of these levels will be explained further below. *But see* Jacques Pelkmans, *The Institutional Economics of European Integration*, in 1 INTEGRATION THROUGH LAW: EUROPEAN AND THE AMERICAN FEDERAL EXPERIENCE 318, 321, 324–25 (Mauro Cappelletti, et al. eds., 1986) (arguing that the five stages outlined by Balassa miss the important distinction between negative integration—the removal of barriers—and positive integration—the transfer of economic decision-making to the union level).

175. *See* BALASSA, *supra* note 115, at 6. Balassa also notes that integration could help counteract increased state intervention in the economy and help mitigate cyclical fluctuations. *See id.* The belief that economic integration also leads to political stability is also important. *See, e.g.*, Robert Schuman, *The Schuman Declaration* (1950) *reprinted in* BRENT F. NELSEN & ALEXANDER C-G. STUBB, THE EUROPEAN UNION 11 (1994).

176. *See* GATT, *supra* note 51. Note, however, that the WTO would probably be considered some form of economic integration because of the inclusion of GATS and TRIPS. GATS and TRIPS are a widening, versus a deepening, of the traditional trade agreement by including services and intellectual property. *See* John M. Fontecchio, *The General Agreement on Trade Services: Is It the Answer to Creating a Harmonized Global Securities System?*, 20 N.C. J. INT'L L. & COM. REG. 115 (1994); *see also* Symposium, *Intellectual Property Law in the International Marketplace: Trade Related Aspects of Intellectual Property Rights: Enforcement and Dispute Resolution*, 37 VA. J. INT'L L. 275 (1997); Michael J. Chapman & Paul J. Tauber, *Liberalizing International Trade in Legal Services: A Proposal*

not to coordinate policies, but rather to trade off economic benefits between members.[177] These basic reciprocal rights, such as most-favored-nation status and national treatment rights, are the relatively uncontroversial backbone of these agreements.[178]

2. Free Trade Agreement

The second level of a trade agreement is a free trade agreement. A free trade agreement entails the reduction and eventual elimination of tariffs between the member states on the goods covered by the agreement.[179] The typical free trade agreement also proposes the elimination of other quantitative restrictions on trade including quotas and bans. Finally, a free trade agreement permits the member states to maintain their respective tariffs with regard to the remainder of the trading community. Most agreements still exempt certain strategic or otherwise important goods from the free trade agreement.

3. Customs Union

The next level of integration is the customs union in which the member states eliminate tariffs between themselves, and unify their tariff levels with respect to the rest of the trading community.[180] A customs union increases the integration between the member states and, arguably, creates a more powerful trading bloc. Outside states must now negotiate tariffs and other trade barriers with several states rather than just the single state. Some examples of customs unions include the Benelux customs union prior to its becoming part of the EU and the

for an Annex on Legal Services Under the General Agreement on Trade in Services, 16 MICH. J. INT'L L. 941 (1995).

177. *See* GATT, *supra* note 51 (noting in the Preamble that the method of achieving GATT's goals was "[b]y entering into reciprocal and mutually advantageous arrangements directed to the substantial reduction of tariffs. . ."). Similar purposes also exist in bilateral or other multilateral tariff reduction agreements. *See, e.g.*, African, Caribbean and Pacific States-European Economic Community: Final Act, Minutes, and Fourth ACP-EEC Convention of Lome, Dec. 15, 1989, 29 I.L.M. 783 (1990) [hereinafter Lome Convention] (providing preferential access to the EEC market). Ironically, it is this convention which is now under attack at the WTO level for providing unfair benefits in the Banana War between the U.S. and EU. *See* sources cited *supra* note 49.

178. *See* THE GATT LEGAL SYSTEM, *supra* note 95, at 20.

179. *See* BALASSA, *supra* note 115, at 2; *see* NAFTA, *supra* note 2, art. 302(2); U.S.-Israel Free Trade Agreement, Apr. 22, 1985, U.S.-Isr., 24 I.L.M. 657 [hereinafter U.S.-Israel FTA]; Central European Free Trade Agreement, Dec. 21, 1992, 34 I.L.M. 3.

180. *See* BALASSA, *supra* note 115, at 2; *see also* GATT, *supra* note 51, article XXIV, sec 8 (discussing the definition of a customs union in GATT).

relatively recent customs union between the Czech Republic and the Slovak Republic.[181]

4. Common Market

The fourth level of integration is the common market. For many years, this was the appellation used to refer to the European Economic Community.[182] The common market is a customs union that moves beyond free trade in goods, eliminating barriers to the free movement of the "factors" affecting the free movement of goods. This includes the free movement of services, capital and labor.[183] By eliminating barriers to free movement of services, including banking, insurance, travel agencies, health care, and other professions, the common market promotes a more integrated and open trade between the member states.[184] The free movement of capital between the states permits the true establishment of cross-border enterprises and facilitates the free movement of goods and services. Finally, the free movement of labor (often the most controversial part of the common market) permits the workers in each of the member states to go where the jobs are. The free movement of goods and services will be facilitated by the ability of the citizens of this common market to work in any of the member states.

5. Economic Union

The fifth level of integration is the economic union. The economic union builds on the common market structure by beginning the harmonization of national economic policies.[185] Those policies could

181. Czech Republic-Slovak Republic Customs Union Agreement between the Czech Republic and the Slovak Republic dated October 28, 1992, entered into force January 1, 1993. *See* World Trade Organization, TRADE POLICY REVIEW: CZECH REPUBLIC 23–24 (Geneva, June 1996); *Czechs, Slovaks To Form Customs Union, But Policies Seen Diverging After Time*, 44 Int'l Trade Rep. 1885 (Nov. 4, 1992); *Czech Parliament Starts to Discuss Agreements with Slovakia*, CTK NEWS WIRE, Nov. 24, 1992.

182. See, for example, the Journal of Common Market Studies and the Common Market Law Reports. There are also common markets in other regions. In Latin America, there is the Andean Common Market (ANCOM) between Columbia, Venezuela, Bolivia, Ecuador and Peru in the Agreement on Andean Subregional Integration, May 26, 1969 28 I.L.M. 1165 [Treaty of Cartagena]; the Caribbean Common Market (CARICOM), created through an Annex to the Treaty Establishing the Caribbean Community, July 4, 1973, 946 U.N.T.S. 17; the Central American Common Market (CACM), General Treaty on Central American Economic Integration, Dec. 13, 1960 455 U.N.T.S. 3 [Treaty of Managua], between El Salvador, Honduras, Nicaragua, Costa Rica and Guatemala; and MERCOSUR, *supra* note 6. There is also the African Common Market between Algeria, Egypt, Ghana, Guinea, Mali and Morocco, dated April 1, 1962.

183. *See* BALASSA, *supra* note 115, at 2; Treaty of Rome, *supra* note 5, article 3.

184. *See* BALASSA, *supra* note 115, at 80–98.

185. The EU would be considered well on its way to full economic union. *See* Treaty on European Union, *supra* note 5.

include fiscal (i.e., inflation and interest rates), taxation, monetary (i.e., exchange rates), and social (i.e., employment policies and welfare). Clearly, this level of integration requires more than coordination between the commerce departments because it involves regular executive consultations about economic planning. This planning would most likely be done through a separate organizational body with its own bureaucracy to coordinate the myriad policies of the states.[186]

6. Economic Integration

The final level of integration is full economic integration between the member states.[187] All of the economic policies—fiscal, monetary and social—would be coordinated. This level of integration would also require a supranational authority to oversee implementation and compliance with the rules, regulations, and decisions pertaining to economic integration.[188] At this level of integration, there would no doubt be additional laws to the constituent treaty with which compliance would be necessary. Whereas the lower levels of integration usually only require government action, integration at this level would also impose restrictions and guidelines on private citizens to eliminate all economic barriers between the member states. Foreign and security policy could remain outside the realm of full economic integration but almost every other type of policy could be affected.[189]

The level of economic integration desired is the third variable—along with sovereignty concerns and function of the international organization—which is decided by member states based on their national interests when creating an international trade organization. These first three variables are dependant upon the goals of the member states. The next three variables discussed look at the realities of the member states in the organization. Each of these variables—number of members, economic development, and political and legal structure—clearly affect the potential goals of any trade organization and impact on what type of dispute resolution regime is most appropriate.

---

186. See, for example, Mesoinstitutions, *supra* note 113, at 21–27 on efficiency gains from producing organizations. An economic union would have to be considered under this category of organizations.

187. Examples of complete economic integration of constituent states include the United States, Canada and Brazil.

188. *See* BALASSA, *supra* note 115, at 2.

189. For example, EU expansion into the subject areas of education, environment, immigration, abortion, and human rights could all be used as signs of progress toward complete economic integration.

D. *Number of Member States*

The importance of the number of member states to an international trade treaty comes from two different disciplines. First, negotiation theorists have determined that multiparty negotiations are clearly more complex than bilateral negotiations.[190] Understandably, the structure created in an international organization must take account of the negotiating complexities. An increased number of member states will affect how decisions are made both in the creation of rules and in the resolution of disputes.

Second, the economic gains of state cooperation are also affected by the number of states involved. As Joel Trachtman writes, "we assume that states enter the market of international relations in order to obtain gains from exchange."[191] Two of the potential sources of economic gain from trade are economies of scale and economies of scope.[192] Economies of scale come from global business, global regulation or technological economies of scale.[193] Economies of scope come from centralized production and regulatory economies of scope.[194] Both the benefits of economies of scale and scope increase over time and with increased frequency of transactions. And all of these benefits depend on the size of the potential economy concerned.[195]

1. Bilateral Treaty

A bilateral treaty is often the simplest to understand and interpret. Rarely will the states involved feel the need to create an additional body under the treaty to interpret or monitor the treaty. The rules of the treaty are relatively straightforward, as in a free trade agreement[196] or in a bilateral investment treaty.[197] The treaty might also deal with specific

190. *See, e.g.*, HOWARD RAIFFA, THE ART AND SCIENCE OF NEGOTIATION, 251–355 (1982); *see also* INTERNATIONAL MULTILATERAL NEGOTIATION (I. William Zartman ed., 1994); DOUBLE-EDGED DIPLOMACY (Peter B. Evans, et al. eds., 1993) (focusing on the problems of international bargaining and domestic politics as two-level games).

191. *The Theory of the Firm*, *supra* note 19, at 489. See Alan O. Sykes, *Comparative Advantage and the Normative Economics of International Trade Policy*, 1 J. INT'L ECON. L., 49 (1998) for an excellent primer on the economics of trade.

192. *See The Theory of the Firm*, *supra* note 19, at 493.

193. *See The Theory of the Firm*, *supra* note 19, at 494. Global regulation decreases inefficient regulatory disharmony or evasion and encourages global business.

194. *See The Theory of the Firm*, *supra* note 19, at 494–95. Economies of scope occur through "spillover" of international regulation. "Once several areas of international regulation are established, economies of scope may be realized by regulating other areas." *Id.*

195. *See*, BALASSA, *supra* note 115, at 35–39 (discussing the impact of the size of the union on economic gains).

196. *See, e.g.*, U.S.-Israel FTA, *supra* note 179.

197. *See, e.g.*, Argentina-U.S. BIT, *supra* note 61.

sectors of the economy.[198] Usually the aims of the treaty will be limited vis-a-vis integration[199] to narrow trade goals. As in non-trade bilateral agreements, if compliance does not occur, the states would renegotiate the agreement on an ad hoc basis, rather than submit the dispute to any oversight body.

2. Several States

More recently, agreements among several states have proliferated as neighboring states draft and join smaller international trade organizations in order to boost their own economies.[200] Again, the goals of these agreements can vary from simple investment treaties to new organizations, as in the case of MERCOSUR. The structure of these agreements starts to become more complex. The concern with monitoring, harmonization, and compliance will lead certain of these organizations to create oversight bodies, and even judicial bodies.[201]

3. Regional Agreements

At the next level up, trade agreements become even larger by attracting members from the entire region. The clearest examples of this level agreement are the European Union and the proposed Free Trade Agreement of the Americas. With membership above 15 to 20 states, a separate institution is a necessary to at least coordinate meetings of the states if not to monitor compliance with the laws.[202]

4. Global Treaties

The largest type of trade organization is the World Trade Organization with the implicit goal of global membership.[203] The type of dispute resolution mechanism required at this level is the subject of ongoing

---

198. *See, e.g.*, Agreement Between the Government of United States of America and the Government of Ghana for Sales of Agricultural Commodities, Feb. 8, 1990, U.S.-Ghana, 90 U.S.T. 77, KAV No. 2905; Statement Regarding the Agreement Between the United States and Morocco Relating to the Agreement of June 25, 1987 for Sale of Agricultural Commodities, October 20, 1988, U.S.-Morocco, 88 U.S.T. 355; KAV No. 1417.

199. *But see* Treaty Regarding the Inclusion of the Principality of Liechtenstein in the Swiss Customs-Area, Mar. 29, 1923, Liech.-Switz., 2 L.T.S. 231. Liechtenstein is now considered part of Switzerland for economic purposes.

200. *See, e.g.*, Treaty of Cartagena and Treaty of Managua, *supra* note 182.

201. *See, e.g.*, MERCOSUR, *supra* note 6.

202. This would be consistent with the role of a facilitating organization as described above.

203. In fact, current membership of the WTO is 134. WTO home page, (last visited Sep. 20, 1999) <http://www.wto.org>.

discussion.[204] Again, as the number of states grow, the need for oversight, information exchange, and general organization has also multiplied. There is also no doubt that the number of potential disputes is increased.

The number of member clearly impacts other variables. For example, exit—the ability to either leave the organization or ignore decisions from the dispute resolution mechanism—is clearly more difficult at the extremes in the range of member states. In a bilateral agreement, exit could result in the collapse of the underlying agreement. A blatant breach of a bilateral treaty legally suspends the other state's duties under the treaty.[205] At the other extreme, few states could afford to completely withdraw from (or never join) a global organization. The jockeying over China's accession to the WTO is only one example of this concern.[206] The number of member states will also determine the necessity for additional organizational structures. Again, a global organization, even if it is facilitative, will most likely set up a secretariat. The number of member states also affects the level of economic of integration possible. Finally, in terms of legal factors discussed in the first part of this article, standing is the factor most affected by the number of member states. The argument has already been made that expanding standing under the WTO would overwhelm the system.[207]

E. *Similarity in Economic and Social Levels*

Economic theories and cost-benefit analysis of international organization also require an examination of the economic and social development of the member states.[208] In a cost-benefit analysis, states enter organizations in order to reap an advantage.[209] The international

204. *See, e.g.*, Special Issue, *WTO Dispute Settlement System*, 1 J. INT'L ECON. L. 175 (1998); *Symposium on the First Three Years of the WTO Dispute Settlement System*, 32 INT'L LAW. 609 (1998); John H. Jackson, *Dispute Settlement and the WTO: Emerging Problems*, 1 J. INT'L ECON. L. 329 (1998).

205. *See* Vienna Convention, *supra* note 47, art. 60.

206. *See, e.g.*, Erik Eckholm, *U.S. and China Trying Hard for Breakthrough on Trade*, N.Y. TIMES, Feb. 24, 1999, at A8; Erik Eckholm, *China's Entry into World Trade Organization Is Called Unlikely*, N.Y. TIMES, June 21, 1998, at A10.

207. *See* Philip M. Nichols, *Participation of Nongovernmental Parties in the World Trade Organization*, 17 U. PA. J. INT'L ECON. L. 295, 318–19 (1996) (arguing that providing standing to private actors in the WTO would create significant logistical problems).

208. *The Theory of the Firm*, *supra* note 19, at 495–98 (compares economic theories in explaining why international organizations are created); *see also* Richard A. Posner, *The New Institutional Economics Meets Law and Economics*, 149 J. INST'L THEOR'L ECON 73 (1993) (compares two economic theories and notes that there is significant overlap).

209. Jay Smith uses the relative economic power of member states vis-à-vis one another as a determining factor in how dispute resolution will be structured. Smith argues that treaty value is determined by potential economic gain and increased by the security that the

system is like a market and states can choose whether to engage in transactions. The comparative economic levels between member states impacts the evaluation of these costs and benefits to be gained by trading.[210] Although all states are ostensibly equal under international law,[211] it would be naïve to think that economic power and social development can be ignored.

1. Approximately the Same

Some trade treaties are signed among states with similar economic development. Examples of this type of treaty could include the original Treaty of Rome, creating the European Economic Community[212] and the US-Canada Free Trade Agreement.[213] While differences clearly existed between these states at the time of signing,[214] these differences are small compared to the rest of the global economy. If the economic strength of the states is relatively similar, the goals of the treaty are also more likely to be similar.[215] Creating economies of scale and eliminating tariff barriers

---

agreement will be followed. The more binding the dispute resolution, the more trade benefits will be realized. Treaty value must be balanced against the loss of policy discretion which occurs as organizations are made more binding. Thus, he argues, the more trade-dependent the economy is of a member state, the more binding the dispute resolution mechanism that this state will favor. He also examines the states' relative global economic power. Smith, *supra* note 124.

210. *But see* Joel Trachtman, *Trade and . . . Problems, Cost-Benefit Analysis and Subsidiarity*, 9 EUR. J. INT'L. L. 32 (1998) (discussing the limitations of cost-benefit analysis when applied to the conflict between trade values and other values).

211. *See* JANIS, *supra* note 18, at 179; *see also* UN Charter, *supra* note 16, art. 2(1) ("The [U.N.] is based on the principle of the sovereign equality of all its members.")

212. Treaty of Rome, *supra* note 5.

213. Canada-United States: Free-Trade Agreement, Jan. 2, 1988, Can.-U.S., 27 I.L.M. 281.

214. For example, in 1988 the per capita gross domestic product was $19,488 in the United States and $18,058 in Canada. *See* 42 STAT. Y.B. 161, 175, U.N. Sales No. E/F. 97.XVII.1.

215. For example, the Preamble to the United States-Canada Free Trade Agreement resolves: " . . . .TO STRENGTHEN the unique and enduring friendship between their two nations; TO PROMOTE productivity, full employment, and a steady improvement of living standards in their respective countries" U.S.-Canada FTA, *supra* note 213.

Accompanying legislative history also shows the goals of the agreement:

> Mr. President, I would like to express my strong support for the United States-Canada Free-Trade Agreement [FTA] which will not only serve to strengthen our important economic and political ties with our great ally, Canada, but it will also serve as an important model for our trading relations with the rest of the world.

134 CONG. REC. 24422 (Sep. 19, 1988) (statement of Mr. Bumpers).

> . . .The United States-Canadian Free Trade Agreement or [FTA] which we have before use today is, in short, a comprehensive plan to pull down most of the existing barriers to trade between our two countries. If the FTA is approved, it will truly be a watershed event in modern economic history.

are primary goals; opening new markets, tapping cheap labor, or benefiting from less expensive consumer goods are less likely to be goals for one or the other state. Furthermore, similar economic power affects the willingness of each government to leave differences open for further negotiation. Negotiating from equal power is more comfortable for member states; judicial decisions are not viewed as necessary.

2. Clear Imbalance of Economic & Social Development

The alternative situation occurs when a treaty is concluded between states that differ quite significantly in their level of development. NAFTA could be considered one example, since the Mexican economy is clearly weaker than its partners[216]as could treaties between the European Union and Caribbean or South American states.[217] The goals of these treaties will differ from those among states at similar economic levels. Furthermore, the type of dispute resolution mechanism may be subject to more debate. While more powerful states may wish to retain their political clout through a Negotiation Regime, less powerful states would prefer a regime that is more politically neutral.[218]

---

134 CONG. REC. 24421 (Sep. 19, 1988) (statement of Mr. Glenn).

Compare this with the Preamble to the Treaty of Rome:

> DETERMINED to establish the foundations of an ever closer union among the European peoples,
>
> DECIDED to ensure the economic and social progress to their countries by common action in eliminating the barriers which divide Europe.
>
> DIRECTING their efforts to the essential purpose of constantly improving the living and working conditions of their peoples,
>
> RECOGNIZING that the removal of existing obstacles calls for concerted action in order to guarantee a steady expansion, a balanced trade and fair competition,
>
> ANXIOUS to strengthen the unity of their economies and to ensure their harmonious development by reducing the differences existing between the various regions and by mitigating the backwardness of the less favoured. . . .

Treaty of Rome, *supra* note 5, at Preamble.

216. *See* Budgetary and Economic Analysis of the North American Free Trade Agreement, CIS-NO:93-J932-30 (reporting at the time of the NAFTA negotiations, the per capita GDP for the U.S. and Canada were between U.S.$20,000 to $25,000, while Mexico was at $5,000); *see also Dispute Resolution as a Catalyst*, *supra* note 6, at 852–53; Smith, *supra* note 124, at ch. 3.

217. *See, e.g.*, Fourth ACP-EEC Lome Convention, *supra* note 177 (providing preferential access to the EEC market). For a US example, see Gary G. Yerkey, *U.S., Laos Conclude Bilateral Trade, Investment Agreements, USTR Announces*, 14 INT'L TRADE REP. 1420 (Aug. 20, 1997).

218. *See* Smith, *supra* note 124, at 28 (arguing that dispute resolution mechanism in Chapter 20 of NAFTA [close to a facilitated Negotiation Regime] is a direct result of the US's relative power vis-à-vis Mexico and Canada).

3. Assorted Levels of Development

As the number of member states increase, the likelihood is that a simple division between developed and undeveloped economies is not applicable. In the case of the larger regional or global organizations, the member states will be at different stages of development. Even the North-South division or First World-Third World division is too simple a distinction to make since it glosses over many of the differences between states within these groups. Furthermore, simple tracking of the recent WTO cases demonstrates that the disputes do not regularly fall along economic divides.[219]

F. *Government Type and Legal Culture of Member States*

The last pair of variables to examine in determining regimes of dispute resolution is the type of government and concurrent legal culture in a member state. The importance of these variables comes from several different political theories. First, bargaining theory notes that the type of government in a member state affects the government's ability to negotiate and the government's negotiation strategy.[220] Second, the type of government, and particularly the impact of a democracy, has been examined by theorists from Kant to liberal international relations theory. Kant argued that international peace and domestic justice were intertwined.[221] Logically, international organizations would be more stable if comprised of democratic states.[222] The explosion of democracies around the world, may, in time, make the question of treaties among states with

219. *See* WTO Website (last visited Sep. 23, 1999) <www.wto.org/wto/dispute/bulletin.htm>. Overview of the State-of-Play of WTO Disputes reporting to date that complaints filed by developed country Members is 93 matters/120 requests, complaints by developing country Members is 29 matters/31 requests, and complaints by both developed and developing country Members is 4 matters/10 requests. *Id.*

220. *See* Evans, et al., *supra* note 190; *see also* Robert D. Putnam, *Diplomacy and Domestic Politics: The Logic of Two-Level Games*, 42 INT'L ORG. 427 (1988) (noting that the transparency of a democracy requires different behavior when negotiating between states than does totalitarian states).

221. "[T]he mutual self-interest in international commerce 'sooner or later takes hold of every people, and it cannot exist side by side with war.'" Ernst-Ulrich Petersmann, *How to Reform the United Nations: Lessons from the International Economic Law Revolution*, 2 UCLA J. INT'L & FOR. AFF. 185, 186 (1997) (citing IMMANUEL KANT, POLITICAL WRITINGS 114 (Hans Reiss ed. & H.B. Nisbet trans., Cambridge University Press, 2d ed. (1991)) [hereinafter *How to Reform the United Nations*]; *see also* Fernando R. Tesón, *The Kantian Theory of International Law*, 92 COLUM. L. REV. 53 (1992).

222. *See* DEBATING THE DEMOCRATIC PEACE (Michael E. Brown et al. eds., 1996); Michael W. Doyle, *Kant, Liberal Legacies, and Foreign Affairs*, 12 PHIL. & PUB. AFF. 205 (1983); Michael W. Doyle, *Liberalism and World Politics*, 80 AM. POL. SCI. REV. 1151 (1986); R. J. Rummel, *Libertarianism and International Violence*, 27 J. CONFLICT RESOL. 27 (1983) (demonstrating that liberal democracies have not engaged in war with one another).

different types of governments moot.[223] In the meantime, differences among states pertaining to the role of domestic political interests, the power of domestic lobbies, and the independence of the judiciary will continue to affect their involvement in the international economy.[224] Furthermore, the differences between democracies and non-democratic states will be highlighted as free trade is promoted.

Finally, recent literature has addressed the impact of lawyers and litigation strategy in international organizations.[225] It is clear that growth in international trade agreements has boosted the practice of many Washington, D.C. lawyers.[226] Questions, however, are already arising about appropriate representation before international tribunals and the ability of small states as well as individual plaintiffs to find adequate representation.

The recent Banana case in front of the WTO is a classic example of this issue. The WTO panel held that the small Caribbean state of St. Lucia was not entitled to hire private counsel if other states objected.[227] In a landmark decision, the Appellate Body of the WTO held that a state could hire whomever they pleased.[228] Therefore, to ignore the impact of lawyers on the implementation of these agreements would be naïve.

1. Democracies, Open Economies and Strong Legal Cultures

On the one hand, if all member states in an international organization are democracies, the task is made easier. Under the circumstances, states have similar assumptions about the rule of law, the separation of judicial decisions from executive decisions, and underlying beliefs

223. *See How to Reform the United Nations, supra* note 221 (explaining how international economic integration and increased constitutionalization of the United Nations would help encourage the transition to democracy).

224. *See* Goodman, *supra* note 131, at 30 (arguing that democratic government should be preferred globally for the functional reasons of open communication between states and reduced transaction costs).

225. *See* Catherine Barnard, *A European Litigation Strategy: The Case of the Equal Opportunities Commission, in* NEW LEGAL DYNAMICS OF EU 253 (Jo Shaw & Gillian More eds., 1995); *see also* Peter Menyasz, *Attorney Urges Private Party Participation to Protect Commercial Interests at WTO,* 15 INT'L TRADE REP. 1612 (Sep. 23, 1998).

226. For articles on the general growth of trade lawyers in the 1980s, see Alexander Stille & John C. Metaxas, *Trade Lawyers,* NAT'L L. J., Nov. 11, 1985, at 2. *See also* Marcia Coyle, *Once Tranquil Trade Law Hit By New Frenzy,* NAT'L L. J., Apr. 20, 1987, at 1.

227. European Communities—Regime for the Importation, Sale and Distribution of Bananas, May 22, 1997, WT/DS27/R/USA at 7.10–7.12 (1997) (holding that private lawyers would not be admitted to GATT and WTO Dispute Settlement proceedings). Interestingly, it was the United States and Canada who objected.

228. Appellate Body, European Communities—Regime for the Importation, Sale and Distribution of Bananas, Sep. 9, 1997 WT/DS27/AB/R at 5–12(1997) (holding WTO members are entitled to be represented by private counsel and that this allows developing country members to "participate fully in dispute settlement proceedings.")

about the power of the market.[229] Both the EU and MERCOSUR have drafted the requirement of democracy into their membership standards.[230] The disadvantage of a democracy is that domestic interest groups, such as labor, or certain sectors, such as agriculture or the garment industry, may block or change a proposed treaty because of potential economic losses from open markets.[231] Instead of examining the overall economic benefit for the state, each interest group may look at past experience and narrowly focus the debate on whether or not it will help them. Arguably, this type of public debate is skewed in favor of well-organized groups, be it labor or a business association, rather than consumers, the perennially unheard voice of the majority.[232]

Though states that host large numbers of lawyers may well curse their fate,[233] the presence of lawyers is reflective of a state with healthy

---

229. *See* ADAM SMITH, AN INQUIRY INTO THE NATURE AND CAUSES OF THE WEALTH OF NATIONS (1776); *see also* Frederick M. Abbott, *Trade and Democratic Values*, 1 MINN. J. GLOBAL TRADE 9, 17–18 (1992) (explaining Adam Smith's and David Ricardo's economic theories in favor of a liberal trading system).

230. The Treaty of Rome, *supra* note 5, at Preamble; MERCOSUR: Protocol of Brasilia for the Settlement of Disputes, Dec. 17, 1991, 36 I.L.M. 691. In fact, the threatened coup in Paraguay in 1996 was avoided, in part, because of Paraguay's membership in MERCOSUR. *See* Kevin G. Hall, *Failed Coup Made Bloc Stronger*, J. COM., May 1, 1996, at 1A. "Member countries [of MERCOSUR] and the US exerted strong pressure for Paraguay to stick with democracy during the April 1996 stand-off between then- president Juan Carlos Wasmosy and then-general Oviedo. . .". Ken Warn, *Paraguay Rift Set to Mar Trade Summit*, FIN. TIMES, Dec. 8, 1998, at 6.

231. *See* DANIEL VERDIER, DEMOCRACY AND INTERNATIONAL TRADE 275 (1994); BETH V. YARBROUGH & ROBERT M. YARBROUGH, COOPERATION AND GOVERNANCE IN INTERNATIONAL TRADE: THE STRATEGIC ORGANIZATIONAL APPROACH 11 (1992). The debate about fast track authority to negotiate free trade agreements is one example of this split in the U.S. The debate seems to focus on who was helped or hurt by NAFTA with statistics showing both job loss and job gain from the treaty. Furthermore, the divide between business, which is in favor of more free trade, and labor, which fears the further erosion of jobs, can focus the public debate away from the legislative procedures of fast track authority and, instead, on the fear of what fast track authority will bring to each group. *See* Taylor, *supra* note 10; Helen Dewar, *Florida Torn Over 'Fast Track' Trade-Offs: Agricultural and Political Pressures Keep State Straddling the Fence on Global Commerce*, WASH. POST, Nov. 29, 1997, at A1; David R. Francis, *How NAFTA Impacts Flow of US Jobs South of Border*, THE CHRISTIAN SCIENCE MONITOR, Mar. 24, 1997, at 1; James Sterngold, *NAFTA Trade-Off: Some Jobs Lost, Others Gained*, N.Y. TIMES, Oct. 9, 1995, at A1.

232. Public choice theory is helpful in understanding the impact of interest groups in trade. For more general information on public choice theory, *see* DANIEL A. FARBER & PHILIP P. FRICKEY, LAW AND PUBLIC CHOICE (1991); Charles K. Rowley & William Thorbecke, *The Role of the Congress and The Executive in U.S. Trade Policy Determination: A Public Choice Analysis in* NATIONAL CONSTITUTIONS AND INTERNATIONAL ECONOMIC LAW *supra* note 29, at 347; KAY LEHMAN SCHLOZMAN & JOHN T. TIERNEY, ORGANIZED INTERESTS AND AMERICAN DEMOCRACY 339–46 (1986); Paul B. Stephan III, *Barbarians Inside the Gate: Public Choice Theory and International Economic Law*, 10 AM. U.J. INT'L L. & POL'Y 745 (1995); Symposium, *The Theory of Public Choice*, 74 VA. L. REV. 167 (1988).

233. *See, e.g.*, Marc Galanter, *The Faces of Mistrust: The Image of Lawyers in Public Opinion, Jokes, and Political Discourse*, 66 U. CIN. L. REV. 805 (1998).

respect for the rule of law. A flourishing international practice bar can be useful in a variety of ways. First, this bar will probably lobby for new trade agreements in their own self-interest.[234] Second, the bar will be important to implementing the agreement. In any type of structure, the lawyers will be advising their clients on the rights and remedies provided by the agreement. Even with no international dispute resolution structure, the bar may need to provide advice about domestic remedies and lobbying. The plethora of new dispute resolution mechanisms has created a need for legal assistance to wade through the rules and procedures.[235] Therefore, the number of sophisticated lawyers in a state does and should impact the willingness of that state to join trade organizations with more sophisticated dispute resolution regimes.

2. Emerging Democracies with Controlled Economies

For emerging democracies, an international trade agreement will pose other problems. First, it is more likely that the agreement may require change within the economy beyond a tariff reduction. Laws regulating treatment of international companies, the protection of intellectual property, and taxation will probably also need to be changed. This agreement may be part of a larger plan to privatize industries, eliminate wage and price supports, and encourage more free market investment. Second, because of the overall economic change, the potential for severe economic dislocation is greater in the implementation of these trade agreements. If this occurs, the democratic institutions themselves may be at risk as citizens look to renew the stability by returning to the rule of previous governments.[236]

A situation of either limited numbers of lawyers or few lawyers who are actually trained in international trade lead to different problems for those states. First, a much larger burden will fall on the government counsel to explain and implement any trade agreement. In all circum-

234. In fact, the American Bar Association (ABA) supported expanding the right of private parties to bring cases under NAFTA. *See* American Bar Association Section on International Law and Practice, *Reports to the House of Delegates: Dispute Settlement Under a North American Free Trade Agreement*, 26 INT'L LAW. 855, 859 (1992). *See also*, American and Canadian Bar Associations Joint Working Group on the Settlement of International Disputes, *Settlement of Disputes Under the Proposed Free Trade Area Agreement*, 22 INT'L LAW. 879 (1988) (proposing a reference procedure from national courts in which individuals could bring cases to a Joint Canada-United States Free Trade Tribunal).

235. "Not only the size, but also the emphasis of trade law practice has undergone a dramatic shift, lawyers say. Once focused on tariff and quota disputes, lawyers today often are concerned with the complex interplay of rules set by nations and by the WTO." Josh Karlan, *Fifty Years of WTO—and Legal Work*, NAT'L L. J., June 1, 1998, at A14.

236. The threat to democracy in the Russian Federation because of economic instability is a prime example.

stances, private actors are likely to be unfamiliar with a new dispute resolution system. The problem in a state with few lawyers is that the learning curve will be much longer. Informing clients about the new law and training lawyers in the procedures will fall more directly to government counsel or to hired foreign counsel. Companies may move more slowly in adjusting to the new rules or may not take advantage of new rights provided under the agreement.

Moreover, governments of smaller states may feel that it is necessary to hire foreign counsel to represent them in these new global mechanisms.[237] Over time, this situation may both harm the international organization and the state. Countries may not feel so invested in a process which requires them to use foreign counsel. They may also be less comfortable revealing state practices to someone who is not part of the government. Their citizens and their own domestic attorneys may feel cut out of this new dispute resolution process and withdraw in fear, resentment or suspicion rather than learn and actively participate. In the end, this phenomenon can only harm the credibility and integrity of the dispute resolution mechanism. The suspicion that many Europeans have for the European Union would no doubt be magnified if their own domestic attorneys and judges were not involved in the decisions that affected their lives so directly. Therefore, when creating these international dispute resolution mechanisms, member states and the organization itself should think about what type of structure they are creating and the education they will need to provide to their own citizenry in order to truly understand and support the new organization.

3. Totalitarian Governments

The irony is that negotiating with a dictatorship is, in some ways, very simple. If the leader signs the agreement, it is unlikely that any domestic pressure will prevent ratification or implementation. The problem rests more with the type of economy that exists in the state and that state's ability to provide national treatment to foreign companies. When things go wrong, foreign companies will expect remedies at the domestic level that may not be available.[238] In this case, appropriate and effective remedies at the international level are necessary to truly encourage the economic rights and benefits provided for by the international agreement.

In addition, a totalitarian government will address the costs and benefits of trade agreements differently. In a nutshell, states trade off

237. *See supra* notes 227–28 (the Banana case) and accompanying discussion.

238. *See, e.g.*, MASHAALAH RAHNAMA-MOGHADAM ET AL., DOING BUSINESS IN LESS DEVELOPED COUNTRIES: FINANCIAL OPPORTUNITIES AND RISKS (1995).

sovereignty costs for economic gains in these organizations. This calculus for democracies has been well explained by Trachtman, Smith, and others.[239] For totalitarian governments, the trade-off must be calculated differently. First, the economic gains to consumers would arguably be less important to these governments. Without a voting public, leaders will clearly be less inclined to value that impact. Secondly, binding dispute resolution regimes often give more power to the judiciary vis-à-vis the executive branch.[240] The strengthening and increased independence of the judiciary, both domestic and international, is clearly alien and perhaps risky to a totalitarian government. Furthermore, the totalitarian government would find this particular sovereignty cost more expensive and more threatening than a democracy.

IV. Which Regime When?

This article first outlined the four current dispute resolution regimes. Next, the article examined political and economic factors based on a variety of interdisciplinary theories relating to international organizations. The next task is to bring these two segments together and make some conclusions about which dispute resolution regime will be most appropriate given a set of political and economic factors.

A. *Negotiation Regime*

The Negotiation Regime relies on ad hoc rule-making and diplomacy between the states in order to resolve disputes. This regime is used only between states; individuals usually are not granted rights under the trade treaty. Neither supremacy nor transparency are goals of this type of regime. Furthermore, states enforce compliance with the outcomes of negotiation through renewed negotiation, rather than any structural penalties.

1. Concerns with Sovereignty

The Negotiation Regime of dispute resolution makes most sense to those states concerned with their sovereignty. Negotiation provides "voice" directly by ensuring that states are only bound by those interpretations of law to which they expressly agree. Negotiation is the ultimate dispute resolution mechanism for giving parties control over

239. *Essay in Trade Governance*, *supra* note 8; Hainsworth, *supra* note 123; *Theory of the Firm*, *supra* note 19; Smith, *supra* note 124.

240. *See Transformation of Europe*, *supra* note 21, at 2426 (noting why domestic judges were so willing to use the article 177 procedure in the European Union).

the outcome.[241] Negotiation also provides parties with "exit" from the original trade agreement since the negotiation can modify the rules with which the states choose not to comply. A desire to renegotiate could arise because certain trade concessions granted in the agreement are no longer palatable or because one of the economic and social factors discussed below—inter alia, domestic political pressure or fear of a judicial process which does not exist domestically—has become an issue.

2. Type of Organization

A Negotiation Regime is at the heart of a facilitating organization. The dispute resolution described in Abbott and Snidal for facilitating organizations discusses good offices and mediation.[242] Even the functions of convening meetings and providing information would not require any type of dispute resolution beyond a Negotiation Regime.

3. Goals of Economic Integration

This regime would work best when states are not interested in harmonizing their laws and the goals of integration are limited to lowering tariffs and increasing trade. When states have a goal of further integration such as a common market or economic union, the number of rules to be interpreted and applied could overwhelm any ad hoc system. For example, the informal and provisional system at MERCOSUR could clearly be at odds with its goals of integration.[243] At the very least, some oversight body is necessary in order to truly track implementation of the trade agreement and, if desired, to provide interpretations of the rules. The importance of consistent interpretation and efficient dispute resolution is increased exponentially as the trade agreement moves further toward integration. In a case where the rule changes apply simply to tariffs and some non-tariff barriers, ad hoc dispute resolution may be possible.

4. Number of Member States

In a trade agreement with many states, an ad hoc system of negotiation may become unworkable. That is because either the states must negotiate one-on-one sequentially to deal with noncompliance or all the states must convene in order to jointly modify the treaty. Both of these options are time-consuming and inefficient in an agreement with nu-

241. *See, e.g.*, STEPHEN B. GOLDBERG, ET AL., DISPUTE RESOLUTION 3–6 (1992); Frank E.A. Sander & Stephen B. Goldberg, *Fitting the Forum to the Fuss: A User-Friendly Guide to Selecting an ADR Procedure*, 10 NEG. J. 49, 50–51 (1994).

242. *Why States Act*, *supra* note 155, at 22.

243. *See Dispute Resolution as a Catalyst*, *supra* note 6.

merous members.[244] Therefore, a Negotiation Regime works best with a limited number of states.

5. Similarity in Economic and Social Levels

Relying on negotiation for dispute resolution favors those states who are more economically powerful. Because powerful states can link any particular trade dispute to trade in general, economic aid and other economic incentives, weaker states are less likely to prevail in a dispute over trade compliance even when legally their position may be correct. It is, therefore, understandable that when agreements are made between states at different economic levels, the more powerful states will push for a system that relies more on diplomacy.[245] The weaker state may argue strenuously for a more neutral regime of dispute resolution without success. When evenly balanced states are signing a trade agreement, a Negotiation Regime may be less attractive.[246] Once states have agreed on a set of trade rules, having a neutral regime to implement those rules has the advantage of shielding the system from domestic pressure (somewhat)[247] and of being much more efficient than the alternative of requiring the states to sit down and renegotiate each trade dispute.

6. Government Type and Legal Culture

As discussed above, a Negotiation Regime does not shield a government from domestic political interest groups. In a democracy, there will be continuing pressure on the government to protect that industry,[248] continue those subsidies,[249] retaliate

244. *See, e.g.*, RAIFFA, *supra* note 190. The problems with GATT prior to the WTO demonstrate the difficulty of negotiating dispute resolution in a regime with global membership.

245. See for example Smith, *supra* note 124, ch. 3, at 19–23 (discussing Chapter 20 of NAFTA). *See also* James R. Holbein & Gary Carpentier, *Trade Agreements and Dispute Settlement Mechanisms in the Western Hemisphere*, 25 CASE W. RES. J. INT'L L. 531 (1993).

246. *See* Smith, *supra* note 124, at 27–28 (explaining the more adjudicatory regime in the WTO).

247. *See* JANIS, *supra* note 18, at 125 (pointing out that a decision from an international tribunal can be more palatable domestically than negotiating rights away where a government could be held directly responsible).

248. *See* I. M. DESTLER, AMERICAN TRADE POLITICS: SYSTEM UNDER STRESS 69–73 (1986). As a result of the "second oil shock of 1979" the Japanese automobile industry exported a significant number of fuel efficient vehicles into the United States. *Id.* at 69–70. American sales significantly dropped, threatening a "symbol of U.S. economic supremacy." *Id.* at 70. Not only did the Chrysler Corporation, the Ford Motor Company, and the UAW lobby for protection, but so did American politicians and legislatures. *See id.* at 70.

249. *See* JOHN MCCORMICK, THE EUROPEAN UNION: POLITICS AND POLICIES 240–249 (1996) (discussing the problems of trying to reform the common agricultural policy of the

unilaterally,[250] and to link trade policy with foreign policy.[251] While special interests will be in favor of a system that protects their ability to influence their government, the government itself might be more comfortable with a system that could provide cover for politically unpopular decisions.

On the other hand, democracies will also be more comfortable with a judicial system that mirrors their own. The respect for the rule of law and independent judiciary is likely to be far more ingrained in states that already have that system domestically. Non-democratic states are more likely to be suspicious of any judicial system utilizing a "Western" or "foreign" idea.[252] These states may prefer a Negotiation Regime that protects the decision-making power of the national leader. In addition, these states, which almost always have controlled economies, may fear a foreign body imposing change on the domestic economy too quickly.

To the extent that any state feels that it does not yet have a sufficient number of lawyers trained in international trade, this Negotiation Regime will clearly be preferred. The responsibility for knowledge of the law will be limited to the government. The need for additional education and awareness about the legal procedures of the new trade agreement will be nonexistant. Therefore, for developing states, this regime may be the easiest to implement in the short term.

B. *Investor Arbitration*

The second regime for dispute resolution is investment arbitration. Under this regime, individuals have some rights under the trade treaty and have the ability to bring an arbitration case against the state violating the rules under the treaty. These arbitration decisions are binding as to the damages awarded but do not provide for changing the law of the violating state. These decisions have no supremacy over domestic law.

EU); *see also* Chad Bowman, *Agriculture Lags in World Trade Reform, A Priority in '99, U.S. Trade Official Says*, 15 INT'L TRADE REP. 2025 (Dec. 2, 1998).

250. *See, e.g., The Limits of Economic Power, supra* note 94.

251. *See, e.g.,* Cuban Liberty and Democratic Solidarity (LIBERTAD) Act of 1996 (Helms-Burton Act), 104 Pub. L. No. 114, 110 Stat. 785; Iran and Libya Oil Sanctions Act of 1996, 104 Pub. L. No. 104-172, 110 Stat. 1541; MASS. GEN. LAWS ch. 7, § 22G (1997) (the "Massachussetts Burma Law" which prohibited procurement from any business doing business with Myanmar). This law was held to be an unconstitutional violation of the federal government's prerogatives in foreign policy. *See* National Foreign Trade Council v. Baker, 26 F. Supp. 2d 287 (D. Mass. 1998).

252. For example, see discussion *supra* note 206 on China's accession to the WTO. Only the more Western Arab countries such as Bahrain, Egypt, Kuwait, Qatar, and the United Arab Emirates are members of the WTO. Oman and Saudi Arabia are observer states that have applied to officially join the WTO. *See* Members of the WTO, WTO Website (last visited October 20, 1999) <www.wto.org>.

Arbitration decisions, depending on the procedure chosen, may have some transparency in terms of rule publication but may not provide for publication of the decision and the legal reasoning. Enforcement of arbitration decisions depends on whether the violating state provides for judicial enforcement of arbitration decisions.

1. Concerns with Sovereignty

Admittedly, being subject to arbitration is a novel step for many states. Even if states were willing to enforce arbitration awards in their own courts, states rarely waived their sovereign immunity to any type of case against them. Only with the creation of ICSID and the evolution of the restrictive immunity theory, did states begin to accept arbitration against them.[253] Even then, the waiver of immunity occurred on case-by-case basis.[254] In the 1990's, the United States began to use ICSID as the dispute resolution mechanism of choice in many of its bilateral investment treaties (BIT's).[255] These agreements, and NAFTA, now provide a blanket waiver of immunity for any case arising under the relevant treaty.[256]

The sovereignty given up in Investor Arbitration Regime is minimal. "Exit" in terms of selective non-compliance does become more and more difficult (and would result in an economic backlash on the part of investors). On the other hand, "voice" is maximized in that the state has the ability to frame the questions open to arbitration and certain remedies are completely precluded. Arbitration panels do not order a state to change its laws. By virtue of the extremely low level of integration that usually applies in this regime, the limited remedies, and possible prob-

---

253. Under the traditional theory of immunity, states had absolute immunity for all acts. Under the restrictive theory of immunity, only public acts of the state are immune. When the state acts as a trader in the market, those private commercial acts are not immune. *See, e.g.*, the Foreign Sovereign Immunities Act, *supra* note 77.

254. See the discussion of the SOABI case in front of the French Court of Cassation for an example of the pitfalls of immunity rules that may interfere with the execution of ICSID awards. Parties should address the issue of immunity directly by means of appropriate waivers of immunity. *See* George R. Delaume, *Decisions of Regional and Foreign Courts*, 86 AM J. INT'L L. 138, 142 (1992).

255. *See, e.g.*, Treaty Between the Government of the United States of America and the Government of the Republic of Albania Concerning the Encouragement and Reciprocal Protection of Investment, Jan. 11, 1995, U.S.-Alb., S. TREATY DOC. NO. 104-19 (1995), art. IX, §§ 4, 6. "Each Party hereby consents to the submission of any investment dispute for settlement by binding arbitration . . . ." Id. at § 4. "Any arbitral award rendered pursuant to this Article shall be final and binding on the parties due to the dispute. Each Party shall carry out without delay the provisions of any such award and provide in its territory for the enforcement of such award." *Id.* at § 6.

256. *See* NAFTA, *supra* note 2, art. 1122 (Consent to Arbitration).

lems of enforcement in the courts, this regime of dispute resolution has the most "voice" of the adjudicatory methods.

2. Type of International Organization

As states determine that they desire an organization that produces law, the dispute resolution regime must also move along that continuum. Investor arbitration is the first step in terms of providing "binding intervention."[257] This function ensures that the rules and norms as outlined by the underlying treaty will be enforced.

3. Goals of Economic Integration

Where the goals of integration are minimal, investor arbitration provides a remedy for aggrieved individuals. This remedy is provided by forfeiting the ability of the arbitration panel to further push integration. In arbitration, the questions for dispute will be narrowly construed to deal with only the dispute at hand. When the level of integration is minimal, a consistent body of law that provides precedent and transparency is not as important as when the level of integration is higher.

4. Number of Member States

Because arbitration is done on a case-by-case basis, this system could work well regardless of the number of states involved. Furthermore, if decisions are publicized between the member states, some transparency is provided in the system in order to help states and investors understand the interpretation of the law. However, the ad hoc nature of arbitration panels and their rotating personnel have the potential for creating confusion for investors, thus diminishing predictability and increasing investor insecurity. The greater the number of member states, the greater number of disputes that may arise over interpreting the same rules. The greater number of disputes, the greater number of potential arbitration decisions that may or may not build upon one another. The danger of inconsistent application of the treaty increases exponentially with each new member to the treaty. Therefore, this system would work best in bilateral or small multilateral arrangements.

5. Similarity in Economic and Social Levels

One of the great advantages of this regime is that differences between economic levels is minimized. Clearly these differences will manifest themselves in the content of the treaty itself and may also

---

257. *Why States Act*, *supra* note 155, at 15.

manifest themselves in terms of historic aversion to arbitration. For example, the Calvo Doctrine in Latin America emerged as a response to power imbalances.[258]

Investor arbitration has several elements that prove interesting in terms of state power. First, because each case is brought by an individual investor against another government, a government does not have to make the highly politicized choice of bringing a case. Instead, this is a choice left to the investor who will decide based on his own economic loss and chance of success in arbitration. Second, the domestic courts are left out of the equation until the enforcement stage—again insulating this decision from domestic politics. Third, like any other international adjudication, the decision is from a neutral party and may even provide political cover for the violator. Of course, like any other type of adjudication, those with more resources and more lawyers will have an advantage in the process,[259] but this process is clearly better for the less powerful states than the Negotiation Regime.

6. Government Type and Legal Culture

Under this regime of dispute resolution, the type of government of the member state is also relatively unimportant. As long as each state provides for enforcement of arbitration awards (and really does enforce awards) and has waived its immunity under the treaty, other member states and their investors need not concern themselves with the domestic structure, stability or rule of law (other than how these factors would affect their investment.) In terms of the adjudicatory dispute resolution regimes discussed, this regime relies the least on the existence of a democratic model of government. In a treaty between states with vastly different government types, this regime may well provide the most feasible option. International arbitration is the oldest form of adjudication between states[260] and will probably be most acceptable to those governments which have little experience with an independent judiciary.

258. The "Calvo Clauses" were developed in the mid-1800's in response to European diplomatic intervention in Latin American countries. The doctrine's two basic principles of "national treatment", which provides that foreign nationals will not be accorded greater privileges than citizens, and "no diplomatic intervention", which provides that claims of foreign nationals cannot be pursued through either diplomatic or forceful intervention, are embodied in the constitutions and statutes of Latin American states. These clauses also traditionally prevented a state from submitting to arbitration claims by foreign nationals. *See* Christopher K. Dalrymple, *Politics and Foreign Direct Investment: The Multilateral Investment Guarantee Agency and the Calvo Clause*, 29 CORNELL INT'L L. J. 161 (1996).

259. There have been many articles written about the advantages of litigation for those with money, and the clear disadvantages for those with limited financial resources. *See, e.g.*, Anthony D'Amato, *Legal Uncertainty*, 71 CALIF. L. REV. 1 (1983).

260. *See* JANIS, *supra* note 18, at 109–117.

Lawyers, of course, are happy with any procedure that requires their help. As we move from regime to regime, arbitration is preferred by lawyers over negotiation between states. Furthermore, a growing number of lawyers have experience with arbitration and are more than happy to sell this to both investors and states. Because many lawyers have had experience with domestic arbitration, there is likely to be a sufficient number of trained lawyers in most developed states. Unlike the unfamiliar procedures of an international panel, far less additional training of the bar is necessary to successfully implement this regime of dispute resolution. Therefore, out of the adjudicatory regimes, the Investor Arbitration Regime is best when there are concerns about the experience and training of the lawyers in the member states.

C. *International Adjudication*

Under the International Adjudication Regime, private actors are not granted rights directly. Rights under this regime accrue to states that are also the only ones granted standing before the dispute resolution body. Under this regime, decisions are supreme to domestic law but are not integrated further into domestic law, unless states take steps to give them effect. Transparency in the International Adjudication Regime can be very good. Rules and decisions are published, with decisions providing persuasive authority for future cases. Increasingly, this regime provides for enforcement as well.

1. Concerns with Sovereignty

While the International Adjudication Regime has limited supremacy in that decisions are not integrated into domestic law, there is still clearly the intent that decisions emanating from this regime are supreme and should be followed. The question of sovereignty arises since states are relinquishing their ability to "exit" from the regime. Even with only five years of cases from the WTO, it is apparent that domestic concerns over some of the decisions raise important sovereignty issues and legitimate questions of national interests versus global goals.[261] This

261. *See* Canada—Certain Measures Concerning Periodicals, WT/DS31 (June 30, 1997); European Communities—Measures Concerning Meat and Meat Products (Hormones), United States, WT/DS26/R (June 30, 1997); European Communities—Measures Concerning Meat and Meat Producers (Hormones), Canada, WT/DS48/R (June 30, 1997); United States—Import Prohibition of Certain Shrimp and Shrimp Products, *supra* note 40. The above cases are all clear examples of cultural, social, or environmental issues in which the states have invested a great deal of identity or political commitment. By comparison, NAFTA has a specific cultural industries exception. *See* NAFTA, *supra* note 2, art. 2106; Jeffery Atik, *Identifying Antidemocratic Outcomes: Authenticity, Self-Sacrifice, and International Trade*, 19 U. PA. J. INT'L ECON. L. 229 (1998) (noting the self-sacrificing

regime balances the limited "exit" ability with increased "voice" by granting each state membership in the dispute resolution body. For instance, the WTO agreement demonstrates "voice" by allowing each member state to limit the extent of the tariffs covered under the agreement. The ongoing debates about investment laws and financial services[262] exemplifies the concern with relinquishing yet more sovereignty to a regime that provides for little "exit" once a complaint is lodged.[263]

One last interesting note about this regime is the concept of "loyalty" that Hirschman also uses to explain behavior. Once states have invested in creating an international adjudication regime, the continuation and success of it relies on the states' "loyalty" to the regime. Again, the responses to unpopular decisions of the WTO demonstrates the tug-of-war between following current national sentiment and upholding the integrity of the institution.[264]

2. Type of International Organization

This type of dispute resolution regime is also consistent with the producing organization as outlined by Abbott and Snidal. The organization will use its neutrality and independence in order to bind states and ensure compliance. In terms of enforcement, an International Adjudication Regime has important benefits for strengthening norms and

behavior in which states engage in order to protect certain interests). The battle over certain cultural values continues. *See* Anthony DePalma, *19 Nations See U.S. as Threat to Cultures*, N.Y. TIMES, Jul. 1, 1998, at E1 (discussing the perceived negative impact of U.S. free trade on foreign cultures); *Canada, U.S. Exchange Proposals in Start of Talks Over Magazine Advertising Dispute*, 16 INT'L TRADE REP. 208 (Feb. 3, 1999) (discussing threatened U.S. retaliation for a proposed Canadian law, written in response to the above WTO ruling, which prohibits foreign magazine publishers from selling advertising aimed primarily at the Canadian market).

262. *See* Louis Uchitelle, *Global Tug, National Tether; As Companies Look Overseas, Governments Hold Strings*, N.Y. TIMES, Apr. 30, 1998, at D1 (noting the debate over the Multilateral Agreement on Investments (MAI)); *see, e.g.*, *WTO Financial Services Pact to Enter Into Force March 1*, 16 INT'L TRADE REP. 265 (Feb. 17, 1999).

263. *But see* R.W. Apple, Jr., *Split Over Cuba Is Eased By U.S. and Europeans*, N.Y. TIMES, Apr. 12, 1997, § 1, at 1 (showing the ability of the U.S. to prevent the Helms-Burton act from reaching the WTO Dispute Settlement Body by claiming there was no jurisdiction). *Cf.* David E. Sanger, *Europeans Drop Lawsuit Contesting Cuba Trade Act*, N.Y. TIMES, Apr. 21, 1998, at A8.

264. *See, e.g.*, David E. Sanger, *U.S. Won't Offer Trade Testimony on Cuba Embargo*, N.Y. TIMES, Feb. 21, 1998, at A1 (discussing the impact of bringing the Helms-Burton to the WTO); Thomas E. Skilton, *GATT and the Environment in Conflict: The Tuna-Dolphin Dispute and the Quest for an International Conservation Strategy*, 26 CORNELL INT'L L. J. 455 (1993) (reacting to the GATT decision against the United States' law banning the import of tuna caught with non-dolphin friendly nets). On the other hand, states want to preserve their right of access to the WTO. The U.S., with all of its complaints about the WTO, has already been the plaintiff in 50 cases at the WTO.

encouraging compliance.[265] Furthermore, as a "manager of enforcement", International Adjudication Regimes can ensure that enforcement and retaliation are not disruptive to the larger international community.[266] Because the international organization can clarify, legitimize, and launder retaliation, it strengthens the underlying regime compared to the risks of unilateral and unlimited retaliation under a decentralized system of enforcement.[267]

3. Goals of the Economic Organization

This regime is best used when the goals of integration are limited. Because of the limited standing and supremacy of the regime, real change in the domestic economies is going to be more difficult to achieve. As the EU has demonstrated, it takes numerous domestic cases, an active oversight body in the Commission, and true supremacy in order to accomplish the higher levels of integration. Therefore, tariff reduction and some selective harmonization of non-tariff barriers is probably most realistic for this type of regime where states may bring cases dealing with issues at the federal or national level. While states could attempt to use this regime if a higher level of integration were desired, such as a common market, the restrictions on standing and limited impact of decisions would require active state support and continued intervention in order to accomplish that level of integration. The convergence of these factors is unlikely.

4. Number of States

One of the benefits of an International Adjudication Regime is its ability to handle a large number of states. Once an agreement is negotiated (clearly a more arduous task with more states), the regime itself is relatively easy to operate regardless of the number of states involved. The limited standing afforded by this regime actually helps in this regard in that the docket is much smaller than if standing were permitted for private actors.[268] The clear rules of the regime also make it easy for states to use it simultaneously. Cases can proceed along separate schedules and on timelines established by the regime rather than requiring the maneuvering and coordination that is necessary under, for example, the Negotiation Regime. States are not dependent upon the domestic political cycles or national negotiations of every member state but are able to

265. *See Why States Act*, *supra* note 155, at 26–27.

266. *See id.* at 27.

267. *See id.* at 27.

268. *See*, Nichols, *supra* note 207.

pursue complaints between themselves on a one-on-one basis by using the International Adjudication Regime.

5. Similarity in Economic and Social Levels

The similarity in economic levels—if the states are approximately the same, imbalanced, or mixed—is only an indirect variable for this regime. The economic level matters more regarding the goals of the trade agreement that typically choose an International Adjudication Regime rather than the operation itself. In other words, if the goals of integration are more limited (i.e., selected tariff reduction) a mixture of economic levels may well be the catalyst that promotes such an agreement.[269] States may desire this type of agreement expressly because their economic levels differ and there could be joint benefits to opening their respective economies to each other.

On the other hand, states may desire further integration at the free trade level or a customs union, in which case the number of states involved begins to exponentially make the initial trade agreement much more difficult to attain. This does not directly affect the type of dispute resolution regime chosen but does make it more likely that an International Adjudication Regime, if established globally, would be used at a lower level of integration.

6. Government Type and Legal Culture

The International Adjudication Regime is based on the concept of an independent judiciary and a respect for the rule of law. Therefore, it will probably work better with states that include these concepts in their own domestic system. While we have seen a wide variety of government types in the membership of the WTO, [270] it is unclear how much these states really agree with the use of this type of adjudication. Of course, the point could be that it is irrelevant—states make a determination to join based on economic needs and a cost-benefit analysis and are forced to accept the type of dispute resolution regime. Furthermore, while it might be incongruous or inconsistent for a state to accept independent adjudication at the international level and resist it domestically, there is nothing that says it cannot be done.[271] In the end, however, I be-

269. In other words, industrialized states would benefit from new markets while less advanced states would benefit from cheap exports. *See, e.g.*, Smith, *supra* note 124; *A Theory of the Firm*, *supra* note 19; BALASSA, *supra* note 115.

270. For example, WTO members include non-democracies such as Bahrain, the Democratic Republic of the Congo, Kenya, Kuwait, Malaysia, Myanmar, and Nigeria.

271. *See, e.g.*, Oil Platforms (Iran v. U.S.), 1996 I.C.J. 803 (Dec. 12, 1996); Maritime Delimitation and Territorial Questions between Qatar and Bahrain (Qatar v. Bahr.) 1991

lieve that it is more likely that the International Adjudication Regime will work better with democratic states committed to upholding the rule of law. This impacts other factors including concerns with sovereignty—a democratic state will have more "loyalty" to this type of regime—and with the ability of its lawyers to operate in the regime, as discussed below.

Because the International Adjudication Regime is only open to states, government lawyers will be the most involved in this regime. Skilled lawyers who understand the international trade system will be needed in order for states to successfully pursue their cases in front of international tribunals. Concern with lack of training has already led some states to hire private lawyers in order to represent them.[272] Clearly, this type of dispute resolution regime places a burden on states in which the government lawyers have not been adequately exposed to trade law. Unlike the Negotiation Regime where governments can rely on the traditional diplomatic corps, this regime shifts the responsibility to those with legal training and expertise. This type of shift could also raise additional sovereignty concerns, in particular with governments that have been more comfortable using diplomats rather than lawyers to resolve disputes. Furthermore, if the lawyers are hired from other states, the sovereignty concerns could increase. Under that scenario, cases of national importance would be handled by non-nationals and, arguably, with less supervision than in the Negotiation Regime. Clearly, this could make states more uncomfortable with the International Adjudication Regime.

D. *Supranational Court Regime*

The final regime currently used in the international trading system is the Supranational Court Regime best exemplified by the European Union. Under this regime, individuals are directly granted rights under the trade agreement (and EU legislation) and have standing to bring cases to protect these rights in their domestic courts, if not the European Court of Justice. The rulings of the ECJ have supremacy over national law and are often integrated into the domestic law by the use of national court references. The procedures of the Supranational Court Regime are well-understood and its decisions are regularly published providing excellent transparency. Finally, enforcement under this regime is the most stringent of all types of regimes since domestic courts are used to

I.C.J. 50 (Oct. 11, 1991) (examples of two current ICJ cases where non-democratic states have brought cases).

272. *See supra* notes 227–28 and accompanying discussion.

enforce the law. Additionally, the use of damages has provided real punishment for states not adhering to the law.

1. Concerns Over Sovereignty

The Supranational Court Regime asks member states for the greatest relinquishment of sovereignty in a number of ways. First, the member state gives up sovereignty to the supranational court, which has supremacy over domestic courts. Second, the member state gives up sovereignty from the executive branch, which previously controlled trade policy, to the judiciary—both domestic and international. Third, the member state relinquishes its centralized power to its citizens by granting private actors rights and remedies under this regime. When trying to craft a new international trade regime, each of these forfeitures of sovereignty can be nerve-wracking at best and deal-breaking at worst.

Under the Supranational Court Regime, unlike under other regimes, the state loses virtually all power to "exit"—not comply with a rule. In exchange, it retains "voice" because it can influence what laws are passed under the trade agreement. Yet even here, the extent of the economic integration promoted by the regime works to erode the separate "voice" of the member state. Under this regime, the best explanation of state behavior relies on Hirschman's definition of "loyalty" where states find that the general advantages of the organization are worth the loss of voice and exit. One only has to look at the history of the EU and the goals of economic integration to understand the impact that "loyalty" may have. The visionaries of the Treaty of Rome sought to prevent another Franco-German war, to tie Germany into Europe, and to bolster the Western European economy in the face of communism.

Furthermore, where "loyalty" exists, states choose to remain in the organization and change it from within rather than leave. The history of change in the EU demonstrates this hypothesis since it is the member states that have worked in the last fifteen years to change the focus and dynamics of the EU. Furthermore, the example of the United Kingdom and Denmark's opting out of some of these changes demonstrates both the sovereignty concerns of losing "voice" and "exit."

2. Type of International Organization

A Supranational Court Regime is part of an international organization that is at the far end of the range from facilitation to producing. An organization that is highly producing—high levels of norm coordination, centralization, and independence—will prefer a dispute resolution regime that complements these intentions. A Supranational Court Regime has the ability to provide the highest level of rule centralization and coordination through its oversight and enforcement of the trade rules. This regime centralizes the interpretation and application of the underlying treaty rules. Rather than leaving each state to interpret the law or leaving interpretation to ad hoc panels, the supranational court is the central and supreme interpreter of the law. Furthermore, the enforcement through the domestic system under a Supranational Court Regime ensures an even higher level of compliance.

A supranational court also maintains a high level of legitimacy. In its role as arbiter, the supranational court is respected for its high levels of autonomy and independence.[273] A court can act as an enforcer in addition to the monitoring role it plays through its case load. Instead of acting solely as a manager of state-to-state enforcement, it has an additional level of enforcement—the ability to provide punishments on its own.

3. Goals of the Economic Organization

A Supranational Court Regime only becomes necessary when a high level of economic integration is desired. While we could argue that the Supranational Court Regime would be useful even at lower levels of economic integration, it is clearly necessary when issues beyond simple tariff relief are involved. When the member states choose to coordinate their economies to the extent that the EU has and create a common market, it is apparent that some federal structures must be created. As the goals of integration begin to include movement of people, capital, and services, in addition to the free movement of goods, the importance of integrating this law into the domestic fabric with supremacy becomes more pressing. Similarly, it is equally important to involve individuals in protecting the array of rights and concerns covered by an agreement establishing such a high level of integration.

4. Number of States

As the EU continues to expand, the question of the optimal number of states under this regime becomes of current, not just hypothetical, importance. The structures required for a Supranational Court Regime could be overburdened by a global membership. The ECJ would no doubt need further screening mechanisms for cases or additional lower

273. "Courts as independent institutions also formulate and express community policy. By enunciating, elaborating, and applying rules publicly, they educate the community and strengthen underlying norms." *Why States Act*, *supra* note 155, at 25 (citing Kenneth Abbott, *GATT as a Public Institution: The Uruguay Round and Beyond*, 31 BROOKLYN J. OF INT'L L. 31 (1992)).

courts. At the other extreme, such an elaborate structure would be unnecessary for a bilateral or trilateral agreement.

5. Similarity of Economic and Social Levels

Because of the level of harmonization required under this regime, it is probably better if the member states have somewhat similar economic levels. And while it is clear that the states in the EU vary significantly,[274] these states are all considered to be of the First World rather than the Third World. Even the requirements for new members coming from Eastern Europe set certain standards of economic and social development before integration in the EU is possible. Arguably, the areas in which the EU is having the most trouble (i.e. free movement of labor and open borders) are the areas where the member states differ most from one another in terms of levels of employment, wages and benefits.[275]

6. Government Type and Legal Culture

Again, we can look to the EU to provide a current example of what is required under this regime. New members in the EU must have a democratic form of government. Not only does this advance the overall goals of the EU in securing a democratic continent and peaceable neighbors, this also makes sense in terms of the structure of the EU. A regime which provides individual rights, standing for private actors, and relies on respect of the judiciary must be comprised of states which hold those values in high regard at the domestic level. The structures and procedures of a Supranational Court Regime would clearly be frustrated by member states which did not permit their citizens such powers vis-à-vis domestic structures and were not willing to relinquish their sovereignty to their citizens.

The Supranational Court Regime relies the most of any of the regimes on the skill and involvement of private lawyers. The involvement of domestic lawyers in strengthening the EU system is obvious to most EU observers. Again, the provision of rights and standing to private ac-

---

274. For example the gross domestic product per inhabitant in 1997 ranged from 33,035 ECU in Luxembourg to 8,919 ECU in Portugal. The average was 18,983 ECU. European Union web server (last visited Oct. 16, 1999) <http://europa.eu.int/ en/ comm/ eurostat/ indic/indic16.htm>.

275. *See* Kimberly Green, *Labor Standards in the European Union: The Effects on Multinationals*, 18 HOUS. J. INT'L L. 497, 498–518 (1996) (discussing the harmonization of standards under the EU's Social Charter and Protocol on Social Policy). Unemployment rates as of August 1998 averaged 10 percent in the EU ranging from 18.7% in Spain to 2.2% in Luxembourg and 4.5% in Austria. European Union web server (last visited Oct. 16, 1999) <http://europa.eu.int/en/comm/eurostat/indic/indic14.htm>.

tors can only be utilized with the cooperation of lawyers in each of the member states who are adept at bringing cases to both the domestic and supranational courts.[276] The right of representation in the Supranational Court Regime is of paramount importance in assuring that legitimate cases are pursued regardless of a state's interest in bringing the case. As new states join the EU, it is important that their domestic lawyers are trained sufficiently in order to take full advantage of this regime. Without a core of lawyers who understand the procedures of the Supranational Court Regime, this regime would not be as effective in promoting the harmonization goals of the organization.

V. Directions for Future Work

An analysis of the four types of regimes of dispute resolution would not be complete without recognizing some of the weaknesses of this type of organization and the methodology chosen. There are at least four flaws with discussing dispute resolution regimes in this way. First, these regimes are only based on international trade organizations. Second, the evolution of these international trade organizations is an ongoing process. In particularly examining the WTO and NAFTA at this stage of development may be premature. Third, the political and economic variables are all treated equally in the analysis to help determine an appropriate regime. Finally, the analysis of the legal factors and political variables assumes that these factors are taken into account at the time of negotiating the original trade agreement. In fact, the legal factors such as supremacy or direct effect may evolve over time and well beyond the original intention as we have seen, for example, in the EU.

A. *Only International Trade Agreements Used*

While this study has limited itself to trade agreements for simplicity and cohesiveness, one could clearly argue that not including human rights organizations or other types of international organizations makes the analysis somewhat problematic. After all, human rights regimes such as the European Convention on Human Rights,[277] the Inter-American

276. *See, e.g.*, Louise L. Hill, *Lawyer Publicity in the European Union: Bans are Removed But Barriers Remain*, 29 Geo. Wash. J. Int'l L. & Econ. 381 (1995) (discussing the practice of lawyers in each member state).

277. *See* Convention for the Protection of Human Rights and Fundamental Freedoms, Nov. 4, 1950, 213 U.N.T.S. 221, 234–48 (entered into force Sept. 3, 1953); *see generally* J. G. Merrills, The Development of International Law by the European Court of Human Rights (2d ed. 1993).

Convention on Human Rights,[278] the African Charter of Human Rights,[279] and the International Labor Organization[280] all deal with the legal factors set forth in section II. Each of these regimes has debated and decided issues of direct effect, standing, supremacy, transparency, and enforcement. It would clearly be revealing to study the differences between these human rights regimes and to reflect upon the political and economic variables of their respective memberships.[281] Arguably, the lessons from these regimes would be helpful for international trade and should not be overlooked. A full study of regimes would also include the new Law of the Sea regime,[282] environmental treaties,[283] and perhaps look at security or general regional organizations as well.

---

278. *See* American Convention on Human Rights, Nov. 22, 1969, arts. 52–73, 1144 U.N.T.S. 123, 157–61 (discussing the Inter-American Court of Human Rights in Chapter 8 of the Convention). *See* Dinah Shelton, *The Jurisprudence of the Inter-American Court of Human Rights*, 10 AM. U.J. INT'L L. & POL'Y 333 (1994).

279. African Commission on Human and Peoples' Rights, Articles 47–54 of the African Charter on Human and Peoples' Rights, adopted June 27, 1981, O.A.U. Doc. CAB/LEG/67/3/Rev. 5 21 I.L.M. 58, 65–66 (1981) (entered into force Oct 21, 1986). *See* Rose M. D'Sa, *Human and Peoples' Rights: Distinctive Features of the African Charter*, 29 J. AFR. L. 72 (1985).

280. The International Labor Organization (ILO) utilizes a tripartite system divided into government, employment, and labor to promote the global recognition of human and labor rights. The governing body consists of 28 government members, 14 employer members, and 14 worker members. Committees and delegations for annual conferences are similarly structured. The ILO is unique in allowing organizations of employers or workers to allege non-compliance complaints against the contracting states. Although private individuals are not allowed direct access without the backing of an established organization, the democratic process is strengthened by the employers' and workers' involvement. *See How to Reform the UN, supra* note 221, at 433–34 (commenting that the increase of private individual participation "reflect[s] the democratic functions of international liberal rules and organizations for the participation of individual rights"). *See generally* HECTOR BARTOLOMEI DE LA CRUZ, ET AL., THE INTERNATIONAL LABOR ORGANIZATION 3 (1996) (providing an overview of the ILO procedures).

281. *See, e.g.*, Helfer and Slaughter, *supra* note 25, (drawing lessons from Europe for the UN).

282. United Nations Convention on the Law of the Sea, *opened for signature* Dec. 10, 1982, U.N. Doc. A/Conf.62/122, S. Treaty Doc. No. 39, 103d Cong., 2d Sess. (1992), 21 I.L.M. 1261. As a guiding principle, the parties to a dispute can agree to select any dispute settlement method they wish. If the parties cannot agree to a method of settlement, then more complex provisions of the Convention apply. *See, e.g.*, Lakshman D. Guruswamy, *Should UNCLOS or GATT/WTO Decide Trade and Environment Disputes?*, 7 MINN. J. GLOBAL TRADE 287 (1998); Jonathan I. Charney, *The Implications of Expanding International Dispute Settlement Systems: The 1982 Convention on the Law of the Sea*, 90 AM. J. INT'L L. 69 (1996).

283. *See* Janet McDonald, *Trade and the Environment: Greening the GATT: Harmonizing Free Trade and Environmental Protection in the New World Order*, 23 ENVTL. L. 397, 457 (1993); Chris Wold, *Multilateral Environmental Agreements and the GATT: Conflict and Resolution?* 26 ENVTL. L. 841, 858 (1996); Naomi Roht-Arriaza, *Shifting the Point of Regulation: The International Organization for Standardization and Global Lawmaking on Trade and the Environment*, 22 ECOLOGY L.Q. 479, 484 (1995).

Moreover, focusing only on international trade casts the political and economic variables through an economic interest prism. Arguably, states would be willing to give up some sovereignty for security, as in NATO, but they may not be willing to relinquish sovereignty for economic reasons. Then again, states might be willing to trade some sovereignty for clear economic benefit and might not be willing to give up sovereignty in the human rights arena. We must recognize that these regimes and the choices behind them are merely snapshots and may not be characteristic of all decisions or all organizations.

B. *International Trade Organizations are New Organizations*

Another problem with the regime analysis set forth is that it is based on some organizations that have existed for less than a decade. While we could write about the Negotiation Regime and the Supranational Court Regime ten years ago, the International Adjudication Regime really did not exist prior to the WTO and the Investment Arbitration Regime was rarely used. Therefore, we are relying on relatively few years and few cases in order to make determinations about these regimes, describe how they operate, and explore the motivations of the member states participating in them. The WTO is already debating changes to its dispute resolution system.[284] NAFTA may well be subsumed in the FTAA, if it ever comes to fruition.[285]

On the other hand, this remarkable evolution is exactly what makes this study so interesting. We are witnessing a dramatic change in how disputes are resolved. There is no doubt that the WTO and NAFTA will continue to evolve as will the EU, MERCOSUR, and other new organizations. Therefore, we must again recognize that this study is a snapshot of international dispute resolution regimes today. We should expect continued change and growth in international trade.

C. *All Factors Have Equal Weight*

This analysis of the dispute resolution regimes has treated both the legal factors and the political variables as equally important within each group. This equal treatment is probably problematic in three ways. First, in selecting the type of dispute resolution regime, some of the legal factors are more important than others. For example, direct effect

284. *See e.g.* Menyasz, *supra* note 225; *WTO Begins Contentious Talks on Reform of Dispute Resolution Rules; Delays Expected*, 15 INT'L TRADE REP. 1788 (Oct. 28, 1998); Daniel Pruzin, *Four Nations Submit Proposals to Reform WTO Dispute Settlement Process*, 15 INT'L TRADE REP. 2024 (Dec. 2, 1998); *USTR Will Seek to Clarify WTO Rules on Dispute Settlement at Ministerial Meeting*, 16 INT'L TRADE REP. 137 (Jan. 27, 1999).

285. *See* O'Hop, *supra* note 115; *Essay in Trade Governance*, *supra* note 8.

distinguishes the Supranational Court Regime more than any of the other legal factors and may influence its choice of that regime. The lack of enforcement distinguishes the Negotiation Regime from the other three. And, while transparency is important, it is probably not as important as the other factors when determining which regime to choose.

Second, certain political and economic variables are probably more important than others for states that are negotiating over a dispute resolution regime. A concern over sovereignty may result in a Negotiation Regime despite the existence of other factors that would point to the selection of other types of regimes. States with a limited economic agenda may choose an Investor Arbitration Regime regardless of the number of states or the type of government involved.

Third, some of the factors are linked. Standing for private actors presupposes that private actors are granted rights. Similarly, we can only discuss effective enforcement once we have assumed supremacy and compliance. This linkage of variables also occurs in the political and economic arena. It is clearly more likely that democratic states will have lawyers better trained in using an independent court system. Similarly, states with free market economies are more likely to have a higher economic and social development level. Thus, treating the legal factors or the political variables separately may grant them too much independence and importance.

D. *Assume Factors Evaluated During Original Negotiations*

The final flaw in this analysis may well be that this study assumes that states know in advance how far their regimes will evolve. We can clearly learn from the history of the EU that states may not, and probably cannot, evaluate fully their dispute resolution options because these regimes will change over time. For instance, only after the Van Gend en Loos decision in 1963, was it clear that the EU was going to provide direct effect of treaty rights. Supremacy was not confirmed until a year later in the Costa v. ENEL decision. These decisions occurred five and six years respectively after the creation of the EEC and began the constitutionalization of the EU. We may or may not see that type of evolution in MERCOSUR, NAFTA, and the WTO. Furthermore, NAFTA and the WTO may also play off one another in that there is interaction between the two systems.[286] Parties have a choice of the forum in which to bring a claim. Instead of stronger enforcement guidelines under NAFTA between the states, the parties left open the option of

286. *See, e.g.*, Michael S. Valihora, *NAFTA Chapter 19 or the WTO's Dispute Settlement Body: Hobson's Choice For Canada?* 30 CASE W. RES. J. INT'L L., 447 (1998).

going to the WTO, except in cases where the NAFTA standards are stronger (i.e. environmental) or controversial (the 3rd party to NAFTA would prefer the case under NAFTA).[287]

Of course, we could assume that states that wish to limit the direct effect or supremacy of their dispute resolution regime can do so. On the other hand, as we compare the EU and the Supranational Court Regime with the Investment Arbitration Regime and the International Adjudication Regime, we should recognize that those regimes are in their comparative infancy. Arguably, if we compared the EU in 1963 with NAFTA and the WTO today, that would be a more valid comparison of the states' intentions in creating a dispute resolution regime.

Conclusion

Now that the analysis of the dispute resolution regimes has been started, the question remains what do we do with the information gathered. One step is to complete further analysis dealing with some of the weaknesses outlined above in this initial study. For example, we could weigh factors differently and spend time specifically analyzing which factors are important to which states during the negotiation of the dispute resolution regime. We should continue to analyze the EU and how its evolution reflects the weight of the legal factors involved in selecting a regime and the importance of each of the political variables to that selection as well. This in-depth study could shed more practical light on some of the theoretical assumptions concerning the relationship of the political variables to the appropriate dispute resolution regime. Furthermore, this kind of examination of the evolution of the EU might help shed additional light on how the WTO, NAFTA, or MERCOSUR might evolve in the future.

We should continue to compare dispute resolution regimes across subject matter. As discussed above, the variety of regimes and the varying levels of effectiveness of human rights organizations could provide additional insight into the political and economic variables at stake when creating dispute resolution regimes, as well as the relative importance of the legal factors to choosing these regimes.

Finally any of the factors or variables could be studied more closely. Additional legal factors could also be added to flesh out further differences (i.e. whether the dispute resolution body was rotating or standing) or additional political variables could be examined, such as the power of certain domestic interest groups. My hope in presenting

287. *See* NAFTA, *supra* note 2.

this analysis is to create an initial template of different types of dispute resolution regimes from which we can start to better understand the similarities and differences, as well as the advantages and disadvantages of each regime.

This article does not conclude by exalting one of the theories discussed over the others; the value of an analysis using each of them should be clear. An economic analysis as to why states join international organizations and how dispute resolution may be based upon those desires is crucial, yet insufficient. The level of economic integration and the structure of the organization are affected by other factors such as domestic concerns with sovereignty, history, type of government, relations between the member states and the goals of improving foreign policy, and the desire to stabilize one's own or neighboring governments and economies. All of these variables should enter into any calculation of organizations and dispute resolution. An appropriate review of these variables is necessary before either undertaking the design of a new dispute resolution mechanism or the reform of an existing one. One theory, from political science, economics or traditional legal analysis, is only one side of a multifaceted decision.

It is also too simplistic to expect just one theory to explain the existence of any given regime. For example, a Negotiation Regime could be established due to any one of several variables. A more powerful state might refuse to yield its advantages. In a treaty between only two or three states, member states might decide a more complicated dispute resolution mechanism is not necessary. Finally, there could be domestic concerns with sovereignty which prevent involvement in a more constitutional regime, something that happens in the United States. In terms of explaining the Supranational Court Regime at the other end of the continuum, it is not a story of one theory triumphing over the others. To reach this level of constitutionalization, all of the variables from each of the multidisciplinary theories must be present. In the EU, there was a desire for significant economic integration—for economic gains, political stability and foreign policy goals. There was a desire for a highly producing organization which, at the time, was not as concerned with the loss in sovereignty as it was with reigning in the excesses of sovereignty. All of these variables need to be present in order to arrive at a Supranational Court Regime.

By examining organizations in this way, it becomes easy to see which variables are then missing in other organizations and why other regimes evolve. For example, MERCOSUR ostensibly establishes an organization pursuing a high level of economic integration, desiring political stability, and having the potential for economic gain. We can see, however, the missing variables. The problem in MERCOSUR is clearly on the domestic level of each member state, with the type of each government, the legal and political culture, and each state's concerns with sovereignty. These variables, based on the history and politics of the states, are weighted more than economic goals at this point. Lack of one or two of these variables then explains why states choose not to move along the continuum of constitutionalization. In order to move along in terms of legal factors, states need the coalescing of all of the political, economic and social variables that are brought forth by the multidisciplinary theories explained in this article.

As more and more regional organizations are created, this analysis of dispute resolution regimes could provide useful guidelines, if not answers, about how the states might choose to set up a dispute resolution regime. Recognizing some of the legal differences between the dispute resolution regimes might encourage clearer debate about the advantages and disadvantages of each of the regimes. Similarly, candid review of the political and economic variables between the member states could encourage states to evaluate the weight of each of the variables and to make clearer decisions about their priorities in setting up a dispute resolution regime.

Part II
New Processes: Institutions, Informal and Hybrid Dispute Processes

[10]

The Problem-Solving Workshop in Conflict Resolution

Herbert C. Kelman

THE idea that face-to-face communication among parties in conflict, in a context other than diplomatic negotiations, may contribute to conflict management and resolution is certainly not new. The American Friends Service Committee, in particular, has pioneered in such endeavors. In the last few years we have seen some exciting new experiments in this type of international communication, based on concepts and techniques from the behavioral sciences. Notable among these are the exercises in "controlled communication" of John Burton and his associates at the Centre for the Analysis of Conflict at University College, London,[1] and the Fermeda Workshop, organized by Leonard Doob and his associates at Yale University.[2] Both approaches are designed to bring together representatives of nations or national (ethnic) communities involved in an active conflict, for face-to-face communication in a relatively isolated setting, free from governmental and diplomatic protocol. Discussions, following a relatively unstructured agenda, take place under the guidance of social scientists who are knowledgeable both about group process and about conflict theory. The talks are designed to produce changes in the participants' perceptions and attitudes and thus to facilitate creative problem-solving.

This chapter summarizes the Burton and Doob approaches and then compares, evaluates, and attempts to integrate them.[3] The ge-

1 See John W. Burton, *Conflict and Communication: The Use of Controlled Communication in International Relations* (London: Macmillan, 1969).

2 See Leonard W. Doob, ed., *Resolving Conflict in Africa: The Fermeda Workshop* (New Haven: Yale University Press, 1970).

3 This chapter is a product of a research program on social influence and

neric term "problem-solving workshop"[4] is used to refer to both approaches, since it emphasizes the fact that these approaches utilize "workshop" techniques, but that their orientation is toward problem-solving rather than sensitivity training or personal growth as such.

The workshop approach (and psychological analysis more generally) is often greeted with skepticism; indeed, I share some of that skepticism myself. Before turning to the work of Burton and Doob, therefore, let me clarify some assumptions that I bring to this analysis—and with which, I believe, Burton and Doob generally concur.

(1) I do not assume that most international conflicts are simply products of misunderstanding and misperception that can be cleared up through improved communication.[5] Real conflicts of interest or competing definitions of national interest are often at the center of such disputes. In such cases, improved understanding may demonstrate more clearly that the goals of the conflicting parties are indeed incompatible. Communication may still be useful, in that it may reveal more precisely to each party what the costs of pursuing various alternative policies are likely to be. Nevertheless, more accurate perception would clearly not alter the realities of the underlying conflict.

Moreover, even where there is misperception, face-to-face communication can directly affect only the perceptions and attitudes of the participating individuals. International conflicts, however, usually involve not only individual misperceptions, but also institutionalized ones—that is, misperceptions that are built into and perpetuated through the decision-making apparatus. Vested interests and organizational commitments become attached to a given perception of a conflict situation at various levels in the decision-making bureaucracy, making it difficult for changed perceptions to penetrate.

Clearly, then, problem-solving workshops are not meant as panaceas or as total solutions. They are merely inputs into a more complex resolution process. They are not alternatives to diplomatic and political negotiations, but supplementary or preparatory to them. Burton argues that his procedures of controlled communication are potentially significant and central inputs into conflict resolution; yet

commitment to social systems, supported by U.S. Public Health Service Research Grant Number MH–17669–02 from the National Institutes of Mental Health.

4 Richard E. Walton, "A Problem-Solving Workshop on Border Conflicts in Eastern Africa," *Journal of Applied Behavioral Science* 6, no. 4 (October–December 1970): 453–89.

5 I have discussed some of these issues in the introductory and concluding chapters of *International Behavior: A Social-Psychological Analysis*, ed. Herbert C. Kelman (New York: Holt, 1965); and in "The Role of the Individual in International Relations: Some Conceptual and Methodological Considerations," *Journal of International Affairs* 24, no. 1 (1970): 1–17.

he too speaks of these procedures as preparing the ground for negotiation and as establishing the preconditions of agreement—not as substituting for negotiation.

(2) The problem-solving workshops discussed here are not to be equated with T-groups or sensitivity training as usually defined. They do use some of the techniques and approaches derived from T-group experience. The Fermeda Workshop utilized fairly standard T-groups during its first phase, although in retrospect its organizers are inclined to view this decision as a mistake. In any event, the main task of these workshops is not to increase personal sensitivity, or even interpersonal trust and understanding of the other side; nor is there any assumption that international conflict can be redefined and resolved at an interpersonal level. Workshops are designed to promote trust and openness in communication. However, these are seen not as ends in themselves, but as means toward the development of an atmosphere in which creative problem-solving becomes possible. Unlike the standard T-group, the problem-solving workshop is oriented toward carrying out a concrete task and achieving a usable product.

THE BURTON EXERCISES IN CONTROLLED COMMUNICATION

John Burton's book[6] and other papers on controlled communication draw on experiences gained in two workshops, one involving an international conflict and the other an intercommunal conflict. I was on the panel of social scientists in the second exercise, and I base my impressions of the approach on that experience. It differed in several ways from the first exercise and from further ones that Burton and his associates are currently planning—both because of different circumstances and because the technique itself is still evolving—but it illustrates Burton's general orientation.

The exercise dealt with the conflict between the Greek and Turkish communities in Cyprus. It was held in the fall of 1966, in a university setting in London. It lasted a week. The participants included two representatives of the Greek community and two of the Turkish community. They were selected by the top decision-makers in their respective communities, but they participated essentially as private citizens rather than as official representatives. The exercise was presented to them basically as an academic project, which would meet

6 Burton, *Conflict and Communication.*

the interests of the sponsoring organization in the analysis of concrete conflict situations. At the same time, the organizers indicated that the communication between the two parties might also contribute to resolution of their conflict. The exercise's potential relevance to conflict resolution was clearly understood on all sides, but the organizers made no promises—nor did the parties, in agreeing to participate, commit themselves to anything other than a contribution to an academic enterprise.

In addition to the four Cypriots, a panel of six social scientists (one of whom served as chairman) participated in the discussions. Meetings were held each morning and afternoon during the week (and continued informally during lunch and tea). The discussions were relatively unstructured and designed to encourage participants to share their definitions of the conflict, their perceptions of their own and others' goals and actions, and their assessments of the costs and benefits of alternative conflict resolutions. The chairman and the panel tried to move the discussion away from mutual accusations and legalistic attempts to assign blame and toward a behavioral analysis of the conflict's causes, escalation, and perpetuation, as well as toward efforts to explore possible solutions.

The discussions can be roughly divided into three phases. In the first, the conflicting parties presented their respective views of the conflict; the social scientists generally intervened only to ask questions of detail, which sometimes helped sharpen and clarify an issue or lay the groundwork for subsequent analysis. During the second phase, the social scientists presented various models of conflict. The discussion following each focused first on the origins and processes of conflict in general, and then on the specific conflict at hand. Applicability of the various models to the Cyprus situation was explored, largely by the parties themselves. The social scientists intervened to inform and elaborate, and to propose tentative interpretations of the conflict in terms of the models presented. The social scientists used conflict theory and other theoretical concepts as a psychotherapist might use personality theory: they provided general models for analyzing conflict and then encouraged the parties to confront possible implications of these models for their situation. Where relevant, they drew on these models to raise questions about the two parties' differing perceptions of the same situation.

During the third phase, the parties considered various approaches to resolving the conflict. The social scientists contributed to this phase in two ways: by bringing in relevant experiences from the resolution of other international or intercommunal conflicts, especially through the development of patterns of functional cooperation; and by systematically attempting to explain why solutions that seemed very reasonable to one party caused anxiety and rejection in the other. The social scientists did not themselves propose solutions, nor did they convey the expectation that an agreed-upon solution was to be found. The assumption was that solutions would eventually have to be achieved through formal channels of negotiation, but that new insights about the conflict and new ideas for its resolution emerging from the workshop would be communicated to the relevant decision-makers and might thus influence the negotiation process.

The outcome of the workshop is difficult to assess. The parties seem to have communicated to each other some new and potentially important facts about their respective goals and intentions. Some new insights about the origins and escalation of the conflict have apparently been developed. Certainly by the end of the sessions the parties were able to communicate with each other more freely and within a shared frame of reference. Moreover, there is no doubt that the new information and insights acquired by the participants were transmitted to the top leaders of their own groups, because of the relationship of the participants to the decision-making process. We can only speculate, however, about the extent to which and the way in which these entered into subsequent negotiations. At the time of the exercise, the two parties had not been in official communication with each other for some time. Shortly after the exercise, communication between them was resumed. It is quite likely that the exercise played some role in this development, though we cannot be certain. At the very least, it may have provided a mechanism for the two sides to test each other out in a noncommittal fashion and an opportunity to learn whether resumption of negotiations would be fruitful.

THE FERMEDA WORKSHOP

The Fermeda Workshop was named after a hotel in the mountains of South Tyrol, where the Yale team of Leonard W. Doob, William J. Foltz, and Robert B. Stevens organized a workshop focusing on the border disputes in the horn of Africa between Somalia and its two neighbors, Ethiopia and Kenya. I did not witness this workshop firsthand. My information is based on various written accounts[7] and on

7 Leonard W. Doob, William J. Foltz, and Robert B. Stevens, "The Fermeda Workshop: A Different Approach to Border Conflicts in Eastern Africa," *Journal of Psychology* 73, no. 2 (November 1969): 249–66; Doob, *Resolving Conflict in Africa*; Walton, "Problem-Solving Workshop."

personal communications with several of the participants, particularly with Leonard Doob and Richard Walton. In this connection, I also benefited from a working conference sponsored by the United Nations Institute for Training and Research in May, 1970, in which experiences from both the Fermeda Workshop and the controlled communication exercises were presented, discussed, and evaluated in detail.[8]

The African participants in the Fermeda Workshop included six Somalis, six Ethiopians, and six Kenyans. The Ethiopian and Kenyan participants all held academic posts; the participants from Somalia—which had no university—were professionals or civil servants working in areas unrelated to foreign policy. Plans for the workshop were cleared with the three governments, but the participants were selected by the organizers and came as private individuals, rather than as official representatives. Participants from the same country did not constitute a team and, as far as is known, did not even communicate with each other in anticipation of the workshop. They were told that the workshop would follow the format of sensitivity-training groups, and that some innovative solutions to the countries' border problems were hoped for. They knew this was a highly exploratory effort, which might or might not yield significant results. In addition to the African participants and the three Yale organizers, the workshop included four American specialists in sensitivity training and related techniques, who came in the roles of "trainers" or "process consultants."

The workshop lasted two weeks, with a two-day break in the middle. From the beginning, the participants were broken up into two T-groups, each including three Somalis, three Kenyans, three Ethiopians, two trainers, and one or two of the organizers. During the first few days, the groups, which met intensively, followed standard T-group procedures, aimed at developing self-awareness and open communication among the participants. The trainers did not structure or lead the discussions, but functioned as observers and interpreters of group process. During this period, there were also several meetings of the total group in which theoretical notions about leadership styles and about cooperative and competitive strategies were presented by the trainers and illustrated through simulation exercises. These sessions were designed both to improve the working processes within the T-groups and to provide concepts that could be drawn upon in later discussions of the border disputes.

8 See "Social Psychological Techniques and the Peaceful Settlement of International Disputes," *UNITAR Research Reports*, no. 1 (1970).

During these first few days, the meetings did not deal at all with the substantive issues relating to the border disputes. They focused on individual and group development instead. During the second phase, the workshop turned specifically to the border disputes. First, participants met in their three separate national groups; each group was asked to list its own grievances and the grievances of the other two national groups, as they perceived them, and to present these lists to the total group. The procedure did not work too well, since two of the groups failed to engage in the requested role reversal. In general, the total group seemed to make little progress at this point, and the participants' planning committee (which had since been formed) decided to revert to the original T-groups to work out concrete solutions. The general assembly was used during this phase for presentation and practice of brainstorming techniques and for reports of the activities of the individual T-groups.

Within each of the two T-groups, proposals were developed that all group members, regardless of their national affiliations, were willing to endorse. These proposals were then brought to the general assembly with the aim of achieving a joint solution. However, this particular effort did not succeed, apparently because the trust developed in the T-groups did not carry over to the larger group. National differences came to the fore; participants who had agreed to a solution hammered out in their individual T-group sometimes reverted to rigid defenses of their national position; in some cases, participants from one T-group accused fellow nationals from the other group of betraying their national cause by subscribing to a detrimental proposal. The workshop closed without being able to meet the staff's original goal of developing a joint proposal supported by the total group.

Though the workshop did not arrive at a joint proposal, it did have some positive outcomes. Within the T-groups, trust and an openness of communication developed. These yielded, in each group, a proposal for resolving the conflict that was generally supported by all group members. In response to a questionnaire, the participants indicated (on the whole) that they had acquired new knowledge about the cultures and problems of the other countries, that they had gained a better understanding of the other countries' views of the disputes, and that they were somewhat more open now to alternative solutions. Participants did not feel that the workshop yielded many innovative ideas for solving the border disputes. About a year after the workshop, Doob carried out follow-up interviews with thirteen of the eighteen African participants to gain some impressions of the impact the workshop had on them and on their respective countries.[9] On the whole, their reactions to the experience (and in some cases to the workshop techniques) were positive: they felt close to the other participants, regardless of nationality, and eager to remain in touch with them, and they showed an understanding of the intense emotional meanings that their respective positions had for each of the parties. On the other hand, their own attitudes on the best ways to resolve the conflict were not appreciably affected. News of the workshop reached important officials in each of the three countries, although most of the participants did not make extensive efforts to communicate their experiences.

THE TWO APPROACHES COMPARED

In comparing the two approaches—and particularly in noting the differences between them—we must keep in mind that neither one represents a "closed system," a set of established and tightly defined procedures. Both are seen by their inventors as exploratory, as requiring further refinement, and as open to change, extension, and recombination. In this spirit, differences between the two approaches do not necessarily reflect incompatible views, but rather different starting-points and experiences. There is every reason to suppose that the two approaches can borrow from each other and be combined in various ways, and to treat them as two variants of a more general model, each applicable to a special set of circumstances.

The two approaches have several important features in common:

(1) *Setting.* In both approaches, workshops are held in settings isolated from political and diplomatic environments. The Fermeda Workshop was held in a physically isolated setting; the London exercise was held in an academic setting, removed from the pressures and publicity that typically surround official negotiations. The isolation is partly to reduce distraction and permit participants to concentrate intensively on the task. More important, it allows participants to explore issues while free of constant preoccupation with the public statements they must issue and the impressions they will be making on their various constituencies.

(2) *Sponsorship.* Both types of workshops are sponsored by academic organizations, independent of governmental or intergovernmental agencies. The governments concerned were informed and

9 Leonard W. Doob, "The Impact of the Fermeda Workshop on the Conflicts in the Horn of Africa," *International Journal of Group Tensions* 1, no. 1 (1971): 91–101.

consulted and, in fact, gave their approval of the workshops, but the workshops had no official status whatsoever. The sponsors' legitimacy depended entirely on their status as scholars and people of good will, whose interest in the exercise derived from their research concerns and their desire to make a constructive contribution to the resolution of a violent conflict. The organization of the Fermeda Workshop was greatly aided, however, by the backing of the United Nations Institute for Training and Research.

(3) *Participants.* Although the two approaches differed significantly in the criteria for selecting participants, both sets of participants had two characteristics in common. On the one hand, they were prestigious members of their respective communities, who at least potentially (in the London workshop quite clearly and, indeed, by the nature of their selection) had access to their top decision-makers. On the other hand, they participated in the sessions as private citizens who spoke only for themselves. Even the participants in the London workshop, who were almost certainly briefed by their respective administrations, did not come as official, instructed delegates.

(4) *Interpersonal atmosphere.* In both workshops the discussions and the environments were designed to create an informal atmosphere in which participants would be free to express their views openly and to get to know and respect each other as individuals. The atmosphere fostered mutual trust, a sense of shared values, and commitment to a common task, cutting across national or ethnic divisions.

(5) *Discussion format.* Central to both workshops was the opportunity for direct, face-to-face communication among the conflicting parties. The agenda for discussion was relatively unstructured. The initiative for introducing issues—or for following up on inputs from the third parties—was largely left to the participants themselves. Third parties refrained from imposing their definitions of the situation and their interpretations of actions and events on the participants; rather, they encouraged participants to speak for themselves—to describe their own motives and perceptions, express their own hopes and fears. In particular, both workshops were committed to the idea that solutions must emerge from the group discussions, rather than be imposed from the outside.

(6) *Role of third parties.* Both workshops were under the general guidance of third parties, defined in terms of their professional skills and knowledge as theoretical or applied behavioral scientists rather than in terms of some official capacity as mediators. Though they

participated in the proceedings, their primary task was to provide tools that the participants could utilize in their discussions and analyses, to offer relevant information and suggest interpretations, and to facilitate the group process in other ways. In short, they played a role similar to that of the psychotherapist. And like psychotherapists, they tried to maintain analytical rather than evaluative attitudes toward the participants' pronouncements.

These common features of the two approaches are essentially designed to achieve two ends. First and foremost, they are designed to give participants the freedom, opportunity and impetus to move away from a rigid reiteration of official positions and from efforts to justify their own sides and score points against the other side, and, instead, to absorb new information, explore new ideas, revise their perceptions, reassess their attitudes, and engage in a process of creative problem-solving. The isolated setting, the academic sponsorship, the participants' nonrepresentative roles, the informal atmosphere, the development of trust, the encouragement of self-expression and of an analytical orientation, and the inputs and attitudes of the social scientists all are geared to facilitating these processes.

Second, some common features of both approaches are designed to enhance the probability that the new information and ideas, the changed perceptions and attitudes, and the innovative proposals for solutions generated by the workshop will be fed into the policy process. The selection of potentially influential participants, the coordination with their governments, and a format that allows the definition of the issues and the development of solutions to emerge out of group discussions, rather than being externally imposed (thus discouraging analyses and solutions that go considerably beyond what the decision-makers are prepared to entertain), are geared to achieving this end. Both approaches, it seems to me (as I shall elaborate later), are more effectively designed to produce changes in participants than to feed such changes into the policy process—although the balance between these two ends is one respect in which the two approaches differ from each other.

Let me turn to some of the differences between the two approaches. In terms of the six categories used to describe common features of the two approaches, several distinctions can be drawn. (1) The Fermeda Workshop, held in a physically isolated setting, placed greater emphasis on the creation of a "cultural island" and on the psychological insulation of workshop participants. (2) The London workshop was sponsored by a research center concerned with international relations theory, diplomacy, and the analysis of conflict, representing a research project within that center's ongoing program; the Fermeda Workshop was sponsored by social scientists interested in African studies and staffed by specialists in group process, representing an experimental application of the human-relations training laboratory to conflict resolution. (3) Participants in the London exercise were considerably closer to foreign policy decision-making and came as a team; those in the Fermeda Workshop were more removed from the foreign policy process and came as individuals, thus manifesting greater diversity and division within each national contingent. (4) The Fermeda Workshop placed more deliberate emphasis on creating an interpersonal atmosphere marked by emotional involvement, group solidarity, and mutual trust, and in forging cross-national bonds within the working group. (5) To facilitate discussion of the substantive issues of the conflict, the London workshop made greater use of theoretical models of conflict and of illustrative cases, while the Fermeda Workshop focused more extensively on the ongoing group process and interpersonal behavior; in discussion of the substantive issues themselves, the Fermeda Workshop made more deliberate efforts than the London workshop to hammer out an agreed-upon proposal for resolving the conflict. (6) In the London workshop, the social scientists made more theoretical inputs, both in their own presentations and in their interventions, and they were generally more active in the course of the discussion itself; in the Fermeda Workshop, they provided more feedback on the basis of their observations of group process and were more active in programming the workshop activities—in setting the tasks to which the participants were to devote themselves.

These differences in detail reflect certain underlying differences between the two approaches, both in their conception of the enterprise as such and in their definition of the workshop task. They differ in their views of the workshop's relationship to the larger process of conflict resolution, and in their views of precisely what ought to be happening within the workshop itself. My formulation of these differences may be overly sharp, but it should be helpful in pointing up the unique contributions of each approach.

How do the two approaches differ, first, in their conceptions of the enterprise? As I have indicated before, both are concerned with creating an atmosphere in which change—in the form of revised perceptions and attitudes and innovative solutions—can take place, in the hope that this change can be fed into the political processes of conflict resolution. However, the two approaches differ, it seems to me, in their conceptions of precisely where the workshop fits into these political processes and what it is intended to accomplish.

In Burton's conception, the workshop is much more closely linked to national and international political processes. The concept of controlled communication flows out of a theoretical orientation toward international relations, containing such propositions as these: that "international conflict is a spill-over from internal or communal strife";[10] that "the starting point in analysis and resolution of conflict is at the systems level of highest transactions";[11] that "conflict occurs as a result of ineffective communication, and that its resolution, therefore, must involve processes by which communication can be made to be effective";[12] and that "since the resolution of conflict depends upon effective communication, it can come only from the parties themselves. Processes are required that alter perceptions, and promote the points of view of the parties, and not of third parties."[13] In Burton's view, then, procedures like those of controlled communication represent crucial steps in the conflict resolution process.

In keeping with this conception, Burton's workshops are closely coordinated with the relevant decision-makers. The participants must be individuals who are fully aware of the positions of these decision-makers. Though they need not be officials themselves (and do not come to the workshop in any official capacity), they are nominated by the top decision-makers and are in touch with them both before and after the workshop. Burton himself, both before and after conducting a workshop, tries to establish and maintain contact with the relevant governmental and intergovernmental agencies. In the first project conducted by the London Centre, the meetings themselves extended over a period of several months: after an initial week of intensive discussions, the group reconvened under the Centre's auspices whenever the parties felt that a session would be useful. In principle, then, controlled communication is not a one-shot exercise, but can be tied into a continuing process of conflict resolution at various points in time. Of course, such coordination of workshops with ongoing political processes is greatly facilitated when the sponsoring organization is specifically devoted to research on international conflict.

The Fermeda Workshop was further removed from the political process. Though the organizers communicated with the governments

10 Burton, *Conflict and Communication*, p. 17.
11 Ibid., p. 19.
12 Ibid., p. 49.
13 Ibid., p. 55.

concerned, their purpose was to inform the governments and get their approval, rather than to coordinate directly with decision-making bodies. Though the participants were potentially influential members of their societies, they were selected by the organizers and could not be viewed as even unofficial representatives of their respective governments. Both Burton and Doob took pains to hold the workshop itself in a setting isolated from the pressures of political and diplomatic environments, but Doob placed greater emphasis on separating the total enterprise from the political process.

In Doob's conception, as I understand it, a workshop can contribute to conflict resolution by creating certain products that can then be fed into the political process. In other words, the workshop itself is not directly linked to national decision-making or diplomatic efforts at conflict resolution, but its products may well be relevant to these activities. The workshop's potential products are of two kinds: they may take the form of attitude changes in influential persons, which would be reflected over time in the inputs these individuals make into their national policy debates; and they may be documents, setting forth possible solutions that would not have emerged as readily from the usual political procedures.

The difference between Burton's and Doob's conceptions of the enterprise thus has some clear implications for what the workshop is intended to accomplish. For Doob, it is a more self-contained enterprise, standing or falling on the immediate products that emerge from it. There is, therefore, more emphasis on the personal learning of the participants—on whether they come away from the workshop with demonstrably greater knowledge and insight. There is also more emphasis on producing an agreed-upon solution, in the form of a document that can serve as an input to the policy debate. For Burton, too, it is important to produce changes in the participants and to promote problem-solving; however, these effects are viewed as steps in the conflict-resolution process more than as ends in themselves. There is less emphasis on the personal learning of the participants, except insofar as it influences the new information and insights that they can feed into the policy process. Similarly, there is less emphasis on the production of agreed-upon documents within the workshop itself. The presumption is that the actual working out of solutions must happen elsewhere; the workshop will have made its contribution if it has brought some new possibilities for solutions to the attention of the relevant decision-makers.

If we look at the two ends of the enterprise that are central to both approaches—creating an atmosphere in which change can take place, and feeding new information and insights into the policy process—we can probably say, at the risk of some oversimplification, that Doob's conception places relatively more emphasis on creating the conditions for *change*, while Burton's places relatively more emphasis on creating the conditions for *transfer*. In selecting independent participants, in insulating the workshop on a "cultural island," in breaking up the national groupings, in encouraging group solidarity and emotional involvement, and in emphasizing group process and personal learning, the Fermeda Workshop made it more probable that participants would experience changes, but by the same token it made the transfer of such changes once the participants returned to their home settings—and particularly the penetration of the changes into the policy process—less likely. On the other hand, the London exercise, by working more closely with the decision-making agencies, by selecting participants more directly tied to the decision-making process, by maintaining the national teams as the basic unit and avoiding divisions within it, and by keeping the discussions more fully at an intellectual and substantive level, took less advantage of the workshop's potential for producing changes, but increased the probability that any changes that did occur would be transferred to the policy process.

Given these somewhat distinct conceptions of the enterprise, how does each approach define the task of the workshop itself? What are the means by which the workshop brings about the desired changes, and what roles do the participants and the social scientists have to enact if these changes are to take place?

Both approaches are designed to create the conditions for effective problem-solving. To this end, participants must learn to communicate with each other in new ways, to revise perceptions distorted by a long history of conflict, and—in Burton's words—to see "the conflict as a problem to be solved and not as a contest to be won."[14] In relation to each other, they must move from the roles of antagonists engaged in a zero-sum game, in which neither party dares to yield a point, to the role of collaborators searching for a positive-sum solution to a common problem. The social scientists' role is to facilitate this movement. The two approaches diverge in emphasis in their views of how this movement comes about.

In Burton's approach, the primary mediating process is the behavioral analysis of conflict. The workshop is designed to draw the participants into this process of conflict analysis along with the panel of social scientists. Anthony de Reuck, a member of the Centre for

14 Ibid., p. 157.

the Analysis of Conflict, has distinguished three roles that participants may play in a workshop: combatant representative, conflict analyst, and cooperative representative. He points out:

> An essential part of the controlled communication technique is to divest the parties of their roles and inhibitions as combatant representatives, and to offer them alternative roles, first as conflict analysts and later as cooperative representatives. In their roles as combatant representatives, the parties' reference groups are their governments and people at home. In their analytical roles, each party's reference group is that physically present around the conference table. At first, no doubt, it comprises only the academic panel, but as the meeting proceeds, I believe it could be shown to expand to include also the opponent party.[15]

The role of conflict analyst, fostered by the definition of the situation, gradually guides participants into that of cooperative representative. It also remains as an alternative when the cooperative process becomes too difficult or threatening: participants can retreat into the more intellectual role of general conflict-analyst.

The role of conflict analyst is readily available insofar as the workshop is presented—as was the case in the London workshop—as a research project. The research context, more generally, can facilitate entry into communication and broaden the content of what is communicated. Thus, when research serves as the context of the encounter, it becomes possible to bring together conflicting parties who until now refused to communicate, because to do so would have meant to yield a political point or to take unacceptable risks. The research context permits communication with minimum commitment and minimum risk. Similarly, within the situation, the research context allows participants to discuss issues and entertain ideas that they would have to avoid if they were speaking "for the record." Having agreed to collaborate in an ongoing research program, to which their conflict is relevant as a case in point, they can graciously defer to the wishes of the "professors" and pursue certain lines of discussion that would otherwise have met with objection. The combination of research with conflict resolution thus creates an ambiguity that may greatly help to move the process along. As Burton points out:

15 Anthony de Reuck, "Controlled Communication: Rationale and Dynamics," paper prepared for UNITAR Workshop on Social Psychological Aspects of Peaceful Settlement, New Paltz, N.Y., May 15–17, 1970.

> The ambiguity of the role of representatives—whether they are acting as official representatives in expressing viewpoints, or whether as honorary academics participating in an exercise designed to examine conflict—is itself an asset. It provides a reason for exploration even on matters on which official policy has been firmly stated, it makes possible a working relationship between the participants as persons, and it removes any implications of official commitments. Traditional means of peaceful settlement require commitment: this procedure depends for its success on the absence of any commitment, and the establishment of relationships that do not require it.[16]

In short, the research context can surmount some of the barriers to communication that characterize the relationship of conflicting parties—provided, of course, that the sponsors of the workshop are genuinely interested in conflict research and not just using it as a device to bring the parties together. At the same time, the research context makes the role of conflict analyst particularly natural. After all, conflict analysis is the substance of the research in which the participants have agreed to help out. They are acting as informants, providing data for the social science panel, and gradually entering into the process of analysis itself. Thus the research context creates not only a general readiness to engage in communication, but a natural occasion for the specific process that Burton considers to be a crucial step in conflict resolution. Furthermore, insofar as both parties are working with the social science panel in a research effort, they can more readily come to regard each other as collaborators in a common enterprise.

In line with Burton's definition of the workshop task, the primary role of the social scientists is "to inject into discussion new information, not about the dispute in question, but about conflict, its origins and processes drawn from theoretical analyses and empirical studies."[17] Later in the workshop, when solutions are under discussion, the social scientists also contribute information designed to extend the range of integrative mechanisms and possibilities for functional cooperation that the participants can consider. The social science panel, and particularly the discussion chairman, are by no means oblivious to the group process. They try to encourage movement away from the role of combatant representative and toward the role of conflict analyst and increasingly toward that of cooperative

16 Burton, *Conflict and Communication*, p. 43.
17 Ibid., p. 157.

representative. But the key professional input of the social scientists is at the level of theory and empirical findings.

In the Fermeda model, the primary mediating process is sensitization of participants to their own interpersonal behavior and to group process. The workshop essentially offers training in the skills of effective communication through the use of the "laboratory approach to learning." The training is designed to enhance participants' awareness of ways in which their own emotional commitments and the nature of group interaction may hinder effective communication and problem-solving, and to increase their ability to overcome these obstacles. The trainers convey the process of analyzing the ongoing interaction through demonstration, exposition, and the use of special exercises, and they draw the participants into active involvement in this process. As one of the trainers at Fermeda describes it, "The basic feature of this approach is that participants learn through analysis of, and generalizations from, their own experience and that of others with whom they interact. Laboratory participants, in different words, must first participate (interact, behave); then they are encouraged to reflect upon the meaning and impact of that behavior in relation to both themselves and others."[18] To adapt de Reuck's terminology, in the Fermeda model the participants move from the role of combatant representative to that of cooperative representative through adopting the role of process analyst—a role calling for self-conscious attention to what is happening in the group and what each participant is contributing to that process, and thus mediating change from self-defeating to more constructive modes of interaction.

Adoption of the process-analyst role is facilitated by definition of the workshop as essentially a learning experience—a training laboratory. In this context, participants are more prepared to go along with procedures (such as the T-group) that have no obvious connection to the substantive issues with which they are concerned, and to accept exercises (such as simulation and brainstorming) that might otherwise strike them as overly artificial. (Even so, some of the participants in Fermeda apparently resented procedures that had no clear and immediate relationship to the objective that had brought them to the workshop.) Furthermore, the context of a training laboratory—like the context of a research project in the London exercise—permits communication with relatively little commitment and risk. In this playful, protective, and insulated environment, the in-

18 Thomas E. Wickes, "The African Context and the Schedule," in Doob, *Resolving Conflict in Africa*, p. 26.

dividual is moved to pursue and express ideas that would be unacceptable in other settings, and he feels free to do so without worrying that he will be held accountable for it. In the Fermeda T-groups, participants felt free to consider and support positions that deviated from the normative positions of their own national groups. It is interesting, however, that when the two T-groups came together in the general assembly and participants were exposed to fellow nationals, with whom they had not shared the common T-group experience, they tended to revert to a nationalistic stance. The learning context, which had served to reduce inhibitions, was overwhelmed by the real-life context provided by the presence of "outsiders" (particularly from one's own national group) and by the approaching end of the workshop and anticipated return home. As long as the learning context is maintained, however, the freedom to explore with a minimal sense of risk can greatly facilitate creative problem-solving.

Other important features of the training laboratory situation can help to push the problem-solving process forward. The development of a sense of solidarity an openness of communication, and warm personal bonds within the learning group not only contributes to the learning process; it also constitutes an important element of the problem-solving that this learning process is designed to facilitate. A cohesive group can more readily approach the conflict to be resolved as a joint task for the conflicting parties, to be tackled in a collaborative spirit. Similarly, the deliberate utilization of the here and now as a source of insights, through observation and analysis of ongoing interaction, facilitates both the learning process and the conflict-resolution process itself. The T-group, according to a Fermeda trainer, "replicates in microcosm the dynamics of the real system without acting it out. It focuses on an examination of its own process, analyzing and learning from what is happening right here and now. It provides an instrument to 'see' problems or divisions between people more clearly because they are projected and illustrated in the group and to accelerate the search for solutions that personal and shared identification with problems stimulates."[19] Insofar as participants can draw on the here and now in analyzing the conflict, they can partly overcome constraints imposed on the problem-solving process by formulations of the conflict that are rooted in historical arguments and the public positions of their respective governments.

In line with the Fermeda Workshop's definition of its task, the

19 Charles K. Ferguson, "Appraisal by a Trainer," in Doob, *Resolving Conflict in Africa*, p. 133.

primary role of the social scientists is to encourage the development of sensitivity to group process and effective communication patterns among the participants. As the group turns to direct efforts at problem-solving, the social scientists' role is to facilitate the process —to help the group identify snags when the process seems to break down and to develop strategies that would keep it moving. In both the training and the problem-solving phases (which need not be temporally separated), they help the group observe and analyze the interaction in which members are currently engaged. As in Burton's exercises, the social scientists may inject relevant theoretical considerations or empirical information, but their major inputs in the Fermeda model consist of observations and interpretations of the ongoing group process.

The differences between Burton's and Doob's approaches are mostly differences in emphasis. Despite their different origins, both approaches are built on a surprisingly similar set of insights about the use of "clinical" procedures to promote change and collaborative problem-solving among conflicting parties, and about the potential contributions of these procedures to conflict resolution at the political level. Both are concerned with producing change, and with its feedback to national and international decision-making; to facilitate change, both use inputs from conflict theory and from group-process analysis. They differ essentially in their ways of maximizing the unique strengths of the workshop approach and of minimizing its limitations.

In the following sections, I consider some of these strengths and limitations of the workshop approach. In each case, I try to show how insights from both Burton's and Doob's experiences might be combined to utilize the workshop most effectively. My general assumption is that workshops, though rooted in the same basic principles, may vary along a number of dimensions—such as the degree of emphasis on personal probing or theoretical analysis, the proximity of participants to the decision-making process, or the specific attributes of third parties present. The Burton and Doob experiments occupy different positions on some of these dimensions and thus represent different combinations of the possible features by which a workshop might be defined—different cells, as it were, in a multidimensional matrix of workshop types. Various other combinations should be possible, each best suited to a particular set of circumstances. Further conceptualization and experimentation in this area can help us specify the circumstances in which a workshop is likely to be useful and, if so, the combination of techniques most likely to be effective, given the nature of the particular conflict, the occasion for convening a workshop, and the relationship of both the organizers and the participants to the various decision-making units.

UNIQUE STRENGTHS OF THE WORKSHOP APPROACH

In the most general terms, the unique strength of the workshop approach is that it allows certain processes of communication that are almost impossible to achieve in the settings (particularly the more public and formal ones) where conflicting parties usually interact. The workshop facilitates such interactions, first, by providing a novel *context* for communication and, second, by using a unique set of *techniques* and third-party inputs to guide the communication process.

In many conflict situations, the very fact that communication is taking place may be seen, by one or both sides, as a concession—because it suggests that the other side may have a valid claim, or even because it constitu es recognition of the other side's existence as a legitimate entity. Communication may also be avoided because it represents unacceptable risks: decision-makers may be afraid that their willingness to talk would be taken as a sign of weakness, or that talks would reduce the pressure on the opponent, or that they would inevitably lead to compromises which would weaken the regime's domestic and international standing, or that they would end in failure with a resulting loss in credibility and prestige. Conflicting parties may, therefore, refuse to communicate at all, or at least to engage in meaningful communication. Once such a pattern has been established, public commitments and private fears make it difficult for the parties to break out of it—even when they have come to feel that something might be gained from communication. In this type of situation the workshop may be particularly helpful by providing a context in which parties can enter into discussion with minimum commitment and risk. If the outcome of the workshop seems promising, decision-makers can continue discussions through more formal channels; if it yields nothing useful, they can ignore it without feeling discredited; if, for some reason, it blows up, they can easily disown it, since it was merely an academic exercise to which they had no formal commitment.

These considerations suggest one criterion for determining whether mounting of a workshop is indicated. When there is some desire for communication among the conflicting parties but the official channels for communication are unavailable, or their use entails unacceptable risks at this point, a workshop may provide the needed alternative mechanism. It may allow decision-makers to transmit and receive information otherwise unobtainable, and to see whether officially acknowledged initiation or resumption of communication is likely to have more positive than negative consequences. In the limiting case, a workshop may serve as dress rehearsal for more formal negotiations.

For the individual participants, the workshop also offers an opportunity to communicate with minimum commitment and risk. This fact has a bearing not only on their willingness to participate, but also on the type of communication they are prepared to engage in. I have already indicated how the context of both Burton's and Doob's workshops enhances the participants' freedom to entertain and express ideas that they would be inclined to eschew in settings marked by greater public accountability. The usual norms against deviating from the position of one's own side, so pervasive in a conflict situation, are relaxed in the workshop context. More than that, an opposing set of norms, calling for uninhibited exploration of all possibilities, is generated in this setting. In Burton's workshop it derives from the requirements of the research for careful analysis of all dimensions and ramifications of the conflict; in Doob's, from the requirements of the laboratory method for open and honest communication. Having committed themselves to the enterprise, the participants feel a sense of obligation to abide by its norms.

To provide a novel context, it seems to me, the workshop must be held under the auspices of some institution independent of the political process which can bring an overarching set of norms to bear on the proceedings. In other words, there needs to be some institutionalized basis for the norms governing the workshop, if the participants are to regard them (while they are in the situation) as binding and as superseding their national norms. A workshop held under the auspices of a body such as the United Nations Security Council, for example, might not provide the necessary novel context, since it does not claim a set of norms independent of those of the member-states.[20] An agency more nearly transnational in character—set up to perform a function that cuts across (rather than coordinates) national interests—would be more suitable. Burton's and Doob's experiences suggest that such a transnational institution for conflict resolution might be most effective if it included research and training as part of its mission.

20 Burton discusses other limitations of the Security Council as a possible institutional base for conflict resolution. See his *Conflict and Communication*, p. 235.

For both the London and the Fermeda workshops, the institutional base was the university. They provided the novel normative context of a research project in one case and of a training laboratory in the other. The research project seems to me to present a very useful context, particularly when the participants are relatively senior and high in status, and when the workshop requires the cooperation of decision-making agencies. Both the decision-makers who are asked to approve or support the enterprise and the participants themselves can usually understand and accept a research-linked workshop without difficulty, and they can readily justify their cooperation with such an effort. It is quite evident why students of conflict would want to meet with representatives of conflicting parties in a face-to-face encounter, and why the parties themselves would be prepared to support such a scholarly enterprise and to regard it as a source of potentially useful findings. Another virtue of the research context is that it offers the workshop participants the roles of expert informant and research collaborator—roles that are inherently rewarding and in keeping with their status. Finally, the research context allows a continuing relationship between the sponsors and the conflicting parties, and a resumption of the workshop if the need and opportunity arise: the natural life of the research project coincides with the natural life of the conflict.

The training-laboratory context strikes me as somewhat less powerful on all of these counts. Doob and his associates themselves seem to have concluded that the rationale and value of workshops within this context are not always manifest to governments and participants, and that the role of trainee is resented by some participants as insulting and out of keeping with their status. The training-laboratory context is also less amenable to a continuing relationship, since repeated workshops presumably offer diminishing returns from a training point of view. Finally, this context is more vulnerable to failure: a workshop that produces little learning and problem-solving can be assimilated in a research context, since (regardless of outcome) it provides grist for the research mill, but it may be quite demoralizing to both participants and staff in a training context. Nevertheless, there are occasions on which the training laboratory context may be highly appropriate and productive. Thus, a workshop might be organized specifically to serve an educational purpose—involving as its participants, for example, groups of students representing conflicting parties or diplomats seeking to gain insight into the nature of conflict and the techniques of its resolution. Furthermore, it must be kept in mind that training, in some fashion, is at least a *component* of all workshops. Thus even in the Burton model participants must gradually learn the language and the attitudes required for the role of conflict analyst, and the hope is that this learning will generalize to their post-workshop behavior.

The context of the workshop, as we have seen, helps overcome some of the barriers to communication that are so prevalent in conflict situations. The relative lack of commitment gives participants the *freedom* to talk more openly and honestly, and the norms of the setting create an *expectation* that they will do so. The fact that the parties have come together for a task defined, essentially, by a third party, makes it possible and necessary for them to abandon, to some degree, their competitive stance toward each other and to adopt a more trusting and collaborative one. To capitalize on this favorable context for communication, the workshop approach utilizes a set of techniques and interventions to guide the communication process. Some of these are more pronounced in Burton's approach; others, in Doob's.

Interactions between conflicting parties are usually highly repetitive and stereotyped. Alternative versions of the historical record are recited, old accusations and justifications are rehearsed, and fine legalistic points about rights and wrongs are debated. The workshop approach is designed to cut through this type of argumentation and to set a more constructive communication process into motion. The social scientists contribute to this end by setting the stage for a different communication process, by keeping the process moving and preventing a reversion to less-productive exchanges, and by injecting ideas, observations, and information on which new learning and insight can be built.

In setting the stage, the social scientists communicate the ground rules that are to govern the proceedings. In both word and action, they try to make clear that discussions will be mostly unstructured, that the basic raw material for analysis and problem-solving will have to emerge from the participants, and that the norms of the situation call for honest communication of perceptions and motives and for free exploration of a wide range of ideas. Through the attitudes they convey in their own interventions, they try to create a task-oriented, collaborative atmosphere, and an analytical, nonevaluative approach to the conflict. Stage-setting is mostly done at the beginning, but it has to continue throughout the proceedings. The social scientists must periodically remind the group of the ground rules. Furthermore, they must reinforce the norms and the atmosphere they have tried to convey whenever the opportunity arises—by the kinds of questions they ask, by their reactions to what the participants say and do, and by the way they handle participants' efforts to induce them to assume leadership, to take sides, or to make authoritative pronouncements.

To keep the discussions moving in constructive directions, the social scientist injects observations about the ongoing group process whenever the group seems to have reached an impasse. He may simply point out that the discussions have stalled or that the participants have reverted to the standard pattern of argumentation among conflicting parties. He may describe what has been happening in the group, thus bringing to the members' attention some of the interactions that may have failed to register on them, but leaving up to them the interpretation of these events. At times, he may himself offer possible interpretations of the dynamics of the group process that seem to be impeding progress. Such interpretations, in my view, ought to be relatively infrequent. Moreover, they must be presented in the form of tentative hypotheses, recognizing that they may be wrong or (even if they are perfectly accurate) that the group may not be quite ready for them. (These considerations are similar to those governing a psychotherapist's tentative allusions to his patient's unconscious defenses in interpreting his resistances to the therapeutic work.) Finally, such interpretations in a problem-solving workshop must be at the level of group process, rather than personality dynamics.

Group process observations are useful, not only in keeping the discussions moving in constructive directions, but also in transmitting to the participants a potentially effective tool for problem-solving. Participants are encouraged to engage in process analysis themselves and thus to acquire a more analytic stance concerning their own and other members' interactions in the group. The ability to step aside and observe the ongoing interaction process is particularly valuable in the resolution of intergroup conflicts, which by their very nature inhibit effective communication and problem-solving.

The purpose of initiating and facilitating new patterns of communication in the workshop is to provide opportunities for the emergence of ideas, observations, and information on which new learning and insight can be built. It is such new learnings and insights that make it possible, and sometimes necessary, for participants to reassess their attitudes and reformulate the issues in ways more conducive to problem-solving. Some of the new information is injected directly into the discussion by the social science panel. Much of the information is specifically introduced by participants, or emerges from their discussions, or is generated by their interactions; but the social scientists contribute to the process by helping to elicit the information, by encouraging the participants to focus on it, and by suggesting some of its implications.

One can distinguish at least three sources of new information in the workshop situation from which potentially new learnings and insights may emerge:

(1) In the course of the discussions, participants may acquire new information about the perceptions and intentions of the other side. The relatively private and relaxed setting may induce them to express sentiments that have not previously been acknowledged in public statements. Such information is bound to be useful, by adding depth to one's understanding of the other side's position, but there is also some danger in overemphasizing the significance of this information: the public positions of a government may be better indicators and predictors of policy than the private sentiments of individuals, even if these individuals are high officials (particularly since public pronouncements set constraints on future action). The workshop setting not only encourages the transmission of such new information, but also increases the probability that others will be receptive to it, to the extent that a degree of openness and mutual trust has developed. The social scientists contribute to the transmission and reception of this type of information by creating an atmosphere in which there is greater openness to new information and setting a task around which trust can be built. Moreover, when new information is introduced, the social scientists can call attention to it and make it a focus for discussion. They can encourage the participants to confront the information, making sure that it is neither avoided nor distorted and that its implications are duly drawn.

(2) The workshop can introduce the participants to a new conceptual framework for the analysis of conflict, a set of theoretical propositions, and a body of empirical findings, all of which may be applicable to their own situations. In the London workshop, such information was provided fairly systematically by the panel of social scientists, who then drew the participants into discussion of the theoretical models and their implications for various conflicts. The participants thus acquired some new insights into the nature of conflict, as well as a common language and frame of reference for analyzing specific conflict situations. The learning process may be aided, as in the Fermeda Workshop, by the introduction of games and simulations when such procedures might help illustrate and give experiential meaning to a theoretical proposition. In any event, the

application of the new concepts and analytical tools to their own situations must be left largely to the participants themselves. The social scientists can encourage the participants to make such efforts; they can ask leading questions, engage in gentle probings, and suggest tentative hypotheses to explain the nature and course of the conflict. But, in the final analysis, the application must be made *by the participants* if it is to have major impact on the resolution process. The timing of interpretations is also crucial, even if they are presented in tentative fashion. Again, one can take a leaf from the psychotherapist's book: an experienced therapist does not offer an interpretation unless he feels confident that the patient is ready for it.

(3) As the participants interact with each other and with the third parties in the course of the workshop, they may be illustrating—here and now—some of the underlying dynamics of the conflict between the communities they represent. Their behavior in the group may reflect the nature of the relationship between their communities and the self-perpetuating pattern of interaction that they have adopted. For example, in the course of the London workshop, I developed (but was unable to explore) the hypothesis that some of the interactions of the Greek-Cypriot and Turkish-Cypriot participants, with each other and with the social science panel, could be understood in terms of their statuses as members of the majority and minority populations respectively. The exploration of such hypotheses, based on ongoing interactions, can be a source of profound insight, since the participants can see the conflict in operation. They can observe its concrete manifestations in the very situation in which they are still actively involved and almost at the very moment that the interaction occurs. This type of experience has much in common with the "corrective emotional experiences" that many psychotherapists see as the heart of the therapeutic process.[21] In the context of psychotherapy, "the essence of a corrective emotional experience is the fact that the patient's examination of his attitudes and behavior patterns occurs simultaneously with their actual manifestation at a real-life level of emotional intensity. He examines his attitudes and behavior while he is still experiencing the relevant feelings, which makes this more than a mere intellectual exercise."[22] Like the psychotherapist, the social scientist in a workshop can facilitate such insights by calling attention to ongoing interactions that might illuminate

21 Franz Alexander and Thomas M. French, *Psychoanalytic Therapy* (New York: Ronald Press, 1946), pp. 66–68.

22 Herbert C. Kelman, "The Role of the Group in the Induction of Therapeutic Change," *International Journal of Group Psychotherapy* 13, no. 4 (October 1963): 415.

the relationship between the conflicting parties, and by helping participants explore their implications. Again, of course, his interventions must be tentative and sensitively timed.

In sum, I have described three major types of new information and insight that the workshop can provide and that can facilitate attitude change and problem-solving: direct information about the perceptions and sentiments of the other side, theoretical concepts for conflict analysis with potential applicability to the specific conflict under discussion, and analysis of ongoing interactions that might reflect the relationships between the conflicting parties. The first was common to both the London and the Fermeda experiences, the second was more prominent in London, and the third in Fermeda.

The combination of Burton's systematic use of theoretical inputs with Doob's greater emphasis on analysis of group process and on emotional learning would, in my view, maximize the workshop's potential for producing change. Process analysis can promote change, not only by facilitating movement in the group, but also by utilizing the ongoing interactions as a source of new insights. However, problem-solving workshops in conflict resolution ought not to be equated with sensitivity training in the usual sense of that term. Though they encourage interpersonal trust and personal learning among the participants in order to achieve their goals, their purpose is not to promote personal growth or strong in-group feelings. Their purpose is to facilitate creative problem-solving in a specific conflict situation. It is essential that this task-orientation and problem-solving emphasis be reflected in the organization of the workshop and all of its components. In line with this view, I would agree with the tentative conclusion of Doob and his associates that it would be inadvisable, in future workshops, to separate "training" from work on the substantive issues.[23] The substantive issues ought to be the focus of attention throughout, with group process observations, as well as special laboratory devices (simulations, role reversals, brainstorming, or the setting of operational goals or subgoals), brought in whenever they become relevant and the participants seem ready for them.

23 The first few days of the Fermeda Workshop were devoted to T-groups in order to prepare participants for subsequent collaborative efforts to find solutions to their border disputes. The organizers concluded that "the sharp temporal distinction . . . between training in behalf of developing self-awareness and, more especially, communication skills on the one hand and the discussion of the substantive issues may have been a mistake and ought, therefore, to be blurred in the future. . . . It would . . . perhaps be better to begin a workshop with the substantive issue as the thesis and to let personal probing creep in slowly but inevitably as the antithesis." See Doob, *Resolving Conflict in Africa*, p. 122.

LIMITATIONS OF THE WORKSHOP APPROACH

The ultimate goal of a problem-solving workshop is to feed the changes and solutions it has generated into the policy process. As I have already pointed out, however, it is more effectively designed to *produce* changes in its participants and to generate innovative solutions than it is to *transfer* these products to the policy process. Much of the workshop's strength derives from its separation from the policy process. It is held under independent auspices, in a setting removed from decision-making agencies, with participants acting as relatively uncommitted individuals, and according to ground rules that encourage the transcendence of official positions. All of these features, by removing some of the usual barriers to change, make its occurrence more probable, but by the same token they make its transfer more difficult.

The problem of transfer actually involves two interrelated questions. First, if an individual changes in the workshop setting—that is, if he reassesses his attitudes and accepts a new approach to resolving the conflict—what is the likelihood that he will maintain these new attitudes and formulations once he returns to his home setting? Second, assuming he does—or to the extent that he does—maintain these changes, what is the likelihood that he will be able to bring his new attitudes and formulations effectively to bear on the policy process?

The first question is common to all types of workshops, ranging from those primarily oriented toward individual change to those oriented toward organizational problem-solving. It refers to what has been called the "reentry" problem. The workshop takes the individual into a different world, frees him from the usual pressures and constraints that bind him to a limited perspective, and thus allows him to reexamine his assumptions and to develop new ways of looking at things. But once he leaves this more open and protective environment and returns to the real world, there is a great danger of backsliding. The old pressures will come into play, and the dominant frame of reference will begin to reassert itself. Moreover, the individual may find that the new ideas he expresses are met with hostility and that the proposals he puts forth are systematically shot down. Of course, the severity of the reentry problem varies as a function of many factors. But I think it can be fairly said that, given an influence attempt that removes an individual or a small group from their usual environments, any feature that enhances the probability for change almost invariably compounds the problem of reentry.

Workshops involving conflicting nations or communities may well present serious reentry problems, because here the issue of group loyalty is particularly salient. An individual who returns with a less militant view of the conflict may find himself treated as one who has been coopted by the other side, who has betrayed his own group, or who has inadequately defended its position. These pressures may make it difficult for him to express and ultimately to maintain his new attitudes.

The ease of maintaining changes produced in the workshop depends partly on the nature of the setting and the experiences it provided for the participants. The more different the setting and experiences are from those in which the participants habitually find themselves, the greater the likelihood that the workshop will present novel inputs, break up old thought-patterns, and produce change. These same conditions make the probability of transfer less likely, however. New attitudes may be closely associated with the unique stimuli of the workshop setting and fail to generalize to the home environment's radically different stimuli. Furthermore, a setting so different that it removes all reminders of home fails to prepare the individual for the reactions his new attitudes are likely to elicit upon his return. By keeping reminders of the home setting to a minimum, the workshop may reduce resistance to change, but at the same time fail to build immunity against the pressures to which the new attitudes will later be exposed.

These considerations must enter into the decision of how much the workshop should insulate its participants from family, work, and political distractions. As Walton points out, comparative insulation "allows for a deeper immersion in the mental and emotional processes of the workshop and permits the development of a 'cultural island,' which in turn encourages participants to challenge cherished assumptions, break old thought processes, and modify attitudes." But it also has its disadvantages:

> Because the attitudes, views, and products generated by the workshop must eventually be persuasive also to countrymen who have not attended the workshop, it is possible for the cultural island effect to be too complete, if it leads to proposed solutions which will later be dismissed out-of-hand back home as unrealistic or idealistic. Similarly, some would consider the cultural island too complete if upon returning home a participant expresses conciliatory atti-

> tudes which are so deviant from the national norms that he loses credibility.[24]

Thus changes are more likely to take place in a cultural island, but more difficult to maintain once the individual returns to the mainland. Another workshop feature that is relevant in this connection is the extent to which participants are functioning as members of a national team or as individuals. If they function in teams, they are more likely to stick to the official positions of their respective groups longer. If they function as individuals, variations in point of view within each national group can emerge more quickly and a wider range of ideas thus becomes available for discussion and problem-solving. Also, participants can learn more quickly that the other side is not monolithic, and they can come to appreciate some of the diversity in its views. Thus change may occur more readily in workshops where national contingents are not treated as units.[25] At the same time, however, such a procedure may make transfer of new attitudes more difficult. Positions developed without having to achieve consensus within the national contingent may be more vulnerable to attack and rejection by fellow nationals once participants return home. In fact, this possibility became apparent at the Fermeda Workshop even before the participants left; changes achieved in the intimacy of the T-groups did not quite survive "reentry" into the general assembly.

The ease of maintaining changes produced in the workshop depends not only on the conditions of the workshop itself, but also on the nature of the setting and experiences to which the participants return. If they come back to fairly conservative settings that are committed (ideologically or organizationally) to the official group position, then the changes they underwent are less likely to maintain themselves. Thus, for example, changes are more likely to be maintained among participants who return to an academic setting, since diversity in views on national issues is more readily accepted there.

24 Walton, "Problem-Solving Workshop," pp. 482–83.

25 Walton argues that when participants (as in the Fermeda Workshop) come as individuals rather than in national teams, and when the representatives from the same national group do not know each other or have not previously worked together, it would be best—even when trying to maximize change—to meet with each national contingent separately before bringing members together in a multinational grouping. Such a procedure would help develop trust within each national group and make it easier for it to "tolerate and indeed encourage differences in viewpoints among its members" ("Problem-Solving Workshop," p. 479), thus "improving the quality of the deliberations . . . and the likelihood that the community would converge on some areas of substantive agreement" (p. 486).

On the other hand, participants returning to government agencies, which are committed to a particular way of formulating the conflict, may find their new attitudes and formulations ignored or rejected. As they continue to work under these pressures and within the built-in framework of assumptions, they are more likely to revert to the official position on the conflict.

The question of participants' organizational background leads us directly to the second problem involved in the transfer of changes generated by a workshop: what is the likelihood that participants will be able to bring their new attitudes and formulations (assuming these have been maintained) to bear on the policy process? Since the workshop is, by its nature, removed from the policy process, the problem of feeding its products back into that process must inevitably arise. The ease of achieving such feedback depends largely on the participants' characteristics and their relationships to the policy process.

In general, it stands to reason that if the decision-makers are involved in the plans for the workshop, if the workshop organizers consult with them both before and after, and if the participants themselves are close to the center of decision-making and are at least informally acting as representatives of the decision-makers, then the opportunity for feedback will be greater. There is probably less *change* in this case than in a workshop where the participants act purely as private citizens. The closer the participants are to decision-making agencies, the more likely they are to be constrained by official positions and decision-makers' expectations, and the less likely they are to be open to change. Whatever changes *do* occur, however—whatever new learnings and insights the participants acquire—will come to the attention of the decision-makers much more readily in this case. Thus it would again appear that there is a reciprocal relationship between change and transfer: the closer the participants are to the center of decision-making, the less open they are to change, but the more capable they are to feed whatever changes they do experience into the policy process.

On closer examination, it seems to me that the picture is considerably more complicated than the one I have drawn so far. Whether or not participants closest to the locus of decision-making are most likely to inject their changes into the policy process may well depend on the nature of the changes in question, as well as on the precise relationship of the participants to the decision-making units. For example, if change takes the form of some new learning about the intentions of the other side, then the proposition no doubt holds. Say a workshop participant concludes from the discussions that the other side may be willing (despite previous public pronouncements) to entertain certain new lines of negotiation; he would be in a much more favorable position to carry this information to the decision-makers and to persuade them to act on it if he is close to the decision-making unit and has in fact been sent to the workshop by that unit (presumably to obtain just this kind of information). On the other hand, if the change he experienced is more fundamental—if he comes away from the workshop convinced that the whole policy pursued by his government is inappropriate, and committed to a thorough reformulation of the issues and the possibilities for solution—then his proximity to the locus of decision-making may make little difference. It may not enhance his ability to inject his new insights into the policy process and may, in fact, reduce it, depending on the exact nature of his relationship to the decision-making bureaucracy.

In conceptualizing this problem, I start with the assumption that the workshop approach can change *individual* perceptions, attitudes, and formulations of problems and solutions. Thus workshop techniques can be most useful when directed at those points in the decision-making process at which individual perceptions and formulations of the conflict become relevant and important. It can be argued that diplomats and foreign-policy officials do *not* represent such points in the process. They are relatively unlikely to act as individuals, bringing their own attitudes and perceptions to bear on their official role performance. They tend to act within a highly institutionalized conceptual framework; the assumptions of that framework are built into the routine operations of the decision-making apparatus and are constantly reinforced by the interactions of its various units. Perceptions and attitudes certainly enter into the role performance of diplomats and foreign-policy officials, but they are most likely to be the shared and frozen perceptions and attitudes that pervade the decision-making bodies. Diplomats and officials are usually not in a position to reexamine them or to call for their reexamination. Thus, it is not too likely that (acting within their roles) these individuals would effectively use changes gained through a workshop experience.

On the other hand, the situation might be quite different for legislators or their staff assistants, or for the leaders or executives of various powerful pressure groups. These are individuals whose task in the foreign-policy process is to formulate and define issues in keeping with the interests (at least as they interpret these) of the constituencies they represent. Though they can generally be counted on to support the administration's foreign policy, they are not necessarily bound by the perspectives of the decision-making units and are relatively free to promote changes in direction or emphasis of existing policy. If they revise their perceptions and attitudes, their own inputs into the policy process may well be affected. These inputs, in turn, while not determining policy, may influence it considerably. I would hypothesize that individuals in these kinds of roles might be best able to make effective use of changes resulting from a workshop experience, because it is their business (unlike that of the diplomat or foreign-policy official) to bring their own perceptions and attitudes to bear on the policy process.

Thus my analysis tentatively suggests that the ideal participants in a workshop (even if its goal is to have maximal impact on the policy process) are not necessarily those closest to the locus of decision-making. Such individuals may not only be less likely to experience substantial changes in attitude, when compared to individuals more remote from the locus of decision-making, but they may also be less able to inject the changes they do experience into the policy process. Perhaps the ideal candidates for workshops are individuals at some intermediate distance from the decision-making apparatus. They must be influential members of their societies, preferably with an active interest in foreign-policy issues, but—if our criterion is their ability to feed the products of the workshop into the policy process—it may be better if their role is to influence and evaluate foreign policy, rather than to make it or carry it out.

There is, of course, more than one type of workshop and more than one model of the "ideal participant." Perhaps, if my argument is correct, individuals at such intermediate positions in the foreign-policy process as legislators or lobbyists may be the most "natural" candidates for workshop participation, but there are sure to be occasions when a very different type of participant—closer to the policy process or farther removed from it—would be highly appropriate. Selection of appropriate participants depends on the purpose of a particular workshop and on its place in the larger context of efforts at conflict resolution. The proper matching of participants and occasions is one of the major issues for further conceptualization and experimentation.

CONCLUSION

The pioneering work of Burton and Doob has demonstrated the feasibility and suggested the potential usefulness of problem-solving workshops as inputs to international conflict resolution. Their experiments have pointed to the unique strengths and limitations of this approach, and they have revealed some of the dimensions along which workshops may vary. There is now a need for further experimentation, along with theoretically based efforts to specify just where the workshop approach can fit into the conduct of international relations and thus contribute to processes of conflict resolution. Such efforts, in turn, require a conceptualization of international politics in terms of the entire range of interactions that culminate in official state behavior.

I have argued that the workshop approach can have significant impact at those points in the policy process at which individual perceptions and attitudes play a determining role. To assess the potential of the approach, therefore, we must look beyond the points at which the final, official foreign-policy steps are taken—in other words, beyond the foreign-policy bureaucracy and the diplomatic corps—since at these points individual perceptions and attitudes are unlikely to play a major part (except perhaps in influencing style and detail of policy execution). Instead, we must take a more total view of the international political process and its ramifications. It involves multiple actors—individual and collective, official and unofficial—all of whom influence foreign policy and the shape of international relations. Within this larger process, there are many points at which individual perceptions and attitudes may have major impact, both on short-term decisions and on long-term trends. The analytical task required now is identification of these points and specification of the types of individuals who are located at them and of the nature of their contributions to the policy process. Such an analysis would provide a systematic basis for determining the occasions on which problem-solving workshops may produce useful inputs to conflict resolution and for selecting the participants appropriate to a given occasion.

The occasions on which a workshop may contribute to conflict resolution vary widely. The relevance of workshops is perhaps most apparent in situations where conflict has reached violent proportions, but communication between the conflicting parties has never been initiated, or has broken down, or has reached an impasse, with each side frozen into a position totally unacceptable to the other side. Typically, in such situations, the decision-making units on each side are boxed in by a set of images of the other side, assumptions about the nature of the conflict, commitments to a national posture, and real or imagined constraints that prevent them from breaking out of their conceptual prisons and exploring new alternatives. New ideas and insights are desperately needed to cut into these self-perpetuating processes, and problem-solving workshops may be uniquely able to provide these. On such occasions, it seems to me, the most appropriate participants would be (as I suggested before) individuals at an intermediate distance from the foreign-policy apparatus, who are politically powerful and widely respected and whose loyalty to the national cause is beyond question, but who are not themselves completely caught up in the existing policy framework.

Other occasions for workshops may be tied much more specifically and closely to the process of diplomatic negotiations. There are moments in the interaction between conflicting parties when a workshop might be precisely the mechanism needed to facilitate negotiations—to bridge a specific gap between the position at which the parties find themselves and the one they know they want to reach. For example, a workshop may provide a context for exploring (with minimum risk) whether there is a basis for resuming broken-down negotiations; or for running a "dress rehearsal" before making a final commitment to formal negotiations; or for discussing certain new proposals in a relatively noncommittal fashion, away from the limelight in which official negotiations may be simultaneously proceeding; or, finally, for working out certain technical details of an agreement, which can be handled more effectively in a problem-solving format than in a diplomatic one. Participants in workshops of this type would most likely be diplomats, foreign-policy officials or advisers, or technical experts, depending on the specific occasion for the workshop.

At the other end of the continuum are workshops that are primarily educational. Such workshops may be occasioned by a specific conflict. They may bring together influential members of the two conflicting nations or communities, such as leaders of civic associations, journalists, intellectuals, business or labor leaders—or perhaps future influentials, such as students. The purpose might be modest and entirely long-range: to develop new ways of conceptualizing the conflict among elite segments of the populations, in the hope that these would eventually contribute to changes in public opinion and thus help create an atmosphere for alternative policies. Needless to say, such a workshop would probably contribute little to averting an imminent crisis. Educational workshops may also be organized independently of any specific conflict, to sensitize the participants to the nature of conflict and provide insights into its resolution. Diplomats or students of international relations in particular might benefit from such exercises.

The occasion for the workshop should help determine not only the types of participants selected, but also the mix of individuals composing the group. Various possibilities for composing the national groups and the total group suggest themselves, calling for experimentation and conceptual clarification. Depending on the purpose of the workshop, the national contingents may be selected to be homogeneous or they may be deliberately composed to represent different segments within each nation. In selecting the parties, an interesting possibility, particularly (though not exclusively) germane to general educational workshops, would be to include participants representing several pairs of conflicting nations or communities. Such a format would permit comparisons, would bring in a range of empirical inputs, and would allow participants to develop insights and to sharpen their conceptual tools through analysis of conflicts other than their own.

The criteria for selecting the parties in any given conflict situation are by no means self-evident, since the definition of the parties is itself often a matter of controversy. In selecting the Greek-Cypriot and Turkish-Cypriot communities—rather than Greece and Turkey—as the parties for the London workshop, the organizers took a position on the nature of the conflict. So did the organizers of the Fermeda Workshop in selecting Somalia, Ethiopia, and Kenya—the three nation-states—as the parties, rather than the Somali people and neighboring ethnic groups. The definition of the parties is even more controversial in conflicts in which one party is reluctant to recognize the other as a legitimate entity. Workshop organizers cannot avoid deciding how the parties are to be defined and thus indirectly taking a position in the controversy, but in making this decision it is important to analyze the relevance of different sets of parties to the workshop's particular purpose.

A workshop may be a way of establishing communication between parties unwilling or unable to communicate through official channels. However, if one party has refused to communicate, as a matter of policy, because of an unwillingness to recognize the other as a legitimate entity, then it may be equally reluctant to participate in a workshop. Communication, even in the context of an unofficial workshop, may represent too great a concession, particularly if the other party has *favored* a policy of communication. Thus, the organization of a workshop—creating the conditions under which both parties could participate without feeling that they are compromising their positions—is a complex problem in its own right, requiring some experimentation. To overcome some of the barriers to initiating a workshop, it may be useful to think of it in stages. In some situations, it may be necessary to start with separate workshops for the national groups, paving the way for joint meetings. Such preparatory workshops may also confront divisions within the national groups and select the teams to represent them at the joint workshop. It may also be useful, by the same token, to experiment with separate follow-up workshops for each national group, preferably augmented by other participants from the same society.

One final set of issues requiring further conceptual and experimental analysis concerns the role of the social scientists in the problem-solving workshop. I have discussed their possible inputs to the proceedings in some detail. It would be useful to specify which of these inputs are most appropriate on what occasions. It is also important to keep in mind that these inputs are never mere scientific statements or process observations, devoid of value presuppositions. The organizers bring to the situation their own definitions of the nature of the conflict, their own assumptions about the possibilities for resolution, and their own preferences for the directions resolution should take. It would be well to make these explicit for themselves and for the participants.

[11]

ADJUDICATING IN ANARCHY: AN EXPRESSIVE THEORY OF INTERNATIONAL DISPUTE RESOLUTION

TOM GINSBURG*
RICHARD H. MCADAMS**

ABSTRACT

Frequent compliance with the adjudicative decisions of international institutions, such as the International Court of Justice (ICJ), is puzzling because these institutions do not have the power domestic courts possess to impose sanctions. This Article uses game theory to explain the power of international adjudication via a set of expressive theories, showing how law can be effective without sanctions. When two parties disagree about conventions that arise in recurrent situations involving coordination, such as a convention of deferring to territorial claims of *first possessors*, the pronouncements of third-party legal decision makers—adjudicators—can influence their behavior in two ways. First, adjudicative expression may construct *focal points* that clarify ambiguities in the conven-

* Associate Professor of Law and Political Science, University of Illinois.

**Visiting Professor, Yale Law School; Guy Raymond Jones Professor of Law, University of Illinois. The authors thank Todd Allee, Ian Ayres, David Caron, Robert Cooter, Paul Diehl, Karim Medjad, Eric Posner, Duncan Snidal, Paul Stephan, and Tom Ulen for comments and discussions, and workshop participants at the 2002 Midwest Law and Economics Meeting, the 2003 American Law and Economics Association Meeting, Northwestern University Law School and the University of Illinois Political Science Department. Thanks also to Claudia Acosta, Nykhana Chambers, and John Palchak for excellent research assistance and to Richard Snyder for sharing his data on shared U.N. policy positions.

tion. Second, adjudicative expression may provide *signals* that cause parties to update their beliefs about the facts that determine how the convention applies. Even without the power of sanctions or legitimacy, an adjudicator's focal points and signals influence the parties' behavior. After explaining the expressive power of adjudication, this Article applies the analysis to a range of third-party efforts to resolve international disputes, including a comprehensive review of the docket of the International Court of Justice. We find strong empirical support for the theory that adjudication works by clarifying ambiguous conventions or facts via cheap talk or signaling. We claim that the theory has broad implications for understanding the power of adjudication generally.

TABLE OF CONTENTS

INTRODUCTION

In 1872, an international arbitral tribunal set up by treaty ruled that Great Britain had to pay $15.5 million to the United States for damages caused by a ship, the *Alabama*, built in Britain and sold to the Confederacy during the Civil War.[1] The panel had no means of enforcing its judgment, but Great Britain duly complied, launching the modern era of interstate dispute resolution.[2] Almost a century later, the International Court of Justice (ICJ) decided a case that facilitated the delimitation of the continental shelf between Germany, Denmark, and the Netherlands, ending a high stakes dispute and allowing those countries to proceed in developing gas and mineral resources.[3] Quite recently, the ICJ helped resolve a diplomatic feud related to Belgium's attempt to arrest a former Minister of Foreign Affairs from the Congo.[4] In each of these cases, and many more, international adjudication successfully resolved significant conflict between nations. Adjudication generated compliance notwithstanding the absence of external sanctions to *enforce* the decisions. Compliance without centralized sanctions contradicts our conventional image of how legal systems operate. The result is a puzzle at the heart of international law. Given the so-called "anarchic"[5] environment of international relations, why would nations bother to comply with the decisions of international tribunals?

This question is part of a larger one. In recent years, political scientists and international lawyers have identified compliance with international law as the central problem for analysis.[6] Despite high

1. *See* 1 J.G. WETTER, THE INTERNATIONAL ARBITRAL PROCESS 27-173 (1979).

2. *See* JOHN G. COLLIER & VAUGHAN LOWE, THE SETTLEMENT OF DISPUTES IN INTERNATIONAL LAW: INSTITUTIONS AND PROCEDURES 33 (1999).

3. North Sea Continental Shelf Cases (F.R.G. v. Den., F.R.G. v. Neth.) 1969 I.C.J. 3 (Feb. 20).

4. Case Concerning the Arrest Warrant of 11 April 2000 (Congo v. Belg.) 2002 I.C.J. 1 (Feb. 14), *available at* http://www.icj-cij.org.

5. HEDLEY BULL, THE ANARCHICAL SOCIETY: A STUDY OF ORDER IN WORLD POLITICS xii (1964).

6. ABRAM CHAYES & ANTONIA HANDLER CHAYES, THE NEW SOVEREIGNTY: COMPLIANCE WITH INTERNATIONAL REGULATORY AGREEMENTS 1-29 (1995); George W. Downs et al., *Is the Good News About Compliance Good News About Cooperation?*, 50 INT'L ORG. 379, 379-80 (1996); Andrew Guzman, *A Compliance Based Theory of International Law*, 90 CAL. L. REV.

profile instances of noncompliance, most writers seem to agree with Louis Henkin's famous assessment that "almost all nations observe almost all principles of international law and almost all of their obligations almost all of the time."[7] Scholars disagree, though, on precisely *why* nations do so. Traditional international lawyers contend that international law works because it is perceived largely as morally authoritative and legitimate.[8] Realists have long contended that international law is epiphenomenal, that nations generally comply only because their international obligations are usually congruent with national interests.[9] Finally, institutionalists claim that international institutions influence state behavior by facilitating communication and disseminating information about member nations.[10] The choice between these theories goes to the heart of whether international law matters: only by knowing the

---

1823, 1825 (2002); Oona Hathaway, *Do Human Rights Treaties Make a Difference?*, 111 YALE L.J. 1935 (2002); Daniel Ho, *Compliance and International Soft Law: Why do Countries Implement the Basle Accord?*, 5 J. INT'L ECON. L. 647, 647 (2002); Harold Hongju Koh, *How Is International Law Enforced?*, 74 IND. L.J. 1397 (1999); Harold Hongju Koh, *Why Do Nations Obey International Law?*, 106 YALE L.J. 2599 (1997); Kal Raustiala & Anne-Marie Slaughter, *International Law, International Relations and Compliance*, *in* HANDBOOK OF INTERNATIONAL RELATIONS 538-58 (Walter Carlsnaes et al. eds., 2002); Beth A. Simmons, *Compliance with International Agreements*, 1 ANN. REV. POL. SCI. 75, 75 (1998).

7. LOUIS HENKIN, HOW NATIONS BEHAVE 47 (1979) (emphasis omitted); *see also* Charles Kegley & Gregory Raymond, *International Legal Norms and the Preservation of the Peace 1820-1964*, 8 INT'L INTERACTIONS 171, 173 (1981) (providing empirical support for assertion that national behavior is consistent with international law); David G. Victor & Kal Raustiala, *Conclusions*, *in* THE IMPLEMENTATION AND EFFECTIVENESS OF INTERNATIONAL ENVIRONMENTAL COMMITMENTS: THEORY AND PRACTICE 659, 661 (David G. Victor et al. eds., 1998). *But see* Peter M. Haas, *Choosing to Comply: Theorizing from International Relations and Comparative Politics*, *in* COMMITMENT AND COMPLIANCE 43, 44 (Dinah Shelton ed., 2000) (explaining that "empirical studies suggest that national compliance is uneven at best").

8. *See, e.g.*, THOMAS FRANCK, THE POWER OF LEGITIMACY AMONG NATIONS 41-49 (1990).

9. John J. Mearsheimer, *The False Promise of International Institutions*, 19 INT'L SEC. 5, 6 (1995); *see also* 5 THUCYDIDES, THE HISTORY OF THE PELOPONESSIAN WAR, *reprinted in* THE LANDMARK THUCYDIDES 352 (Richard Crawley trans., Robert B. Strassler ed., 1998) (quoting the Athenians in a Melian dialogue, "right ... is only in question between equals in power, while the strong do what they can and the weak suffer what they must").

10. *See* ROBERT KEOHANE, AFTER HEGEMONY: COOPERATION AND DISCORD IN THE WORLD POLITICAL ECONOMY 49-64 (1984); Robert Axelrod & Robert O. Keohane, *Achieving Cooperation Under Anarchy: Strategies and Institutions*, *in* COOPERATION UNDER ANARCHY 226 (Kenneth A. Oye ed., 1986); Robert O. Keohane & Lisa L. Martin, *The Promise of Institutionalist Theory*, 20 INT'L SEC. 39, 45 (1995); Beth Simmons, *See You in "Court"? The Appeal to Quasi-Judicial Legal Processes in the Settlement of Territorial Disputes*, *in* A ROAD MAP TO WAR: TERRITORIAL DIMENSIONS OF INTERNATIONAL CONFLICT 205, 208 (Paul F. Diehl ed., 1999) (using the term "rational functionalism" for the concept).

reasons for compliance can we assess whether international law has the potential to become a powerful independent force in world affairs.

To date, however, the focus of the compliance literature has been almost exclusively on *primary* compliance with international norms, embodied either in customary international law or in treaty obligations.[11] Relatively neglected is the question of *secondary* compliance: why states comply with decisions rendered by international courts. This is the question we address. Stated differently, this Article seeks to explain why some states are willing to comply with their primary international obligations *only after* a third party adjudicator has articulated those obligations.

Our approach is both theoretical and empirical. The explanation we offer is rooted in game theory, which has been used successfully in a variety of problems in international organization. With few exceptions, however, the central game concept has been the prisoners' dilemma. This Article focuses on a different concept— coordination. Coordination games describe situations where parties have fully or partially common interests that can be achieved only if they coordinate their strategies among multiple possible equilibria.[12] Below, we explain why we think this model more closely approximates many strategic situations in the real world. This Article seeks to move coordination to a central place in the evolving study of international law and institutions.

A focus on coordination produces the Article's principle theoretical contribution—an *expressive* theory of adjudication. Our expressive claim has four steps. First, we contend that the need for coordination is pervasive, even in situations of international conflict. For example, when the value of disputed territory is low relative to the costs of military action, international competition for territory takes the form of a coordination game known as Hawk/Dove. In this case, each nation prefers to gain the territory by having the other side defer to its claim, but each considers the worst possible outcome to

11. *See* Simmons, *supra* note 6, at 78 (characterizing "compliance with standing, substantive rules often embodied in treaty arrangements" as first order compliance as contrasted with second order compliance with third-party decision making) (citations omitted).

12. ERIC RASMUSEN, GAMES AND INFORMATION: AN INTRODUCTION TO GAME THEORY 29 (3d ed. 2001).

be a military conflict resulting from mutual claims to the territory. Thus, despite their conflicting interest over territory, the parties may have a common interest in avoiding war.

Second, we use evolutionary game theory to explain how conventions emerge over time—*even in a state of anarchy*—from the interactions of players in coordination situations.[13] Such conventions often benefit players by avoiding conflict and maintaining cooperation. For example, for those territorial disputes that take the form of the Hawk/Dove game, nations may come to expect that the first possessor of a territory will play Hawk and that others will play Dove. As long as every nation can determine who the first possessor is, the property-like convention will avoid conflict.

Third, we describe why conventions are inevitably imperfect. Ambiguities in the underlying expectations, and in the facts the convention makes relevant, prevent players from coordinating in every situation. For example, a first possession convention regarding territory will fail to coordinate expectations in cases where there are divergent understandings of what constitutes possession, divergent understandings about possible exceptions to the possession convention, or divergent beliefs about the particular facts that define possession. Uncoordinated expectations will lead to conflict, as two nations play Hawk expecting the other to play Dove.

Finally, we explain how a third party's expression can resolve ambiguity, in the convention or the facts, and thereby influence behavior of players in a coordination game. We do not place any reliance on the nations' ideological commitments, such as a perceived obligation to obey legitimate adjudicative determinations. Instead, expression works partly as cheap talk[14]—by constructing a *focal point* around which parties coordinate—and partly because third-party *signals* cause players to update their beliefs about the state of the world. In either case, expression can change the action a selfish party chooses to play. We also identify why adjudication combining cheap talk and signaling exerts a more powerful influence on the parties' behavior than either type of expression can achieve in isolation. The resulting theory of adjudication has broad application, not only explaining international adjudication but also

13. *See infra* Part II.B.1.

14. *See infra* Part II.C.1.a.

broader comparative questions of dispute resolution and the origins of domestic systems of adjudication.

On the empirical side, we test our theory by considering a variety of evidence about international adjudication. We examine the early history of international dispute resolution, provide three extended case studies of major adjudications prior to the creation of the ICJ, and conduct a quantitative analysis of the decisions of this latter tribunal. Indeed, we have conducted the most comprehensive empirical review to date of the contentious docket of the ICJ, which we contend provides considerable support for our expressive theory of adjudication.

The Article proceeds as follows: Part I begins by stating more carefully the puzzle of compliance with international adjudication. Part II presents the expressive theory of adjudication. This part claims that coordination games can be used to describe a broad range of international phenomena. It also explains how third-party dispute resolution resolves coordination problems expressively. Part III discusses various examples of international dispute resolution from the perspective of this expressive theory with special attention to the docket of the ICJ. We argue that dispute resolution processes help parties resolve the underlying and ubiquitous problem of coordinating among multiple equilibria. The last Part provides a conclusion.

I. THE PUZZLE OF COMPLIANCE WITH INTERNATIONAL ADJUDICATION

A. Unexplained Compliance with International Dispute Resolution

Studying compliance with international norms raises certain methodological issues. Oran Young defines compliance as "occur[ing] when the actual behavior of a given subject conforms to prescribed behavior, and non-compliance or violation occurs when actual behavior departs significantly from prescribed behavior."[15] Measuring the level of compliance with international norms, however, is not straightforward. As Beth Simmons notes: "[C]ompliance

15. Simmons, *supra* note 6, at 77 (quoting ORAN R. YOUNG, COMPLIANCE AND PUBLIC AUTHORITY 104 (1979)).

is rarely a transparent, binary choice. Actors' behavior is often intentionally ambiguous, dilatory, or confusing, and frequently takes place under conditions in which verification ... is difficult.... [and] highly context-specific."[16] Compliance with, for example, a ruling of the ICJ may be decades in coming, with a different outcome than the one the court required, albeit one that still satisfies the parties.

Notwithstanding these problems, studies of international adjudication find a high degree of compliance. In the introduction we gave three noteworthy illustrations—compliance with the decisions rendered in the *Alabama* (1872), *North Sea Continental Shelf* (1969), and *Case Concerning the Arrest Warrant of 11 April 2000* (2002).[17] More generally, previous scholars have claimed there is complete or nearly complete compliance with final decisions (on the merits) of the ICJ.[18] In a later section, we present an exhaustive review of the ICJ docket and conservatively estimate compliance with ICJ decisions to be sixty-eight percent, although some real noncompliance also is identified.[19] Similarly, studies of General Agreement on Tariffs and Trade (GATT) and World Trade Organization (WTO) dispute resolution find "quite high" levels of compliance.[20]

This high level of compliance is a puzzle for rational choice theory. Rationalist approaches fail to predict compliance with international judicial institutions, such as the ICJ, because they

16. *Id.* at 78-79 (citations omitted); *see also* Richard Bilder, *Beyond Compliance: Helping Nations Cooperate*, *in* COMMITMENT AND COMPLIANCE, *supra* note 7, at 65, 67 ("Obligation and no-obligation, compliance and breach, shade imperceptibly into one another .... Issues of compliance and breach are frequently part of the ongoing game or process of international interaction rather than something subsequent to and apart from it."); Haas, *supra* note 7, at 61-64 (discussing constructivism and compliance).

17. *See supra* notes 1-4 and accompanying text.

18. COLLIER & LOWE, *supra* note 2, at 178 (claiming that previously "all decisions were, sooner or later, complied with") (citation omitted); COMPLIANCE WITH JUDGMENTS OF INTERNATIONAL COURTS 35 (M.K. Bulterman & M. Kuijer eds., 1996) (explaining that most decisions are complied with).

19. *See infra* note 239 and accompanying text.

20. *See, e.g.*, ROBERT E. HUDEC, ENFORCING INTERNATIONAL TRADE LAW: THE EVOLUTION OF THE MODERN GATT LEGAL SYSTEM 286 (1993); Warren F. Schwartz & Alan O. Sykes, *The Economic Structure of Renegotiation and Dispute Resolution in the World Trade Organization*, 31 J. LEGAL STUD. 179, 200 (2002) (finding "the level of compliance with trade commitments is quite high").

lack the power to sanction a nation for failing to comply.[21] In the absence of centralized sanctions, a rationalist must wonder why there is *any* compliance with the adjudications of international institutions.

One possible answer is selection bias. If the only cases that go before international bodies for dispute resolution are those most capable of resolution, either because of their stakes or the issue area involved, then high compliance is unsurprising. Some argue, therefore, that the fact of compliance cannot tell us much about compliance in general or the power of international law to constrain state behavior.[22]

Selection bias exists, but it does not resolve the puzzle of adjudicatory compliance. Even if international dispute resolution draws the "easy cases," selection biases leave unexplained what it is about certain cases that make them easy to resolve. If one believes the realist critique that international law is epiphenomenal, then there should be no easy cases. A realist might, of course, maintain that parties would undertake the same behavior in the absence of dispute resolution. But this is implausible; if parties knew in advance the precise solution to their dispute, based on their relative power, they would not bother going through the process of third-party dispute resolution, which is costly and time consuming. States would not turn to third parties unless they played some role in helping the states to resolve problems. Consequently, if states do not know in advance the precise solution to their dispute, then the process of international dispute resolution has had some effect and has generated compliance.

A second possible answer to the puzzle of compliance is reputation.[23] Andrew Guzman argues that concerns about reputation can

21. In contrast, traditional international lawyers who focus on legitimacy as the primary determinant of compliance tend to overpredict compliance. *See* Downs et al., *supra* note 6, at 380-82.

22. *See id.* at 383 (noting that "we do not know what a high compliance rate really implies").

23. *See* P. K. Huth, *Deterrence and International Conflict*, 2 ANN. REV. POL. SCI. 25, 41-42 (1999) (explaining that there are relatively few studies on international reputations); Beth Simmons, *International Law and State Behavior: Commitment and Compliance in International Monetary Affairs*, 94 AM. POL. SCI. REV. 819, 820 (2000) ("[G]overnments make commitments to further their interests and comply with them to preserve their reputation for predictable behavior in the protection of property rights."); Simmons, *supra* note 10, at 210

secure compliance, particularly where stakes are low.[24] With low stakes, the reputation benefits that states will obtain from compliance will offset the costs of noncooperation. Reputation is, however, an incomplete way of explaining compliance with international adjudication. If reputation were strong enough to compel compliance with adjudication, one wonders why it was not also strong enough to resolve the dispute *without* adjudication. Why is reputation too weak to induce compliance before a third party pronounces a nation's legal obligations, but still strong enough to induce compliance after such a pronouncement?

A related problem with the reputation explanation is the fact that reputation may be compartmentalized across states.[25] The United States might flout international obligation *X* owed to, say, Iran but at the same time fulfill obligation *X* to India, Peru, and Germany. If so, what will the latter three states infer about a judicial decision that finds the United States failed to observe the obligation vis-à-vis Iran? The states might infer that the United States is less likely to cooperate with *them* in the future, which means they might find it worthwhile to diminish their cooperation with the United States at the present time. This reaction would constitute a reputation *sanction* for the United States' breach of its obligation to Iran. But there is another possibility. India, Peru, and Germany might perceive that the United States has strong interests in maintaining cooperation with *them* that do not exist for Iran. The three states may then reason that they can safely ignore the United States' breach of its legal obligations to Iran. If so, the United States suffers no loss of reputation among any states other than the one to whom it breaches its obligations. If breaching its obligations to Iran creates no reputation spillover to its relationship with other countries, then the United States should also be willing to ignore its legal obligations to Iran, both before and after international adjudication.

(arguing that states comply because long-run reputational cost outweighs short-term gain).

24. Guzman, *supra* note 6, at 1883 ("The likelihood that reputational effects will be sufficient to ensure compliance grows smaller as the stakes grow larger.").

25. *See* George W. Downs & Michael A. Jones, *Reputation, Compliance, and International Law*, 31 J. LEGAL STUD. 95, 108-09 (2002) (describing how segmented reputations develop).

In the end, perhaps reputation will have a role to play in explaining adjudication, but not without a greater understanding of how third-party expression changes the reputation calculus. The puzzle of compliance thus remains. We need to understand why and for what cases states turn to international institutions for dispute resolution.

B. The Broader Puzzle of Compliance Without Sanctions

Compliance with international adjudication is actually only one illustration of the more general problem of explaining compliance in contexts where a tribunal lacks coercive enforcement power. Obvious examples include certain alternative forms of dispute resolution, such as nonbinding arbitration. Even in a nation's courts, however, enforcement is often less effective than deterrence theorists might think necessary to compel compliance. Historically, we know of at least one legal system that shared many features with the current system of international law. For several hundred years, Iceland had a stable legal system not unlike the current international system.[26] It had a type of legislature to make laws, and courts to decide cases, but no public enforcement of the courts' decisions. In other words, Icelandic institutions made law and declared rights, but no governmental institutions existed to enforce those declarations.

When someone won a court case in Iceland, enforcement would be left to private parties.[27] Typically, legal cases involved killing of an individual for which blood money had to be paid. If one failed to pay damages as determined by an adverse judgment, the original claimant could come back to the adjudicator, who would then declare the defaulting defendant an outlaw (meaning the defendant could be killed without the killer incurring legal liability).[28] Consider the puzzle though: The immunity granted to the killer of an outlaw is merely the right to be free from judgments issued by

26. *See* DAVID FRIEDMAN, LAW'S ORDER 263-67 (2000); Richard Posner, *Medieval Iceland and Modern Legal Scholarship*, 90 MICH. L. REV. 1495, 1496-97 (1992) (reviewing WILLIAM I. MILLER, BLOODTAKING AND PEACEMAKING: FEUD, LAW AND SOCIETY IN SAGA ICELAND (1990)).

27. FRIEDMAN, *supra* note 26, at 264.

28. *Id.*

a court that had *no power* to enforce its judgments. Without adjudicatory enforcement power, it is not apparent why the defendant would feel any more protected when his death would produce a judicial declaration of liability than when it would not. Yet, despite the purely expressive power of the court, the Icelandic system provided sufficient incentives for many people to pay judgments.[29]

The legal institutions in the international system are similar to those in medieval Iceland. Several international institutions are quasi-legislative in their power to create law, while a proliferating number of judicial institutions adjudicate disputes. But international law still famously lacks a central enforcer, in other words, an executive. This so-called "anarchic"[30] situation means that laws must be enforced frequently through self-help. Yet, like the pronouncements of the court in medieval Iceland, the decisions of international tribunals are still largely effective in the cases presented to them.[31] Compliance with international adjudication will help explain the Icelandic courts and more generally provide insights into the evolution of domestic court systems. In the next Part, we offer a theory that explains judicial compliance in both contexts.

29. While this system would seem to allow the stronger parties to avoid paying judgments rendered against them, Iceland had a market in claims, so that a successful but weak claimant could transfer his claim to a stronger party for enforcement of the judgment. This system worked so long as power asymmetries among the players were not too great. Apparently Iceland had some social surplus, but not an enormous one. There were enough resources to support a few public officials. There were not enough resources, however, so that a powerful individual could hire enough other powerful people as retainers to form a state. Presumably, whenever one faction would gather a number of powerful individuals so as to try to coerce others, it would lose judgments. As the number of judgments against the prospective ruler rose, so did the incentive for other powerful individuals to challenge the person so as to gain the payment due earlier but weaker plaintiffs. This may have created a mechanism for internal stability and an equilibrium of power. *See id.* at 263-67.

30. BULL, *supra* note 5, at 130.

31. Of course, there are some important distinctions. Arguably, inequality of power is more severe in the international system than in a society of individuals. *See* FRIEDMAN, *supra* note 26, at 265-67.

III. APPLYING THE MODELS: THE EXPRESSIVE EFFECT OF INTERNATIONAL DISPUTE RESOLUTION

This Part discusses how interstate dispute resolution exploits the power of third parties to influence outcomes in coordination games. Section A briefly reviews the history of third-party involvement in the resolution of disputes between nations. Section B then provides three case studies drawn from dispute resolution prior to the establishment of the ICJ in 1946, demonstrating how the signaling and focal point models usefully explain the various functions being served. Section C turns specifically to the ICJ, describing and explaining countries' compliance with the court's decisions. Our comprehensive review of the ICJ docket reveals that the court receives a wide variety of types of claims. The disputes the court *resolves*, however, include a large number of what are essentially international property disputes that can be resolved either by providing a signal of the state of the world or clarifying the underlying international conventions. This theory thus explains which disputes are ultimately resolved by the court and how the court resolves them.

A. A Brief History of Interstate Dispute Resolution

Interstate dispute resolution originated in ancient times.[127] It was particularly well developed in the form of arbitration among the ancient Greek city-states.[128] The Greeks attributed the origin of arbitration to the gods of Olympia, whose interactions paralleled the relations among city-states.[129] Arbitration was sometimes carried

127. *See, e.g.*, DAVID BEDERMAN, INTERNATIONAL LAW IN ANTIQUITY 16 (2001).

128. *See* SHEILA AGER, INTERSTATE ARBITRATIONS IN THE GREEK WORLD 337-90 B.C. (1997); BEDERMAN, *supra* note 127, at 8 n.14, 93-94 (noting that arbitration was not practiced much among Romans or other ancient civilizations, with the exception of Persia).

129. This religious sanction was used to legitimate the practice. BEDERMAN, *supra* note 127,

out by intergovernmental organizations, known as *amphictyones*, which were formed among several states that shared religious sites, as well as by city-states.[130] The disputes they resolved typically involved issues of territory, with historical and mythic evidence of title arrayed against claims of use or possession.[131] The arbitrators did not rely on centralized enforcement. We do not know precisely how many of these decisions were enforced, but there seems to be evidence of substantial compliance in the absence of centralized enforcement.[132]

In the modern period, an important juncture in the development of routine procedures for use in international dispute resolution was the *Alabama* arbitration between the United States and Britain, concluded in 1872 and referred to at the outset of this Article.[133] The *Alabama,* built in Britain and sold to the Confederacy, sunk many Union merchant ships. The United States claimed that the sale of the ship violated Great Britain's obligations of neutrality, and Britain disagreed. Several years after the end of the Civil War, the Washington Treaty of May 1871 called on the parties to submit the dispute to arbitration. The arbitral tribunal, involving one national of each party and three neutrals, found that Britain violated its

at 82.

130. The object was to preserve these sites from violence; the organizations could arbitrate disputes among its members as well as provide protection in wartime. *Id.* at 61. The Oracle of Delphi served as one such arbitrator early on, but was not particularly good at it. Bederman notes the case of Clazomenae and Cyme who were fighting about the ownership of a temple between their two territories. The Oracle ruled that ownership would go to the first to make a sacrifice at the temple. Rather than resolve the dispute, this expression intensified it as both city-states raced to the temple to physically possess it. The Oracle was also apparently a poor signaler, and the city-states ultimately secularised arbitral practice accordingly. *Id.* at 83 (claiming that the Oracle's awards "typically lacked the clarity and precision needed to settle the matter authoritatively").

131. *See* AGER, *supra* note 127, at 4; BEDERMAN, *supra* note 127, at 84.

132. BEDERMAN, *supra* note 127, at 8 n.14.

133. *See supra* notes 1-2 and accompanying text; *see also* SHABTAI ROSENNE, THE WORLD COURT 5 (5th ed. 1995); Henry T. King, Jr. & James D. Graham, *The Origins of Modern International Arbitration*, 51 DISP. RES. J. 42, 48 (1996); Monroe Leigh et al., *International Law Societies and the Development of International Law,* 41 VA. J. INT'L L. 941, 941 n.1 ("It was widely held at the time that the Geneva Arbitration of 1872 averted a potential armed conflict between the United States and United Kingdom ...."). *But see* David Caron, *War and International Adjudication*, 94 AM. J. INT'L L. 4, 9 (2000) (arguing that claims that the award averted war are "somewhat exaggerated").

obligations and further specified the obligations of neutral states in wartime.[134]

In terms of the framework set out in Part II, this dispute arose over fuzziness in the convention on neutrality. The laws of war are of ancient origin, and included not only obligations on the parties to a conflict, but also obligations on neutral states not to support either party militarily. Ordinary commercial transactions with combatant parties, however, were generally considered to be legal. How extensive were the obligations of a neutral government to ensure that ordinary commercial transactions did not involve war material? This issue was fuzzy: There were multiple possible solutions, and the parties held different views as to which solution should be adopted. The United States claimed that Britain was under an obligation by virtue of her neutrality not to sell warships to either side; the British government argued that the *Alabama* had been built as a merchant ship and had been fitted at sea as a warship, after which it had escaped from Britain.[135] Britain did not consider itself to have provided war material to the Confederacy.

In this case, there was no real factual dispute, but rather a question as to whether the conventions governing the obligations of neutral states rendered Britain liable for the damage caused by the *Alabama*. The Tribunal found that Britain was indeed liable and required to pay $15.5 million in compensation to the United States, which Britain duly paid.[136] The arbitration thus generated compliance in the immediate dispute before it and also clarified the scope of the convention, holding that a neutral government in wartime is obligated to use due diligence to prevent the equipping or building, within its jurisdiction, of any vessel that it should believe is intended to participate in war, and to prohibit belligerent powers from using its ports or waters as the base of naval operations or military supply.[137]

Inspired by this successful arbitration, the Hague Peace Conferences of 1899 and 1907 sought to facilitate the peaceful settlement of interstate disputes, providing for commissions of inquiry,

134. King & Graham, *supra* note 133, at 48.
135. *Id.*
136. *Id.* at 49.
137. *See* Eric C. Bruggink, *The "Alabama" Claims*, 57 ALA. LAW. 339, 342 (1996).

conciliation, mediation, arbitration, and adjudication and a Permanent Court of International Arbitration (PCIA).[138] The PCIA maintains lists of arbitrators available to states, publishes rules governing arbitration and other procedures, and holds international conferences on arbitration.[139] Although states frequently resorted to the PCIA before the first World War,[140] its caseload declined after the 1922 creation of the Permanent Court of International Justice (PCIJ), and the PCIA has not heard an interstate case since 1932.[141] Its docket has been limited to a handful of ad hoc arbitrations since that time.[142]

The creation of the PCIJ marked a turning point in the institutionalization of international dispute resolution.[143] For the first time, a standing body existed that could hear the entire range of interstate claims. This institutionalization into a standing body allowed the development of a reputation for quality and gave the dispute resolver an incentive to signal accurately. The PCIJ heard a wide range of cases before World War II suspended its operations,[144] and the court heard its last case in 1939.[145] Nevertheless, in its lifetime it decided many important issues and laid the foundation for the establishment of the ICJ in 1946.[146]

138. *See* COLLIER & LOWE, *supra* note 2, at 35-36.

139. *Id.* at 36.

140. ROSENNE, *supra* note 133, at 17 (stating that fourteen disputes were handled by the PCIA between 1902 and 1920).

141. COLLIER & LOWE, *supra* note 2, at 36-37. It has, however served as a registry for interstate arbitrations.

142. Arbitration is also needed in a number of international trade and investment agreements. Prominent examples include NAFTA's Chapter 11, which provides for arbitration of disputes between individual investors and states, and the ICSID regime, which hosts arbitration of disputes involving foreign investors. In addition, there is an extensive practice of international commercial arbitration that is beyond the scope of this paper.

143. *See* BROWNLIE, *supra* note 75, at 709-10.

144. *Id.* at 710.

145. 1 J.H.W. VERZIJL, THE JURISPRUDENCE OF THE WORLD COURT 599 (1965).

146. BROWNLIE, *supra* note 75, at 17-19; VERZIJL, *supra* note 145, at 57-58.

CONCLUSION

This Article pursued Professor Abbott's suggestion to "reason forward from a theoretical understanding of particular issue areas to richer explanations of the meaning and function of international agreements, procedures and institutions."[291] The game theory concept of coordination explains compliance with international tribunals. Even in a state of anarchy, when nations face repeated games of coordination, conventions emerge. The coordinated expectations underlying a convention allow nations to avoid conflict. Ambiguity inevitably prevents the convention from perfectly coordinating expectations, however, and in this situation adjudication can work expressively, without sanctions, by clarifying the convention and the state of the world to which it applies. Adjudication can both construct a focal point and provide a signal that causes national leaders to update their beliefs, both of which can influence their behavior.

International adjudication should therefore be understood for what it is. Rather than serving as a utopian institution that can end all international conflict, international adjudication such as that provided by the ICJ can only provide solutions to parties faced with coordination problems. Compliance with ICJ decisions can occur, even absent centralized enforcement mechanisms, because the decisions make one outcome focal or provide an important signal of the state of the world, either of which facilitates the parties in

291. Abbott, *supra* note 34, at 2.

ordering their own affairs. The law as declared by the ICJ and other international institutions is *merely* expressive, but expressive law often works to resolve or avoid disputes. In arguing that coordination problems deserve more attention in international relations and international legal scholarship, we have used realist/rational choice assumptions of optimizing behavior and self-interest to expand the understanding of the functions law can play. But our approach is clearly institutionalist in character, seeking to understand how institutions can resolve conflicts and what purposes they serve.

[12]

Restorative Justice: What Is It and Does It Work?

Carrie Menkel-Meadow

Georgetown University Law Center, Washington, DC 20001;
email: meadow@law.georgetown.edu

Key Words

reconciliation, reintegration, community, victims, offenders, criminal law, crime and punishment, human rights, reparations, international law

Abstract

This article reviews the now extensive literature on the varied arenas in which restorative justice is theorized and practiced—criminal violations, community ruptures and disputes, civil wars, regime change, human rights violations, and international law. It also reviews—by examining empirical studies of the processes in different settings—how restorative justice has been criticized, what its limitations and achievements might be, and how it might be understood. I explore the foundational concepts of reintegrative shaming, acknowledgment and responsibility, restitution, truth and reconciliation, and sentencing or healing circles for their transformative and theoretical potentials and for their actual practices in a variety of locations—family abuse, juvenile delinquency, criminal violations, problem-solving courts, indigenous-colonial-national disputes, ethnic and religious conflicts, civil wars, and liberation struggles. Restorative justice, which began as an alternative model of criminal justice, seeking healing and reconciliation for offenders, victims, and the communities in which they are embedded, has moved into larger national and international arenas of reintegration in political and ethnic conflicts. This review suggests that there are important and serious questions about whether restorative justice should be supplemental or substitutional of more conventional legal processes and about how its innovations suggest potentially transformative and challenging ideas and "moves" for dealing with both individual and group transgressive conduct, seeking peace as well as justice.

INTRODUCTION: CONCEPTS, DEFINITIONS, AND PURPOSES OF RESTORATIVE JUSTICE

To its conceptual and practical founders (John Braithwaite, Howard Zehr, and Mark Umbreit, among others), the field of restorative justice is an effort to transform the way we think of punishment for wrongful acts. When a crime or serious bad act (which may include more classes of activity than those legally labeled criminal) occurs, it affects the victims, offenders, interested bystanders (such as family members, employees, or citizens), and the larger community in which it is embedded. To paraphrase one of the field's founders (Zehr 2002, Zehr & Mika 1998), these bad acts or ruptures in human interaction create needs and responsibilities for the direct participants in the act, as well as for the larger society in which their act(s) occur. Restorative justice is the name given to a variety of different practices, including apologies, restitution, and acknowledgments of harm and injury, as well as to other efforts to provide healing and reintegration of offenders into their communities, with or without additional punishment. Restorative justice usually involves direct communication, often with a facilitator, of victims and offenders, often with some or full representation of the relevant affected community,[1] to provide a setting for acknowledgment of fault by the offender, restitution of some sort to the victim, including both affective apologies and material exchanges or payments, and often new mutual understandings, forgiveness, and agreed-to new undertakings for improved behaviors. In its most idealized form, there are four Rs of restorative justice: repair, restore, reconcile, and reintegrate the offenders and victims to each other and to their shared community.

Restorative justice raises deep philosophical, sociological, and empirical issues. The philosophical literature focuses on the purposes and nature of wrongdoing and punishment (Gabbay 2005, Blumenson 2006) and is only briefly reviewed here. At both the philosophical and sociological level, restorative justice raises important questions about who should have power, control, and possession over crime, acts of wrongdoing, punishment, restitution, reconciliation, and community interests (Christie 1977, Menkel-Meadow 1995, Von Hirsh 2003). When an act of wrongdoing is committed, who has an interest in its rectification: the victim, the community, the offender, those affected by the act, or the larger society? Who decides what justice is: the victim (who might want vengeance or restitution), the state (who will want to deter future crimes and acts of wrongdoing, set precedents for others, and establish social control), or the community in which the wrongdoing is embedded (where motivations may vary from revenge to the desire to reclaim every community member)? Who has the power to forgive and accept restitution or reconciliation: the victim, the victim's family, the community in which the wrong occurred, or the state? What if acts of wrongdoing affect both individuals and a larger community, such as hate crimes or genocides? If crime or other acts of wrongdoing are a collective hurt or tear in the social fabric, can individuals forgive on behalf of anyone besides themselves? Are crime victims adequate proxies for the rest of a society that may define justice differently (more harshly, less harshly)? How are we to know what the proper unit of analysis is for measuring appropriate forms of punishment or restitution? What is the proper balance between victim-offender reconciliation, community peace, and social order or justice? (Similar issues have been raised in the civil sphere of dispute processing; see Menkel-Meadow 1995, 2006.) How should we integrate both the public and private aspects of crime and wrongdoing? Should right-making of wrongdoing be backward facing (punishment and legal justice) or future facing (reconciliation, restoration, and social justice)?

[1]The notion of what the community is in restorative justice is one of some controversy (Weisberg 2003).

Whatever one's views on these important philosophical and criminological issues, the question remains: Does restorative justice work? Does it meet its own claims of reduced recidivism, restored communities, and reintegrated offenders? Is restorative justice more efficient (less costly, more deterrent, more restitutionary) than more conventional forms of punishment? Is it more fair or just (as perceived by participants or as analyzed by external, objective, and professional measures of these illusive concepts)? This article reviews the extant findings, which do demonstrate some support for restorative justice claims, while also raising questions about the (limited) conditions under which restorative justice may be most effective. The next major issue of evaluation in the field is whether even successful victim-offender restorative justice can be scaled up to national levels of political and civic reconciliation, either through truth and reconciliation–like processes or through reparations (Bradford 2005, Brooks 1999, Brophy 2006).

Restorative justice as a social practice and movement began, in its modern incarnation, in the 1970s as a response to what was considered to be an overly harsh criminal justice system that neither effectively deterred crime nor successfully rehabilitated offenders. Championed by social workers, progressive criminal treatment professionals (including police officers and prison reformers), some lawyers and judges, psychologists, and community and peace activists, restorative justice was practiced first (Lerman 1999), and theorized later, most eloquently by John Braithwaite (1989, 1995, 1999, 2002, 2003, 2006). Restorative justice proponents suggested that by providing structured environments in which offenders and victims met and explained their injuries and hurts to each other, offenders could acknowledge and explain their bad acts, apologize, and make restitution to victims who could forgive and feel safe again. With family members or community representatives present, there would be public accountability, an inquiry into root causes of criminal or wrongful acts, and, at its best, suggestions for creative, tailored solutions. Restitutionary possibilities would emerge from facilitated dialogue. Through structured shaming (Kahan 1996, 2006; cf. Markel 2007), responsibility taking, and acknowledgment of injury done, offenders might be effectively reintegrated into their communities, and victims would no longer be frightened or traumatized by what had happened to them.

From the beginning, restorative justice practices were intended to heal at both the individual and group or social level. Attention in both practice and theory was placed on healing those directly affected by a crime or bad act and on institutional and social reform. At its most aspirational or utopian, restorative justice has been seen as a potentially transformative social practice that could, under the right conditions, obviate the need for harsh criminal punishment and incarceration. In this conception, restorative justice was linked as a social movement to community organizing, criminal justice and prison reform, the civil alternative dispute resolution (ADR) movement (Menkel-Meadow et al. 2005), and the peace movement in that it sought alternative processes for different and more humane and tailored outcomes. In its more grounded and practical institutionalized forms, restorative justice was often supplemental, not substitutive, to conventional criminal proceedings. In an early core definition of restorative justice, it is a "process that brings together all the parties affected by an incident of wrongdoing to collectively decide how to deal with the aftermath of the incident and its implications for the future" (Marshall 1998, Roche 2004). Although some think restorative justice is most appropriate in the context of small, interpersonal wrongful acts, such as petty thefts, simple assaults, drug- or alcohol-related crimes, and family abuse, restorative justice has been adapted for cases involving murder, rape, genocide, and other serious transgressions against large groups or even a whole society (Umbreit et al. 2005, Wellikoff 2004). It has also been used effectively as a model for pre- or nonlegal disputes in schools, organizational and corporate conflict management, neighborhoods, communities, and families (Llewellyn & Howse 1998).

What began as a domestic social reform movement (simultaneously developed in Australia, New Zealand, Canada, the United States, the Netherlands, Austria, and others), restorative justice and its basic principles became a process of international interest when Desmond Tutu (1999) led a truth and reconciliation process to transform and heal South African society's transition from apartheid to a just, multiracial society. Variations on indigenous [such as Rwandan *gacaca* (Honeyman 2004, Bolocan 2004, Raper 2005) and Ugandan *mato oput* (Blumenson 2006)] and newly minted restorative processes (Avruch & Vejarano 2001) have now been used in more than 25 national efforts to move more peacefully through political, racial, ethnic, and civil wars and transitions to more peaceful, democratic, and just states. Restorative justice principles thus helped form a new field of international law and political structure: transitional justice (Teitel 2000).

Restorative justice has several foundational concepts that have now been elaborated and extended to many arenas of social and political interaction:

- Personalized and direct participation in a process of speaking and listening of both a wrongdoer (offender) and a victim of an act of wrongdoing;
- Narration of what an act of wrongdoing consisted of and the harm or injury it caused to those affected (including both direct victims and often others, including bystanders and the larger community);
- Explanation by the offender of what was done and why;
- Acknowledgment and acceptance of fault for the wrong committed by the offender with recognition of the harm caused (with apology, if not coerced);
- Opportunity for appreciation or understanding of why the wrong occurred (root causes) and, in some cases, forgiveness of the individual, without forgetfulness of the act;
- Consideration of appropriate outcomes or restitution to those wronged by all participants, including victim, offender, family members, and/or larger community, often with expert facilitation;
- Reintegration of the wrongdoer into the larger community, through apology, restitution, and/or support and social services provided (alone or in conjunction with formal punishment as well);
- Reconciliation of wronged and wrongdoer, within a renewed commitment to shared social norms (often reconstituted within the restorative process);
- An orientation to the wrongdoer that treats the act separate from the person so that the person may be redeemed as the victim/community is repaired;
- An orientation to the future, to the extent possible, to make right what was wrong and to rebuild new relationships and new communities.

These foundational concepts come from a belief that conventional legal processes (criminal, international tribunals, and even civil processes) are often ineffective in their bureaucratic separation of offender from the actual consequences of acts, in the timing of any remedial actions (delayed incarcerations or other punishments), and in the inattention to the personal nature of the wrong (both for rehabilitation of the offender and restitution of the particular harm suffered by the victim), not to mention in their failure to deter or reduce crime. Restorative justice hopes to harness the commission of wrongful acts to the making of new opportunities for personal, communal, and societal growth and transformation through empowerment of both victims and offenders in direct and authentic dialogue and recognition. It also hopes practically to reduce recidivism and reintegrate wrongdoers into more positive roles and relationships.

At the theoretical level, most proponents of restorative justice claim that such processes reclaim the property of the crimes or conflicts from their ownership and mismanagement by the state (Christie 1977) and return them to the victims and offenders whose lives are most affected. As with the civil ADR movement, restorative justice proponents claim that outcomes can be creatively tailored to meet the requirements and needs of the situations and the parties. Thus, there will be higher rates of compliance and greater satisfaction with the process itself, encouraging belief in its legitimacy and its ability to rectify wrongs and repair broken or harmed social relationships. Restorative justice is designed to remove negative stigmatization of the individual and replace it with recognition of the wrongfulness of an act, with shaming of the act, and with reintegration of the person (Braithwaite 2002; Strang 2001, 2004). As an ideology and as a practice, restorative justice often appeals across the political spectrum, with liberals seeking criminal justice reform through personalized treatment, compassion, and understanding for socially disadvantaged offenders, and conservatives approving of offender accountability, responsibility, and restitutionary payments to victims (Barnett 1977). When it works most effectively, restorative justice enhances participatory and deliberative democracy and can promote community building, political legitimacy, and the development of new social and legal norms. Progressive theorists and practitioners see in restorative justice another form of participatory deliberative democracy; conservative theorists see devolved and localized governance for crime control.

Although there are many contested theoretical and practical issues in the uses of restorative justice at its different levels (personalistic wrongs, less serious crimes, serious crimes, state crimes, crimes or wrongs against humanity) that are reviewed below, recent scholarship (Strang 2004, Johnstone 2003, Roche 2004, Strang & Braithwaite 2000, Minow 1998) on these issues has enabled a relatively coherent set of issues, research questions, and objections to be developed across levels of analysis and uses of restorative processes. Such issues include:

1. Whether restorative justice processes are effective in meeting their own claimed advantages, such as reduced recidivism rates; increased rates of reintegration to a nonoffender life; movement toward reconciled, postconflict societies;
2. Whether victims feel coerced or blackmailed to participate, forgive, forget, and forego (desires for revenge or other retributivist goals) (Acorn 2004, Brown 1994);
3. Whether offenders feel coerced to confess, apologize, and waive the rights of the criminally accused (Dolinko 2003, Delgado 2000, Brown 1994);
4. Whether restorative processes—like other alternative processes that focus on direct, but informal, narrative—privilege some (the articulate, the verbal) and disadvantage others [the less verbal; the racially, gendered, or class-based disadvantaged (Young 1990, 2000; Daly 2002, 2005; Cahn 2006)];
5. Whether certain classes of wrongdoing should never be submitted to restorative processes, e.g., serious crimes such as murder, rape, or wrongdoing in which society as a whole, not just individuals, is affected, such as genocide or hate crimes (Robinson 2006, Rugge & Cormier 2005);
6. Whether particular wrongdoers or offenders (or victims) should be excluded from restorative processes, e.g., repeat offenders, the mentally impaired, those who are remorseless;
7. Whether psychological or socially based communication technologies at the individual level are effective for macro institutional, national, and larger social problems;
8. Whether restorative justice can or should substitute entirely for state and

formal criminal sanctions and punishments or whether it should be a totally informal and voluntary supplementary process;

9. Whether restorative justice is more economically and criminologically efficient (less costly, more deterrent) than conventional criminal justice methods;
10. Whether a focus on future remediation or right-making diminishes important concerns about blame for past wrongs (Menkel-Meadow 2004, Grillo 1991);
11. Whether individualized forms of restorative justice can meet the requirements of equity-based justice or equality when similarly situated offenders are provided with differential outcomes (Robinson 2006);
12. Whether privatization of justice in the criminal context (whether individual or at larger state levels) deprives us of the public function of courts, tribunals, punishments, and precedent-setting (Luban 1995);
13. Whether private criminal justice can operate within the shadow of the law, with both the potential coercion of the state as a threatened alternative, or as a weak substitute where there is no formal law enforcement (international criminal law);
14. Whether participation in restorative justice procedures enhances both individual and communitarian sensibilities for empowerment, fairness, legitimacy, satisfaction, and social justice;
15. Whether restorative justice is a spiritual, utopian project, with a faith in human ability to be transformed, at both individual (Katz 1990) or group levels (Gibson 2004a), and whether it can be harnessed to practical, institutional, large-scale social and legal change.

This article reviews the claims made for restorative justice and the difficult and compelling issues raised by its use and offered by its critics to discount its achievements and possibilities. I begin by recounting some of the history of restorative justice in its various forms, with its differentiated claims. I then explore some of the most trenchant critiques that have been made of restorative justice at philosophical, social, political, jurisprudential, and practical levels. Next, I report on what we know to date about how restorative justice actually works from a variety of empirical sources, including several meta-analyses performed by others. Finally, I suggest what issues and challenges lie ahead for both the use and assessment of restorative justice efforts in individual, community, national, and international efforts to deal effectively with human-inflicted harm.

FORMS AND MODELS OF RESTORATIVE JUSTICE

Although in one sense restorative or restitutionary justice is as old at least as the earliest forms of classical justice in Greek, Arab, and Roman legal culture (Braithwaite 2002), modern restorative justice traces its origins to objections to both retributivist and failed rehabilitative models of criminal law and punishment. Victim control of the prosecution of wrongful acts was a common practice before the modernization of the criminal justice system in the late Middle Ages in Europe (Langbein 2003) relocated the management of crime from private citizens to the state. State control of crime developed to provide revenue for the state (in fines and punishments) and more order and control (and equity) in the treatment of offenders. State control of criminal acts was also a product of the fear of vigilante or vengeance motives on the part of victims, which actually perpetuated violence, as needs for less bloodthirsty and more orderly outcomes were required, not only as religious, social, and humanitarian values evolved, but also to provide some predictability for the growing commercial society and increasingly centralized political order (Thompson 1976). Although fines and jail terms began to substitute for blood feuds in postmedieval Europe, elements of violent retributivist and vengeance-seeking systems of justice continued to coexist with local restorative forms of community moots or mediation in many cultures. The history of criminal justice and punishment is one of increasing state control and surveillance (Foucault 1979), with concomitant increased costs of public institutions and public responsibility, with little demonstrated reduction of crime, violence, or antisocial acts (cf. Zimring 2006).

The twentieth century was certainly the most violent of all centuries at nation-state, group, and individual levels, even with the modern criminal and penological apparatus that had developed by then. Aside from Anglo and middle European criminal justice models of punishment (incapacitation, incarceration, retribution, rehabilitation), other legal cultures have long focused on restorative, reparative, or restitutionary forms of justice, including community moots, wise elder mediation, religious forms of repentance and reparation, and various forms of communal conferencing (*nanante*, *ubuntu*, *gacaca*) in the Middle East, Africa, and Asia and peace circles in indigenous American (both North and South) cultures. All these forms of justice or dispute resolution involve some narration before victims, offenders, family members, supporters, community members, and leaders, with communally arrived at outcomes (fines of animals, crops, other goods, or money; reparative work; and often ritual ceremonies of healing and forgiveness, including the sharing of common food and drink, as well as dances, songs, and other expressive activities). Most reparative forms of justice were scaled to smaller communities where mobility for both offenders and the community was limited and continuing face-to-face contacts with community members were the norm.

As state control embraced more social control of criminal offenders, both through formal legal processes and therapeutic intervention models, reformers began to experiment with new forms of handling (I never say managing) wrongdoing. In the early 1970s, both in Canada and the United States, contemporaneously with similar movements in civil and family law toward mediation, experimental programs in victim-offender reconciliation programs (VORP) or victim-offender mediation (VOM) (Umbreit 1994) were established alongside or within progressive court systems, some as diversionary programs for minor crimes, others as independent processes. By the mid-1990s, there were hundreds of programs in many states and provinces of the United States and Canada. These early programs focused on facilitated conversations of wrongdoers, victims, and family members both as supporters and as possible disciplinarians or enforcers. These programs sometimes served as alternatives to state prosecutions (dismissals if victims agreed and were otherwise made whole). VORP and VOM were often founded by social reformers, progressive criminal law professionals (including police, probation and parole officers, and social workers and some lawyers and judges), and, notably, by religious groups, such as the Mennonites, who brought their reparative philosophy to bear on all forms of conflict resolution (Zehr 1990, Lederach 1997).

Some of the developments in the 1970s were sparked by First Nation practices in Canada (Stuart 2001) for "peace or sentencing or family circles" used both for internal wrongs committed within tribes and then later expanded to First Nation land and other disputes with the larger nation-state (Bradford 2005). These practices enlarged the notion of who was a proper participant or stakeholder in conflicts involving harm to other members of the community. A more flexible, tailored, and communitarian sense of justice or fairness, including group responsibility for bringing individuals back into the community, characterized many of these programs. "Healing or peace circles" of a variety of North American native groups, including the Navajo (Yazzie & Zion 1996), brought native practices to the attention of conventional court systems. Processes including "talking sticks" that rotate among participants and equalize who will talk (especially in leaderless groups) are radically different from legalistic and adversarial confrontations. The purpose of such conferences is often not to assess fault or guilt (with fact-finding), although there is narration of what happened and why, because usually fault or guilt is admitted. The purpose of the circle or conference is to consider the best ways to make the victim whole or compensated and to consider various forms of treatment or reintegration of the wrongdoer. With the emphasis on remedial approaches (for both victims and offenders), considered from a collectivity (the community, tribe, family, or other representatives), power is not located in a single judge, and the norms that are referenced may be negotiated and interpreted for particular cases, with less emphasis on formal rules and standards. These processes have many variations, including referral back to courts if wrongdoers do not admit fault or victims are not satisfied with apologies or restitutionary offers when laws have been violated. In other cases, the state may defer to some other form of authority (Indian tribes, local law enforcement, etc.), provided there is full participant consent or other legal authorization.

Perhaps the greatest and deepest impact of these new processes was seen in New Zealand, where family conferencing modeled on both traditional Maori and modern practices developed into a mandatory model for juvenile justice (Maxwell & Morris 1993). Here the movement represents collaboration among mainstream conservative and social democratic political parties, Christian profamily groups, and Maori philosophy and participation (Braithwaite 2002). In such family conferences, alternative structures to conventional adversary adjudication involve the juvenile offender, teachers, social workers, family members, victims, and others who jointly develop a package of restitutionary payments or service, apologies, and plans for future behavior, often in lieu of incarceration. In sentencing circles, a community group helps develop programs and proposals for compensating victims and preparing behavioral plans for amelioration of the conduct of the offender. Such programs, of course, have their critics (see below), both for coercing compliance and also for reduction of criminal defendant rights in nations with strong civil liberties protections (Delgado 2000). There is also some evidence that, when used in smaller, homogeneous communities (which are felt to be more oppressive to some adolescents than the cold state), there is an increased risk of flight from the community (Marshall 1998).

In the United States, the states making most use of these programs are Minnesota, Vermont, Wisconsin, Maine, New Mexico, Pennsylvania, and Montana, which employ various forms of victim-offender programs for juveniles and for postconviction, probation, parole, and "creative" sentencing. Less use is made currently at the federal criminal level because of determinate sentencing laws (Beale 2003), although in earlier periods, the federal courts varied by region in how they delivered tailored justice to particular offenders, with contrasting retributivist and rehabilitative goals (Utz 1978). A new development includes "problem-solving courts" (Kaye 1997, Berman et al. 2005) in which restorative and rehabilitative principles have made their way into the formal justice system, as specialized courts in drug offenses, vice, abuse, neglect, and other family issues have developed more reparative sentences, including personalized treatment programs, some elements of restorative shaming, and some structured encounter with victims, as well as regular reporting and accountability (e.g., drug tests) to the court itself (Dorf & Sabel 2000).

Restorative justice programs are intended, in ideology, to be purely voluntary, but aspects of restorative justice have been co-opted into mandatory diversionary and formal court programs, raising questions of philosophical purity and efficacy and challenging efforts to measure the impact of these programs. Some models of restorative justice have been used in prisons, concurrent with and adjunct to formal punishment, and observers fear that some offenders may pay twice with formal criminal sanctions and demands for less formal restitutionary or shaming rituals that reduce their human dignity (Nussbaum 2004). Restorative justice processes can also be used following release, as conditions of parole or probation, connecting the offender to agreements with victims or the community for social service, compensation, or accountability for behavioral change. Although restorative justice is motivated by those seeking humanistic integration, it is easy to see how some restorative justice forms can appear oppressive, reducing freedom of action and individual agency and requiring intrusive surveillance and accountability that can devolve into counterproductive resentment.

Restorative justice has, in recent years, informed a variety of other legal and political processes. John Braithwaite argues for its effectiveness as responsive regulation in matters of corporate and public policy regulation. When state regulators engage in negotiated conversations with managers of corporations and industries (such as nursing homes, trade groups, commercial enterprises), Braithwaite (2002) argues, compliance is greater and dialogues allow more realistic, flexible, and contingent enforcement of important legal standards (see also Hawkins 1984).

Dispute resolution theorists and practitioners have argued that public and deliberative encounters in regulatory, civil, and criminal matters can be seen as a new form of governance, promoting healthy democratic deliberation that is more participatory, legitimate, and flexible in its legal and social problem solving when matters are openly negotiated with many stakeholders and when multiple issues and multiple parties are involved in the deliberations (Menkel-Meadow 2004, Elster 1995, Bohman 1996).

In the 1990s, restorative justice practices moved outward from individual acts of wrongdoing to the systematic wrongdoing of civil and ethnic wars (by both intra- and international state and nonstate actors) and illegitimate regimes such as apartheid. The use of TRCs and similar public panels of encounters of victims and offenders and the larger nation-state and international community has given rise to whole new institutions of justice (Avruch & Vejarano 2001, Minow 1998, Stromseth et al. 2006). These truth commissions are intended to provide a new national narrative as victims seek answers and information about their individual family members [what happened to the disappeared (Argentina, Chile), the murdered, or the incarcerated (Guatemala, Rwanda, South Africa)], as well as the truth about state-sanctioned violence and harm (Sierra Leone, East Timor). As discussed more fully below, the challenge for these various and quite diverse TRCs has been to ensure participation by both victims and perpetrators, which in many cases is not a direct encounter as in more conventional criminal restorative justice practices, in settings where there is mostly talk or testimony and not real punishment or restitutionary relief.

At the national or institutional level of restorative justice, the goals may be quite different than in more individualized acts of wrongdoing. The commissions are designed to heal the nation-state or civil community by allowing many narratives of hurt and harm to be told and by creating new collective narratives of the truth so that a society can begin anew with transformative understandings of both its past and its future. Like the use of restorative justice in more individual settings, the efficacy and effectiveness of these processes have been debated and questioned (see below), but these processes are clearly evolving and offer great promise of adapting to different political, cultural, and historical contexts and may ultimately transform our conceptions of international justice. As is more fully explored below, as scholars and political activists assess and debate their effectiveness, there are particularly rich encounters between the international human rights community (with rights-based conceptions of justice) and the international conflict resolution and peacekeeping communities (with more realist and pragmatic conceptions of post-conflict regimes). Differences of theoretical paradigms, of assumptions about human behavior, of philosophies, and of commitments (such as to the rule of law or to pragmatic, informal actions of nongovernmental organizations) and practices may themselves have to be mediated to make these new forms of justice meet their aspirational goals, either alongside conventional legal structures (with conventional international or national prosecutions of the most serious atrocities) or as substitutes for them (in less serious cases in which redemption, reassimilation, or even co-optation of past aggressors may be possible or desirable for security and continuity of regimes). The newer forms of truth and reconciliation practices combine tiered systems of prosecution (for most serious crimes) and confession and restorative justice for less serious offenses (Honeyman 2004, Hayner 2001). Whether these alternative institutions are public or private is also a crucial issue. The South African TRC proceedings were televised to the whole nation, but virtually all of the Latin American commission proceedings (Argentina, Chile, and Guatemala) were privately conducted (even with publication of formal reports).

CRITIQUES OF RESTORATIVE JUSTICE

Most proponents of restorative justice appeal in visionary, optimistic, and aspirational terms for a new human sensibility to emerge from the transformative effects of dialogue, conversation, empowerment, and understanding, from individual juvenile offender advocates to architects of the most complex truth and reconciliation governmental processes or formal state institutions, such as problem-solving courts. The claims made on behalf of restorative justice are simultaneously instrumental, incremental, and grand:

- Restorative justice enhances understanding of the root causes of crime and conflict;
- Outcomes reached in restorative justice are more likely to be complied with;
- Restorative justice processes reduce recidivism rates;
- Restorative justice offers the possibility of reclaiming, repairing, and transforming individual wrongdoers and reintegrating them into productive activity;
- Participants in restorative justice processes are more likely to develop fellow-feeling, empathy, and a sense of moral responsibility, mutuality, and reciprocity;
- Restorative justice processes enhance community building, community norm development, and democratic participation by increasing the number of stakeholders who are involved in its deliberations;
- Restorative justice permits more real, less formal, less stylized or legal human communication and interaction, producing more authentic understanding;
- Restorative justice processes are richer at expressing a variety of often competing justice values simultaneously—acknowledgment of fault, recognition of consequences that flow from wrongful activity (punishment, remorse), compensation to victims, social learning and healing, mercy, as well as moral judgment—and are thus more creative and flexible and represent a form of responsive justice (Nonet & Selznick 1978) that is humanely civilized and not as brittle as formal adversarial justice structures;
- Processes using restorative justice values are more likely to engage individuals in voluntary commitments for undertakings to others and self and to encourage self-empowerment and self-esteem;
- The underlying values of restorative justice promote a positive redemptionist and ameliorative view of human behavior, with a positive hope that even the worst among us can be transformed to consider the common good and the best for other human beings;

- Outcomes produced by participatory restorative justice processes are more tailored to the specific needs of individuals, groups, communities, and nations; they can be bargained for with more nuance, detail, and accountability than those produced by formal and overbooked systems of justice;
- Restorative justice is potentially less costly and more efficient both in monetary and deterrent effects than conventional penological practices;
- If the principles of restorative justice were to gain ascendancy, the criminal justice system would be radically transformed (less punitive and more responsive), if not eliminated.

Since the practices of restorative justice in all of the forms described above have been developing and attempting to express these aspirational values, a core of critiques of restorative justice has emerged at different levels and from the perspectives of different disciplines. There are empirical claims that restorative justice does not meet its own claims (see next section) (Braithwaite 2002, Daly 2002, Van Ness 1993); philosophical and sociological claims that humans continue to carry base retributivist and vengeful motivations that are impervious to so-called transformative processes (Acorn 2004); legalistic claims that restorative justice unfairly coerces and manipulates its participants to forgive (victims) or confess and accept harsher terms (offenders) than legal rights and rules would permit in formal justice institutions and that restorative justice does not deliver equitable or equal justice (Dolinko 2003, Delgado 2000); anthropological critiques that concepts in restorative justice ideology are culturally specific and not universal (Avruch & Vejarano 2001) and that notions of community are social constructs and can be manipulated for bad ends (Weisberg 2003); and political claims that restorative justice processes will be manipulated, corrupted, co-opted, and deformed to produce oppression, more state surveillance and discipline, and more inappropriate social control (Abel 1982, Levrant et al. 1999).

In addition to these critiques, specific critics have suggested that, like civil ADR, restorative justice privatizes that which should be public (Luban 1995), prevents precedents and rule generation for community norm development, and hides its outcomes from measurement and evaluation. The location of restorative justice (whether in or alongside courts or as private conferencing sessions) problematizes the relation of the state to law enforcement and shared governance with private entities (a larger issue that clearly implicates more than restorative reforms in this age of public-private partnerships).

Criminologists worry that restorative justice will lead to subjective, nonobjective, and nonrational assessments of harm and need and will produce great inequities for both victims and offenders. What is extremely painful to one victim may be tolerable for another. Whether victims receive recompense and restitution will depend not on the quality of the offense, but on the resources of the offender. Philosophers such as Nussbaum (2004) decry the potential degradation and loss of humanity that can come from compelled shaming. Acorn (2004) argues similarly about the effects of coerced compassion on the part of victims, who have been seriously harmed and are made to feel ashamed about their desires for punishment, vengeance, and retribution. In these claims, we see that the very promise of restorative justice to be more authentic has the potential to be less authentic than other forms of structured and rule-based discourse because of its compelled or expected narratives. When the harm is not only personal but social, how can the offender satisfy the needs of the community for rectification and safety with a simple (even if authentic) apology (Robinson 2003, 2006)?

Within the restorative justice movement itself, practitioners and theorists have their own worries (Braithwaite 2002, pp. 137–68) that offenders may be stigmatized in a different, but harmful, way than they are stigmatized in formal court proceedings; that victims can feel revictimized in their retelling of pain or injury suffered [comparable to the rape victim's dilemmas in the formal adjudication system (Matoesian 1993)]; that oppressive or false communities in societies that are actually heterogeneous will attempt to impose their own values on participants in the process; or that even with community homogeneity more conservative or majoritarian values may gain ascendancy and dampen individual freedoms (Weisberg 2003). Although conceived as a part of a progressive movement for social justice, the appeal of restorative justice to the Christian Fundamentalist Right in the United States has caused some to be concerned about whether restorative processes will be used for antiprogressive ends (imposing conservative, antiliberationist, narrowly religious, or monocultural values). Or, with less conservative ends, governments may simply co-opt such processes to achieve their ends (diversionary programs, docket clearing, more social control and surveillance devolved to nonstate actors) and thus routinize and make less authentic the human encounter and engagement contemplated by restorative justice proponents. Like civil forms of ADR in such processes as consensus building, collaborative governance, negotiated rulemaking, and multi-agency mediation, some worry that the separation of powers and accountability in constitutional governments will be obscured and made difficult to monitor. Lawyers, in particular, worry about how informal processes, while serving some ends of responsive and flexible justice, can erode other important values—individual civil rights, standards for convictions, rights of appeals, written opinions, and accountability of decision makers.

Feminists have been strong critics (and proponents in other contexts) of restorative justice models that decriminalize violence against woman and seek lesser punishments and no incarceration for wrongful acts that have only recently achieved some form of legal recognition (Daly 2005, Stubbs 1995). Practitioners worry that processes that are structured around dialogue and narrative (Young 2000) may privilege the verbal and well educated and disempower those without education or other resources. And others worry that restitution commodifies crime and wrongdoing by allowing offenders to buy their way out if they can (Kahan 2006). Imprisonment, at least in theory, is a great equalizer in incapacitation.

Finally, restorative justice requires well-intentioned, nonmanipulative participants and sufficient resources to allow authentic encounters and dialogue to occur. Thus, even for some proponents of restorative justice, there is a fear that restorative justice can only work with large commitments of time, resources, and skilled individuals and must necessarily be deformed and watered down to ritualized imperfections if it is assimilated, aggregated, and institutionalized without sufficient care and resources.

EMPIRICAL ASSESSMENTS OF RESTORATIVE JUSTICE: DOES IT WORK?

There are many challenges in assessing the claims of both proponents and critics of restorative justice at the conceptual and methodological levels. Most importantly, as in assessments of all comparative forms of justice or legal case processing, including civil dispute resolution, it is virtually impossible to conduct controlled experiments or treatments of submitting the same matter to different treatment conditions for comparison. In both criminal justice matters and larger conflicts, ordinarily there is only one treatment of the matter or, if several treatments are used, the treatments are used for different purposes or at different times [such as use of VOM for remedy but not guilt assessment, triaging, or grading of crimes against humanity that are assigned to formal prosecution or more restorative processes, such as *gacaca* in Rwanda (Bolocan 2004)]. So, although a few controlled studies are emerging in which there is random assignment of cases to either restorative justice or more conventional models of process, the bulk of empirical evaluations of restorative justice efforts focus on aggregate comparison data, with attempts at matched cases or data sets of different forms of treatment or intervention. Examples include efforts to assess (*a*) comparative compliance rates with agreements or judgments; (*b*) satisfaction rates for victims, offenders, professionals, and the larger community with different processes and outcome possibilities; (*c*) reoffender or recidivism rates; (*d*) reduction of violence generally [community measures beyond those of participants in the process (Zimring 2006)]; and (*e*) in the case of TRCs, whether postconflict societies build efficacious systems of governance with legitimacy, compared with societies that have not used such processes (Stromseth et al. 2006).

The second challenge is to define and operationalize the meaning of variables assessed. As several new meta-analyses have shown, over the course of many years of study, such variables as reoffense rates vary enormously from study to study, thereby greatly confounding analysis. In some studies reoffense is measured in short time intervals (six months), in others longer (up to two years or more). Some studies cut finely and look at degrees of severity of offense (simple and single property offenses, simple to repeated assaults), and others look only at whether there is a subsequent conviction or, quite differently, simply another arrest. Because it is easiest to measure, with exit interviews or follow-up methods, the most common factor studied is a crude measure of satisfaction with the process (and/or outcome), tracking the now rich and robust findings of procedural justice attitudes (MacCoun 2005, Thibault & Walker 1975). These findings demonstrate that the processes generally favored are informal processes that give participants voice and that have some cathartic effect in response to the dispute or act of wrongdoing. And these informal processes are favored even when parties lose (or do not gain much) in outcomes. Here again, the comparisons are analogical, rather than experimental.

Aggregate studies compare satisfaction rates of those who have used the conventional justice system with those who have attended some alternative process (Kakalik et al. 1996, Lind et al. 1989), but it is virtually impossible for the same participant to compare treatment in the two types of processes in the same case, leaving open the possibilities that case factors and other variables may account for process satisfaction. For example, in one of the most rigorously designed tests of comparative civil case processing, LaFree & Rack (1996) found that race and ethnic matching of third-party neutrals (whether mediators or judges) with participants (Anglo-white, Hispanic, or African American) accounted for some of the comparative satisfaction rates of disputants (and also explained some of the variance in outcomes in the two processes, mediation or adjudication).

At the level of assessing the more ambitious truth and reconciliation or societal restorative processes, measurements are even more complex and difficult to assess. Should individuals be polled about satisfaction (those who have participated and those who have not)? Is it possible, as some political scientists have attempted, to compare rates of internal conflict and civil wars over time and between nation-states and also to measure aggregate levels of international conflict (Stein 1993) when different conflict resolution processes are used? As the growing literature on TRCs and postconflict interventions indicates, there are great variations in the purposes, structures (direct or indirect encounters and testimonies, amnesties or punishment, types of matters subject to informal processes, publicity and accessibility of such processes, location, type of third-party interventions or facilitations), and functioning of these innovations in justice. Comparisons across widely different political, social, and cultural contexts may be quite difficult.

Despite these methodological problems, the emerging data often provide not only confirming or disconfirming information about the claims and hypotheses about restorative processes, but also, in some cases, information about new and perhaps unintended effects of such processes, such as Gibson's (2004a,b) findings on the development of human rights consciousness among those who viewed (on national television) the South African Truth and Reconciliation process, even if they did not participate directly (see below).

Here I present an overview of what studies to date have revealed about how restorative justice is working or is perceived to be working, in a variety of locations, with great variations in purpose, structure, and use.

The greatest claims for restorative justice, in its most conventional forms in criminal justice—that it creates greater compliance with agreements or judgments, reduces imprisonment (and therefore costs to the system), provides greater satisfaction for both victims and offenders, and reduces recidivism rates—have all been substantiated in a variety of different studies on at least three continents (North America, Australia and New Zealand, and Europe), despite methodological difficulties in almost all settings. Comparisons between systems (restorative and conventional-retributivist) are difficult when the participants do not engage in both types [and satisfaction rates with informal processes tend to be high, whether in civil cases (mediation, arbitration, or other forms of ADR) or criminal cases (see Lind et al. 1989, Kakalik et al. 1996)].

Some studies focus on participation rates, noting that even when referred by courts (in less than voluntary settings) many offenders choose to admit guilt and attend mediation with their victims. (In virtually all court programs, defendants who do not admit guilt and instead seek trial are not referred to VOM. Thus, how voluntary a guilt admission is remains a worrisome issue.) Participation rates for victims range from 40% to 60% of those referred. Interestingly, participation rates for victims go up when more time elapses between referral and participation in cases involving personal injury (assault), but decrease when more time elapses in cases involving property (theft, vandalism) (Umbreit et al. 2005). There is a curvilinear relationship for participation rates of victims and the seriousness of the offense, with participation rates lowest for less serious offenses ("I can't be bothered") and for the most serious (fear of the offender or reliving the trauma in serious bodily harm cases) (Coates & Gehm 1985, Wyrick & Costanzo 1999).

Many studies have demonstrated high satisfaction rates on the part of both offenders and victims who feel they were treated better in restorative justice processes than in the criminal justice system (Poulson 2003, reviewing 7 selected studies out of 100 on psychological outcomes of restorative justice), often with satisfaction rates greater by a factor of 3 to 4. Studies in such diverse locations as Bethlehem, Pennsylvania (McCold & Wachtel 1998); Brooklyn, New York (Davis et al. 1980); Canberra, Australia (Strang et al. 1999, Strang 2001); Israel (Umbreit & Ritter 2006); a multi-state U.S. study (Umbreit & Coates 1992, Umbreit et al. 2001); Canada (Umbreit 1995); and the United Kingdom (Umbreit & Roberts 1996, Marshall & Merry 1990); along with meta-analysis of multiple studies (Latimer et al. 2001), with diverse sets of victims (female, young, old, low and middle socioeconomic classes) and offenders (most, but not all of the studies focus on juvenile offenders, with increasing attention to adult offender programs as restorative justice practices expand) all find that victims have satisfaction rates higher than what they had expected to gain from a process following injury and harm. Offenders are much more likely to feel they have been treated fairly. Offender satisfaction rates with restorative justice compared with court processes tend to be higher than victims' satisfaction (typically because, in minor offenses, participation in restorative justice proceedings may eliminate other forms of punishment, including incarceration, although in some programs offenders might have had their cases totally dismissed in a more conventional setting).

Both victims and offenders report satisfaction with their ability to narrate and explain more fully both the harm and injury that wrongdoing caused in particular circumstances and the reasons for committing bad acts. On the victim side, there is a slightly lower perception that their opinions were taken more seriously in restorative justice than in court, compared with offenders (Poulson 2003). And, in an important and rigorous analysis in Australia, victims whose restorative justice proceedings were badly handled or did not take place were the least satisfied [less satisfied than court users and participants in more successful restorative justice proceedings (Strang 2001)]. Thus, the quality of the restorative justice process may be especially important when there are high expectations about what it can accomplish. Participants generally expressed satisfaction with the fairness of mediators or third-party facilitators over judges [by a factor of 2.3 for victims and 6.0 for offenders (Poulson 2003)].

Victims have been satisfied with what they perceive to be greater accountability in restorative justice (Poulson 2003), and, not surprisingly, victims were more likely to forgive the offender in restorative justice processes than in court proceedings, probably because offenders are much more likely to apologize [6.9 times more likely according to Poulson's (2003) meta-analysis] than in court proceedings.

Since the beginning of the 1990s, researchers have attempted to track compliance rates with reparation and compensation agreements. Although many argue that restorative justice does not require an agreement but rather seeks understanding and dialogue, studies document that agreements for some sort of restitution are highly likely to occur [more than 90% in VOM programs in which there is face-to-face contact, with some form of restitutionary agreement being reached in the vast majority of cases (Umbreit et al. 2005, Umbreit 2001, Umbreit & Coates 1992)]. Compliance rates range from a high of 100% to usually no lower than about 75%, in comparison with control groups with diversionary or other sentences from courts (see, e.g., Haley & Neugebauer 1992, Marshall 1998, Kuhn 1987, McCold & Wachtel 1998). Latimer et al.'s (2001) meta-analysis of eight studies with a control group found that restitutionary compliance was 33% higher in restorative justice cases than in the control cases (in court). Other studies in the United States have found comparisons of compliance of 81% completion rates in restorative justice with 58% completion in court cases (Umbreit et al. 2005). And in a randomly assigned treatment evaluation of six different programs, 89% completion was found in restorative justice, compared with 75% completion in courts (Ervin & Schneider 1990).

Satisfaction rates for victims are often attributed to the nonmaterial or human aspects of the process—the ability to explain in regular language (not court-stylized admissible evidence) what the harm caused has meant for the individual, to learn facts relating to the wrongdoing, and to learn a little bit about why an offender does bad things. In his meta-analysis of seven studies, Poulson (2003) found that victims who participated in restorative justice proceedings were half as likely to feel upset about the crime afterwards than were victims who went to court. In the places where restorative justice is used in very serious crimes, such as murder or serious felonies, the effects of restorative justice are often only in this nonmaterial realm—accountability and apology by the wrongdoer and some relief in the form of closure or forgiveness for the survivors (Umbreit et al. 2003), because in very serious cases (murder, rape, and serious assault) restorative justice is ancillary or supplemental, not substitutionary, to formal adjudication. In its most spiritual forms, restorative justice is experienced as a cathartic event, both for victims and offenders. As one participant described it, "Today I have observed and taken part in justice administered with love" (Braithwaite 2002, p. 53).

Indeed, some have asked whether an apology from a murderer might provide greater psychological closure (at least for some) than the death penalty (Hirsch 2006).

Perhaps the greatest empirical effort has been expended on examining what concrete and measurable effects restorative justice has had on recidivism rates. In a meta-analysis of 19 studies with 9307 offenders (juveniles), Nugent et al. (2003) found that VOM participants were 33% less likely to reoffend within six months than those who had not participated in VOM. This rigorous meta-analysis recognizes important categorical and coding issues—different studies define reoffense differently (arrest, conviction, any new contact with the criminal justice system), and the time period in which an offender is followed can have important effects on the findings. Generally speaking, over longer periods of time (as the offender moves further and further away from the VOM event), recidivism rates move closer together for restorative and conventional criminal justice participants (Nugent et al. 2003). These data must be compared with the general rates of decline in juvenile delinquency with the ordinary life course (which some estimate at as much as 50% who no longer offend when they grow older; see McCord 2000). Victimless crimes (like some forms of drunk-driving and some drug offenses) may be less subject to restorative justice–court differences as the encounter with a victim is minimal (with a state official standing in for the harm the crime caused) (Strang 2001). And comparisons of recidivism rates are subject to great selection biases, with the more minor crimes or those committed by juveniles more likely to be assigned to restorative, not conventional adjudicative, treatment conditions (Braithwaite 2002, Bazemore & Walgrave 1999, Bradshaw et al. 2006, Pfeiffer 1998). Finally, empirical studies, with rare exception, tend to homogenize offenders and do not capture the offender who commits crime "for the thrill of it" and may not be deterred by either restorative justice or conventional criminal processes (Katz 1990).

John Braithwaite and other researchers studying regulatory enforcement have documented that compliance with regulations is often higher (and rates of repeated noncompliance lower) when regulated industries and corporate actors are actively engaged in discussions of compliance and allowed to talk with their regulators (Braithwaite 2002, Hawkins 1984). Inspections of mine safety (in the United States and the United Kingdom) that involved exit conferences with dialogues and plans for reparation were much more likely to lead to compliance with rules and increased safety standards. Braithwaite found that persuasion worked much more effectively in the corporate compliance context than did punitive measures. Similar results have been noted in nursing home regulation, special education (Handler 1986), and nuclear power regulation in a field now internationally called "communitarian regulation" (Rees 1988, 1994) [not unlike American reg-neg (negotiated rulemaking); see Harter 1982].

Uses of restorative justice in controversial arenas such as domestic abuse have met with criticism by feminists and some child advocates, but in fact many studies do report some success with nonrecidivism in some forms of family conferencing and other forms of restorative justice (Burford & Pennell 1998). There has been less rigorous demonstration of successful uses of school peer mediation or antibullying to reduce school violence (Braithwaite 2002, pp. 59–61), although such efforts continue, especially in the wake of recent violent school shootings. Most of the United States was treated to its first public display of restorative justice when the Amish families who lost children in a school shooting in Pennsylvania forgave the wrongdoer, prayed with his widow, and created an image of freedom as "the freedom from vengeance, which is forgiveness" (Fleming 2006, Arendt 1998). Although not a restorative justice process with the actual offender (those who prayed together were all families of either the murderer or his victims and were, thus, all survivors), this demonstration of religious forgiveness was quite contrary to the images presented of more vengeful parents in other school shootings (such as Columbine, Colorado).

With the expansion of restorative justice to specialized reparative courts, like drug courts, vice courts, and unified family courts, researchers have just begun to explore rigorously whether new treatment models with less punishment reduce recidivism, increase employment, or have other ameliorative effects for both individuals and the larger community. Dorf & Sabel (2000), for example, have studied drug courts' effectiveness and have argued that these experiments in local social control should be allowed to flourish and vary as evaluators seek to discover what works (such as ongoing relations with social workers and accountability to judges and other court personnel) in which contexts [big cities with larger budgets and more resources or smaller communities with more *gemeinshaft* or surveillance (depending on whether one has a Weberian or Foucaldian perspective)]. Courts that treat defendants as members of a community have been documented as being perceived to be more fair than conventional courts (Frazer 2006), and perceptions of fairness are linked to increased compliance (Tyler & Huo 2002). These efforts to evaluate problem-solving courts are controversial, especially among those who see restorative justice institutions as formally abrogating legal rights in the name of remedial creativity (Thompson 2002). With restorative justice's analogue in the debate about use of bargaining processes for negotiated rulemaking in administrative regulation and civil law (Harter 1982, Coglianese 1997, Freeman 1997), critics fear that softer processes will undermine legal formality, separation of powers, formal legal accountability, and enforcement, as well as ordered norm and rule creation.

Evaluation of restorative justice's rehabilitative potential recapitulates the historical dialectic of all judicial reform. Nineteenth-century reformers created juvenile courts to be a more responsive, less punitive, paternalistic institution for wayward youths. Civil libertarian litigation in the 1960s produced, among other cases, *In re Gault* (1967), which infused juvenile criminal proceedings with legal rights, such as the right to legal counsel and, some would argue, more punitive outcomes. Restorative justice, like its analogues in civil justice, is a reaction to an over-rigidified, bureaucratized, punitive, and ineffective (at crime reduction) criminal law system, which now has its own critics for drawing different lines around individual and collective, formal and informal, material and spiritual, rights-based and interest-based values. Where restorative processes are supplemental, not substitutional, of the conventional legal process, they are more likely to be accepted. Yet some would prefer other reforms of the criminal justice system to remedy its problems. Some argue for less plea bargaining and faster, more responsive trials to allow defendants and victims to come to formal justice faster. Others argue for less draconian sentencing, both in length of time and severity, to return to earlier reform efforts at more rehabilitative notions of criminal remediation. Still others argue for decriminalization of certain offenses (minor property crimes, drug offenses) or more localization of criminal law enforcement, whereas more conservative forces argue for harsher sentences and criminalization of more offenses. In the political standoffs surrounding criminal justice policy, restorative justice appears to be one reform that appeals to both sides of the political spectrum, if for different reasons.

Beyond the conventional criminal justice system, efforts to expand restorative and reparative processes to larger acts of wrongdoing (Elster 2006) [state violence, genocide, civil wars, ethnic conflicts, international human rights violations, and past wrongs such as slavery and internment (Brophy 2006)] have also pitted restorative reformers against more formal rights-based reformers. The activity of nongovernmental organizations, the United Nations, and other organizations in enunciating and enforcing human rights standards has created whole new institutions of formal prosecution at the international level [the International Criminal Tribunal for the Former Yugoslavia (Hagan 2003) and for Rwanda and the International Criminal Court, among others]. Proponents of enforcement of international human rights argue for strict criminal prosecution, whereas others argue that some forms of reparative justice [whether individualized (Godobo-Madikizela 2003) or more collective (Keller 2007)] are more likely to lead to healed and functioning postconflict societies, replicating timeless philosophical debates about the relative efficacy of principle, adjudication, and rights versus interest- or needs-based bargaining (Elster 1995; Menkel-Meadow 1984, 2003). The rapid execution of Saddam Hussein after prosecution in a state (not international) tribunal, cutting off further testimony, information, and maybe public remorse, has reignited debates about how justice is delivered in such contexts. Whereas some tribunals have been international and other TRCs are nation-state based, other efforts have experimented with more mixed combinations of international and state-based institutions (Sierra Leone, East Timor). Meanwhile, complex legal issues of whether international bodies, such as the International Criminal Court, should bend to national policies of amnesty or forgiveness remain unresolved (Blumenson 2006).

Attempts to study the aftereffects of TRCs and more local, indigenous restorative processes, such as *gacaca* in Rwanda, now abound, with heated debate and controversy (Borer 2006, Henkin 2002, Rotberg & Thompson 2000, Kritz 1995, Avruch & Vejarano 2001, Hayner 2001) as many nations have filed formal truth reports with a variety of reparative conditions (Guatemala, Argentina, Chile, El Salvador, South Africa, Sierra Leone, East Timor). Questions of whether international or local principles of justice should govern are now being raised as well (for their effects on postconflict legitimacy of the legal processes used and the creation of new postconflict national identities, see Ivković & Hagan 2006). International tribunals are often viewed as aligned with one side in ethnic conflict, as some have argued has occurred in the International Criminal Tribunal for the former Yugoslavia, thus prolonging hostility and promoting continuing desires for vengeance.

Some decry the lack of participation by important perpetrators, such as Dyzanhaus's (2003) exposure of the absence in the South African TRC of apartheid-era judges, who failed even to narrate and acknowledge their crimes against humanity in upholding the legality of the apartheid regime. Others more forcefully critique the absence of any real punishment, accountability, or reparative compensation (Andrews & Ellmann 2002, Abel 1995) for horrific wrongs, not to mention the failure to confront more long-lasting harms—not only discrimination, wrongful murders and incarceration, and removal of civil liberties, but also continuing gross economic injustice, with little effort to ameliorate, even with well-written and democratically approved constitutions, the continuing conditions of inequality, poverty, and increasing crime among the have-nots. Some fear that having written a report and formally repented as a government, instead of "nunca mas!" (never again), Argentina and Chile, among others, could just as easily fall again into the clutches of brutal dictators (especially as Pinochet successfully avoided full accountability for his crimes). Whether postconflict or postdictatorship societies can put aside their past hostilities and sharp divisions and seek more moderate third ways or alternative strategies without fully coming to terms with the past remains to be seen. Democratically elected regimes are certainly fragile in the former Soviet Union and parts of Eastern Europe, whereas Latin America appears, as of this writing, to have turned a democratic corner, even while left and right cleavages remain strong in many countries. Optimistic citizens hope that past atrocities of military dictatorships have inoculated civil societies against ever again permitting them to exist, but history cautions against definitive conclusions, especially when economies are so volatile and inequality remains so pervasive, if not worse than in earlier decades. In the United States, arguments are made for truly restorative justice, not only in the nonmaterial form of apologies for slavery, Japanese American internment, and Native American genocide and property expropriation (Bradford 2005), but for material reparations to be paid to descendants of the victims of these social and political crimes (Brophy 2006, Ogletree 2002). Indigenous groups throughout the world have begun to make similar claims and to file national civil and international claims and lawsuits, seeking a variety of forms of justice, including land claims, monetary compensation, and self-determination and self-governance.

Nevertheless, as the debate between the past and future continues in the practices of truth and reconciliation panels or other forms of transitional justice and in the pages of scholarly reports, some rigorous empirical analysis has suggested that, as with the law of unintended consequences, other effects may be generated by such alternative justice systems. Gibson's (2004a,b) recent study of post-TRC South Africa demonstrates powerfully that those who viewed at least some of the televised Truth and Reconciliation proceedings were much more likely to adopt a human rights consciousness than were those who did not view any of the proceedings. Even in a setting with racially differentiated beliefs in the efficacy of the rule of law, exposure to the wrongful acts of apartheid and their public condemnation increased some perceptions of the need for political and racial tolerance and respect for minorities within a majoritarian rule of law conception. Thus, the transformative, educational effects of such processes may have benefits for those outside of the victim-offender dyad (and are why so many restorative justice projects seek to include community representation and some form of publicity or transparency). These processes are not only for the active participants or victims of the specific act of wrongdoing or harm. To the extent that formal justice systems are about providing public norms and accountability and remedying harm to the larger community, public restorative justice processes have been empirically demonstrated to provide educative, participatory, democracy-enhancing potential, through radically different formats and with potentially wider reaching effects.

THE FUTURE OF RESTORATIVE JUSTICE: CHALLENGES AND OPPORTUNITIES

Restorative justice is more of an idea, philosophy, set of values, or sensibility than a single concrete and uniform set of practices or processes. In some settings, there is direct communication, confrontation, and reconciliation of victims and offenders; in others, there is more indirect restorative justice (Tickell & Akester 2004, *Utah Law Review* 2003, *Marquette Law Review* 2005), using procedures similar to caucusing or separate meetings, as in civil mediation, especially when direct communication between offenders and victims might make things worse or too painful (as in some murder, rape, and other serious crimes). In some settings, restorative justice is only for the victim and offender, promising safety, confidentiality, and tailored, individualized, reparative, and conciliatory outcomes. In other settings, more public participation is crucial [by those affected by the wrongful conduct, family members, supporters, treating or representative professionals, the larger community, and, in its most public forms such as TRCs, the larger society (O'Hear 2004, 2006)].[2] What began as an idea to reduce the punitive nature of conventional criminal punishment (especially for juvenile offenders and victimless crimes) and to improve the outcomes of criminal justice has developed into

[2]Restorative justice processes have been demonstrated in documentary films, focused on the actual operation of a variety of processes, or actually televised for an entire society, as with the South African TRC. More recently, restorative justice was depicted in a 2006 British film, *Breaking and Entering* by Anthony Minghella, which concludes with a juvenile criminal family conference in London.

a social and political movement seeking to use restorative or reparative sensibilities to heal not only single acts of misconduct, but civil wars, genocides, and international, multi-ethnic, political, and religious conflict.

Restorative justice as a social movement has been both constituted by and works in collaboration with other political movements—peace studies, nonviolence advocates and practitioners, civil ADR and conflict resolution process proponents, international human rights activists, participatory and deliberative democracy theorists and practitioners (Menkel-Meadow 2005), and those who believe in responsive or dialogic regulation and justice (Pavlich 1996, 2005). What these movements have in common is a belief that more flexible, humane, dialogic, conversational, and authentic human engagement can end a cycle of misconduct, punishment, retribution, vengeance, and more bad acts and violence by both individualized and systematized processes of turning the other cheek, including authentic responsibility taking, accountability, and restitutionary outcomes leading to forgiveness, reconciliation, and reintegration. These are large, aspirational, almost utopian ideas and goals, informed by a basic optimism about humans' ability to engage in social learning and behavior modification at both individual and large group levels. Efforts to operationalize such grand notions at so many different levels are still experimental, evolving, and fragile. As social scientists and political leaders try to assess whether notions of reconciliation and reintegration can substitute for more punitive and retributivist institutions, they will have to confront a variety of challenges to these processes, including:

- Whether processes that may work on smaller scales (juvenile criminal offenders, community sentencing circles) can be scaled up to national and international conflict settings without compromising the basic ideas of restorative justice;
- Whether restorative justice requires shared values at the community, nation-state, or international level to be effective, or whether something less than unanimity or consensus can be appealed to in seeking human reconciliation after acts of wrongdoing;
- Whether the informality, confidentiality, and flexibility of restorative justice threatens important human and legal rights (publicity, representation, due process, anticonfessional rules, equity and proportionality in punishment) or whether human rights and human problem-solving processes can be reconciled;
- Whether informality, confidentiality, and flexibility in the sanctioning of wrongdoing compromises needs for public processes, public norm generation and enforcement, and transparency and equity;
- Whether restorative justice processes should be supplemental or substitutionary to more conventional processes of punishment and prosecution;
- Whether restorative justice processes themselves privilege some over others (the verbal, well resourced, represented, willing, clever, or manipulative);
- Whether authentic participation in restorative processes and rituals is possible in any mass, multi-valued, and diversely constituted community or society and whether participation in more micro, specific case situations can transform individuals and societies on a macro level to engage in more deliberative and responsive solutions to bad situations;
- Whether the basic philosophy of separating bad acts from bad people can be an effective notion for dealing with modern, group, and mass-level harmful acts.

These challenges are many and profound. Not listed above are the more practical challenges of structuring, supervising, and monitoring the operation and effectiveness of restorative justice programs. As restorative justice ideas are propelled from one domain to another, both ideas and institutionalized practices are themselves transformed to meet the needs of particular communities. There is always the danger of co-optation, both by the larger system and by individuals who learn to work the system with insincere apologies, offers of restitution or reparation, or other inauthentic performances. How insincere participation can and should be discovered and disciplined (in a nonfact-finding environment) remains a serious conundrum for restorative justice advocates. Whether rules, standards, and best practices can or should be generated to assure quality of process or some uniformity across or within domains remains an important policy issue in this field.

Yet, with all these challenges, we know that restorative justice has reduced recidivism and reoffense rates in many programs (with both juveniles and adults); that restorative justice processes, with more direct and responsive communication and negotiation, can generate new norms that are more reflective of changed circumstances or enhanced human understanding; and that even merely observing a restorative justice process or ritual can have social learning and transformative effects on how human beings conceive of their rights and responsibilities in a modern and diverse world. As social scientists develop rigorous evaluations of how these programs work in different settings, at different levels, with different purposes and structures, and with comparisons to relevant conventional processes, we will learn more about how restorative and reparative philosophies and practices may transform punitive forms of social control with more optimistic ideas about human empowerment, understanding, problem solving, and reconciliation after events of individual and group fissures. If, as the saying goes, you can get more bees with honey than with vinegar, perhaps we can get more social progress, peace, and justice with healing than with punishment.

DISCLOSURE STATEMENT

The author is not aware of any biases that might be perceived as affecting the objectivity of this review.

LITERATURE CITED

Abel R. 1982. The contradictions of informal justice. In *The Politics of Informal Justice:* Vol. 1. *The American Experience*, ed. RL Abel, pp. 267–320. New York: Academic

Abel R. 1995. *Politics by Other Means (After the Law).* London/New York: Routledge

Acorn A. 2004. *Compulsory Compassion: A Critique of Restorative Justice.* Vancouver: Univ. B.C. Press

Andrews P, Ellmann S. 2002. *The Post-Apartheid Constitutions: Perspectives on South Africa's Basic Law.* Johannesburg, So. Afr: Witwatersrand Univ. Press

Arendt H. 1998. *The Human Condition.* Chicago: Univ. Chicago Press. 2nd ed.

Avruch K, Vejarano B. 2001. Truth and reconciliation commissions: a review essay and annotated bibliography. *Soc. Justice: Anthropol. Peace Hum. Rights* 2(1–2):47–108

Barnett R. 1977. Restitution: a new paradigm of criminal justice? *Ethics* 87:279–301

Bazemore G, Walgrave L, eds. 1999. *Restorative Juvenile Justice: Repairing the Harm of Youth Crime.* Monsey, NY: Crim. Justice Press

Beale SS. 2003. Still tough on crime? Prospects for restorative justice in the United States. *Utah Law Rev.* 2003:413–37

Berman G, Feinblatt J, Glazer S. 2005. *Good Courts: The Case for Problem Solving Justice*. New York: New Press

Blumenson E. 2006. The challenge of global standard of justice: peace, pluralism and punishment at the International Criminal Court. *Columbia J. Transnatl. Law* 44:801–74

Bohman J. 1996. *Public Deliberation: Pluralism, Complexity and Democracy*. Cambridge, MA: MIT Press

Bolocan MG. 2004. Rwandan gacaca: an experiment in transitional justice. *J. Disput. Resolut.* 2004(2):355–400

Borer TA, ed. 2006. *Telling the Truths: Truth Telling and Peace Building in Post-Conflict Societies*. Notre Dame, IN: Notre Dame Press

Bradford W. 2005. Beyond reparations: an American Indian theory of justice. *Ohio St. Law J.* 66:3–104

Bradshaw W, Roseborough D, Umbreit MS. 2006. The effect of victim offender mediation on juvenile offender recidivism: a meta-analysis. *Confl. Resolut. Q.* 24(1):87–98

Braithwaite J. 1989. *Crime, Shame and Reintegration*. Cambridge, UK: Cambridge Univ. Press

Braithwaite J. 1995. Reintegrative shaming, republicanism and policy. In *Criminology and Public Policy: Putting Theory to Work*, ed. H Barlow, pp. 191–205. Boulder, CO: Westview

Braithwaite J. 1999. Restorative justice: assessing optimistic and pessimistic accounts. *Crime Justice* 25:1–127

Braithwaite J. 2002. *Restorative Justice and Responsive Regulation*. Oxford: Oxford Univ. Press

Braithwaite J. 2003. Holism, justice and atonement. *Utah Law Rev.* 2003:389–412

Braithwaite J. 2006. Narrative and "compulsory compassion." *Law Soc. Inq.* 31(2):425–46

Brooks RL, ed. 1999. *When Sorry Is Not Enough: The Controversy Over Apologies and Reparations for Human Injustice*. New York: NY Univ. Press

Brophy AL. 2006. *Reparations: Pro and Con*. London/New York: Oxford Univ. Press

Brown JG. 1994. The use of mediation to resolve criminal cases: a procedural critique. *Emory Law Rev.* 43:1247–309

Burford G, Pennell J. 1998. *Family Group Decision Making Project:* Vol. 1. *Outcome Report*. St. John's: Memorial Univ. Newfoundland, Sch. Soc. Work

Cahn N. 2006. Women in post-conflict reconstruction: dilemmas and directions. *William Mary J. Women's Law* 12:335

Christie N. 1977. Conflicts as property. *Br. J. Criminol.* 17:1–5

Coates RB, Gehm J. 1985. *Victim Meets Offender: An Evaluation of Victim-Offender Reconciliation Programs*. Valparaiso, IN: PACT Inst. Justice

Coglianese C. 1997. Assessing consensus: the promise and performance of negotiated rulemaking. *Duke Law Rev.* 46:1255–349

Daly K. 2002. Restorative justice: the real story. *Punishm. Soc.* 4(1):55–79

Daly K. 2005. Feminist engagement with restorative justice. *Theor. Criminol.* 9(4):9–28

Davis RC, Tichane M, Grayson D. 1980. *Mediation and Arbitration as Alternatives to Prosecution in Felony Arrest Cases: An Evaluation of the Brooklyn Dispute Resolution Center*. New York: VERA Inst. Justice

Delgado R. 2000. Goodbye to Hammarabi: analyzing the atavistic appeal of restorative justice. *Stanford Law Rev.* 52:751–75

Dolinko D. 2003. Restorative justice and the justification of punishment. *Utah Law Rev.* 2003:319–42

Dorf MC, Sabel CF. 2000. Drug treatment courts and emergent experimentalist government. *Vanderbilt Law Rev.* 53:831–83

Dyzenhaus D. 2003. *Judging the Judges: Judging Ourselves: Truth, Reconciliation and the Apartheid Legal Orders*. Oxford: Hart

Elster J. 1995. Strategic uses of argument. In *Barriers to Conflict Resolution*, ed. K Arrow, RH Mnookin, L Ross, A Tversky, R Wilson, pp. 236–57. New York: Norton

Elster J, ed. 2006. *Retribution and Reparation in the Transition to Democracy*. Cambridge, UK: Cambridge Univ. Press

Ervin L, Schneider AL. 1990. Explaining the effects of restitution on offenders: results from a national experiment in juvenile courts. In *Criminal Justice: Restitution and Reconciliation*, ed. B Galaway, J Hudson, pp. 183–206. Monsey, NY: Crim. Justice Press

Fleming AT. 2006. The tender face of religion. *National Public Radio*, Oct. 6

Foucault M. 1979. *Discipline and Punish: The Birth of the Prison*. New York: Vintage Books

Frazer MS. 2006. *The Impact of the Community Court Model on Defendant Perceptions of Fairness: A Case Study at the Red Hook Community Justice Center*. New York: Cent. Court Innov.

Freeman J. 1997. Collaborative governance and the administrative state. *UCLA Law Rev*. 45:1–98

Gabbay Z. 2005. Justifying restorative justice: a theoretical justification for the use of restorative justice practices. *J. Disput. Resolut*. 2005(2):349–97

Gibson JL. 2004a. *Overcoming Apartheid: Can Truth Reconcile a Divided Nation?* New York: Russell Sage Found.

Gibson JL. 2004b. Truth, reconciliation and the creation of a human rights culture in South Africa. *Law Soc. Rev*. 38(2):5–40

Godobo-Madikizela P. 2003. *A Human Being Died That Night: A South African Story of Forgiveness*. Boston: Houghton Mifflin

Grillo T. 1991. The mediation alternative: process dangers for women. *Yale Law J*. 100:1545–81

Hagan J. 2003. *Justice in the Balkans: Prosecuting War Crimes in the Hague Tribunal*. Chicago: Univ. Chicago Press

Haley J, Neugebauer AM. 1992. Victim-offender mediation: Japanese and American comparisons. In *Restorative Justice on Trial: Pitfalls and Potentials of Victim-Offender Mediation—International Research Perspectives*, ed. H Messner, HU Otto, pp. 105–30. Dordrecht/Boston: Kluwer Acad.

Handler J. 1986. *The Conditions of Discretion: Autonomy, Community, Bureaucracy*. New York: Russell Sage Found.

Harter P. 1982. Negotiating regulations: a cure for the malaise. *Georgetown Law J*. 71:1–113

Hawkins K. 1984. *Environment and Enforcement: Regulation and Social Definition of Pollution*. Oxford: Clarendon

Hayner PB. 2001. *Unspeakable Truths: Confronting State Terror and Atrocities*. New York: Routledge

Henkin A, ed. 2002. *The Legacy of Abuse: Confronting the Past, Facing the Future*. New York: Aspen Inst. Justice Soc. Program

Hirsch SF. 2006. *In the Moment of Greatest Calamity: Terrorism, Grief and a Victim's Quest for Justice*. Princeton, NJ: Princeton Univ. Press

Honeyman C. 2004. Potentials for participatory justice in Rwanda: the gacaca jurisdictions. *Peace Confl.: J. Peace Psychol*. 10:1–24

In Re Gault, 387 U.S. 1 (1967)

Ivković SK, Hagan J. 2006. The politics of punishment and the siege of Sarajevo: toward a conflict theory of perceived international (in)justice. *Law Soc. Rev*. 40:369–410

Johnstone G. 2003. *A Restorative Justice Reader: Text, Sources, Context*. Cullompton, Devon, UK/Portland, OR: Willan

Kahan DM. 1996. What do alternative sanctions mean? *Univ. Chicago Law Rev*. 63:591–653

Kahan DM. 2006. What's really wrong with shaming sanctions. *Texas Law Rev*. 84:2075

Kakalik JS, Dunworth T, Hill LA, McCaffrey D, Oshiro M, et al. 1996. *An Evaluation of Mediation and Early Neutral Evaluation Under the Civil Justice Reform Act*. Santa Monica, CA: RAND Corp.

Katz J. 1990. *Seductions of Crime*. New York: Basic Books

Kaye J. 1997. Changing courts in changing times: the need for a fresh look at how courts are run. *Hastings Law J.* 48:851–66

Keller LM. 2007. Seeking justice at the international criminal court: victim's reparations. *Thomas Jefferson Law Rev.* In press

Kritz N, ed. 1995. *Transitional Justice: How Emerging Democracies Reckon with Former Regimes*. Washington, DC: US Inst. Peace Press

Kuhn A. 1987. A review and assessment of victim-offender reconciliation programming in West Germany. In *Criminal Justice, Restitution and Reconciliation*, ed. B Galaway, J Hudson, pp. 109–24. Monsey, NY: Crim. Justice Press

LaFree G, Rack C. 1996. The effects of participants' ethnicity and gender on monetary outcomes in mediated and adjudicated civil cases. *Law Soc. Rev.* 30:767–97

Langbein JH. 2003. *The Origins of Adversary Criminal Trial*. Oxford: Oxford Univ. Press

Latimer J, Dowden C, Musie D. 2001. *The Effectiveness of Restorative Justice Practices: A Meta-Analysis*. Ottawa: Res. Stat. Div., Dep. Justice

Lederach JP. 1997. *Building Peace: Sustainable Reconciliation in Divided Societies*. Washington, DC: US Inst. Peace Press

Lerman D. 1999. Restoring justice. *Tikkun* 14:13–15

Levrant S, Cullen FT, Fulton B, Wozniak JF. 1999. Reconsidering restorative justice: the corruption of benevolence revisited. *Crime Delinq.* 45:3–27

Lind EA, MacCoun RJ, Ebener PA, Felstiner WLF, Hensler DR, et al. 1989. *The Perception of Justice: Tort Litigants' Views of Trial, Court-Annexed Arbitration and Judicial Settlement Conferences*. Santa Monica, CA: RAND Corp.

Llewellyn J, Howse R. 1998. *Restorative Justice: A Conceptual Framework*. Ottawa, ON: Law Comm. Can.

Luban D. 1995. Settlements and the erosion of the public realm. *Georgetown Law J.* 83:2619

MacCoun RJ. 2005. Voice, control and belonging: the double-edge sword of procedural fairness. *Annu. Rev. Law Soc. Sci.* 1:171–201

Markel D. 2007. Still wrong? Professor Kahan on the fall of shaming and the rise of restorative justice. *Texas Law Rev.* In press

Marquette Law Rev. 2005. Symposium: restorative justice in action. *Marquette Law Rev.* 89:247–358

Marshall TF. 1998. *Restorative Justice: An Overview*. Minneapolis, MN: Cent. Restorat. Justice Peacemak.

Marshall TF, Merry S. 1990. *Crime and Accountability: Victim Offender Mediation in Practice*. London: Home Office

Matoesian GM. 1993. *Reproducing Rape: Domination Through Talk in the Courtroom*. Chicago: Univ. Chicago Press

Maxwell GM, Morris A. 1993. *Families, Victims and Culture: Youth Justice in New Zealand*. Wellington: Victoria Univ. Wellington, Inst. Criminol.

McCold P, Wachtel B. 1998. *Restorative Policing Experiment: The Bethlehem Pennsylvania Police Family Group Conferencing Project*. Pipesville, PA: Community Serv. Found.

McCord J. 2000. A theory of motivation and the life course. In *Social Dynamics of Crime and Control: New Theories for a World in Transition*, ed. S Karstedt, K Bussman, pp. 229–42. Oxford: Hart

Menkel-Meadow C. 1984. Toward another view of legal negotiation: the structure of problem solving. *UCLA Law Rev.* 31:754–849

Menkel-Meadow C. 1995. Whose dispute is it anyway? A philosophical and democratic defense of settlement (in some cases). *Georgetown Law J.* 83:2663–91

Menkel-Meadow C. 2003. Introduction: from legal disputes to conflict resolution and legal problem solving. In *Dispute Processing and Conflict Resolution: Theory, Practice and Policy*, ed. C Menkel-Meadow, pp. xi–xlii. Aldershot, UK: Ashgate-Dartmouth

Menkel-Meadow C. 2004. Remembrance of things past? The relationship of past to future in pursuing justice in mediation. *Cardozo J. Confl. Resolut.* 5:97–115

Menkel-Meadow C. 2005. The lawyers' role in deliberative democracy. *Nev. Law Rev.* 5:347–69

Menkel-Meadow C. 2006. Peace and justice: notes on the evolution and purposes of legal processes. *Georgetown Law J.* 94(2):553–80

Menkel-Meadow C, Love LP, Schneider AK, Sternlight J. 2005. *Dispute Resolution: Beyond the Adversarial Model.* New York: Aspen

Minow M. 1998. *Between Vengeance and Forgiveness: Facing History After Genocide and Mass Violence.* Boston: Beacon

Nonet P, Selznick P. 1978. *Law and Society in Transition: Toward Responsive Law.* Berkeley: Univ. Calif. Press

Nugent W, Williams M, Umbreit MS. 2003. Participation in victim-offender mediation and the prevalence and severity of subsequent delinquent behavior: a meta-analysis. *Utah Law Rev.* 2003:137–66

Nussbaum M. 2004. *Hiding from Humanity: Disgust Shame and the Law.* Princeton, NJ: Princeton Univ. Press

Ogletree CJJ. 2002. Reparations: a fundamental issue of social justice. *Black Coll.* 33:118–22

O'Hear MM. 2004. Revisiting informal justice: restorative justice and democratic professionalism. *Law Soc. Rev.* 38:139

O'Hear MM. 2006. Victims and criminal justice: What's next? *Fed. Sentencing Report.* 19(2):83–90

Pavlich G. 1996. The power of community mediation: government and formation of identity. *Law Soc. Rev.* 30:707–33

Pavlich G. 2005. *Governing Paradoxes of Restorative Justice.* London: Glasshouse

Pfeiffer C. 1998. Juvenile crime and violence in Europe. *Crime Justice* 23:255–328

Poulson B. 2003. A third voice: a review of empirical research on the psychological outcomes of restorative justice. *Utah Law Rev.* 2003:167–203

Raper J. 2005. The gacaca experiment: Rwanda's restorative dispute resolution response to the 1994 genocide. *Pepperdine Dispute Resolut. Law J.* 5:1–56

Rees JV. 1988. *Reforming the Workplace.* Philadelphia: Univ. Penn. Press

Rees JV. 1994. *Hostages of Each Other: The Transformation of Nuclear Safety Since Three Mile Island.* Chicago: Univ. Chicago Press

Robinson PH. 2003. The virtues of restorative processes, the vices of "restorative justice." *Utah Law Rev.* 2003:375–88

Robinson PH. 2006. Restorative processes & doing justice. *Univ. St. Thomas Law J.* 3:421–29

Roche D, ed. 2004. *Restorative Justice.* Aldershot, UK/Burlington, VT: Ashgate-Dartmouth

Rotberg RI, Thompson D, eds. 2000. *Truth v. Justice: The Morality of Truth Commissions.* Princeton, NJ: Princeton Univ. Press

Rugge T, Cormier R. 2005. Restorative justice in cases of serious crimes: an evaluation. In *New Directions in Restorative Justice: Issues, Practice and Evaluation*, ed. E Elliott, RM Gordon, pp. 266–77. Cullompton, Devon, UK: Willan

Stein AA. 1993. *Why Nations Cooperate: Circumstances and Choice in International Relations.* Ithaca, NY: Cornell Univ. Press

Strang H. 2001. *Victim Participation in a Restorative Justice Process.* Oxford: Oxford Univ. Press

Strang H. 2004. *Repair or Revenge: Victims and Restorative Justice.* Oxford: Clarendon

Strang H, Barnes GC, Braithwaite J, Sherman LW. 1999. *Experiments in Restorative Policing: A Progress Report on the Canberra Reintegrative Shaming Experiments (RISE).* Canberra: Aust. Natl. Univ. **http://www.aic.gov.au/rjustice/rise/progress/1999.html**

Strang H, Braithwaite J. 2000. *Restorative Justice: Philosophy to Practice.* Aldershot, UK/Burlington, VT: Ashgate-Dartmouth

Stromseth J, Wippman D, Brooks R. 2006. *Can Might Make Rights? Building the Rule of Law After Military Interventions.* Cambridge, UK: Cambridge Univ. Press

Stuart B. 2001. Guiding principles for peacemaking circles. In *Restorative Community Justice: Repairing Harm and Transforming Communities*, ed. G Bazemore, M Schiff, pp. 219–41. Cincinnati, OH: Anderson

Stubbs J. 1995. Communitarian conferencing and violence against women: a cautionary note. In *Wife Assault and the Canadian Criminal Justice System*, ed. M Valverde, L MacLeod, K Johnson, pp. 260–89. Toronto: Cent. Criminol., Univ. Toronto

Teitel RG. 2000. *Transitional Justice.* New York: Oxford Press

Thibault JW, Walker L. 1975. *Procedural Justice: A Psychological Perspective.* Hillsdale, NJ: Erlbaum

Thompson AC. 2002. Courting disorder: some thoughts on community courts. *Wash. Univ. J. Law Policy* 10:63–99

Thompson EP. 1976. *Albion's Fatal Tree.* New York: Pantheon

Tickell S, Akester K. 2004. *Restorative Justice: The Way Ahead.* London: Justice

Tutu D. 1999. *No Future Without Forgiveness.* New York: Doubleday

Tyler TR, Huo YJ. 2002. *Trust in the Law.* New York: Russell Sage Found.

Umbreit MS. 1994. *Victim Meets Offender: The Impact of Restorative Justice and Mediation.* Monsey, NY: Crim. Justice Press

Umbreit MS. 1995. *Mediation of Criminal Conflict: An Assessment of Programs in Four Canadian Provinces.* St. Paul: Cent. Restor. Justice Mediat., Univ. Minn.

Umbreit MS. 2001. *The Handbook of Victim Offender Mediation: An Essential Guide to Practice and Research.* San Francisco: Jossey-Bass

Umbreit MS, Coates RB. 1992. *Victim Offender Mediation: An Analysis of Programs in Four States of the US.* Minneapolis: Citizen Counc. Mediat. Serv.

Umbreit MS, Coates RB, Vos B. 2001. The impact of victim offender mediation: two decades of research. *Fed. Probat.* 65:29–35

Umbreit MS, Coates RB, Vos B. 2005. Victim offender mediation: evidence-based practice over three decades. In *The Handbook of Dispute Resolution*, ed. ML Moffitt, RC Bordone, pp. 455–70. San Francisco: Jossey-Bass

Umbreit MS, Ritter R. 2006. Arab offenders meet Jewish victims: restorative family dialogue in Israel. *Confl. Resolut. Q.* 24(1):99–109

Umbreit MS, Roberts AW. 1996. *Center for Restorative Justice & Mediation, Mediation of Criminal Conflict in England: An Assessment of Services in Coventry and Leeds.* St. Paul: Cent. Restor. Justice Mediat., Univ. Minn.

Umbreit MS, Vos B, Coates RB, Brown K. 2003. *Facing Violence: The Path of Restorative Justice and Dialogue.* Monsey, NY: Crim. Justice Press

Utah Law Rev. 2003. Symposium: the practice of restorative justice. *Utah Law Rev.* 2003:1–533

Utz PJ. 1978. *Settling the Facts: Discretion and Negotiation in Criminal Court.* Lexington, MA: Lexington Books

Van Ness DW. 1993. New wine and old wineskins: four challenges of restorative justice. *Crim. Law Forum* 4:251–76

Von Hirsh A, ed. 2003. *Restorative Justice and Criminal Justice: Competing or Reconcilable Paradigms?* Portland, OR: Hart

Weisberg R. 2003. Restorative justice and the danger of "community." *Utah Law Rev.* 2003:343–74

Wellikoff I. 2004. Victim offender mediation and violent crimes: on the way to justice. *Cardozo Online J. Confl. Resolut.* 5:2

Wyrick P, Costanzo M. 1999. Predictors of client participation in victim-offender mediation. *Mediat. Q.* 16:253–57

Yazzie R, Zion JW. 1996. Navajo restorative justice: the law of equality and justice. In *Restorative Justice: International Perspectives*, ed. B Galaway, J Hudson, pp. 144–51. Monsey, NY: Crim. Justice Press

Young IM. 1990. *Justice and the Politics of Difference.* Princeton, NJ: Princeton Univ. Press

Young IM. 2000. *Inclusion and Democracy.* Oxford: Oxford Univ. Press

Zehr H. 1990. *Changing Lenses: A New Focus for Crime and Justice.* Scottdale, PA: Herald

Zehr H. 2002. *The Little Book of Restorative Justice.* Intercourse, PA: Good Books

Zehr H, Mika H. 1998. Fundamental concepts of restorative justice. *Contemp. Justice Rev.* 1:47–55

Zimring FE. 2006. *The Great American Crime Decline.* New York: Oxford Univ. Press

[13]

Accountability for Atrocities: Moving Forward by Looking Backward?

Jane Stromseth, David Wippman
and Rosa Brooks

Atrocities cast a long shadow. In post-intervention societies, reestablishing security, reconstructing governance institutions, and reforming the justice system are all crucial steps in promoting the rule of law, but important as they are, they are rarely sufficient to grapple with the legacy of past abuses. In most of the post-conflict societies discussed in this book, severe abuses were widespread in the period prior to intervention. The Balkan wars, for instance, were characterized by brutal massacres, mass rapes, and ethnic cleansing. Sierra Leone's civil war was characterized by the forced recruitment of child soldiers, widespread rapes and murders, and the gruesome mutilation of civilians. Afghanistan, Iraq, and East Timor also have had bloody pasts marked by severe abuses.

In such societies, the traumatization caused by widespread past atrocities does not end when the guns fall silent. Although nothing can undo the suffering caused by atrocities, ensuring that perpetrators face some reckoning may be critical to moving forward in countries recovering from violent conflict. Ensuring accountability may help victims move on and can also help signal to all members of post-conflict societies that, henceforth, such abuses will not be permitted to recur. Just as important, the process of ensuring accountability may, in some circumstances, reinforce broader efforts to reform the justice system.

As with every challenge discussed in this book, however, "ensuring accountability" is more easily said than done. In the wake of violent conflicts, national justice systems, if they function effectively at all, usually have only limited ability to address the claims and needs of victims or render fair justice. More often than not, citizens may view existing legal institutions skeptically because of corruption, systematic bias, association with abusive past regimes, failure to effectively address past grievances, or severe shortfalls in human and other resources. Those who have committed atrocities, moreover, may still wield political power or exert influence behind the scenes. Even when criminal trials are initiated against perpetrators, those facing trial and their political allies may view the proceedings as illegitimate forms of "victor's justice." And in some situations accountability mechanisms may actually trigger further violence. Meanwhile, it is not always clear how victims can best be served: although some victims may demand trial and punishment of perpetrators, others may place greater emphasis on public acknowledgment of their suffering and on reparations or some tangible form of assistance. In such contexts, both interveners and domestic leaders – confronted by limited resources and other urgent reconstruction challenges – must struggle to balance justice, reconciliation, and other compelling goals.

Yet the challenge of accountability cannot be ignored. As we argued in Chapter 6, establishing a credible and functioning justice system that serves the goals of the rule of law is a central part of the challenge of moving forward after violent conflict. Even more fundamentally, strengthening the rule of law depends on building the public's confidence that they will be protected from predatory state and nonstate actors, that they can resolve disagreements fairly and reliably without resorting to violence, and that legal and political institutions will function in ways that protect rather than violate basic human rights. Only then is the rule of law, as we defined it in Chapter 3, likely to take hold: a state of affairs in which most people, most of the time, choose to resolve disputes in a manner that is consistent with fair rules and fundamental human rights norms, in which modern legal institutions and laws exist, and in which there is a widely shared cultural and political commitment to the values underlying those institutions and laws.

This chapter explores the following question: can the pursuit of accountability for atrocities through criminal prosecutions and other supplementary methods help build the rule of law and strengthen domestic justice systems?

At a broad level, this question has divided scholars and practitioners alike. A *rights-based approach* argues that major perpetrators of atrocities must be held legally accountable if a country is to make an effective transition to a society marked by the rule of law. Defenders of criminal prosecutions see the biggest barrier to sustainable peace as legal impunity and argue that vigorous prosecution of at least major offenders is the only real way to remove the stain of impunity from traumatized societies. Fair trials affirm that atrocities are wrong and unacceptable – drawing a clear line for all to see – and incarceration prevents the guilty from repeat offenses and potentially serves as a deterrent to others.[1] Trials can also give victims a sense of justice that helps them move forward without a need to seek personal vengeance. Truth

[1] *See, e.g.*, M. Cherif Bassiouni, *Accountability for Violations of International Humanitarian Law and Other Serious Violations of Human Rights*, in POST-CONFLICT JUSTICE (M. Cherif Bassiouni, ed., 2003) at 3, 4, 54.

commissions can supplement trials and acknowledge more fully the truth of what occurred and the pain and needs of victims and, many argue, may potentially contribute to reconciliation over time.[2] Even if accountability efforts are inevitably imperfect responses to the suffering caused by atrocities, they can symbolize a society's desire to confront its past, to reject patterns of impunity, and to move in a new direction.

An alternative, *realist view* disputes the beneficial impacts of trials and argues instead that criminal prosecution of major perpetrators can be destabilizing. Proponents of this view argue that conditional amnesties may be necessary to remove "spoilers" and thus help create a better prospect for peace and long-term development of the rule of law. Once political bargains are struck among contending groups, they argue, "institutions based on the rule of law become more feasible."[3] Pursuing accountability without establishing "political and institutional preconditions," they contend, "risks weakening norms of justice by revealing their ineffectiveness and hindering necessary political bargaining."[4]

Neither camp is without its vulnerabilities. If some proponents of the rights-based approach are at times too starry-eyed about the practical benefits of trials and truth commissions or sometimes unpragmatic in acknowledging real-world constraints, the realists are prone to overstate the downsides of prosecution by focusing on the perspectives of self-interested ruling elites rather than on a broader segment of post-conflict societies, including victims and civil society organizations. The realists also tend to overstate the practical benefits of amnesties: even if high-ranking individuals are given an amnesty as the price for peace, there is no assurance that the amnesty will in fact be sufficient to sustain peace. In Sierra Leone, for instance, the amnesty given to Revolutionary United Front (RUF) forces and other groups in the 1999 Lome Agreement did not stop the conflict, rooted in greed and self-interest, from continuing.[5] An international intervention led by Britain was

[2] *See* Priscilla B. Hayner, UNSPEAKABLE TRUTHS: CONFRONTING STATE TERROR AND ATROCITY (2001), for an extremely thoughtful discussion of truth commissions. In both East Timor and Sierra Leone, truth commissions sought to contribute to reconciliation through community-based reconciliation procedures that we examine in this chapter.

[3] Jack Snyder & Leslie Vinjamuri, *Trials and Errors: Principle and Pragmatism in Strategies of International Justice*, 28 INT'L SEC. 5, 6 (Winter 2003/04). Snyder and Vinjamuri argue that "[j]ustice does not lead; it follows... [and] a norm-governed political order must be based on a political bargain among contending groups and on the creation of robust administrative institutions that can predictably enforce the law." Id. Although they "agree that the ultimate goal is to prevent atrocities by effectively institutionalizing appropriate standards of criminal justice," they argue that "the initial steps toward that goal must usually travel down the path of political expediency." Id., at 6–7.

[4] Id., at 6–7.

[5] The text of the Lome Agreement is *available at* http://www.sierra-leone.org/lomeaccord.html. Article IX of the agreement provided that "[i]n order to bring lasting peace to Sierra Leone, the Government of Sierra Leone shall take appropriate legal steps to grant Corporal

necessary. Realist critics also understate the degree of innovation and pragmatism that is already reflected in more recent efforts to link accountability for past atrocities to forward-looking reforms.

Trends on the ground, to some degree, are overtaking this broad theoretical debate. Advocates of the rights-based approach increasingly have recognized the need to supplement trials with noncriminal accountability mechanisms that offer alternatives to trials for lesser offenders. The community reconciliation process in East Timor (now Timor Leste) is one recent example.[6] Furthermore, the normative acceptability of amnesties for serious offenses is more contested today, both internationally and domestically.[7] In Afghanistan, for instance, amnesty provisions proposed by the Northern Alliance were not included in the Bonn Agreement, and a majority of Afghans surveyed oppose amnesties for serious offenses.[8] Furthermore, devising amnesty arrangements that effectively remove spoilers and

Foday Sankoh absolute and free pardon." That article also provided for the Government of Sierra Leone to "grant absolute and free pardon and reprieve to all combatants and collaborators in respect of anything done by them in pursuit of their objectives, up to the time of the signing" of the Lome Agreement. In addition, "the Government of Sierra Leone shall ensure that no official or judicial action is taken against any member of the RUF/SL, ex-AFRC, ex-SLA or CDF in respect of anything done by them in pursuit of their objectives as members of those organizations, since March 1991, up to the time of the signing of the present Agreement."

[6] Upon attaining independence in May 2002, East Timor became the Democratic Republic of Timor Leste. Because this book and chapter refer to multiple time periods, pre and post independence, we use the term East Timor for ease of reference, but we recognize that Timor Leste is the country's preferred English name today. The community-based reconciliation procedures developed by the Commission for Reception, Truth and Reconciliation are discussed in detail in its report, *Chega!: Final Report of the Commission for Reception, Truth and Reconciliation in East Timor* (2005), *available at* http://www.etan.org/news/2006/cavr.htm (hereinafter *Chega!: Final Report of the CAVR*). "Chega!" means "Enough!" in Portuguese.

[7] *See* The Secretary-General, *Report of the Secretary-General on the Rule of Law and Transitional Justice in Conflict and Post-Conflict Societies*, para.10, *delivered to the Security Council*, U.N. Doc. S/2004/616 (August 3, 2004) ("United Nations-endorsed peace agreements can never promise amnesties for genocide, war crimes, crimes against humanity or gross violations of human rights"); Charles T. Call, *Conclusions*, in CONSTRUCTING JUSTICE AND SECURITY AFTER WAR (Charles T. Call, ed., 2006).

[8] *See* Afghan Independent Human Rights Commission, *A Call for Justice: A National Consultation on Past Human Rights Violations in Afghanistan* (hereinafter *A Call for Justice*), at 21, 41–43, *available at* http://www.aihrc.org.af/rep_Eng_29_01_05.htm (noting that views varied regionally, but that 60.5 per cent overall of those surveyed rejected the idea of "amnesties or pardons for anyone who confessed their crimes before an institution created for transitional justice"). As the report explains, the Bonn Agreement "affirms accountability as a principle" but provides for no particular mechanisms. Although an amnesty provision proposed by the Northern Alliance was not adopted, a clause prohibiting amnesty for war crimes and crimes against humanity supported by the United Nations "was deleted." Id., at 43. More recently, however, the Afghan government has agreed that "no amnesty will be granted for gross violations of human rights." Press release, Afghan Independent Human Rights Commission, *Truth-seeking and Reconciliation in Afghanistan* (December 15, 2005), at 2.

genuinely help to create conditions for strengthening the rule of law – rather than just permitting impunity – is enormously difficult in practice.

Nevertheless, the realists do have an important point. Moving forward after atrocities does require a clear-eyed assessment of the underlying forces that impede stability and reform. Holding key perpetrators criminally accountable – especially before international tribunals miles away – may advance international standards of justice; but it may have very little, if any, impact on strengthening the domestic rule of law in a post-conflict society. Just as we cannot assume that such trials will be destabilizing domestically – or that amnesties will effectively neutralize spoilers and clear the way for genuine reform – neither can we assume a positive spillover effect on domestic rule of law-building from criminal trials.

Indeed, the question of whether and how accountability proceedings can contribute to strengthening domestic justice systems and to building the rule of law in post-conflict societies is surprisingly underanalyzed.[9] For too long, the practical division of the fields of "transitional justice" and "rule of law reform" into two largely separate communities of scholars and practitioners has impeded efforts to explore systematically how accountability processes might, concretely, contribute to forward-looking rule of law reforms.[10] If this gap can be overcome, opportunities for valuable synergies between accountability efforts and rule of law reform programs can be pursued more effectively. To be sure, we are relatively early in the process of understanding the longer-term impacts of accountability processes – such as criminal prosecutions, truth commissions, reconciliation proceedings, vetting – in different post-conflict societies; furthermore, the unique circumstances and obstacles in each society attempting to overcome horrific atrocities make generalizations risky. Still, more systematic thinking and empirical research on the impact of accountability proceedings in specific post-conflict societies is a critical need and an increasingly important area of inquiry.[11]

[9] Scholars advocating a variety of approaches to accountability acknowledge that we need more systematic analysis of the impact of accountability proceedings on strengthening the rule of law prospectively. For a helpful recent effort to explore the potential impact of accountability efforts on forward-looking justice reform, *see* CONSTRUCTING JUSTICE AND SECURITY AFTER WAR, *supra* note 7, especially the Introduction and Conclusion by Charles T. Call.

[10] One scholar and practitioner who spans both fields and has worked hard to bring them together is Neil Kritz of the U.S. Institute of Peace. *See, e.g.*, Neil J. Kritz, *The Rule of Law in the Postconflict Phase: Building a Stable Peace*, in TURBULENT PEACE: THE CHALLENGE OF MANAGING INTERNATIONAL CONFLICT (Chester A. Crocker et al., eds., 2001); Neil J. Kritz, *Progress and Humility: The Ongoing Search for Post-Conflict Justice*, in POST-CONFLICT JUSTICE, *supra* note 1, at 84–87.

[11] For thoughtful recent assessments of East Timor's community reconciliation proceedings, for example, *see* Spencer Zifcak, The Asia Foundation, *Restorative Justice in East Timor: An Evaluation of the Community Reconciliation Process of the CAVR* (2004); Piers Pigou, United Nations Development Programme, *The Community Reconciliation Process of the Commission for Reception, Truth and Reconciliation* (2004).

This chapter aims to clarify what we know – and don't know – about the impact of accountability processes on domestic justice systems and the rule of law in post-intervention societies. We aim to look backward and forward at the same time and to explore systematically the relationships, if any, between retrospective accountability proceedings and prospective domestic capacity-building and reform. Before examining the experiences in a number of post-intervention societies, we first consider some of the broad trends that have influenced choices made in these situations regarding particular accountability mechanisms and goals. We then offer a theory about how accountability processes may contribute to building the rule of law in post-conflict societies through their demonstration and capacity-building effects. The chapter then examines the empirical record, looking in particular at the practical impact of the international tribunals for former Yugoslavia and for Rwanda; at the hybrid national/international tribunals in Kosovo, East Timor, and Sierra Leone; at domestic prosecutions particularly in Bosnia; and at the truth and reconciliation commissions in a number of post-intervention societies. We also discuss the trials only just beginning in Iraq's special tribunal for crimes against humanity, as well as the prospects for accountability in Afghanistan.

We argue that the long-term impact of accountability proceedings on the rule of law depends critically on three factors: first, the effective disempowerment of key perpetrators who threaten stability and undermine public confidence in the rule of law; second, the character of the accountability proceedings pursued, particularly whether they demonstrate credibly that previous patterns of abuse and impunity are rejected and that justice can be fair; and third, the extent to which systematic and meaningful efforts at domestic capacity-building are included as part of the accountability process. In a number of countries studied here, we argue that trials have not been as influential as advocates had hoped and seem to have had little impact at all on forward-looking efforts to strengthen justice systems and the rule of law. But in other cases, accountability processes, particularly those located within affected countries that enjoy considerable public support and engage in systematic outreach, are contributing to national capacity-building and may be reinforcing domestic expectations of accountability and demands for fairer justice processes in the future. We identify some of the features of the more effective processes, such as Sierra Leone's Special Court and East Timor's Commission for Reception, Truth and Reconciliation, but we also acknowledge their limitations and emphasize the challenge of sustaining their impact and legacy.

First, however, we must provide some essential background – on broad trends in efforts to seek accountability for atrocities since the 1990s, and on key goals and specific mechanisms that have been pursued in different cases.

I. "TRANSITIONAL JUSTICE" IN EVOLUTION: THE ACCOUNTABILITY LEARNING CURVE

When international and local leaders pursue accountability for atrocities, they have many goals in mind beyond contributing to domestic legal reform.[12] Bringing major perpetrators to justice – demonstrating that their conduct is wrong and unacceptable – is an immediate and fundamental goal. Prosecuting and punishing major offenders affirms and reinforces the core international legal rules prohibiting genocide, crimes against humanity, and war crimes.[13] Holding individual perpetrators legally accountable can also provide some sense of justice and relief to victims and their families and potentially help to defuse grievances and curtail cycles of vengeance.

Prosecution of major offenders, it is also hoped, may help to deter future perpetrators by setting an example and making clear that wrong-doers will be held accountable. But because prosecutions inevitably are selective and because many factors contribute to individual decisions to commit atrocities, the issue of deterring future abuses is a complex and often uncertain matter.[14] Although it would be a mistake to claim too much for accountability proceedings, alone, in preventing future atrocities, they can be a central part of a larger effort to strengthen and to begin institutionalizing normative commitments to accountability – rather than impunity – in post-conflict societies.

The selective and focused nature of criminal trials after massive atrocities, however, means that they are limited mechanisms for achieving a number

[12] *See* Jane E. Stromseth, *Introduction: Goals and Challenges in the Pursuit of Accountability*, in ACCOUNTABILITY FOR ATROCITIES: NATIONAL AND INTERNATIONAL RESPONSES (Jane E. Stromseth, ed., 2003) at 1, 5–13. For analysis of accountability goals, methods, and concrete experiences, *see* POST-CONFLICT JUSTICE, *supra* note 1; Martha Minow, BETWEEN VENGEANCE AND FORGIVENESS: FACING HISTORY AFTER MASS VIOLENCE (1998); Hayner, UNSPEAKABLE TRUTHS, *supra* note 2; Steven R. Ratner & Jason S. Abrams, ACCOUNTABILITY FOR HUMAN RIGHTS VIOLATIONS IN INTERNATIONAL LAW: BEYOND THE NUREMBERG LEGACY (2nd ed. 2001); Ruti G. Teitel, TRANSITIONAL JUSTICE (2000); Miriam J. Aukerman, *Extraordinary Evil, Ordinary Crime: A Framework for Understanding Transitional Justice*, 15 HARV. HUM. RTS. J. 39 (2002); David A. Crocker, *Reckoning with Past Wrongs: A Normative Framework*, 13 ETHICS & INT'L AFF. 43 (1999); Neil J. Kritz, *Coming to Terms with Atrocities: A Review of Mechanisms for Mass Violations of Human Rights*, 59 LAW & CONTEMP. PROBS. 127 (1996).

[13] *See generally* Ratner & Abrams, ACCOUNTABILITY FOR HUMAN RIGHTS VIOLATIONS IN INTERNATIONAL LAW, *supra* note 12; Bassiouni, *Accountability for Violations of International Humanitarian Law and Other Serious Violations of Human Rights*, *supra* note 1.

[14] On the difficulties of deterrence, *see* David Wippman, *Atrocities, Deterrence, and the Limits of International Justice*, 23 FORDHAM INT'L L. J. 473 (1999); David Wippman, *Exaggerating the ICC*, in BRINGING POWER TO JUSTICE: THE PROSPECTS OF THE INTERNATIONAL CRIMINAL COURT (Joanna Harrington, ed., 2005); Gary Jonathan Bass, STAY THE HAND OF VENGEANCE: THE POLITICS OF WAR CRIMES TRIBUNALS (2000), at 290–295; Payam Akhavan, *Beyond Impunity: Can International Criminal Justice Prevent Future Atrocities*, 95 AM. J. INT'L L. 7 (2001).

of other important goals, such as a comprehensive account of a conflict and its causes. In contrast, truth commissions are more likely than trials to be effective in compiling a comprehensive "truth" that addresses the broader context of a conflict and provides a fuller account of the factors contributing to atrocities. Truth commissions can provide a greater opportunity for direct participation by a larger number of victims and may also – as in East Timor and Sierra Leone – seek to promote reconciliation and reintegration of lesser perpetrators into the community through reconciliation agreements and rituals. Unlike trials, truth commissions can make far-reaching policy recommendations, and they may be better able to advance goals of "restorative" or "reparative" justice by focusing directly on the concrete needs of victims.[15] Sierra Leone's truth commission, for instance, has recommended free health care and education for amputees, victims of sexual violence, and other injured by the conflict.[16] East Timor's Commission for Reception, Truth and Reconciliation likewise has proposed an ambitious reparations program (calling on Indonesia and other states to contribute), as well as a broad array of innovative reforms.[17]

No single mechanism or approach can satisfy the many – sometimes conflicting – goals of justice, truth, prevention and deterrence, reconciliation, and domestic capacity-building in the aftermath of severe atrocities. Recognition of this fact has contributed to a significant recent trend toward "mixed" approaches to accountability that combine multiple mechanisms designed to advance a number of different goals. These mechanisms may include criminal prosecutions but also truth commissions, reconciliation procedures for lesser offenders, and vetting (restrictions on access to government positions), for instance. Generally, the more deeply rooted the causes of atrocities, the more pressures accountability processes will face to be not only the arbiter of justice in specific cases but also to become an agent for achieving more systemic social change.

A second trend in transitional justice is to move away from remotely located international tribunals toward hybrid courts with national participation situated directly in affected countries. In both East Timor and Sierra Leone, for instance, defendants have been prosecuted for war crimes and crimes against humanity before mixed panels of national and international judges, with the prosecutorial staff likewise composed of international and national lawyers. Although purely international tribunals may sometimes be necessary, international courts – like the international criminal

[15] For a thoughtful discussion of reparative justice, *see* Rama Mani, BEYOND RETRIBUTION: SEEKING JUSTICE IN THE SHADOWS OF WAR (2002), at 173–178.

[16] *See Witness To Truth: Report of the Sierra Leone Truth and Reconciliation Commission*, Vol. 1, para. 51 (2004), *available at* http://www.trcsierraleone.org/drwebsite/publish/index.shtml (hereinafter *Witness to Truth*).

[17] *See Chega!: Final Report of the CAVR, supra* note 6, *Part 11: Recommendations.*

tribunals for former Yugoslavia and for Rwanda – are physically and often psychologically distant from the people most affected by the atrocities they are prosecuting; these tribunals are also not designed to contribute resources or training directly to the domestic justice system. In contrast, hybrid tribunals located within post-conflict societies may be viewed as more legitimate by domestic audiences, have greater potential for domestic capacity-building by involving domestic jurists directly in the work of the court, and may be better able to demonstrate the importance of accountability and fair justice to local populations.[18] These potential benefits, in theory at least, have contributed to the trend toward hybrid arrangements, a trend that may well continue even with the arrival of the International Criminal Court.[19]

A third, and overdue, trend is a more systematic effort to understand the specific goals and priorities of domestic populations who, after all, are the people who endured the atrocities and must chart a new future. The question of how best to face the past – and what forms of accountability to pursue – is a difficult one, and different societies ultimately may have quite different goals and priorities. Within those societies, moreover, various actors and groups may disagree, possibly quite strongly, over priorities. In East Timor, for example, President Xanana Gusmao has long stressed the importance of reconciliation and forward-looking social justice, whereas others (including the Commission for Reception, Truth and Reconciliation in its recent report) also emphasize the continuing importance of criminal prosecution of major offenders.

International actors, moreover, have their own priorities. Even when international commitment to accountability is reasonably strong, which it sometimes is not, international actors may not give sufficient attention to the concrete problems and obstacles to achieving meaningful accountability in specific post-conflict countries. Domestic leaders often perceive international leaders and donors as more concerned about sending a general deterrent message regarding atrocities than about the specific, long-term needs of the particular post-conflict society directly involved.[20] Yet these needs, as well as the often deep-seated grievances, inequalities, and systemic problems that contribute to violence and instability, must be addressed if a stable rule of law is to take root.

The growing recognition of the importance of understanding local goals and priorities is evident in Afghanistan. With international support, the Afghan Independent Human Rights Commission (AIHRC) conducted a

[18] *See* Laura A. Dickinson, *The Promise of Hybrid Courts*, 97 AM. J. INT'L L. 295 (2003).

[19] *See* Jenia Iontcheva Turner, *Nationalizing International Criminal Law*, 41 STAN. J. INT'L L. 1 (2005); Stromseth, *Introduction: Goals and Challenges in the Pursuit of Accountability*, in ACCOUNTABILITY FOR ATROCITIES, *supra* note 12, at 32.

[20] *See, e.g.*, Jason Strain & Elizabeth Keyes, *Accountability in the Aftermath of Rwanda's Genocide*, in ACCOUNTABILITY FOR ATROCITIES, *supra* note 12, at 98–99, 130.

countrywide survey and series of 200 focus groups to determine the priorities of the Afghan people regarding accountability. In its report, *A Call for Justice*, the AIHRC documents overwhelming Afghan support for removing from power those who committed serious abuses during Afghanistan's long years of conflict, many of whom continue to wield power today.[21] Strong public support for criminal trials for the most serious offenders is accompanied by widespread support for vetting and removing other offenders from power. Afghans, though generally unfamiliar with "truth commissions" as such, also expressed a strong desire for some truth-seeking mechanism as well as deep support for "reparations" or compensation to those victims most in need. Afghans also expressed a strong preference for conducting criminal trials in Afghanistan – not outside the country – and for a hybrid tribunal that includes both Afghan as well as international jurists. This impressive effort to understand what the people of Afghanistan want holds out the potential for tailoring accountability processes to fulfill deep domestic aspirations; but whether, in fact, these aspirations will be fulfilled remains an open question fraught with obstacles, as we discuss below.

II. THE CHALLENGE OF DEMONSTRATING AND INSTITUTIONALIZING ACCOUNTABILITY NORMS

If the trends discussed above underscore the need for multifaceted accountability procedures, they also signify a growing determination on the part of both international and domestic actors to leave behind a continuing legacy – facilities, skills, new habits of thought and practice – when accountability proceedings conclude. But the impact of different accountability initiatives on strengthening the domestic rule of law in post-conflict societies is not straightforward. Much depends on how accountability processes are conducted, the uncertainties of unintended consequences, and the extent to which local perceptions of justice are altered by the proceedings. The potentially salutary impacts of accountability proceedings fall into at least two categories: their demonstration effects and their capacity-building effects. We consider each in turn.

A. Demonstration Effects

First, accountability proceedings can contribute to strengthening the rule of law in post-conflict societies through their *demonstration effects*.[22] Most

[21] *A Call for Justice*, *supra* note 8, at 17–21, 27–29, 34, 46–47.

[22] The idea of "demonstration effects" has been discussed by others as well. *See* International Center for Transitional Justice & United Nations Development Programme, *The "Legacy" of the Special Court for Sierra Leone*, 2003, at 12, *available at* http://www.ictj.org/downloads/LegacyReport.pdf. We try in this chapter to develop the concept and amplify the ways in which accountability proceedings can have positive demonstration effects on

tangibly and directly, by removing perpetrators of atrocities from positions in which they can control and abuse others, criminal trials (and processes such as rigorous vetting) can have a cathartic impact by assuring the population that old patterns of impunity and exploitation are no longer tolerable. Barring known perpetrators from again committing atrocities and delegitimizing them in the eyes of the public helps to break patterns of rule by fear and begins to build public confidence that justice can be fair. Many Afghans, for instance, have made clear that their trust in justice and in government institutions depends on removing serious abusers from positions of power and that they view this as essential for, not contrary to, security and long-term stability.[23]

Such cathartic processes can, nevertheless, be wrenching and traumatic in the near term. As powerful figures and their allies see their authority slip away, they may choose to mount resistance, which can aggravate existing instabilities. Also, in circumstances where vetting processes have been extensive, if inconsistent, as in Iraq, there is a risk that so many individuals may be removed from their positions that it undermines the stability of existing institutions or the prospects for building new ones in a timely manner.

In addition to disempowering perpetrators, the demonstration effects of accountability processes will depend on their character and credibility. Accountability proceedings – particularly trials but also truth commissions – aim to demonstrate that atrocities are unacceptable, condemned, and not to be repeated. They aim to substantiate concretely, and to demonstrate, a norm of accountability. If the proceedings that lead to conviction for major offenses – or the reconciliation rituals for lesser offenses – are widely viewed as fair and legitimate, they are more likely to demonstrate credibly that previous patterns of impunity have been rejected, that law can be fair, and that political position or economic clout does not immunize a person from accountability. If a norm of accountability is demonstrated credibly, it may provide meaningful justice to victims, reducing the chances of personal vengeance-seeking and eliminating impunity as a source of grievance more broadly. Providing a model of fair justice – through fair criminal prosecutions or through balanced reconciliation agreements for lesser offenders, for instance – can give citizens legitimate reason to expect (and to demand) better accountability and fairer processes in the future in other areas of life as well.

Of course, if accountability proceedings are widely viewed as biased, or if big fish go free while much lesser offenders are held accountable, those

building the rule of law in post-conflict societies. For an interesting analysis of the "political effects" of criminal tribunals, including their impact in delegitimating offenders and their possible stabilizing or destabilizing effects, *see* William W. Burke-White, A SYSTEM OF MULTILEVEL GLOBAL GOVERNANCE IN THE ENFORCEMENT OF INTERNATIONAL CRIMINAL LAW (forthcoming), Chapter IV.

[23] *A Call for Justice*, *supra* note 8, at 17, 41–44.

proceedings may have negative, counterproductive demonstration effects. They may send a message that justice is not fair, that previous patterns of impunity are continuing, and that deep-seated grievances will not be addressed. The complete failure to pursue accountability at all can send a similar message. In Afghanistan, for example, impunity is still rampant in those parts of the country where regional commanders and warlords function as a law unto themselves. Accountability for current abuses is probably of greater immediate concern for many Afghans than accountability for the past, but the two are clearly related when, in many instances, warlords who grew accustomed to operating with impunity in the past brazenly continue to do so in the present.[24]

Pursuing accountability fairly and credibly can have *empowering ripple effects* in a post-conflict society. By putting the issue of accountability on the national agenda, credible accountability proceedings can be a focal point for local and international nongovernmental organizations who advocate for related domestic reforms. Interveners involved in accountability proceedings can stress the importance of accountability norms to local elites generally,[25] and local and international NGOs can magnify these effects by working to inform and empower ordinary citizens about the importance of accountability and fair justice and by keeping pressure on post-conflict governments.[26] To effectively strengthen the domestic rule of law in the long term, accountability proceedings must demonstrate the value and importance of accountability and fair justice to local leaders and ordinary citizens alike: positive domestic change is more likely if pressure can be applied both from above and below.[27]

[24] On the problem of impunity in Afghanistan, *see* Rama Mani, Afghanistan Research and Evaluation Unit, *Ending Impunity and Building Justice in Afghanistan* (2003); *A Call for Justice, supra* note 8, at 17 ("Many persons who committed gross human rights violations remain in power today. This has provoked a profound disappointment in Afghans together with an almost total breakdown of trust in authority and public institutions").

[25] For a helpful general discussion of the importance of socializing elites in achieving norm change, *see* G. John Ikenberry & Charles A. Kupchan, *Socialization and Hegemonic Power*, 44 INT'L ORG. 2283 (1990).

[26] Political scientists have developed various models of norm diffusion and human rights advocacy. These include a "spiral model" through which local and international NGOs put pressure on domestic governments – from above and below – to abide by human rights principles, and a process of "norm cascades" as values gain credence broadly through a society after reaching a certain "tipping point." *See* Thomas Risse & Kathryn Sikkink, *The Socialization of International Human Rights Norms into Domestic Practice*, in THE POWER OF HUMAN RIGHTS: INTERNATIONAL NORMS AND DOMESTIC CHANGE (Thomas Risse, ed., 1999), at 1 (spiral model); Martha Finnemore & Kathryn Sikkink, *International Norm Dynamics and Political Change*, 52 INT'L ORG. 887 (1998) (norm cascades).

[27] This analysis is consistent with Risse and Sikkink's "spiral model." On the critical importance of socializing elites, *see* Ikenberry & Kupchan, *Socialization and Hegemonic Power, supra* note 25. On the importance of empowering citizens, especially the poor, in building the

Accountability proceedings, in short, can strengthen the fabric of a post-conflict society by helping to build and spread domestic support for a norm of accountability. As political scientists have argued, at some point in the development of a new norm, a "tipping point" is reached where the norm, enjoying broad acceptance, "cascades" through a society.[28] Before this point is reached, active efforts at persuasion by norm advocates, including local and international NGOs, are essential. Accountability proceedings can serve as a focal point for these efforts. Indeed, building toward an accountability cascade – in which expectations of accountability become the norm – is critical to overcome the legacy of a previous and pervasive impunity cascade in which order and accountability simply broke down (an example of an impunity cascade is Sierra Leone's situation in 1991, when many factors together tipped the country toward violence with impunity).[29] The slow and enormously hard work of building new normative expectations of accountability – rooted in a real capacity to deliver it, at least at a basic level – is often the key to establishing a viable domestic rule of law after conflict. The demonstration effect of accountability proceedings can be an essential, though not sufficient, component of that long-term effort.

B. Capacity-Building Effects

A second, related way that accountability proceedings can influence development of the rule of law domestically is through concrete *capacity-building*. Accountability proceedings cannot simply be an "aside" – standing totally apart from ordinary and ongoing processes of reform. Instead, over time, accountability norms – the condemnation of brutal atrocities, the importance of fair proceedings for determining responsibility, and the need for effective and impartial procedures for resolving future disputes more generally – must become *embedded in domestic practices*. Some accountability mechanisms,

rule of law, *see* Stephen Golub, *Beyond Rule of Law Orthodoxy: The Legal Empowerment Alternative,* Carnegie Endowment for International Peace, Democracy & Rule of Law Project, Rule of Law Series, No. 41, 2003.

[28] *See* Finnemore & Sikkink, *International Norm Dynamics and Political Change, supra* note 26, at 895.

[29] Sierra Leone's Truth and Reconciliation Commission has argued as follows: "While there were many factors, both internal and external, that explain the cause of the civil war, the Commission came to the conclusion that it was years of bad governance, endemic corruption and the denial of basic human rights that created the deplorable conditions that made the conflict inevitable. Successive regimes became increasingly impervious to the wishes and needs of the majority.... Government accountability was non-existent. Political expression and dissent had been crushed. Democracy and the rule of law were dead. By 1991, Sierra Leone was a deeply divided society and full of the potential for violence. It required only the slightest spark for this violence to be ignited." *Witness to Truth, supra* note 16, Vol. 1, para. 11, at 10.

by virtue of their location and degree of local participation, can help build domestic capacity directly by increasing the skills and experience of local professionals and through outreach efforts designed to educate and empower citizens and civil society organizations more broadly. International tribunals can serve important goals – such as providing justice for victims and conveying a strong international statement about fundamental international principles, including due process – even if their domestic impact in post-conflict societies is less clear. But unless norms of accountability are *institutionalized domestically* in a sustainable manner by strengthening national legal institutions and encouraging fairer processes and greater substantive accountability more broadly, the longer-term impact of accountability proceedings for past atrocities is likely to be uncertain.

Even though accountability proceedings can contribute to such domestic capacity-building, they also can compete with and divert resources from domestic legal systems. Prosecutions for serious violations of international humanitarian law are complex, costly, and time consuming, and competing priorities – for example, between international and domestic actors – can generate sharp tensions. In Rwanda, for instance, the government and ordinary citizens alike resent the millions of dollars spent on the international tribunal in Arusha, Tanzania, while Rwanda's own domestic legal system languishes desperately in need of aid. Even when hybrid courts are established, as in Sierra Leone and East Timor, the contrast between the facilities and resources of war crimes tribunals and the regular justice system is stark and sobering. The long-term needs of "ordinary" justice institutions generally cry out for attention, while international funding typically flows more generously to the more dramatic accountability proceedings.

This potential tension highlights the need to think more systematically from the start about designing processes that can both advance fundamental goals of accountability and develop domestic capacity for fair justice. Criminal trials, of course, must focus on their core purpose of bringing individual perpetrators to justice in fair and impartial proceedings. But modest efforts to enhance their domestic rule of law impact (for example, through early and well-planned outreach to local populations explaining the proceedings and the principles underlying them) can potentially make a real difference.

Based on the framework we have outlined here, one would expect that international trials held far from the people most affected by atrocities – and lacking in any direct domestic capacity-building or outreach efforts – are unlikely to have a substantial impact on strengthening the domestic rule of law in post-conflict societies. Even if they prosecute and thereby remove major perpetrators from domestic power structures, these trials must also be seen domestically to be doing justice if they are to have positive demonstration effects. Hybrid tribunals or truth commissions located in the affected country – with strong domestic participation and outreach – are more likely to leave a tangible legacy, at least if the bulk of the population views them as legitimate and fair. Either approach will have a limited long-term impact, however, if strategic efforts at domestic capacity-building are never undertaken or if underlying domestic conflicts (whether ethnic tensions or deep-seated perceived injustices) are simply left to fester or are even exacerbated by proceedings regarded as biased.

But what more specific conclusions can we draw, from recent experience, regarding the impact of accountability proceedings on building the rule of law domestically? It is to this challenging question that we now turn.

III. INTERNATIONAL TRIBUNALS AND THEIR IMPACT ON DOMESTIC RULE OF LAW: THE ICTY AND THE ICTR

The international community had good reason, at the time, to establish special international tribunals for Yugoslavia and Rwanda. Both conflicts involved egregious and widespread violations of international humanitarian law, and many states were determined to convey an emphatic international message that such conduct was unacceptable. In neither case were domestic legal systems in a position to provide fair and impartial justice. The Balkans were in the throes of a bitter conflict, and violence and ethnic hostilities precluded chances of fair and unbiased domestic prosecutions. Rwanda's legal system was devastated and overwhelmed in the face of massive genocide. The risks of "victor's justice" in both situations were substantial. In these circumstances, international tribunals held out a better prospect of independent and impartial proceedings and also of gaining custody over perpetrators beyond national borders.[30]

Established by the UN Security Council and funded largely by member states, the International Criminal Tribunal for the former Yugoslavia (ICTY)[31] and the International Criminal Tribunal for Rwanda (ICTR)[32] both have accomplished a great deal. They have each brought to justice, in fair trials, at least some of the individuals most responsible for egregious atrocities. Rwanda's former prime minister, Jean Kambanda, for instance, pled guilty and was convicted of genocide before the ICTR and is serving a life

[30] *See* Kritz, *The Rule of Law in the Postconflict Phase, supra* note 10, at 816.

[31] S.C. Res. 827, U.N. Doc. S/Res/827, May 25, 1993; *see* International Criminal Tribunal for the Former Yugoslavia, *ICTY at a Glance*, General Information, *available at* http://www.un.org/icty/glance-e/index.htm (last accessed February 4, 2006).

[32] S.C. Res. 955, U.N. Doc. S/Res/955 (November 8, 1994).

sentence.[33] At the ICTY, General Radislav Krstic – Commander of the Drina Corps – was found guilty of genocide in the 1995 Srebrenica massacres of as many as 8000 Muslim men and boys. The trial of former Yugoslav president Slobodan Milosevic before the ICTY was plagued by delay and other difficulties before his death in March 2006 brought the proceedings to an end without a final verdict; but his indictment for crimes committed in Bosnia, Croatia, and Kosovo – the first indictment ever to be brought against a sitting head of state – sent a clear message that nobody is above the law and contributed to his ultimate fall from power.[34] Both tribunals have also set some groundbreaking legal precedents contributing to the development of international criminal law, and they have played an educational role in focusing world attention on fundamental rules of international law. In bringing major perpetrators to justice, both tribunals have established an official record of the horrendous crimes committed and the criminal responsibilities of those involved.

Yet, despite these significant steps, both international tribunals may be remembered in the end as much for their shortcomings as their accomplishments. For one, they are geographically and psychologically distant from those most affected by the atrocities they are investigating and prosecuting. This distance, coupled with only belated and limited attempts at outreach, has undercut their legitimacy in the eyes of critical domestic audiences. Limited accurate information about the tribunals' proceedings, at least at first, undermined the tribunals' potential impact among local populations. For example, despite working hard to provide an impartial forum, the ICTY has suffered from a crisis of legitimacy – especially among Serbs – many of whom do not regard the tribunal as an embodiment of neutral justice.[35] These various factors have limited the ability of the international tribunals

[33] He was also convicted of conspiracy to commit genocide, direct and public incitement to commit genocide, complicity in genocide, and crimes against humanity. The ICTR also has brought a number of other high-level perpetrators to justice, including cabinet members and mayors.

[34] *See* Case Information Sheet: Milosevic (IT-02–54), *available at* http://www.un.org/icty/cases-e/index-e.htm (last accessed February 5, 2006). For a discussion of the indictment's impact, *see* Burke-White, A SYSTEM OF MULTILEVEL GLOBAL GOVERNANCE IN THE ENFORCEMENT OF INTERNATIONAL CRIMINAL LAW, *supra* note 22, Chapter IV, at 231–234. For information on the Krstic case, see Prosecutor v. Krstic, Case No. IT-98-33-A, Judgment in the Appeals Chamber, April 19, 2004, *available at* http://www.un.org/icty/krstic/Appeal/judgment/index.htm. As of May 2006, important ICTY indictees – such as Ratko Mladic and Radovan Karadzic – still remained at large.

[35] *See* Jelena Pejic, *The Yugoslav Truth and Reconciliation Commission: A Shaky Start*, 25 FORDHAM INT'L L. J. 1 note 6 (2001). Others, including a group of Bosnian Serb and Bosnian Croat judges and prosecutors, have also expressed skepticism regarding the neutrality of the ICTY. *See* Report, *Justice, Accountability and Social Reconstruction: An Interview Study of Bosnian Judges and Prosecutors*, 18 BERKLEY J. INT'L L. 102, 104 (2000) (hereinafter *Justice, Accountability, and Social Reconstruction*).

to demonstrate fair justice and accountability for atrocities in a way that resonates with the people most directly affected.

The ICTY and the ICTR also have contributed very little to building domestic judicial capacity in the Balkans or Rwanda, respectively. Although this was never their main purpose or preoccupation, both tribunals could have done much more to assist domestic capacity-building. The ICTY and ICTR are in a position to try only a limited number of high-level cases, so domestic legal systems have a critical role to play if significant accountability for atrocities is to be realized. But neither tribunal, until they began focusing systematically on their completion strategies (for wrapping up their own trials and investigations), had done very much to help strengthen the ability of local courts to deal with the substantial number of potential suspects remaining to be tried. More has been done since 2003, when the Security Council called for greater international assistance to improve the domestic capacity in relevant states and encouraged the ICTY and ICTR "to develop and improve" their outreach programs.[36]

A. The ICTY's Impact on Domestic Rule of Law: Kosovo and Bosnia

The ICTY's limited impact on domestic capacity-building is especially unfortunate in light of the more than a billion dollars spent on the tribunal.[37] Despite the start of an outreach program in 1999 and other periodic contacts between ICTY personnel and legal communities in the region, systematic and sustained efforts to share the tribunal's technical expertise with justice systems in the region were not pursued, illustrating a general lack of priority placed on such efforts.[38] As David Tolbert, former senior legal adviser at the ICTY and later deputy prosecutor, put it: "principally due to a failure in design and, to a lesser extent, in implementation, the tribunal's long-term impact on the systems of justice in the area of conflict has been minimal."[39]

Take the situation in Kosovo, for instance. The ICTY has devoted enormous energy and resources to investigating war crimes committed in Kosovo in 1998–1999, but so far the ICTY and the UN Mission in Kosovo (UNMIK) have not developed formal arrangements for sharing information or

36 S.C. Res. 1503, U.N. Doc. S/Res./1503 (August 28, 2003), para 1. For discussion of ICTR outreach, *see* Victor Peskin, *Courting Rwanda: The Promises and Pitfalls of the ICTR's Outreach Program*, 3 J. INT'L CRIM. JUS. 950 (2005). For examples of ICTY outreach, *see* the Calendar of Events at http://www.un.org/icty/bhs/outreach/events.htm (hereinafter *ICTY Calendar of Events*).

37 Total expenditures through 2005 equaled slightly more than $1 billion. An additional $276.5 million has been authorized for 2006 and 2007. *See* ICTY at a Glance, *supra* note 31.

38 David Tolbert, *The International Criminal Tribunal for the Former Yugoslavia: Unforeseen Successes and Foreseeable Shortcomings*, 26 FLETCHER F. WORLD AFF. 7, 13–15 (2002).

39 Id., at 8.

enhancing cooperation.[40] And although ICTY staff have shared their expertise with Kosovo jurists in periodic outreach activities, the ICTY failed to develop systematic, formalized plans to help enhance the capacity of local institutions to try such complex cases.[41] Because of the substantial funds invested in the Tribunal's work, its "lack of impact on at least preparing and buttressing the local courts" to conduct war crimes prosecutions is "troubling,"[42] leaving more recent efforts associated with ICTY's completion strategy with considerable ground to cover.

The ICTY has played a somewhat greater role in Bosnia. To provide some ICTY oversight of domestic prosecutions, Rules of the Road were agreed on in 1996 between the ICTY and Bosnia, Serbia, and Croatia, respectively. Under this arrangement, ICTY prosecutors review domestic warrants and indictments to ensure their fairness.[43] On this basis, trials of lesser war crimes suspects have been taking place in the two entities of Bosnia-Herzegovina.[44] The number of cases handled domestically is expected to increase sharply as the ICTY progresses with its completion strategy, putting an already weak domestic justice system under serious strain.

[40] Legislation evidently is being developed. *See* press release, UNMIK/PR/1123, United Nations Mission in Kosovo, Legislation on Cooperation with ICTY Can Only Be Promulgated by UNMIK, February 20, 2004.

[41] The outreach program in Kosovo has included ad hoc seminars and information sessions during which specialists from The Hague share their expertise with Kosovar jurists. *See* Int'l Crisis Group, *Finding the Balance: The Scales of Justice in Kosovo* 23 (2003); ICTY Calendar of Events, *supra* note 36.

[42] Tolbert, *The International Criminal Tribunal for the Former Yugoslavia, supra* note 38, at 12. Tolbert argues that with modest resources, the ICTY could have helped build domestic capacity by training local prosecutors, monitoring court proceedings in war crimes cases, training judges, and providing advice on victims' issues. Id., at 16. Instead, despite all the money spent on the ICTY, "there is virtually no effective enforcement of these important laws in the courts that ultimately matter the most, i.e., the region's domestic courts." Id., at 8.

[43] Paragraph 5 of the Rome Agreement of February 18, 1996, provides that "Persons, other than those already indicted by the International Tribunal, may be arrested and detained for serious violations of international humanitarian law only pursuant to a previously issued order, warrant, or indictment that has been reviewed and deemed consistent with international legal standards by the International Tribunal," *available at* www.ohr.int/ohr-dept/hr-rol/thedept/war-crime-tr/default.asp?content_id=6093.

[44] As of November 2003, thirteen war crimes trials were taking place before entity courts. *See* Amnesty International, *Shelving Justice: War Crimes Prosecutions in Paralysis* 5 (2003), *available at* http://web.amnesty.org/library/Index/ENGEUR630182003?open&of=ENG-BIH (hereinafter *Shelving Justice*). *See also* International Crisis Group, *Courting Disaster: The Misrule of Law in Bosnia and Herzegovina* 31 (2002) (hereinafter *Courting Disaster*) (reporting that, as of March 2002, approximately thirty-five verdicts had been entered against accused in courts of the Federation). As of May 2002, an estimated 3000 people in the Republika Srpska and 6000 in the Federation were suspected of war crimes. *Shelving Justice,* at note 1. By February 2006, the cantonal prosecutor for Sarajevo and the surrounding area reported about 2100 war crimes suspects in the region and about 1600 individuals were the subject of requests for investigation by local authorities. *Bosnian TV Reports Prosecutor Outlines Progress in War Crimes Processing*, BBC INTERNATIONAL REPORTS, February 6, 2006.

Yet concerns about fairness and about impunity have been endemic in Bosnia from the start. Bosnian cantonal or entity courts have dispensed justice that has proven highly inadequate, triggering frequent allegations that trials have been tainted by "ethnic justice" and are being used to exact revenge.[45] All too often, instead of promoting justice, war crimes prosecutions in Bosnian courts have been yet another means of continuing ethnic conflict, undermining the goals of justice both for victims and for the accused.[46] With a few notable exceptions, a disturbing pattern has emerged with members of each of the three ethnic groups engaged in attempts to arrest, prosecute, and punish for war crimes members of their rival ethnic groups, who often are still viewed as heroes by their respective communities.[47] Thus far, the majority of war crimes trials have taken place in the Federation, with Muslim areas targeting almost exclusively Bosnian Serbs and Croats, and Croatian areas targeting primarily Serbs and Muslims.[48] Rather than promoting healing and confidence-building among the parties, trials often end up exacerbating divisions and mutual suspicion.[49] The record so far has been discouraging but some improvements have occurred.[50] Moreover, the creation of a special hybrid War Crimes Chamber within the national State Court of Bosnia and Herzegovina holds real promise.

This special War Crimes Chamber is now composed of national and international judges, prosecutors, and other staff, but the international participation will gradually phase out over a period of years.[51] This arrangement is designed to build local capacity to conduct fair trials in accordance with international standards, and ICTY staff have provided briefings and materials to judges and lawyers. The tribunal's location in Sarajevo means that

[45] *See* Michael Bohlander, *Last Exit Bosnia: Transferring War Crimes Prosecution from the International Tribunal to Domestic Courts*, 14 CRIM. L. F. 59, 67 (2003). According to the International Crisis Group, "[p]ublic debates and mutual accusations of pursuing 'ethnic justice' with the aim of eliminating political competitors or protecting one's brethren continue[s], involving a wide range of politicians, judges and human rights' activists," and "[a] leitmotif of the controversy [is] a widely shared recognition that the local judiciary [is] incapable of handling war crimes cases either competently or fairly." *Courting Disaster, supra* note 44, at 33.

[46] Aram A. Schvey, *Striving for Accountability in the Former Yugoslavia*, in Stromseth, ACCOUNTABILITY FOR ATROCITIES, *supra* note 12, at 67.

[47] Id., at 48–49.

[48] Id. The first war crimes trial in the Republika Srpska started only in September 2003. *See* Human Rights Watch, *Bosnia: Massacre Trial Highlights Obstacles to Justice in the Balkans*, January, 2004, *available at* http://hrw.org/english/docs/2004/01/15/bosher6939.htm.

[49] *See* Kritz, *Coming to Terms with Atrocities, supra* note 12, at 136–137.

[50] *See* OSCE, *War Crimes Trials before the Domestic Courts of Bosnia and Herzegovina: Progress and Obstacles*, March 2005, at 51.

[51] For a description of the special War Crimes Chamber, *see* S/2005/458, *Report to the Secretary-General of the Commission of Experts to Review the Prosecution of Serious Violations of Human Rights in Timor-Leste (then East Timor) in 1999*, May 26, 2005 (hereinafter *Commission of Experts Report*), Annex II to letter dated June 24, 2005, from the Secretary-General addressed to the president of the Security Council, July 15, 2005, at 109–110, 112–113.

its proceedings are more accessible to the local population and the prospects for direct outreach are greater. Compared to the problems that have plagued local trials, the special War Crimes Chamber has a greater capacity to render, and to be seen as rendering, impartial justice. The court began its first trial in September 2005 and received its first transfer of an indictee from the ICTY two weeks later.[52] The ICTY prosecutor's office has sought the transfer of an additional twelve defendants, and the local courts continue to send sensitive war crimes prosecutions to the special chamber.[53] Hybrid panels within the State Court also address difficult cases involving organized crime, economic crime, and corruption, with international participation and assistance that will gradually be phased out leaving purely domestic actors in place.

Compared to the distant ICTY and the often problematic local trials, the trials before the State Court's special chamber may be able to demonstrate impartial justice more directly and effectively to domestic audiences. The capacity-building effects of this arrangement are also substantial and vitally important. Even so, several concerns remain. For one, the schedule for the phase-out of international participation, driven substantially by funding realities, may be more rapid than is ideal for effective capacity-building. Furthermore, the entity-level Bosnian courts, rather than the State Court's special chamber, will continue to handle the bulk of war crimes cases, and if they do not receive greater assistance, there is a risk that some of the same problems that have confronted the ICTY may be "replicated at the national level."[54] Finally, although trials before the State Court's special chamber can help provide a model of fair and effective justice at the national level, systematic outreach and dialogue will still be needed as different segments of Bosnian society react to the prosecutions, including of figures who retain substantial loyalty and support within their respective communities.

B. The ICTY and Serbia

The ICTY's contribution to improving the domestic justice system and building the rule of law has been even more complicated in the case of Serbia. For many Serbs, the international prosecution of Milosevic robbed Serbia of the opportunity to hold him accountable in domestic courts. Milosevic's decision to defend himself and to challenge the very terms of reference of the international tribunal resonated in many quarters within Serbia, and a substantial segment of the public questioned whether he was getting a fair trial.[55]

52 Council of Europe, *Bosnia and Herzegovina: Compliance With Obligations and Commitments and Implementation of the Post-Accession Co-Operation Program*, SG/Inf(2005)21, November 3, 2005, para. 54.

53 Id.

54 Amnesty International, *Shelving Justice, supra* note 44, at 8.

55 According to opinion polls, less than one-fourth of Serbs believed Milosevic was getting a fair trial, and his approval rating doubled at the outset of his trial; he went from being a

Several factors have undercut the ICTY's ability to demonstrate to the Serbian population that the tribunal has been fair and impartial in its pursuit of accountability for atrocities. For one, many Serbs take a different view of the history of the breakup of the former Yugoslavia, rejecting the view of predominant Serb responsibility taken by NATO states supporting the ICTY. The tribunal's failure to indict leaders such as Croatian President Tudjman, who is now dead, has left the ICTY open to perceptions within Serbia of an anti-Serb bias. For many Serbs, this perception was reinforced by the tribunal's decision not to investigate NATO's actions during the Kosovo war. The circumstances surrounding the domestic handover of Milosevic to the ICTY also remain controversial, and many Serbs view the government's cooperation with the tribunal as strictly a function of monetary pressures rather than of justice. Finally, Milosevic sought to use his trial as a platform to influence public opinion in Serbia and was surprisingly effective in representing himself in court and portraying himself as an underdog.

All of these perceptions have been compounded by the ICTY's lack of effective outreach within Serbia. If the ICTY had provided Serbs with a clearer idea of its operations and purpose, early on, they might have been less prone to view the tribunal so skeptically. The ICTY did establish an outreach office in 1999 to inform people of the region about its work, but in crucial earlier phases, the ICTY's work was subject to "gross distortions and disinformation" in many parts of the former Yugoslavia.[56] As ICTY official David Tolbert notes, "the tribunal became a political football for certain unscrupulous politicians in the region who cynically manipulated... misunderstandings."[57] The ICTY should have anticipated this potential opposition and taken steps to ensure that the Serbian population would hear the truth about its operations from the very start.

The ICTY's contribution to capacity-building within Serbia has also been sorely lacking. Although more than a billion dollars has supported the ICTY since its inception,[58] relatively little has been done to share the tribunal's technical expertise or to assist local courts, even though they are expected to bring to justice many perpetrators not tried in The Hague. Even though

reviled individual to the fourth most admired Serb. Michael P. Scharf, *The ICTY at Ten: A Critical Assessment of the Major Rulings of the International Criminal Tribunal Over the Past Decade*, 37 New Eng. L. Rev. 915, 930–931 (2003). Public opinion within Serbia has varied over the years, and there is some indication that public opposition to the ICTY diminished after release of the Scorpions video showing members of a Serbian police unit executing Bosnian Muslims in cold blood. *See, e.g.*, Nicholas Wood, *Videotape of Serbian Police Killing 6 Muslims From Srebrenica Grips Balkans,* The New York Times, June 12, 2005, at A1.

56 Tolbert, *The International Criminal Tribunal for the Former Yugoslavia, supra* note 38, at 13.

57 Id.

58 *See* ICTY at a Glance, *supra* note 31.

sharing its expertise and assisting local courts is not formally part of ICTY's mandate, more efforts to do this could have earned the ICTY considerable goodwill in Serbia and helped to better prepare local courts to continue prosecutions after the ICTY concludes its operations.

Yet, despite these problems, attitudes in Serbia – at least among some groups – may gradually be changing, and the ICTY may yet have a positive impact over the longer term. Although Serbia had completed only four domestic war crimes trials by January 2003, despite a large number of suspected war criminals within its borders, Serbia created a new Special Court for Organized Crimes and War Crimes later that year.[59] An exclusively domestic court, Serbia's Special Court receives international support, and the law establishing the Court provides for cooperation with the ICTY. In the Special Court's first case, the "Ovcara trial," in which a number of Serbs were accused of executing 192 Croatian prisoners of war at the Ovcara pig farm in the Croatian city of Vukovar in 1991, ICTY's prosecutor Carla del Ponte provided at least eight boxes of evidence to the Court, and Croatia provided exhumation records.[60] The ICTY's support to the Special Court in this case and in other potential cases is an important development as the ICTY begins to bring its own work to a close over the next few years. In December 2005, the Special Court completed the Ovcara trial, handing down lengthy prison sentences for fourteen of the sixteen defendants.[61]

Also in 2005, the emergence of a videotape showing members of the Serbian police unit known as the Scorpions callously executing Muslims at Srebrenica was aired extensively in Serbia and internationally after first being played at the Milosevic trial on June 1, 2005.[62] As of late 2005, one member of the unit depicted on the tape had been convicted in Croatia, and five others were on trial in Serbia.[63]

Serbia's Special Court has only recently begun its work and its long-term impact within Serbia remains to be seen. The Ovcara trial, at least initially, received considerable domestic attention, and it may have helped to encourage greater public dialogue and awareness regarding war crimes, at least to

[59] The law, passed on July 2003, is *available at* http://www.osce.org/documents/fry/2003/07/446_en.pdf

[60] Milanka Saponja Hadzic, Institute for War and Peace Reporting, *Serbian Judiciary Facing Key Test* (2004), *available at* http://www.iwpr.net. The Ovcara trial began on March 9, 2004. Press release, *Humanitarian Law Center, "Ovcara" Case: A Trial Is Professional but the Indictment Is Amiss*, April 6, 2005, *available at* http://www.hlc.org.yu/english/War_Crimes_Trials_Before_National_Courts/index.php.

[61] *Serbian Court Jails 14 Over 1991 "Execution" of Prisoners in Croatia*, BBC NEWSFILE, December 12, 2005.

[62] Nicholas Wood, *Videotape of Serbian Police Killing 6 Muslims from Srebrenica Grips Balkans*, THE NEW YORK TIMES, June 12, 2005, at A12.

[63] *Serb Jailed over Srebrenica Video*, BBC NEWS, December 29, 2005, *available at* http://news.bbc.co.uk/2/hi/europe/4567704.stm.

some extent. The release and repeated broadcast in Serbia of the Scorpions video has added to that public discussion. Domestic debates over the ICTY still remain highly charged – and prone to opportunistic manipulation by political factions – but the ICTY's legal support to domestic prosecutions like the Ovcara case may help, over time, to demonstrate accountability and build domestic capacity in a manner more widely viewed as credible within Serbia.

C. The ICTR: An Ambivalent Domestic Impact

The ICTR's impact within Rwanda has likewise been a mixed one.[64] The tribunal's relationship with the Rwandan government was uneasy from the start. After seeking international assistance in bringing perpetrators of Rwanda's devastating genocide to justice, Rwanda was the only state on the UN Security Council to vote against establishing the ICTR. Rwanda's objections – which still fester – included the failure to locate the tribunal within Rwanda, the lack of a provision for capital punishment, and limits on the time frame of the court's jurisdiction.[65] Significant management problems early on at the ICTR, coupled with the over one billion dollars spent on the ICTR while Rwanda's domestic system struggles to try thousands of suspects, have also been a source of resentment and tension. The limited number of individuals that the ICTR is able to try, the slow pace of proceedings at the tribunal, and the limited role for, and attention to, needs of victims have all been criticisms raised by Rwandan political leaders.[66]

In the face of these criticisms, the ICTR has had a difficult time establishing broad credibility among the Rwandan public. "Constantly exposed to such bitter criticism highlighting the imperfections of the Tribunal, many Rwandans tend to hold an overwhelmingly negative opinion of international justice," notes Aloys Habimana.[67] For many Rwandans, moreover, the individuals who directly committed atrocities in front of their own eyes matter as much as the more distant architects of the genocide.

The ICTR should have done more from the start to explain its purpose and its proceedings broadly within Rwanda and to address concerns raised by citizens. Instead, the tribunal's outreach has been belated and its physical

[64] Although Rwanda is not a case involving a major international military intervention (quite to the contrary) and therefore is not the focus of other chapters of this book, we discuss it here because of its importance for understanding the potential impact of accountability processes on building the rule of law.

[65] Aloys Habimana, *Judicial Responses to Mass Violence: Is the International Criminal Tribunal for Rwanda Making a Difference Towards Reconciliation in Rwanda?*, in INTERNATIONAL WAR CRIMES TRIALS: MAKING A DIFFERENCE? 83, 84–85 (Steven R. Ratner & James L. Bischoff, eds., 2003).

[66] Id., at 85.

[67] Id., at 86.

presence within Rwanda is limited.[68] Created in 1994, with its first trials commencing in 1997, the ICTR established an outreach project only in 1998 and an Information Center in Rwanda in 2000.[69] The ICTR's own Web site has improved, and several Web sites managed by international NGOs publish good information and analysis on the ICTR, but very few Rwandans have Internet access, so this information is largely available only to foreigners.[70] Radio Rwanda reports from the tribunal in Arusha, Tanzania, and a number of organizations, including the European Commission and some NGOs, support outreach efforts that include distributing documents and showing documentary films about the ICTR in the Rwandan countryside.[71] But much more needs to be done if the ICTR expects to have a longer-term impact within Rwanda.

Still, despite a slow start, the ICTR has the potential to demonstrate the importance of accountability and fair justice to audiences within Rwanda in a number of ways. For one, the tribunal has brought high-level perpetrators of genocide to justice. This sends "a clear message to victims, victimizers, and bystanders that leaders who commit gross violations of human rights are not always invincible," which is a message that "is fundamental for ensuring the rule of law in a post-conflict society like that of Rwanda," as Aloys Habimana argues.[72] In addition, these trials reveal how self-interested leaders exploited ethnic differences for their own purposes – which

[68] All of the courtrooms for the ICTR are in Arusha, Tanzania, and the ICTR's main formal presence in Rwanda is with the Office of the Prosecutor (formerly Carla del Ponte, now Hassan Jallow from the Gambia). The ICTY opened an Information Center in Kigali in 2000.

[69] Peter Uvin & Charles Mironko, *Western and Local Approaches to Justice in Rwanda*, 9 GLOBAL GOVERNANCE 219, 221 (2003). The Information Center, *Umusanzu mu Bwiyunge* ("Contribution to reconciliation"), in Rwanda's capital, Kigali, is open to "students, journalists, civil servants, judges and lawyers, as well as ordinary citizens." U.N. Doc. S/2003/707, A/58/140, International Criminal Tribunal for Rwanda, *Report of the International Criminal Tribunal for the Prosecution of Persons Responsible for Genocide and Other Serious Violations of International Humanitarian Law Committed in the Territory of Rwanda and Rwandan Citizens Responsible for Genocide and Other Such Violations Committed in the Territory of Neighbouring States between 1 January and 31 December 1994*, July 11, 2003, *available at* http://65.18.216.88/ENGLISH/annualreports/a58/140e.pdf (hereinafter *ICTR Report*).

[70] Uvin & Mironko, *Western and Local Approaches to Justice in Rwanda, supra* note 69, at 219.

[71] Id. The U.S.-based Internews media organization, for example, has produced documentary films about ICTR and domestic war crimes trials, which are then shown in rural communities, sometimes accompanied by Rwandan ICTR outreach officers. Peskin, *Courting Rwanda: The Promises and Pitfalls of the ICTR's Outreach Program, supra* note 36, at 960. Peskin urges the ICTR to establish partnerships with Rwandan civil society leaders and academics, some of whom have tried to secure ICTR's commitment, so far unsuccessfully, "to hold post-trial seminars in Rwanda with ICTR officials to discuss the significance of recent trials," which could be a foundation for further Rwandan-initiated outreach. Id.

[72] Habimana, *Judicial Responses to Mass Violence, supra* note 65, at 88.

may contribute to a greater domestic understanding of the causes of the genocide and possibly lay some foundation for reconciliation over time.[73] Finally, through fair trials that follow fundamental principles of due process, the tribunal can help demonstrate to Rwandans "what 'fair justice' should look like,"[74] potentially providing a point of reference for future domestic reforms.

But to have any sustainable long-term impacts along these lines will require more effective and convincing outreach within Rwanda than has occurred thus far. This is an uphill battle given the skepticism about the tribunal among many audiences in Rwanda. The tribunal, in short, faces a major challenge "not only to render justice, but also to make sure that Rwandans, in all their complex categories, see that justice is being done."[75] Yet, so far, the ICTR has been reluctant to partner with independent civil society organizations to engage in sustained outreach, thereby missing opportunities for empowering ripple effects; instead, the ICTR has preferred to interact with the Rwandan government and "government-backed survivor groups," whose cooperation the tribunal needs.[76]

The ICTR also needs to do more, before its work comes to an end, to contribute to capacity-building within the domestic justice system. But, to date, the ICTR has done almost nothing to contribute to the capacity of the Rwandan judiciary.[77] One of the few activities led by the ICTR involving the Rwandan judiciary was a September 2003 visit by twenty senior Rwandan judicial officials (judges, prosecutors, and senior officials) to the tribunal in Arusha.[78] The focus was primarily on issues related to the pursuit of justice at the ICTR (e.g., witness protection, pace of proceedings, and completion strategy) rather than on capacity-building for the Rwandan justice system itself.[79] One is left wondering whether some of the millions of dollars spent annually on the ICTR could have been better spent on direct domestic

[73] Id., at 89.

[74] Id.

[75] Id., at 90.

[76] Peskin, *Courting Rwanda: The Promises and Pitfalls of the ICTR's Outreach Program, supra* note 36, at 961. Peskin notes that despite overtures from leading academics and human rights activists, including Aloys Habimana, the ICTR has not embarked on cooperative partnerships with them to engage in more extensive outreach. Id., at 960–961.

[77] Id., at 957–958.

[78] The ICTR Registrar extended the invitation, and two groups of ten officials spent one week each at the tribunal. The purpose was "to strengthen the co-operation between the Rwandan judicial system and the Tribunal in what is called *appui judiciaire* to the national Rwandese judicial bodies." Press Release, ICTR/INFO-9-2-360. EN, International Criminal Tribunal for Rwanda, *Rwandan Judicial Officials Visit the ICTR*, September 26, 2003, *available at* http://65.18.216.88/ENGLISH/PRESSREL/2003/360.htm. The ICTR has also organized visits to the tribunal by Rwandan law students, as well as some internships. Peskin, *Courting Rwanda, supra* note 36, at 955–956.

[79] Press release, *supra* note 78.

capacity-building, particularly given Rwanda's desire to undertake domestic criminal prosecutions and community-based accountability proceedings.

In short, both the ICTR and the ICTY have faced obstacles in leaving a positive, long-term legacy in the countries most affected by the atrocities they are prosecuting. In future international prosecutions, some of these difficulties could be addressed by earlier, more effective outreach to domestic audiences, and by more systematic efforts to design focused, well-conceived domestic capacity-building programs. Still, international tribunals located far from the affected country with little or no involvement by national judges, prosecutors, and defense counsel are inherently limited in the direct impact they are likely to have domestically in post-conflict societies. But purely domestic proceedings may not be the answer either – at least in cases where national justice systems are devastated by conflict or unlikely to deliver fair or impartial justice. Hybrid, or mixed, tribunals with both national and international participation may, in some instances, hold more promise.

IV. HYBRID TRIBUNALS AND THEIR IMPACT ON DOMESTIC RULE OF LAW

Hybrid tribunals first emerged toward the end of the 1990s as an alternative to purely international or purely domestic courts. In a number of countries – Kosovo, East Timor, Sierra Leone, and Bosnia – hybrid arrangements have been established to try individuals for violations of international and sometimes also domestic law. In addition to combining national and international staff – judges and prosecutors, among others – these hybrids are located directly in the country that experienced the atrocities.

Hybrids, in many ways, are like a piece of clay that can be molded to fit the challenges and circumstances at hand. But they have been shaped by political necessity and compromise as much as by any grand theory. In the case of Kosovo, for instance, biased domestic trials provoked outcries from Kosovo's Serbian population and led the United Nations to design a hybrid system in which panels comprised of a majority of international judges would address war crimes and other sensitive cases and international prosecutors could revive cases dismissed by domestic prosecutors.[80] In other situations – East Timor and Cambodia – hybrids were negotiated because key states simply did not want to create new international tribunals even in the face of major atrocities.[81]

[80] Michael E. Hartmann, U.S. Institute of Peace, *International Judges and Prosecutors in Kosovo* 13 (2003), *available at* http://www.usip.org/pubs/specialreports/sr112.html. Hartmann was the first international prosecutor to serve under this arrangement.

[81] The Cambodian government together with China, for instance, rejected calls by a group of experts for an international tribunal to try former Khmer Rouge leaders. Yet Cambodian domestic courts were in no position to provide impartial justice in such cases. So the United

Though they differ in form and origins, hybrids have at least the potential to overcome some of the limitations of purely international or purely domestic proceedings.[82] They may, for instance, enjoy greater legitimacy among affected local populations than either international prosecutions far away or domestic prosecutions before a justice system of limited means or credibility. International participation and resources can help ensure that the proceedings satisfy international standards of due process, while domestic participation can give citizens of the country most affected a greater stake and sense of ownership. Thus, hybrids may demonstrate accountability in a way that resonates more effectively with local populations.

Second, hybrids may have advantages in contributing to domestic capacity-building and institutionalization of accountability norms. Locating tribunals directly in countries that endured atrocities – and including national participation in their work at all levels – provides an opportunity to build capacity and leave behind a tangible contribution to the national justice system, including resources, facilities, and training. Finally, by providing for direct interaction between national and international jurists and by enhancing opportunities for outreach to the local population, hybrids may be more effective than either international or national processes alone in fostering awareness of, and encouraging respect for, fundamental principles of international law and human rights at the domestic level among citizens and officials of the country involved. They may, to borrow from political science terminology, be more effective at "norm diffusion."[83]

But whether recent hybrids are actually achieving these results is a much more complicated question. The demonstration effects and capacity-building impact of these diverse hybrids, in fact, have varied widely.

A. Kosovo's Hybrid Arrangement: Mixed Results

In Kosovo, UNMIK established a hybrid judicial arrangement in 2000 to prosecute and try war crimes cases. The ICTY has primacy over such cases arising in the conflict in the former Yugoslavia, but it cannot try them all, so domestic courts also have a critical role to play in achieving

Nations and Cambodia – with U.S. involvement along the way – negotiated a compromise hybrid tribunal with a majority of Cambodian judges, although this agreement is only now slowly being implemented. *See* Rachel S. Taylor, *Better Late Than Never: Cambodia's Joint Tribunal*, in Stromseth, ACCOUNTABILITY FOR ATROCITIES, *supra* note 12, at 237. In East Timor, the United Nations together with key states opted for a hybrid arrangement – joint national/international judicial panels within East Timor and domestic prosecutions in Indonesia – even though there were good reasons to doubt whether high-level Indonesian military officials would ultimately face justice under such an arrangement, at least absent sustained international pressure on Indonesia.

[82] For a thoughtful analysis, *see* Dickinson, *The Promise of Hybrid Courts, supra* note 18.

[83] For a discussion of norm diffusion, *see generally* Finnemore & Sikkink, *International Norm Dynamics and Political Change, supra* note 26.

accountability.[84] In Kosovo's case, however, the local judicial system was seriously incapacitated. Most of the local judges and lawyers – of predominantly Serb ethnicity – fled the province or refused to serve in the UN-established judicial system, and newly appointed Kosovar Albanian judges lacked professional experience because of their decade-long exclusion as a result of officially sanctioned discrimination. But in ethnically divided Kosovo, the virtually monoethnic, UN-appointed judiciary was not perceived as providing – nor could it deliver – impartial justice. Only after mounting pressure from ethnic Serbs in what was increasingly viewed as a biased justice system did UNMIK introduce international judges and prosecutors to serve in Kosovo's judicial system.

The initial deployment of these international jurists in 2000 was "crisis driven" and improvised, rather than the result of a carefully designed and implemented strategy.[85] Appointed to most, but not all, war crimes and other sensitive cases, including ethnic crimes and high-level organized crime, the international jurists initially had little impact: they were in the minority on judicial panels and were invariably outvoted by Kosovar Albanian judges. This only reinforced perceptions of "victor's justice" among Kosovo's Serbian population – now with the involvement of the international community – which reinforced resentments and ethnic tensions rather than helping to defuse them. In the face of these clear shortcomings, UNMIK issued regulations in December 2000 providing for the introduction of majority international judicial panels and empowering international prosecutors to reactivate cases abandoned by their Kosovar counterparts.

These "64 panels" – named after UNMIK's Regulation 2000/64 establishing them – have helped to reduce perceptions of bias in the justice system and have redressed some earlier miscarriages of justice. Nevertheless, shortcomings in implementation and some subjective aspects of this arrangement have undermined their potential impact. Introduced by UNMIK without consulting and involving local judges, the arrangement has faced widespread resistance by local judges, and some have refused to participate in majority international panels.[86] Moreover, the grounds for participation of international judges and prosecutors have been criticized as overly vague and subjective,

[84] The ICTY has jurisdiction over serious violations of international humanitarian law committed in the former Yugoslavia since January 1, 1991, including war crimes, genocide, and crimes against humanity. The ICTY's jurisdiction is concurrent with national courts, but it enjoys primacy and can request a national court to defer to it. Statute of the International Criminal Tribunal for the Former Yugoslavia, Art. 9, *annexed to Report of the Secretary General Pursuant to Paragraph 2 of Security Council Resolution 808 (1993)*, UN SCOR, 48th Sess., U.N. Doc. S/25704 (1993) (hereinafter ICTY Statute); ICTY R.P. & Evid. 9–11 (July 21, 2005), *available at* http://www.un.org/icty/legaldoc-e/index.htm.

[85] Hartmann, *International Judges and Prosecutors in Kosovo, supra* note 80.

[86] David Marshall & Shelley Inglis, *The Disempowerment of Human Rights-Based Justice in the United Nations Mission in Kosovo*, 16 HARV. HUM. RTS. J. 95, 130 (2003).

contributing to a perception, especially among Albanians, that the system is a "parallel justice system" vulnerable to political influence and maneuvering. Also, because the regulation does not guarantee prosecution by an international prosecutor before a majority international panel, Kosovo Serb defendants also view the arrangement as vulnerable to double standards and unequal treatment.[87] Thus, the "64 panels" have only partially been able to address public perceptions of bias in ethnically charged Kosovo.

Viewed over the long term, the demonstration effects of the hybrid panels within Kosovo clearly have been mixed. On the one hand, the majority international panels' ability to consider particularly delicate and divisive cases, coupled with the international prosecutors' ability to revive and pursue cases abandoned by local counterparts, has, over time, helped to address systemic biases and miscarriages of justice in the largely monoethnic local justice system. On the other hand, UNMIK's belated, ad hoc introduction of the "64 panels" was a missed opportunity to demonstrate a commitment and a capacity for impartial justice from the start. As the first international prosecutor in Kosovo, Michael Hartmann, has observed, international participation in the judiciary would have been more successful had it been "immediate and bold" rather than "incremental and crisis driven."[88] Early prosecutions and trials before majority international panels could have enhanced the real and perceived impartiality of the judiciary, increasing its legitimacy among the different sectors of the population. Rather than empowering local jurists and belatedly stripping them of their "monopoly" over sensitive cases, such a policy also would have been easier and likely less contentious to implement. Finally, beginning with a more systematic international role in the local judicial system could have had a broader impact by helping to limit the destructive influence and entrenchment of criminal power structures and their linkages to extremist ethnic and nationalist groups.[89]

Not surprisingly, the capacity-building results of Kosovo's hybrid panels also have been less than hoped for. Despite the potential for mutual learning when international jurists serve besides local judges, a number of the international judges, especially early on, had little background or training in international humanitarian law, which limited their ability to contribute to local capacity-building in this area.[90] Language barriers, the intensive workload, and the lack of systematic mentoring mechanisms all hampered potential capacity-building more generally. The hybrid arrangement in

[87] Id., at 134.

[88] Hartmann, *International Judges and Prosecutors in Kosovo, supra* note 80, at 13.

[89] Id.

[90] Marshall & Inglis, *The Disempowerment of Human Rights-Based Justice in the United Nations Mission in Kosovo, supra* note 86, at 129 ("Of the internationals that were appointed between 1999 and 2001, few had conducted trials involving serious criminal offenses and none had any practical experience in, or knowledge of, international humanitarian law . . . ").

Kosovo – which places the most sensitive cases before the "64 panels" – also has delayed the day when Kosovo's local judges have to take full responsibility for adjudicating such cases.

All of this suggests that hybrids are more likely to be effective in demonstrating accountability and fair justice – and in developing local capacity – if they are designed in a more strategic way than was the case with Kosovo's early experiment. It may well be, at least in circumstances where local legal capacity is absent or devastated, that turning to international jurists early on – if they possess the necessary legal background and skills – makes sense as an initial response, while local jurists are trained effectively and expeditiously to join, as soon as possible, in the task of adjudicating sensitive and difficult war crimes cases. In any event, creating standing panels with clear jurisdiction – rather than ad hoc discretionary panels – to address war crimes and other sensitive cases may be less vulnerable to perceptions of political malleability by affected populations.

B. Timor Leste: "Independence Is a Form of Justice"

East Timor's hybrid tribunal for serious crimes has faced tough challenges in pursuing accountability amidst the political complexities associated with the nation's transition to independence, yielding deeply ambivalent demonstration effects. During East Timor's historic referendum in 1999, militias operating with the aid and support of the Indonesian army perpetrated atrocities – murders, rapes, looting, burning – against Timorese independence supporters. An international commission of inquiry established at the UN Human Rights Commission in 1999 called for an international tribunal to bring those responsible to justice. But critical states and UN leaders – involved in delicate negotiations with Indonesia to secure its consent to the deployment of an international military force, INTERFET, to stabilize East Timor after the referendum – instead pressed Indonesia to bring those responsible for the violence to justice domestically.[91] In opting not to establish an international tribunal for this purpose, many no doubt hoped that persistent international pressure on Indonesia might produce meaningful domestic accountability; but, at the same time, the absence of an international accountability mechanism with clear enforcement authority undermined the prospects of trying leading Indonesian suspects if Indonesia itself chose not to do so.

[91] In an April 2000 MOU between Indonesia and the UN, Indonesia agreed to share information and transfer indictees to East Timor. *Memorandum of Understanding Between the Republic of Indonesia and the United Nations Transitional Administration in East Timor Regarding Cooperation in Legal, Judicial and Human Rights Related Matters*, Indon.-UNTAET, April 6, 2000, *available at* http://www.jsmp.minihub.org/Reports/MOU.htm. INTERFET, a UN-authorized military force (with Indonesian consent) led by Australia deployed in August 1999 to restore stability to East Timor, followed by a UN provisional administration – the UN Transitional Administration in East Timor (or UNTAET) together with a UN peacekeeping force. S.C. Res. 1272, U.N. Doc. S/RES/1272, October 25, 1999.

Within East Timor, the UN Transitional Administration (UNTAET) established an innovative hybrid tribunal in June 2000 (in lieu of an international tribunal per se). The Special Panels for Serious Crimes – hybrid judicial panels within the Dili District Court consisting of two international judges and one Timorese judge – were created to try cases of crimes against humanity, war crimes, and other atrocities.[92] UNTAET also established the Serious Crimes Unit, a UN-funded prosecutorial and investigatory office for serious crimes, to serve as the prosecutorial and investigations arm of the hybrid tribunal.[93] Although both the Special Panels and Serious Crimes Unit received UN funding, defense counsel received more limited, ad hoc support – an imbalance of concern from the start.[94] In 2002, the successor UN mission (UNMISET) established a Defense Lawyer's Unit to provide more resources and expertise to assist in defense of suspects before the Special Panels.[95] Overall, however, neither political support (international or domestic) nor resources for East Timor's hybrid tribunal were ever as forthcoming as many originally had hoped.

These limitations seriously constrained the tribunal's impact both in achieving accountability for the atrocities surrounding the referendum and in capacity-building. The special tribunal faced chronic shortages of administrative, legal, and linguistic support, particularly at the beginning. In early trials, for instance, no court reporters or other means were available to produce records of the proceedings.[96] Interpreters frequently were unavailable in some of the four languages (Portuguese, Bahasa Indonesia, Tetum, and English) in which proceedings were conducted. Resources for defense counsel were particularly limited, and no defense witnesses were called at all in a number of the early trials.[97] Significant improvements certainly occurred over time, but a shortage of resources and support personnel continued to

[92] The panels were given jurisdiction over genocide, torture, crimes against humanity, and war crimes; in addition, they had jurisdiction over murder and sexual offenses committed from January 1, 1999, through October 25, 1999 – the period leading up to and following the referendum and before the UN became administering authority in East Timor. UNTAET Reg. 2000/15, U.N. Doc. UNTAET/REG/2000/15, June 6, 2000. Although the jurisdiction over crimes against humanity and the other international crimes was not time limited, the Serious Crimes Unit focused its prosecutions on the crimes surrounding the 1999 referendum.

[93] UNTAET Reg. 2000/16, U.N. Doc. UNTAET/REG/2000/16, June 6, 2000.

[94] *See* David Cohen, *Seeking Justice on the Cheap: Is the East Timor Tribunal Really a Model for the Future?*, ASIA PACIFIC ISSUES (August 2002) at 5, *available at* http://www.eastwestcenter.org/stored/pdfs/api061.pdf; Suzanne Katzenstein, *Hybrid Tribunals: Searching for Justice in East Timor*, 16 HARV. HUM. RTS. J. 245, 251, 262–264 (2003).

[95] For analysis of the Defense Lawyer's Unit, *see* Commission of Experts Report, *supra* note 51, at 36–37.

[96] Cohen, *Seeking Justice on the Cheap, supra* note 94, at 5; Katzenstein, *Hybrid Tribunals, supra* note 94, at 260.

[97] Cohen, *Seeking Justice on the Cheap, supra* note 94, at 5–6; Katzenstein, *Hybrid Tribunals, supra* note 94, at 253.

hamper the tribunal, which concluded its last trials in 2005, with appeals to be completed in 2006.[98]

Substantively, the hybrid tribunal's impact in terms of demonstrating accountability and fair justice has been ambiguous, at best. On the one hand, the tribunal tried a significant number of individuals for crimes against humanity and other offenses in proceedings that an international commission of experts concluded generally accorded with international standards.[99] A total of eighty-seven defendants were tried, with eighty-four convicted and three acquitted.[100] The Serious Crimes Unit also issued many indictments – a total of 95 against 440 defendants – including some against high-level Indonesian military officials.[101] On the other hand, the vast majority of the accused (339 individuals) are beyond the physical jurisdiction of the court (mostly in Indonesia), and they are unlikely ever to be either extradited to East Timor for trial or credibly tried in Indonesia – absent sustained international pressure on Indonesia, which has not been forthcoming, particularly since 9/11. The net result is that East Timor's hybrid tribunal tried only mid- and lower-level indictees, mostly Timorese ex-militia members involved in the violence surrounding the referendum, but did not reach the higher-level suspects in Indonesia. When those at the top never face justice, it sends a very mixed message about accountability to Timorese citizens.

The situation of Indonesia's General Wiranto illustrates this dilemma. Wiranto, who was defense minister and commander of the armed forces of Indonesia at the time of the Timorese referendum, is charged, along with six

[98] The UN Security Council decided to conclude the mandate of the special panels in May 2005 when UNMISET's mandate ended, and it urged that all trials be concluded by then. S.C. Res. 1543, U.N. Doc. S/RES/1543, May 14, 2004. In fact, some appeals were handled subsequently and, as of February 2006, two defendants still had appeals pending. *See* Judicial System Monitoring Programme, *available at* http://www.jsmp.minihub.org/ (follow hyperlinks under SPSC Case Information).

[99] Commission of Experts Report, *supra* note 51, para. 357, at 86.

[100] *See* Judicial System Monitoring Programme, *The Special Panels for Serious Crimes Hear Their Final Case, Justice Update*, May 12–May 20, Issue 12/2005, *available at* http://www.jsmp.minihub.org (hereinafter *JSMP Justice Update*). For information on cases, *see* the JSMP Web site, as well as American University, War Crimes Research Office, Special Panels for Serious Crimes in East Timor Status Updates, *available at* http://www.wcl.american.edu/warcrimes/easttimor_status.cfm.

[101] *JSMP Justice Update, supra* note 100. Those indicted include General Wiranto (former Defense Minister and Commander of the Armed Forces of Indonesia), Major General Zacky Anwar Makarim (Security Task Force Advisor), Major General Adam Damiri (former chief of the Regional Military Command), Brigadier General Suhartono Suratman (former Military Commander for East Timor), Colonel Mohmanned Noer Muis (Commander of the Sub-Regional Command 164), Brigadier General Timbul Silaen (former Chief of Police for East Timor), and Lieutenant Colonel Yayat Sudrajat (Commander of the Intelligence Task Force of Sub-Regional Command 164). Amnesty International & Judicial System Monitoring Programme, *Justice for Timor-Leste: The Way Forward,* April 2004, *available at*: http://news.amnesty.org/library/index/engasa210062004.

other high-ranking Indonesian military officers and the former governor of East Timor, with committing crimes against humanity – murder, deportation, and persecution – in 1999.[102] After many months, the special court issued a warrant for his arrest, but East Timorese officials refrained from handing the warrant to Interpol for international action. Key Timorese leaders, including President Xanana Gusmao, have placed a higher priority on forward-looking reconciliation and on building a strong relationship with Indonesia than on seeking judicial accountability for the 1999 atrocities.[103] Gusmao, in particular, has argued that pressing Indonesia might produce a military backlash just at a moment when the country was struggling to solidify its own democratic reforms.[104] Indeed, Gusmao met with Wiranto – then a candidate for president of Indonesia – in 2004, just before the Indonesian elections, proclaiming that bygones should be bygones.[105] Although other Timorese officials, such as Foreign Minister Jose Ramos-Horta, were critical of this meeting and its timing,[106] few Timorese leaders are comfortable pressuring their powerful neighbor to hand over top figures given their strong desire to improve East Timor's economy, to resolve border issues, and generally to build cordial relations with Indonesia. Even East Timor's prosecutor-general, who earlier had emphasized the importance of bringing Wiranto to justice, later backed off.[107]

Timorese political leaders consistently have emphasized the importance of consolidating East Timor's independence and building a strong relationship with Indonesia. Ramos-Horta has stressed, moreover, that "independence is a form of justice."[108] This is an important point from someone who, along with Gusmao and many others, devoted his career to East Timor's long and historic struggle for independence. Independence for the Timorese people

[102] Wiranto is charged under the principle of command responsibility. The February 2003 indictment is available on the JSMP Web site at http://www.jsmp.minihub.org/index.htm (follow link to SPSC Case Information for 2003).

[103] President Gusmao was elected overwhelmingly as East Timor's first president, and he has placed a strong emphasis on looking forward. Gusmao has focused on pursuing economic development and "social justice" in East Timor – and on achieving reconciliation and reintegrating resistance fighters and remaining remnants of opposing militias into Timorese society. *See* Rachel S. Taylor, *Justice and Reconciliation in East Timor, Interview: East Timorese President Xanana Gusmao*, WORLD PRESS REVIEW, October 1, 2002, *available at* http://www.worldpress.org/Asia/743.cfm. Gusmao has also sought to establish constructive relations with Indonesia – East Timor's powerful neighbor and key trading partner.

[104] *See, e.g.*, Letter dated June 22, 2005 from the President of Timor-Leste to the Secretary-General, Annex I to letter dated July 14, 2005 from the Secretary-General addressed to the President of the Security Council, U.N. Doc. S/2005/459, July 15, 2005, at 3.

[105] *East Timor's Foreign Minister Questions Gusmao's Meeting With Wiranto*, ASSOCIATED PRESS (May 30, 2004).

[106] Id.

[107] *Forwarding Wiranto Warrant to Interpol Not in E. Timor Interest: Prosecutor*, AGENCE FRANCE PRESS (May 25, 2004).

[108] Interview with Foreign Minister Jose Ramos-Horta in Dili, Timor Leste (November 2003).

does provide tangible vindication for their struggle and their suffering. And East Timor clearly needs to consolidate its long-sought independence and to build constructive relationships with its neighbors.

Yet lack of accountability has been a bitter pill to swallow. As many human rights advocates, church leaders, and civil society organizations in East Timor and elsewhere emphasize, the victims and survivors of the brutal atrocities in 1999 – and during the much longer quarter century of Indonesian occupation – deserve to know the truth about who was responsible, and those who bear the greatest responsibility need to be held accountable in some way. East Timor's Commission for Reception, Truth and Reconciliation has argued that "the crimes committed in 1999 were far outweighed by those committed during the previous 24 years of occupation and cannot be properly understood or addressed without acknowledging the truth of the long conflict"; the Commission also urges that the mandate of the Special Panels and Serious Crimes Unit be renewed so that they can concentrate on key cases from the longer period of 1975–1999, and it calls for a serious effort on Indonesia's part to hold major perpetrators accountable as well.[109] Realistically, this will only happen if there is much stronger and more consistent international pressure on Indonesia to live up to its earlier commitment to pursue accountability domestically, as well as international support for an international accountability mechanism of some kind if this does not occur.

Within Indonesia, however, the recent trend has been in the exact opposite direction. In August 2004, an Indonesian court overturned the convictions of four Indonesian security officials previously found guilty of crimes against humanity in the violence in East Timor.[110] No reasons were given for the court's reversal. These acquittals mean that no Indonesian security officials are serving time for the horrific violence and brutality perpetrated against the East Timorese in the period surrounding its referendum.[111]

109 *Chega!: Final Report of the CAVR, supra* note 6, Part 11: Recommendations, at 23–25.

110 Evelyn Rusli, *Indonesia Court Voids 4 Convictions in 1999 East Timor Strife*, THE NEW YORK TIMES, August 7, 2004, at A2.

111 In the end, all those tried before Indonesia's Ad Hoc Human Rights Court "were acquitted either at trial or on appeal except for one, Eurico Guterres, whose appeal has yet to be heard." Commission of Experts Report, *supra* note 51, at para.171. The August 2004 acquittals triggered sharply divergent reactions. They caused an outcry among human rights NGOs, both domestic and international, and provoked strong statements by a number of governments. But many Timorese officials took a very different view. Foreign Minister Ramos-Horta expressed support for an international truth commission but opposed an international criminal tribunal. Prosecution of Indonesian officials, he argued, could be destabilizing within Indonesia and would undermine East Timor's efforts to improve its relations with Indonesia. Dan Eaton, *East Timor Urges End to Push for UN Tribunal*, REUTERS, August 9, 2004; *East Timor's Foreign Minister Opposes Rights Tribunal*, ASSOCIATED PRESS, September 8, 2004. For a discussion and critique of the Indonesian prosecutions before the Ad Hoc Human Rights Court, *see* Commission of Experts Report, *supra* note 51, at 38–80.

Meanwhile, in East Timor, the capacity-building impact of the hybrid tribunal, like its accountability record, has been mixed. Valuable experience clearly has been gained by Timorese judges serving on the Special Panels and by Timorese investigators and prosecutors working in the Serious Crimes Unit. The fact that the Timorese judges serving on the trial and appellate panels are also part of the domestic justice system and likely will continue to serve there means that their experience on the Special Panels – in trial procedures, opinion-drafting, and so forth – will be of direct benefit to the national courts.[112] This is valuable capacity-building. Nevertheless, language barriers among the national and international judges limited the opportunities for exchange of ideas and mutual learning. Also, salary and support arrangements made Timorese judges on the Special Panels sometimes feel like second-class citizens.[113] A lack of systematic and well-planned training early on also constrained the capacity-building potential of the hybrid tribunal.[114]

On the prosecution side, few Timorese were integrated into top positions in the serious crimes prosecutorial office. More generally, the stark contrast in resources between the Serious Crimes Unit and East Timor's "ordinary crimes" capacity presented a constant struggle for East Timor's prosecutor-general, Longuinhos Monteiro, who headed both components and whose five district prosecutors had no land phone lines by which to communicate.[115] Monteiro expressed concern that when the tribunal's mandate ended (as it did in 2005) and the UN departed, equipment and resources on which Timorese prosecutors in the Serious Crimes Unit had come to depend would also leave with the UN, despite the considerable domestic legal challenges that would remain.[116] As of February 2006, the wrap-up arrangements, including provisions for storage of the Serious Crime Unit's files, were being

[112] Although, as we discussed in Chapter 6, Timorese judges failed their exams to move beyond probationary status, they are engaged in intensive training programs and many passed their midterm evaluation. *See* U.N. Doc. S/2006/24, *Progress Report of the Secretary-General on the United Nations Office in Timor-Leste,* January 17, 2006, para. 19.

[113] The United Nations pays the salaries of international judges, prosecutors, and investigators. Timorese counterparts are paid at local rates by the Timorese government. It is not so much salary differentials but rather some differences in basic support – such as computers and other resources – that has grated on some Timorese judges, for instance.

[114] This has been a more general problem in the East Timorese judicial system. *See* Katzenstein, *Hybrid Tribunals, supra* note 94, at 265–268.

[115] Interview with Prosecutor-General Longuinhos Monteiro in Dili, Timor-Leste (November 2003).

[116] Id. In the end, the UN-funded Serious Crimes Unit was able to investigate only less "than half of the estimated 1,450 murders committed in 1999." U.N. Doc. S/2005/533, *Progress Report of the Secretary-General on the United Nations Office in Timor-Leste,* August 18, 2005, para. 49. Arrangements for storing the Serious Crime Unit's original files in Timor Leste, and for storing a complete copy of these records at the United Nations are being finalized. Id., at paras.12–14. For discussion of the conclusion of the tribunal's mandate, see *supra* note 98.

finalized. On the defense side, the capacity-building has been more limited. Internationals largely handled the defense in serious crimes cases, while providing some training for Timorese public defenders.[117] In short, important local capacity-building clearly has taken place, but the potential offered by East Timor's hybrid arrangement has been realized only partially.

To sum up: The mixed results of East Timor's Special Panels reflect the broader ambivalence of Timorese leaders, UN officials, and major governments about pressing Indonesia too hard. Other goals – consolidating independence, forging political and economic ties, resolving outstanding border issues, counterterrorism cooperation – have consistently taken higher priority. Given how closely East Timor's fate is tied to that of Indonesia, and taking into account the broader international unwillingness to pressure Jakarta, the path chosen by East Timor's leaders is understandable. Nevertheless, disappointment within East Timor about the limited accountability for the 1999 atrocities, and more broadly for atrocities throughout the long Indonesian occupation, may fester unless more is done to seek meaningful accountability.[118] Furthermore, Indonesia's unwillingness to acknowledge the responsibility of specific Indonesian military leaders and militia forces for the violence in East Timor perpetuates a pattern of impunity that bodes poorly for its human rights accountability in other contexts.

Against this background, it is hardly surprising that the decision of East Timor and Indonesia to establish a bilateral Commission of Truth and Friendship (CTF) in late 2004 has evoked ambivalent responses within East Timor.[119] According to its terms of reference, the CTF aims to "resolve residual problems of the past" and to "establish the conclusive truth" regarding "the events prior to and immediately after the popular consultations," including the "nature, causes and the extent" of the human rights violations, and to do so through "a forward looking and reconciliatory approach"

[117] Katzenstein, *Hybrid Tribunals, supra* note 94, at 263, 267. *See also* Commission of Experts Report, *supra* note 51, at 36–37.

[118] As we discuss below, many Timorese participating in the community-based reconciliation proceedings have expressed strong disappointment that many of those who committed serious crimes have not been prosecuted at all. *See Chega!: Final Report of the CAVR, supra* note 6, Part 9: Community Reconciliation, at 48 (para. 170); Zifcak, *Restorative Justice in East Timor, supra* note 11, at 41; Pigou, *An Evaluation of the Community Reconciliation Process, supra* note 11, at 100–101; Commission of Experts Report, *supra* note 51, at 89 (para. 381) (citing 2004 opinion poll in which "52 per cent of the population responded that justice must be sought even if it slows down reconciliation with Indonesia, while 39 per cent favoured reconciliation even if that meant significantly reducing efforts to seek justice").

[119] The leaders of Indonesia and East Timor met in Bali on December 14, 2004, to establish the Commission of Truth and Friendship. Information about the Commission, including its terms of reference and members, is available on its Web site at http://www.ctf-ri-tl.org. The Commission has ten members, five of whom are Indonesian and five Timorese, including the Chair of East Timor's CAVR.

that "will not lead to prosecution and will emphasize institutional responsibilities."[120] The CTF ultimately will issue a report that will establish a "shared historical record" and recommend measures to "heal the wounds of the past." Human rights and victims groups in East Timor, however, have expressed deep concern about aspects of the CTF's mandate, particularly the idea of "amnesty for those involved in human rights violations who cooperate fully in revealing the truth."[121] There is also concern that the Commission will face pressure from the Indonesian side not to call senior military leaders at all, and that it will backtrack on what has already been accomplished thus far in documenting the historical record and issuing indictments.

C. East Timor's Innovative Community Reconciliation Procedures

Within East Timor, it is the Commission for Reception, Truth and Reconciliation (CAVR) that may ultimately have the greater domestic impact, particularly through its innovative community reconciliation procedures and through its comprehensive report and recommendations. An independent body supported by voluntary contributions, the CAVR included seven national commissioners and twenty-nine regional commissioners and was chaired by Aniceto Guterres Lopes, an accomplished and widely respected Timorese human rights lawyer.[122] From 2001 until it completed its over-2000 page report in 2005, the Commission worked diligently to seek the truth regarding human rights violations in East Timor during the period between April 1974 and October 1999, reaching out to citizens throughout East Timor, gathering testimony from victims, and holding a series of major public hearings.[123] The CAVR was also charged with assisting the reception and reintegration of individuals into their communities after the long period of political conflict in East Timor.

The Commission's community reconciliation process made a unique contribution to this goal. The Commission's staff traveled throughout the country to visit communities affected by violence during the Indonesian

[120] Terms of Reference for the Commission of Truth and Friendship, paras. 7–14, *available at* http://www.ctf-ri-tl.org.

[121] Id., at para. 14.b.i.

[122] The commission was supported by voluntary contributions from states, nongovernmental organizations, and individuals. Established by UNTAET in 2001, the commission's mandate was negotiated with Timorese leaders. *See* UNTAET Reg. 2001/10, U.N. Doc. UNTAET/REG/2001/10, July 13, 2001; Carsten Stahn, *Accommodating Individual Criminal Responsibility and National Reconciliation: The UN Truth Commission for East Timor*, 95 AM. J. INT'L L. 952 (2001). The commission was headquartered at Dili's former Balide Prison, the site of horrific torture and atrocities during Indonesian rule – a location that will become a museum once the commission's work is finished.

[123] *See Chega!: Final Report of the CAVR*, *supra* note 6.

occupation. Working with community leaders, the Commission established panels composed of a regional commissioner and local leaders before which community-based reconciliation proceedings took place. The involvement of traditional local leaders helped provided legitimacy within communities, but the Commission also took pains to ensure that women and young people were included in the process.[124] This helped to empower some new voices in traditional community settings.

Under a carefully devised procedure, individuals who committed lesser offenses – such as looting or minor assault – were able to acknowledge what they had done in a public hearing before their community, express contrition, and enter into a "community reconciliation agreement" (CRA). Prosecutors in the Serious Crimes Unit reviewed written statements from these individuals before the community hearings even took place in order to determine whether the person was eligible to participate or, instead, potentially liable for prosecution for more serious crimes. Eligible individuals who concluded CRAs are immune from civil liability or criminal prosecution for the acts underlying the agreement. The CRAs were registered with district courts, however, providing a link to the formal justice system in the event of non-compliance.

The Commission received more than 1500 statements from individuals (called deponents) wishing to participate in the process. Ultimately, 1371 deponents completed the community reconciliation process, and the CAVR estimates that up to 3000 more might have participated had the process continued for a longer time. Over 40,000 Timorese – nearly 5 percent of the total population – attended the community hearings held throughout the country.[125]

These community reconciliation proceedings have had three results or accomplishments, in the view of the Commission's chair, Aniceto Guterres Lopes.[126] First, they helped to stabilize the situation in rural areas after a turbulent period. Second, they provided a sense of justice processes in communities throughout the country that have limited access to formal courts. The proceedings "reinforced the value of the rule of law, and contributed to the fight against impunity by resolving a significant number of cases that could not realistically have been dealt with through the formal justice system."[127] Third, the community reconciliation process encouraged local cultural traditions of reconciliation and conflict resolution. They

[124] The CAVR followed the requirement of its mandate "that a minimum 30% of all Regional Commissioners be women" and that community reconciliation panels have "appropriate gender representation." Id. Part 9: Community Reconciliation, at 43 (para. 154).

[125] *Chega!: Final Report of the CAVR*, *supra* note 6, Part 9: Community Reconciliation, at 29, 43, 47.

[126] Interview with CAVR Chair Aniceto Guterres Lopes in Dili, Timor-Leste (Nov. 2003).

[127] *Chega!: Final Report of the CAVR*, *supra* note 6, Part 9: Community Reconciliation, at 47.

also provided some valuable mediation training and capacity-building to panel members and other participants. These accomplishments are steps in building a foundation for further development of the rule of law in East Timor.

Not surprisingly, the community-based reconciliation procedures were more successful in some communities than in others. The hearings attracted significant numbers of people in many communities. Some participants confessed to specific offenses such as looting, whereas others acknowledged only a general association with Indonesian police or authorities. Some community reconciliation agreements required individuals to provide concrete restitution to victims – such as rebuilding a destroyed home, returning stolen goods, or repaying a victim for lost livestock – or to engage in forms of community service such as working on damaged school buildings or assisting orphanages or churches.[128] Many CRAs, however, simply involved a formal, public apology before the community.[129] Some individuals seemed genuinely contrite in these reconciliation proceedings, others far less so. The impact of the proceedings thus no doubt has varied in different communities and among different participants.

Most of the deponents who entered into community reconciliation agreements have expressed clear satisfaction with the process. A number of former militia members, for instance, have felt that the procedures helped them integrate more effectively into their communities.[130]

The response among victims has been more mixed, however, for a number of reasons. For some, the confessions of the deponents were not as forthright as hoped for, and the CRAs in many cases were not very demanding.[131] Victims hoping for more information about the fate of their loved ones were sometimes disappointed. Some victims found the proceedings and the public apology before the community to be a constructive and affirming experience, but others felt a certain sense of pressure or community expectation that they

[128] Pigou, *The Community Reconciliation Process of the Commission for Reception, Truth and Reconciliation, supra* note 11, at 56.

[129] Id. As Zifcak explains, as the reconciliation process unfolded over time, "simple apology" became more common as the basis of reconciliation agreements: "A straightforward apology embodied in a legal document signed by all parties combined with a commitment not to take part in any similar activities became, then, the quickest and easiest means of obtaining some form of closure, which in turn signaled 'success.'" Zifcak, *Restorative Justice in East Timor, supra* note 11, at 22. For additional reflections on why only apology was required in many CRAs, *see Chega!: Final Report of the CAVR, supra* note 6, Part 9: Community Reconciliation, at 33.

[130] Pigou, *The Community Reconciliation Process of the Commission for Reception, Truth and Reconciliation, supra* note 11, at 81; *Chega!: Final Report of the CAVR, supra* note 6, Part 9: Community Reconciliation, at 33–34.

[131] Pigou, *The Community Reconciliation Process of the Commission for Reception, Truth and Reconciliation, supra* note 11, at 81–83; Zifcak, *Restorative Justice in East Timor, supra* note 11, at 20–22, 25–26.

would reconcile with perpetrators.[132] The CAVR acknowledges that clearer guidelines regarding the role of victims in the proceedings and a greater focus on their needs would have been beneficial.[133]

Despite the range of reactions to the community reconciliation procedures, they do seem to have brought some sense of justice procedures to rural communities that have little access to the country's formal justice system. The emphasis on confession, forgiveness, and reconciliation also had deep cultural resonance in predominantly Catholic East Timor. Problematic, however, is a lingering sense of injustice and inequity that many Timorese feel because of the failure of the Serious Crimes Unit and Special Panels to bring to justice many who committed more serious offenses. For many Timorese, support for the community reconciliation process was tied to expectations that serious offenders living within their communities would be brought to justice. Yet the vast majority have not been investigated or charged. When lesser offenders conclude reconciliation agreements but more serious offenders often face no process at all, the resulting "justice deficit" has disappointed public expectations of fair accountability.[134]

Unfortunately, the circumstances surrounding the release of the CAVR's final report have also created a sense of injustice in East Timor. In late 2005, the CAVR completed and presented its report to President Gusmao, who subsequently presented it to the Timorese parliament. But, as of February 2006, the report had not been publicly released within East Timor, despite the fact that it had been presented to UN Secretary-General Annan and was available in full or in part on various Web sites.[135] The fact that the

[132] Zifcak, *Restorative Justice in East Timor, supra* note 11, at 20–22, 25–26. *See also Chega!, Final Report of the* CAVR, *supra* note 6, Part 9: Community Reconciliation, at 39.

[133] *Chega!: Final Report of the CAVR, supra* note 6, Part 9: Community Reconciliation, at 39 (para. 33) (noting that "[g]uidelines establishing a right of victims to a say in the decision on what 'acts of reconciliation' the perpetrator should perform, and a stronger place for victims in the formal decision-making structure of the CRP would have helped to ensure that their interests were not overlooked.").

[134] For analysis of this problem, *see Chega!: Final Report of the CAVR, supra* note 6, Part 9: Community Reconciliation, at 48 (para. 170); Zifcak, *Restorative Justice in East Timor, supra* note 11, at 41; Pigou, *The Community Reconciliation Process of the Commission for Reception, Truth and Reconciliation, supra* note 11, at 100–101. Less than half of the 1450 murders estimated to have been committed in 1999 were ultimately investigated by the Serious Crimes Unit. U.N. Doc. S/2005/533, *Progress Report of the Secretary-General on the United Nations Office in Timor-Leste,* August 18, 2005, para. 49.

[135] The commission submitted its report to President Gusmao on October 31, 2005, who presented it to East Timor's parliament and cabinet in November 2005. In January 2006, President Gusmao presented the report to UN Secretary-General Annan. Yet, as of February 2006, the report had not been publicly released in East Timor, even though the CAVR's mandate provides that the report "shall be immediately available to the public and shall be published in the Official Gazette." UNTAET Reg. 2001/10, U.N. Doc. UNTAET/REG/2001/10, July 13, 2001, section 21.3. The report has been available in full on the Web site of the International Center for Transitional Justice since January 30, 2006, *see* http://www.ictj.org in

report has not been presented publicly in East Timor – when it is otherwise widely available – is perplexing and upsetting to many Timorese human rights and victims organizations and to members of the public. It remains to be seen whether and how this will be rectified, and whether many of the Commission's important and innovative recommendations are taken up by the Timorese government and by other states.

D. Sierra Leone's Special Court: A Promising Hybrid

Though it faces many challenges, Sierra Leone's Special Court is probably the criminal tribunal that has been best able, thus far, to begin realizing in practice the potential benefits of a hybrid accountability mechanism. The tribunal has made a reasonably strong start in its primary mission of seeking justice and accountability for the brutal atrocities that marked Sierra Leone's decade-long civil war – a war that claimed the lives of an estimated 75,000 people and displaced a third of the country's population.[136] Two major trials began in summer 2004. These include the trial of three leaders of the RUF – the Revolutionary United Front – who are accused of horrific crimes against humanity and war crimes, including terrorizing the civilian population, rape, murder, amputations, abduction of women into forced "marriages," and forced recruitment of child soldiers.[137] Also on trial are three leaders of the CDF – Civilian Defense Forces – who are on trial for multiple counts of crimes against humanity and war crimes, including murder, inhumane acts, terrorizing the civilian population, and conscripting child soldiers.[138] A third trial against three members of the AFRC – Armed Forces Revolutionary Council – for similar crimes began in March 2005. One year later, in March 2006, former Liberian President Charles Taylor was finally taken into custody by the Special Court, where he stands charged with eleven

English and Bahasa Indonesia, but, as of February 2006, translation of the Report's introduction into Tetum had not been completed.

[136] Institute for Transitional Justice, *The Special Court for Sierra Leone: The First Eighteen Months*, 2004, at 1, *available at* http://www.ictj.org/downloads/SC_SL_Case_Study_designed.pdf. For a discussion of the conflict, *see* Avril D. Haines, *Accountability in Sierra Leone: The Role of the Special Court, in* ACCOUNTABILITY FOR ATROCITIES, *supra* note 12, at 176.

[137] The RUF leaders on trial are Issa Hassan Sesay, Morris Kallon, and Augustine Gbao. *See* http://www.sc-sl.org/RUF.html. In his opening statement, Special Court prosecutor David Crane described a meeting on February 27, 1991, in which Liberia's Charles Taylor, along with RUF General Foday Sankoh and others, planned the invasion of Sierra Leone and the capture of its diamond-rich areas – an invasion that set in motion the devastating decade-long conflict in Sierra Leone.

[138] Sam Hinga Norman, former Commander of the Civilian Defense Force (CDF) and former Deputy Defense Minister and Minister of Internal Affairs, is one of the three accused in this case. The other two accused are Allieu Kondewa and Moinina Fofana. *See* http://www.sc-sl.org/CDF.html. The three members of the AFRC on trial are Alex Tamba Brima, Brima Bazzy Kamara, and Santigie Borbor Kanu. *See* http://www.sc-sl.org/AFRC.html.

counts of crimes against humanity, war crimes, and other serious violations of international humanitarian law, including terrorizing the civilian population, murder, rape, sexual slavery, and use of child soldiers.[139]

The Special Court, established in 2002 by agreement between the government of Sierra Leone and the United Nations, was a deliberate effort to design a tribunal that could overcome some of the limitations of purely international or purely domestic proceedings.[140] In many ways, the Court's structure and mandate reflected the lessons – the "accountability learning curve" – of the previous decade. As a hybrid tribunal supported by the United Nations – with both international and domestic judges, prosecutors, investigators, defense counsel, and administrators – the Special Court has greater resources and credibility than Sierra Leone's struggling domestic justice system.[141] Yet the Court's physical location in Sierra Leone, with nationals participating in each of its components, provides important opportunities for building domestic capacity – and for extensive outreach efforts designed to deepen public understanding and expectations of accountability and fair justice, producing a more direct impact on the local population. In contrast to the enormous expense and open-ended time frames of the ICTY and ICTR, Sierra Leone's Special Court has a mandate focused on those who bear "the greatest responsibility" for serious violations of international humanitarian law – a mandate that the Court's original prosecutor, David Crane, argued is manageable and achievable in a time frame that he believes should allow both justice to be done and wounds to begin to heal as Sierra Leone moves forward.[142]

[139] Taylor's indictment, and a summary of the charges against him, are available on the Web site of the Special Court for Sierra Leone, *available at* http://www.sc-sl.org/Taylor.html. Taylor was taken into custody by the Special Court on March 29, 2006, and he was arraigned on April 3, 2006.

[140] The court's design also reflected political compromises as, for example, in the time frame of its jurisdiction. Haines, *Accountability in Sierra Leone, supra* note 136, at 214–215; *see also* J. Peter Pham, *Politics and International Justice in a World of States*, 4 HUM. RTS. & HUM. WELFARE 119, 131–32 (2004).

[141] The court has primacy over Sierra Leone's domestic courts and is a "mixed" or "hybrid" tribunal in at least two ways: its staff includes both international and national personnel, and it has authority to prosecute certain offenses under international law and under Sierra Leonean law. As a treaty-based court explicitly empowered to try those bearing "the greatest responsibility for violations of international humanitarian law" committed in Sierra Leone since November 30, 1996, the tribunal can prosecute those shielded from domestic prosecution by the amnesty of the 1999 Lome Agreement. Haines, *Accountability in Sierra Leone, supra* note 136, at 213.

[142] Interview with prosecutor David Crane in Freetown, Sierra Leone (June 2004). Crane argued that the mandate, in his view, was achievable within a time frame of three to five years. Id. *See also* David Crane, *Dancing with the Devil: Prosecuting West Africa's Warlords, Current Lessons Learned and Challenges*, in COLLOQUIUM OF PROSECUTORS OF INTERNATIONAL CRIMINAL TRIBUNALS, ARUSHA (2004) at 4–5, *available at* http://65/18/216/88/ENGLISH/colloquim04/04 (hereinafter Crane, *Dancing*).

The Special Court has faced some but not all of the practical challenges of earlier hybrid tribunals. Maintaining adequate and reliable funding has been an ongoing concern, because the Special Court depends primarily on voluntary donations.[143] Nevertheless, starting up its operations with voluntary rather than UN-assessed funding actually proved to be beneficial because it gave the Court flexibility in hiring, enabling it to assemble an extremely talented staff very quickly. The Court has also managed to blend national and international staff quite well,[144] avoiding some of the disparities in salaries and support that created tensions, for instance, in East Timor.[145] Language barriers between international and national staff have not been an issue here, so easier exchange and give-and-take between staff is more possible. The Special Court's Defense Office also represents an important (and earlier) effort to achieve greater equality between the prosecution and the defense than has been the case in other tribunals.[146] Still, the many practical disparities between support for the prosecution and for the defense have been a continuing issue.[147]

[143] For instance, insufficient voluntary contributions led to a budget shortfall of about US $20 million in the tribunal's third year of operations, requiring a one-time UN contribution of over $16 million. Commission of Experts Report, *supra* note 51, at 29, para. 103.

[144] Each of the Special Court's four components – chambers, office of the prosecutor, defense office, and registry – is an interesting blend of international and national staff. As of June 2004, for example, the Trial Chambers included three judges: a Sierra Leonean national appointed by the government of Sierra Leone and a Canadian and a Cameroonean appointed by UN Secretary-General Annan. The Appeals Chamber included five judges: a Sierra Leonean and a British/Australian jurist, both appointed by Sierra Leone, and three judges – a Nigerian, a Sri Lankan, and an Austrian – appointed by the Secretary-General. The prosecutor was an American, and approximately 50 percent of the prosecutor's office (which includes investigators) was Sierra Leonean. The first registrar was an experienced British court administrator. The head of outreach is a Sierra Leonean, as are almost all of her staff. The defense office, an innovative component of the court, includes as part of its structure three duty counsel (two were Sierra Leonean and one Gambian, as of June 2004).

[145] The fact that living allowances for local Sierra Leonean jurists are less than for international judges has nevertheless been criticized by some Sierra Leoneans.

[146] The Special Court's registrar, Robin Vincent, was a strong early advocate of establishing a defense component modeled on a public defender's office. His evaluation of the ICTR influenced his views about the need for a more robust defense capacity in Sierra Leone. At Sierra Leone's Special Court, duty counsel in the defense office assist defendants before they have obtained independent counsel; they also provide research support to defense counsel and assist in building a defense and formulating arguments. In addition, the defense office has established a list of qualified defense counsel, and it administers contracts for attorneys appointed to represent indigent defendants and for defense investigators. Still, the Court's administrators will frankly acknowledge that they wish they had built up the defense office earlier and provided it with a greater budget. Nevertheless, it is a considerable and dramatic improvement over the limited support offered to the defense in other tribunals, both hybrid and international.

[147] *See* James Cockayne, *The Fraying Shoestring: Rethinking War Crimes Tribunals*, 28 FORDHAM INT'L L. J. 616, 699–674 (2005).

Sierra Leone's Special Court is very much a work in progress, so it is too early to determine whether, in fact, it will ultimately succeed in delivering meaningful justice to the people of Sierra Leone or in helping to improve domestic capacity for fair justice and the rule of law. A number of positive signs already exist, but there are also areas of concern. In any event, the theoretical benefits of an in-country hybrid do not flow automatically; they require astute planning, considerable resources, and sensitivity to the many practical and political challenges that can arise when a tribunal locates directly in the country most affected by the atrocities.[148]

So far, the glass is at least half full. By indicting those who bear the greatest responsibility for starting and orchestrating the brutal conflict in Sierra Leone, the tribunal helped to disempower and prevent them from again committing such atrocities. Sierra Leoneans agree to a remarkable extent who these people are. In outreach meetings all across the country held by the Special Court's prosecutor, Sierra Leoneans put former Liberian president Charles Taylor at the top of the list. He was followed by two others: RUF commander Foday Sankoh and General Sam Bockarie. All three have been indicted, but only Taylor is still alive to stand trial. (Sankoh died of natural causes in custody; Bockarie was killed in Liberia as was his family, allegedly on Taylor's orders.[149])

Charles Taylor presents the biggest challenge in the struggle for accountability and for peace in West Africa. Virtually everyone agrees that he bears the greatest responsibility for the violence that engulfed Sierra Leone and much of the rest of West Africa. Preventing him from ever again exercising power directly in Liberia – or behind the scenes – is a critical goal in bringing lasting peace to the region. Throughout Sierra Leone, people overwhelmingly support prosecuting him before the Special Court. [150] For two and a half years, however, Taylor was in Nigeria under a grant of asylum brokered as part of his departure from power in Liberia. During this period, the Nigerian government, along with some other African and international leaders, resisted handing Taylor over, arguing that to do so would undermine

[148] *See, e.g.*, id., at 674–675.

[149] The chief of investigations for the Special Court stated in May 2003 that he had "credible information" that Bockarie's family had been killed on orders from Taylor, which "casts serious doubts about [Taylor's] claims regarding the circumstances of Sam Bockarie's death." Press release, *Bockarie's Family Alleged Murdered; Office of the Prosecutor Demands Full Cooperation from Taylor*, Special Court for Sierra Leone, Office of the Prosecutor, May 15, 2003, *available at* http://www.sc-sl.org/Press/prosecutor-051503.html. *See also* U.S. State Department, Bureau of Intelligence & Research, *Background Note on Sierra Leone*, May, 2006, *available at* http://www.state.gov/r/pa/ei/bgn/5475.htm (stating Taylor "probably" directed Bockarie's killing to keep him from testifying).

[150] Sierra Leone's Parliament in February 2006 unanimously adopted a resolution calling for Taylor's trial before the Special Court. Press release, *Prosecutor Welcomes Sierra Leone Parliamentary Resolution Supporting Taylor's Trial at the Special Court*, Special Court for Sierra Leone, Office of the Prosecutor, February 9, 2006, *available at* http://www.sc-sl.org/Press/prosecutor-020906.pdf.

future negotiated departures of dictators as a way to end conflicts.[151] Others, in contrast, argued strongly that ending the impunity of high-level leaders for atrocities – such as those of which Taylor is accused – is an essential step in preventing their recurrence in the region.[152] In the end, as international pressure grew for holding Taylor to account, and after a newly elected government in Liberia called for his prosecution, Nigeria handed Taylor over to the Special Court in March 2006.

As Taylor arrived and was taken into custody in Sierra Leone, hundreds of Sierra Leoneans gathered in the hills of Freetown near the Special Court to commemorate this dramatic day. Yet, whether Taylor's trial would, in fact, be held in Sierra Leone, as many hoped, or instead would take place in The Hague before a panel of the Special Court for Sierra Leone assembled there, was yet to be determined. Taylor's trial raises special issues of security and stability as a result of his role in West Africa's conflicts. In the end, the Special Court and the government of Sierra Leone requested that his trial be held at The Hague, and Taylor was transferred there in June 2006.

Although it has made considerable progress, the Special Court faces some distinct challenges in demonstrating meaningful accountability for atrocities to the people of Sierra Leone. To demonstrate credibly that justice is fair, the court's proceedings much be widely viewed as legitimate both in terms of their substance (who is being prosecuted for what offenses) and in terms of process. The fact that the prosecution indicted Charles Taylor as well as leaders from all the major groups in Sierra Leone's conflict – the RUF, the AFRC, and the CDF – is important in demonstrating that no one is above the law and in avoiding the perception of victor's justice.

Still, there are difficult, lingering issues that may affect the perceived legitimacy of the trials among the Sierra Leonean population. For one, Charles Taylor's long-awaited prosecution before the Special Court has raised public expectations of accountability that may be disappointed, at least to some extent, by the decision to hold the trial outside of Sierra Leone, thus making the proceedings less accessible to the local population.[153] Second, the trial of CDF leader and former Interior Minister Sam Hinga Norman has generated controversy, at least initially: many regard him as a hero who acted to

[151] For discussion of the controversy over the Special Court's unveiling of the sealed indictment against Taylor during a peace negotiation in Ghana and subsequent differences of view over Nigeria's offer of amnesty to Taylor, see Pham, *Politics and International Justice in a World of States*, *supra* note 140, at 131–133.

[152] *See* Zainab Bangura, op-ed., *Flouting the Rule of Law*, The Washington Post, June 25, 2004, at A29.

[153] *See* John E. Leigh, op-ed, *Bringing It All Back Home*, The New York Times, April 17, 2006, at A25. Leigh, who is Sierra Leone's former ambassador to the United States, argues that transferring Taylor to The Hague for trial "would defeat a principal purpose behind the establishment of the special court in Sierra Leone – namely, to teach Africans, firsthand and in their own countries, the fundamentals of justice and to drive home that no one is above the law." Id.

defend Sierra Leone from the RUF, and the court's outreach staff has had to work hard to explain that he is being tried for serious atrocities in violation of international law – that regardless of one's cause, there are clear limits on how one can fight. Third, many Sierra Leoneans express frustration that many individuals who did the actual chopping, raping, and killing remain free. As one amputee put it, "the person who chopped off my hand lives down the street; if there is no justice, my children may seek vengeance."[154] Or as one local TV journalist, critical of the peacekeeping forces of the Economic Community of West African States, exclaimed: "ECOMOG forces killed my brother and raped my sister, so why aren't they being tried?"[155] In other words, although Sierra Leoneans support trying those who bear "the greatest responsibility" for the atrocities, there remains frustration that other, lower-level offenders are not being held accountable as well.

The Special Court's processes also need to be perceived as fair to credibly demonstrate a norm of accountability and impartial justice. The fact that both international and national jurists and staff participate in the work of the Special Court has enhanced its legitimacy among the local population. But even so, the Special Court's local outreach officers have encountered skepticism in both directions: some Sierra Leoneans, based on negative perceptions of the country's own judicial system, needed reassurance that the Sierra Leonean jurists on the court would, in fact, be impartial; others wondered whether the court was being forced upon Sierra Leone by international actors. Still, the tribunal seems to enjoy considerable support and legitimacy in Sierra Leone.[156]

To sustain this perception, the tribunal needs to conduct demonstrably fair trials. The prosecution team is extremely skilled and well resourced. A significant concern is whether defense counsel will be effective enough and have sufficient resources to mount a high-quality defense or to effectively assist defendants who have opted to represent themselves, such as former Interior Minister Sam Hinga Norman. Ensuring that the defense has the personnel and resources to present a credible defense will be important to the legitimacy of the proceedings. But beyond the issue of a technically skilled defense, whether Sierra Leoneans ultimately will regard the Special Court

[154] Town hall meeting with Amputee Association in Freetown, Sierra Leone, June 2004.

[155] Interview in Freetown, Sierra Leone, June 2004. ECOMOG is the acronym for forces of the Economic Community of West African States (ECOWAS) that deployed to Sierra Leone in response to the conflict. *See ECOMOG: Peacekeeper or Participant?*, BBC NEWSFILE, February 11, 1998, *available at* http://news.bbc.co.uk/2/hi/africa/55719.stm.

[156] For example, in one poll conducted by the Campaign for Good Governance (CGG), a Sierra Leonean NGO, before the trials even began, 67 percent of those surveyed had heard of the court, 62 percent found it necessary, and 61 percent thought the court was intended to benefit the people of Sierra Leone. Cited in International Crisis Group, *The Special Court for Sierra Leone: Promises and Pitfalls of a "New Model,"* 2003), at 17, *available at* http://www.crisisgroup.org/home/index.cfm?id=1803&l=1.

as demonstrating meaningful accountability and fair justice will depend on whether they are convinced – through outreach and other efforts – that defendants such as Sam Hinga Norman are fairly and appropriately being tried for conduct that violates agreed rules.[157] Finally, the trial of Charles Taylor raises a whole host of issues that will demand an extremely disciplined handling of the proceedings by the Special Court's judiciary. The tumultous trials of former leaders Slobodan Milosevic and Saddam Hussein have made clear that such proceedings face the ever-present risk of turning into highly-charged political drama, and thus require judges who can walk a fine line between protecting the accused's rights to speak and maintaining courtroom dignity, order, and efficiency.

1. Outreach: Demonstrating Accountability and Fair Justice

Even though Charles Taylor's trial poses special challenges, it also provides a long-awaited opportunity to demonstrate meaningful accountability and fair justice to the people of Sierra Leone. In fact, systematic outreach to the population of Sierra Leone has been central to the Special Court's work from the very beginning. In September 2002, shortly after he arrived in Freetown, prosecutor David Crane began traveling throughout the country to hear what the Sierra Leonean people had to say about who bore "the greatest responsibility" for the atrocities committed during the brutal conflict. A month later, the office of the prosecutor and the registry conducted outreach together. In the spring of 2003, a chief of outreach was hired, and the outreach office, under the registry, now also has ten district offices throughout Sierra Leone. This substantial outreach program has been vital in engaging the Sierra Leonean people in the work of the court and stands in contrast to the lack of systematic outreach in other post-conflict contexts.

The explicit goal of the Special Court's countrywide outreach program is to "promote understanding of the Special Court and respect for human rights and the rule of law in Sierra Leone."[158] Thus, in addition to providing basic information about the court – how it came about, its authority, structure and procedures, who is indicted for what offenses, and an update on the trials – the outreach office raises broader issues as well. In community town hall meetings and focused workshops around the country, outreach officers aim to demonstrate and illustrate, based on the actual proceedings before

[157] For a skeptical assessment emphasizing the political nature of accountability proceedings, *see* Tim Kelsall, *Politics, Anti-Politics, International Justice: Notes on the Special Court for Sierra Leone*, October 15, 2004 (Submitted at the conference "Settling Accounts: Truth, Justice and Redress in Post-Conflict Societies," Weatherhead Centre for International Affairs, Harvard University, November 1–3, 2004, *available at* http://www.wcfia.harvard.edu/conferences/truthjustice/Papers/KelsallFullPAPER.pdf).

[158] Special Court for Sierra Leone, Outreach Mission Statement.

the court, that no one is above the law, that law can and should be fair, and ultimately that the rule of law is more powerful than the rule of the gun.[159] In a society with limited mass media and a strong oral tradition, these meetings are critical to convey the importance of accountability.

Outreach meetings and workshops frequently involve lively, intense, and wide-ranging conversations on vital, difficult issues. The court's outreach officers work hard, for example, to explain what "fair justice" looks like. A prosecution and defense before an impartial tribunal is an important concept to convey to a population deeply skeptical of the fairness of justice systems and inclined, from bitter experience, to believe that people are simply "on the take." The outreach staff uses the concrete cases before the Special Court to illustrate key principles. For instance, when the appellate chamber ruled that Charles Taylor was not entitled to immunity from prosecution as head of state, this illustrated the concept that no one is above the law. The indictment and trial of former Interior Minister Sam Hinga Norman – controversial in some quarters – illustrates, the outreach officers stress, that the Special Court is not a court controlled by the government. When pressed – as they often are – by victims who ask why the person who chopped off their hand is not being prosecuted, the outreach staff discusses the principle of command responsibility to explain that somebody is answering for the crime. These discussions – led by dynamic Sierra Leoneon outreach officers – are often not easy, but they do wrestle forthrightly with the difficult challenges of justice and accountability.

There is no doubt that these outreach efforts are having an impact. In a society where travel to rural areas is difficult and access to media is limited, the outreach staff has reached out to engage the population on critically important issues. Opinion polls indicate that significant majorities are aware of the court and view its work positively.[160] As the three combined trials of RUF, CDF, and AFRC leaders have proceeded, moreover, the Special Court's public affairs office has produced weekly audio summaries highlighting critical developments in the proceedings, which are widely broadcast over the radio throughout Sierra Leone.

The outreach and public affairs efforts have not been immune from criticism. Some members of the defense staff at the Special Court have expressed

[159] With a chief of outreach and substantial staff in Freetown and ten district offices, the Special Court's outreach office conducts its outreach in a variety of ways. These include "community townhall meetings," held after making arrangements with local chiefs; workshops for special groups (for instance, school pupils and university students, military forces, police, market women, victims, ex-combatants, youths, teachers); and radio discussion programs, among others. Sierra Leonean outreach officers lead these discussions in the local dialects that allow them to best communicate with the participants. Interviews with the chief of outreach and with district outreach officers, Freetown, Sierra Leone, June 2004. *See also* http://www.sc-sl.org/outreach.html.

[160] *See The Special Court for Sierra Leone, supra* note 156, at 17.

frustration that they have not had more opportunity to engage in outreach, particularly after the early efforts by the prosecution.[161] The weekly radio broadcasts of trial proceedings have not been as frequent as some observers would like. And the ability of most Sierra Leoneans to actually attend Special Court proceedings in the capital remains limited, despite court-sponsored programs to bring groups of citizens to Freetown to attend the trials.[162]

More fundamentally, whether the demonstration effects of the trials – and the outreach office's efforts to convey norms of accountability and fair justice throughout the country – will have a longer-term impact within Sierra Leone remains to be seen and is linked to the broader issue of capacity-building and institutionalization of accountability norms.

2. Capacity-Building in Sierra Leone

The Special Court, by virtue of its location and substantial local participation, is in a position to help build domestic capacity directly by increasing the skills and experience of local professionals. The Sierra Leoneans who work at the court as prosecutors, investigators, defense counsel, judges, administrators, outreach officers, and other staff are learning a great deal about international humanitarian law and its basic principles, about the conduct of fair trials, and about substantive issues in their specific areas of responsibility. Interactions between international and national staff are a valuable two-way street of mutual learning – as the international investigators who work hand in hand with their Sierra Leonean counterparts are the first to attest. The unanswered question, however, is how many of the local judges, prosecutors, defense counsel, investigators, and other court staff actually will remain in Sierra Leone after the court completes its work – and consequently continue to use their valuable skills in the national justice system.

The Special Court engages in a second kind of capacity-building, namely, working with NGOs that share a common commitment to accountability. By linking up with organizations committed to advancing fundamental human rights principles, the court can potentially have larger ripple effects within Sierra Leone and help to educate and empower citizens and civil society organizations more broadly.

Two examples illustrate these effects. First, the Special Court's outreach officers worked hard to help establish "Accountability Now Clubs" across the country – clubs of university students to discuss issues of accountability, justice, human rights, and good governance, with the expectation that club members will visit secondary and elementary schools to address these issues and communicate the critical importance of accountability past, present,

[161] Cockayne, *The Fraying Shoestring, supra* note 147, at 672–673.

[162] Human Rights Watch, *Bringing Justice: The Special Court for Sierra Leone: Accessibility and Legacy*, 2004, at 2, *available at* http://hrw.org/reports/2004/sierraleone0904/8.htm.

and future.[163] Second, the outreach staff, along with other court personnel, participate in the Special Court Interactive Forum, a gathering of local and international NGOs that focus primarily on the work of the court and how it can be improved, but that also can network on additional accountability and human rights issues.

Finally, the Special Court is in a position to contribute expertise and training to Sierra Leone's domestic justice system. International investigators at the Special Court, for instance, have trained a number of Sierra Leonean police officers in witness management and protection – a critical issue given the long-term dangers that witnesses take on in coming forward to testify before the Special Court. A number of the court's judges and other legal professionals have lectured on law reform and related topics at local universities and bar associations. More generally, the Special Court has worked with the Sierra Leone Bar Association and with various organizations, both domestic and international, to identify and develop projects aimed at "helping to rebuild a devastated judiciary."[164] The Special Court's resources and the time of its personnel are understandably focused on its core mission of trying those who bear the greatest responsibility for the atrocities committed in Sierra Leone; but there is no doubt that more systematic efforts to provide training and to share expertise with participants in the local justice system would be beneficial.[165]

Ultimately, however, whether the Special Court's capacity-building efforts – the professional skills development of its own staff, the ripple effects of working with local NGOs, and the training and sharing of expertise with local jurists and legal personnel – will make a lasting and sustainable impact on Sierra Leone's domestic justice system and political culture will depend on longer-term reforms within Sierra Leone. The jury clearly is still out on

[163] These clubs exist at eight universities throughout Sierra Leone. *See* http://www.sc-sl.org/outreach.html.

[164] Crane, *Dancing, supra* note 142, at 6–7.

[165] A joint UNDP/ICTJ report recommends that as part of its "legacy" efforts, the Special Court should focus additional attention on substantive law reform in Sierra Leone, on professional development for domestic justice personnel, and on programs to raise greater awareness in the provinces of the Special Court as an example of fair, effective legal process. ICTJ & UNDP, *The "Legacy" of the Special Court for Sierra Leone, supra* note 22, at 1–2. The Special Court's outreach staff has provided training, for instance, to lay personnel working in the customary law system. Working together with the UN Development Programme, the Special Court's outreach staff offered training on fundamental human rights principles to lay magistrates, court clerks, court bailiffs, and other participants in the customary law system. The outreach staff provided information on the Special Court and linked principles that are supposed to govern the application of customary law ("equity, good conscience, and natural justice") to human rights principles of equality, independence, and impartiality. Interview with the director of outreach, Special Court for Sierra Leone, Freetown, Sierra Leone (June 2004). Developing a fairer, more transparent, more equitable system of dispute settlement in the customary law system remains a very long-term challenge, however.

this, and the challenges are immense, as the previous chapter discussed. The degree of outreach and serious dialogue about accountability that the Special Court has inspired is impressive and has indeed sent some ripples of hope through Sierra Leonean society. But the enormous challenge of institutionalizing principles of accountability – including strengthening a weak and underresourced domestic justice system and addressing deep and pervasive problems of corruption and governance – ultimately will determine how sustainable these efforts prove to be.

E. Sierra Leone's Truth and Reconciliation Commission

Sierra Leone's Truth and Reconciliation Commission (TRC) highlighted these broader challenges in its final report. The commission focused on the deeper and more systemic causes of grievance in Sierra Leone – such as lack of transparency and accountability in the use of governmental power, few opportunities for young people, and pervasive corruption.[166] Stressing that many of these causes of conflict have not yet been addressed adequately, the commission recommended reforms to strengthen Sierra Leone's legal and political system, including greater transparency and public access to information and greater accountability of government officials.[167]

As in East Timor, Sierra Leone's TRC gained significant national participation in its work, collecting over 8000 statements from civilians and combatants in Sierra Leone and neighboring countries.[168] Local NGOs and human rights leaders supported creation of the TRC, in part to address the complexity of the conflict and its devastating effects, including on children who often were victimized and forced to take up arms. A Sierra Leonean NGO estimates that up to 70 percent of combatants were children.[169] Moreover, 72 percent of combatants claimed to have been forcibly conscripted, with more than 80 percent of the female soldiers reporting that status.[170]

[166] The commission emphasized that "it was years of bad governance, endemic corruption and the denial of basic human rights that created the deplorable conditions that made conflict inevitable," that "[d]emocracy and the rule of law were dead" by the start of the conflict, and that only the "slightest spark" was required for "violence to be ignited." *Witness to Truth, supra* note 16, Vol. 1, para. 11. Sierra Leone's TRC submitted its report to the Security Council in October 2004, *available at* http://www.trcsierraleone.org/drwebsite/publish/index.shtml.

[167] Id., para 12.

[168] International Center for Transitional Justice, *The Sierra Leone Truth and Reconciliation Commission: Reviewing the First Year* (2004), at 3, *available at* http://www.ictj.org/downloads/SL_TRC_Case_Study_designed.pdf; *The Special Court for Sierra Leone, supra* note 156, at 10.

[169] International Center for Transitional Justice & Post-Conflict Reintegration Initiative for Development and Empowerment, *Ex-Combatant Views of the Truth and Reconciliation Commission and the Special Court in Sierra Leone*, September, 2002, at 13, *available at* http://www.ictj.org/images/content/0/9/090.pdf.

[170] Id.

[14]

From Nuremberg

John Hagan

"Collectively," Louise Arbour remarked as chief prosecutor at The Hague, "we're linked to Nuremberg. We mention its name every single day."[1] It was characteristic of the Canadian Arbour to begin a public statement about the tribunal with a reference to a shared experience. Robert Jackson was the charismatic U.S. Supreme Court justice who prosecuted the Nazi leadership at Nuremberg. His efforts to "stay the hand of vengeance" helped make Nuremberg the lasting influence Arbour described. Yet Jackson also shared prevailing prejudices of his day, and he notes in his oral history that "I had a great deal of argument and difficulty about the staff, particularly with Jewish people."[2] This bias coincided with an insular tendency in Jackson's leadership.

Jackson reasoned that having too many Jewish lawyers at the Nuremberg trial would undermine its objectivity. He acknowledged that "we had a good many Jewish persons on the staff" and that "some of them did excellent work." He rationalized, however, that "most of them felt . . . they ought to do their work in the background and not be put forward into places of great prominence in order to avoid the impression that it was a Jewish enterprise."[3] This kind of attitude made Jackson's leadership appear more singular than collective in character.

Jackson's views are the more striking today given that Louise Arbour *in part* was selected as prosecutor at The Hague because her gender was thought to be an *asset* in responding to rape as a war crime. In any case, a result of Jackson's attitude is an underappreciation of the roles played by others at Nuremberg who contributed to the collective creation of his charismatic image. Among the lesser-known Jewish contributors are the former Harvard University law professor Sheldon Glueck and his student Ben Ferencz. Glueck was the prescient author of *War Criminals: Their Prosecution and Punishment,*[4] and Ferencz assisted Glueck as a law student before going off to war and later becoming a Nuremberg prosecutor. Their experiences are instructive with regard to international legal activism and its early development at Nuremberg.

FROM WAR TO WAR CRIMES

Fresh out of law school, Ferencz arrived on the beaches of Normandy immediately after D-Day. The Germans had retreated and he at first was perched on a hill, manning a machine gun to guard against attack from the rear. This may have been the last time Ferencz looked back in a lifelong struggle for international criminal justice that has stretched from Nuremberg into the new millennium. I pulled Ferencz away from his computer late one evening. After updating me on his schedule, he lamented, "My wife says I have no time to live. I say I have no time to die."

Ferencz served under General Patton. "If the Germans had counterattacked, we had relatively little way of repelling them, but they didn't, so off we went."[5] They chased the retreating Germans across France, Luxembourg, Belgium, and then Germany.

Back at Harvard, in the winter of 1944, Sheldon Glueck got a call from Washington asking him to suggest someone to work in a new war crimes program that preceded the Nuremberg trials. Promises were being made to do something about the execution of downed Allied flyers. Jewish victims of the Holocaust were still of less urgent concern. Glueck recommended Ferencz, and he was transferred to a new Judge Advocate section, where a colonel informed him, "We've been instructed to set up a war crimes branch and your name has been forwarded to us as a man who knows about this." The colonel knew nothing about war crimes, and Ferencz's first job was to brief him. "I swear to you," Ferencz recalls, "that's exactly how the war crimes program started in the United States Army."[6]

Ferencz knew the topic from his work on Glueck's book. "I had read everything that had been written about war crimes . . . and my job was to make summaries." Perhaps more significant, however, Ferencz also had read reports Glueck received about what had happened to the Jews in Poland beginning in 1939. "We knew that the Jews were being rounded up and sent to camps where they were being exterminated."[7] Now he would observe the results at first hand.

The new unit had five colonels, and Ferencz was the only enlisted man. None of the others were lawyers. Soon one Private Nowitz arrived, covered in mud from building a bridge but bringing the encouraging news that he was a Yale law graduate. Later a few other enlisted men with law degrees, never more than a half dozen in total, joined Ferencz and Nowitz. As Ferencz put it, "we were the war crimes team."[8] Ferencz and Nowitz were the nucleus of a nascent investigation and eventual trial team whose form is still today recognizable as the dominant organizational nexus of war crimes work at the Hague tribunal.

The work was grim enough at first when it involved finding bodies of downed Allied flyers. Then they began to encounter the concentration camps. Buchenwald was the first, but they soon were moving through a horrifying succession of camps. A report would come into headquarters that a tank division was approaching or had just overrun an area and had "come upon people who looked very strange, they were wearing pajamas, all looking like skeletons." Ferencz or Nowitz would jump into a jeep and join the unit going into the camp. They soon learned that to be most effective, two things are required before all others: the evidence and the perpetrators. The best chance of getting both was to be on the scene as quickly as possible. This was the importance of "real-time" war crimes investigation, a priority in Louise Arbour's later efforts at the Hague tribunal.

The scenes Ferencz encountered in the German concentration camps have been with him ever since. The memories come in a torrent: "Well, I'm sure that everybody by this time has seen the photographs of what the camp looked like and bodies lying in the dust, naked, a little item of clothing on, many of them not moving, some of them stirring, mostly bones; human beings, men weighing 50, 60 pounds. . . . And then, of course, the piles in front of the crematoria, stacked up like cordwood, and on the carts that were dragging them to the crematoria, these open carts just loaded with bodies, hands and arms hanging out on the sides."[9] Ferencz found that one defense against these horrendous images was to concentrate on the legal requirements of his job.

Conditions in the camps were chaotic. The American soldiers as well as the inmates would often vent their emotions by destroying everything, including those who ran the camps and their records. "It was bedlam, chaos everywhere, everything was destroyed, the inmates would go crazy, they would catch the guards and kill them, beat them up, burn them alive. I've seen all that, and so you have to move very fast . . . as soon as I got the evidence that I thought I needed I got out of the camp." From there it was on to the next camp. "We were moving fast . . . from one to the next, Abenzie and Muthausen and a whole string of camps." Ferencz noted that it usually took two to three days to get the material they needed.

In his movement through the camps, Ferencz also met up with Russian soldiers who wondered why he bothered with evidence. They asked incredulously, " 'What's the matter with you Americans—are you crazy? You know what they did, why do you ask them what they did? You're crazy! Kill 'em. Kill 'em.' And they did!"[10] As we will see later, this Russian attitude would prove crucial to what the Nuremberg trials eventually could and could not accomplish.

Ferencz and Nowitz kept on with their work, which was not only gruesome but seemingly endless. They kept finding more camps. "What we didn't know was all these sub-camps that were scattered all around. There were hundreds of them! Everywhere! . . . I have a list of over a thousand concentration camps run by the Germans and German industry. . . . We added three or four hundred later; I don't know how many thousand we have by now."

Throughout, Ben Ferencz felt a sense of the urgency; the fact that Ben and Jack were working together helped to hold off feelings of despair. Ferencz described putting himself "into a mental cocoon which was surrounded by an ice barrier which just enabled me to go on." He emphasized that working toward a shared goal with Jack Nowitz was important. "Interestingly enough," he added, "it was not somber in the sense that we never laughed . . . there were light moments as well."[11]

Ferencz explained that Nowitz was sometimes "exuberant" in his descriptions of crime scenes and that he would have to temper his prose. "He would come upon a typical concentration camp scene and had to write a report. He would say, 'These sadistic beasts, guards were murdering the people in cold blood, and it was outrageous and a violation of every act of human decency.' And I would have to calm him down and say, 'Look, Jack, we're just preparing legal documents to draw up an indictment. You refer to them as accused, you don't refer to them as dirty bastards. . . . Just describe the facts and the facts will speak for themselves.' We had a lot of fun actually together on that. We were good friends." The friendship and the humor helped both to deal with the horror and atrocity they were pursuing in ways that, as we will see, were important not only for them but also for others we will encounter throughout this book.

The first of the resulting war crimes trials were conducted in the Dachau concentration camp. Ferencz couldn't help but think there was ironic justice in hammering up a sign announcing their presence as "United States Army, War Crimes Unit, Dachau." The procedures were informal, but they had prisoners and something had to be done. The trials were conducted under rules developed for military court martials. There were three judges, the one with the highest rank presiding.

Ferencz freely acknowledges that their methods were flawed. They were in "hot pursuit," and "I wasn't going to take any crap from these SS officers. I had witnessed their deeds." Not proud that threats of coercion sometimes were used, he recalled, "When I got a confession I would take it and go out and find myself an officer and say to him, 'Here, I got a confession out of that son-of-a-bitch, you go in and be nice to him, give him a cigarette, have him write it and bring out the second edition. And if it's consistent with the first then we'll destroy the one that I got.'"

Although the trials may have been a rough form of victor's justice, they served an urgent need. Gary Bass, the political historian of international criminal tribunals, identifies this inclination as the beginning of a commitment to "liberal legalism."[12] Ferencz reasoned that "anytime you bring anybody to justice even if it is in an inadequate court, it's better than not bringing them to justice at all." His point of comparison was with the Russians, "who just shot them."[13] This was the comparison that Ferencz' former professor, Sheldon Glueck, was also pursuing in anticipation of the more important trials to come at Nuremberg. Glueck was the scholar behind Ferencz the activist, and his contribution was to better articulate liberal legal principles as a foundation for the work at Nuremberg.

LIBERAL LEGALISM AT HARVARD

Sheldon Glueck began teaching at Harvard University in the early 1940s and developed an understanding of at least three crucial factors: that the European Jews were nearly entirely powerless victims of the Nazis, that the Soviet Union was a powerful yet dubious partner at Nuremberg, and that these realities would make the use of international criminal law to punish German crimes against humanity a challenging undertaking.

Glueck was a pragmatist whose Jewish immigrant background gave him a direct interest in the war.[14] Glueck's involvement, however, unlike Ferencz's, lasted for less than a decade. His early contribution was to recognize the significance of the formal legal punishment of German war crimes. Writing before the war's end, Glueck urged as a fundamental principle of liberal legalism that "it is desirable that the United Nations set up an International Criminal Court . . . as a concrete token of the determination of civilized peoples to vindicate the rule of law in international affairs."[15]

In framing his position, Glueck did not reject out of hand the popular challenge to liberal legalism.[16] In fact, he accepted the early views of Churchill and Roosevelt that in disposing of the Nazi leaders "the United Nations have a perfect right to do as they please. . . . They can shoot them without any legal proceedings." But he also argued that "solemn arraignment followed by trial in an international court is to be preferred . . . in order to inform public opinion . . . and to fix the record of history."[17] Thus Glueck supported an international law of crimes against humanity. He joined the London Assembly in endorsing an early definition built on Hersh Lauterpacht's[18] conception of "crimes against humanity," which included "all crimes committed either within an Axis country or outside such country for the extermination of a race, nation or political party."[19]

The inclusion of "extermination" in this conception of crimes against humanity predated the Geneva Convention definition of genocide as "acts which were intended to destroy, in whole or part, a national ethnic or racial group."[20] Samantha Power notes that Raphael Lemkin first introduced this concept of genocide and then struggled to get it into the Nuremberg indictment.[21] Like those of Glueck and Ferencz, Lemkin's roots were European and Jewish. He placed an almost Talmudic faith in the power of law. Ferencz would later encounter Lemkin in the halls of the Nuremberg tribunal. He remembers that "this new idea of his was not something we had time to think about" and that "we wanted him to just leave us alone so we could convict these guys for mass murder."[22] Lemkin lost almost all of his family to the Holocaust and literally worked himself to death lobbying for the concept of genocide. The formal definition of genocide was ultimately provided in the 1948 Convention on the Prevention and Punishment of the Crime of Genocide, with Lemkin there to tirelessly assist.

The Hague tribunal's definition of crimes against humanity is summarized today as "inhumane acts of a very serious nature committed as part of a widespread or systematic attack against a civilian population on political, ethnic or religious grounds, whether committed in times of peace or war."[23] The distinction between "widespread or systematic attack against a civilian population," as a crime against humanity, and the "intentional destruction in whole or in part of a national ethnic or racial group," as the crime of genocide, is elaborated in the tribunal's Foca and Srebrenica trials, considered in the later chapters of this book.

First and probably foremost, Glueck did not want to see the results of World War I, when few and minor punishments were imposed on German war criminals at the Leipzig trials, repeated. Glueck served in France during World War I and knew that only twelve persons were tried and six convicted by the German Supreme Court, receiving sentences from two months to four years. Glueck set out his well-formulated arguments in influential and widely read articles, in his early book, and in a statement for congressional hearings.[24]

Glueck was unabashed in his pragmatism, insisting in his congressional statement that "the time for such clear-cut and level-headed policy-framing and program-implementing is getting short." He argued that politics must sometimes intrude on law, saying, "The issues to be faced cannot successfully be dealt with by regarding the absolute separation between the political and the legal as something sacrosanct for all times." Instead, he reasoned, "in the early stages of any system of law the executive and the judicial are not sharply differentiated."[25]

Glueck also rejected national sovereignty and claims of sovereign immunity as defenses, maintaining that national sovereignty was a privilege of power. Glueck argued that "to allow the fact that many atrocities were committed inside Germany . . . to prevent the trial of Germans for such atrocities, would be a triumph of bookish legalism and the death of both common sense and justice. There is nothing sacrosanct about the territorial theory of jurisdiction."[26] Subsequent decisions favorable to a broader, more universal conception of jurisdiction and hostile to the defense of national sovereignty have been distinguishing features of the Hague tribunal.

FROM WASHINGTON TO LONDON

Glueck contacted Jackson when he learned that he would be the American prosecutor.[27] Following the March 1945 congressional testimony and promulgation of the resulting resolution, events began to move rapidly. By spring, Glueck was in regular communication with the Office of Strategic Services (OSS) in Washington, headed by General William J. "Wild Bill" Donovan,[28] who was in charge of planning for Nuremberg.

With the end of the semester at Harvard, Glueck joined the OSS team in Washington. Jackson had just submitted a report to the president. Although this report noted "atrocities and offenses, including . . . persecutions on racial or religious grounds," it omitted specific mention of the Holocaust's primary victims, the Jews of Europe. Instead, for Jackson, the point of greater urgency was that "it is high time that we act on the juridical principle that aggressive war-making is illegal and criminal."[29] His report concluded with a lengthy review of the international law of war and its aggressive violation; Donovan was more focused on evidence of the Holocaust.

Glueck joined the group of seventeen lawyers, secretaries, and assorted staff that accompanied Jackson on a June 26 flight from Washington to London, where final planning began for the Nuremberg trial. Within two days of arriving at London's Claridge Hotel, Jackson issued work assignments. Glueck was appointed as the Consultant Supervising Installation of the Control System for the collection and classification of evidence. He saw the challenge before him with regard to evidence of the Holocaust. Many if not most of those involved in planning the Nuremberg trial were unconvinced about the Holocaust, and some were dismissive. Henry Stimson, the cabinet-level architect of Nuremberg, had earlier remarked to Roosevelt, "I have great difficulty in finding any means whereby military commissions may try and convict those responsible for excesses committed within Germany both before and during the war which have no relation to the conduct of war."[30]

Gary Bass observes that Stimson "was a rather mild and genteel anti-Semite, no worse but no better than the bulk of the American establishment in the 1930s and 1940s."[31] Jackson noted that most Americans simply didn't comprehend the enormity or significance of the Holocaust, saying, "The interest was greatest among people who had relations in Europe who had been persecuted, and the refugees. But the crimes of the Hitler regime were all a little remote to this country."[32] Americans were more focused on the Pacific theater and the defeat of Japan. Telford Taylor, who prosecuted the High Command case and who later became chief prosecutor after Jackson departed, readily acknowledged that "like so many others, I remained ignorant of the mass extermination camps in Poland, and the full scope of the Holocaust did not dawn on me until several months later at Nuremberg."[33] It was Taylor who in turn brought Ben Ferencz to Nuremberg to prosecute perhaps the most important Holocaust case after Jackson returned to the United States.

In an evidence planning meeting held the day after their arrival in London and attended by Glueck, the role of Jewish refugee groups was quickly discounted. The minutes of this meeting record that "the view was expressed that their materials are mostly gossip and that their evaluations are very emotional. It was considered that they are not a useful source for evidence."[34] There clearly was an evidentiary challenge to be met.

The control system devised by Glueck for collecting and managing evidence involved separately developed digest forms. These forms were numbered and began with the name of the defendant and the subject matter. Each numbered record of evidence was then cross-referenced in terms of other proof and data required, the point of law or possible defense at issue, connected OSS or other study material, and an indication of the subheading of the count and instrument of accusation to which the evidence was linked. Finally, each digest form ended with an open-ended prompt for "quotable material to be used by the prosecutor in summing up."[35] These forms were crucial in organizing the extraordinary volume of evidence left by the highly bureaucratized German war machine.

In the end, the overwhelming nature of the evidence of the Holocaust prevailed in shifting the focus of the trial from charges of waging aggressive war to crimes against humanity. Donovan, Glueck, and others foresaw this from the outset, but especially as the pictorial, witness, and interrogation accounts accumulated, Jackson as well was persuaded and turned the emphasis in court to the presentation of this evidence.

After the war, Jackson noted how essential Glueck's superbly organized efforts were to the trial's outcome: "When negotiations for a Four-Power agreement for the trial of Nazi war criminals began in London in June 1945, Professor Glueck's book was one of the few published studies of the problems involved in trial. . . . As captured documents began to pour in, he also devised a system for summarizing and indexing them, so that a large mass of material could be readily available on any particular point. His original plan is substantially the system pursued throughout the Nuremberg trial."[36] Glueck's evidence control system was a masterful organizational contribution and a reflection of his pragmatism and persistence. By these means, Glueck played a crucial role in translating the principles of liberal legalism into living law. He was not chosen to go on from London to Nuremberg for the trial. His legacy nonetheless continued through the lifelong work of his student, Ben Ferencz.

BETWEEN BERLIN AND NUREMBERG

Ferencz left the war crimes trials in Dachau in 1946, happy to be out of the army and looking forward to marrying Gertrude, the young woman he had pursued in the years before the war. Yet he wasn't home more than a matter of weeks before he received a telegram from General Mickey Marcus asking him to return to Dachau. Ben phoned Gertrude and asked, "How would you like to go to Europe for a honeymoon?" She was dismayed but agreeable, convinced they would be back in no more than six months.

Next Telford Taylor called from Washington with a more compelling offer. "I'm going back to Nuremberg, I've been over there, the International Military Tribunal is already in process, Justice Jackson is there, we're winding up that trial but I'm going to take over after him and we're going to set up a whole series of subsequent trials. I'm going to be in charge and I need staff and I've heard about you and I'd like you to come with me."[37] Taylor noted that the first trial was dealing with the highest-level Germans who presided over the war and the Holocaust. There remained the hierarchy below these leaders who were also responsible: the ministerial bureaucrats, industrialists, generals, SS members, doctors, and lawyers. This was a larger vision of the trial than Glueck had assumed possible.

Taylor picked Ferencz for his legal training and investigative experience. The team structure of this undertaking was especially attractive to Ferencz. They knew that much of the documentary evidence must be in Berlin, the core of the German war machine. Ferencz was assigned a team of fifty investigators, but he initially was given only a basement office. When he arrived he found a dusty picture of President Truman on the floor, which he promptly signed "To my friend Benny, from Harry." He framed and hung the picture and then placed a call to the colonel in command of the Berlin sector.

Ferencz asked the colonel to come by his office, explaining, "I'm here on assignment from the President of the United States to carry on a war crimes commission. . . . I want you to come over right away." When the colonel arrived, Ferencz asked, "You don't expect me to carry on this job in this office?"[38] Maybe it was the picture of the president. In any case, the colonel soon put half a building at his disposal.

The staff was a close-knit group. It included Ben's new bride, Gertrude, and a large number of German-speaking refugees, many of whom were Jewish, who knew the German scene and were uniquely motivated. An enormous stockpile of eight to ten million records was soon found in a bunker under a small chateau in Dahlem.

Ferencz next reencountered the influence of Glueck, specifically the digest forms he developed, which now were used to coordinate the investigative research. These forms became a crucial "way of funneling information from a document to the hands of a person who can see its merit and its relationship." Ferencz and Taylor were also flying between Berlin and Nuremberg during this time (and at one point wound up parachuting to safety).

A remarkable event in the first Nuremberg trial had involved the testimony of the SS general Otto Ohlendorf, who had headed a part of the *Einsatzgruppen* (EG), the extermination squads that followed the German troops as they invaded Poland and the Soviet Union. These squads included three thousand men whose assignment was to annihilate Jews, Gypsies, and others. At the first trial, Ohlendorf was a witness rather than a defendant. When he was asked how many people his soldiers had killed, he matter-of-factly responded, "In the year between June 1941 and June 1942 the *Einsatz* troops reported ninety thousand people liquidated."[39] Yet Ohlendorf was not among the targeted defendants for Taylor's subsequent Nuremberg trials. Ferencz could not believe that "we had trials against some SS officers, the *Reichssicherheitshauptamt,* but we hadn't planned an Einsatzgruppen trial."[40]

One nearly complete set of EG records was discovered in the burnt-out Gestapo basement headquarters. "One of my researchers came in with these Leitz folders, three or four of them, with all these daily reports from the front: how many Jews they'd killed in which towns, and the reports would read, you know, 'Today we entered the town of So-and-So. Within the first 24 hours we succeeded in eliminating'—they never—they always used euphemisms—'in eliminating 14,312 Jews, 127 Communist officials, 816 Gypsies' and they would list them. . . . I looked at it and said, 'My God, we have here a chronological listing of mass murder.' "[41] These records showed that the EG had slaughtered more than a million men, women, and children. Ferencz took the next plane to Nuremberg to inform Taylor.

Taylor was astonished but did not know where to fit this devastating information into the planned new trials. Ferencz protested, "It's enough for a separate trial by itself. Look, here we've got the names of all the commanding officers. There were 3000 men there, we have four big commands, Einsatzgruppen A, B, C, D, and each one with ten or twelve different units under them." Ferencz finally said that he would prosecute the case himself and Taylor responded, "Well, you've got your other job; you've got to do it in addition to your other job." Ferencz agreed and thus became the prosecutor in the case that a United Press article called "the biggest murder trial in history."[42] Ferencz was at this time still only twenty-seven years old.

The Einsatzgruppen case involved twenty-two defendants, including six SS generals, one of whom was Ohlendorf. The trial lasted nine months, although the prosecution presented its case in just three days. Thirteen of the accused were sentenced to death, but only four were actually executed. The maximum penalty at the Hague tribunal is life imprisonment.

BEYOND NUREMBERG

The victory of the Allied forces in World War II opened a window of political opportunity that lasted barely long enough for cooperation in prosecuting the captured Nazi leadership at Nuremberg. From the outset the American government had its doubts about how far the Nuremberg tribunal should go in imposing international criminal law on Germany, and this evolved into concerns about how this body of law could be institutionalized vis-à-vis the Soviet Union or, later, in relation to the use of American power in response to the cold war threat from the Soviets. The conflicting spheres of American and Soviet influence soon loomed large as the dominant postwar concern and added to problems that plagued the relationship between the Soviet Union and the other Allies from the beginning of the tribunal.[43] Not until this mentality subsided in the 1990s would there be sufficient global consensus to initiate another international tribunal.

This was the geopolitical context in which Justice Robert Jackson as prosecutor developed the Nuremberg tribunal. The responses of Glueck and Ferencz to their differing involvements with the tribunal offer hints about this kind of experience and its effect on individuals working in the area of international criminal justice and human rights. After writing his second book about war crimes and the Nuremberg tribunal following the war,[44] Glueck soon returned to his better-remembered longitudinal research on delinquency.[45] He did not have the experience of being a direct participant in Nuremberg, and he sensed that the geopolitical climate was not conducive to building a career in international law.

Ben Ferencz persisted in making international criminal law and human rights his life's work. After finishing at Nuremberg in 1948, Ferencz became director-general of the Jewish Restitution Successor Organization, which filed claims for more than one hundred sixty-three thousand properties in Germany. This effort led to further work with a German program of restitution and indemnification that eventually provided more than $60 billion and is still providing aid for victims of the Holocaust. Ferencz did not finally return to the United States until 1956, ten years later than he originally promised his wife.

Following a decade of legal practice with Telford Taylor in a prominent New York firm, and during the lead-up to the American involvement in Vietnam, Ferencz became heavily involved in work with the United Nations to more rigorously define international aggression and to make the case for an international criminal court. When his children left home and he had saved enough money, Ferencz turned back to his international work full-time. In the late 1970s he wrote a book titled *Less Than Slaves,* which established the liability of German industrialists who profited by working concentration camp inmates to their deaths.

In the early 1990s, nearly fifty years after Nuremberg, the geopolitics of international criminal law changed. The catalysts were the demise of the Soviet Union and the end of the cold war. A new public awareness also resulted from televised and eyewitness accounts of atrocities in the Balkans and later in Rwanda. The tacit acceptance of human rights violations on both sides of the cold war divide became simultaneously more visible and less tolerable. Human rights and women's organizations were able to work on their own and later through a UN commission of experts, discussed in the following chapter, to establish the International Criminal Tribunal for the Former Yugoslavia and later for Rwanda. This and the 1998 Rome Treaty to establish a permanent international criminal court were major steps toward the goals of liberal legalism to which Ferencz had devoted his adult life.

The trajectory of the cold war and the attention of the media to war crimes in the past decade tell us much about why international criminal law advanced so dramatically at Nuremberg and now has a renewed life at The Hague. This was the political opportunity structure in which the liberal legalism of international criminal justice first flourished, then failed, and recently has flourished anew.[46] It may be harder to explain why Ben Ferencz has persisted in his efforts throughout his life, while the pragmatic Sheldon Glueck and most others shifted their interests to other issues when the cold war made progress in this area so difficult. The firsthand exposure of Ferencz to the consequences of the Holocaust and the Nuremberg tribunal likely had much to do with his persistence.

The initial frenetic work of Ferencz with Jack Nowitz to enact some early form of justice in the concentration camps that they discovered during the German defeat and retreat may provide a further clue about the role of legal teamwork in fostering lifelong activism. We have seen that Ferencz then went to Berlin, where he became the leader of a larger team effort that linked Jewish refugee investigators with American lawyers to develop the evidence for the second set of postwar prosecutions. His early and later investigative work and the linkage of the latter to a historic trial anticipated the organization of investigation and trial teams at the Hague tribunal. The current study is able to more fully examine the organization of parallel efforts in the real-time unfolding of the Hague tribunal, with the goal of better appreciating and understanding how one person working with others can make an important difference of the kind made by Ferencz in World War II and beyond.

LEGAL ACTIVISM AS AGENCY

At little more than five feet in height, and now more than eighty years old, few today would call Ben Ferencz charismatic. Yet in his ninth decade he is clearly an example of human agency in action. Carol Heimer notes that social scientists use the term *agency* in two ways, both of which are relevant to legal and human rights activism.[47]

Sociologists use *agency* to analyze ways individuals autonomously enact meaningful choices that make a difference in their own and others' lives. Economists use the term to refer to effective methods for the selection and direction of others who act on the behalf of a principal. The latter usage is often referred to as the principal-agency problem—which can be a source of opportunity as well as a problem. Agency in the sociologists' sense can involve acting autonomously with respect to the wishes of a principal, and this may include developing these wishes in new and unexpected ways. Agency in this sense can be an ongoing process of negotiation and sponsorship with a principal or principals.

Robert Jackson was charismatic, and in many ways he was the salient figure at Nuremberg. His charisma mainly derived from his association with this tribunal and its accomplishments even after he left. Yet we have seen that the legacy of Nuremberg also benefited enormously, and perhaps ironically, from the agency of lesser-known figures such as the pragmatic Sheldon Glueck and his legal activist student, Ben Ferencz. Jackson's gate-keeping role at Nuremberg nicely illustrates the point that the principal-agent relation can be a source of both problems and opportunities. The way in which Jackson was a captive of the biases of his structural and cultural time and place and allowed these biases to limit Jewish participation at the tribunal illustrates the extent to which the principal-agent relation is as much socially shaped as it is individually determined. The contingency and dependence of charisma on agency and its structural and cultural dimensions is a persistent theme in this study of the Hague tribunal.

This chapter has featured several elements of the Nuremberg experience that illustrate the highly contingent influence of a charismatic figure such as Justice Jackson. These elements are all salient considerations in the sociological study of social movements,[48] and the identification of these elements makes the point that legal activism is in important ways a special form of social activism.

The first of these factors involves political opportunity. In this instance political opportunity presented itself in the form of the shaky alliance with the Soviet Union that allowed the Nuremberg tribunal to emerge. The beginning of the cold war subsequently closed off this opportunity and prevented the evolution of the IMT into a more permanent international criminal court. The Hague tribunal, the much-delayed next step toward such a court, had to await the new political opportunities presented by the end of the cold war.

The second factor involves investigation and trial teams as mobilization structures. Ben Ferencz started in the concentration camps with an investigation team that consisted of little more than himself and Jack Nowitz, but his work evolved in Berlin into a fifty-person investigation team, and then into a Nuremberg trial team that prosecuted the genocidal murders of more than a million people. We will see in following chapters how investigation and trial teams have emerged again as essential mobilization structures at the Hague tribunal. We will consider the crucial role that experiences in such teams have played in the advancement of the emerging field of international humanitarian and criminal law.

The third factor involves the emergence of liberal legalism as a cultural or interpretive framework featuring a normative commitment to the rule of law as the foundation of an institutional response to war crimes. Stalin, as well as Churchill and Roosevelt at early stages, endorsed more vengeful sentiments that form the background and sometimes the foreground challenges to the principles of liberal legalism. The Hague tribunal represents a renewed commitment to liberal legalism's rule of law.

The fourth factor is what social movement theorists have called an alternation experience,[49] in this instance involving the firsthand exposure of Ferencz and others to the conditions of the concentration camps. Although alternation includes "changes of life" that can be as common as movement from high school to college, the social movement theorist Doug McAdam notes that such experiences can also be "key turning points in life" that produce "powerful and enduring changes."[50] Whereas others were often simply shell-shocked by their exposure to the war and the concentration camps, Ferencz responded with a form of agency that was shaped by his exposure to liberal legalism while at Harvard University. Legalism became activism in the work of Ben Ferencz. The events in Croatia, Bosnia, and Kosovo have more recently created the circumstances of parallel alternation experiences for individuals and teams at the Hague tribunal.

When I closed my interview with Ben Ferencz at about ten o'clock in the evening, he offered a parting lecture on why I should press the case in this book for a permanent international court. "You have to do this," Ben implored. "The greater goal is for a permanent court where these principles apply equally to everyone and lead to a more humane and peaceful world." Then he concluded, "That's the story of my life. What I'm working on. What I was working on all day today. Probably doing all day tomorrow. People say, 'When are you going to take a vacation?' and I say, 'What's a vacation?' They say, 'When are you going to retire?' and I say, 'What's a retirement?' And my wife says, 'You have no time to live' and I say, 'I have no time to die.' "

[15]

Rwandan Gacaca: An Experiment in Transitional Justice

Maya Goldstein Bolocan[*]

I. Introduction

For new democracies emerging from destructive violence and massive human rights abuses, reckoning with the past remains the most challenging question. The difficulty lies in crafting a response that can strike the necessary—but inherently problematic—balance among the victims and their families, the perpetrators of horrendous crimes who demand that they be treated humanely and fairly, and a nation that wants to see its past acknowledged while struggling to move forward towards durable peace and democracy.

With the introduction of the state-run Gacaca jurisdictions[1] in June 2002, Rwanda embarked upon what President Paul Kagame has described as "the only way forward."[2] The law setting up the Gacaca jurisdictions was passed in 2000[3] by the Rwandan transitional government, and most recently amended in June 2004,[4] to try thousands of genocide suspects by means of a decentralized, community-based system of courts inspired by local traditions. Attempting to reduce delays in the overburdened criminal justice system, while at the same time seeking justice and reconciliation, the Gacaca jurisdictions represent one of the boldest

---

* Maya Goldstein Bolocan has served as a Human Rights Officer and a Legal System Monitor with the United Nations Mission in Kosovo/OSCE Pillar in 1999-2001, and has worked on rule of law and technical legal assistance programs in transitional countries with the American Bar Association Central European and Eurasian Law Initiative (ABA/CEELI), in Washington, D.C. She holds an LL.M. from Georgetown University (with Distinction); an LL.M. in International Human Rights Law from Essex University (with Distinction); and a J.D. from the State University of Milan (with Distinction). The author would like to thank Professor Carrie Menkel-Meadow for her invaluable, insightful guidance and encouragement throughout the process of writing this article, as well as Lisa Bhansali, Professor Jane Stromseth, and the editors of the *Journal of Dispute Resolution* for very useful comments and suggestions. The author is solely responsible for the content of the article. Email: mayagolds@yahoo.com.

1. The word "Gacaca" indicates in Kinyarwandan—Rwandan local language—the lawn or grass where communities assemble to resolve community disputes. Although the new system is officially called Inkiko-Gacaca (where the term Inkiko means "jurisdictions"), this article will refer to it by using the terms "Gacaca," "Gacaca courts," or "Gacaca jurisdictions."

2. Interview with Paul Kagame, President of Rwanda (July 16, 2002) (cited in Gacaca Jurisdictions: Interim Report of Observations June 10 – Aug. 8, 2002), *available at* http://www.fas.harvard.edursocstud/rwanda/introduction.html#_ftn4 (last visited Oct. 24, 2004) [hereinafter *Gacaca Jurisdictions*]. *See generally* the official web site of the Republic of Rwanda *at* http://www.rwanda1.com/.

3. Organic Law No. 40/2000 of 26/01/2001 setting up "Gacaca jurisdictions" and Organizing Prosecutions for Offenses Constituting the Crime of Genocide or Crimes Against Humanity Committed Between October 1, 1990 and December 31, 1994, *available at* www. Inkiko-gacaca.gov.rw/textes legaux.html (last visited Oct. 24, 2004).

4. Organic Law No. 16/2004 of 19/6/2004 Establishing the Organization, Competence and Functioning of Gacaca courts Charged with Prosecuting and Trying the Perpetrators of the Crime of Genocide and Other Crimes Against Humanity, Committed Between October 1, 1990 and December 31, 1994, *available at* www.Inkiko-gacaca.gov.rw/ (last visited Oct. 24, 2004).

and most original "legal-social"[5] experiments ever attempted in the field of transitional justice. By blending retributive and restorative approaches in an innovative way, Gacaca courts represent a unique opportunity to seek justice in an open, accessible, and participatory fashion. Nonetheless, several deficiencies are present in the Gacaca law—especially with respect to fair trial standards—that, coupled with the prevalent political and human rights climate in Rwanda, may seriously impair the effectiveness of the Gacaca jurisdictions in seeking justice.

Far from being irreconcilable, both a degree of retribution and reconciliation are possible, and are indeed desirable, under Gacaca. This paper argues that shifting the emphasis from the retributive nature of Gacaca to its restorative potential may, in the long term, offer better perspectives of peace and reconciliation to a deeply wounded society. It also argues that, where Gacaca retains its retributive element, it should do so while trying to respect the human rights of those brought before it. Part II of this paper briefly discusses the dominant model of transitional justice, namely the prosecutorial approach of criminal trials, and its effectiveness vis-à-vis alternatives that emphasize the search for truth and reconciliation instead of retribution. Part III provides a brief background on the genocide in Rwanda and examines the major shortcomings of criminal prosecutions by both the International Criminal Tribunal for Rwanda (ICTR) and by the Rwandan government in seeking justice and reconciliation. Part IV considers the newly conceived role of the Gacaca jurisdictions in trying genocide-related cases. This section first briefly reviews the traditional Gacaca as a community-based, informal dispute resolution mechanism. It then presents the modernized, state-mandated Gacaca jurisdictions and their role in complementing the ordinary criminal justice system. Part V critically assesses the unique retributive and restorative nature of this system, highlighting the tension between the two. It ponders some of the major benefits (provision of accessible, participatory justice) and shortcomings (lack of due process guarantees and adequate punishment), as well as the socio-political context in which Gacaca courts operate. Part VI proposes ways to strike a balance between these two conflicting approaches. It argues that if Gacaca is to retain a retributive element, efforts should be made to minimize due process concerns. At the same time, if the purpose is to achieve accountability while seeking reconciliation, the emphasis on restorative justice should be strengthened. This section of the paper also suggests that Gacaca could be used in conjunction with a truth commission. The conclusion highlights the potential benefits of Gacaca and its contribution to devising future accountability mechanisms in the aftermath of mass atrocities. It stresses that an approach that combines retributive and restorative justice measures may better suit the complex needs of transitional societies.

II. TRANSITIONAL JUSTICE: THE ONGOING DEBATE

In the aftermath of mass violence and gross human rights abuses, both the concerned societies and the international community struggle in finding responses

5. *See* Peter Uvin, The Introduction of a Modernized Gacaca for Judging Suspects of Participation in the Genocide and the Massacres of 1994 in Rwanda (June 2000) (discussion paper) (prepared for the Belgian Secretary of State for Development and Cooperation), *available at* http://fletcher.tufts.edu/humansecurity/scholarpapers.html (last visited Oct. 24, 2004).

that adequately address multiple, challenging, and often competing goals. While seeking justice—in the strict sense of obtaining punishment for perpetrators and redress for victims—is often the most immediate goal, there are other, critically important, objectives that should be considered in devising mechanisms of accountability. These include: rendering a truthful account of the past, pursuing reconciliation, deterring and preventing the occurrence of future violence and abuses, and advancing the rule of law while strengthening the foundations of the new democratic order.[6]

While several approaches to accountability exist, this chapter focuses on two often conflicting, but not irreconcilable, perspectives: retributive justice, and restorative justice.[7]

III. SETTLING ACCOUNTS: THE RETRIBUTIVE JUSTICE MODEL

Since the Second World War, the dominant paradigm for dealing with past human rights abuses has been the retributive form of justice embodied in the Nuremberg trials.[8] This model of individual accountability forms the basis of modern human rights law, which has now evolved to recognize the existence of a duty to prosecute—at the international or national level—for crimes against humanity, war crimes, genocide, and torture.[9]

International criminal tribunals for the former Yugoslavia and for Rwanda, new hybrid international-national war crimes courts, the ever-growing list of countries exercising universal jurisdiction over crimes against humanity committed in other nations, and the establishment of the International Criminal Court, have all contributed to the 'globalization' of the retributive approach, reinforcing the view that the primary road to justice is through criminal prosecutions.[10]

Proponents of this form of accountability rightly observe that justice is all too often bartered away for political settlements, with impunity as the bitter price to be paid to secure an end to ongoing violence and repression.[11] They seem to share the basic assumption that, although not always feasible, prosecuting perpetrators

---

6. *See* Jane E. Stromseth, *Introduction: Goals and Challenges in the Pursuit of Accountability*, *in* ACCOUNTABILITY FOR MASS ATROCITIES: NATIONAL AND INTERNATIONAL 1, 5-11 (Jane E. Stromseth ed., 2003) (for a general discussion of goals of accountability efforts).

7. *See generally* M. Cherif Bassiouni, *Accountability for Violations of International Humanitarian Law and Other Serious Violations of Human Rights*, *in* POST CONFLICT JUSTICE 3, 26-39 (M. Cherif Bassiouni ed., 2002) (classifying accountability measures according to their goals: truth, justice and redress). Accountability options include: international prosecutions, international and national investigatory commissions, truth commissions, national prosecutions, national lustrations mechanisms, civil remedies, and mechanisms for the reparation of victims. *Id.*

8. *See* Ruti Teitel, TRANSITIONAL JUSTICE 31-39 (2001).

9. For a general discussion of the duty to prosecute gross human rights abuses amounting to *jus cogens* crimes under international law see Bassiouni, *supra* note 7, at 26. *See also* Diane F. Orentlicher, *Settling Accounts: The Duty to Prosecute Human Rights Violations of a Prior Regime*, 100 YALE L.J. 2537 (1991).

10. *See* Mark A. Drumbl, *Sclerosis: Retributive Justice and the Rwandan Genocide*, 2 PUNISHMENT & SOC'Y 287, 296-97 (2000) [hereinafter Drumbl, *Sclerosis*] (stating that the "law and order" western paradigm is "going global"). *See also* Peter E. Harrell, RWANDA'S GAMBLE: GACACA AND A NEW MODEL OF TRANSITIONAL JUSTICE 40 (2003) (referring to the prevalence of the "liberal-prosecutorial" model in transitional justice).

11. Bassiouni, *supra* note 7, at 7-8 (stating that, in such instances, justice becomes the "victim of realpolitik").

of mass atrocities is the optimal, preferable method for dealing with past injustices.

Prosecutions for gross human rights abuses of a prior regime can indeed serve several important functions. They can discourage future human rights abusers, curtail vigilante, retaliatory justice, and foster respect for the rule of law and the new democratic order.[12]

Establishing individual accountability by way of criminal trials is not only essential to achieve some degree of justice, but is also an effective way of demarcating the past from the present. As observed by Neil Kritz, trials communicate that the "culture of impunity" that permitted heinous abuses to be perpetrated in the first place is being replaced by a "culture of accountability," providing some degree of security to victims while at the same time admonishing and deterring potential future abusers.[13] Criminal prosecutions of human rights violators may provide some victims with a "sense of justice and catharsis," a sense that, by having addressed their grievances, their suffering can at last, more easily, come to an end.[14]

By assigning individual responsibility, criminal trials significantly point out that specific individuals have committed the crimes in question, not an entire ethnic or religious group. The individualization of accountability and punishment may not only be just, but also necessary to overcome dangerous "patterns of vengeance and collective blame."[15] Thus, prosecutions may help curtail the recurrence of vigilante justice and promote social peace in the long term.[16] Dispensing justice through criminal trials may also favor reconciliation between victims and offenders.[17] Failing to do so, on the other hand, fosters resentment and contempt for the law and is deemed as one of the main reasons for the continued perpetration of grave human rights violations throughout the world.[18] Trials may also provide a public account and acknowledgment of the past. When they are conducted in accordance with full due process, they are deemed to represent "the most authoritative" (if not the only) version of the truth.[19]

---

12. Michael P. Sharf & Nigel Rodley, *International Law Principles on Accountability*, *in* POST CONFLICT JUSTICE 89, 90 (Cherif M. Bassiouni ed., 2002).

13. Neil Kritz, *Progress and Humility: The Ongoing Search for Post-Conflict Justice*, *in* POST CONFLICT JUSTICE 55, 58 (Cherief M. Bassiouni ed., 2002) [hereinafter Kritz, *Progress and Humility*]. *See also* Orentlicher, *supra* note 9, at 2542 (identifying criminal punishment as "the most effective insurance against future repression").

14. Neil Kritz, *The Rule of Law in the Postconflict Phase*, *in* MANAGING GLOBAL CHAOS: SOURCES OF AND RESPONSES TO INTERNATIONAL CONFLICT 587, 595 (Chester A. Crocker & Fen Osler Hampson eds., 1996) [hereinafter Kritz, *Postconflict Phase*].

15. *See* Stromseth, *supra* note 6, at 7. *See also* MARTHA MINOW, BETWEEN VENGEANCE AND FORGIVENESS: FACING HISTORY AFTER GENOCIDE AND MASS VIOLENCE 122 (1998) (asserting that trials may "convert the impulse for revenge into state-managed truth-seeking and punishment").

16. Chandra Lekha Sriram, *Revolutions in Accountability: New Approaches to Past Abuses*, 19 AM. U. INT'L L. REV. 301, 382 (2003).

17. *See* ANTONIO CASSESE, INTERNATIONAL CRIMINAL LAW 6 (2003).

18. Sharf & Rodley, *supra* note 12, at 90 (referring to the conclusion of a report of the U.N. Commission on Human Rights and its Sub-Commission on Prevention of Discrimination and Protection of Minorities).

19. *Id.* (stating that "criminal trials can generate a comprehensive record of the nature and extent of the violations, how they were planned and executed, the fate of individual victims, who gave the orders and who carried them out").

While prosecutions can reinforce the rule of the law by discouraging personal vendettas, failure to adequately punish former human rights abusers breeds cynicism and distrust towards the new political order. As stated by Ruti Teitel, where trials are in keeping with the "full procedural legality associated with working democracies . . . [they] express public condemnation of aspects of the past, as well as public legitimization of the new rule of law."[20]

At a minimum, beyond any utilitarian justification, criminally prosecuting individual violators represents a moral duty owed to the victims of atrocious acts. In particular, it affords them a partial remedy for their injuries and helps them restore their dignity.[21]

Prosecutions should be initiated, first and foremost, at the local level. Nevertheless, international prosecutions for gross human rights abuses may be able to provide justice where the concerned national systems are unwilling or unable to do so.[22] International prosecutions present some advantages over national ones. Unlike local trials, international justice may be less subject to allegations of bias—or victor's justice.[23] Justice dispensed through international forums will also have a broader, more powerful impact than a domestic process.[24] First, from a deterrence point of view, it emphatically communicates to potential perpetrators of atrocious crimes, not only in the country concerned, but worldwide, that they will not escape international stigma and condemnation for such atrocities.[25] Second, it contributes to the development and interpretation of international criminal and human rights laws.[26]

IV. THE LIMITS OF CRIMINAL PROSECUTIONS

The ability of the punitive approach to promote justice, social reunion, and reconciliation through criminal trials has been questioned by some observers.[27] Due to either lack of political will or scarcity of resources, transitional justice in the form of criminal trials has been sporadic and selective, both at the local and

---

20. Ruti Teitel, *Transitional Jurisprudence: The Role of Law in Political Transformation*, 106 YALE L.J. 2009, 2037 (1997). *See also* David Dyzenhaus, *Debating South Africa's Truth and Reconciliation Commission*, 49 U. TORONTO L.J. 311 (1999) (stating that the "pursuit of retributive justice in a transition to democracy is thought to be important, not only because of the intrinsic worth of doing justice, but also because the enactment by the courts of the rituals of retributive justice will educate society in the practices of the rule of law that are crucial to the stability of democracy").

21. Sharf & Rodley, *supra* note 12, at 90.

22. *See* Rome Statute of the International Criminal Court, U.N. Diplomatic Conference of Plenitpotentiaries on the Establishment of an International Criminal Court, U.N. Doc. A/CONF.183/9, art. 17, Annex II (1998).

23. *See* Kritz, *Progress and Humility*, *supra* note 13, at 58.

24. *Id.*

25. *Id.*

26. *Id.*

27. *See generally* Miriam J. Aukerman, *Extraordinary Evil, Ordinary Crime: A Framework for Understanding Transitional Justice*, 15 HARV. HUM. RTS. J. 39 (2002); Erin Daly, *Transformative Justice: Charting a Path to Reconciliation*, 12 INT'L LEGAL PERSP. 73 (2002) [hereinafter Daly, *Transformative Justice*]; David Little, *A Different Kind of Justice: Dealing with Human Rights Violations in Transitional Societies*, 13 ETHICS & INT'L AFF. 65 (1999); MINOW, *supra* note 15, at 25-51 (for a general discussion of shortcomings of criminal prosecutions).

international level.[28] Because massive human rights violations are often perpetrated by a great number of people, far from fostering stability and reconciliation, prosecution of every single perpetrator may be "politically destabilizing, socially divisive, and logistically and economically untenable."[29] Where criminal prosecutions have taken place, they have been time-consuming and incremental, invariably subject to compromise and pragmatism.[30] Moreover, they have frequently been conducted in disregard of international due process guarantees. This has made them subject to claims of partisan, victor's justice. Thus, prosecution of a small number of perpetrators will be the best available option in most circumstances. Understandably, this selectivity has seriously undermined perceptions of fairness.[31]

Criminal trials may also be incapable of producing a comprehensive version of the truth both because of the circumscribed scope of each trial's inquiry with its focus on specific, individual facts and events, and because of the manipulation and misuse of rules of evidence characterizing their adversarial nature.[32] In this setting, a victim's opportunity to tell her full story is often denied. By placing justice in the hands of lawyers and impartial administrators, trials may have a disempowering effect on victims, leaving them with the sense that justice has not been done.[33]

Because of their focus on the individual responsibility of voluntary perpetrators, criminal prosecutions may be ill-suited to deal with gross human rights

28. *See* MINOW, *supra* note 15, at 122 (observing that, at best, tribunals can try only a small percentage of those involved in collective violence on the scale of what happened in Bosnia, Rwanda, Argentina and Cambodia). *See also* Carnegie Council on Ethics and International Affairs, Evaluating Justice and Reconciliation Efforts (statements of Paul van Zyl excerpted from the panel discussion "Memory, Justice and Reconciliation: Coming to Terms with the Past"), *available at* www.cceia.org/viewMedia.php (last visited Oct. 24, 2004) (arguing that in transitional scenarios it is often impossible to prosecute more than a tiny fraction of those responsible for a variety of reasons: collapse or incapacitation of the criminal justice system; impossibility of prosecution according to due process in criminal justice systems that have long functioned under authoritarian rule; the difficulty of making policy choices as to whether to prosecute past or current crimes; challenges faced by practical difficulties of prosecuting crimes of the state as opposed to ordinary crimes; difficulty in allocating scarce economic resources; high cost of trials and their time consuming nature; difficulties linked to the issue of jurisdiction in international trials).

29. Aukerman, *supra* note 27, at 51-52 (citing Neil J. Kritz, *Coming to Terms with Atrocities: A Review of Accountability Mechanisms for Mass Violations of Human Rights*, 59 LAW & CONTEMP. PROBS. 127, 138-39 (1996)).

30. *See* Daly, *Transformative Justice*, *supra* note 27, at 103 (arguing that criminal prosecution "does nothing to tell the anxious population that something is being done now to ease the pain" and that "a strategy of extensive criminal trials is not an appropriate resolution for most current transitions").

31. *See* MINOW, *supra* note 15, at 40-45. *See also* Mark A. Drumbl, *Toward a Criminology of International Crime*, 19 OHIO ST. J. ON DISP. RESOL. 263, 270-71 (2003) (arguing that selectivity also compromises the deterrent value of prosecution) [hereinafter Drumbl, *Criminology*].

32. *See* Daly, *Transformative Justice*, *supra* note 27, at 103. *See also* Drumbl, *Sclerosis*, *supra* note 10, at 293 (affirming that courts create "microscopic and logical truths" emerging from carefully controlled situations and based on a sequential proof of facts beyond a reasonable doubt); Donald W. Shriver, *Truth Commissions and Judicial Trials: Complementary or Antagonistic Servants of Public Justice?*, 16 J.L. & RELIGION 1, 8-9 (2001) (arguing that the prohibition of hearsay, rumor, and even references to previous criminal records may "screen out many version of fact," and comparing the courtroom to a playing field in which the "most skilful, rather than the most truthful, side will win").

33. *See* Drumbl, *Sclerosis*, *supra* note 10, at 294 (stating that criminal trials may paradoxically lead to a "conflict between victims and due process," where protecting the defendant's due process rights may irremediably affect the scope, content and form of the victim's account).

abuses committed by mass segments of the population. In such cases, in fact, often individuals act collectively "with varying degrees of responsibility and under varying degrees of coercion," which makes it difficult to apply ordinary principles of criminal law.[34] The focus on selected individuals cannot account for the structural, inner causes of the violence or uncover the complex connections existing between people that made the massacres possible.[35]

Finally, due to their adversarial and divisive nature, trials are not likely to succeed in producing reconciliation, or at least stability, in highly polarized, post-conflict societies.

International trials, while suffering from many of the shortcomings attributed to domestic ones, also suffer the problems associated with "externalized" justice due to their physical and psychological disconnect with the local population.[36] This makes it more difficult for them to have an educational and deterrent impact, provide victims with the sense that justice is being done, as well as foster new democratic values.[37]

V. ALTERNATIVES TO THE PROSECUTORIAL MODEL: RESTORATIVE JUSTICE

In the aftermath of mass violence, the exclusive recourse to criminal trials, adjudication, and imprisonment as mechanisms of individual accountability may do little to promote justice and societal regeneration. Advocates of a different approach question the offender-specific, backward-looking, and strictly punitive nature of the kind of justice normally associated with criminal trials, and suggest alternative methods of reckoning with past abuses.[38] In their view, this type of violence may require a "broader form of justice that includes reparations for victims, shaming for ambivalent bystanders, apologies from aggressors, and giving some voice to victims."[39]

Unlike retributive justice, which considers crime primarily as an act against the state and a violation of its laws, restorative justice views crime as a conflict between individuals that results in injury to the victims, as well as the community

34. Daly, *Transformative Justice*, *supra* note 27, at 105. *See also* Aukerman, *supra* note 27, at 41 (arguing that mass atrocities such as genocide may be "qualitatively" different from ordinary crime because of the number of victims involved and because they are typically undertaken, or at least supported, by state or quasi-state actors for political reasons).

35. *See* MINOW, *supra* note 15, at 47 (stating that trials are not an "ideal" tool in helping to achieve consensus over controversial, complex events). *See also* Drumbl, *Sclerosis*, *supra* note 10, at 298 (arguing that situations of mass violence like the Rwandan genocide, where the deviant behavior is not the exception but the rule, pose a significant challenge to criminal law, which is predicated upon punishing only deviant behavior, and that the characteristic dichotomy between innocence and guilt produced by trials downplays the importance of collective wrongdoing).

36. *See* Sriram, *supra* note 16, at 379-90.

37. *Id.*

38. *See* Carnegie Council on Ethics and International Affairs, *supra* note 28 (statements of David Little).

39. *See* Mark A. Drumbl, *The (Al)lure of the Genocide Trials*, *in* EFFECTIVE STRATEGIES FOR PROTECTING HUMAN RIGHTS 217, 219 (David Barnhizer ed., 2001) [hereinafter Drumbl, *(Al)lure of Genocide Trials*]. *See also* Jennifer J. Llewellyn & Robert House, *Institutions for Restorative Justice: The South African Truth and Reconciliation Commission*, 49 U. TORONTO L.J. 355, 388 (1999) (generally arguing that restorative justice is "model" justice in transitional contexts).

and the offenders themselves.[40] This approach envisions crime as a "violation of people and relationships" that "creates obligations to make things right," and justice as an interactive process that engages the victim, the offender, and the whole community in a search for solutions which promote reintegration, repair, reconciliation, and reassurance.[41] Because crime is seen as an injury that violates personal and communal harmony, restorative justice adopts a process of "bringing together the individuals who have been affected by an offense and having them agree on how to repair the harm caused by the crime" in an attempt to restore victims, offenders, and communities in a way that all stakeholders can agree is just.[42] These principles seem to situate restorative justice between vengeance and forgiveness. Unlike retribution, restorative justice is forward-looking—it tries to repair the relationships that have been broken by the offense and to reduce the causes of hostility and estrangement through reparations and compensation.[43] It is also a victim-centered process, as it provides a forum in which offenders listen to victims and answer their questions.[44] In this way, "victims can hear offenders explain the circumstances behind the crime, express remorse, and take responsibility."[45] In order to achieve healing, restorative justice calls for restitution to the victim by the offender.[46] This is intended to restore the victim's status to the extent that is possible and to stop the cycle of violence, instead of escalating it through retributive, or forceful, responses.[47] Restitution is also an act of account-

40. *See* Laura Stovel, When the Enemy Comes Home: Restoring Justice After Mass Atrocity 2-3 (June 2003) (paper presented at the Restorative Justice Conference, Vancouver), *available at* www.sfu.ca (last visited Oct. 24, 2004).

41. HOWARD ZEHR, CHANGING LENSES: A NEW FOCUS FOR CRIME AND JUSTICE 181 (1990). *See also* Stovel, *supra* note 40, at 2. The two approaches to justice reflect two distinct ethics. "The ethic of the dominant legalistic justice system emphasizes obedience to moral principles presumed to be partly reflected in the law. *Id.* It views crime as law breaking and a violation against the state and accountability as punishment for breaking the law." *Id.* Restorative justice, on the other hand, reflects an ethic of care according to which people are ethically responsible for people with whom they have a relationship. *Id.* While legalistic justice views justice primarily as procedural equality, and appropriate punishment for the crime by impartial adjudicators, restorative justice assumes that humans are relational beings who need to live in community with others, and sees a crime as a violation of another person. *Id.* at 3. The injury thus caused not only violates the victim and those close to him, but also creates "rifts" between the community, and both the victim and the offender. *Id.* When a crime occurs, the victim feels less secure in the community and needs to heal from the shock, while the "offender has lost the trust of both the victim and the community and has to work to earn that back." *Id.* at 3-4.

42. David Dolinko, *Restorative Justice and the Justification of Punishment*, 2003 UTAH L. REV. 319, 320 (discussing John Braithwaite's approach to restorative justice). *See* Carrie J. Niebur Eisnaugle, Note, *An International "Truth Commission": Utilizing Restorative Justice as an Alternative to Retribution*, 36 VAND. J. TRANSNAT'L L. 209, 214 (2003) (arguing that restorative justice focuses on dialogue between individuals or groups that are in conflict by encouraging them to deal with each other directly, face to face, rather than through an advocate such as a lawyer or a diplomat). The two main approaches to restorative justice are family group conferencing and victim-offender mediation. Stovel, *supra* note 40, at 4.

43. Carnegie Council on Ethics and International Affairs, *supra* note 28 (statements of David Little).

44. Stovel, *supra* note 40, at 5-6.

45. *Id.* at 6. Stovel argues that, "Beyond testifying, victims are rarely considered in criminal trials processes." *Id.* at 5. "Their needs to have input in the trial, receive information, ask offenders questions and receive compensation from him are rarely met." *Id.* "[O]ffenders have no incentive to cooperate in the process of truth telling." *Id.* at 6. "Trials are ill-suited to bring out plentiful and context rich information." *Id.*

46. Eisnaugle, *supra* note 42, at 215.

47. *Id.*

ability, where the offender takes responsibility for the harm caused and takes action to repair it.[48] Restorative justice may also be the best way to reintegrate offenders back into their communities and allow them to make amends for their actions.[49] Finally, it empowers communities to seize and deal with conflicts and tensions that arise between them.[50]

In recent years, some commentators have seen restorative justice as having the potential to address—at least in part—the needs of the victims of mass atrocities, while providing some degree of accountability and enhancing the prospects of a peaceful transition.[51] This different kind of justice may be used in alternative, or better in parallel to, normal judicial procedures, normally in the form of truth commissions.[52] The benefits of this approach in the context of transitional societies emerging from violence seem to be significant. "It is the form of justice most directly concerned with reconciliation [because] [i]t addresses the reintegrative needs of both victims and perpetrators."[53] In poor countries with weak, inefficient, and corrupt judicial systems, it offers an alternative to lengthy and expensive trials that often lack any public credibility.[54] In such cases, full public disclosure of government sponsored crimes, coupled with sincere apologies and compensation, may be preferable to the unrealistic prospect of destabilizing mass criminal prosecutions. Finally, as is sometimes the case, this form of justice may draw on pre-existing restorative justice practices that are deeply embedded in the local culture.[55]

Truth commissions have thus been able to provide an appealing middle ground between retribution and amnesia, while at the same time representing an avenue through which a more holistic notion of accountability for human rights abuses can be pursued.[56] Although different models exist, the purpose of most truth commissions is to investigate widespread human rights abuses and provide an accurate, official account of the past, and of the broader context in which the violence occurred, while at the same time offering victims a forum to tell their stories and be vindicated, thus achieving some sense of closure.[57]

---

48. *Id.*

49. Stovel, *supra* note 40, at 7.

50. *Id.* at 8 (arguing that professionalized justice "steals the conflicts" from the community and robs it of its power, ability, and confidence to face trouble and restore peace).

51. *See* Aukerman, *supra* note 27, at 81 (stating that restorative justice as a form of conflict resolution is certainly relevant to transitional justice, where the latter's aim is to achieve "enough forgiveness, reconciliation, or healing to make coexistence possible").

52. Eisnaugle, *supra* note 42, at 222.

53. Stovel, *supra* note 40, at 1.

54. *Id.*

55. Truth and reconciliation commissions established in South Africa and, more recently, in East Timor and Sierra Leone rely on, and incorporate—to a certain extent—customary practices and traditions reflecting a restorative justice philosophy.

56. *See* Eisnaugle, *supra* note 42, at 215 (observing that restorative justice offers "a more 'holistic' approach to conflicts than other forms of justice because it is not directed at primarily inflicting suffering on the offender, but rather focuses on the needs of all parties involved in the crime"). *See also* Llewellyn & House, *supra* note 39, at 356 (arguing that the restorative justice philosophy permeating the South African Truth and Reconciliation Commission offered not only a different, but also a superior model of justice).

57. *See* Aukerman, *supra* note 27, at 82 (stating that truth commissions "can focus on victims, craft a shared narrative about the past as the basis for a [common] future," and return conflicts to those concerned by "active[ly] involv[ing] victims, perpetrators, and the larger community"). *See also* Eis-

While several truth commissions have proliferated around the world over the last twenty years, the most successful to date has been the South African Truth and Reconciliation Commission (TRC)—a semi-judicial body established in 1995 to investigate apartheid era crimes—that expressly endorses a restorative justice philosophy in its mandate.[58] The fruit of political compromise and broad-based consultations, the TRC was seen as representing a bridge between the past of a violent and divided society, and a "future founded on human rights, democracy and peaceful coexistence" for all South Africans.[59] Trading truth for amnesty, the TRC's main goals were to uncover the truth concerning victims and perpetrators, to restore the dignity of victims and survivors, as well as to search for healing and national reconciliation.[60] While granting amnesty to selected individuals was a controversial aspect of the TRC, it proved to be an extremely effective mechanism in identifying responsibility for human rights abuses.[61] Over a period of two years, the TRC gathered testimonies from approximately 24,000 victims of human rights abuses.[62] It also received amnesty applications and statements from thousands of perpetrators.[63] This narrative process gave victims a chance to relate their suffering, thus providing them with the specific acknowledgment and vindication they had long been denied and, in most cases, with cathartic and psychologically beneficial effects.[64] It helped relatives of those victims to uncover the specific truth regarding abuses committed on their loved ones.[65] Finally, the same

---

naugle, *supra* note 42, at 224 (reporting that more than twenty truth commissions have been established around the world over the last two decades).

58. This was based on the belief that transcending the divisions of the past required "understanding but not . . . vengeance . . . reparation but not . . . retaliation." DION A. BASSON, S. AFR. INTERIM CONST., TEXT AND NOTES 1, 339 (1993). The notion of African ubuntu (i.e. the recognition of humanity in everyone) pervades the TRC. Unlike previous truth commissions, the TRC had the power to compel testimony, to stimulate participation by perpetrators in exchange for amnesty, and to link victim testimony to subsequent reparations.

59. Charles Villa-Vicencio, *Restorative Justice in Social Context: The South Africa Truth and Reconciliation Commission*, *in* BURYING THE PAST: MAKING PEACE AND DOING JUSTICE AFTER CIVIL CONFLICT 207, 207-08 (Nigel Biggar ed., 2001) (quoting Postamble to the [S. AFR]. INTERIM CONST. (Act No. 200 of 1993)).

60. *Id.* at 209. The TRC was composed of the following committees: the human rights committee, the amnesty committee, and the reparations and rehabilitation committee. MINOW, *supra* note 15, at 60.

61. Paul van Zyl, *Unfinished Business: The Truth and Reconciliation Commission's Contribution to Justice in Post-Apartheid South Africa*, *in* POST CONFLICT JUSTICE 743, 751 (Cherif M. Bassiouni ed., 2002). Amnesty from criminal and civil prosecutions was granted upon full disclosure of one's involvement in political crimes. The amnesty provisions created an enormous incentive on prospective applicants to reveal their responsibility in past abuses, due to their fear of being implicated by their accomplices. *Id.* Due to its reliance on self-incrimination, it permitted the TRC to obtain invaluable evidence about past human rights violations without being burdened by due process requirements. *Id.* at 751-52. Requiring the applicant to prove that the acts had been politically motivated, as opposed to being motivated by personal consideration (which would have resulted in the denial of the grant of amnesty), often caused a "chain reaction" with applicants implicating senior political or other leaders. *Id.* at 752.

62. *Id.* at 746.

63. *Id.* at 751.

64. *Id.* at 747-48. *See also* Jonathan Allen, *Balancing Justice and Social Unity: Political Theory and the Idea of a Truth and Reconciliation Commission*, 49 U. TORONTO L.J. 315 (1999) (generally arguing that the TRC conferred on victims dignity, consideration, and respect by providing them with a forum where they could recount their stories of oppression in a way that forensic constraints of a courtroom would not permit).

65. van Zyl, *supra* note 61, at 748.

process also contributed towards the establishment of a social truth regarding the nature and the impact of human rights abuses on the victims and their families, making it almost impossible to refute and distort such reality.[66]

The TRC hearings allowed both the victims and the perpetrators to tell their side of the story, ask questions, and talk about the impact and consequences of the violence on their lives in order to try to achieve healing. The punishment imposed on those found guilty of apartheid crimes—where they were given amnesty—was not retributive punishment, but was expressed in terms of shame, ostracism, and moral opprobrium.[67] The assumption was that, given an admission of guilt on the part of those involved in various crimes, the process of forgiveness and, ultimately, reconciliation would be significantly advanced, funding the basis for a new moral relationship.[68] In the most optimistic views, public testimonies and acknowledgments of the past provided an opportunity for individuals and the nation as a whole to heal.[69] Importantly, the TRC also held a series of institutional hearings to inquire into the acquiescence and responsibilities of professions and institutions deeply implicated in the apartheid.[70] Though some of those called to participate failed to come forward, these hearings nonetheless highlighted the corrupt and vicious nature of the regime, thus providing a wider context to the uncovered individual abuses.[71] While the commission rightly focused on crimes committed by the apartheid regime, it also made important statements concerning the responsibility of members of the liberation movement for human rights abuses committed by them.[72]

The TRC has sometimes been criticized for denying justice to victims, because it let those responsible of horrible crimes walk away with impunity and without showing any remorse—the TRC legislation only required truth.[73] It has

66. *Id.* at 746-47.

67. Daly, *Transformative Justice*, *supra* note 27, at 154. *See also* Llewellyn & House, *supra* note 39, at 357 (stating that, "The [TRC's] emphasis [was] on reintegrative measures that . . . rebuild social bonds, as opposed to measures such as imprisonment that isolate and alienate the perpetrator from society").

68. *See generally* MINOW, *supra* note 15; Allen, *supra* note 64.

69. MINOW, *supra* note 15, at 61.

70. van Zyl, *supra* note 61, at 749, 751-52.

71. David Dyzenhaus, With the Benefit of Hindsight 1-3 (June 7-9, 1999) (paper delivered at the conference, "TRC: Commissioning the Past," University of the Witwatersrand, Johannesburg), *at* www.trcresearch.org.za/papers99/dyzenhaus.pdf (last visited Oct. 24, 2004) (reporting that the institutional hearings were held into the role of the media, the health sector, business and labor, religious organizations and the prisons). In October 1997, the TRC held a three day hearing into the role of the legal community during the apartheid regime. *See id.* Partly prompted by the judges' refusal to attend the hearing, this focused on their responsibilities and the abdication of their duty to respect the rule of law during the apartheid era. *Id.*

72. van Zyl, *supra* note 61, at 752-53. *See also* Dyzenhaus, *supra* note 71, at 26 (reporting that the idea for the TRC originated in the context of an African National Congress initiative in the early 1990s to appoint commissions to inquire into the brutalities committed by its own soldiers in training camps).

73. Stephen A. Garrett, Models of Transitional Justice: A Comparative Analysis (Mar. 14-18, 2000) (paper prepared for the International Studies Association 41st Annual Convention) (stating that the central ethical dilemma posed by the TRC was whether those who are guilty of brutal crimes should be allowed to go free simply by offering a potentially hypocritical and false contrition for past wrongs), *at* www.ciaonet.org/isa/gas02/gas02.html (last visited Oct. 24, 2004). *But see* MINOW, *supra* note 15, at 56 (stating that, far from granting blanket amnesty, the TRC left the door open for prosecutions and civil suits to be brought against those who did not apply for, or were not granted amnesty). *See also* Benjamin N. Schiff, *Do Truth Commissions Promote Accountability or Impunity? The Case of the*

also been criticized, rightly, for having failed to provide adequate reparation to apartheid victims.[74] While the failure of the current South African government to vigorously prosecute those who failed to seek, or those who were denied, amnesty has been held by some observers as reflecting the limits of the TRC, it rather seems to underscore the inadequacy, weaknesses and biases of the legal system.[75]

Despite these criticisms, the TRC was an overall success. Notably, the TRC condemned and fully revealed a heinous regime, restored victims' dignity by giving public legitimacy to their stories, laid the foundations for the promotion of a human rights-based culture, and instilled in ordinary South Africans a determination that the injustices of the past should never happen again.

VI. STRIKING THE BALANCE: JUSTICE, TRUTH, AND RECONCILIATION

Truth and accountability are essential if societies traumatized by mass atrocities are to limit destructive ethnic, religious, political and racial conflicts and to recover a degree of stability and peace. What means a society chooses to deal with the past will reflect the balance between competing, multiple goals and will be necessarily context-driven. A combination of factors—social, political, economic, and cultural—should determine what form of justice is not only desirable, but also pragmatically feasible and realistic, in a particular transitional context.[76] These factors include the gravity of the violation, the extent and severity of the victimization, the number of and those who are the accused, the extent to which the violence has subsided, the community's will, as well as the type and nature of the new government.[77] As observed by Mark Drumbl, in the aftermath of broad-based violence involving thousands of victims and perpetrators, like in Rwanda,

South African Truth and Reconciliation Commission, *in* POST CONFLICT JUSTICE, 325, 331 (Cherief M. Bassiouni ed., 2002) (arguing that fears that the TRC would be too generous in granting amnesty are unfounded since, by late 2000, while the commission had received 7,112 applications for amnesty, it had granted only 849 of these; arguing also that the de facto impunity for most of the "architects of apartheid" was due to the "bias and incapacity" of the legal system, not to the TRC's failure).

74. Those who were granted amnesty were under no obligation to make any compensation to victims or the society. This aspect was criticized even by the most fervent supporters of the TRC. *See* Llewellyn & House, *supra* note 39, at 388 (arguing that "removing reparation from the amnesty process [not only] seriously limits the connection between amnesty and restoring the victim [but also that], as far as the perpetrator is concerned, amnesty without any way to make amends for one's actions could result [in a] 'shaming machine,' serving to stigmatize, rather than reintegrate, perpetrators"). *See also* Daly, *Transformative Justice*, *supra* note 27, at 156 (stating that the TRC "produced an imbalance of justice: it granted amnesty to some perpetrators but did not secure meaningful reparations to any victims"); Naomi Roth-Arriaza, *Reparations Decision and Dilemmas*, 27 HASTINGS INT'L & COMP. L. REV. 157, 174 (reporting that, in 2003, South African President Mbeki proposed a one-time grant of about $3,500 to each victim, a fact that has been strongly criticized by victims' groups).

75. *See* Schiff, *supra* note 73, at 341 (observing that the TRC's effect upon impunity appears "mixed" and that, if considered vis-à-vis a weak legal system, it has the merit of having exposed at least violations committed by some perpetrators).

76. *See* Aukerman, *supra* note 27, at 92; MINOW, *supra* note 15, at 50 (stating that trials should not be pursued "where there is no chance for or perception of fairness or where there are overwhelming disparities between the resources and will needed"). *See also* Erin Daly, *Between Punitive and Reconstructive Justice: The Gacaca Courts in Rwanda*, 34 N.Y.U. J. INT'L L. & POL. 355, 367 (2002) [hereinafter Daly, *Punitive and Reconstructive Justice*] (stating that "[a]ny response Rwanda develops not only must be consistent with principles of justice but also be pragmatically feasible," and that "[j]ustice that exists only in theory is no[t] justice at all").

77. Bassiouni, *supra* note 7, at 41-42.

the "social geography" of the society in question, including its demographic composition, dynamic of group relations, and political makeup, should play a central role in the consideration and selection of accountability responses.[78] While some form of retribution for the most paradigmatic abusers seems necessary to avoid trivializing victims' suffering and to achieve a degree of justice, this will generally not suffice. Far from being mutually exclusive, blended response and mixed policies, including trials for the most paradigmatic violations, public inquiries, mediation, amnesties, and truth commissions, may be more effective in providing a degree of justice and the necessary societal reconciliation.[79]

Rwanda represents an interesting test case where solutions have been creatively devised to remedy shortcomings of the criminal trials paradigm. The Gacaca law adopts an innovative and unique approach by combining the punitive-retributive goals normally associated with criminal trials, with restorative measures promoting reconciliation and rehabilitation. This poses the main question of how to strike the right balance between the backward-looking, reactive nature of retribution, and forward-looking, restorative justice principles.

VII. JUSTICE IN THE AFTERMATH OF THE GENOCIDE: JUSTICE DENIED

In the aftermath of the genocide, both the international community and the Rwandan government have sought to achieve accountability for unspeakable crimes by way of the Western retributive model of justice embodied in criminal prosecutions. Given the magnitude of the genocide, including the fact that thousands were involved as victims and perpetrators, and the inadequacies and shortcomings characterizing both the international and the domestic trials, the general perception is that justice, accountability, and reconciliation have not been achieved.

78. *See* Drumbl, *(Al)lure of Genocide Trials*, *supra* note 39, at 219 (advocating for blended responses and policies to redress genocidal violence); Aukerman, *supra* note 27, at 41. Aukerman questions the applicability of the "ordinary crime" prosecution paradigm to "massive human rights atrocities" involving numerous individuals, and challenges the view that prosecutions are the best way of redressing criminal actions in the context of transitional justice. *Id.* The author concludes that "[We] must first determine the goals of transitional justice, and then decide on the priority to be given to prosecution." *Id.* at 92. *See also* Jeremy Sarkin, *The Tension Between Justice and Reconciliation in Rwanda: Politics, Human Rights, Due Process and the Role of the Gacaca Courts in Dealing with the Genocide*, 45 J. AFR. L. 143, 288-89 (2001) (stating that "[u]niversal application of a retributive justice model runs the risk of devaluating the importance of context in determining whether such a model will be effective in redressing mass atrocity in the affected society" and that "if retributive justice is implemented without a pre-existing contextual inquiry, a disjuncture might . . . emerge between the imperative to implement trials and the consequences these trials may have on the post-genocidal society").

79. *See* Drumbl, *(Al)lure of Genocide Trials*, *supra* note 39, at 219. This heterogeneous approach seems to be confirmed by the Velasquez-Rodriguez judgment, in which the Inter-American Court of Human Rights holistically defined justice to encompass the needs of the victims, as well as the imperative to reform state institutions to prevent future abuses. In that case, the Inter-American Court of Human Rights stated that a state is bound to fulfill the following obligations in response to the commission of a gross violation of human rights: conduct an investigation to establish the truth regarding the violation suffered by the victim and capable of identifying the perpetrators of such violation; prosecute those responsible for the violation; provide reparation or compensation to the victims of human rights violation; take steps to ensure that the violation does not recur in the future. *See* Velasquez-Rodriguez, Inter-Am. C.H.R. (ser. C) No. 4 (1988).

VIII. BACKGROUND TO THE GENOCIDE AND POLITICAL CONTEXT

Between April and July 1994, an estimated 800,000 Rwandans[80]—roughly ten percent of the entire population—were ruthlessly massacred in what was a "carefully planned and orchestrated slaughter, coordinated at the highest level of the state."[81] The genocide was triggered by the assassination of the Rwandan Hutu President Habyarimana on April 6, 1994 when the plane on which he was flying was shot down as it was approaching Kigali airport.[82] Although the country had experienced waves of violence since it obtained independence in 1962,[83] what was strikingly unique to the 1994 aggression were its savage brutality and the extent of the involvement of both victims and perpetrators. Relying on massive government-sponsored propaganda dehumanizing the Tutsi, and on the subservience of Rwanda's highly hierarchical society, the meticulously planned, efficient genocidal campaign was led by all the main actors within the then Hutu dominated government. These included the Presidential Guard, the Rwandan Armed Forces (RAF), as well as local politicians and administrators whose main task was to mobilize and involve thousands of Hutu citizens in slaughtering their own neighbors.[84] The killings were carried out with the most shocking, sadistic cruelty by using machetes, clubs, axes, knives, grenades, and guns.[85] Those responsible for the violence beat their victims to death, amputated their limbs, buried them alive, raped, and killed them.[86] Victims included women, men, and children, as "[n]o survivors were to be left to tell the story."[87]

---

80. A recent census conducted by the Rwandan government reports that 937,000 Rwandans died in the genocide. Integrated Regional Information Networks, *Rwanda: Census finds 937,000 died in genocide*, RELIEFWEB, Apr. 2, 2004, *available at* http://www.reliefweb.int/w/rwb.nsf/s/F308B7EC241 68C9885256E6A00558A7D (last visited Oct. 24, 2004). Although the number of victims will never be known with certainty, even the most conservative estimates indicate that over three quarters of the entire Tutsi population were killed. *See* Organization of African Unity, Rwanda, the Preventable Genocide § 14.80 (July 2000) [hereinafter O.A.U. Report].

81. *See* RWANDA AND SOUTH AFRICA IN DIALOGUE: ADDRESSING THE LEGACIES OF GENOCIDE AND CRIMES AGAINST HUMANITY 2 (Charles Villa-Vincencio & Tyrone Savage eds., 2001) [hereinafter RWANDA AND SOUTH AFRICA IN DIALOGUE].

82. In the plane crash, the President of Burundi was also assassinated.

83. Prior to the genocide, the population of Rwanda consisted of an estimated 85 percent Hutu, 14 percent Tutsi, and 1 percent Twa. Past ethnic and political divisions between Hutu and Tutsi, fostered and fueled by the colonial "divide and rule" policy, led to large scale massacres mostly perpetrated against Tutsi in 1963 and 1966. *See* RWANDA AND SOUTH AFRICA IN DIALOGUE, *supra* note 81, at 4-7. About 10,000 Tutsi were killed and 170,000 were driven into exile between 1959 and 1961 when a Hutu supported by the Belgians deposed the Tutsi monarchy. Following several attempts by the Tutsi to overthrow the Rwandese government, some 20,000 Tutsi were massacred. Amnesty International, Rwanda Gacaca: A Question of Justice 4 (Dec. 2002) [hereinafter Amnesty International, *Question of Justice*].

84. The genocide was "so routine, so sustained, that the perpetrators simply called it "work" . . . [it] was—according to its very design—a highly public affair, whose organizers actively sought to enlist in its deadly "work" the maximum possible number of Hutu participants. *See* Helena Cobban, *The Legacies of Collective Violence: The Rwandan Genocide and the Limits of Law*, *available at* http://boston review.net/BR27.2/cobban.html (last visited Oct. 24, 2004). *See also* Daly, *Punitive and Reconstructive Justice*, *supra* note 76, at 364 (reporting that an estimated 650,000, about one tenth of the Hutu population, participated in the killings).

85. O.A.U. Report, *supra* note 80, § 14.26.

86. *Id.* §§ 14.26-27.

87. *Id.*

The genocide was stopped only in July 1994, when the Rwandan Patriotic Army (RPA)—primarily composed of Tutsi émigrés in Uganda—took control of Kigali and ousted the Hutu regime, establishing the Rwandan transitional government of National Unity.[88] The government has since been dominated by the main Tutsi party—the Rwandan Patriotic Front (RPF)—whose leader, Paul Kagame, won a landslide victory in elections held in August 2003.[89]

In the aftermath of the genocide, Rwanda was a wrecked country with no functioning institutions or infrastructure. Of the seven million inhabitants before the genocide, about three quarters had been killed, displaced, or fled.[90] The rest were like walking dead, left to grasp with a bewildering reality.

It is in this scenario that the transitional government was confronted with the daunting task of dealing with the masses of alleged perpetrators in an attempt to break the vicious cycle of impunity that had permitted the genocide to happen in the first place.[91] To be effective, any legal response to such broad-based violence needed to achieve the multiple, competing goals of justice, reconciliation, and deterrence. Despite progress in the country's reconstruction since the genocide, Rwanda remains a deeply divided, traumatized society, where ethnic polarization runs high beneath tight government control.

IX. The International Criminal Tribunal for Rwanda

Established under Chapter VII of the United Nations Charter in 1994, the International Criminal Tribunal for Rwanda (ICTR) was conceived to bring to justice the most serious perpetrators of the genocide, and other violations of international humanitarian law, by way of an impartial forum that would avoid the perception of victor's justice in Rwanda.[92] With its creation, the international community was to send to the world the unequivocal message that the appaling crimes committed in Rwanda clearly violated international law and would not be tolerated in the future.[93] Finally, it was hoped that trials before the tribunal could ultimately contribute to the process of national reconciliation, the restoration of peace, and the prevention of future genocide in Rwanda.[94]

88. *See* Drumbl, *Sclerosis*, *supra* note 10, at 288. The RPA is the army of the rebel Tutsi political party Rwandan Patriotic Front. *See generally* Mark A. Drumbl & Kenneth S. Gallant, *Appeals in the Ad Hoc International Criminal Tribunals: Structure, Procedure, and Recent Cases*, 3 J. APP. PRAC. & PROCESS 589, 604 (2001).

89. Paul Kagame, the Tutsi RPF's leader responsible for stopping the 1994 genocide, won 95 percent of the votes. *See Kagame Won, a little too well*, THE ECONOMIST, Aug. 28, 2003, *available at* www.economist.com (last visited Oct. 24, 2004) [hereinafter *Kagame Won*].

90. O.A.U. Report, *supra* note 80, § 17.3.

91. Harrell, *supra* note 10, at 37 (stating that justice was seen both as a moral duty to the survivors and as necessary to break the cycle of impunity while seeking reconciliation).

92. U.N. SCOR, 49th Sess., 3453d mtg., U.N. Doc. S/RES/955 (1994). *See also* Statute of the ICTR, S.C. Res. 955, U.N. SCOR, 3453d mtg., Annex, art. 1-4, U.N. Doc. S/RES/955 (1994).

93. *See* Jason Strain & Elizabeth Keyes, *Accountability in the Aftermath of Rwanda's Genocide*, *in* ACCOUNTABILITY FOR ATROCITIES: NATIONAL AND INTERNATIONAL RESPONSES 87, 98-99 (Jane E. Stromseth ed., 2003).

94. Statute of the ICTR, S.C. Res. 955, U.N. SCOR, 3453d mtg., at preamble, U.N. Doc. S/RES/955 (1994).

Significantly, the ICTR was the first international court ever to deliver verdicts in relation to genocide.[95] But, while the tribunal has made some relevant contributions by setting new important legal precedents in the field of human rights and humanitarian law,[96] it has nonetheless been looked upon with growing skepticism, not only by the Rwandan government, but also by some foreign observers.[97] Since its establishment, managerial, administrative and logistical deficiencies have compromised its ability to deliver justice effectively and swiftly.[98] As of September 2004, only nineteen judgments have been handed down involving twenty-three accused.[99] Rwanda's disappointment with the slow pace of justice has been further exacerbated by the realization that the tribunal consumes disproportionately conspicuous resources at the expense of the national judicial system.[100] Recent plans to complete all tribunal's activities by 2010 further contribute to the bitterness felt by many Rwandans vis-à-vis an international community perceived as indifferent to their quest for justice.[101]

The tribunal has also been regarded by the majority of Rwandans as the embodiment of victor's justice, in that it has failed to investigate war crimes committed by the RPF, despite the fact that these fall within its mandate.[102]

Furthermore, the tribunal has been criticized for failing to deliver to its "primary audience"—i.e. the society victimized by the violence.[103] The effectiveness of the tribunal in delivering justice while seeking peace and reconciliation has

95. ICTR, General Information, *available at* http://www.ictr.org/default.htm (last visited Oct. 24, 2004) [hereinafter ICTR, General Information].

96. The ICTR has delivered the first conviction in history of a former head of government, former Prime Minister Kambanda, for genocide; has recognized that rape and sexual violence constitute genocidal acts when committed with the intent to destroy a protected group; and has defined the contour of rape as a crime against humanity. Roman Boed, *The International Criminal Tribunal for Rwanda*, *in* POST CONFLICT JUSTICE 487, 493 (Cherif M. Bassiouni ed., 2002).

97. Rwanda, at the time a member of the Security Council, was the only country to vote against the resolution establishing the ICTR. Among the reasons for this position, the limited temporal jurisdiction of the ICTR and its refusal to impose the death penalty. *See* Strain & Keyes, *supra* note 93, at 104-09. For a critique of the ICTR performance, see Drumbl, *(Al)lure of Genocide Trials*, *supra* note 39, at 227 (criticizing ICTR proceedings for being slow, very expensive, selective, subject to due process challenges and widely perceived as illegitimate by Rwandans). *See also* Makau Mutua, *From Nuremberg to the Rwanda Tribunal: Justice or Retribution?*, BUFF. HUM. RTS. L. REV. 77, 78-79 (2000) (arguing that the contribution of the ICTR to the protection of human rights as well as the process of peace and normalization inside Rwanda is "marginal, if not entirely irrelevant," and that the tribunal is alien to "political realities and removed from both the individual and national psyches of the victims as well as the victors in the Rwanda conflict").

98. Pernille Ironside, *Rwandan Gacaca: Seeking Alternative Means to Justice, Peace and Reconciliation*, 15 N.Y. INT'L L. REV. 31, 35 (2002).

99. ICTR, Fact Sheet No. 1, The Tribunal at a Glance, *available at* http://www.ictr.org/default.htm (last visited Oct. 24, 2004) [hereinafter ICTR, Fact Sheet No. 1].

100. Former Rwandan General Prosecutor Gerald Gahima, Re-establishing the Rule of Law and Encouraging Good Governance (Sept. 9, 2002) (presented at the 55th Annual DPI/NGO Conference) [hereinafter Gahima] (condemning the manifest bias of the international community towards international mechanisms at the expense of national systems). In 2002-2003, the UN General Assembly allotted to the ICTR a total budget of $177,739,400. *See* ICTR, General Information, *supra* note 95.

101. The ICTR first submitted its completion strategy to the UN Security Council in July 2003. According to the plan, ICTR's investigations are due to be completed by the end of 2004, while all trials and appeals are expected to be terminated by, respectively, 2008 and 2010. *See* ICTR, Fact Sheet No. 1, *supra* note 99.

102. On the jurisdiction of the ICTR, see Statute of the ICTR, S.C. Res. 955, U.N. SCOR, 3453d mtg., at preamble, arts. 1-4, U.N. Doc. S/RES/955 (1994).

103. *See* Kritz, *Progress and Humility*, *supra* note 13, at 59.

indeed been frustrated by its inaccessibility to ordinary Rwandans. While its location in "neutral" land—Arusha, Tanzania—was to send a message of impartiality, it makes it in fact impractical—if not impossible—for Rwandans to attend court proceedings or hear news of ICTR trials.[104] This, and the virtually total exclusion of victims from the tribunal proceedings, has led some critics to see the tribunal as being largely inaccessible, distant, and as having a minimal and disempowering impact on victims' lives.[105] It is no surprise, therefore, that Rwandans regard the tribunal as a "foreign and removed body alien in procedure, whose slow pace of trials is proof of UN inefficiency, or worse, indifferent to Rwandan needs."[106]

Given the limited capability of the ICTR to deliver justice, the Rwandan government has turned to the national judicial system as the principle means to deliver accountability and end the cycle of impunity.

X. ENDING IMPUNITY IN POST-GENOCIDE RWANDA: THE 1996 GENOCIDE LAW

Despite its almost complete human and physical incapacitation, and the impossible challenge posed by having to deal with the genocide on such a widespread scale, the prosecution of genocide suspects was looked upon by the Rwandan government as the only way of ending impunity and as an essential precondition to achieving stability and reconciliation.[107] This determination was to be faced by a crude reality. In the aftermath of the genocide, the Rwandan provisional government of National Unity was faced with the enormous and urgent challenge of re-building the judicial system virtually from scratch.[108] The events of the spring 1994 had in fact devastated the already limited judicial infrastructure

104. Strain & Keyes, *supra* note 93, at 107 (reporting that only recently have Rwandans been able to get news from the ICTR in Kinyarwanda, the national language of Rwanda). *See* Kritz, *Progress and Humility*, *supra* note 13, at 59 (stating that the victim's groups and local society were long ignored by the two ad hoc international criminal tribunals, and outreach to the local population on their work took years to begin). Some progress is currently being made as the ICTR is currently building a courtroom in Kigali. *Id.*

105. Victims cannot constitute themselves civil claimants in proceedings before the tribunal. Stef Vandeginste, *Victims of Genocide, Crimes against Humanity, and War Crimes in Rwanda: The Legal and Institutional Framework of Their Right to Reparation*, *in* POLITICS AND THE PAST 249, 53 (John Torpey ed., 2003) [hereinafter Vandeginste, *Victims of Genocide*]. While the statute of the tribunal provides for the possibility that reparation in the form of restitution be ordered in the judgments, this has never happened to date. *Id.* On the other hand, the ICTR has launched, in 2000, an aid program for victims, which includes the provision of legal advice, psychological counseling and rieducation, as well as financial assistance for resettlement. *Id. See also* David Rawson, *Coping with Chaos while Acting Justly: Lessons from Rwanda*, *in* EFFECTIVE STRATEGIES FOR PROTECTING HUMAN RIGHTS 125, 132 (David Barnhizer ed., 2001) (stating that the ICTR remains "geographically distant and conceptually estranged from the people it purports to serve").

106. *See* Ironside, *supra* note 98, at 36.

107. *See* Jean De Dieu Mucyo (former Rwandan Minister of Justice), RWANDA AND SOUTH AFRICA IN DIALOGUE, *supra* note 81, at 49 (stating that the eradication of impunity was a precondition for peace). *See also* Gahima, *supra* note 100, at 4 (stating that prosecutions were undertaken to address the victims' demands for justice, issues of accountability and impunity, to foster the rule of law, and to promote peace and reconciliation).

108. *See* Cara J. Ferstman, *Domestic Trials for Genocide and Crimes Against Humanity: The Example of Rwanda*, 9 AFR. J. INT'L & COMP. L. 857, 861 (1997).

and decimated most of its personnel.[109] According to post-genocide statistics, over 80 percent of the country's legal personnel—including judges, prosecutors and magistrates—had either been killed or fled the country following the outbreak of the violence in April 1994.[110] These difficulties were exacerbated by the challenge of establishing the rule of law in a context where none ever existed in the first place.[111]

With the help of the international community, the Rwandan government started the rehabilitation and introduced important reforms of the justice system in a relatively short period of time.[112] Approximately 324 magistrates, 100 deputy prosecutors and 298 judicial police officers and inspectors were trained prior to the reopening of the court system in 1996, though these numbers still fell considerably short of what was needed for the system to operate under normal circumstances.[113] It is in this context that the government of Rwanda proceeded with an unrealistic program of maximum accountability with the aim of prosecuting all those responsible for genocide-related crimes, thus assigning to the justice system an impossible task.[114]

In 1996, the government passed Organic Law No. 08/96 on the organization of prosecution for offenses constituting the crime of genocide or crimes against humanity committed since October 1, 1990.[115] The special legislation was conceived "to bring about justice, retribution, and the end of impunity" by setting up specialized chambers within the ordinary jurisdictions of the first instances courts to try genocide-related cases.[116]

---

109. Chris Mburu, Challenges Facing Legal and Judicial Reform in Post-Conflict Environments: Case Study from Rwanda and Sierra Leone 11, 17-18 (July 8-12, 2001) (paper presented at the World Bank Conference "Empowerment, Security and Opportunity through Law and Justice") (reporting the destruction of courthouses and of the most basic legal documents and materials). *See* William A. Shabas, *Justice, Democracy and Impunity in Post-Genocide Rwanda: Searching for Solutions to Impossible Problems*, CRIM. L.F. 524, 533 (1996). *See also* Madeline H. Morris, *The Trials of Concurrent Jurisdiction: The Case of Rwanda*, 7 DUKE J. OF COMP. & INT'L L. 349, 353 (1997).

110. There are different estimates as to the number of legal personnel present in the country at that time. *See* O.A.U. Report, *supra* note 80, § 18.4 (reporting that there were only five judges in the country and fifty lawyers). *But see* Mburu, *supra* note 109, at 11 (reporting that out of 750 judges in early 1994, only 244 were left after the genocide; out of 87 prosecutors, 14 were present in post-genocide Rwanda; out of 193 investigators only 39 survived).

111. *See* Gahima, *supra* note 100, at 2 (stating that the pre-genocide justice administration system was "largely manned by unqualified people . . . judges were appointed on the basis of political patronage, [and that] corruption in the judiciary was rife"). *See also* Schabas, *supra* note 109, at 531 (reporting that, in 1993, the Rwandan justice system comprised about seven hundred judges and magistrates, of whom less than fifty had any formal legal training).

112. Institutional reforms included the establishment of the Supreme Council of Magistrates and the reestablishment of the Supreme Court, which had been suppressed since 1978. *See* Amnesty International, *Question of Justice*, *supra* note 83, at 12.

113. *Id.*

114. *See* Mark A. Drumbl, *Rule of Law Amid Lawlessness: Counseling the Accused in Rwanda's Domestic Genocide Trials*, 29 COLUM. HUM. RTS. L. REV. 545, 630 (1998) [hereinafter Drumbl, *Lawlessness*].

115. *See* Organic Law No. 08/96 of Aug. 30, 1996 on the Organization of Prosecutions for Offenses Constituting the Crime of Genocide or Crimes Against Humanity Committed Since 1 October 1990, *available at* www.preventgenocide.org/law/domestic/rwanda.htm (last visited Oct. 24, 2004) [hereinafter Genocide Law].

116. *See* Ferstman, *supra* note 108, at 863 (discussing the Genocide Law).

The law created four categories of offenses and corresponding punishments.[117] Category 1, which carried the death penalty,[118] included those who masterminded the genocide (e.g. the planners, instigators, organizers, and leaders of the genocidal campaign; persons who acted in positions of authority; notorious murderers; and those who committed particularly heinous acts or sexual torture).[119] Category 2, which carried the penalty of life imprisonment,[120] comprised the perpetrators, conspirators, or accomplices of intentional homicide or serious assault resulting in death.[121] Category 3, which carried the penalty of imprisonment for a number of years,[122] comprised persons accused of "other serious" but non-lethal assaults.[123] Category 4 comprised persons who committed offenses against property[124] and must pay civil damages.[125] The specialized justice program established by the Genocide Law also relied heavily on a "fast-track . . . confession procedure."[126] This offered all perpetrators in the genocide—other than those in Category 1—a substantial sentence reduction subject to a full and detailed confession, a guilty plea and an apology to the victims.[127] This system was conceived to accelerate preliminary investigations, speed up and reduce the number of trials, and enhance reconciliation through public admission of guilt.[128]

XI. THE RWANDAN GENOCIDE TRIALS: PROBLEMS AND CHALLENGES IN DELIVERING JUSTICE

Since their start in 1996, the Rwandan trials for genocide have been subject to extensive criticism directed at the lack of experience and independence of the judges,[129] as well as their disregard of due process rights.[130] By the end of 2002,

117. Genocide Law, *supra* note 115, arts. 2, 14.
118. *Id.* art. 14.
119. *Id.* art. 2.
120. *Id.* art. 14.
121. *Id.* art. 2.
122. *Id.* art. 14.
123. *Id.* art. 2.
124. *Id.*
125. *Id.* art. 14(d).
126. *See* Drumbl, *Lawlessness*, *supra* note 114, at 586-87.
127. Genocide Law, *supra* note 115, arts. 4-16. *See* Morris, *supra* note 109, at 359 ("[a] greater penalty reduction is made available to perpetrators who confess and plead guilty prior to prosecution than to perpetrators who confess only after prosecution has begun").
128. Lawyers Committee for Human Rights, Prosecuting Genocide in Rwanda: The ICTR and National Trials 51 (1997), *at* http://www.humanrightsfirst.org/pubs/descriptions/rwanda.htm#. *See also* Morris, *supra* note 109, at 360 (commenting that the requirement of a detailed confession was important for establishing a "truthful historical record" of the genocide, and in facilitating investigations and prosecutions of genocide related crimes).
129. When the trial started, most judges in the Specialized Chambers had no trial experience and little training. *See* Drumbl, *Lawlessness*, *supra* note 114, at 594. *See also* Ferstman, *supra* note 108, at 862 (stating that some of the judges presiding over genocide trials were lay persons with only four months training).
130. *See* Drumbl, *Lawlessness*, *supra* note 114, at 614 (stating that when the trials started in 1996, only 54 percent of the defendants had defense counsel). *See also* MINOW, *supra* note 15, at 124 (arguing that, rather then ending the cycle of revenge, Rwandan trials were revenge). *But see* United States Department of State, Country Report on Human Rights Practices: Rwanda (2001) (reporting that, from 1999 through 2002, the vast majority of genocide trial met international fair trial standards) [hereinafter Country Report].

approximately 7,331 persons had been judged on genocide-related charges, mostly through group trials.[131] Although the quality of genocide trials has considerably improved over time, they are still carried out in a highly charged political context and by scarcely qualified personnel.[132] The judiciary continues to suffer from a dearth of resources, inefficiency, corruption, and executive influence.[133] Its "Tutsification,"[134] coupled with the virtual wholesome impunity of the RPF for war crimes committed during and after the civil war, raises serious questions regarding its legitimacy and impartiality.[135]

The credibility of the domestic system of justice is further called into question by the desperate prison situation in Rwanda. In the aftermath of the genocide, a massive campaign of arrest associated with a dysfunctional judiciary led to the unlawful, prolonged detention of thousands of individuals.[136] As of April 2004, some 80,000 inidividuals were still detained on genocide-related charges.[137] Due to the overcrowding and the appalling sanitary situation, most prisoners live in life threatening conditions.[138] This grim situation is not likely to drastically change, as even the most optimistic estimates indicate a prison population of 60,000 by 2005.[139]

While the genocide trials have permitted the Rwandan government to individualize culpability for the genocide and to send a strong deterrent message to

---

131. *See* Amnesty International, *Question of Justice, supra* note 83, at 16 (estimating that, by the end of 2001, only 6 percent of genocide suspects had been tried).

132. *Id.* at 15-16.

133. *Id.* at 13-14. *See also* Stef Vandeginste, *Rwanda: Dealing with Genocide and Crimes against Humanity in the Context of Armed Conflict and Failed Political Transition*, *in* BURYING THE PAST: MAKING PEACE AND DOING JUSTICE AFTER CIVIL CONFLICT 223, 235 (Nigel Biggar ed., 2001) [hereinafter Vandeginste, *Dealing with Genocide*] (reporting that in some cases suspects have been released by corrupting the judges and that this has led to popular vendetta).

134. *See* Marc Cousineau, L'etablissement de l'Etat de droit au Rwanda: un but irrealisable, 28 OTTAWA L. REV. 171, 180 (1997) (stating that in 1996, 85 percent of those trained to become magistrates were Tutsi). *See also* Fillip Reyntjens, *Chronique Politique du Burundi et du Rwanda*, *in* L'AFRIQUE DES GRANDS LACS ANNUAIRE 1999-2000, at 112 (F. Reyntjens et S. Marysse ed., 2000) (reporting that in 1999, the majority of presidents of tribunals of first instance, court of appeals and Supreme Court were Tutsi, as well as most of the prosecutors); O.A.U Report, *supra* note 80, § 18.38 (stating that, "as virtually all other sectors of Rwandan public life, the justice system was dominated by Tutsi").

135. *See* Strain & Keyes, *supra* note 93, at 116. *See also* Press Release, Human Rights Watch, *Rwanda: Deliver Justice for Victims of Both Sides*, Aug. 12, 2002 (reporting that thousands were killed in human rights abuses propagated by the RPF), *available at* http://www.hrw.org/press/2002/08/rwanda081202.htm (last visited Oct. 24, 2004).

136. *See* Amnesty International, *Question of Justice, supra* note 83, at 6-8. *See also* Country Report, *supra* note 130, § 1(d) (reporting that, in 2001, ninety-five percent of approximately 110,000 individuals detained were awaiting trial on genocide-related charges, the majority of whom had incomplete files).

137. *See* Amnesty International, Rwanda: The Enduring Legacy of Genocide and War (Apr. 6, 2004), *available at* http://web.amnesty.org/library/index/engafr470082004 (last visited Oct. 24, 2004) [hereinafter Amnesty International, *Enduring Legacy*].

138. *See* Commission on Human Rights Report on the Situation of Human Rights in Rwanda submitted by the Special Representative, Mr. Michel Moussalli, E/CN.4/1999/33, at 30. *See also* Amnesty International, *Question of Justice, supra* note 83, at 8 (reporting 11,000 deaths between 1994 and 2001 due to "preventable disease, malnutrition and the debilitating effects of overcrowding").

139. Peace and Reconciliation in Africa, (Nov. 8-12, 1999) (paper presented at the All-Africa Conference on African Principles of Conflict Resolution and Reconciliation, Addis Ababa, Ethiopia) [hereinafter *Peace and Reconciliation*].

those convicted,[140] they have failed to achieve other equally important goals. As observed by Mark Drumbl, "By focusing on individual guilt or innocence in a situation of broad societal complicity, the importance of collective wrongdoing and the structural causes of the genocide are ignored, if not negated."[141] According to Drumbl, the trials have also strikingly failed to generate feelings of individual responsibility and guilt among prisoners, with most of them regarding themselves simply as prisoners of war ending up on the losing side.[142] This, coupled with the general distrust of the Tutsi-dominated judicial system, may explain why the trials have failed to produce a full, reliable record of what happened in 1994, despite the thousands of criminal prosecutions undertaken by the Rwandan government.[143] Further, the slow pace, the inaccessibility of court proceedings, and lack of reparation through trials have been of little benefit to the victims.[144] The Rwandan justice system has thus been deemed to be a "lethargic, and arbitrary enforcement procedure" that denies justice to alleged perpetrators and victims alike and hinders the process of reconciliation.[145]

XII. SEARCHING FOR ALTERNATIVE FORMS OF JUSTICE: THE GACACA JURISDICTIONS

Acknowledging the inability of the ordinary justice system to deal with the sheer number of perpetrators, the Rwandan government started to question the efficacy of a "Western-style, highly individualized prosecutorial approach" and to consider alternative ways of overcoming the judicial impasse.[146] It thus decided to introduce Gacaca jurisdictions to try genocide cases. These consist of a community-based, highly decentralized system of local courts inspired by the traditional dispute resolution mechanism existing in Rwanda since pre-colonial time.[147]

140. Strain & Keyes, *supra* note 93, at 111 (stating that the trials "brought to justice" those responsible for the genocide while exonerating those who did not participate in the eye of the state and, more importantly, of their communities).

141. *See* Drumbl, *Sclerosis*, *supra* note 10, at 295 (arguing that the simplistic categories of "innocent" or "guilty" created by trials contribute to reinforcing the "dualistic nature" of Rwanda post-genocidal society).

142. Drumbl, *(Al)lure of Genocide Trials*, *supra* note 39, at 227-28. Several observers have noted that Hutu prisoners usually deny the genocide ever happened and refer to the events taking place between April and July 1994 as the civil war. *Id.* at 228.

143. *See* Drumbl, *Sclerosis*, *supra* note 10, at 295 (quoting Carrie Gustafson, *International Criminal Courts: Some Dissident Views on the Continuation of War by the Penal Means*, 21 HOUS. J. INT'L L. 1, 26 (1998)).

144. *See* Vandeginste, *Dealing with Genocide*, *supra* note 133, at 237 (stating that victims are often unaware that court hearings are taking place, and that the process of obtaining certificates and of estimating the damage is cumbersome and expensive for them). *See also* Vandeginste, *Victims of Genocide*, *supra* note 105, at 256-57 (although compensation for victims has been awarded in 50 percent of civil verdicts, in none of these cases were the verdicts awarded against the state or against those found criminally guilty).

145. Drumbl, *Lawlessness*, *supra* note 114, at 600.

146. *See* Cobban, *supra* note 84, at 8-10. *See also* African Rights, Gacaca Justice: A Shared Responsibility 1 (Jan. 2003) [hereinafter African Rights] (estimating that, at the current pace, it will take about twenty years to complete genocide-related trials).

147. Reyntjens, *supra* note 134, at 95. According to the government, the new Gacaca jurisdictions rely on the use of arbitration traditionally embodied in Gacaca to achieve goals of retribution, rehabilitation of victims, reconciliation and construction of a "new Rwandan national identity." *See* Cobban, *supra* note 84, at 11 (citing Richard Sezibera, Rwandan Ambassador); Gahima, *supra* note 100 (speak-

While the new system was primarily conceived to remedy the slow pace with which justice was being meted out by the ICTR and the domestic courts, it also purported to respond to their lack of inclusiveness by engaging individuals and communities in the process of justice and reconciliation.[148] The Gacaca jurisdictions—which have been promoted by the government as a synthesis of the traditional Gacaca and a formal, Western-style court system—are expected to have an approximate lifespan of five to eight years.[149]

XIII. THE ROLE OF TRADITIONAL GACACA

In its original form, Gacaca is an informal, community-based, localized system of dispute resolution that has ancient roots in Rwanda, with origins in pre-colonial times.[150] Acting as a "local healing . . . mechanism that is cheap and accessible," Gacaca's indigenous forums are used by villages' inhabitants as an alternative to the formal state courts to resolve minor disputes arising among them.[151] Gacaca is an expression of the culture and reflects the close-knit nature of rural communities from which it originated.[152] It operates on an informal, ad hoc basis, through meetings convened whenever the need arises.[153] Traditionally, unless women are a party to the conflict, only male adults take part in the meetings which are chaired by respected community elders, acting as arbitrators.[154] Gacaca embodies restorative justice principles because it does not seek to achieve justice by punishing the perpetrator, but to restore social order by finding communal, compromised solutions, and by reintegrating the offender within the community.[155] As with other African traditional dispute resolution systems, Gacaca aims

ing of "extraordinary laws" to respond to an "extraordinary event"-i.e. the genocide); *Rwandan To Resurrect Traditional Justice System*, AGENCE FRANCE PRESSE, June 17, 2002, *available at* www.globalpolicy.org/intljustice/general/2002/0617ga.htm (last visited Dec. 9, 2004).

148. Strain & Keyes, *supra* note 93, at 117. *See also On a Patch of Grass*, THE ECONOMIST, May 17, 2003, at 42 (characterizing Gacaca as "rough, cheap and the main means of Hutu-Tutsi reconciliation").

149. *Genocide Suspects' List to Swell to Over 500,000*, HIRONDELLE NEWS AGENCY, Sept. 2, 2004, *available at* http://www.hirondelle.org/arusha.nsf/0/4E338483245F4F2D43256F04005708F8?OpenDocument [hereinafter *Genocide Suspects' List*].

150. *See* Daly, *Punitive and Reconstructive Justice, supra* note 76, at 370-71. In many African countries, colonial powers introduced their own system of courts while allowing indigenous systems of dispute resolution to continue operating. This resulted in a dual, parallel system of laws and courts called legal pluralism. Penal Reform International, Access to Justice in Sub-Saharan Africa: the Role of Traditional and Informal Justice Systems 51 (2000) [hereinafter *Access to Justice*].

151. *See* Sarkin, *supra* note 78, at 159-60.

152. Informal dispute resolution mechanisms generally exist in small, rural communities dominated by "multiplex relationships," i.e., "relationships which are based on past and future economic and social dependence, and which intersect ties of kinship." In such communities a dispute between two individuals is perceived as a conflict belonging to the whole community. *See Access to Justice, supra* note 150, at 22.

153. Stef Vandeginste, Justice, Reconciliation and Reparation after Genocide and Crimes against Humanity: The Proposed Establishment of Popular Gacaca Tribunals in Rwanda (Nov. 8-12, 1999 Addis Ababa) (paper presented to the All Africa Conference on African Principles of Conflict Resolution and Reconciliation) [hereinafter Vandeginste, *Justice*]

154. *Id.* at 15, 17.

155. *Id.* at 15. *See also Peace and Reconciliation, supra* note 139, at 7 (stating that arbitrators' decisions are based more on the "need to restore social harmony rather than ascertaining innocence or guilt").

at restoring peace and social harmony within the community affected by the conflict.[156] Although most of the disputes dealt with by Gacaca have a civil nature, some conflicts amounting to minor criminal offenses are also referred to it, resulting not in a criminal sanction but in some sort of civil settlement.[157] Conflicts dealt with by Gacaca include disputes over land use and land rights, cattle, marriage, inheritance rights, loans, damage to properties or animals, theft, as well as light bodily injuries.[158] Reflecting its restorative, reconciliatory nature, the sentences it imposes must be accepted by all of the parties involved.[159] In cases where an agreement between the parties cannot be reached, the case can be referred to the local "Cantonal Tribunal." Gacaca meetings have over time become more formalized, being held at regular intervals and with local administrative authorities sometimes acting as arbitrators in the dispute.[160] Although most Gacaca forums ceased to operate during the 1994 genocide, they were reinstated shortly thereafter and are currently active in many areas of the country.[161]

XIV. The Contemporary Gacaca: Between Traditional and State Justice

Faced with the slow pace of justice in the aftermath of the genocide, the Rwandan government devised a creative solution by reviving and adapting the traditional Gacaca system of informal dispute resolution to try genocide-related cases.[162] The Gacaca courts are village-based, quasi-judicial forums designed to complement and remedy the failure of the classical system of justice by achieving multiple, ambitious goals.[163] These consist of the reduction of delays in the overburdened criminal justice system, the uncovering of the truth, and the achievement of justice and reconciliation through a highly participatory strategy.[164] In a unique way, Gacaca are set to do so by means of retributive and re-integrative measures.

By involving ordinary Rwandans in the process of justice, Gacaca is based on the assumption that the offenses "were publicly committed before the very eyes of the population, which thus must recount the facts, disclose the truth and participate in prosecuting and trying the alleged perpetrators."[165] Under the new system, genocide trials take place in the afflicted communities "for whom reconciliation is

156. *Access to Justice*, *supra* note 150, at 24.

157. *See* Fillip Reyntjens, *Le Gacaca ou la justice du gazon au Rwanda*, 40 POLITIQUE AFRICAINE 34 (1990).

158. *Id.*

159. *See* Vandeginste, *Justice*, *supra* note 153, at 15.

160. *Id.* at 16.

161. Jennifer Widener, *Courts and Democracy in Postconflict Transitions: A Social Scientist's Perspective on the African Case*, 95 AM. J. INT'L L. 64, 66 (2001). *See also Access to Justice*, *supra* note 150, at 78-79.

162. *See* African Rights, *supra* note 146, at 1 (stating that the traditional Gacaca system "was shaped to suit the needs of contemporary Rwanda").

163. On the failures of the formal justice system to deliver justice, see Gahima, *supra* note 100, at 6 (acknowledging the limited number of Rwandan courts; the cumbersome procedures; the slowness of the system; the impossibility to participate in the judicial process of the society at large).

164. Manuel Explicatif sur la Loi Organique Portante Creation des Jurisdictions Gacaca 8, Cour Supreme (Departements de Jurisdictions Gacaca).

165. *See* Organic Law No. 16/2004 of 19/6/2004, *supra* note 4, at preamble.

not an abstract goal but a constant daily struggle."[166] Unlike the formal justice system and the ICTR, Gacaca jurisdictions operate in the absence of legally qualified judges, prosecutors, and legal counsel.[167]

The recourse to the traditional Gacaca as an ad hoc mechanism to complement the ordinary justice system was first proposed in 1998 by a Commission largely composed of members of parliament, prefects and representatives of the Ministry of Justice.[168] Although studies conducted in the phase of conceptualization of the Gacaca jurisdictions indicate that they were widely supported by Rwandans,[169] real understanding about their functioning appeared to be very limited, with individuals who are the most knowledgeable about the law expressing skepticism regarding the courts' effectiveness in trying genocide cases.[170]

XV. ORGANIZATION, JURISDICTION AND POWERS OF THE GACACA JURISDICTIONS

First adopted by the Rwandan Transitional Assembly in January 2001,[171] the law devising and regulating the Gacaca courts system was recently amended by Organic Law No. 16/2004 of 19/6/2004 (Gacaca law).[172] Following a two year pilot phase in which Gacaca courts were established and operated on a circumscribed basis,[173] the amended version of the Gacaca law addresses some of the system's shortcomings by streamlining and simplifying the Gacaca process and by reducing the overall number of judges involved in it.[174] The Gacaca law estab-

166. *See* Strain & Keyes, *supra* note 93, at 118.

167. Amnesty International, *Question of Justice, supra* note 83, at 37.

168. *See* Vandeginste, *Justice, supra* note 153, at 1.

169. According to a survey, conducted in 2000, by a Rwandese NGO, 93 percent of the Rwandese population was in favor of establishing the Gacaca jurisdictions to try genocide related cases and considered them to be the appropriate instrument to promote national reconciliation. *See* Special Gacaca, LE VERDICT No. 15/16, July 2000. *But see* Sarkin, *supra* note 78, at 160 (reporting that at least one group, the Rally for the Return of Refugees and Democracy in Rwanda, has rejected the Gacaca courts); Vandengiste, *Justice, supra* note 153, at 14 (reporting that a sociological enquiry conducted in 1996 indicated that people generally rejected the use of traditional Gacaca to deal with the genocide cases).

170. *See* S. GABISIREGE & S. BABALOLA, PERCEPTIONS ABOUT THE GACACA LAW IN RWANDA: EVIDENCE FROM A MULTI-METHOD STUDY 11 (Johns Hopkins Univ. Sch. of Public Health, Center for Communications Programs 2001).

171. Organic Law No. 40/2000 of 26/01/2001, *supra* note 3 (setting up the "Gacaca jurisdictions" and organizing prosecutions for offenses constituting the crime of genocide or crimes against humanity committed between Oct. 1, 1990 and Dec. 31, 1994).

172. Organic Law No. 16/2004 of 19/6/2004, *supra* note 4 (establishing the organization, competence and functioning of Gacaca courts charged with prosecuting and trying the perpetrators of the crime of genocide and other crimes against humanity, committed between Oct. 1, 1990 and Dec. 31, 1994).

173. *See* Hirondelle News Agency, *Gacaca Tribunals Officially Launched in Rwanda*, June 24, 2004 (reporting that the 751 Gacaca courts involved in the pilot phase have so far collected information on the genocide in their respective communities, classified the alleged perpetrators, and completed lists of the victims), *available at* http://hirondelle.org/arusha.nsf/English?OpenFrameSet (last visited Oct. 24, 2004).

174. The June 2004 amendments reduced the overall number of Gacaca judges from 258,209 to 169,400; reduced the number of judges on each Gacaca bench from 19 to 9; eliminated the two highest levels of Gacaca courts as established by Organic Law No.40/200 of 26/01/2001, namely those at the district and the province level; and introduced measures to protect the identity of rape victims. *See* IRIN News, *Rwanda: Traditional Courts Inaugurated*, June 24, 2004, *available at* www.irinnews.org/

lishes a hierarchical system of "Gacaca courts" in the country's two lowest administrative units—notably the cell and the sector—and introduces a Gacaca court of appeal in each sector.[175] The Gacaca courts are supervised and coordinated by the newly established National Service.[176] The new law classifies genocide suspects into three categories according to the degree of their responsibility and the seriousness of the crimes they committed, and confers on the Gacaca courts the competence to try middle-low level suspects in Categories 2 and 3.[177] Category 2 includes perpetrators and accomplices of homicide and other serious attacks causing death; those who injured or attempted to kill their victims; as well as those who committed assaults without the intention to kill.[178] Category 3 includes those suspected of having committed offenses against property.[179] Category 1 suspects—which includes the instigators and organizers of the genocide, notorious murderers, rapists and those who committed acts of torture against their victims—will continue to be tried by the ordinary courts.[180] General assemblies at the cell and sector level (composed of all adult residents in the respective communities) elect nine adults of "integrity" from within themselves to serve as "judges" in the Gacaca courts, and five deputies.[181] Gacaca judges are not required to possess any legal qualifications.[182] The Gacaca courts combine the powers of the prosecution and of the ordinary tribunals. At the cell level, the general assembly exercises the functions of a prosecutor: it identifies the crimes, the victims, the alleged perpetrators and gives evidence to the bench.[183] On the basis of this information, the bench compiles lists of the cell's residents, victims, and suspects; gathers evidence and testimonies; makes all necessary investigations; and receives confessions, guilty pleas and apologies.[184] In order to conduct hearings, Gacaca jurisdictions are vested with powers similar to those conferred upon ordinary criminal tribunals.[185] Gacaca benches at the cell level determine the categorization of all sus-

report.asp?ReportID=41860 (last visited Oct. 24, 2004) [hereinafter IRIN News, *Traditional Courts Inaugurated*].

175. Organic Law No. 16/2004 of 19/6/2004, *supra* note 4, arts. 3-4. Each Gacaca court is composed of three organs: a General Assembly, a Seat (or bench), and a Coordination Committee. *See id.* art. 5.

176. *Id.* art. 50.

177. *Id.* art. 2. A previous version of the Gacaca law classified genocide suspects into four categories in accordance with the 1996 Genocide Law (Organic Law No. 08/96 of August 30, 1996), and conferred on the Gacaca courts the task to try Category 2-4 suspects. *See* Organic Law No. 40/2000 of 26/01/2001, *supra* note 3, art. 51.

178. Organic Law No. 16/2004 of 19/6/2004, *supra* note 4, art. 51(2).

179. *Id.* art. 51(3).

180. *Id.* art. 51(1).

181. *Id.* art. 13. The General Assembly for the Sector level elects, within itself, nine persons of integrity and their five deputies to make up the Seat both of the Gacaca court of appeal, and of the Gacaca court of the sector. *See also id.* art. 8.

182. See *id.* art. 14. According to this provision, Rwandans of "integrity" who are at least twenty-one years of age can be elected as Gacaca judges under condition that they have not participated in the genocide; are free from the spirit of "sectarianism"; have not been sentenced to a penalty of at least six months of imprisonment; are of high morals and conduct, truthful and honest; and are characterized by a spirit of speech sharing.

183. *Id.* art. 33. *See also* Daly, *Punitive and Reconstructive Justice*, *supra* note 76, at 373.

184. *Id.* art. 34.

185. *See id.* art. 39. Benches at the cell level may compel testimony, order searches, take temporary protective measures against the property of those accused of genocide, sentence the convicted person to pay compensation, summon the alleged perpetrators, and order detention or release on parole where necessary. *Id.*

pects who lived in the cell during the genocide; try suspects of the least serious crimes, those against property (Category 3 suspects); and forward Category 1 and 2 suspects' files to, respectively, the public prosecutor and Gacaca courts at the sector level.[186] Category 2 suspects are tried by the sector-level Gacaca courts.[187] The Gacaca law offers strong sentence reductions as an incentive to confess, and the possibility to commute half of the defendant's sentence into community service.[188] Gacaca hearings are public, except for rape related proceedings and other exceptional cases in which hearings are conducted in camera.[189] The Gacaca law prescribes penalties for individuals who refuse to testify and for those who have threatened or otherwise exercised illicit forms of pressure on witnesses.[190] The Gacaca jurisdictions can impose sentences as severe as thirty years of imprisonment for Category 2 defendants who have killed or attempted to kill their victims and refuse to confess, whereas Category 3 defendants can only be ordered to pay civil compensation for damages to victims' property.[191] Under the law, there is a limited right of appeal only for Category 2 defendants; a right to present opposition against a sentence for those against whom the latter has been pronounced in absentia; and a right to obtain review of a judgment in circumscribed cases.[192] The new system started to be implemented throughout Rwanda in June 2004, following a two-year pilot phase that involved 751 of the nation's 9,010 Gacaca jurisdictions.[193] After considerable delays on the initial government's timeline, thousands of cases are now ready to be tried by the 169,400 popularly elected judges.[194]

XVI. A CRITIQUE OF THE NEW GACACA JURISDICTIONS: PROSPECTS AND CHALLENGES

The new Gacaca jurisdictions represent an innovative, attractive blend between retributive and restorative justice. While acknowledging that, to a certain extent, justice in the form of punishment is indispensable to help victims come to terms with the past, the participatory and restorative nature of the Gacaca process

186. *Id.* art. 34(6)(7)(9)(10). *See also id.* art. 41.

187. *Id.* arts. 36(4), 42.

188. *Id.* art. 73. Confessions can be made at any stage during the proceedings. Sentence reductions are greatest when the confession is done before the name of the suspect appears on the list of accused compiled by Gacaca benches at the cell level. For example, Category 2 suspects accused of murder or attempted murder who do not confess incur a prison sentence ranging from twenty-five to thirty years of imprisonment; this sentence is reduced to twelve to fifteen years in case of confession after the name of the accused appears on the list, down to seven to twelve years where the confession is made prior to the appearance of the name on the list of accused persons. *Id.*

189. *Id.* arts. 38, 21.

190. See *id.* arts. 29, 30. According to art. 29, every Rwandan citizen has a "duty to participate" in Gacaca courts activities, and persons who omit or refuse to testify can be prosecuted by Gacaca courts and be sentenced to up to one year imprisonment. *Id.* art. 29.

191. *Id.* arts. 73-74. If the author of the offense and the victim have reached an amicable settlement, either privately or before the public authority or other witnesses, prosecution of the former is banned. *See id.*, art. 51.

192. *Id.* art. 85.

193. *See* IRIN News, *Traditional courts Inaugurated*, *supra* note 174.

194. According to some sources, Gacaca trials are scheduled to begin in January 2005. *See* Hirondelle News Agency, *Beginning of Gacaca trials moved to 2005*, Sept. 21, 2004, *available at* http://fr.allafrica.com/stories/200409210921.html (last visited Oct. 24, 2004).

makes it an instrument potentially suitable to uncover the truth and foster sustainable peace and reconciliation in the long term. While laudable, both goals are fraught with challenges.

XVII. GACACA JURISDICTIONS AS ACCESSIBLE, PARTICIPATORY, RESTORATIVE JUSTICE

In the face of divisive genocide trials that have prolonged the determination of accountability, Gacaca holds the promises of a system geared towards societal justice and reconciliation.[195]

The new system presents the advantage of dispensing with many of the cumbersome, time-consuming procedures and formalities characterizing conventional trials.[196] Its functioning does not require the intervention of qualified, professional lawyers and judges, but instead relies exclusively on lay judges with a minimum of training, and the communities they represent.[197] The extensive network of Gacaca courts throughout the country makes it possible for the bulk of genocide trials to be held on a large scale and in several places simultaneously.[198]

Procedural simplicity and the speedy disposal of cases may appease the quest for justice of genocide victims and suspects alike because it would send the message that justice is being done. For the rural communities most affected by the genocide, the highly decentralized system of local courts seems to remedy the feeling of alienation caused by geographic distance, technicalities, and lack of communication vis-à-vis the genocide trials conducted to date by the ICTR and the specialized chambers.[199] From the suspects' view, those who have been locked up in horrible prisons for years will at last appear before a jury of their

195. Strain & Keyes, *supra* note 93, at 118.

196. Daly, *Punitive and Reconstructive Justice*, *supra* note 76, at 375 (generally discussing the January 2001 version of the Gacaca law. The same observations apply to the 2004 amended version of the Gacaca law).

197. *See id.*

198. *Id.* By introducing Gacaca courts and decentralizing the process of justice, the Rwandan government had initially hoped to drastically reduce the court caseload, the enormous prison population, and to speed up the trials. According to initial government estimates, with the operation of Gacaca, approximately 110,000 prisoners would have been turned over from the formal justice system to the new courts. *See* RWANDA AND SOUTH AFRICA IN DIALOGUE, *supra* note 81, at 42. These predictions have soon proven to be unrealistic, and there are currently widespread concerns, among the government and observers alike, about the "multiplying effect" that the Gacaca process might have on the number of genocide cases. *See Genocide Suspects' List*, *supra* note 149 (reporting that, contrary to initial government estimates, the number of suspects might increase from about 100,000 to 500,000-600,000 as a result of the Gacaca process. Out of this number, some 50,000 are expected to be tried by the ordinary courts. Despite these estimates, the Rwandan government still maintains that all genocide trials will be completed in a period between five and eight years).
According to a 2004 report by Amnesty International, the 32,000 confessions received by the Ministry of Justice by the end of 2002 incriminated an additional 250,000 individuals. *See* Amnesty International, *Enduring Legacy*, *supra* note 137. As of March 2004, there have been 32,000 additional confessions, likely to implicate many more individuals. *Id.* Finally, the few Gacaca courts that have operated during the pilot phase have also identified thousands of new genocide suspects, foreshadowing a "logistical nightmare" that Gacaca will most likely be unable to tackle. *Id. See also* Lars Waldorf, Human Rights Watch Country Representative for Rwanda, Panel Discussion at the presentation of the film "Gacaca: Living Together again," Washington, D.C., (June 3, 2003) (estimating that 100,000 to 250,000 new incriminations may possibly follow the introduction of gacaca).

199. *See* Ironside, *supra* note 98, at 48-49.

peers, rather than having to face courts deemed to be the expression of victor's justice.[200] Further, the Gacaca law introduces the possibility for victims to obtain reparation for the harm suffered in the form of compensation by allowing them civil intervention in the course of Gacaca proceedings, while at the same time acknowledging their status as victims.[201]

Aside from dramatically increasing access to justice for all parties involved, the Gacaca jurisdictions hold the promises of other important goals. The new state-mandated jurisdictions are characterized by an appealing, highly participatory approach, where participation is seen as the only sustainable way to achieve longer-term peace and societal transformation.[202] Despite being a state creation, the new system delegates as much power as possible to ordinary people in their communities, a fact that may enhance the trust people have in the process and its outcomes.[203] The trials indeed take place "at the heart of the community,"[204] with ordinary Rwandans actively involved in the process by electing and acting as judges, collecting and processing information, and gathering evidence in what is a collectively shared and experienced search for justice and truth.[205] Similar to what has been observed for the South African TRC, it is the process that matters, not just the result. Public hearings that gather the testimony of perpetrators and victims alike become crucial both "as communal experiences and as sources of information."[206] Reflecting its restorative approach, truth in Gacaca emerges communicatively in a dialogue involving all community members, including victims, offenders, supporters and other interested parties. Importantly, victims and survivors of unspeakable crimes are potentially given the opportunity to play a central

200. *Id.* at 50.

201. On the right to reparation under Gacaca, see Vandeginste, *Victims of Genocide*, *supra* note 105, at 258, 263 (referring to the task conferred upon Gacaca judges of determining the damages to be awarded in each judgment in accordance with a scale foreseen under the law creating the Compensation Fund). The Fund will be responsible for the implementation of this part of the verdict, and will be financed by annual contribution from the state budget, as well as voluntary contributions from foreign countries and profit from community service work. *Id.* Compensation will be made either in cash or through actions and interventions to benefit the beneficiary. *Id.* In 1998, a National Fund for Assistance to Survivors of Genocide was also established with the task to assist the most vulnerable survivors. *Id.* This measure has mostly proven ineffective due to instances of misappropriation and embezzlement involving the fund's administrators. *Id.*

202. Strain & Keyes, *supra* note 93, at 121. *See* Daly, *Transformative Justice*, *supra* note 27, at 178-79 (stating that Gacaca has the potential to transform the Rwandan society because it addresses the very deficiencies in the country's social and political fabric that allowed the genocide to happen). According to Daly, "Whereas that society was characterized by a highly centralized administration, the gacaca process will be localized. Law [then virtually absent] will make its comeback in a highly feasible and accessible way . . .[with] people . . . control[ling] the process and the outcome." *Id. See also* Ironside, *supra* note 98, at 49 (observing that the new Gacaca, unlike its original form, provides also for the participation of women, many of whom were elected as judges). This is particularly important given that women have suffered the heaviest repercussions as a result of the genocide. *Id.*

203. Daly, *Punitive and Reconstructive Justice*, *supra* note 76, at 376-77 (stating that, "Rwandans of all stations will literally be defining justice . . . rather than having it defined for and imposed on them"). *See also* Harrell, *supra* note 10, at 60 (observing that the greater legitimacy of local forums is likely to be pronounced in dualist postgenocidal societies, which are frequently suspicious of the central government).

204. African Rights, *supra* note 146, at 2.

205. *See* Daly, *Punitive and Reconstructive Justice*, *supra* note 76, at 376.

206. MINOW, *supra* note 15, at 127-28 (discussing benefits of truth commissions). *See* Vandeginste, *Victims of Genocide*, *supra* note 105, at 260-61 (describing the participatory nature of Gacaca process as amounting to a form of reparation both for victims of the genocide and their communities).

role in Gacaca, challenging those who inflicted pain upon them. Community dialogue may also provide an opportunity to affirm and discuss—and perhaps change—societal norms in a public and participatory setting, even in a context where "social relations and acted-out values have been massively distorted."[207] This is critically important in Rwanda, where the "moral tone of the community" has been tainted by widespread and horrendous crimes.[208] In Rwanda the violence did not arise out of anarchic chaos, but was largely driven by the shared conviction, fostered by the government's propaganda of ethnic hatred, that the Tutsi had to be eliminated for the country to become a better place.[209]

Holding trials at the local, grassroots level empowers ordinary people to pursue justice, and could encourage the perpetrators—who are judged by their peers and within their communities—to contribute to the search for truth, with a potentially "cathartic . . . effect on fragmented communities."[210] For those who confess to, and acknowledge, their crimes before Gacaca, community shaming may have potential re-integrative effects, given the interdependence and close-knit nature of the Rwandan community.[211] Unlike the South African experience with the TRC, confessions in Gacaca need to be accompanied not only by full disclosure of the facts, but also by an apology to the victims, thus possibly helping them to achieve a sense of closure.[212]

The restorative aspects of Gacaca enable perpetrators of the genocide "to make amends for their actions in a way that establishes a human relationship between them, victims and others in the community."[213] Returning perpetrators to face shaming by their own communities, communities made up not only by victims, perpetrators and their respective supporters, but also by those who opposed, or were ambivalent about, the violence, may exercise a considerable pressure on the perpetrators and thus deter recidivism.[214] It may also promote moral education of the perpetrators and their communities. Taking these individuals back to destroyed communities, and confronting them with the harm they have inflicted, thus humanizing it, may further break down the widespread societal complicity while preventing future violence.[215] Although this process may not always be easy or possible, it may still be more effective than criminal trials, the main result

207. Stovel, *supra* note 40, at 9.

208. *Id.* (reporting that First National healing circles in Hollow Water, Manitoba, led to the detection and acknowledgment of widespread social abuse within the community and to the latter capacity to address the problem and reaffirm positive values).

209. *See* Drumbl, *(Al)lure of Genocide Trials*, *supra* note 39, at 220.

210. Ironside, *supra* note 98, at 49 (stating that "by bringing victims and perpetrators face to face to tell their stories [Gacaca] will . . . create moral pressure on perpetrators to confess to their crimes and seek forgiveness" and that "the confession itself will be an important source of justice for victims"). *See also* Daly, *Punitive and Reconstructive Justice*, *supra* note 76, at 376 (stating that trials by the Gacaca jurisdictions may "replace the divisive experience of the genocide with the cohesive experience of securing justice").

211. *See* Drumbl, *(Al)lure of Genocide Trials*, *supra* note 39, at 222-23.

212. *See* Organic Law No. 16/2004 of 19/6/2004, *supra* note 4, art. 54 (requiring those resorting to the "procedure of confession, guilty plea, repentance and apologies" to address apologies "publicly" to the victims in case they are still alive and to the Rwandan society).

213. Stovel, *supra* note 40, at 7 (generally referring to restorative justice benefits for offenders).

214. Drumbl, *(Al)lure of Genocide Trials*, *supra* note 39, at 222-23 (discussing John Braithwaite's theory on reintegrative shaming and its potential relevance in the context of the highly interdependent Rwandan society).

215. *Id.*

of which seems to be to encourage prisoners' persecutory feelings, far from creating any remorse or shame for what they have done. Instilling shame on offenders, rather than imposing guilt on them, may in turn fortify communities, favoring peace and reconciliation in the long term.

By potentially encouraging participants to reveal more contextual information than conventional trials do, Gacaca may also well contribute to establish an historical record of the genocide and its causes well beyond the imperfect, partial versions of truth furnished by the ICTR and the specialized chambers.[216] "Information that would be ruled irrelevant in legalistic criminal trials [may potentially be] very relevant for healing victims, offenders, and their communities, and [for] addressing the social or systemic conditions that led to, or enabled the [genocide to happen]."[217] This truth may be passed on from generation to generation within each and every community, replacing partisan versions of the same tragedy. While, in the most optimistic scenario, Gacaca will involve the entire community in truth-telling, shaming of perpetrators, and broad discussion about the underlying causes of the genocide—in the least, and despite its potential failure—it may uncover the truth in individual situations.[218]

Unlike trials before the ICTR and the specialized chambers, Gacaca is explicitly designed to achieve reconciliation.[219] This is crucial, given that Rwanda is a "dualist post-genocidal society," one in which victims and aggressors must unavoidably coexist, living geographically intermingled and in close economic interdependence.[220] It is also important in the face of trials that are seen as exasperating social division and prolonging the determination of accountability. By bringing justice at the local level—which is where the most people, especially in the rural communities, experienced the genocidal violence—justice becomes visible, by facilitating a process of coming to terms with the past through the emergence of truth.[221] This in turn, may favor the minimum indispensable degree of reconciliation necessary for communities to continue to coexist, in a context where reconciliation is not an option, but a necessity.[222] If successful, the maximum involvement of individuals would not only make them contribute to a process of "national and historical significance . . . but could also strengthen community ties by fostering mutual cooperation."[223]

Gacaca provides both moral and practical incentives for perpetrators to confess their crimes and seek forgiveness, as well as the ability to flexibly fashion

---

216. *See* Strain & Keyes, *supra* note 93, at 125 (observing that, despite the informal nature of Gacaca, its truth-telling aspect cannot be underestimated in a country with an important oral tradition). The Rwandan government hopes that Gacaca trials will help find out how many died in the genocide with more accuracy. *See* IRIN, *Rwanda: Census finds 937,000 died in genocide*, April 2, 2004, *available at* www.allafrica.com (last visited Oct. 24, 2004).

217. Stovel, *supra* note 40, at 9 (discussing benefits of restorative justice).

218. See Drumbl, *Sclerosis*, *supra* note 10, at 301.

219. Strain & Keyes, *supra* note 93, at 125.

220. Drumbl, *(Al)lure of Genocide Trials*, *supra* note 39, at 220.

221. Idi T. Gaparayi, *Justice and Social Reconstruction in the Aftermath of Genocide in Rwanda: An Evaluation of the Possible Role of the Gacaca Tribunals*, 1 AFR. H.R. L.J., 78, 104 (2001).

222. Daly, *Transformative Justice*, *supra* note 27, at 168-69 (arguing that it is at the local level that the hard work of reconciliation needs to be done, and that it is up to the communities to "make sense of what happened" and to find a way of leaving together again).

223. *Id.* at 177.

sentences and remedies.[224] Category 2 suspects who confess can in fact choose to spend half of a considerably reduced sentence by performing community service.[225] This will include administrative tasks, maintenance of public buildings, construction of schools, roads, and community buildings, crop cultivation, education, and first aid activities.[226] Again, performing activities in the interest of victims and the community as a whole may provide perpetrators with an opportunity to compensate the victim and others harmed for the damage done, as well as facilitate their gradual reintegration into the community.[227]

XVIII. Due Process and Human Rights Concerns

Far from embodying a pure restorative philosophy, Gacaca also delivers justice in its most traditional form, through punishment and retribution. Because of this, it has been extensively criticized by some human rights observers on the ground that it restricts international fair trial standards that the Rwandan government is bound to respect under the international and regional conventions it has ratified.[228] Such standards, it is argued, should apply to the Gacaca jurisdictions for a combination of reasons. First, despite the participation of lay judges, Gacaca courts have been created through state legislation and are vested with many of the same powers as ordinary courts (including trying cases as serious as murder and imposing severe criminal sentences); second, they are called upon to apply state legislation; third, enforcement of decisions and supervision of the Gacaca courts is carried out through the state machinery.[229] Some observers have expressed fears that, as currently conceived, Gacaca will amount to an "expedited criminal justice process . . . without the requisite due process safeguards."[230] The lack of respect of fair trial standards could arguably weaken the very democratic foundation of the system by undermining its legitimacy and credibility.

XIX. Competence, Independence and Impartiality of Gacaca Judges

The right to be tried by a "competent, independent and impartial tribunal established by law" is guaranteed under the International Covenant on Civil and

224. *See* Organic Law No. 16/2004 of 19/6/2004, *supra* note 4, arts. 72-73. Category 1 suspects who choose to confess and apologize can see their death or life imprisonment sentence commuted into long prison terms, *see id.* art. 72. *See also* Drumbl, *Sclerosis*, *supra* note 10, at 301.
225. *See* Organic Law No. 16/2004 of 19/6/2004, *supra* note 4, arts. 51, 73.
226. *See* Vandeginste, *Victims of Genocide*, *supra* note 105, at 261.
227. *Id.* (describing aspects of the draft presidential decree foreseeing the creation of Committees for Community Service at the national, provincial and local level).
228. *See* Press Release, Amnesty International United Kingdom, Rwanda: Gacaca Tribunals Must Conform With International Fair Trial Standards (Dec. 17, 2002), *available at* www.amnesty .org.uk/news/press/14258.shtml (last visited Oct. 24, 2004); Leah Werchick, *Prospects for Justice in Rwanda's Citizens Tribunals*, 8 Hum. Rts. Brief 15 (2001) (generally arguing that the use of Gacaca tribunals to try genocide cases as envisaged in a 1999 government's proposal violated both domestic and international due process guarantees).
229. *See* Gaparayi, *supra* note 221, at 95; Vandeginste, *Justice*, *supra* note 153, at 25.
230. Ironside, *supra* note 98, at 51; Gaparayi, *supra* note 221, at 95. *See also* Sarkin, *supra* note 78, at 164-66.

Political Rights (ICCPR)[231] and the African Charter on Human and Peoples' Rights.[232] It is an "absolute right, suffering no exceptions."[233] Internal standards articulating such rights require that those who perform judicial functions be selected on the basis of their integrity and ability, and that they have appropriate training *or* qualifications in law.[234] Although the Gacaca lay judges have been subject to six days of intensive training on a variety of subjects, both the quality and duration of the training have been criticized as being inadequate and insufficient in view of the difficult functions they are called to exercise.[235] Gacaca judges are indeed expected to interpret and apply state legislation, to pronounce judgments in complex and sensitive cases, and to impose harsh sentences involving long prison terms.[236] Categorization of the accused (including Category 1 defendants, liable to the death penalty) is made at the lowest gacaca court level—the cell—where most of the judges are illiterate.[237] Trainees have also not been provided with basic resources and materials, such as the Gacaca law and explicative materials, and the training has not covered fundamental topics, such as those of compensation and community service either.[238]

Serious concerns also exist regarding the actual independence and impartiality of the Gacaca judges. As stated by the Honorable Sandra Oxner, "[J]udicial independence is about personal integrity and about institutions and mechanisms put in place to create an environment best suited for personal integrity to flourish."[239] In its articulation, this concept encompasses such diverse things as an adequate salary, "substantive" or "decisional" independence in making decisions without pressure from external sources—being it state organs, litigants, or the powerful—and "institutional" or "collective" independence of the judicial body as a whole, i.e. administrative and financial independence.[240] Impartiality, on the

231. International Covenant on Civil and Political Rights (ICCPR), Dec. 19, 1966, G.A. Res. 2200A (XXI), 999 U.N.T.S. 171, art. 14(1) (Rwanda acceded on Apr. 16, 1975).

232. African [Banjul] Charter on Human and People's Rights, June 26, 1981, 21 I.L.M. 58, arts. 7(1), 27.

233. Gonzalez del Rio v. Peru (263/1987), Oct. 28, 1992, Report of the Human Rights Committe, vol. II, at 20, U.N. Doc. A/48/48/1993 (1993).

234. United Nations, Basic Principles on the Independence of the Judiciary, at Principle 10, U.N. Doc. A/Res/40/146 (Dec. 13, 1985) [hereinafter *Basic Principles*]. Although such principles are not legally binding, they represent authoritative interpretations of states' due process obligations under international law.

235. The training was held between April and May 2002 and covered matters such as basic principles of law, group management, conflict resolution, judicial ethics, trauma, human resources, equipment and financial management. *See* Amnesty International, *Question of Justice, supra* note 83, at 27. *See also* African Rights, *supra* note 146, at 4-9 (reporting that trainers who included judges, human rights defenders, second year law students and government officials, had been trained themselves for ten days, and were each assigned a group of fifty to seventy trainees).

236. Gaparayi, *supra* note 221, at 90.

237. *See* African Rights, *supra* note 146, at 5-6 (commenting that, since the Department of Gacaca courts did not expect illiterate judges, the training was not designed to take their special needs into account).

238. *Id.* at 4-5, 9.

239. Sandra Oxner, The Quality of Judges § 4 (July 8-12, 2001) (paper presented at the World Bank Conference "Empowerment, Security and Opportunity through Law and Justice," Saint Petersburg).

240. *Id.* § 3. *See also Basic Principles, supra* note 233, at Principle 2. "The judiciary shall decide matters before them impartially, on the basis of facts and in accordance with the law, without improper influences, inducements, pressures, threats or interferences, direct or indirect, from any quarter or for any reason." *Id.*

other hand, requires that judges (professional or lay judges)[241] be free of bias or prejudice in each individual case.[242] The Gacaca law requests that all Gacaca judges be "Rwandans of integrity . . . free from the spirit of sectarianism . . . of high morals and conduct . . . [and] honest."[243] It further establishes that they be removed from their functions in cases where they encourage "sectarianism" or have performed acts "incompatible with the quality of a person of integrity."[244] Grounds of incompatibility of the role of a judge with some professions are also established by the law.[245] Finally, both the secret nature of judges' deliberations, and the exclusion of judges from cases involving defendants to whom they are related or with whom there is a relationship of enmity or friendship,[246] should also guarantee their independence. However, despite such provisions, both the unique magnitude of the offenses committed, and the polarized nature of Rwandan society, pose serious challenges to the integrity of the most well-intentioned judges. Given the broad-based perpetration of genocidal violence, it is likely that most judges could be related to the victims in particular cases, compromising their impartiality in judging the suspects.[247]

Dangers related to the actual lack of impartiality and independence of the Gacaca courts do not only reflect on the defendants, but also on the victims. Communities that are predominantly Hutu, for instance, might very well favor defendants even where they have allegedly committed atrocities.[248] In general, there is a risk that, as they are currently conceived, Gacaca jurisdictions will replicate and amplify, "local political or ethnic dynamics [and may therefore] favor victims or the accused accordingly."[249] Given the ongoing ethnic and political tension and the resulting strong polarization of the Rwandese communities, issues of lack of independence and impartiality may be seen as pervading the whole system, raising concerns as to the overall fairness and legitimacy of Gacaca trials.[250]

Finally, there are material factors that may pose a risk to the judge's independence. Gacaca judges are indeed expected to exercise their functions without perceiving any form of remuneration, despite the risks and the level of commit-

241. Communication 387/1989, Karttunen v. Finland, Decision of Oct. 23, 1992, U.N. Doc. CCPR/C/46/D/387/1989 (1992).

242. *Basic Principles*, *supra* note 233, at Principle 2.

243. Organic Law No. 16/2004 of 19/6/2004, *supra* note 4, art. 14. Elected judges must be at least twenty-one years old and, in addition to other requirements, must not have participated in perpetrating offenses constituting genocide or crimes against humanity. *Id.*

244. *Id.* art. 16(3), 16(6).

245. *See id.* art. 15. Judges cannot be: state officials; persons exercising political activities; active members of the national police or the army; members of religious groups and governmental organizations; or career magistrates. *See id.* art. 15.

246. *Id.* arts. 10, 21.

247. Ironside, *supra* note 98, at 52-53.

248. *Id.* at 55.

249. *Id.* at 52. *See also* Sarkin, *supra* note 78, at 161 (quoting Alison des Forges, "the fairness of the proceedings will vary enormously . . . [and] the result in any one community will be determined by the local balance of power").

250. Amnesty International, *Question of Justice*, *supra* note 83, at 37. Appearance of independence relates to the question of whether litigants have a legitimate doubt about the tribunal's independence, thus affecting the confidence that the courts must inspire in a democratic society. *See* Gaparayi, *supra* note 221, at 92.

ment that this implies.[251] This has been seriously criticized by external observers and the judges alike, as it may compromise their independence and integrity by making them susceptible to corruption.[252]

XX. RIGHT TO DEFENSE

The procedural simplicity characterizing the Gacaca jurisdictions denies the very principle of equality of arms in criminal cases in several ways that favor the prosecution.[253] First, the Gacaca law does not entitle defendants to be represented by a lawyer, contrary to international fair trial standards.[254] It only provides an opportunity for the defendant to speak for himself, and for individuals at the hearings to speak for or against the defendant.[255] This may be problematic, as the majority of defendants have a low educational background and very limited, if any, awareness of their rights.[256]

The Rwandan government purports that the nature of Gacaca as a community forum ensures a procedurally equal position for both plaintiff and defendant.[257] According to this interpretation "the defense will be based on facts, possibly with the help of people giving evidence for the defense. The judges, not being jurists themselves, will not be bogged down with complicated principles of procedure. The accused, the judge, and witnesses, are on equal footing, and recourse to professional lawyers will merely upset the balance."[258]

The defendant's position may be further compromised by the fact that the majority of cases will be judged on the basis of the files prepared and handed over to the Gacaca judges by the public prosecutor's offices, making it difficult for lay judges and defendants—both of whom lack legal skills—to challenge the information contained in them.[259] The position of the defendant may be further compromised by the fact that Gacaca courts may, whenever necessary, be assisted by legal experts appointed by the National Service[260] whom, by virtue of their legal qualifications, may exercise considerable influence over the Gacaca judges. Defendants who choose not to confess are particularly vulnerable, as Gacaca courts can hear evidence from the public prosecutor.[261] Finally, defendants do not have

251. *See Gacaca Jurisdictions*, *supra* note 2 (stressing the difficulties faced by judges in administering justice in highly traumatized communities still deeply divided by mistrust, and the multiple sources of community pressure they are subject to—i.e. by the perpetrators, the survivors and their families). *See also* African Rights, *supra* note 146, at 14 (reporting that, despite early government promises, the Gacaca law does not provide for any compensation).

252. *Id.*

253. *See* Amnesty International, *Question of Justice*, *supra* note 83, at 32, 36-37 (discussing the implications of such principle).

254. The right to defense includes the right to defend oneself in person or through a lawyer. International Covenant on Civil and Political Rights, Dec. 19, 1966, G.A. Res. 2200A (XXI), 999 U.N.T.S. 171, art.14 (3)(d); African Charter, art. 7(1).

255. Organic Law No. 16/2004 of 19/6/2004, *supra* note 4, arts. 64-65, 68.

256. *See* Gaparayi, *supra* note 221, at 97.

257. Amnesty International, *Question of Justice*, *supra* note 83, at 36.

258. Jean de Dieu Mucyo (former Rwandan Minister of Justice), *Gacaca Courts and Genocide*, *in* RWANDA AND SOUTH AFRICA IN DIALOGUE, *supra* note 81, at 53.

259. *See* Organic Law No. 16/2004 of 19/6/2004, *supra* note 4, arts. 46(3), 47. *See also* Amnesty International, *Question of Justice*, *supra* note 83, at 36.

260. *See* Organic Law No. 16/2004 of 19/6/2004, *supra* note 4, art. 26.

261. *Id.* art. 65(5)(c).

access to their case file prior to the hearings, and will not be able to present witnesses in their defense nor to cross-examine witnesses.[262]

XXI. Right to Review by a Higher Tribunal

Under international fair trial standards, individuals convicted of a crime are entitled to have their conviction and sentence reviewed by a higher competent and impartial tribunal according to procedures established by law.[263] The Gacaca law provides for three means of appeal: opposition, appeal, and review of judgments passed by Gacaca courts.[264] While opposition can be made by defendants against judgments pronounced by any Gacaca court in their absence,[265] only Category 2 defendants have the right to appeal their sentence to the Gacaca court of appeal.[266] Judgments relating to offenses against property are not subject to appeal.[267] While the original Gacaca law allowed defendants to appeal their categorization before the Gacaca jurisdiction competent to try their case, this possibility no longer seems to be provided for by the amended version of the law.[268]

Review of judgments pronounced by Gacaca courts are allowed in the following cases: when an individual was acquitted in a judgment passed in the last resort by an ordinary court, but is later found guilty by a Gacaca court; when an individual was convicted by an ordinary court, but is later found innocent by a Gacaca court; when the sentence pronounced against a defendant contradicts the legal provisions of the offenses for which he is convicted.[269] The Gacaca court of appeal is competent to review such judgments. The fact that no appeal can ever be made to the ordinary courts is particularly troubling in the case of Category 2 defendants, some of whom are liable to severe sentences involving long prison terms. As it has been observed, "[b]y containing all hearings and appeals within . . . Gacaca . . . concerns about the absence of fair trial guarantees pervade the entire system."[270]

---

262. *Id.* arts. 64-66, 68 (describing Gacaca hearings and judgments). While defendants are allowed to "comment on the accusations" made against them, "respond to the plaintiff's declarations," and "answer questions" put to them by "any person taking the floor," no explicit reference is made to a right of defendants to cross-examine witnesses or present witnesses in their defense. *Id.* *See also* Ironside, *supra* note 98, at 54.

263. International Covenant on Civil and Political Rights, G.A. Res. 2200A (XXI), U.N. GAOR, 21st Sess., Supp. No. 16, at 54, U.N. Doc. A/6316 (1966).

264. *See* Organic Law No. 16/2004 of 19/6/2004, *supra* note 4, Chap. VI, arts. 85-93.

265. *Id.* arts. 41-43, 86-88.

266. *Id.* arts. 43, 89-91. Judgments passed by the Gacaca court of the sector in the first instance are appealed before the Gacaca court of appeal which gives a ruling in the last resort. *Id.*

267. *Id.* arts. 41, 89. However, other judgments pronounced by the Gacaca court of the cell—such as those pronounced in cases involving tampering of witnesses—are subject to appeal before the Gacaca court of the sector. *Id.* art. 89.

268. *Compare* Organic Law No. 40/2000 of 26/01/2001, *supra* note 3, art. 86, *with* Organic Law No. 16/2004 of 19/6/2004, *supra* note 4, art. 92 (providing that, "if the Gacaca court to which an appeal is referred finds that the appellant has been classified in an inaccurate category, it classifies him or her in the category corresponding to offenses of which he or she is accused, and tries him or her at first and last resort").

269. Organic Law No. 16/2004 of 19/6/2004, *supra* note 4, art. 93.

270. Ironside, *supra* note 98, at 54.

XXII. GACACA IN THE RWANDAN SOCIO-POLITICAL CONTEXT

The Gacaca jurisdictions cannot be seen in isolation, but rather they must be seen in the civil-political context characterizing transitional Rwanda.[271] Despite improvements over the last few years, the Tutsi dominated Rwandan government is still generally perceived as being neither pluralistic nor genuinely democratic.[272] The ruling party, RPF, dominates all the levers of power: the security services, the bureaucracy, the judiciary, banks, universities and state-owned companies.[273] The perceived exclusion of the majority Hutu from many government institutions, including the judiciary, makes the issue of genuine power-sharing a particularly pressing one.[274] This, in turn, fuels continuing political instability and social-ethnic tension, exacerbating dangers that the Gacaca jurisdictions may be vulnerable to local, political, and ethnic dynamics.[275]

In this context, some of the prisoners fear that the introduction of Gacaca courts may legitimize "popular retribution" on those presumed to be responsible for the genocide.[276] Moreover, the Rwandan government's position that the Gacaca courts will not hear accusations of war crimes and crimes against humanity committed by soldiers of the Rwandan Defense Forces (RDF, previously RPA), which must be taken to the regular courts, reinforces the perception of Gacaca as political justice and has been questioned by ordinary Rwandans as well as international observers.[277]

---

271. Sarkin, *supra* note 78, at 159. *See also* Vandeginste, *Victims of Genocide*, *supra* note 105, at 249 (observing that the context in which Gacaca jurisdictions operate is not "neutral," but one characterized over time by intermitting armed conflict, genocide and political transition).

272. *See* Human Rights Watch, World Report 2003: Rwanda (2003), *available at* http://www.hrw.org/wr2k3/africa9.html (last visited on Oct. 24, 2004) [hereinafter Human Rights Watch, *World Report*] (reporting that the Rwandan government . . . demonstrated continuing hostility towards political dissent, press freedom and an independent civil society"). According to THE ECONOMIST, "Rwanda is tranquil: a staggering achievement. But the way the government enforces peace is disturbing." *Rwanda ten years on*, THE ECONOMIST, Mar. 25, 2004. Indeed, perhaps inevitably given the circumstance under which it came to power, "Rwanda's government is unique in Africa in that it tries to control not only what its citizens do, but also what they think [and] the RPF exercises tighter control over the country than perhaps any other African ruling party. There is no freedom of the press, because that might allow "divisionists" to spread once more their foul ideology. There is no freedom of association, either. Anyone who tries to set up a serious opposition party is subject to harassment, arrest and threats . . . . Membership of the RPF is not compulsory, but prominent Rwandans come under great pressure to join." *The Road out of Hell*, THE ECONOMIST, Mar. 27, 2004. *See also* Amnesty International, Rwanda: Deeper into the Abyss - Waging war on civil society (July 6, 2004), *available at* http://www.amnestyusa.org/countries/rwanda/document.do?id=80256DD400782B84802 56EC900405DD4 (last visited Oct. 24, 2004).

273. *See Kagame Won*, *supra* note 89.

274. *See* Sarkin, *supra* note 78, at 152 (stating that "Hutus, for the most part, have been completely marginalized both politically and economically"). *See also* Charles Bigirimana, *It's tension all over as Kigaly heads for elections*, May 12, 2003, ALL AFRICA GLOBAL MEDIA, *at* http://www.allafrica.com /stories/200305140605.html (last visited Oct. 24, 2004).

275. Uvin, *supra* note 5, at 7.

276. *See* Penal Reform International, Research on the Gacaca—PRI Report V (Sept. 2003), *available at* www.penalreform.org/english/gacaca_research.htm (last visited Oct. 24, 2004) [hereinafter PRI Report V] (reporting that, at least in one case, allegations were made that survivors had plotted to denounce all Hutus as *genocidaires* regardless of their actual participation in the killings).

277. *See* Human Rights Watch, *World Report*, *supra* note 272 (stating that the government tried to prevent the ICTR from investigating RDF suspects); Amnesty International, *Question of Justice*, *supra* note 83, at 28-29 (indicating this as a factor of reduced community participation during the Gacaca

On the other hand, there is widespread fear among survivors' groups that Gacaca may amount to *de facto* amnesty for those who committed terrible crimes.[278] Fear is sometimes compounded by frustration at the realization that, in many instances, prisoners may confess to their crimes with defiance and without showing the slightest remorse.[279] In general, there are concrete risks that Gacaca trials will be manipulated and "used for settling personal scores, political issues, issues of land and property, and family issues."[280]

The genocide has profoundly changed the social geography and composition of Rwandese communities. About 800,000 people were killed during the genocide, and some 80,000 individuals are currently still imprisoned as genocide suspects. Moreover, about 700,000 "old caseload refugees" recently returned to the country after decades of exile.[281] In total, the UN High Commissioner for Refugees has estimated that 3.2 million refugees returned to Rwanda in the period between 1993 and 2002.[282] These factors, coupled with the policy of forced collective resettlement pursued by the government since 1996, have radically altered the makeup of most Rwandan communities, possibly irremediably compromising the participatory and active role they should play to guarantee the effective functioning of the Gacaca jurisdictions.[283] The degree of public engagement necessary for the new Gacaca jurisdictions to function effectively might be further hampered by survivors' concerns for their security, and fears that they might be victimized

pilot phase); Amnesty International, *Enduring Legacy*, *supra* note 198 (reporting that justice officials' claims that 1,800 members of the RPA were serving sentences for human rights abuses as of Oct. 2003 were contradicted by information obtained from the Military Prosecutor's Office indicating that only a few dozen of them had actually been prosecuted, and that those found guilty served minimal sentences). *See also* Catherine Honeyman et al., *Establishing Collective Norms: Potentials for Participatory Justice in Rwanda*, 10 PEACE & CONFLICT: J. OF THE AMER. PSYCHOLOGICAL ASS'N. 1, 13 (2004) (lamenting the "corrosive effects of [the] assumed disregard for Hutu lives" where people in a village realized that "Inkiko-Gacaca could not even record the names of Hutus who had died in the cellule").

278. *See* Waldorf, *supra* note 198. *See also* Vandeginste, *Justice*, *supra* note 153, at 24 (stating that some survivors' groups have expressed concerns that genocide crimes will be "trivialized" through trials under Gacaca).

279. *See* PRI Report V, *supra* note 276, at 9 (observing that, in many instances, individuals suspected of genocide related crimes do not seem to be willing to take responsibility for their acts—which they attribute to "bad policy of the former government"—even when they confess to having committed them).

280. Sarkin, *supra* note 78, at 161. *See also* CAGEP Consult for USAID/Rwanda and Ministry of Justice and Institutional Relations, *Assessment of the Judicial Sector in Rwanda*, Nov. 2002 [hereinafter CAGEP Consult, *Assessment of the Judicial Sector*] (warning that judges could be subject to pressure from a variety of sources including administrative authorities, wealthy individuals, security services, as well as families of victims and alleged perpetrators).

281. Uvin, *supra* note 5, at 10. Old caseload refugees are Tutsi refugees who have lived outside Rwanda for decades. *Id.*

282. *See* United Nations High Commissioner for Refugees, Voluntary Repatriation in Africa: Levels and Trends 1993-2002 Table 2 (Mar. 4, 2004), *at* http://www.unhcr.ch/cgi-bin/texis/vtx/home/opendoc.pdf?tbl=SPECIAL&page=events&id=404886df4 (last visited Oct. 24, 2004).

283. Vandeginste, *Justice*, *supra* note 153, at 1 (stating that the Rwandese "social tissue . . . has broken down"). *See also* Daly, *Punitive and Reconstructive Justice*, *supra* note 76, at 380 (stating that in many parts of Rwanda "there may be no such thing as community," and that the Gacaca jurisdictions may prove ineffective in communities largely composed of people who were not part of them during the genocide); African Rights, *supra* note 146, at 41 (estimating that it might be almost impossible to uncover the truth in regions predominantly inhabited by old caseload refugees or where there are barely any genocide survivors).

again.[284] This, in turn, may lead to further violence, instead of fostering peace. In March 2004 alone, fourteen people were sentenced to death and three to life imprisonment for having killed genocide survivors who were expected to testify before the Gacaca courts.[285] Not surprisingly, all these factors seem to have played a role in the so far low community participation in Gacaca, with the government estimating absenteeism in eight out of twelve jurisdictions during the pilot stage.[286] According to Penal Reform International—a Paris-based NGO involved in monitoring Gacaca—Rwandans are somehow still extremely skeptical of the courts, with more than half the population unwilling to participate actively in the process.[287]

While the government has reacted to the reluctant engagement of Rwandans by creating a "duty to participate" in the court's activities,[288] it is doubted that this will favor genuine commitment to the system. There is a risk that, although Gacaca provides an opportunity for ordinary people to be involved in the administration of justice to an unprecedented degree, "this is not a role with which they are familiar, nor one of their own choosing. The [new] Gacaca courts do not have [the] prior credibility of . . . an acknowledged traditional authority or belief system [common to] customary approaches to justice" remaining, instead, a state creation.[289] Finally, concerns have been raised that—similar to colonial uses of indigenous dispute resolution systems—a state-mandated use of Gacaca to deal with genocide cases may undermine its original value as an informal, spontaneous dispute resolution mechanism.[290]

XXIII. SEEKING JUSTICE, MOVING FORWARD: PROPOSALS TO MITIGATE SHORTCOMINGS IN GACACA

This section of the paper tries to strike a balance between justice and reconciliation, punishment and restorative measures. Where justice in the form of retribution and punishment is sought, it is argued, fundamental due process rights should be respected. On the other hand, if Gacaca is not to become simply "an-

---

284. Nicole Itano, *Rwandan Community Courts Slow to Bring Justice*, CHRISTIAN SCIENCE MONITOR, Nov. 8, 2002, *available at* http://www.csmonitor.com/2002/1108/p08s01-woaf.html (last visited Oct. 24, 2004). *See also* PRI Report V, *supra* note 276, at 5 (observing that, in some areas, survivors and witnesses are reluctant to testify as they fear for their personal security).

285. UN Office for the Coordination of Human Affairs, *Rwanda: Nine sentenced to death over killing of genocide survivors*, Mar. 8, 2004, *available at* www.irinnews.org/print.asp?ReportID=39896 (last visited Oct. 24, 2004).

286. Waldorf, *supra* note 198.

287. *See also* PRI Report V, *supra* note 276, at 18 (reporting that more than half of the population do not wish to participate actively in the Gacaca sessions).

288. Organic Law, No. 16/2004 of 19/6/2004, *supra* note 4, art. 29. Article 29 states:

> Every Rwandan citizen has the duty to participate in the Gacaca courts activities. Any person who omits or refuses to testify . . . shall be prosecuted by the Gacaca court . . . [and] incurs a prison sentence from three (3) months to six (6) months. In case of repeat offence, the defendant may incur a prison sentence from six (6) months to (1) one year.

Id.

289. African Rights, *supra* note 146, at 3. *See also* Uvin, *supra* note 5, at 10 (stating that the government's process of "sensitization" to the Gacaca jurisdictions has been, at least initially, mostly "top-down" and one-sided, neglecting the adoption of a more "horizontal," participatory approach, and reporting the lack of involvement of NGOs in the formulation and design of the courts).

290. Vandeginste, *Justice*, *supra* note 153, at 22-23. *See also* Sarkin, *supra* note 78, at 170.

other layer in the implementation of genocide trials,"[291] a shift in the emphasis from a predominantly retributive scheme to one more restorative is needed.

While fraught with challenges, the best contribution Gacaca may make is to prove that, far from being mutually incompatible, both the quest for justice and reconciliation are indeed possible and can be reconciled in some way.

While human rights activists have strongly criticized the disregard of due process rights in Gacaca, other observers have regarded this as the price to be paid in view of its purported restorative, therapeutic, communitarian approach.[292] The truth is that in transitional societies recovering from atrocities perfect justice will more likely be a utopia. This is even more so in the case of Rwanda, where no system in the world would be able to deliver model justice if challenged by a comparable situation.[293] This does not mean that Rwanda should abdicate completely its obligations. While justice may not necessarily be equated with Western principles, as the experience with the South African TRC has shown, there are some measures that the Rwandan government could adopt if Gacaca is not to become a "vehicle for summary and arbitrary justice that fails defendants and genocide survivors alike."[294] These measures would imply both amendments to the Gacaca law and other concrete steps to ensure that dangers implicit in Gacaca are minimized.

XXIV. DUE PROCESS RIGHTS

Under the Gacaca law defendants are not entitled to be represented by a lawyer.[295] The law should be amended to include such a possibility, to conform with international fair trial standards. These standards establish the right to have legal counsel assigned by the state to indigent defendants where the interest of justice so requires.[296] Such determination is primarily based on the seriousness of the offense and the potential maximum punishment.[297] Category 2 defendants who

291. Drumbl, *(Al)lure of Genocide Trials*, *supra* note 39, at 224.

292. *Id.* (arguing that "the more legal or juridical [G]acaca is pressured by the international community to become, the less effective it may be in stripping away the silence of complicity, barriers to shame, and resistance to the therapeutic discussion so needed to heal Rwanda"). *See also* Ironside, *supra* note 98, at 57-58 (stating that "Gacaca offers a promising means for Rwandans to draw together and gain a greater sense of justice and healing than experienced thus far," and that "as very little justice has been achieved to date for Rwandans under the status quo . . . Gacaca offers a solution . . . albeit an imperfect one").

293. *See* Ironside, *supra* note 98, at 57.

294. Press Release, Amnesty International, Rwanda: Gacaca - Gambling with Justice (June 19, 2002), *available at* http://web.amnesty.org/library/Index/ENGAFR470032002?Open&of=ENG-RWA (last visited Oct. 24, 2004).

295. *See* discussion *infra* Part XX.

296. International Covenant on Civil and Political Rights, Dec. 19, 1966, G.A. Res. 2200A (XXI), 999 U.N.T.S. 171, art.14 (3)(d). According to this provision, everyone shall be entitled, in the determination of any criminal charge against him ". . . to defend himself in person or through legal assistance of his own choosing . . . and to have legal assistance assigned to him, in any case where the interest of justice so require, and without payment by him in any case if he does not have sufficient means to pay for it." *Id.*

297. *See* Manfred Nowak, U.N. Covenant on Civil and Political Rights, CCPR Commentary 259-60 (N.P. Engel, Arlington 1993). For instance, the Human Rights Committee has held that any person charged with a crime punishable by death must have counsel assigned. *See* Henry v. Jamaica (571/1994), July 25, 1996, Report of the Human Rights Committee, ¶ 9.2, U.N. Doc. CCPR/C/57D/57

are liable to lengthy prison terms, up to 30 years imprisonment—i.e. those accused of murder or attempted murder—should be entitled to legal counsel at the expense of the state. Given the still acute shortage of legal personnel in Rwanda, a legal aid scheme could be set up that would include not only full-fledged lawyers, but also other categories such as legal advisors, law professors, law students, and representatives of NGOs that have a background and experience in human rights in general and fair trial standards in particular. To encourage their participation, the Rwandan government, with the assistance of the international donor community, could make some form of benefits available.

Alternatively, for the same crimes under Category 2, the recourse to the Gacaca jurisdictions could be made conditional upon consent of the defendants themselves. Should they not consent they should be tried by the ordinary courts, where respect for due process rights is at least nominally guaranteed.

Given the difficult and professional nature of the task imposed upon Gacaca judges, it appears that provisions should be made to grant them some form of compensation,[298] either in the form of a "salary-type remuneration" or other form of non-monetary compensation, such as the payment of primary care assistance or primary school fees for their children.[299] While the first option may be unattainable given the high number of judges, and the fact that it is less akin to the philosophy of Gacaca courts as instruments of popular justice, symbolic forms of compensation may satisfy direct needs of individuals while at the same time contribute to longer-term prospects of societal development.[300] A recent initiative by the Rwandan government directed at providing free medical insurance to families of the Gacaca judges should be welcomed as a first step in this direction.[301] Such arrangements reduce the risk and perception of corruption, enhance the status and prestige of judges in the eyes of the community, as well as represent an incentive favoring their long-term commitment to the Gacaca process.

Additional training should also be provided to all judges in order to enable them to best perform their difficult mandate. This training should be particularly targeted at members of the cell Gacaca benches, who perform the crucial function of categorizing all accused.

XXV. STRIKING A BALANCE: JUSTICE VERSUS RECONCILIATION

In the aftermath of the genocide, the exclusive recourse to criminal trials, adjudication and imprisonment as mechanisms of individual accountability have

1/1994 (1996).

298. Compensation proportionate to the responsibility and social status conferred by the judicial office is an important requirement to support individual judicial integrity. *See* Oxner, *supra* note 239, at 23.

299. *See Gacaca Jurisdictions, supra* note 2. *See also* CAGEP Consult, *Assessment of the Judicial Sector, supra* note 280, at 75 (reporting that 41.5 percent of judges think the provision of some form of remuneration is necessary to guarantee the success of Gacaca).

300. *See Gacaca Jurisdictions, supra* note 2. While the majority of Gacaca judges are in favor of some form of compensation, some of them favor such compensation to be in the form of "free transport, health expenses, school fees for their children . . . [or anything else] that will . . . confer [some] standing on them." *See* African Rights, *supra* note 146, at 15.

301. Zac Nsenga, Rwandan Ambassador to the United States, in a personal communication to the author (Nov. 11, 2004).

failed to promote justice and societal reconciliation.[302] There is a risk that, fully implementing the project of popular retribution as currently envisaged in the Gacaca jurisdictions may further antagonize what is an already deeply divided society, and compromise the many potential strengths of Gacaca as a vehicle of participatory, restorative justice.

While prosecuting and punishing the worst perpetrators of genocide in Rwanda (i.e. the leaders and organizers as well as those who committed the killings) seems to be necessary to instill a culture of accountability and break the cycle of impunity, "it may be insufficient to strike on its own at the root" the inner social and political factors which made such large scale atrocity possible, and which can, if left unaltered, determine its recurrence.[303]

As it has been argued, the nature of Rwanda as a dualist post-genocidal society characterized by unavoidable Hutu-Tutsi interdependence and commingling, coupled with the high degree of public participation and complicity in the genocide, make it well-suited to benefit from restorative justice approaches that prioritize the restoration of peace in local communities by repairing injuries, encouraging repentance, promoting rehabilitation, and, eventually, facilitating reintegration.[304] Shifting the emphasis from the retributive to the restorative paradigm, within or outside Gacaca, may indeed better guarantee justice and individual accountability without compromising the achievement of peace and stability in the long-term.[305] It would also considerably offset human rights concerns linked to Gacaca's disregard for due process rights of defendants.

XXVI. Complementing the Prosecutorial Model: Establishing a Truth Commission

Trials by Gacaca may become more effective where they are complemented by the functioning of a truth commission.[306] The commission would be an independent body comprised of individuals from all ethnic groups, each with objective credibility for their moral integrity, impartiality, and fairness.[307] The mandate of such commission should be all-encompassing, by investigating not only crimes committed by the Hutu population in the context of the genocide, but also human rights violations committed by the RPF in the context of the civil war. Like in South Africa, this would send the message that the government respects human rights so much that it would respect the rights of even those who supported the

302. *See* Drumbl, *Sclerosis*, *supra* note 10, at 288. *See also* Sarkin, *supra* note 78, at 288; Minow, *supra* note 15, at 51 (calling for an "honest modesty" about the transformative potential of trials).

303. *See* Kritz, *Progress and Humility*, *supra* note 13, at 60.

304. *See* Drumbl, *(Al)lure of Genocide Trials*, *supra* note 39, at 221-25, 229.

305. *Id.* at 229 (arguing that a restorative justice model may create in Rwanda "fertile ground" for the growth of much needed multi-ethnic power-sharing structures and institutions).

306. Some authors have recommended that Rwanda establish a truth commission to investigate genocide-related crimes. *See* Sarkin, *supra* note 78, at 166-70 (arguing against the role to be played by Gacaca in trying genocide suspects, and proposing, instead, the exclusive prosecution of the main leaders of the genocide together with the establishment of an independent truth commission). *See also* Drumbl, *Sclerosis*, *supra* note 10, at 296 (proposing the establishment of a truth commission involving not only victims and perpetrators, but also international actors who—directly or indirectly—enabled the violence).

307. *See* Kritz, *Progress and Humility*, *supra* note 13, at 61 (discussing proposals to create a Truth and Reconciliation Commission in Bosnia and Herzegovina).

genocide and personally committed atrocities.[308] Addressing such crimes would also pose the basis for mutuality and full historical accuracy. It could also critically confer the commission much needed legitimacy, altering the so far widespread perception that victor's justice is being pursued in Rwanda. Similar to the South African TRC, the commission would travel the country providing Rwandans, victims and perpetrators alike, with an impartial forum to recount their history and give their version of the truth. While the commission would call on perpetrators to give their side of the story and to repent for their actions, it would not, like the TRC, exchange truth for amnesty.

Such a forum could help Rwanda in establishing a much needed historical account not only of what happened but also of why it happened. The striking extent of public participation in the atrocities, and the fact that so many Rwandans were complicit in the face of their public nature, strongly argue for the need to shed light on the underlying factors that made these atrocities possible. The "open, discursive nature" of a truth commission would arguably better address the problem of widespread complicity in the genocide.[309] In order to establish as truthful and comprehensive a picture as possible, the commission would not only investigate individual abuses, but also focus on the broader socio-political context in which they occurred. In particular, it would examine the role played by various sectors of the society, like the religious leadership, the media, and the political establishment that actively supported and encouraged the genocidal violence.[310] In South Africa, an entire volume of the TRC's Final Report was dedicated to the findings of institutional hearings, and proved to be indispensable in ascribing important political responsibilities to the government and political-societal apparatus.[311] Likewise, in Rwanda, this would somehow permit to hold whole sectors—that will never be the subject of criminal prosecutions—accountable for the genocide, as well as create an historical record of the causes and wider context of an otherwise inexplicable violence. Not doing so, on the other hand, would perpetuate mutual distrust, engender the ethnic divide and irremediably compromise any prospect of genuine, lasting peace in Rwanda.

In a unique and innovative way, the commission would also substantially expand its mission of truth gathering by calling attention not only to the atrocities committed, but also by documenting the positive stories of "ordinary heroes," those who, at great personal risk, maintained their humanity and protected Tutsi neighbors and others who were targeted in the frantic wave of violence.[312]

Most importantly, such a truth seeking process could help the Rwandan society move towards a common and consensual account of the causes and character of wrongdoing before, during, and after the genocide. This would create an unde-

308. See Daly, *Transformative Justice*, supra note 27, at 155 (commenting on the benefits of the South African TRC).

309. *See* Aukerman *supra* note 27, at 82 (generally discussing benefits of truth commissions).

310. *See* Little, *supra* note 27, at 77 (discussing the mandate of the proposed Truth and Reconciliation Commission in Bosnia and Herzegovina).

311. *See* van Zyl, *supra* note 61, at 749 (discussing the South African TRC).

312. This aspect was included in the project for the establishment of a Truth and Reconciliation Commission in Bosnia Herzegovina. Despite the promises it held, the establishment of the commission was aggressively opposed by senior officials within the International Criminal Tribunal for the Former Yugoslavia who were concerned about its future interaction and competition with the tribunal's role and activities. *See* Kritz, *Progress and Humility*, *supra* note 13, at 61-67.

niable, irreversible truth in a country where even the teaching of history is seen as controversial. As it has been observed, the development of a "common national historical narrative" based on a shared interpretation of the facts is indispensable if perpetrators and victims are to continue to live together.[313] By providing a national forum for victims from all sides of the conflict, the commission would facilitate a national dialogue between Rwandans on the genocide, its causes and, hopefully, the kinds of reforms—both at the institutional and political level—needed to prevent its recurrence. The commission would complement, not replace, trials for the most egregious violations before the special genocide chambers. It would also work in parallel with trials conducted by Gacaca, although these would be conducted differently from their current design.

XXVII. Enhancing the Restorative Aspect of Gacaca

The restorative potential of Gacaca proceedings could be enhanced by partly drawing on the approach taken by the Commission for Reception, Truth and Reconciliation (CRTR), which was established in East Timor with the assistance of the United Nations in 2001. Besides being tasked with establishing the truth about human rights violations committed in East Timor under Indonesian rule, the CRTR has been responsible for an innovative "Community Reconciliation Process" directed at favoring the reintegration into local communities of persons accused of having committed less serious crimes in the context of the political violence infesting the territory between 1974 and 1999.[314] This process has been regarded as representing "less an amnesty solution . . . than a model for conflict management permitting [perpetrators of lesser crimes] . . . to return to their homes" upon taking responsibility for their actions and carrying out some form of community service to the benefit of the local population.[315]

Under the new scheme, Gacaca courts would continue to try Category 2 defendants (i.e. the perpetrators, or accomplices of homicide or serious assault resulting in death, those who attempted to kill, and those responsible for other assaults). These courts would, on the other hand, be stripped of their retributive functions and reconfigured to fashion sentences in a more flexible, creative way for the lesser offenses committed by Category 2 defendants (comprising persons who committed assaults or who were accomplices in committing assaults without the intention to kill their victims). Doing so would enhance the restorative nature

313. *See* Susan Dwyer, *Reconciliation for Realists*, 13 ETHICS & INT'L AFF. 81, 89-90 (1999). *See also* Aukerman, *supra* note 27, at 89 (stating that, by articulating "many sides of the same story . . . [truth commissions] may be . . . better at fostering social solidarity in societies where guilt runs in multiple directions").

314. *See* Carsten Stahn, *Accommodating Individual Criminal Responsibility and National Reconciliation: The UN Truth Commission for East Timor*, 95 AM. J. INT'L L. 952, 953 (2001) [hereinafter Stahn]. For a description of the Community Reconciliation Process, see UNTAET Regulation No. 2001/10, Part IV (July 13, 2001) (on the establishment of a Commission for Reception, Truth and Reconciliation in East Timor), *available at* http://www.easttimor-reconciliation.org.

315. *See* Stahn, *supra* note 314, at 957. Perpetrators of lesser crimes are in this way granted immunity from civil and criminal prosecution. Under this scheme, serious criminal offenses, such as crimes against humanity, murder, torture, and rape, are prosecuted by special panels of the Dili District Court, while for minor offenses such as theft, minor assault, arson, or the killing of livestock, the individual may request to participate in the Community Reconciliation Process. *Id.* at 960-61, 964.

of Gacaca and also eliminate most due process concerns linked to its current implementation.

In these cases, and partly mirroring the procedure before the East Timorese CRTR, the accused individual may apply to participate in a Community Reconciliation Process by submitting a statement to Gacaca that includes a full description of the relevant acts, an admission of responsibility, and a renunciation of the use of violence for ethnic and political motives.[316] The case would then be examined by the Gacaca judges. At the public Gacaca hearing, the judges will hear from the applicant, the victim, and other members of the community, as it is currently envisaged. In a variation of the process, and upon hearing suggestions made by the victim and the applicant alike, the judges will then inform the perpetrator of the act of reconciliation deemed most appropriate in the specific case. This may include the performance of community service, reparation, public apology, and/or any other "act of contrition," along with a prescribed time limit for performance.[317]

In determining the most appropriate act of reconciliation, the Gacaca judges will consider not only the actual nature of the crime, but also the total number of acts committed by the applicant, as well as his role in the commission of the crime. In the latter case, special emphasis will be put on whether the applicant was actively involved in the planning, organization, or ordering of the crime, or was following the orders of others in carrying it out.[318] If accepted by the applicant, the act of reconciliation would be confirmed in a Community Reconciliation Agreement signed by him and by the Gacaca panel and then registered in the district court. The district court would have the discretion to reject an agreement if it finds that the act of reconciliation exceeds what is "reasonably proportionate" to the acts disclosed or that it violates human rights principles.[319] Should the perpetrator subsequently fail to fulfill the terms of the agreement, the case will be returned to Gacaca for normal adjudication.

In cases where either the victim or the applicant disagree with the act of reconciliation proposed by the Gacaca panel, the procedure and penalties currently envisaged for perpetrators of lesser crimes belonging to Category 2 would continue to apply.[320] Unlike the current Gacaca process, as a result of which different prison terms and/or community service are automatically applicable—in the latter case upon the confessor's approval—the new process would actively involve victims and perpetrators, with their community supporters, to decide the form accountability will take. It would thus empower all people concerned to "determine their needs at the most local level."[321]

Allowing the community to creatively and flexibly fashion sentences for the least serious crimes would importantly recognize that victims have different recovery needs, and would arguably give them a more powerful voice than what is

316. *See* UNTAET Reg. No. 2001/10 § 23.

317. *See id.* § 27.7. See also Kritz, *Progress and Humility*, *supra* note 13, at 79 (generally describing the CRTR's Community and Reconciliation Process).

318. *See id.* Schedule I.

319. UNTAET Reg. No. 2001/10 §§ 27.8, 28.2.

320. *See* Organic Law No. 16/2004 of 19/6/2004, *supra* note 4, arts. 54, 56, 58, 62-65, 73.

321. *See* Daly, *Punitive and Reconstructive Justice*, *supra* note 76, at 391 (suggesting that the Gacaca law be amended to empower the courts to grant selective and conditional amnesty).

currently envisaged in the Gacaca process. It would also better reflect—in a situation where government hate propaganda and manipulation have had such a devastating impact—the different gradations of individual and collective responsibility that may emerge from the Gacaca hearings. Shifting the focus from the possibility of retribution in the form of imprisonment and/or performance of community service, to a variety of optional restorative measures would also enhance chances that the defendant will effectively reintegrate into the community. By focusing more closely on the needs of all parties involved in the crime, including the victim and the community where it took place, the restorative nature of Gacaca would guarantee a genuinely holistic approach to justice and, hopefully, increase the chances of peaceful coexistence in the future.

XXVIII. CONCLUSION

The challenging task of combining retribution with reconciliation is most daunting in transitional societies recovering from mass violence. The Rwandan experience shows the limits of the conventional prosecutorial approach in achieving these goals, and points towards the need for innovation and flexibility as part of a comprehensive response to horrendous crimes.[322]

Through Gacaca, Rwanda has courageously taken an unexplored path. Rwanda's unconventional experience in prosecuting genocide suspects through the use of village courts extends beyond its context by setting a new precedent in the field of transitional justice and in the search of pragmatic approaches to accountability for atrocities. It represents a test case in creatively shaping and adapting traditional dispute resolution systems to address the competing, partly conflicting goals of justice and reconciliation. Gacaca has a lot of potential: through a highly inclusive approach, it makes accountability, in the wider sense of justice and social reconciliation, the ultimate aspiration of every Rwandan. By acknowledging the suffering of individual victims and their families, and by allowing individuals on both sides of the ethnic and ideological divide to publicly relate their stories, the Gacaca proceedings may dissipate feelings of collective guilt, foster a rule of law supportive culture, facilitate reconciliation, and give to participants a much needed sense of dignity, empowerment and, to some degree, closure. It also indicates that pragmatic and context-sensitive solutions may potentially achieve more goals than the traditional approach of criminal prosecutions. Nonetheless, there are serious flaws in the system that may irremediably compromise the achievement of these objectives and reinforce the perception of many that a partisan version of justice is taking place in the shadows of the genocide.

With retribution retaining a central role in Gacaca, efforts must be made to respect the due process rights of those brought before it. Although the Rwandan government still views individual prosecutions—by the ordinary or Gacaca courts—as the only way of achieving justice, there are a series of alternatives that could assist in increasing Gacaca's credibility and legitimacy. In this view, a mixed, multi-dimensional approach combining restorative initiatives—such as the creation of a truth commission and the reconfiguration of Gacaca to emphasize its restorative approach for lesser offenses—with trials for the most egregious viola-

322. Strain & Keyes, *supra* note 93, at 131.

tions, may better suit the partly conflicting goals of justice and societal regeneration. More importantly, the credibility and ultimate practicability of any post-genocide accountability mechanism is predicated upon its perceived legitimacy and, ultimately, even-handedness and ability to deliver genuine justice to all segments of the population, victims and perpetrators alike. While serious political and social challenges face the Gacaca jurisdictions, only time will tell whether these have truly been the last best chance for justice, stability and social reunification in a deeply wounded nation.

Part III
Issues in New Forms of International and Transnational Dispute Resolution

[16]

Current Illusions and Delusions about Conflict Management— In Africa and Elsewhere

Laura Nader
Elisabetta Grande

This paper provides a critical perspective on the use of U.S. alternative dispute resolution (ADR) approaches for managing conflict in African and other communities. It argues that imposition of American ADR as a condition for foreign aid or capital investment is deeply problematic, and urges a more sophisticated analysis of the power dimensions and ideological basis of ADR. When viewed as an ideologically laden paradigm for how conflict should be resolved (i.e., a conflict paradigm), ADR can be seen as carrying troubling baggage. For example, ADR approaches imported from the United States deal with dispute resolution simply in terms of mechanisms or techniques, ignoring substantive issues central to conflict management in African and other communities. The entire discourse surrounding ADR pays insufficient attention to problems with terms such as modern or traditional, and encourages an ingenuous denial of the effects of inequality in power and money on conflict resolution. This ideological baggage renders unreflective imposition of ADR incompatible with the best interests of African communities. The authors urge a more complete and objective analysis of the global ADR revolution—one that takes a broader perspective.

This era has created the first global, or planetary, technical civilization, but it has reached the limits of its potential, the point beyond which the abyss begins . . . . Man's attitude to the world must be radically changed. We have to abandon the arrogant belief that the world is

Laura Nader is professor of anthropology, Department of Anthropology. University of California, Berkeley. **Elisabetta Grande** is professor of comparative legal systems, Piedmont Eastern University, Alessandra, Italy.

merely a puzzle to be solved, a machine with instructions for use waiting to be discovered, a body of information to be fed into a computer in the hope that sooner or later it will spit out a universal solution.

—V. Havel, *The End of the Modern Era*

In recent decades, U.S.-style dispute resolution (ADR) techniques have been exported to and imposed on communities in other parts of the world. ADR approaches such as mediation may have immediate appeal, appearing to foster harmonious and consensual resolution of conflict. However, they can in fact do more harm than good when forced on communities in which underlying understandings and situations do not fit well with the assumptions and epistemology that undergird ADR. In addition, the use of ADR has power dimensions that have not been adequately analyzed or understood. An accurate and sophisticated analysis would consider these problems as well as the input of nationalism; of political, economic, and religious processes; and of the wide range of players involved—politicians, businessmen, missionaries, arms dealers, ethnic groups, and victims. In short, policy initiatives in this area must proceed from a thorough understanding of conflict management in grounded contexts. This more careful, respectful, and contextual analysis might at times favor constraint over consensus, or more formal law over lawlessness or informal dispute resolution techniques.

HISTORY OF CONFLICT PARADIGMS AND IDEOLOGIES

Anyone who has followed the conflict resolution literature over the past 40–50 years cannot help but notice certain themes that wax and wane. The constellation of certain ideas that has emerged as part of the contemporary, burgeoning conflict resolution industry has a history. By the late 1950s there was already a reactive trend against the equilibrium theorists, those who romanticized consensual and harmonious models, or those who saw a silver lining in every conflict. Two schools of thought predominated. In British anthropology the Manchester school led by Max Gluckman (1959) represented the idea that social conflict was functional for the maintenance of social systems. In the United States anthropologists Bernard Siegal and Alan Beals (1960) saw conflicts as dysfunctional phenomena, produced by strains and stresses in the social system caused by internal and external pressures. Both schools used an integrative approach.

In an early review of the literature (LeVine 1961), the sources of conflict, its functional value, and the patterns of conflict control and resolution were conceptualized in terms of broad understandings of social organization, religion, economic interdependence, and political structures. Some of the article titles in that special issue are instructive: "Land Shortage, Social Change, and Social Conflict in East Africa," "Feuding and Social Change in Morocco," "Extension of Conflict as a Method of Conflict Resolution among the Suku of the Congo." The approach was holistic and not geared to mechanical recipes for dispute resolution.

In 1968 Ralf Dahrendorf extended the earlier work to argue that social conflict is a creative force, suggesting a complete theoretical about-face. In his words, "not the presence but the absence of conflict is surprising and abnormal, and we have good reason to be suspicious if we find a society or social organization that displays no evidence of conflict . . . we must never lose sight of the underlying assumption that conflict can be temporarily suppressed, regulated, channeled, and controlled, but that neither a philosopher-king nor a modern dictator can abolish it once and for all" (1968, 127).

Nevertheless, by the 1970s the dialogue over conflict was shifting once again, and in the United States it was publicly led by the chief Justice of the U.S. Supreme Court, Warren Burger. Alternative Dispute Resolution (ADR) burst onto the scene and was institutionalized (Nader 1989). Conflict, as epitomized by the adversary system, was now portrayed as uncivilized: Lawyers were pictured as hired guns, peace (not conflict) was the goal, and harmony (not contentious behavior) was extolled. ADR, a means for containing the rights movements of the 1960s was (among other things) a movement institutionalized at the national level and then exported. By the 1990s, ADR was a major industry composed of professionals from many fields: law, economics, psychology, political science, peace and conflict, psychotherapy, and religious movements.[1] In spite of early success, the movement was always more attractive to ADR professionals than to its potential consumers, who here and abroad were skeptical about the philosophy and purpose of ADR, as well as about its mechanisms for achieving peaceful solutions. By 1996, those interested in alternative conflict resolution had bifurcated into scholars and practitioners, with the latter being in the greatest number. It is to the practitioner that this paper is principally dedicated.

In Africanist scholarship, the trends followed similar directions. The ethnographic and social anthropological schools of structural functionalism contributed an enormous body of scholarship about "traditional" African societies (see, e.g., Gluckman 1995; Gulliver 1963; Bohannon 1957; Schapera 1959; Nadel 1942). For many anthropologists, traditionalism was good or functional, and modernism (westernization) was disruptive. Today, some refer to the work of the colonial period as written in the "noble savage" tradition because of observations that anthropologists in their protec-

1. One has only to scan the programs of annual meetings of the Society of Professionals in Dispute Resolution (SPIDR) or follow the contents of the *Negotiation Journal* for proof of this.

tionist attitudes sought to preserve African cultures, which ipso facto committed them to preserving the status quo (see, e.g., Marcus and Fischer 1986). Although there were exceptions, the structural-functionalist orientation emphasizes equilibrium, integration, harmony, and consensus. African societies were, however, often neither integrated nor harmonious, either in precolonial conditions (where they were often embroiled in military conquests), or in the colonial period, characterized as it was by economic, political, and racial conflicts.

Some anthropologists portrayed the peoples they studied as if they were culturally homogenous, and spoke about them without adequate attention to the wide degree of structural variation and cultural pluralism. That is, they essentialized, to use a favorite term. We might add that anthropologists were also among the first to criticize this early work, and often in the lead with correctives. A further result of the critical literature was the abandonment of the view of society as harmonious and its replacement by a model that emphasized conflict and dissension in all of its bewildering complexity and dynamism: new nations; new classes; changing roles for men, women, and children; religious transformation; and the transformation of kinship and marriage, nationalism, and transnationalism.

The recognition that Africa was undergoing profound and rapid changes that incorporated indigenous and foreign elements led to an interest in historical ethnography, which examined conflicts of interests and values that surfaced due to the spread of Islam and Christianity, and due to European conquest, which introduced legal transplants and multinational interests. The heritage of colonialism was still being felt in the independence and postindependence period as well as in expressions of Pan-Africanism. There are ties that bind Africans and others that separate them.

With these historical highlights in mind we might see current interdisciplinary policy literature as being of a different sort. Ethnographically rich descriptions of conflict resolution in situ by anthropologists (e.g., Hirsch 1998) commonly are replaced by descriptions of conflict resolution techniques by other disciplines (e.g., political science, law, psychology) that come closer to shreds and patches reporting, work that generally ignores anthropological work on "traditional" conflict resolutions and that seeks to problematize "tradition." Historicized ethnographies become historicized accounts, absent context. Today, the biases of practical, or policy-oriented, scholarship include interdisciplinary searches for peace recipes; these recipes often stem from political considerations that are bipartisan, nationalist, pan-African, religious, or internationalist (see Zartman 2000).

If colonialism was basically ignored as part of anthropological work a half century ago, today neo-colonialism and globalization are also inadequately incorporated, even though interdisciplinary development research is sometimes linked with both alternative dispute resolution and legal implants. But anthropological reflexivity and the self-critiques of the sixties and earlier also now permit us to critically examine scholarship—ours and others', Euro-American and African—with attention to such mundane questions as, Who is providing funding? Who is asking the questions? Who benefits? We can also question whether disciplinary concepts have contributed to "ethnographic error" and to inadequate policy research that ignores root causes of conflict and avoids discussion of Euro-American impositions that may play a part in conflict generation or its absence.

In what follows we talk about four issues that are often neglected in interdisciplinary discussions of dispute resolution policies in Africa: (1) the problem with terms like "traditional" and "modern" dispute resolution; (2) the problem with thinking about dispute resolution in terms of mechanisms or techniques that are specialties; (3) the ingenuousness of speaking about conflict resolution without speaking to and about power; without integrating information on arms dealings, its source, and its distribution; or without including multinationals as they pertain to resource competition; and (4) the ideological bases of conflict management paradigms and the hegemonies that accompany law or alternative dispute techniques.[2] Adequate analysis of these ideologies requires sophisticated understanding of tradition and power. Our goal is to at least round out the picture of "internal" dissensions in Africa, conflicts that are thinly portrayed on the media's front burner as if only explained by "ancient tribal conflicts or rivalries."

TRADITION AND POWER

The symbolic uses of tradition for purposes of legitimization have been widely discussed. Peter Worsley in *The Three Worlds: Culture and World Development* summed it up this way:

> Culture traits are not absolutes or simply intellectual categories . . . . They are strategies or weapons in competition over scarce social goods. What is mistakenly often seen as tradition—attachment to the past as a value in itself—is better viewed as a way of maintaining title to power, wealth and status in the present, or as a nostalgic spiritual contrast to present disprivilege. (1984, 249)

For example, in the Native American context, Michael Tsosie (n.d.) outlines a description of the process in which traditional culture is used to exclude competitors by reducing ethnic identity to a finite trait list. In the

2. Although some practitioners of conflict resolution such as John Paul Lederach, reach for a broader, more holistic paradigm, the result, as in the case of Lederach, is far from its stated aims. Early in his book *Building Peace*, he reiterates the narrower view of sustainable reconciliation in divided societies within a framework of conflict as "internal rather than international . . . competition between sharply defined identity groups" (1997, 10).

same arena, others have noted the application of tradition and culture concepts to pan-Indian militancy as tools for garnering power (see Nader and Ou 1998).

Thinking about tradition and power in the African context is even more tricky. Fifteen years ago, Martin Chanock (1985) documented what some had articulated before him: the European source of what anthropologists had been calling customary law. Chanock drew attention to the role of Christian missionaries in the establishment of local courts that employed a blend of English procedural law and Christian rules of behavior drawn from Bible scriptures. As argued elsewhere, political colonialism and Western Christianity spread the harmony legal model in a manner that resembles the modern ADR movement. Both emphasized compromise and consensus as a preferred way of decision making—peace over justice being a mandatory result (Nader 1990). Missionaries carried forward the "civilizing mission" in two ways: by teaching the "savages" about peaceful resolution of conflict through law courts, and by teaching them the rules of a good Christian life (which among other things excluded polygyny, and included the turning of the other cheek—acquiescence, or the opposite of militancy—something that probably suited the colonial powers since it supported the political agendas of colonialism).

Today, tradition is up for grabs by any person or group interested in garnering power, and anthropologists are analyzing the many ways tradition is "reinvented" for current contexts and purposes (see, e.g., Castillo, Aida, and Nigh 1998; Hobsbawm and Ranger 1985). Again in the Native American context, it has been noted that federal officials and native advocates actively use linguistic, ethical, moral, cultural, and political traditions to sell nuclear waste disposal to Native Americans by means of ADR (Ou 1996). In Africa and elsewhere, traditional symbols and institutions are regularly used by politicians to reach both rural and urban populations. If politicians can manipulate tradition or reinvent tradition, so might strategists in conflict management.

A central dilemma revolves around the observation that experts generally look for standardized solutions, while traditional conflict resolution is often particularistic or situational. For example, in a recent note "Are Alternative Dispute Resolution (ADR) Programs Suitable for Africa?" anthropologist Laurel Rose (1996) addresses some of the conceptual problems of reinvented tradition by comparing contemporary American ADR with conflict resolution in African communities. Rose points out that modern mediators are formally trained, are strangers to the disputants, and are expected to be neutral, private, formal, and structured. By contrast African communities use mediators informally trained through "life experience," who are known to the disputants, are not expected to be neutral, and operate collectively within a council of elders in a public setting. While the

American ADR specialists operate with a limited range of relevance, the African process is characterized by a wide range of relevance, with full communication and public disclosure. Consensus between the parties is not what is sought; rather, the ideal outcome satisfies the whole community, usually placing community interests before the disputants' personal interests.[3]

Under the auspices of the USAID program, Rose visited postwar Rwanda in 1994 to conduct research into the condition of the local justice system (customary institutions know as the *gacaca*) as preparation for a larger ADR research team. The long-term goal was to support a Rwandan ADR initiative to train mediators in the (temporary) absence of courts. Rose found that the *gacaca* survived the war, that people were seldom without operational *gacaca*, and that they adapted to circumstances of refugee camps or other temporary or permanent circumstances. Rose also noted that the *gacaca* took on functions beyond dispute resolution, such as the resettlement of large numbers of displaced persons. Those *gacaca* implicated in war-related events suffered a loss of legitimacy; nevertheless, Rose makes the point that Rwanda's "customary institution" had risen to the challenges of their war-ravaged country and that an ADR initiative, even one making use of traditional institutions like the *gacaca*, would weaken local self-management or customary law. Rose refers to the cultural baggage that travels with American ADR, even when (or especially when) it is tied to a restructuring of indigenous systems. Moreover, she addresses the important issues of tradition and power, raising questions about an American ADR style that has much the flavor of earlier missionizing efforts of religious evangelists.

Technical dispute-resolution missions are of little use in societies where social structures might potentially promote conflict escalation. The other side of this picture appears when local peoples desire to keep control, by means of customary proceedings, in the light of external powers against whom they may be complaining. Under these conditions, localized ADR forums cannot substitute for strong national laws with international appeal capacities.

THE POWER DIMENSION

If any single generalization has emerged from the anthropological research on disputing processes (Nader and Todd 1978), it is that mediation and negotiation require conditions of relatively equal power. In other words, negotiation and mediation cannot be used for all disputes and all conflicts.

3. The dispute resolution style that Laurel Rose describes for Africa resembles practices in preindustrial Protestant New England villages of the seventeenth and eighteenth centuries. See also Rose 1997, which examines conflict-management training as religious proselytization in Papua, New Guinea.

The adversary model was created to deal with uneven playing fields, made even by each party having an advocate in a court of law. In real life things are not so neat. In Africa and elsewhere, there are courts where mediation predominates or at least where a third party can judge whether to mediate, negotiate, or adjudicate a case.

In Euro-American societies, harmony law models recently have been valorized over adversary models—a reversal of the earlier trend, as we mentioned in our historical survey of the literature. But history is clear on one point. During the heyday of European colonialism, courts were valorized over moots, and the colonized were reminded regularly that the *rule of law* was a most important sign of civilized society. Its presence indicated the right to participate in the international law of nations. The presence of courts was a sign of development and social complexity. The World Court was a standard of civilized behavior. Yet, in the latter part of the twentieth century, harmony legal models began to be thought of as more civilized than courts. Now that the "primitives" have courts, practitioners often value ADR or international negotiations as more "civilized." In this worldview, the "civilized" first worlders who wish to go to court are "barbarians," while "primitives" and the natives are considered a model of what it is to be truly human (Nader 1994).

For example, in a piece called "Dispute Resolution Notes from the Kalahari" anthropologist William L. Ury (1990) declares that the Bushman of the Kalahari may have been more peaceful than we who call ourselves "civilized." In his concluding comments he articulates an imaginary purity devoid of the power dimension:

> The Bushman of the Kalahari are a truly interdependent society: they are socialized from birth to be acutely aware of and sensitive to one another's needs. . . . In these people's lives—and presumably in our ancestors' lives as well—cooperation more than competition becomes the order of the day. In our modern economies, based as they are on competition among individuals and groups, it is easy to see the human adventure as a struggle for survival in which you must win at all costs at the expense of others. Our way of life is a few centuries old; the Bushman's has lasted tens of millennia. Life may in fact be about the "survival of the fittest," but what makes people truly "fit," as the Bushman remind us, is their ability to cooperate and to settle disruptive disputes. (199, 237–38)

We can see both the power and the illusory character of such a biased picture. For example, the board of anthropological advisors to a documentary about a Kung woman resigned in the late 1970s after viewing the film because it included shots of not so peaceful Bushmen who did not fit the idyllic picture that Ury and other anthropologists have portrayed.

The most serious illusions and delusions appear when we examine the history of what really happens when disputes are mediated or negotiated. An article called "Civilization and its Negotiators" (Nader 1994) traces the history of international dispute resolution from the World Court to international negotiating teams in the settlement of international river disputes. Lon Fuller argued that when disputes can be reasoned through logical argument, they are appropriately adjudicated (1978, 368–69), yet only a few international water disputes have been settled by adjudication. Before Fuller's article appeared, two international law specialists had argued, specifically in reference to international river disputes (Laylin and Bianchi 1959), that without the possibility of third-party decision makers, the more powerful disputant can use ADR negotiation to greater advantage.

A review of the role of adjudication and negotiation in international river disputes (the Ganges, Jordan, Colorado, Duoro, and Danube rivers) characterized by power asymmetry and upstream-downstream issues reveals preference by the less powerful nations for World Court adjudication, while the more powerful countries prefer negotiation (Nader 1994). In light of the skewing effects of power asymmetries on informally negotiated outcomes, it is understandable why powerful parties have preferred negotiation and ADR over the International Court of Justice.[4]

The United States joined the World Court in 1946 after congressional debates over whether doing so would threaten national sovereignty. Since 1946, the Court's composition and the types of cases it considers have changed. In 1946 two-thirds of the judges were either Americans or West Europeans. With the addition of over 100 states, including many Third World states, attitudes among judges shifted to reflect this changed composition, and newer judges may be sympathetic to the causes of the newer nations. Indeed, this change was reflected in a number of rulings in favor of Third World nation plaintiffs—as, for example, in the case of Nicaragua against the United States in 1984 (see Franck 1986). In 1985, the Reagan administration withdrew the U.S.'s 1946 agreement to voluntarily comply with the jurisdiction of the World Court. As Nader put it, "The Soviet Union in the mid-1960s and the U.S. in the mid-1980s both withheld dues, thereby abdicating their financial responsibility and evincing a mood of indifference to international law" (1994, 44). Furthermore, there has been a gradual divergence between the World Court's decisions and the national interest of the developed countries. Interestingly, the trivialization of international adjudication came at the height of the ADR explosion in the United States and national attacks on domestic adjudication.

4. While studies also suggest that richer and more powerful parties do better in formal proceedings because they can afford to pay for legal costs and outlast the opposition, such proceedings are at least public and open to public scrutiny, while negotiation proceedings are not.

We need to think about these issues before recommending any policies—national or otherwise—for the peoples of Africa. If the spread of ADR is born of a contempt for law and if the International Court is to be replaced by international negotiation, using justifications of efficiency or stability, then what hope is there for the justice issues that should be foundational here? Take, for example, the problem of famine (Lappe and Collins 1978; Schusky and Abbott n.d.). One shocking fact that came to light in the research on the Sahel famine of the 1980s was the extent of food exports from the Sahel. In the peak period of drought and famine, peanuts, cotton, vegetables, and meat were being exported. Sixty percent of the food exports went to Europe and the United States. Food corporations made vast profits at the height of the famine. Furthermore, California-based agribusiness (the world's largest iceberg lettuce growers) had in 1972 established subsidiaries in Senegal. The Senegalese government supplied police to clear away villagers who presumed the land was theirs to grow millet and other needed food. All the alternative dispute mechanisms in the world will not replace the just rule of law (state or international) in such a situation.

Nor can dispute resolution replace the rule of international law or public opinion sanctions in a country like Mozambique, which in 1992 agreed to a settlement that put an end to war. But peace did not bring prosperity; it brought poverty, which some say was caused by IMF-imposed stabilization policies (Hanlon 1996). Some Mozambicans call this economic colonialism, different from earlier colonialism because it does not have a face. In face-to-faceless conflict, the indigenous paradigm of face-to-face dispute resolution has no place, because "in trade negotiations, dispute resolution proceedings are conducted in complete secrecy with all documents unavailable to the public except through leaks to the press. Business groups have traditionally had far greater access to the trade negotiating arena than have environmental and other public interest groups" (French 1993).

One last dimension of power in Africa has to do with military power, which as far as we know is not commonly reported in academic writings on conflict management.[5] The topic was highlighted in a recent issue of *Harper's* in a piece titled "An Army of One's Own—In Africa, Nations Hire a Corporation to Wage War" (Rubin 1997). The author writes about a corporation that provides clandestine warfare, combat air patrol, battle handling, and sniper training to those who can pay. The company—Executive Outcomes—in exchange for $15 million and a share of Sierra Leone's diamond mines—was able to do what no one else had been able to do before:

5. For an excellent discussion of arms dealing and the African continent, see Boutwell, Klare, and Reed 1995. As the authors note, President Mandela of South Africa is well aware of the relation between the global flow of arms and the causes of ethnic conflict and repression. His position on banning weapons sales to countries engaged in civil conflict, however, was opposed by his regime's practical commitment to South Africa's arms industry—that is, by the socioeconomic pressures of post-apartheid reform.

"No one—not the United Nations, not the Organization of African Unity, not the international-conflict-resolution experts who filled up the abandoned tourist hotels in Freetown, Sierra Leone's capital—was able to bring the fighting under control." According to Rubin, Executive Outcomes was to "combat and destroy the 'terrorist enemies of the state'; to restore internal security; and to help build and maintain an economic climate where new investment could be attracted and allowed to flourish"(1997, 45). Sierra Leone, long viewed as a disaster, became a West African "success," so much so that the mercenaries became respected heroes because they had replaced banditry with security. Such occurrences are more than a shift in the nature of war, they indicate a shift in the nature of law. As in the premodern period, military and economic functions will be reunited by means of the booming security business that in the case of Sierra Leone and other African countries is taking over the state, or at least recolonizing, with private armies clearing the way for business firms—the "privatization of violence" Rubin calls it, a shift from geo-politics to geo-economics.

Rubin ends her story by noting that Executive Outcomes is accountable to no nation and no legal body. The marketplace is the law. This is the underside of conflict management in Africa and elsewhere. It is what eventually happens when we abandon the just rule of law in exchange for international negotiation based on economic efficiency of feel-good principles of psychology, rather than focusing on principles of law. It is what happens when the frame is narrow, when the role of foreign and national businesses are not included in the paradigm. As Laurel Rose points out, the locals are pretty adept at inventing tradition to take care of local situations. What they cannot do is deal with grossly unequal power, which is one role for national and international law, if we are civilized that is. ADR specialists have defined their domain in too limited a frame. They need to enlarge the scope. And when they do, they will also realize that it is not possible to have a universal paradigm for conflict management.

One of the cleverest propaganda concepts invented after colonialism, whether consciously or not, was the term *postcolonial*. It is, as with *tradition*, a concept up for grabs. When we say traditional was followed by colonial, and that was followed by postcolonial, it appears as if discontinuities prevailed over continuities. Yet if we look at the factors presently destabilizing the world at an accelerated rate, we find many of the same economic interests that fueled the colonial regimes still in the lead. This article is not the place to review the sources of destabilizations. However, specialists in dispute resolution could develop more realistic frames for specific disputes or conflicts if they understood the message of increasing numbers of businessmen who speak and write about globalization and destabilization by means of such activities as global free trade, intensive agriculture, energy policies, management's bottom line, or marketplace ideology (Korten 1995; Goldsmith 1994; Estes 1996; Soros 1997; Stiglitz 2000).

THE POWER OF IDEOLOGY

Ideologies that are forces of change go beyond the law to link law, business, and community constituencies in modern nation-states. However, the principal vehicle for the transmission of ideological forces has been and continues to be state or international law.

Historian Jerold Auerbach (1983) details ideological progressions in the United States as part of the transformation of American society dating at least from the end of the past century: "Amid the social dislocations that accompanied the rapid concentration of wealth and power in the age of industrial expansion, the full force of law was asserted to protect the new social order" (1983, 139–40). Competing pockets of authority originating in tribalism, religion, ethnicity, and class were stripped of dispute-settlement processes that had contributed to internal cohesion but that now competed with the legal supremacy of the state.[6] He explains the current enthusiasm for delegalization as an effort to deal with the legitimacy dilemma: The law is designed to protect the Haves as well as the Have-nots. The problem is that the ideal of equal justice is incompatible with the social realities of unequal power, so that, as I have said elsewhere, disputing without the force of law is doomed to failure (Nader 1979). In the United States, Auerbach continues, "The historical progression is clear: from community justice without formal institutions to the rule of law, all too often without justice." He concludes that "the pursuit of justice without law does incalculable harm to the prospect of equal justice" (Auerbach 1983,146).

Other scholars during the early 1980s iterated the same line of criticism and elaborated the problems with ADR (Abel 1980; Harrington 1985; Hofrichter 1987). Nevertheless, ADR marched on to become institutionalized and internationalized, despite continued critiques that more recently stress the irreconcilability between problem-solving mediation and transformative mediation (Milner 1996; Bush and Baruch 1996). Scholars have by now documented the ills of problem-solving alternatives that do not address social justice issues, since the core feature of most alternative processes is that they address and resolve individual cases on individuated criteria. Some, like Sally Merry, un-self-consciously argue that "popular justice introduces a new ideology of conflict resolution based on nonviolence and opposition to the violence of law" (Merry and Milner 1993, 62). Others

6. See Nader and Yngvesson 1974 for a discussion of key legal pluralism issues, as well as Merry's (1988) more recent elaboration. However, also note that legal pluralism is not the central issue concerning us here; hegemonies, both legal and epistemological, are.

think that one can tinker with present alternatives to make them more responsive actors in issues of social transformation (Bush and Baruch 1994).

While scholars meditate on the possibilities of popular justice or models of legal pluralism, the real consequences of ADR policies are harsh. The most hard-hitting critique of American ADR is that of the late Trina Grillo (1991), a law professor and mediator, who understood better than most—because she was a practitioner—the ideological nature of ADR mediation in family cases, and the process dangers for women. Grillo's points revolve around the notions that mandatory mediation abridges freedom because it is often outside the law, eliminates choice of procedure, removes equal protection before an adversary law, and is generally hidden from view. In spite of growing awareness of consequences, ADR ideology is intact and diffusing worldwide, in hegemonic splendor.

There is more to American ADR ideology than the obvious congruencies between trade ideology and harmony ideology (i.e., harmonizing), or even the missionizing that was also a central part of European colonization and the pacification of indigenous peoples.[7] There is in American culture such a yearning for an idealized equality that the very ideology of equality creates a denial of unequal power.[8] This in itself inspires the "soldiers" of movements like ADR, those who make it happen: the experts, the practitioners, and sometimes the scholars who feed the narrative.

But serious problems arise when the "soldiers" of a movement like ADR go abroad with such ideological baggage to deal with different sets of legal ideologies among people with different histories. The Horn of Africa seems a perfect place to see how legal stratification creates complexity at various levels (Grande 1995). First, the legal system in the Horn is made of legal "layers" imposed one on the other in the course of history. Religious law (such as Islamic *Sharia*) is superimposed on local customary law (Anderson 1970). Colonial law, either rooted in the common law or in the civil law, is superimposed on both these previous layers. And on top of everything, the law of the modern independent state (sometimes socialist) creates a new layer. In the Horn no legal order has effective power to substitute itself for previous layers. Between the layers of a pluralist legal system (which are all alive and operative in the contemporary world), competition is at play (Merry 1988; Mattei 1990; Bussani 1996).

Even the customary informal legal system results from a historical process of superimposition and mixing of components. What is often referred to

7. The legacy of legal formalism and of the separation between law and politics in Western societies may result in a legal discourse that is separated from power. This becomes even more of a legal fiction when observing legal systems outside the Western legal tradition.

8. Legal formalism, a movement born in Germany in the nineteenth century and not yet challenged in Europe, is accountable more than any other ideological movement for the making of the law as an autonomous, rational, and logical system, enabling lawyers to separate law from power.

as the customary layer is usually made of a large plurality of customs that have been interacting with each other in the course of historical events as experienced by the local population (Sacco 1996). Although the absence of written sources makes it difficult to know the details of the history of different ethnic groups, we know that in the Horn, migrations, conquests, and invasions were experienced after which the customs of both the victors and the defeated groups were mutually changed. Much the same happened in Europe with the clash of legal cultures in medieval times.

Sometimes pluralism is recognized and law is applied in accordance with its status (e.g., colonial law). Sometimes the domain of application depends on the nature of the legal transaction (e.g., family law—customary; business law—modern). Other times states declare a unified option. For example, the state may attempt to disregard or ban traditional law (this approach is typical of socialist Africa). Even in these systems, however, customary law flourishes de facto as soon as the state ceases to invest enough resources to oppose its operation or offer an alternative option. The same phenomenon pertains to the organization of justice. The judicial system is usually unified, but within it, different tribunals apply different law (state law, customary law, Islamic law). The legal culture of the judge and even the process of forum selection may change according to the law that is to be applied.

The relationship between traditional law and modern law is also dynamic and difficult to capture. It is always true that modern law corresponds to an imported one (Grande 1995), and occasionally the outcome of the competition among the different legal ideologies creates original solutions. It is also not necessarily true that traditional law is of ancient and spontaneous origin. Sometimes, a tradition is invented for the purpose of political manipulation (Guadagui 1998). In the process of stratification, a legal system that is imposed on another does not cancel it; instead, it cohabits, officially or unofficially, with older legal orders. Sometimes it restricts the area of application of the old law; sometimes it modifies and/or is in turn modified by it. Susan Hirsch's 1998 ethnography on women's use of coastal Kenyan courts provides an in situ ethnographic account of this process.

It would be difficult to give a precise account of all the legal transplants that produced the law in the Horn. The region has witnessed the evolution of humankind from the stage of hunters to that of farmers, with all the changes in the law that different social organizations carry with them. Even today, populations in the Horn live under varying economic conditions with very different traditional law: Many nomadic populations still live alongside the farmers (see Grande 1995). The law of the Afar people of the desert or of the Somali nomadic shepherds differ from that of the Bela Shangul, a Nilotic population of gatherers and hunters living at the Sudan border. Tiny Eritrea has at least nine major ethnic groups, with recognized and known history. Transplants are by no means excluded at this "traditional layer" of the legal system.

Another important system is at play, although in a nonuniform way, in the Horn. Islamic law in Somalia has competed with the *Xeer* (traditional law), and in certain areas it has even accepted some elements of traditional law. In Ethiopia, where an estimated one-third of the population is of the Islamic religion, a full-fledged system of Islamic courts was established in 1944. The relationship between this law and others has been thereby formalized after centuries of informal relationship, including the religious law of the kings (*Fetha Negast*), which was introduced in the seventeenth century to rule the Christian population (the majority) in Ethiopia.

The colonial experience caused a great wave of legal imports all around the Horn. Elements of the Western legal tradition, both of the common law and of the civil law, found their way in the Horn. In the north of Somalia, British Somaliland became a common law jurisdiction. The Italian colonization made the civil law tradition reach most of Somalia and Eritrea. The civil law can be found also in Djibouti as a transplant from France. The short period of Italian colonization did not relevantly affect the law in Ethiopia. But the "modernization" encouraged transplants from England (criminal procedure code), France (civil code and commercial code), Switzerland (penal code) and even from the Japanese Meiji constitution, itself patterned on the German model. The mixed nature of modern law in Ethiopia was never abandoned, and today the clear influence of American law is present, not only in Ethiopia but also in postindependence Eritrea.

Even socialist law constitutes an important dimension of the legal structure of the Horn. The socialist option was followed in Somalia by Siad after the revolution of 1969 and in Ethiopia by Mengistu right after he was able to impose himself on the Derg. Both these legal systems were deeply affected by the party-centered legal structure of socialist law imported from the USSR (Brietzke 1982).

In the Horn, different legal ideologies have shown rather extreme characteristics. Possibly because of the complexity of the political game, itself determined by the strategic position of the Horn, the attempts of each law to defeat the previous one have been very strong. In particular, all of them have tried, unsuccessfully, to get rid of one key characteristic of the dispute resolution process: its collective nature. The history of the Horn shows that each attempt to find an easy and ready device to solve the tragic problems of the area (or maybe only to keep political control over it) has only created a more unmanageable complexity, with tragic and sometimes paradoxical political outcomes (see Grande 1995). Today, a Western-bolstered 10% Tigrin minority of the population has drafted its own tailored constitution in Ethiopia. The result of the Restore Hope Mission of the United Nations—politically sold as aimed to finally bring to Somalia development, democracy, and eventually, the rule of law—is that the only effective law-and-order devices are Sharaitic courts in some areas of Mogadishu. The only exception, modern Eritrea, faces enormous problems with neighboring Sudan and is struggling with the international bureaucracy to get help after 30 years of neglect.

This emphasis on collectivity of the traditional legal process has never been accepted by subsequent legal models, all of which, concerned with the centralization of power, felt threatened by a social organization based on local groups. As is well known, the very idea of the state is Western, foreign to the African tradition and rather arbitrarily imported by the colonial powers to solve problems of relationship between themselves. In the Horn, although a centralized tradition is all but absent, and the colonization experienced in Somalia, Djibouti, and Eritrea has been a very marginal experience in Ethiopia, harsh political battles between Western powers have created an incompatibility between modern political frontiers and ethnic belonging. For example, ethnic Somalis are important minorities in Ethiopia (the Ogaden region has been the object of a terrible war), Kenya (a former English colony), and Djibouti (a former French colony). Yet the surrender to an imported constitutional structure seems everywhere complete.

The failure of the modern conception of the state in Africa is dramatically clear in the Horn. The centralizing logic of the state and the illusion of unlimited power that it grants to the leading elite have been devastating to the social equilibrium of a society based on kinship. According to the simplifying logic of the state, shared by colonial and postcolonial leading elites in the Horn, the illusion is that enactments are the law, and that an enactment backed by the force of the state is enough to solve problems and develop the legal system in a consciously planned way. The complex relationship between legal ideologies can all but be solved within that illusion. It is not in writing a constitution, however perfectly worded, that one solves problems of incompatibility between Western conception of laws, the state, and African reality. The constitution only adds yet another layer of law (the modern international financial institution's one) that starts from an interest in resolving complexity and ends up increasing complexity.

To the degree that "traditions" in the Horn share some kind of conception of a "collective" indigenous structure, they also obviously share a logic of discrimination between those who belong to the group and those who do not. But if this is the essence of the collective logic, it is shared by the modern Western state and is witnessed by its attitude toward noncitizens. Certainly, it is extremely difficult for any African to belong to a Western-invented state, made of random numbers of different ethnic groups, each having its own "real" tradition. As an ethnic group one does not belong to the state. One tries to occupy its structures of power (Grande 1995). Yesterday, this was done by striking deals with either side of the Iron Curtain (the most interesting example in the Horn being the Ogaden war). Today, the deals are made with international financial institutions and multinational corporations.

This picture of legal transplants from Western societies to traditional societies (or the other way around) makes it clear that sometimes the transplants are purely nominal. By this we mean that short of being real institutional borrowings from one legal system to another (Watson 1974), legal transplants may be nothing more than an ideology that depicts a given institutional arrangement as coming from somewhere else (when it didn't). Nothing is more misleading than the claim of a return to a "primitive" way of solving conflicts, where the disputes are given back to the people, who harmoniously (i.e., in a conciliatory way) settle them.

In many "traditional" legal systems, the individual can find in his group the protection he needs; the more powerful his group, the more protection he gets. Through mediation and negotiation, the power of the group is tested: The self-help that will result if there is no settlement outcome is the strongest incentive to solve disputes. Meditation and negotiation in societies in the Horn cannot be understood without bringing into the picture social structure—the relationship between groups, and particularly the relationship between the individual and the group. In the structure of the "traditional" legal process in this region, the individual does not exist except in the group; rights and duties are only ascribed to the group. The failure to acknowledge this deep structural dimension has been a primary reason for the failed attempts to "modernize" the law in Africa. It may also foreclose the understanding of the true nature of alternative dispute resolution in modern societies.

CONCLUDING THOUGHTS

Mediation, negotiation, arbitration, and adjudication all assume different meanings depending on the context, as in the example of predominantly individual-centered or predominantly group-centered legal culture. In the Horn, the imposition of legal transplants, accompanied by the weakness of the modern state has not been able to change the nature of law. The state, both colonial and postcolonial, has been unable to defeat group centeredness, so that the law in action in modern Africa, although deeply changed and structurally modified by the relentless competition of modernities, still maintains a predominantly group-centered flavor.

Stronger constituencies, such as multinational corporations, are practically unaffected by the state, since they mostly carry on their transactions outside state jurisdiction. Under such conditions, it becomes tempting for the state to avoid performing functions related to dispute resolution. The substitution of the confrontational model with a nonadversarial technique (whether in the United States or in the Horn) becomes in practice a complete loss of protection for poor litigants: They cannot rely on the market to buy protection (as the wealthy can), and they have given up the protection of a group that simply is considered irrelevant as far as state law is concerned.

The unevenness of power between litigants becomes once again relevant, and the weak individual finds himself not only without the effective protection of a group but also without the protection of individual rights, a consideration that, in theory, he has received for giving up the group.

We need epistemological models appropriate for understanding the interaction of law, power, and tradition (Hobsbawn and Ranger 1992), "true" or invented: "We have to abandon the arrogant belief that the world is merely a puzzle to be solved, a machine with instructions for use waiting to be discovered, a body of information to be fed into a computer in the hope that sooner or later it will spit out a universal solution" (Havel 1992). No matter how autonomous we may wish the dispute resolution process to be, it is not. It is completely intermingled with political and economic issues, and with ideologies that characterize social conflict or its opposite. No matter how objective we may try to be, when policies are being engineered from Western or Westernized ideas, the impact of Western notions of autonomous systems and the importance of individual rather than collective perspectives cannot be forgotten.

Clearly any ADR scheme needs careful study of the social conditions in which it may operate. The rhetoric of harmony law models is attractive. But the idea that in a conciliatory model, people do not fight but rather harmoniously agree about a common solution is fiction. So also is the belief that such a harmony model exists in "primitive" and idyllic societies. Similarly we need to understand the real dynamics of power that are at play when foreign systems are transplanted.

In another context, Nader and Shugart (1980) concluded that practitioners of dispute management need to think in terms of a complaint chain, one that moves from negotiation to mediation, then to arbitration and adjudication, in a chain of referrals in which the least powerful gains as they move up the chain, thus giving incentive for parties to move toward an outcome. "Disputing without the Force of Law" (Nader 1979) will not work unless the force of a just law is available as a last resort. It is not possible to divorce law and power.

Current illusions and delusions about conflict management can be addressed if there is a will to do so. ADR devices have been around long enough (at least 25 years) to merit a thorough evaluation for their efficacy and their consequences. ADR, as Chief Justice Burger noted, is a legal revolution, one with many ramifications. Yet, a good portion of the attempt at dialogue with the ADR "legal revolutionaries" has remained unanswered, ignored, or dealt with by means of unscholarly think-tank reports. It is long past time for a real dialogue by serious scholars willing to examine evidence for or against plentiful assertions of ADR's success, as they have managed to do for state-centered law. Such critique might eventually lead both scholars and practitioners in the direction of the extended case method as pioneered by Elizabeth Colson in 1953 for African ethnography, or in the direction of excellent extended case stories such as the recent work of Jonathan Harr (1995), who documented the story of water and the Woburn leukemia cluster. Both models are empirical. The result is methodologically similar; in both instances one finds a wide-angled lens, a broadening of the scope, and a more comprehensive understanding of conflict.

In sum, the underside of conflict management includes more than suggestions for new legal transplants and more than a study of techniques of conflict resolution. Today it includes nationalism and its consequences and actors—politicians, businessmen, arms dealers, mercenaries, ethnics, neocolonialists, and of course, victims. The causes of war and conflict are not necessarily endemic. An integrated perspective on the policy directions of conflict management in the face of more grounded contexts will undoubtedly inspire new directions that favor justice over harmony, a recognition of root causes over consensus, and a realization that U.S.-style alternative dispute resolution is being imposed on many unwilling recipients in foreign countries as a requirement for development aid whether they are appropriate or not for the local context, or whether they address problems of arms dealing and state violence.[9]

REFERENCES

Abel, Richard, ed. 1982. *The Politics of Informal Justice*. 2 vols. New York: Academic Press.

Anderson, James. 1970. *Islamic Law in Africa*. London: F. Cass.

Auerbach, Jerold. 1983. *Justice Without Law?* New York: Oxford University Press.

Bohannon, Paul. 1957. *Justice and Judgment among the Tiv*. London: Oxford University Press for the International African Institute.

Boutwell, Jeffrey, Michael Klare, and Laura Reed, eds. 1995. *Lethal Commerce: The Global Trade in Small Arms and Light Weapons*. Cambridge, Mass.: Committee on International Security Studies.

Brietzke, Paul. 1982. *Law Development and the Ethiopian Revolution*. London: Bucknell.

Bush, Robert and A. Baruch. 1996. The Unexplored Possibilities of Community Mediation: A Comment on Merry and Milner. *Law and Social Inquiry*,21(3): 715–36.

Bussani, Mauro. 1996. Tort Law and Development Insights from the Case of Ethiopia and Eritrea. *Journal of African Law* 40:43–60.

9. The authors are grateful to an anonymous reader for pointing out that requirements for development aid include ADR, noting that in Latin America NGOs are being forced to waste scarce resources to conduct seminars based on ADR techniques.

Castillo, Hernandez, Rosalva Aida, and Ronald Nigh. 1998. Global Processes and Local Identity among Mayan Coffee Growers in Chiapas, Mexico. *American Anthropologist* 100(1):136–47.

Chanock, Martin. 1985. *Law, Custom, and Social Order: The Colonial Experience in Malawi and Sabia.* Cambridge, England: Cambridge University Press.

Colson, Elizabeth. 1953. Social Control and Vengeance in Plateau Tonga Society. *Africa* 23:199–212.

Dahrendorf, Rolf. 1968. *Essays in the Theory of Society.* Stanford, Calif.: Stanford University Press.

Estes, Ralph. 1996. *Tyranny of the Bottom Line: Why Corporations Make Good People Do Bad Things.* San Francisco: Berrett-Koehler Publishers.

Franck, T. 1986. *Judging the World Court.* New York: Priority Press Publications.

French, Hilary F. 1993. Costly Tradeoffs: Reconciling Trade and the Environment. *World Watch Paper* 113, March.

Fuller, Lon. 1978. The Forms and Limits of Adjudication. *Harvard Law Review* 92(2):353–409.

Gluckman, Max. 1959. *Custom and Conflict in Africa.* Glencoe, Ill.: Free Press.

———. 1955. *The Judicial Process among the Barotse of Northern Rhodesia.* Manchester, England: Manchester University Press.

Goldsmith, Sir James. 1994. *The Trap.* New York: Carroll and Gray.

Grande, Elisabetta, ed. 1995. *Transplants, Innovation, and Legal Tradition in the Horn of Africa.* Torino: Harmattan-Italia.

Grillo, Trina. 1991. The Mediation Alternative: Process Dangers to Women. *Yale Law Journal* 100:1545–610.

Guadagni, Marco. 1998. Legal Pluralism. In *The New Palgrave: A Dictionary of Economics and the Law. Torino: L'Harmattan Italia.*

Gulliver, P. H. 1963. *Social Control in an African Society: A Study of the Arusha, Agricultural Masai of Northern Tanganyika.* Boston: Boston University Press.

Hanlon, Joseph. 1996. Strangling Mozambique: International Monetary Fund "Stabilization" in the World's Poorest Country. *Multinational Monitor* 17 (7 and 8, July/August):17–21.

Harr, Jonathon. 1995. *A Civil Action.* New York: Vintage Books.

Harrington, Christina B. 1985. *Shadow Justice: The Ideology and Institutionalization of Alternatives to Court.* Westport, Conn.: Greenwood Press.

Havel, Vaclav. 1992. The End of the Modern Era. *New York Times,* March 1.

Hirsch, Susan. 1998. *Pronouncing and Persevering: Gender and the Discourses of Disputing in an African Islamic Court.* Chicago: University of Chicago Press.

Hobsbawm, Eric, and Terence Ranger. 1992. *The Invention of Tradition.* New York: Cambridge University Press.

Hofrichter, Richard. 1987. *Neighborhood Justice in a Capitalist Society: The Expansion of the Informal State.* New York: Greenwood Press.

Korten, David C. 1996. *When Corporations Rule the World.* West Hartford, Conn.: Kumarian Press.

Lappe, Frances M., and J. Collins. 1978. *Food First: Beyond the Myth of Scarcity.* Rev. ed. Boston: Houghton-Mifflin.

Laylin, J. G., and Bianchi, R. L. 1959. The Role of Adjudication in International River Disputes: The Lake Lanoux Case. *American Journal of International Law* 53(1):30–49.

Lederach, Jean Paul, 1997. *Building Peace: Sustainable Reconciliation in Divided Societies.* Washington, D.C.: United States Institute of Peace.

LeVine, Robert A. ed. 1961. *The Anthropology of Conflict: Journal of Conflict Resolution* (special issue) 5(1).

Mattei, Ugo. 1990. Socialist and non-Socialist Approaches to Land Law: Continuity and Change in Somalia and Other African States. *Review of Socialist Law* 16:17–55.

Marcus, George E., and Michael M. J. Fischer. 1986. *Anthropology as Cultural Critique: An Experimental Moment in the Human Sciences*. Chicago: University of Chicago Press.

Merry, Sally. 1988. Legal Pluralism. *Law and Society Review* 22(5):869–96.

Merry, Sally E., and Neal Milner, eds. 1993. *The Possibility of Popular Justice: A Case Study of Community Mediation in the United States*. Ann Arbor: University of Michigan Press.

Milner, Neal. 1996. Mediation and Political Theory: A Critique of Bush and Folger. *Law and Social Inquiry* 21(3):737–59.

Nadel, S. 1942. *A Black Byzantium*. London: Oxford University Press.

Nader, Laura. 1979. Disputing without the Force of Law. *Yale Law Journal* (special issue on dispute resolution) 88(5):998–1021.

———. 1989. The ADR Explosion: The Implications of Rhetoric in Legal Reform. In *Windsor Yearbook of Access to Justice*, 269–91. Windsor, Ontario: University of Windsor.

———. 1990. *Harmony Ideology: Justice and Control in a Mountain Zapotec Village*. Stanford, Calif.: Stanford University Press.

———. 1994. Civilization and Its Negotiators. In *Understanding Disputes: The Politics of Argument*, ed. P. Caplan. Oxford: Berg.

Nader, Laura, and Jay Ou. 1998. Idealization and Power: Legality and Tradition in Native American Law. *New Directions in Native American Law: Oklahoma City University Law Review* (special edition) 23(1).

Nader, Laura, and Chris Shugart. 1980. Old Solutions for New Problems. In *No Access Is Law: Alternatives to the American Judicial System*, ed. Laura Nader. New York: Academic Press.

Nader, Laura, and Harry Todd. 1978. *The Disputing Process: Law in Ten Societies*. New York: Columbia University Press.

Nader, Laura, and Barbara Yngvesson. 1974. On Studying the Ethnography of Law and its Consequences. In *Handbook of Social and Cultural Anthropology*, ed. J. Honigman, 883–921. New York: Rand, McNally.

Ou, C. Jay. 1996. Native Americans and the Monitored Retrievable Storage Plan for Nuclear Waste: Late Capitalism, Negotiation, and Controlling Processes. In *Essays in Controlling Processes*, ed. L. Nader, Kroeber Anthropological Society Papers 80:32–88.

Rose, Laurel L. 1996. Are Alternative Dispute Resolution (ADR) Programs Suitable for Africa? In *Africa Notes*, 5–7. Ithaca, N.Y.: Cornell University Press.

———. 1997. When Conflict Management Training Is Perceived as Religious Proselytization: A Case Study from Papua, New Guinea. *Conflict Resolution Notes* 14(3):28–31.

Rubin, Elizabeth. 1997. An Army of One's Own: In Africa, Nations Hire a Corporation to Wage War. *Harper's*, February, 44–55.

Sacco, Rodolfo. 1996. *Il Diritto Africano*. Torino: UTET.

Schapera, Isaac. 1959. *A Handbook of Tswana Law and Custom*. New York: Oxford University Press.

Schusky, E., and D. Abbott. n.d. Misperception and Misdirection in the Sahel. Paper presented at Symposium on Hunger, Work, and the Quality of Life. International

Congress of Anthropological and Ethnological Sciences post-plenary session, Hyderabad, India, December 1978.

Siegal, Bernard, and Alan Beals. 1960. Conflict and Factionalist Dispute. *Journal of the Royal Anthropological Institute* 90:107–17.

Soros, George. 1997. The Capitalist Threat. *Atlantic Monthly*. February, 45–58.

Stiglitz, Joseph E. 2000. The Insider—What I Learned at the World Economic Crisis. *New Republic*, 17 April 17, 56.

Tsosie, Michael. n.d. Traditional Culture: Issues of Power and Control within Native American Communities. Typescript.

Ury, William L. 1990. Dispute Resolution Notes from the Kalahari. *Negotiation Journal* 6(3):229–38.

Watson, Alan. 1974. *Legal Transplants*. Charlottesville: University Press of Virginia.

Worsley, Peter. 1984. *The Three Worlds: Culture and World Development*. Chicago: University of Chicago Press.

Zartman, I. William. 2000. *Traditional Cures for Modern Conflicts: African Conflict "Medicine."* Boulder, Colo.: Lynn Rienner.

[17]

BETWEEN DIALOGUE AND DECREE: INTERNATIONAL REVIEW OF NATIONAL COURTS

Robert B. Ahdieh*

Recent years have seen dramatic growth in the number of international tribunals at work across the globe, from the Appellate Body of the World Trade Organization and the International Tribunal for the Law of the Sea, to the Claims Resolution Tribunal for Dormant Claims in Switzerland and the International Criminal Court. With this development has come both increased opportunity for interaction between national and international courts and increased occasion for conflict. Such friction was evident in the recent decision in Loewen Group, Inc. v. United States, *in which an arbitral panel constituted under the North American Free Trade Agreement found a Mississippi jury trial to have been "the antithesis of due process."*

Much of the interaction of courts across national borders—including the citation of foreign legal authority, transnational coordination of complex litigation, and the enforcement of foreign judgments—has been analyzed through the metaphor of "dialogue." As suggested by the Loewen *case, however, there is a growing pattern of interaction between international tribunals and national courts for which dialogue is an ill-suited analogy. Contrary to conventional expectations of incapacity and restraint in international adjudication, recent interactions between international tribunals and domestic courts incorporate a significant dimension of "review" in both a literal and a figurative sense. Although such review is not appellate in nature, it shares with appellate review some potential to effectuate its mandate without the consent of the court subject to review. This dimension of "power" further distinguishes emerging cases of international review from transnational dialogue. Standing between the hierarchy of appellate review and the comity of judicial dialogue,* Loewen *and similar occasions for international engagement with national courts represent a distinct pattern of judicial interaction, one I develop and detail as "dialectical review."*

 Associate Professor of Law, Emory University School of Law. A.B. 1994, Princeton University; J.D. 1997, Yale Law School. I am grateful to my colleagues David Bederman, Anita Bernstein, Bill Buzbee, Marc Miller, and Robert Schapiro for their sage counsel and unfailing patience. Many thanks also to Alex Aleinikoff, Karen Alter, Jeff Atik, Vicki Been, George Bermann, Andrea Bjorklund, Jack Coe, Chip Brower, Bill Dodge, Ken Doroshow, Lee Epstein, Tom Ginsburg, Oona Hathaway, Larry Helfer, Ronnie Kann, John Orth, Kal Raustiala, Mark Rosen, Anne-Marie Slaughter, Paul Stephan, Alec Stone Sweet, Michael Van Alstine, Todd Weiler, Bert Westbrook, Keith Whittington, attendees of the Association of American Law Schools's Program on Intersystemic Adjudication and the International Law Association's session on NAFTA Chapter 11—Reflections on Law Making and Breaking, and workshop participants at the University of Connecticut School of Law, for their varied assistance and encouragement. The Emory Law School library staff, the *New York University Law Review* editorial board, and my research assistants, finally, have been instrumental in bringing this Article to fruition.

Defined broadly as a hybrid of appellate review and dialogue, the nature of dialectical review can be elaborated by examining other hybrid judicial interactions—federal habeas review of state criminal convictions and appellate courts' use of dicta as a signaling device to lower courts. In each of these cases, a form of dialectical review serves as a mechanism of legal innovation. In the face of accelerating trends of globalization, a pattern of dialectical review between international and national courts can help to facilitate the emergence, evolution, and internalization of universal norms of due process. The present analysis thus offers international and domestic judges, as well as policymakers, a framework for understanding and facilitating beneficial judicial interaction in an ever-shrinking world.

Introduction

> *By any standard of measurement, the trial involving O'Keefe and Loewen was a disgrace. . . . By any standard of evaluation, the trial judge failed to afford Loewen the process that was due.*[1]

In recent years, a wave of international judicialization has washed over the globe.[2] Whether permanent or ad hoc, human rights oriented or commercial, international or quasi-international, such tribunals have multiplied exponentially. The collective jurisdictional reach of international tribunals has also expanded, both by design and through gradual accretions of judicial authority.[3] Unsurprisingly, the incidence

[1] Loewen Group v. United States, ICSID Case No. ARB(AF)/98/3, 4 J. World Investment 675, 702, ¶ 119 (NAFTA Ch. 11 Arb. Trib. 2003). Publicly released documents on all North American Free Trade Agreement (NAFTA) disputes are available online at http://www.naftalaw.org.

[2] *See* Roger P. Alford, *Federal Courts, International Tribunals, and the Continuum of Deference*, 43 Va. J. Int'l L. 675, 677–79 (2003) (noting array of new international tribunals formed in recent years); Laurence R. Helfer & Anne-Marie Slaughter, *Toward a Theory of Effective Supranational Adjudication*, 107 Yale L.J. 273, 370–73 (1997) (describing growing transnational interaction among judges and increased citation to foreign and international sources); *see also* Sandra Day O'Connor, *Federalism of Free Nations*, *in* International Law Decisions in National Courts 13–14 (Thomas M. Franck & Gregory H. Fox eds., 1996) (acknowledging growing community of courts around globe). It bears noting at the outset that the reference to "international tribunals" herein is intended to be broadly descriptive. For purposes of the immediate analysis, it is not necessary to differentiate "international" tribunals from "transnational" or "supranational" ones. Nor is it necessary to draw a fine line between tribunals, courts, and arbitral bodies.

[3] *See* Jenny S. Martinez, *Towards an International Judicial System*, 56 Stan. L. Rev. 429, 430, 436–37 (2003) (noting recent "flurry of judicialization" in which diverse international tribunals have emerged).

and extent of transnational judicial interaction—including citation of foreign decisions, negotiated divisions of judicial responsibility in complex cross-border litigation, and the enforcement of foreign judgments—has also grown.

Much of this interaction has been explored both descriptively and normatively through the metaphor of "dialogue."[4] The characterization of transnational judicial interaction as dialogue is hardly surprising, given an understanding of international relations as shaped by "passive virtues" of a sort, including respect for national sovereignty and heavy reliance on diplomacy. However, a growing pattern of transnational interactions among courts challenge the adequacy of the dialogic metaphor. In these cases, the relevant judicial engagement incorporates a strong dimension of judicial "review" and at least a threat of meaningful international "power."[5]

In *Loewen Group, Inc. v. United States*,[6] an ad hoc tribunal convened under Chapter 11 of the North American Free Trade Agreement (NAFTA) subjected the judgments and procedures of the Mississippi courts to a searching review.[7] In doing so, the tribunal threatened to impose a massive damages award on the ultimate "deep

[4] *See, e.g.*, Helfer & Slaughter, *supra* note 2, at 323–27, 358–62, 373–87 (describing dialogue between European Court of Justice (ECJ) and European Court of Human Rights (ECHR)); Harold H. Koh, *Transnational Public Law Litigation*, 100 YALE L.J. 2347, 2371 (1991) (proffering that "institutional dialogue" is important characteristic of transnational public law litigation); Martinez, *supra* note 3, at 434 (advocating antiparochial pattern of dialogue between courts).

[5] *See infra* Parts II.B & IV.B.1.

[6] 4 J. WORLD INVESTMENT at 675. For more on the *Loewen* case, see generally William S. Dodge, *International Decision*, 98 AM. J. INT'L L. 155 (2004).

[7] Specifically, the tribunal considered claims of "denial of justice," discriminatory treatment, and indirect expropriation, based on the Mississippi litigation of a civil claim against the Loewen Group. During that trial, repeated suggestions of racism in the Loewen Group's management, irrelevant references to the wealth of its founder (particularly to his yacht), and even an analogy of the Loewen Group's business practices to the Japanese bombing of Pearl Harbor were permitted. *See* Jake A. Baccari, *The* Loewen *Claim: A Creative Use of NAFTA's Chapter 11*, 34 U. MIAMI INTER-AM. L. REV. 465, 468–69 (2003) (describing plaintiff's emphasis on defendant's race, wealth, and nationality); Michael I. Krauss, *NAFTA Meets the American Torts Process:* O'Keefe v. Loewen, 9 GEO. MASON L. REV. 69, 77 (2000) (noting plaintiff's analogy of the Loewen Group's actions to Japanese bombing of Pearl Harbor); *see also* Stefan Matiation, *Arbitration with Two Twists:* Loewen v. United States *and Free Trade Commission Intervention in NAFTA Chapter 11 Disputes*, 24 U. PA. J. INT'L ECON. L. 451, 455 (2003). This collective pattern of misconduct at trial contributed to a jury's award of $500 million in compensatory and punitive damages—the largest damage award in Mississippi history—on contracts worth less than $5 million. *See* Baccari, *supra*, at 468–69 (describing types of damages awarded to plaintiff). Furthermore, the Loewen Group insisted that it was unable to appeal this shocking verdict because of its inability to post the $625 million supersedeas bond that Mississippi law required to stay performance pending appeal—a requirement the Mississippi courts could waive for good cause, but would not. *See* Matiation, *supra*, at 456 (noting trial court's rejection of Loewen Group's motion to post reduced bond amount of

pocket," one capable of placing meaningful pressure on recalcitrant courts—the U.S. government. This prospect of a significant award against the federal government meant that the tribunal's review and critique of the Mississippi courts had real potential to influence those courts, regardless of their immediate receptivity to a dialogue regarding their compliance with international norms of due process.

The pattern of international review of national courts exemplified by *Loewen* is a far cry from the "dialogue" manifest in constitutional courts' citation of one another and in the transnational management of cross-border litigation.[8] As suggested above, this divergence begins with the international tribunal's close and critical *review* of the judgment and procedures of the national court for consistency with due process, non-discrimination, and substantive requirements of international law. Such searching review is not without precedent. Denial of justice claims—which rest on a national court's violation of international legal norms—have a long pedigree, even if the courts of the developed world have rarely been the subject of such review.[9] In recent years, the European Court of Justice (ECJ) and the European Court of Human Rights (ECHR) have engaged in some analogous review, and shades of an international review of national courts also can be found in decisions of the International Court of Justice (ICJ) and the World Trade Organization (WTO).[10] Yet, instances of such review have been rare.[11]

$125 million); *see also* Baccari, *supra*, at 469–70 (citing Mississippi courts' failure to waive or reduce bond requirement among grounds for Chapter 11 claim).

[8] It is interesting to note, in this vein, that Chief Justice Margaret H. Marshall of the Massachusetts Supreme Judicial Court, among the most enthusiastic judicial advocates of conventional judicial *dialogue*, in which courts pay greater heed to foreign decisions, *see, e.g.*, Margaret H. Marshall, *"Wise Parents Do Not Hesitate to Learn from Their Children": Interpreting State Constitutions in an Age of Global Jurisprudence*, 79 N.Y.U. L. REV. 1633 (2004); *see also* Emily Bazelon, *A Bold Stroke*, LEGAL AFF., May/June 2004, at 30, 32–33, has expressed consternation about a recent Chapter 11 decision, *see* Adam Liptak, *Review of U.S. Rulings by NAFTA Tribunals Stirs Worries*, N.Y. TIMES, Apr. 18, 2004, § 1, at 20, in which the tribunal assessed the potential for a denial of justice in the Massachusetts Supreme Judicial Court's dispensation of an appeal by a Canadian real estate company, *see* Mondev Int'l Ltd. v. United States, ICSID Case No. ARB(AF)/99/2, 42 I.L.M. 85, 109–15, ¶¶ 126–156 (NAFTA Ch. 11 Arb. Trib. 2002), *available at* http://www.naftalaw.org; *infra* notes 397–413 and accompanying text.

[9] *See infra* Part V. The claims of interest herein are thus unprecedented because they include denial of justice claims against highly developed countries, and not only developing or underdeveloped countries. *See* Barton Legum, *The Innovation of Investor-State Arbitration Under NAFTA*, 43 HARV. INT'L L.J. 531, 537–38 (2002) (discussing novelty of NAFTA's investor-state claim mechanism between two developed countries).

[10] *See infra* Part VI.B.

[11] Even if Chapter 11 review was simply a replication of the pattern of supranational review in Europe, it would represent an interesting case study because of its application to the United States, a nation traditionally resistant to international judicialization. Given

Even where it has occurred, international review of national courts commonly has not been coupled with any meaningful capacity of the international tribunal to effectuate its judgment without the consent and cooperation of the relevant national court. By contrast, notwithstanding Chapter 11 tribunals' lack of formal authority over national courts, they enjoy just such power. This power arises from the prospect of a substantial damage award to a private litigant, who can readily enforce it against federal authorities.[12] Given this institutional design, Chapter 11 tribunals would appear to enjoy a greater capacity than most international courts to exercise power in their interactions with national courts.[13] Chapter 11 consequently manifests some equipoise of judicial power, in which neither judicial interlocutor can afford to ignore the other.

If dimensions of review and power make Chapter 11 review and similar interactions between international tribunals and national courts more than dialogue, those interactions still do not amount to appellate review. Some alternative paradigm for the design and operation of the growing pattern of international review in Chapter 11 and similar investment agreements, as well as in certain decisions of the ECJ and the ECHR, and even potentially in the work of the ICJ and the WTO, is therefore necessary. By way of response, I offer a model of "dialectical review"—a pattern of judicial *review*, yet one with *dialogue* at its core. Consistent with classical usage, such dialectical review might be said to rest on a recurrent engagement of international and national courts, advancing toward a synthesis of shared norms of due process.

The basic character of dialectical review can be found in its incorporation of distinct elements of dialogue and appellate review. It is a hybrid pattern of judicial interaction, with values of horizontal comity operating alongside elements of vertical hierarchy. This broad pattern can be further elucidated by reference to cases of hybrid judicial interaction outside Chapter 11. I offer two potential analogies: First, I analogize the Chapter 11 interaction of international and national courts to historical patterns of federal habeas corpus review of state criminal convictions. As explored by Robert Cover and Alex Aleinikoff, the interaction of federal and state courts in habeas review has much to offer to our understanding of the growing pattern of

this "innovation" of Chapter 11, the analysis herein proceeds with a particular orientation to U.S. court interactions with international tribunals.

[12] *See* North American Free Trade Agreement, Dec. 17, 1992, U.S.-Can.-Mex., art. 1135, 107 Stat. 2057, 32 I.L.M. 289, 605 (entered into force Jan. 1, 1994) [hereinafter NAFTA] (outlining remedies available under Chapter 11).

[13] *See infra* Parts IV.A.1 & B.1.a.

international–national court interaction in the world today.[14] Second, I draw parallels to appellate courts' use of dicta as a signaling device to other institutions, in forms explored by Alexander Bickel, Guido Calabresi, and Neal Katyal.[15]

This Article's analysis of Chapter 11 and potential domestic analogies points to dialectical review as a distinct form of judicial interaction inadequately captured within available paradigms. Such review begins with an interaction of international and national courts to which each brings a distinct set of perspectives. Each enjoys some capacity to press its views on the other but suffers from an inability to impose its will. Each can force the other to listen but not necessarily to act. Given as much, there arises a recurrent pattern of dialectical engagement, critique, and counsel, from which learning and innovation can emerge. The beginning of such a pattern can already be discerned in the Chapter 11 context, and perhaps in the interaction of other international tribunals and national courts. Hope for such engagement might thus be found in the receptive rejoinder of the Oklahoma Court of Criminal Appeals to the ICJ's recent decision in *Avena and Other Mexican Nationals*.[16]

---

14 *See* Robert M. Cover, *The Uses of Jurisdictional Redundancy: Interest, Ideology, and Innovation*, 22 WM. & MARY L. REV. 639, 648 (1981) (describing opportunities for redundant litigation of norms of constitutional criminal procedure because of concurrent federal and state competency); Robert M. Cover & T. Alexander Aleinikoff, *Dialectical Federalism: Habeas Corpus and the Court*, 86 YALE L.J. 1035, 1036 (1977) (outlining Warren Court's approach to reforming criminal procedure through dialogue between state and federal courts). Ronald Wright and Marc Miller have explored a similar pattern in the habeas review of capital cases using a rubric of "interactive federalism" and stressed the need for each court to reflect on its role in the system. *See* Ronald F. Wright & Marc Miller, *In Your Court: State Judicial Federalism in Capital Cases*, 18 URB. LAW. 659, 660 (1986); *see also id.* at 693–94 (offering cases in which state courts grappled with their relationship with federal courts). The present analysis is an attempt to engage in analogous reflection on the place of national courts and international tribunals in an emerging international judicial order.

15 *See* ALEXANDER M. BICKEL, THE LEAST DANGEROUS BRANCH: THE SUPREME COURT AT THE BAR OF POLITICS 69–71, 197–98 (1962) (identifying various mechanisms of restraint by Supreme Court as important tools in Court's pursuit of its constitutional mission); GUIDO CALABRESI, A COMMON LAW FOR THE AGE OF STATUTES 101–19 (1982) (suggesting that courts can use threat of judicial revision of statutes and sunset language to induce legislative reconsideration of anachronistic laws); Guido Calabresi, *Antidiscrimination and Constitutional Accountability (What the Bork-Brennan Debate Ignores)*, 105 HARV. L. REV. 80, 104 (1991) (suggesting importance of legislative "second-look" at hastily passed legislation in face of constitutional questions); Neal K. Katyal, *Judges As Advicegivers*, 50 STAN. L. REV. 1709, 1711 (1998) ("The combination of 'narrow holding + advicegiving dicta' enjoys a natural advantage over a broad holding in terms of democratic self-rule, flexibility, popular accountability, and adaptability.").

16 (Mex. v. U.S.) 43 I.L.M. 581 (Mar. 31, 2004). The Oklahoma Court of Criminal Appeals granted an indefinite stay of execution and a hearing on Torres's Vienna Convention on Diplomatic Relations claims, following the International Court of Justice's (ICJ) ruling in *Avena*. Torres v. Oklahoma (Torres II), No. PCD-04-442 (Okla. Crim. App. May

The following Part introduces the subject with a description of the nature of Chapter 11 and its application in *Loewen*. Part II considers appellate review and dialogue as alternative paradigms of judicial interaction and suggests the present incompatibility of international review of national courts with either model. Part III explores the desirable ends of a regime of international review of national courts. Drawing on the habeas and dicta analogies, I suggest the particular utility of international review as a source of innovation in the development of legal norms.

Part IV offers a synthesis. Drawing on the respective elements of appeal and dialogue in the international review of national courts, together with the proposed role for such review in fostering innovation, I outline the model of dialectical review. After identifying three core characteristics of such review, I consider their manifestation in the design and operation of Chapter 11 review, both confirming the applicability of the model I propose and helping to flesh out its details. Part V completes the articulation of the paradigm of dialectical review under Chapter 11, positing the development of international norms of due process as an appropriate end of the international review of national courts. Finally, Part VI concludes with some consideration of the future of dialectical review, both under Chapter 11 and similar investment agreements, and in a growing array of other interactions among international tribunals and national courts. In the years ahead, sometimes jarring occasions for intersystemic judicial review—and a resulting need for effective models of such interaction—can be expected to grow.

13, 2004) (order granting stay of execution and remanding case for evidentiary hearing); *see Oklahoma Court Halts Execution*, AUGUSTA CHRON., May 14, 2004, at A14; S. Lynne Walker, *Mexican Man's Death Penalty Lifted: World Court Swayed Oklahoma Execution*, SAN DIEGO UNION-TRIB., May 14, 2004, at A3; *see also infra* notes 556–58 and accompanying text.

II
Between Hierarchy and Comity: The Nature of International Review of National Courts

The international review of national court judgments and procedures represents a relatively unfamiliar pattern of interaction among judicial institutions. Chapter 11 review of the Mississippi trial court's oversight of the litigation against the Loewen Group, and the trial court's and Mississippi Supreme Court's refusal to waive or reduce the Mississippi appeal bond requirement, does not easily fit into conventional categories of court-to-court relations. *Loewen* thus calls attention to the need for better appreciation of such interaction, definition of its ultimate goals, the development of institutional forms that are consistent both with those goals and with a commitment to national sovereignty and judicial autonomy. How should we understand such interaction? How is it best designed, and how best conducted? What exactly, in blunt terms, is going on here?

In assessing how international review of national courts,[58] under Chapter 11 and otherwise, is best understood, designed, and conducted, two alternative paradigms of judicial interaction offer themselves as possible models. The first pattern—appellate review—might be said to be the most familiar pattern of interaction among domestic courts. The second—judicial dialogue—is the most common characterization of transnational interactions among courts. The nature and potential relevance of each alternative is considered in turn.

A. *The Hierarchy of Appellate Review*

I identify four core characteristics of "appellate" review. First, and perhaps foremost, is the authority of an appellate court to undo the determinations of law, and sometimes even the findings of fact, reached by the court subject to review.[59] Following naturally from this phenomenon is the binding nature of that review.[60] Minimally, the judgment of an appellate court binds the trial court in the case at bar. More expansively, decisions on appeal consequently have some

[58] Chapter 11 review extends to domestic tribunals generally. References to "national courts" herein consequently encompass both federal and state courts, including the array of adjudicatory bodies that come within the auspices of state judiciaries. This definitional point calls attention to a necessary point of clarification: The particulars of the analysis herein are directed to the interaction of U.S. courts with Chapter 11 and other international tribunals. The model articulated also has application to the other NAFTA states and beyond. For ease of analysis and discussion, however, I explain the model with reference to the U.S. courts.

[59] *See* Paul D. Carrington et al., Justice on Appeal 2 (1976) (describing role of appellate review in correcting errors made at trial).

[60] *See id.* at 2–3.

formal or informal *stare decisis* effect, binding lower courts in future cases as well.[61] The pattern of review characteristic of the appellate interaction of courts, moreover, is largely unidirectional. With notable exceptions, appellate judgments are not, in the ordinary case, subject to substantive critique in a trial court. Finally, appellate review is constrained in its reach yet expansive in its depth. Appellate review is rarely de novo.[62] Factual findings are subject to an exceedingly deferential standard of review, if they are subject to review at all.[63] As to questions of law, however, courts of appeal possess relatively plenary powers of review and reversal.[64]

The basic purposes of appellate review are in line with these characteristics. Appellate review is commonly described as serving two primary functions: First, appellate review is an effective mechanism of error correction.[65] Second, appellate review enhances consistency both within and across relevant jurisdictions.[66] Following naturally

---

61 *See* RUSSELL F. MOORE, STARE DECISIS: SOME TRENDS IN BRITISH AND AMERICAN APPLICATION OF THE DOCTRINE 34 (1958). Judgments ordinarily do not bind the issuing court itself, which is free to alter its own decision. *See* Brian C. Kalt, *Three Levels of* Stare Decisis*: Distinguishing Common-Law, Constitutional, and Statutory Cases*, 8 TEX. REV. L. & POL. 277, 278 (2004) ("In the common-law context . . . the court has a relatively low barrier for overturning itself.").

62 *See* 5 AM. JUR. 2D *Appellate Review* § 662 (1995).

63 *See, e.g.*, FED. R. CIV. P. 52(a) (stating that federal appellate courts shall set aside only clearly erroneous findings of fact).

64 *See* Salve Regina Coll. v. Russell, 499 U.S. 225, 238 (1991) (holding that questions of law should be addressed anew by appellate courts); *see also* 19 JAMES WM. MOORE ET AL., MOORE'S FEDERAL PRACTICE ¶ 06.04(1) (3d ed. 1999).

65 *See* ROSCOE POUND, APPELLATE PROCEDURE IN CIVIL CASES 3 (1941).

66 *Cf.* Evan H. Caminker, *Precedent and Prediction: The Forward-Looking Aspects of Inferior Court Decisionmaking*, 73 TEX. L. REV. 1, 38–41, 76–77 (1994) (noting importance of jurisprudential consistency). Carrington characterizes these functions as review for correctness and institutional review. *See* CARRINGTON, *supra* note 59, at 2. They have also been described as resolving concrete disputes and providing guidance for future cases. *See* Lisa A. Kloppenberg, *Measured Constitutional Steps*, 71 IND. L.J. 297, 298 (1996) (arguing that U.S. Supreme Court's avoidance doctrine prioritizes resolution of concrete disputes and downplays Court's "important function of providing guidance on federal constitutional questions").

Additional functions of appeal have been identified, but these are best understood as subsumed within the functions mentioned above. *See* ROBERT J. MARTINEAU, MODERN APPELLATE PRACTICE: FEDERAL AND STATE CIVIL APPEALS 18–19 (1983) (other purposes of appeal include protection against outside interference by allowing judicial system to correct itself, provision of psychological relief for losing party, and "doing justice"); W. MICHAEL REISMAN, SYSTEMS OF CONTROL IN INTERNATIONAL ADJUDICATION AND ARBITRATION 4 (1992) (describing functions of "control systems" in adjudication); Philip B. Kurland, *Jurisdiction of the United States Supreme Court: Time for a Change?*, 59 CORNELL L. REV. 616, 618 (1974) (three functions of appellate review include error correction, consistency, and lawmaking). Dramatically different conceptions of the appellate relationship also have been offered. *See generally* Donald R. Songer et al., *The Hierarchy of Justice: Testing a Principal-Agent Model of Supreme Court-Circuit Court Interactions*, 38 AM. J. POL. SCI. 673 (1994) (applying principal-agent model to U.S. Supreme Court's relationship

from these dual purposes, it might be said that appeal serves some legitimization function by enhancing confidence in the judicial system.[67] Efforts to introduce appellate mechanisms into international trade–dispute settlement, for example, have been framed in just these terms.[68]

Collectively, the various characteristics and functions of appellate review enumerated above suggest that some gradation of judicial authority is central to the nature of appellate review. Appellate courts sit in a relationship of superiority to rather than parity with the courts subject to their review.[69] An appellate system of review, as such, is one defined by *hierarchy*. In slightly different terms, appellate courts enjoy some meaningful *power* over the courts subject to their review.[70]

Is Chapter 11 review of national courts a form of appeal? It does have some unidirectional character, given that any domestic "review" that follows on the Chapter 11 process is either limited in scope or arises in the context of a new fact pattern.[71] It also exhibits some of the complex mix of broad and narrow authority in appellate review. Most importantly, as I will outline below, Chapter 11 tribunals possess

---

to federal appeals courts). Finally, Martin Shapiro offers what is perhaps the broadest array of possible functions of appellate review. *See* Martin Shapiro, Courts: A Comparative and Political Analysis 49–56 (1981) (mentioning "allow[ing] the loser to accept his loss without having to acknowledge it publicly," "ensuring against the venality, prejudice, and/or ignorance of trial court judges," facilitating "an independent flow of information to the top on the field performance of administrative subordinates," ensuring that lower courts "are following rules or laws or policies of social control acceptable to the regime," and "sort[ing] out unresolved issues of policy and mov[ing] them toward the top for decision" among possible functions of appellate review).

67 *See* Carrington, *supra* note 59, at 2.

68 This includes the introduction of an "Appellate Body" into the GATT's dispute settlement procedures, *see* Andreas F. Lowenfeld, *Remedies Along With Rights: Institutional Reform in the New GATT*, 88 Am. J. Int'l L. 477, 480 (1994), proposals to include an appellate mechanism in the investment dispute procedures of the FTAA, *see* Valerie Hughes, *Essay on John C. Thomure, Jr.'s Presentation*, 28 U. Miami Inter-Am. L. Rev. 685, 695 (1997), and the formation of a negotiating group under the recently signed Dominican Republic–Central America–United States Free Trade Agreement to draft provisions for an investment dispute appeals mechanism, *see infra* note 523.

69 *See* Ashutosh Bhagwat, *Separate But Equal?: The Supreme Court, the Lower Federal Courts, and the Nature of the "Judicial Power,"* 80 B.U. L. Rev. 967, 967 (2000) ("[J]udges of the lower, or 'inferior,' federal courts are viewed by the Court, and even view themselves, as subordinates who must defer to 'judicial superiors.'"); Caminker, *supra* note 66, at 41–42; Charles H. Koch, Jr., *Envisioning a Global Legal Culture*, 25 Mich. J. Int'l L. 1, 53 (2003) ("Common lawyers are accustomed to great weight being given higher court precedent in lower courts."); *see also* Bhagwat, *supra*, at 982–83 (suggesting that Supreme Court has hierarchical view of appellate process).

70 *See* Susan B. Haire et al., *Appellate Court Supervision in the Federal Judiciary: A Hierarchical Perspective*, 37 Law & Soc'y Rev. 143, 143–49 (2003) (discussing appellate courts' use of review power to control decisionmaking in lower courts).

71 *See infra* Part IV.B.2.b.

a certain degree of power, similar to that possessed by appellate courts but unlike that of many international tribunals.[72] Yet Chapter 11 review deviates from the pattern of appellate review in too many respects to be characterized fairly in that fashion.[73]

Although somewhat unidirectional, Chapter 11 review is constrained by an important dimension of bidirectionality. This bidirectionality is manifested in the prospect of national review of the tribunal's award upon enforcement or petition for review or annulment, as outlined below,[74] as well as the ability of national courts to critique and even reject the Chapter 11 tribunal's view in future decisions. The power of Chapter 11, moreover, is far less than that of a court of appeals.[75] Chapter 11 tribunals do not have the ability to "reverse" national court decisions[76] nor are their awards formally binding on national courts in the same or future cases.[77] Finally, recalling the purposes of appellate review, Chapter 11 review does not appear to be designed to serve as a mechanism of error correction[78] or jurisprudential consistency.[79]

---

72 *See infra* Part II.B.

73 *See* Azinian v. Mexico, Case No. ARB(AF)/97/2, 14 ICSID REV. 538, 568, ¶ 99 (NAFTA Ch. 11 Arb. Trib. 1999) ("The possibility of holding a State internationally liable for judicial decisions does not, however, entitle a claimant to seek international review of the national court decisions as though the international jurisdiction seized has plenary appellate jurisdiction. This is not true generally, and it is not true for NAFTA."), *available at* http://www.naftalaw.org.

74 *See infra* Part IV.B.2.b.

75 Other differences with appellate review might also be noted, including the application of a different body of law by Chapter 11 tribunals and national courts, Chapter 11 tribunals' lack of directive authority vis-à-vis national courts, and the completely independent origins and financing of Chapter 11 and national court adjudication processes.

76 *See* Loewen Group v. United States, ICSID Case No. ARB(AF)/98/3, 4 J. WORLD INVESTMENT 675, 731, ¶ 242 (NAFTA Ch. 11 Arb. Trib. 2003), *available at* http://www.naftalaw.org; *Azinian*, 14 ICSID REV. at 568, ¶ 99; Mondev Int'l Ltd. v. United States ICSID Case No. ARB(AF)/99/2, 42 I.L.M. 85, 110, ¶ 129 (NAFTA Ch. 11 Arb. Trib. 2002), *available at* http://www.naftalaw.org.

77 Rather than a hierarchical relationship, the interaction of Chapter 11 tribunals with national courts appears more in line with that of independent courts. *Cf.* William W. Burke-White, *Regionalization of International Criminal Law Enforcement: A Preliminary Exploration*, 38 TEX. INT'L L.J. 729, 756 (2003) (describing challenges arising from lack of hierarchy in international judicial order). Chapter 11 tribunals are not subject to any law of the case arising from the national adjudication; rather, they apply a distinct body of law and authority.

78 *Cf.* James M. Fischer, *Discretion and Politics: Ruminations on the Recent Presidential Election and the Role of Discretion in the Florida Presidential Election Recount*, 69 U. CIN. L. REV. 807, 815–17 (2001) (describing lower court "discretion" as restraining appellate review). The limitation of Chapter 11 remedies to money damages directed at federal authorities appears ill-suited to error correction. *See* NAFTA, *supra* note 12, art. 1135, at 646 (noting available remedies under Chapter 11).

79 Molly Warren Lien's vertical model of "integrative comity" comes close to the relationship of Chapter 11 tribunals and national courts but remains a doctrine of *comity* and

Given the seeming inconsistency of Chapter 11 with appellate review, it should come as little surprise that Chapter 11 panels have repeatedly rejected any conception of themselves as courts of appeal.[80] They have explicitly done so, in fact, at nearly every opportunity. In *Loewen*, the panel could "find nothing in NAFTA to justify the exercise by this Tribunal of an appellate function parallel to that which belongs to the courts of the host nation."[81] Likewise, in *Mondev v. United States*, the panel held that "it is not the function of NAFTA tribunals to act as courts of appeal."[82]

Yet widespread dismay over Chapter 11's perceived creation of an international court of appeals persists.[83] If the Chapter 11 panels are to be believed, such concerns can be put aside. Is it possible, however, that the lady doth protest too much?

B. *Judicial Dialogue and Transnational Comity*

If a paradigm of appellate review is too strong to capture the interaction of Chapter 11 tribunals with national courts, perhaps judi-

---

thus does not incorporate the dimension of power that is present in Chapter 11 review. *See infra* Part II.B; *see also* Lien, *supra* note 52, at 639 (proposing that where United States has consented to jurisdiction of international tribunal and courts receive decision from that tribunal, "American courts should accord a high degree of comity, deference, and respect for that court and should generally aid it in protection of its jurisdiction and enforcement of its judgments unless to do so would violate a clear and express constitutional or statutory prohibition under U.S. law"); *id.* at 648.

Mirjan Damaska famously has characterized common law regimes as systems of coordinate adjudication, by contrast with the hierarchical adjudicatory system of civil law jurisdictions. *See* MIRJAN R. DAMASKA, THE FACES OF JUSTICE AND STATE AUTHORITY: A COMPARATIVE APPROACH TO THE LEGAL PROCESS 18–28 (1986). *See generally* Mirjan R. Damaska, *Structures of Authority and Comparative Criminal Procedure*, 84 YALE L.J. 480 (1975) (developing theory of coordinate and hierarchical systems). I characterize the U.S. system as hierarchical in a different sense, however, focusing not on the adjudicatory system as a whole, but on the relationship of appellate and trial courts within it. *Cf.* Sarah K. Harding, *Comparative Reasoning and Judicial Review*, 28 YALE J. INT'L L. 409, 452 n.254 (2003) (arguing that, while Mirjan Damaska situates U.S. system as operating under "coordinate" model, functioning of U.S. Supreme Court is in fact more "hierarchical").

80 *See Loewen*, 4 J. WORLD INVESTMENT at 731 ¶ 242; *Azinian*, 14 ICSID REV. at 568, ¶ 99; *Mondev*, 42 I.L.M. at 109, ¶ 126; *cf.* Avena and Other Mexican Nationals (Mex. v. U.S.), 43 I.L.M. 581, 598, ¶ 37 (2004). The United States claimed that Mexico's submission in *Avena* was inadmissible because Mexico sought to have the ICJ function as a court of criminal appeal. *Id.*

81 *Loewen*, 4 J. WORLD INVESTMENT at 731, ¶ 242; *see also Azinian*, 14 ICSID REV. at 568, ¶ 99.

82 42 I.L.M. at 109, ¶ 126.

83 *See, e.g.*, PUB. CITIZEN, NAFTA CHAPTER 11 INVESTOR-TO-STATE CASES: BANKRUPTING DEMOCRACY i (2001) (claiming corporate investors are using Chapter 11 as appeal of domestic judicial decisions), *at* http://www.citizen.org/documents/ACF186.pdf; *Bill Moyers Reports: Trading Democracy* (PBS television broadcast, Feb. 1, 2002) (criticizing Chapter 11 review for disruption of American jury verdicts), transcript *available at* http://www.pbs.org/now/transcript/transcript_td.html.

cial "dialogue," the standard-form model used to capture the interaction of courts across national borders, offers a closer approximation.[84] Articulated most thoroughly by Anne-Marie Slaughter,[85] the dialogic notion of judicial interaction has been offered as a prism through which transnational judicial interactions—such as national court referrals of European law issues to the ECJ,[86] New York and British bankruptcy judges' extended colloquy over jurisdictional and merits issues in the dissolution of the Maxwell Communication Corporation,[87] and, more conventionally, national courts' deference to the jurisdiction of foreign tribunals and enforcement of those tribunals' judgments—can be understood and analyzed.[88] In essence, the dialogic metaphor posits a symbiotic relationship among autonomous judicial institutions. Grounded in a sense of "judicial comity,"[89] it arises where

[84] In fact, various domestic interactions among courts might also be characterized in dialogic terms. *See* Caminker, *supra* note 66, at 54–55; Jay Tidmarsh, *A Dialogic Defense of* Alden, 75 Notre Dame L. Rev. 1161, 1163, 1167 (2000) (proposing dialogic model of relationship between state and federal courts). Various doctrines of U.S. federal–state court relations, from the rules of abstention to the *Rooker-Feldman* doctrine, might then be measured by the extent to which they facilitate or discourage domestic judicial dialogue.

[85] *See, e.g.*, Helfer & Slaughter, *supra* note 2; Anne-Marie Slaughter, *Court to Court*, 92 Am. J. Int'l L. 708, 709–11 (1998) [hereinafter Slaughter, *Court to Court*] (developing theory of "judicial comity"). *See generally* Anne-Marie Slaughter, *A Typology of Transjudicial Communication*, 29 U. Rich. L. Rev. 99 (1994) [hereinafter Slaughter, *Typology*] (describing importance of transjudicial communication to formation of international rule of law). Besides the strong orientation to the metaphor of dialogue in the study of transnational judicial interaction, the latter literature is also characterized by an emphasis on the treatment of international decisions in national courts. *See, e.g.*, International Law Decisions in National Courts (Thomas M. Franck & Gregory H. Fox eds., 1996); Alford, *supra* note 2. Less attention has been given to the treatment of national decisions by international tribunals. *But see* Pippa Tubman, *National Jurisprudence in International Tribunals*, *in* International Law Decisions in National Courts, *supra*, at 107. This "top-down" inquiry is the emphasis of the present analysis.

[86] *See* Slaughter, *Typology*, *supra* note 85, at 101.

[87] *See* Anne-Marie Slaughter, *A Global Community of Courts*, 44 Harv. Int'l L.J. 191, 213–15 (2003) [hereinafter Slaughter, *Community of Courts*] (describing creation of "private insolvency treaty" by U.S. and English judges); Anne-Marie Slaughter, *Judicial Globalization*, 40 Va. J. Int'l L. 1103, 1114 (2000) [hereinafter Slaughter, *Judicial Globalization*] (noting extensive discussions between judicially appointed administrators to resolve issues surrounding liquidation).

[88] *See, e.g.*, Martinez, *supra* note 3, at 465–68 (identifying judicial dialogue as new paradigm reconciling overlap in authority that theories focused on hierarchical judicial enforcement or pure national sovereignty commonly overlook).

[89] *See* Slaughter, *Court to Court*, *supra* note 85, at 711 ("Comity requires more than consultation born of intellectual curiosity. It expresses an appreciation of different assignments and a global allocation of judicial responsibility, sharpened by the realization that the performance of one court's function increasingly requires cooperation with others."); Slaughter, *Judicial Globalization*, *supra* note 87, at 1112 (describing "judicial comity" as "deference not to foreign law or foreign national interests, but specifically to foreign courts"); *see also* Lien, *supra* note 52, at 593–94 ("A common definition of comity, a word derived from the simple Sanskrit verb for 'he smiles,' is that it refers to the informal and

courts actively engage and cooperate with one another. Such dialogue, Slaughter suggests, can help promote acceptance of reciprocal international obligations, encourage the cross-fertilization of ideas and innovations, enhance the legitimacy of individual decisions, and foster patterns of collective deliberation.[90]

While a precise dissection of judicial dialogue is beyond the scope of this Article, several core characteristics capture much of the transnational judicial interaction that the dialogic view seeks to describe.[91] To begin with, intersystemic judicial dialogue is ordinarily prospective rather than retrospective.[92] In judicial dialogue, a court does not seek to critique the prior decision of another. Rather, its orientation is to some future decision or norm. The borrowing that takes place among

---

voluntary recognition that the courts of one nation accord to the judicial decisions of another."); Joel R. Paul, *Comity in International Law*, 32 HARV. INT'L L.J. 1, 3–4 (1991) ("Comity has been defined variously as the basis of international law, a rule of international law, a synonym for private international law, a rule of choice of law, courtesy, politeness, convenience or goodwill between sovereigns, a moral necessity, expediency, reciprocity or 'considerations of high international politics concerned with maintaining amicable and workable relationships between nations.'"); *cf.* Somportex Ltd. v. Phila. Chewing Gum Corp., 453 F.2d 435, 440 (3d Cir. 1971) ("Although more than mere courtesy and accommodation, comity does not achieve the force of an imperative or obligation. Rather, it is a nation's expression of understanding which demonstrates due regard both to international duty and convenience and to the rights of persons protected by its own laws.").

90 *See* Slaughter, *Typology*, *supra* note 85, at 116–19. I would argue that the dialogic model of judicial relations has been applied to a wider variety of interactions than warranted. It has thus come to encompass interactions that have little in common with one another. Slaughter has spoken of a gradation from horizontal to vertical dialogue. *See id.* at 103–11. Horizontal dialogue captures the tendency of national courts, in particular constitutional courts, to look to one another's decisions in similar or related cases. *See id.* at 103–06. The South African Constitutional Court has engaged actively in such dialogue. *See* Slaughter, *Community of Courts*, *supra* note 87, at 195. Even the U.S. Supreme Court has made recent moves in this direction. *See, e.g.*, Lawrence v. Texas, 539 U.S. 558, 573 (2003). Vertical dialogue, by contrast, has been invoked to reference the complex interactions of the ECJ and the ECHR with the national courts of Europe. *See* Slaughter, *Typology*, *supra* note 85, at 106–11 (describing European national courts' referral of European law issues to ECJ under Article 177 of Treaty of Rome and enforcement of ECHR decisions as domestic law). In particular, Slaughter considers the ECJ's extended colloquy with the German Constitutional Court emblematic of this pattern. *See id.* at 100. The analysis herein is intended to challenge the capacity of the paradigm—or metaphor—of dialogue to encompass this broad array of interactions. Rather, I will suggest that the patterns of interaction which Slaughter characterizes as vertical dialogue encompass elements of dialogue, but also aspects of direct review. They demand, as such, some alternative construct for their appreciation. *See infra* notes 103–08 and accompanying text.

91 Given the wide breadth that has been given to the dialogic metaphor, *see supra* note 90, no enumeration of features is likely to capture all its forms. Instead, I focus on what I consider the true pattern of judicial dialogue—what Slaughter terms "horizontal" dialogue. *See* Slaughter, *Typology*, *supra* note 85, at 103.

92 *Cf.* ROBERT E. KEETON, VENTURING TO DO JUSTICE: REFORMING PRIVATE LAW 26–27 (1969) (suggesting potential prospective function of judicial decisions).

constitutional courts is a prime example.[93] In such cases, courts engage one another in the explication of new jurisprudential norms.[94] The explicit negotiation among courts involved in the resolution of multinational litigation or transnational business matters, as in the insolvency proceedings of the Maxwell Communication Corporation, reveals a similarly prospective orientation.[95] In these cases, courts engage one another, not to the end of assessing one another's past decisions or norms, but with an eye to resolving new questions or dilemmas. Stated slightly differently, judicial dialogue does not involve the "review"—in a judicial sense—of one court's decision by another. Given a prospective orientation, past determinations of a court are not the focus of judicial dialogue.[96] The focus of judicial dialogue is instead on the implications for forthcoming decisions.

A second important characteristic of judicial dialogue—and a point of contrast with appellate review—is its bidirectionality. Neither side is privileged in its contribution to a judicial dialogue. European courts may borrow from U.S. courts in one case, while U.S. courts borrow from their European counterparts in another. By contrast, the appeals process involves one court consistently engaging in review while the other is consistently subject to it. This does not mean that every dialogue invariably incorporates multiple voices. Rather, in any given case, only one side may be heard. Even over an array of cases, one court may be more active in the dialogue. At a minimum, however, dialogue must exclude any barrier to the participation of both judicial parties, should they choose to participate.

Finally, judicial dialogue is characterized—unlike appeal—by some dimension of voluntariness.[97] When the South African Constitutional Court draws on the jurisprudence of the U.S. Supreme Court, the German Constitutional Court, or the ECHR,[98] and, at least

[93] *See* Slaughter, *Judicial Globalization*, *supra* note 87, at 1116–19 (citing examples of South African, British, and U.S. national courts looking to decisions of foreign courts for guidance).

[94] The U.S. Supreme Court essentially did just this in *Lawrence*, 539 U.S. at 573, 576–77, a decision that other constitutional courts, faced with related questions of sexual preference, can be expected to consider, cite, and discuss in turn.

[95] *See* Slaughter, *Community of Courts*, *supra* note 87, at 213–15.

[96] It bears restating that others might enumerate a distinct set of characteristics to describe judicial dialogue. For purposes of the present analysis, however, it is enough to argue that the core characteristics I set out capture most of what is commonly intended by references to judicial dialogue.

[97] *See* Martinez, *supra* note 3, at 467 (noting voluntary communication among courts).

[98] *See* Slaughter, *Community of Courts*, *supra* note 87, at 195; Slaughter, *Judicial Globalization*, *supra* note 87, at 1116. In fact, the South African court even has had occasion to cite decisions of the California Supreme Court and the Massachusetts Supreme Judicial Court. *See id.* Among other cases, the South African court looked to foreign and international jurisprudence in its landmark decision on the death penalty. *See* State v.

nominally, even when lower national courts in Europe refer cases to the ECJ,[99] they do so voluntarily.[100] Such voluntary, discretionary engagement would seem to be a *sine qua non* of any conception of dialogue.[101] This voluntariness suggests the limited role of judicial *power* in the dialogic interaction of courts. True dialogue does not depend on, and is arguably inconsistent with, the assertion or exercise of power between the relevant judicial bodies. Neither court enjoys authority over the other; hence, their engagement is a dialogue rather than a monologue.

Given its transnational application, dialogue offers itself as a promising framework for understanding Chapter 11 and similar international review of national courts. I will suggest, in fact, that there is an important dialogic dimension to Chapter 11, given its prospectivity and bidirectionality—the first and second characteristics described above. On the whole, however, Chapter 11 and analogous forms of international review of national courts are difficult to reconcile with the collective character of dialogue, and particularly with the third characteristic of voluntariness. Chapter 11 review is not grounded primarily in judicial comity. Chapter 11 and analogous mechanisms of international review involve a dimension of *power* more in line with appellate review than with dialogue.[102] Even the prospectivity and bidirectionality of Chapter 11 review are limited in important ways.

Makwanyane & Another, 1995 (3) SALR 391 (CC). The court does so, moreover, based on constitutional provision—grounded, perhaps, in the country's long pariah status—for the review of international and foreign case law. *See* Slaughter, *Community of Courts*, *supra* note 87, at 201 n.48.

99 *See* Consolidated Version of the Treaty Establishing the European Community, 2001 O.J. (C 80) 1, art. 234. The "preliminary reference" procedure, by which European national courts refer questions to the ECJ, is voluntary for all courts other than those of last resort. *See id.* Even the high courts of Europe's member states enjoy some scope of interpretation in determining whether to submit a preliminary reference. *See infra* note 586 and accompanying text.

100 *See* Melissa A. Waters, *Mediating Norms and Identity: The Role of Transnational Judicial Dialogue in Creating and Enforcing International Law*, 93 Geo. L.J. (forthcoming 2005) (manuscript on file with the *New York University Law Review*) ("[C]ourts engage in this comparative dialogue not out of a sense of legal obligation.").

101 *The Oxford English Dictionary* defines "dialogue" as "[a] conversation carried on between two or more persons; a colloquy, talk together." 4 The Oxford English Dictionary 601 (2d ed. 1989).

102 To similar effect, Karen Alter has rejected a characterization of the interactions of European institutions, including national courts and the ECJ, as dialogue. *See* Karen J. Alter, Establishing the Supremacy of European Law: The Making of an International Rule of Law in Europe 38 (2001). Instead, she posits a pattern of "doctrinal negotiation":

> A dialogue implies two or more actors talking to each other, using reason to reach a mutually accepted outcome. The notion of a dialogue implies that the outcome reached is the best reasoned outcome, the one that convinces all sides. A negotiation, on the other hand, implies competing interests where

As to the initial element of prospectivity, under Chapter 11 and similar international regimes, the relevant international tribunal is focused on *review*—in an appellate sense of the word—of the national court's judgment and procedure.[103] The international tribunal engages in such review with reference to a particular case brought before it by the aggrieved litigant from the national court proceeding.[104] In *Loewen*, for example, the magnitude of the damages award imposed by the court (by way of the jury) was a focus of review.[105] The tribunal also considered the court's refusal to sustain specific objections and order specific jury instructions and the courts' discretionary judgments regarding a variety of other trial issues.[106] In such an analysis,[107] the international tribunal is not engaged in what can fairly be characterized as a dialogue. Instead, it is explicitly considering *and critiquing* the national court's substantive judgments and procedural determinations.[108] Its analysis is not primarily prospective,

> parties recognize that they may not be able to have it as they most like it. Negotiations usually lead to compromises that take into account the power of the negotiating parties, the conflicting interests of the different actors, and the intensity of those interests.

Id. In essence, Alter's "negotiation" acknowledges the pattern described herein, in which no party to the relevant interaction enjoys complete autonomy. *Compare id. with infra* Part IV.A.1.

103 In *Loewen*, thus, the "claim of injury [was] based upon judicial action in a particular case." Loewen Group v. United States, ICSID Case No. ARB(AF)/98/3, 4 J. WORLD INVESTMENT 675, 708, ¶ 143 (NAFTA Ch. 11 Arb. Trib. 2003), *available at* http://www.naftalaw.org; *see also id.* ¶ 161 (noting "judicial violation of international law"). Similarly, in *Mondev*, "the measure challenged [was] that of a local court." Mondev Int'l Ltd. v. United States, Award, Case No. ARB(AF)/99/2, 42 I.L.M. 85, 103, ¶ 97 (NAFTA Ch. 11 Arb. Trib. 2002), *available at* http://www.naftalaw.org. To related effect, Slaughter has spoken of the growing occasion for judges to evaluate the "independence and quality of fellow judges of other nations." SLAUGHTER, *supra* note 57, at 86.

104 This distinguishes the "review" of Chapter 11 from that of a forum non conveniens determination, in which the court makes a generalized assessment of the subject judicial system. *Cf. Loewen*, 4 J. WORLD INVESTMENT at 708, ¶ 143. While also likely to offend the latter, such broad review raises an entirely different set of concerns than does the Chapter 11 review of a previously adjudicated case.

105 *See id.* at 685, 698–700, 702, ¶¶ 46, 104–114, 122.

106 *See id.* at 685, 693–95, ¶¶ 47, 78–87.

107 In *Mondev*, described in greater detail below, *see infra* notes 397–413 and accompanying text, the Massachusetts Supreme Judicial Court's asserted rationale for official immunity was subject to review, *see Mondev*, 42 I.L.M. at 112, ¶ 139.

108 A separate question concerns the constitutionality of such review under U.S. law. *See* A. Mark Weisburd, *International Courts and American Courts*, 21 MICH. J. INT'L L. 877, 891–92 (2000) (arguing that Article III of U.S. Constitution precludes United States from entering into treaties allowing review of federal court decisions by international tribunals, and that principles of constitutional federalism do not allow federal government to subject state courts to international judicial review). There have been previous incidents of international tribunals undermining decisions of U.S. courts, including the Supreme Court, but even those cases involved limited review of the *Loewen* variety. *See, e.g.*, Martinez, *supra* note 3, at 473 (noting international commission created by United States and Britain

even if, as I will argue, its conclusions ultimately are. The charge of the Chapter 11 tribunal is to review the decision of the national court. At least from the latter's perspective, this is more than a dialogue.

Bidirectionality is also relatively constrained in Chapter 11 and similar review. As I describe below, such bidirectionality does exist; Chapter 11 tribunals review decisions of national courts, but national courts may subsequently review the arbitral award. A general back-and-forth may emerge across cases as national courts respond to prior Chapter 11 reviews of their decisions and Chapter 11 tribunals respond in turn. In this respect, Chapter 11 and analogous international review of national courts exhibits some dialogic character. The response of national courts to Chapter 11 review, however, is distinct from bidirectional dialogue as described above. It is not parallel. As such, it is unlike the reciprocal borrowing amongst constitutional courts or U.S. and British courts' negotiation of the Maxwell bankruptcy.[109] Chapter 11 tribunals' interaction with national courts is more in the nature of seriatim, rather than parallel, interactions.

The ultimate obstacle to squeezing Chapter 11 and similar international review of national courts into the rubric of judicial dialogue is the important place of power in any judicial exchange under Chapter 11 and its analogues.[110] It is worth pausing to consider this feature, as it represents the most important innovation of Chapter 11 review of national courts. In what sense does Chapter 11 review involve the exercise of power? We have already established that the power of Chapter 11 is not that of hierarchical appeal. To understand the power of Chapter 11 more fully, one might begin with the contrast between Chapter 11 review and the engagement of courts in dialogue.

---

following Civil War, which reviewed and reversed several Supreme Court decisions, as well as U.S. courts' enforcement of international arbitration agreements); *see also supra* note 54 and accompanying text.

[109] *See* Slaughter, *Community of Courts*, *supra* note 87, at 213–16; Slaughter, *Judicial Globalization*, *supra* note 87, at 1116–19.

[110] Eric Posner and John Yoo recently have argued that more powerful international tribunals—as defined by greater independence and jurisdiction to hear individual claims, among other features—are actually less effective institutions of international adjudication. *See* Eric A. Posner & John C. Yoo, *A Theory of International Adjudication*, 91 CAL. L. REV. (forthcoming 2005) (manuscript on file with the *New York University Law Review*). Others have challenged their analysis directly. *See, e.g.*, Laurence R. Helfer & Anne-Marie Slaughter, *Of States, Bargains, and Judges: The Limited Role of Dependence in International Adjudication*, 93 CAL. L. REV. (forthcoming May 2005), *available at* http://law.vanderbilt.edu/faculty/helfer.html. It is unclear how Chapter 11 and similar review would fit within Posner and Yoo's typology, as they do not address it directly. For present purposes, it is sufficient to note that the features of Chapter 11's institutional design, which I characterize as introducing a dimension of power, enhance the relative autonomy of Chapter 11 tribunals in their interaction with national courts. Whether this is ultimately more or less effective—in Posner and Yoo's terms—is a question for another day.

Dialogic courts do not stand in a position of authority vis-à-vis one another. In citing decisions of the U.S. Supreme Court or the ECHR, the South African Constitutional Court is not acting out of any sense of obligation. The same can be said of courts deferring to the jurisdiction of a foreign court, or enforcing that court's prior judgment. They do so not because of any mandate held by their counterpart—because of its power—but out of a sense of comity or respect.

Even vertical judicial interactions may lack a significant dimension of power. The historical relationship between the ICJ and U.S. courts may be one example. The ICJ is not completely without persuasive influence in its relations with U.S. courts.[111] In the aftermath of the ICJ's recent decision in *Avena*, national courts—including state courts—have exhibited some broad sense of obligation to at least acknowledge the Court's interpretation of the Vienna Convention on Consular Relations and its critique of the application of the procedural default rule to asserted violations of the Convention.[112] While I will suggest below that *Avena* may signify the stirrings of a power dynamic in ICJ relations with national courts,[113] as it has historically functioned, the ICJ's diffuse influence is different in kind from the manifestation of power that emerges from the design and practice of Chapter 11 review of national courts.[114] The rare occasion on which meaningful political pressure may follow from a decision of the ICJ does not alter this conclusion. Such pressure is more in the nature of political, rather than judicial, pressure.

I would argue that two features of Chapter 11 and similar regimes may contribute to a strengthened dynamic of power in Chapter 11 review of national courts. First is the use of investor-state mechanisms by which individual litigants bring claims directly against national authorities.[115] Eliminating the requirement of espousal, through

[111] *See, e.g.*, Sanja Djajic, *The Effect of International Court of Justice Decisions on Municipal Courts in the United States:* Breard v. Greene, 23 HAST. INT'L & COMP. L. REV. 27, 108 (1999) (arguing that by publicly criticizing U.S. commitment to Vienna Convention on Consular Relations, ICJ placed U.S. citizens traveling abroad at risk of reciprocal treatment, potentially creating incentive for American courts to "introduce transjudicial communication by being responsive to the holdings of the World Court").

[112] *See infra* notes 556–58 and accompanying text.

[113] *See id.*

[114] *See* Tom Ginsburg & Richard H. McAdams, *Adjudicating in Anarchy: An Expressive Theory of International Dispute Resolution*, 45 WM. & MARY L. REV. 1229, 1238–39 (2004) (suggesting generally limited power of international tribunals). In their recent work, Ginsburg and McAdams offer an alternative theory of the power of international tribunals, complementary to, but distinct from, the theory of power in Chapter 11 that I offer herein. *See generally* Ginsburg & McAdams, *supra*.

[115] *See* Ernest A. Young, *The Trouble with Global Constitutionalism*, 38 TEX. INT'L L.J. 527, 536 (2003) (describing private right of action against national governments under Chapter 11 and its potential impact); *see also* José E. Alvarez, *The New Dispute Settlers:*

which individual claims were historically adjudicated in international fora only if taken up by the home state of the aggrieved party, increases the volume of cases before Chapter 11 and similar tribunals. Such an increase offers international judicial actors greater opportunity to speak to, and to influence, national adjudication. Direct access also eliminates the role of political commitments in filtering out sensitive cases before they reach the tribunal.[116] Such cases might include those requiring international review of national courts—the cases of interest herein. In this sense, international tribunals open to individual claims might be said to enjoy greater relative control over their docket. Non-espoused claims also may enhance the power of Chapter 11 tribunals by encouraging the emergence of domestic constituencies committed to effectuating tribunal decrees.[117] Those constituencies can be expected to pursue that goal without the political constraints of amicable foreign relations, which might preclude state action to enforce an international judgment even if they permitted the case to proceed at the outset.

This suggests the somewhat counterintuitive second source of power in the institutional design of Chapter 11. By offering monetary damages as the relevant remedy, rather than injunctive or other direct forms of relief, Chapter 11 dramatically enhances the potential for enforcement of remedial decrees and hence increases the power of Chapter 11 tribunals. By relying on a regime of liability rules of a sort—rather than property rules—Chapter 11 essentially manages to create an effective mechanism of *international* judicial power.[118] By

---

(Half) Truths and Consequences, 38 Tex. Int'l L.J. 405, 415 (2003) (noting rarity of "commitment to dispute settlement" manifest in Chapter 11). In the terms offered by Keohane, Moravcsik, and Slaughter, the power of Chapter 11 review arises from its combined elements of independence, access, and embeddedness. *See* Robert O. Keohane et al., *Legalized Dispute Resolution: Interstate and Transnational*, 54 Int'l Org. 457, 458 (2000). These features come together to create a high degree of delegation, with resulting enhancement of the power of Chapter 11 and similar tribunals. *See id.* at 486.

116 *See* Frederick M. Abbott, *NAFTA and the Legalization of World Politics: A Case Study*, 54 Int'l Org. 519, 543 (2000); Karen J. Alter, *The European Union's Legal System and Domestic Policy: Spillover or Backlash?*, 54 Int'l Org. 489, 517 (2000). For example, early in the development of the European legal community, political concerns caused the European Commission, as well as member states themselves, to be hesitant about pursuing claims against member states. The European legal system consequently remained ineffective at compelling compliance with European law until the development of the direct effect doctrine, which allowed individual litigants to raise European law issues before the national courts. *See* Alter, *supra* note 102, at 11–16 (noting that original European legal system was ineffective at compelling compliance with European law and that scholars and judges attribute increased effectiveness to direct effect doctrine).

117 *See* Keohane et al., *supra* note 115, at 477.

118 *See* Eugene Kontorovich, *Liability Rules for Constitutional Rights: The Case of Mass Detentions*, 56 Stan. L. Rev. 755 (2004) (suggesting potential benefits of liability rules over property rules in constitutional jurisprudence); *see also* Guido Calabresi & A.

contrast with directive judgments of the ICJ, for example, monetary liability is difficult for state respondents to resist.[119] Such relief requires no legislation, regulation, or other domestic reform. It simply requires payment.

Such a payment obligation is especially likely to be met under the Chapter 11 regime because it is directed not to the offending national court or other subnational entity, but rather to the ultimate deep pocket—the federal authorities of the relevant NAFTA state party.[120] Hence, the role of comity in international relations is turned on its head, with the state entity most sensitive to amicable foreign relations charged with the liability for any Chapter 11 award. Lest even federal authorities waver in their commitment to their foreign obligations, the efficacy of a Chapter 11 award, and hence the power of the issuing tribunal, is further enhanced by the relatively ready enforceability of the award in the national courts of the state faced with the payment obligation.[121] Given the private invocation of Chapter 11 dispute settlement and the monetary nature of any resulting judgment, if a liable state party refuses to comply with a Chapter 11 judgment, the private claimant can be expected to take any and all measures necessary to enforce it.[122]

Douglas Melamed, *Property Rules, Liability Rules, and Inalienability: One View of the Cathedral*, 85 HARV. L. REV. 1089, 1106–10 (1972) (arguing that transaction costs and difficulty of assessing damages affect choice between property and liability rules).

119 *Cf.* Stephan, *supra* note 51, at 640 ("[W]here international law rests on explicit commitment, including acceptance of an enforcement process that operates independently of the state subject to the law, we need to take notice."). I will argue below that the interaction of international tribunals and national courts explored herein is analogous to the Warren Court–era interaction of federal and state courts on habeas review, as elucidated by Robert Cover and Alexander Aleinikoff. *See infra* Part III.B.1. Notably, Cover and Aleinikoff cite the Warren Court's failure to invoke equitable remedies in its criminal procedure jurisprudence, as distinct from its reapportionment and civil rights decisions, as one of the critical catalysts behind the non-traditional pattern of intersystemic judicial interaction they observe in habeas review. *See* Cover & Aleinikoff, *supra* note 14, at 1039–40.

120 *See* NAFTA, *supra* note 12, art. 1136, at 646.

121 Such enforcement is not automatic, *see* Abbott, *supra* note 116, at 537, but is easier to accomplish than would be enforcement of any form of injunctive relief, with the likely need for some form of legislative or regulatory intervention.

122 Given the continuing failure of Canada and Mexico to join the ICSID Convention, Chapter 11 awards are enforced in national courts, under the terms of the New York Convention. *See* Jack J. Coe, Jr., *Taking Stock of NAFTA Chapter 11 in Its Tenth Year: An Interim Sketch of Selected Themes, Issues, and Methods*, 36 VAND. J. TRANSNAT'L L. 1381, 1441, 1443 (2003). While the latter allows some room for national tribunals to resist enforcement, primarily on grounds of public policy, the New York Convention ordinarily leads to enforcement of challenged international arbitral awards. *See id.* at 1443; *see also* Abbott, *supra* note 116, at 537. The New York Convention, of course, is the common name for the Convention on the Recognition and Enforcement of Foreign Arbitral Awards, June 10, 1958, 21 U.S.T. 2517, 330 U.N.T.S. 38. On the Convention generally, see Alford, *supra* note 2, at 700–04.

International review under Chapter 11 therefore suggests a capacity for, if not necessarily the overt assertion of, judicial power.[123] Such power is limited, even by comparison with the constrained power of domestic courts. Compared to traditional international adjudication, however, Chapter 11 tribunals possess meaningful judicial power. As outlined, however, the power of Chapter 11 tribunals operates between courts and executive or legislative bodies. Such inter-branch engagement among international courts and national executive and legislative agencies is notable,[124] but is different in kind from the assertion of power among judicial institutions. The capacity of Chapter 11 tribunals to assert power, however, ultimately extends to national courts as well. While I explore this power dynamic between Chapter 11 tribunals and national courts in greater detail below, its essence lies in two factors.[125]

First, Chapter 11 awards have the capacity to undo certain types of national judicial decisions, including any award of exemplary or punitive damages and any denial of the liability of a federal government entity.[126] Second, and perhaps more importantly, by directing its damage awards against the federal government, Chapter 11 creates an institutional mechanism for putting pressure on national courts, whether at the federal or state level.[127] Had the Loewen Group succeeded in winning its $750 million claim against the federal govern-

---

Admittedly, a pattern of engagement grounded in national review upon enforcement (or petition for annulment or revision) has the potential to produce an odd dynamic, with national courts potentially reviewing the decision of an international tribunal, which itself reviewed the decision of a national court. This peculiarity would be especially pronounced where the national court charged to review the international award is either the *same* court that the international tribunal reviewed or is inferior to that court. In the latter dynamic, a lower national court is indirectly called to review the decision of its hierarchical superior. Shades of this occurred in the *Köbler* case, described *infra*, in which an Austrian trial court was forced to review the decisions of an Austrian high court. *See* Case C-224/01, Gerhard Köbler v. Republik Österreich, 41 C.M.L.R. 813 (2004); *see also infra* notes 598–603 and accompanying text.

123 With an eye to the dimensions of power in Chapter 11 review of national courts, Anne-Marie Slaughter has classified Chapter 11 as a form of "enforcement network." *See* SLAUGHTER, *supra* note 57, at 21, 145. In broader terms, Slaughter sees Chapter 11 as part of an emerging pattern of vertical government networks, in which supranational authorities act in tandem with national authorities to effectuate policy ends. The former, in essence, "borrow" authority from the latter. *See id.* at 20–21.

124 This pattern is a significant worry for many. It is not, however, the issue of interest herein.

125 *See infra* Parts IV.A.1 & B.1.a.

126 *See infra* notes 320–22 and accompanying text.

127 In Part IV.B.1.a, I suggest several possible mechanisms of such pressure, including statutorily authorized enforcement of NAFTA's provisions by the executive branch, judicial or legislative steps to eliminate or curtail the complete diversity rule in cases involving aliens, and federal efforts to secure state or local indemnification of Chapter 11 awards.

ment, various pressures on the Mississippi authorities, including the courts, might have been predicted.[128]

Given the manifestation of power in Chapter 11 review of national courts, the recurrent engagement of judicial systems can hardly be said to be voluntary. National courts do not face Chapter 11 review by way of a voluntary dialogue. Rather, such review is forced upon them.[129] Unlike the dialogic interactions noted above, Chapter 11 review of national courts does not arise from the consent of the relevant judicial participants.[130] At the conclusion of such review, moreover, Chapter 11 tribunals enjoy some meaningful capacity to achieve desired results without the cooperation of the counterpart national court. Such power distinguishes Chapter 11 review from most conventional mechanisms of international judicial review, which

---

[128] This is not to deny that the imposition of Chapter 11 awards arising from state- or municipal-court malfeasance on the federal government, as opposed to the offending jurisdiction, if not the court itself, also limits Chapter 11 power in important respects. If imposition of liability on the state or local court were possible, Chapter 11 might be even stronger. By creating a mechanism of effective pressure, however, an award issued against the federal government offers its own dimensions of power, as suggested above and described in greater detail below.

In fact, federal liability may be preferable in at least one respect. As I will suggest below, the efficacy of Chapter 11 review of national courts as a source of judicial innovation depends on the emergence of a regularized pattern of cases. *See infra* Part IV.A.3. Absent a certain volume of decisions, Chapter 11 will be far more limited in its impact. Because of its orientation to federal authorities, however, it is not necessary that Chapter 11 review of national courts occur with the frequency of ordinary appeal if such review is to influence court behavior generally. The direction of Chapter 11 awards to federal authorities may enhance their influence and cause their effects to be felt more widely than if they had been directed to any single state or local jurisdiction. *Cf.* Bhagwat, *supra* note 69, at 985–86 (suggesting that U.S. Supreme Court enjoys meaningful power over lower courts, notwithstanding limited occurrences of review); Caminker, *supra* note 66, at 80–81 (same); Tidmarsh, *supra* note 84, at 1163 (arguing that federal-state dialogue does not require participation of each system in every case: "it is enough that the court has the opportunity to comment over a range of cases"). Even if the federal authorities do not expressly disseminate the lessons of a Chapter 11 judgment, greater public exposure of an award against the federal government might be expected to facilitate that end.

[129] Of course, such review arises out of the voluntary accession to NAFTA or other relevant international agreements. Yet such generalized consent is distinct from the consensual nature of judicial dialogue, a case-specific election to engage another court.

[130] *Cf.* Reem Bahdi, *Globalization of Judgment: Transjudicialism and the Five Faces of International Law in Domestic Courts*, 34 GEO. WASH. INT'L L. REV. 555, 558 (2002) ("[C]ourts speak to each other across jurisdictions not because they have to but because they want to."). That jurisprudential notions of dialogue have some origins in Alexander Bickel's conception of the passive virtues, *see* Stephen L. Carter, *Constitutional Improprieties: Reflections on* Mistretta, Morrison, *and Administrative Government*, 57 U. CHI. L. REV. 357, 378–79 (1990), would seem to confirm the difficulty of reconciling Chapter 11's relatively proactive review with a purely dialogic vision of judicial action.

are obliged to rely on dialogue with national courts for their efficacy and success.[131]

Chapter 11 review of national courts thus sits uneasily with conventional assumptions of the limited authority of international institutions, and of courts in particular. It is not simply another case of transnational judicial dialogue, given elements incompatible with a model of interaction grounded in voluntary exchange and a spirit of comity. It borrows from appellate review some capacity to undo the effects of the relevant national court decision, even if not to reverse it,

131 Examples of judicial institutions that engage in close judicial review of the judgment or procedures of a foreign court or have some meaningful capacity to pursue desired policy outcomes without the consent and cooperation of the court subject to review can be offered. *See also infra* Part VI.B. Chapter 11 is relatively unique in combining both elements. Hence its exploration herein.

As for engagement in close review, I have previously mentioned the sometimes harsh review of forum non conveniens inquiries. *See supra* note 104. Besides its lack of case specificity, however, such review involves a limited assertion of power, because the relevant ends do not encompass the application of any resulting judgment to the subject judicial system. The ICJ's gentle admonishment of the U.S. Supreme Court in the *LaGrand* case, with its suggestion that the Court could have done more to effectuate the ICJ's provisional measures, also might be noted: "[I]t would have been open to the Supreme Court, as one of its members urged, to grant a preliminary stay, which would have given it 'time to consider, after briefing from all interested parties, the jurisdictional and international legal issues involved.'" LaGrand (F.R.G. v. U.S.), 2001 I.C.J. 466, at 508 ¶ 114 (citing Federal Republic of Germany v. United States, 526 U.S. 111, 113 (1999) (Breyer, J., dissenting)). Again, however, the element of power is absent. *See infra* notes 554–55 and accompanying text. A similar case of "review" might be found in the ECJ's encouragement of lower national courts in Europe to disregard directives from their national high courts not to submit questions of European law to the ECJ. *See* Helfer & Slaughter, *supra* note 2, at 310; *see, e.g.*, Case 106/77, Amministrazione delle Finanze dello Stato v. Simmenthal, 1978 E.C.R. 629 (counseling lower Italian court to apply European law rather than Italian constitutional rule, notwithstanding earlier directive from Italian Constitutional Court (ICC) to refer any such conflict to ICC). Besides the indirect nature of such review, the power at work in this case remains limited. *See infra* notes 590–94 and accompanying text (exploring pattern of interaction of ECJ and European national courts).

Perhaps the closest parallel to the invasive review of Chapter 11 comes in decisions regarding the enforcement of foreign judgments. Here, one might even identify some degree of effective "power"—the capacity to prevent enforcement. Such review is worthy of further study. It is at least clear, however, that the power dynamic arising in the enforcement of foreign judgments is a less active (and perhaps less invasive) one than that of Chapter 11.

What about courts that have meaningful power but do not engage in national court review? The best example of this pattern, notably, is another international trade court. The dispute settlement panels of the WTO, as well as its Appellate Body, wield tremendous power. They are more than able to create effective incentives to achieve their desired ends. The WTO dispute settlement process, however, as well as that of the General Agreement on Tariffs and Trade (GATT) before it, have had little occasion to interact with national courts. Rather, WTO review is conventionally directed to the executive and legislative branches of the WTO member states. As with the ICJ, however, there is no institutional bar to the emergence of such review of national courts in the future. *See infra* notes 559–63 and accompanying text (analyzing judicial interactions under GATT and WTO regimes).

and some resulting influence on national court decisions. In its retrospective orientation—its *review* of the prior national court decision—it operates in a unidirectional pattern and exhibits some degree of hierarchy. Moreover, as in appellate review, Chapter 11 tribunals enjoy significant authority within a narrow scope of jurisdiction.

Most importantly, Chapter 11 review of national courts exhibits a dimension of power echoing the relationship between appellate and trial courts. It does not arise from the voluntary consent of the court subjected to review. Effectuation of the ultimate judgment, moreover, may occur even absent the cooperation of the court reviewed.

While Chapter 11 review of national courts consequently amounts to something more than judicial dialogue, it remains something less than a true appeal. For it exhibits important dialogic features as well. Chapter 11 decrees are not binding on national courts in any formal sense. Furthermore, though not bidirectional in a purely dialogic sense, there is some inevitable back-and-forth among Chapter 11 tribunals and national courts, both within and across cases. I will suggest below that Chapter 11 review also has some prospective dimension, coupled with the retrospective character of its substantive analysis. Like judicial dialogue, it is oriented to norm development, at least as much as error correction.

Most importantly, as suggested above and explored in greater detail below, the power of Chapter 11 and similar international review is limited in scope.[132] It is characterized by a distribution of power in which each judicial body enjoys some autonomous capacity to effectuate its will, but not unlimited capacity to do so. Within this dynamic, some pattern of exchange—of discourse—remains essential.

Chapter 11 review of national courts, then, has some hybrid quality, exhibiting important features of both appellate review and judicial dialogue.[133] While the appropriate effectuation and particular characteristics of Chapter 11 and analogous review of national courts, given its hybrid nature, requires greater consideration,[134] it is useful to first consider the ends of such review. What benefits might international review of national courts, in institutional forms such as Chapter 11, have to offer?

---

132 *See supra* notes 75–77 and accompanying text; *infra* Part IV.B.1.a.

133 *See* Wright & Miller, *supra* note 14, at 660–61 (describing similarly mixed nature of federal–state court interaction on habeas review of capital sentences). Frank Cross has posited legal interaction as defined by either hierarchy or dialogue. *See* Frank B. Cross, *Shattering the Fragile Case for Judicial Review of Rulemaking*, 85 VA. L. REV. 1243, 1308 (1999). The present analysis posits something in the middle.

134 *See infra* Part IV.A.

CONCLUSION

While the interaction of judicial institutions is commonly conceived to be shaped by a dynamic of either vertical hierarchy or horizontal comity, this Article outlines a hybrid pattern of interaction, standing between these extremes. Alexander Bickel, Robert Cover,

1. As this example may suggest, however, the power of Chapter 19 panels may ultimately be too substantial, compared to the national administrative adjudicators whom they review, for the Chapter 19 process to operate as a true dialectic.

Yet another international opportunity for dialectical exchange may come in the interaction of national courts and the newly established International Criminal Court, under Article 17 of the Rome Statute, Rome Statute of the International Criminal Court, July 17, 1998, art. 17, 37 I.L.M. 1002, 1012, which provides for complementary jurisdiction in the International Criminal Court if national courts fail to exercise their jurisdiction to prosecute actionable international crimes. Articulation of the detailed implications of the latter standard should offer substantial opportunity for a dialectical pattern of engagement. *See* SLAUGHTER, *supra* note 57, at 148–50; *see also* Bartram S. Brown, *Primacy or Complementarity: Reconciling the Jurisdiction of National Courts and International Criminal Tribunals*, 23 YALE J. INT'L L. 383, 389 (1998) (describing choice between primacy and complementarity in jurisdiction of International Criminal Court).

611 A comparative analysis of the various courts noted above, through a prism of dialectical review, is beyond the scope of this Article, but offers a fruitful avenue for future study.

612 *See* Jacqueline Bhabha, *European Harmonisation of Asylum Policy: A Flawed Process*, 35 VA. J. INT'L L. 101, 102 (1994) (noting that major objective of European leaders has been to create "increasingly connected and interdependent" Europe).

613 *See* Abbott, *supra* note 116, at 522–23; Alvarez, *supra* note 115, at 430 n.113; *see also Committee Statements on the NAFTA: Hearing Before the Senate Comm. on Finance, Statement of the Committee on Finance on S. 1627 The North American Free Trade Agreement Implementation Act (NAFTA)*, 103rd Cong., 139 CONG. REC. 30,201, 30,203 (1993) ("If in the future a NAFTA dispute settlement panel were to determine that a particular U.S. law was inconsistent with the NAFTA, the Congress would retain the full authority to determine whether or not to amend or modify that law.").

Alexander Aleinikoff, Guido Calabresi, Neal Katyal, and others have identified an array of non-conventional forms of judicial communication. I offer "dialectical review" in a similar spirit. Judicial institutions engaged in dialectical review participate in more than dialogue, which each can freely disregard. In dialectical review, as revealed by Chapter 11 and its domestic analogies, both courts enjoy some capacity to assert power, albeit not in so direct or final a form as in appellate review. The intersystemic judicial communication of dialectical review, as a result, is not easily ignored. Besides this distinct power dynamic, an effective regime of dialectical review rests on the presence of diverse legal and institutional perspectives and an institutional design crafted to provide adjudicatory continuity. In tandem, these features make dialectical review a mechanism of beneficial legal innovation through which judicial coordination, jurisprudential harmonization, and norm internalization may arise.

This analysis offers its most immediate recommendations to the judges who are party to these forms of interactions and the policymakers charged with the reform and replication of Chapter 11 and analogous regimes. By only a slight extension, the analysis herein speaks to judicial, legislative, and executive participants in other international dispute settlement regimes, including the ICJ, the WTO, and the ECJ. It may extend further afield, yet closer to home, by its application to the interplay of federal and state courts in habeas and other civil matters, and to the interaction of both federal and state courts with tribal courts in the United States. To the judges who are potential parties to dialectical review, this Article commends an approach characterized by careful but firm assertions of authority, by contextual and casuist analysis, and by efforts to enhance their relevant judicial system's capacity for continuity. Policymakers charged with the reform of existing mechanisms of intersystemic adjudication and the creation of new systems of review should focus particular attention on maintaining an equipoise of power between participating tribunals, thus furthering the dialectical dynamic and the prospect of efficient innovation.

Yet, the ultimate lessons of the present analysis may extend even further. The model of dialectical review proposed herein ultimately speaks to an array of situations in which institutions—including legislative and executive institutions and even broader social institutions—interact without a dominant convention of either hierarchy or comity. Such situations may represent a far greater—and perhaps growing—proportion of the interactions among institutions than the ordinary dichotomy of mandate versus contract might suggest.

Along horizontal dimensions of governance, the pattern of dialectical engagement may offer meaningful guidance for the complex interaction of legislative, executive, and judicial authorities in the modern administrative state. Vertically, dialectical review bespeaks a conception of federal-state relations grounded not in federalism's conventional project of clear jurisdictional segregation, but in a dynamic interaction directed to a fluid distribution of power. Exploration of the interaction of international tribunals and national courts in the novel setting of Chapter 11 may therefore have important implications well beyond NAFTA and international adjudication. This study and its paradigm of dialectical review may offer fruitful guidance for the management of a growing dynamic of coordination among political and social institutions, both at home and abroad.

[18]

Truth, Memory and the Rule of Law

David Dyzenhaus

I listened to the Prosecutor and I saw that he did not have any ideas about us. He was ignorant of our ways and feelings. I looked at the Judge and the prosecutor and the thought came to me that they were ants and in engaging with them we were dwarfing ourselves. It is a curse to be a Judge when you believe that you hold the life of a person in your hand. Only God holds our lives in his hands. He gives it and He alone can take it.

Andrew Zondo, 19-year-old soldier of the African National Congress, after being sentenced to death for planting a mine in 1985 which killed five people in a South African shopping centre.[1]

1. Introduction

This book presents an account of three days at South Africa's Truth and Reconciliation Commission (TRC). It is an account of the Legal Hearing—South Africa's official inquiry into the legal order during the apartheid era and into those who sustained it.

The TRC is meant to form one of the principal building blocks in the "historic bridge" described in the "Post-amble" to South Africa's Interim Constitution of 1993—a bridge "between the past of a deeply divided society characterized by strife, conflict, untold suffering and injustice, and a future founded on the recognition of human rights, democracy and peaceful coexistence and development opportunities for all South Africans, irrespective of colour, race, class, belief or sex".[2]

The Post-amble suggested some of the essential features of the TRC by requiring that the South African Parliament would enact

[1] McBride Submission, 11.

[2] Constitution of the Republic of South Africa Act 1993, s. 232(4).

legislation to carry out the promise of the Constitution to lay "the secure foundation for the people of South Africa to transcend the divisions and strife of the past, which generated gross violations of human rights, the transgression of humanitarian principles in violent conflicts and a legacy of hatred, fear, guilt and revenge". The violations and transgressions, the Post-amble continued, could "now be addressed on the basis that there is a need for understanding but not for vengeance, a need for reparation but not for retaliation, a need for *ubuntu*[3] but not for victimisation".

The legislation itself had to put into effect the following scheme:

> "In order to advance such reconciliation and reconstruction, amnesty shall be granted in respect of acts, omissions and offences associated with political objectives and committed in the course of the conflicts of the past. To this end, Parliament under this Constitution shall adopt a law determining a firm cut-off date, which shall be a date after 8 October 1990 and before 6 December 1993, and providing for the mechanisms, criteria and procedures, including tribunals, if any, through which such amnesty shall be dealt with at any time after the law has been passed".

The Post-amble concluded with the following ringing declaration:

> "With this Constitution and these commitments we, the people of South Africa, open a new chapter in the history of our country.
>
> Nkosi sikelel' iAfrika. God seen Suid-Afrika. Morena boloka sechaba sa heso. May God bless our country. Mudzimu fhatutshedza Afrika. Hosi katekisa Afrika".

However, one should be aware from the outset that the Interim Constitution and its products like the TRC were the result of a compromise negotiated between the various political parties engaged in the process of designing a new order for South Africa. Since the handover of power was negotiated, it was not considered a realistic option to have Nuremberg-type criminal trials where perpetrators, or at least the main perpetrators, of human rights abuses would be punished for their crimes. Those who felt compromised by any kind of inquiry favoured an option of official amnesia about the past, a forgetting underpinned by a blanket amnesty. But this option was neither realistic nor morally acceptable. And so South Africans opted

[3] *Ubuntu* is a word which in this context means both "compassion" and "recognition of the humanity of the other"; see Kader Asmal, Louise Asmal, Ronald Suresh Roberts, *Reconciliation Through Truth: A Reckoning of Apartheid's Criminal Governance*, 2nd edn. (Cape Town: David Philip, 1997), p. 21.

for the truth commission model which had been developed in various forms within other systems of transitional justice, for example, in Chile, Argentina and El Salvador.

These commissions have in common only that they are official inquiries into the past which seek to present an account of the details of the repression inflicted by the old regime. The scope of such an inquiry, the powers given to the commission and the consequences that follow from it depend largely on the extent to which the old regime still holds power during the transition.[4]

As we will see, the TRC has vast powers and it goes well beyond any of its models in the degree to which it is open, driven by public participation, and able to craft and shape its inquiry. For the scope of its inquiry is wide, it has tools to enforce participation, and its reports are supposed to lead to institutional reform and reparations to victims.

The TRC's difference from other models is a result of its beginnings in a debate about how to manage the transition to democracy, and of the fact that it was designed by a parliament after public hearings, rather than by a presidential commission with its eye firmly on not rocking the boat. In addition, the appointment of Archbishop Desmond Tutu as Chair of the TRC resulted in a particular understanding of its role in reconciliation, one which was in no way suggested or required by the official statutory mandate. Under his direction, Commissioners go beyond the statutory mandate and actively seek professions of repentance from perpetrators of abuses and of forgiveness from their victims. The slogan adopted by the TRC—"Truth: the road to reconciliation"—indicates the seriousness with which the TRC takes the aspiration to reconciliation. Finally (and this was anounced early in 1998), once the TRC itself has formally been disbanded, its work will continue through a body known as the "Institute for Change, Memory and Reconciliation"

[4] In a useful comparative article, Priscilla B. Hayner notes the following four characteristics of a truth commission: "First, a truth commission focuses on the past. Second, a truth commission is not focused on a specific event, but attempts to paint an overall picture of certain human rights abuses, or violations of international humanitarian law, over a period of time. Third, a truth commission usually exists temporarily and for a predefined period of time, ceasing to exist with the submission of a report of its findings. Finally, a truth commission is always vested with some sort of authority, by way of its sponsor, that allows it greater access to information, greater security or protection to dig into sensitive issues, and a greater impact with its report": see "Fifteen Truth Commissions—1974 to 1994: A Comparative Study" (1994) 16 *Human Rights Quarterly* 597, 604.

which will focus on advanced research into the TRC's final report and participate in the global debate about the significance of the TRC for transitions in other countries.

The TRC was established in terms of the Promotion of National Unity and Reconciliation Act 1995. Section 3(1)(a) declares its task to be:

> "(a) Establishing as complete a picture as possible of the causes, nature and extent of the gross violations of human rights . . . including the antecedents, circumstances, factors and context of such violations, as well as the perspectives of the victims and the motives and perspectives of the persons responsible for the commission of the violations by conducting investigations and holding hearings".

Gross violations are defined in section 1(1)(xix) as:

> "the violation of human rights through—
> (a) the killing, abduction, torture or severe ill-treatment of any person; or
> (b) any attempt, conspiracy, incitement, instigation, command or procurement to commit an act referred to in paragraph (a),
>
> which emanated from conflicts of the past and which was committed during the period 1 March 1960 to the cut-off date within or outside the Republic, and the commission of which was advised, planned, directed, commanded or ordered, by any person acting with a political motive".

The Commission is divided into three committees. The Committee on Human Rights Violations has the task of conferring victim status on individuals who claim to have been subject to human rights violations.[5] Those who have victim status conferred on them are eligible for government reparations. This committee has also taken it as part of its mandate (in terms of section 3(1)(a)) to hear

[5] 1995 Act, s. 1(1)(xix) defines "victim" as "(a) persons who, individually or together with one or more persons, suffered harm in the form of physical or mental injury, emotional suffering, pecuniary loss or a substantial impairment of human rights—(i) as a result of a gross violation of human rights; or (ii) as a result of an act associated with a political objective for which amnesty has been granted; (b) persons who, individually or together with one or more persons, suffered harm in the form of physical or mental injury, emotional suffering, pecuniary loss or a substantial impairment of human rights, as a result of such person intervening to assist persons contemplated in paragraph (a) who were in distress or to prevent victimization of such persons; and (c) such relatives or dependants of victims as may be prescribed".

Note that not all victims attend victims' hearings. The sheer number of victims results in the TRC selecting "representative" victims to tell their stories in a public forum.

testimony which will establish the "complete picture" of gross human rights violations; and, as we will see, it was a submission at such a hearing which eventually led to the TRC deciding that the Commission, rather than any specific committee, should hold an inquiry into the legal order.

The Committee on Amnesty hears applications for amnesty from those who have committed gross human rights violations. As long as the act fits the criteria set out in section 1(1)(ix) and as long as the applicant has made "full disclosure of all relevant facts",[6] amnesty will be granted. The grant of amnesty carries significant benefits, since it grants the applicant immunity from both criminal and civil liability.[7]

The Committee on Reparation and Rehabilitation has as its main task preparing a report to government which will form the basis for reparations to and rehabilitation of victims.[8] It also participates in one of the most important tasks of the TRC as a whole, the making of "recommendations to the President with regard to the creation of institutions conducive to a stable and fair society and the institutional, administrative and legislative measures which should be taken or introduced in order to prevent the commission of violations of human rights".[9]

In addition, the TRC has an investigating unit with police powers of search and seizure and the TRC itself has the authority to subpoena reluctant witnesses to appear before it.[10]

[6] 1995 Act, s. 20(1)(c). Amnesty can be granted for any politically motivated crime, but only gross human rights violations require an Amnesty Hearing.

[7] 1995 Act, s. 20(7)(a).

[8] 1995 Act, s. 25(1)(b)(i) permits the Committee to make recommendations on urgent interim measures.

[9] 1995 Act, s. 4(h) read with s. 25(1)(b)(ii).

[10] See chapter 6 of the 1995 Act. Section 31(i) provides: "Any person who is questioned by the Commission in the exercise of its powers in terms of this Act, or who has been subpoenaed to give evidence or to produce any article at a hearing of the Commission shall, subject to the provisions of subsections (2), (3) and (5), be compelled to produce any article or to answer any question put to him or her with regard to the subject-matter of the hearing notwithstanding the fact that the article or his or her answer may incriminate him or her.

(2) A person referred to in subsection (1) shall only be compelled to answer a question or to produce an article which may incriminate him or her if the Commission has issued an order to that effect, after the Commission—(a) has consulted with the attorney-general who has jurisdiction; (b) has satisfied itself that to require such information from such a person is reasonable, necessary and justifiable in an open and democratic society based on freedom and equality; and (c) has satisfied itself that such a person has refused or is likely to refuse to answer a question or produce an article on the grounds that such an answer or article might incriminate him or her".

2. The Apartheid Divide

The ordinary day-to-day operation of the apartheid machine inflicted huge suffering on the majority of South Africa's population. In the cause of white supremacy, people were forcibly removed from their homes, their land was taken away from them, family members were separated from each other, they were stripped of their citizenship and consigned to dustbowls ruled by dictatorial puppets, and they were explicitly told that they should have just those rights and just that amount of education that would fit them into an economic system run for the exclusive benefit of the white minority.

Apartheid inflicted violence daily on all those who were the victims of its racist laws. That violence was "ordinary" only in that it was part of the fabric of daily existence. There was also the "extraordinary" violence of apartheid—the beatings, torture, and murder (sometimes amounting to massacre) which the security forces dealt out to political opponents of the ordinary violence.

[11] The 1995 Act has been amended once by Act 84 of 1995 to change the cut-off date from the original one of 10 December 1993 in order to include gross human rights abuses commmitted just prior to the elections of 1994.

[12] In an unpublished paper, Jennifer J. Llewellyn and Robert Howse argue that the justice with which the TRC is concerned is restorative: "Institutions for Restorative Justice: The South African Truth and Reconciliation Commission as a model for dealing with conflicts of the past". I address such an argument briefly in Chapter 4.

4. The Legal Hearing

It is against this background that I wish to examine the TRC's Legal Hearing. This was but one of the hearings into the role of the professions and institutions of apartheid, the others included hearings into

justice to victims of past abuse and the need for reconciliation and rapid transition to a new future; between encouragement to wrongdoers to help in the discovery of truth and the need for reparations for the victims of that truth; between a correction in the old and the creation of a new. It is an exercise of immense difficulty interacting in a vast network of political, emotional, ethical and logistical considerations. It is an act calling for a judgment falling substantially within the domain of those entrusted with lawmaking in the era preceding and during the transition period. The results may well often be imperfect and the pursuit of the truth might inherently support the message of Kant that 'out of the crooked timber of humanity no straight thing was ever made' [Immanuel Kant paraphrased in Isaiah Berlin's essay on "Two Concepts of Liberty" in *Four Essays on Liberty* (Oxford: Oxford University Press, 1969) at p. 170]".

Though note that Mahomed went on to say that there "can be legitimate debate about the methods and the mechanisms chosen by the lawmaker to give effect to the difficult duty entrusted upon it in terms of the epilogue. We are not concerned with that debate or the wisdom of its choice of mechanisms but only with its constitutionality" (1029–30).

[50] Antjie Krog, Afrikaner poet and journalist, has this to say about the TRC after two years of in-depth reporting on its Hearings: "With all [the TRC's] mistakes, its arrogance, its racism, its sanctimony, its incompetence, the lying, the failure to get an interim reparation policy off the ground after two years, the showing off—with all of this—it has been so brave, so naively brave in the winds of deceit, rancour and hate. Against a flood crashing with the weight of a brutalizing past on to new usurping politics, the Commission has kept alive the idea of a common humanity. Painstakingly it has chiselled a way beyond racism and made space for all of our voices. For all its failures, it carries a flame of hope that makes me proud to be from here, of here": Antjie Krog, *Country of My Skull*, n.16 above, p. 278.

the role of the media, the medical profession, business, political parties, and the churches. These hearings were set up by the TRC in terms of its understanding of its broad mandate to establish "as complete a picture as possible of the causes, nature and extent of the gross violations of human rights . . . including the antecedents, circumstances, factors and context of such violations".

What makes these professional and institutional hearings different is that their purpose is not to establish who is a victim or who may get amnesty. Rather, they are meant to be inquiries into how professions and institutions which on the face of it seemed no different than their counterparts in Europe or North America, were deeply implicated in apartheid.

Archbishop Desmond Tutu said in his opening address to the Legal Hearing that it was the "most important of the professional hearings", almost as important as the "victim/survivor hearings". His reason was similar to the one contained in the paradox we saw Chaskalson sketch above; law was used as the instrument of apartheid but also seemed to hold out some promise of curbing its worst excesses.[51]

Indeed, one can say that even the illegal acts of the security forces were "under the cover of the law", since the law made it so difficult to get evidence of what was happening. Even more important, though, is that the Legal Hearing forced the connection to be made between what I have called the ordinary and the extraordinary violence of apartheid. By examining together the administration of statutes which set out the programme of apartheid and the statutes which set up the framework for suppressing opposition to apartheid, the Hearing revealed the continuum between ordinary and extraordinary violence.

In his address, Archbishop Tutu told of what it was like to grow up as a black child in a world of daily humiliation, not only of oneself but, inevitably more painful, of one's parents. That humiliation, he pointed out, was enshrined in the law of the land, laws whose violation demanded the sanctions of the criminal law, branding as criminals people attempting to exercise basic human rights.[52]

[51] "You see, in dealing with human rights violations, you are really concerned with justice, law, order, the disposition of power and authority and how these are regulated within conventional parameters so that they are not abused"; Transcript, p. 2.

[52] Transcript, pp. 3–7. Note that Tutu quoted extensively from Judge Pius Langa's submission, including the extracts reproduced below in Chapter 2, text to n. 59.

Judges and magistrates upheld those laws, even interpreted them so as to give maximum effect to their policy. The Attorneys-General—the civil servants in each province who controlled prosecutions—saw to the prosecution of violations of apartheid law. The legal profession, divided between the Bar of advocates who enjoyed an exclusive right of audience before the Supreme Court and the side-Bar of attorneys whose extra-curial work included instructing the advocates, by and large participated in sustaining apartheid law or did their best to ignore it. And the legal academy managed for the most part to educate their students and to write about the law as if apartheid did not exist.

In other words, the law was not self-executing under apartheid. It required administration, application and interpretation by judges, magistrates, prosecutors, officials of the Departments of Justice and Law and Order, and lawyers, both in the academy and the legal profession. Apartheid law was in large part the statutes enacted by the National Party-controlled Parliament, which enjoyed a legislative supremacy unchecked by any written constitution. But it was also the law that arose out of decisions made by civil servants, the judiciary, and the legal profession. And the great majority of lawyers had a legal education which failed to make apartheid and its law part of the curriculum, and also did not generally give students critical tools for understanding their society.

So at the Legal Hearing two not unrelated questions were put to those who staffed the legal order. How was it that you implemented without protest, and often with zeal, laws that were so manifestly unjust? And how was it that when you had some discretion as to how to interpret or apply the law, you consistently decided in a way that assisted the government and the security forces? And to those whose skills could have been used to resist—if only by criticising—apartheid law, the question was put of why they stood passively by or actively supported the regime.

These questions had a special poignancy for all except the ordinary civil servants in the government ministries who were subject to a rigid sytem of command from above. The judges and magistrates who interpreted the law, the Attorneys-General who directed prosecutions, the advocates and attorneys who argued cases, and the legal academics who trained lawyers and expounded the law, all had in common the following characteristics. They subscribed to the view that the administration of the law is also the administration of justice.

And they jealously wished to maintain the independence of their role from political interference under the new order by claiming that they had maintained independence under the old. The special poignancy comes about in that they seemed to think that their role during the apartheid era had an element of justice to it and that their commitment to independence of role was displayed in the public record of their deeds under apartheid. And, as we will see, the situation of the judges was the most poignant of the group who would not and could not claim that they were just following orders.

5. Trial or Inquiry?

The TRC invited all who had played a role in the apartheid legal order to present written submissions in answer to a set of questions on their role during apartheid. It expected that the most important of these submissions would then be summarised orally before the Commission during the Hearing, so that specific questions could be put to the presenters. At the end of each of the three days, a panel discussion was scheduled, in which representatives of different organisations who had not made an oral submission that day would debate the day's proceedings.

The TRC hoped to construct a different atmosphere from the one that prevailed at a victim or amnesty hearing. No-one would be applying for amnesty in a bid to escape a criminal prosecution, and no-one would be seeking to find out about the details of torture or assassination. No-one would need to be subpoenaed in order to get his or her evidence. Representatives of different parts of the old legal order would come forward to present their views in an atmosphere of inquiry rather than confrontation.

The TRC was thus anxious to assure those whom it invited that it was not concerned with findings of guilt or even with making judgements about what particular individuals or officers or organisations had done. The issue was not about putting a legal order, or any person or organisation, "on trial".[53] But these assurances, while

[53] For example, the letter sent to judges included the following paragraph: "The Commission would like to stress that as it is not the purpose of the hearing to establish guilt or hold individuals responsible, the hearing will not be of a judicial or quasi-judicial nature. The hearing is an attempt to understand the role the legal system played in contributing to the violation and/or protection of human rights and to identify institu-

sincere, proved unfounded. The atmosphere at the Hearing was more often than not confrontational and accusatory, more like a trial than an inquiry.

The stage was set for confrontation before the Hearing started. The magistrates, public servants who staffed the lower courts, and who had done most of the work of judicial administration of the apartheid laws, with one exception simply refused to make written submissions or to come to the Hearing.[54] The General Council of the Bar, the governing body for the different Bars of advocates in South Africa, nearly declined to make a written submission but in the end presented a three volume written submission and participated fully

tional changes required to prevent those abuses which occurred from happening again. We urge all judges both serving and retired to present their views as part of the process of moving forward".

Questions posed varied slightly according to the audience, but the following list of issues put to the judges is indicative of the general scope of the inquiry:

"(a) the relationship between law and justice.
(b) the principles and standards by which to evaluate the legal system;
(c) what informed judicial policy;
(d) what, if any, attempts were made by the Executive or other organisations/individuals to undermine the independence of the Judiciary;
(e) the relationship between the Judiciary and the State i.e.
  (i) the State Security Council;
  (ii) political Parties or organisations;
(f) the role of the judiciary in applying security legislation;
(g) the appointment of members of the Judiciary;
(h) the role of Commissions of Inquiry and the appointment of Judges to serve on these Commissions;
(i) the relationship between the South African Judiciary, legal profession and law schools;
(j) the exercise of judicial discretion;
(k) racial and gender discrimination in the Judiciary, legal profession and law schools;
(l) the role of other functionaries namely:
  (i) the Minister of Justice;
  (ii) the Department of Justice, including line functions and the Justice College;
  (iii) magistrates;
  (iv) Attorneys-General;
  (v) legal Profession: Bar Council, Association of Law Societies, Para-Legal Association;
  (vi) lay assessors;
  (vii) interpreters; and
  (viii) the homelands (self-governing territories and independent states).

* Recommendations on how the legal system can be transformed to reflect a human rights culture and a respect for the rule of law, and which will address the perception that justice is the privileged domain of few in our society."

[54] The Regional Court President of Pretoria, Mr G. Travers, was the exception. In the end, Travers persuaded two magistrates to make submissions, but too late for them to be heard.

in the Hearing. Some Law Faculties made written submissions, but few sent representatives to participate. And we will see that some showed complete indifference towards the work of the TRC.

Several judges did in the end make written submissions. Others indicated contempt. For example, C.F. Eloff, Judge President or most senior judge of the Transvaal Provincial Division, said that that the content of the letter of invitation to participate left him with the "impression that what you plan to do on October 1997 will be a meaningless exercise".[55] Judge David Curlewis, who enjoyed a reputation during the apartheid era as a "hanging judge" and as impervious to arguments about the need for judges to uphold the rule of law, dismissed the invitation as "three pages of waffle".[56] He then proceeded to spark a public outcry by his remarks on sentencing a serial killer to thousands of years of imprisonment. For he expressed his great regret that the death penalty is no longer available in South Africa and condemned politicians for interfering with judicial work by abolishing the death penalty, when in fact it was the Constitutional Court which, in its first decision, found the death penalty in violation of South Africa's Constitution.

No judge was willing to participate in person in the Hearing despite the best persuasive efforts of Archbishop Tutu. Their absence was the most conspicuous feature of the three days of the Hearings. Their presence was perceived to be crucial, so much so that the draft programme issued on 22 October still had them scheduled to appear on 27 October, the first day. It was their failure to appear, combined with the non-appearance or reluctance to appear of others, which set the stage for the confrontational tone of the proceedings.

That tone was cemented by the Hearing itself. Archbishop Tutu, in his opening address, excoriated the judges. Judges, he said, were faced with moral choices under apartheid and generally they had made the wrong one. They had been faced with another choice—whether to appear before the TRC, and again they had made the wrong choice. This showed, he said, that they "had not yet changed a mindset that properly belongs to the old dispensation.".[57]

Four of the five oral submissions which immediately followed his address attacked the judges for failing to be there to account for their

[55] Letter of 10 September 1997.

[56] See the report by Carmel Rickard, *Sunday Times*, 2 November 1997, p. 16.

[57] Transcript, pp. 8–9.

role. In the first, I argued that the judges of the old order should be present to answer a charge of dereliction of duty.

The second, given by Professor Lennox S. Hinds of Rutgers University on behalf of the International Association of Democratic Lawyers, put forward the case for regarding apartheid law as violating international human right standards to the point where apartheid law constituted a gross abuse of human rights. By implication, this case made the judges complicit in gross abuse of human rights, and Professor Hinds suggested, in answer to questions put by Hanif Vally, chief legal officer of the Commission who had the task of leading evidence during the Legal Hearing, that a good technical case could be made for arraigning judges on a charge of complicity in such abuse.[58]

In the third, Ms Paula McBride, a human rights activist, delivered a stinging indictment of the judiciary's role in meting out the death penalty. In the fourth, Ms Liza Key, a documentary film-maker, uncovered an unknown part of South Africa's legal history—the political biography of Dimitrio Tsafendas, assassin of Prime Minister and architect of apartheid Hendrik Verwoerd—which spoke volumes about the phenomenon of apartheid's institutionalised divide. In the fifth, four members of NADEL, the National Association of Democratic Lawyers, provided an account of the apartheid legal order as a whole in which the role of judges in sustaining the order figured prominently.

In all of these submissions, the depth of the critique of judges of the old order was matched by expressions of outrage that the judges of that order considered themselves above the TRC's process of inquiry into truth and attempts at reconciliation. And this issue did not go away. The Minister of Justice, Dullah Omar, pointedly began his oral submission by saying how pleased he was to accept the invitation to submit himself to the TRC's inquiry; even President Mandela, he said, would not be above accepting such an invitation.[59]

All oral submissions took the general form of submissions before the TRC, that is, of an oath or affirmation about the truth of one's testimony, followed by the submission, and then questions from the Commissioners, though the bulk of questions were put by Hanif Vally. The feeling of giving evidence in a court of law also no doubt contributed to the confrontational atmosphere.

[58] Transcript, pp. 47–8.

[59] Transcript, pp. 133–4.

Finally, the sense of confrontation was heightened by the nature of the submissions. Some, like those mentioned above, were deliberately confrontational, attacking judges or other officials. Some others adopted the classic pattern of perpetrators of human rights abuses—rote apologies coupled with exculpatory claims. Thus, just as in the Amnesty Hearings, the Commissioners would sometimes exhort those giving evidence to open their hearts, bare their souls.[60] Little new came to light in these submissions, except from that of the Director-General of Justice, where the officials had clearly been instructed by Minister Omar—a human rights lawyer and former detainee who had escaped one security force assassination attempt—to answer frankly any questions about their administration of security law.[61]

In addition, the Association of Law Societies—that is, of attorneys' associations—made full written submissions and participated fully, as did various groups of lawyers who have formed independent associations because of their dissatisfaction with the conservatism of the professions, most prominently NADEL, and the BLA or Black Lawyers' Association. Some "non-lawyers" made submissions. As we will see, these were among the most powerful of the Hearings. Several Attorneys-General made both written and oral submissions as did some individual practitioners and academics, a group of law students from the University of Natal, a representative of Amnesty International, and the Legal Resources Centre, the non-governmental organisation founded in the late 1970s to mount human rights challenges to apartheid legislation.

Like any trial, however, the bulk of the proceedings were in fact quite tedious. Perhaps as a result of the latitude the TRC had become used to giving victims to tell their story, the presiding Commissioners, Archbishop Tutu on day one, and Ms Yasmin Sooka on days two and three, made little effort to confine the oral submissions to the scheduled times.[62]

But there were electric moments on each day; on day one, the critique of the absent judges; on day two, the presentation by the General Council of the Bar; and on day three, the appearance of the

[60] See, for example, the Transcript, at pp. 472 and 497–8.

[61] The Department revealed the operation of an Internal Board which reviewed detentions. The officials were unable to give a satisfactory account of the workings of the Board, but significant was that some judges participated in its decisions; Transcript, pp. 607–36.

[62] And sometimes an oral submission consisted of largely irrelevant ramblings.

Attorneys-General. It was in those moments that the drama of law's relationship with justice was played out on a live stage. But before we launch into the account of the Hearing itself, it is important to raise one last question about both this work and the Hearing, one which, like the others raised so far, can be addressed fully only at the end.

6. Focusing on Judges

There is a legitimate question about both the Hearing's and my own focus on judges. After all, judges are but a small part of any legal order; indeed, they are a small part of any legal order's judicial system if we conceive such a system as including all those officials charged with making authoritative determinations of the legal rights of those subject to the law. The cutting edge of any legal order—the place where subject meets the law—is going for the most part to be in the enforcement of the law by the police and in the adjudication of disputes about the law by magistrates. For this reason, some thought that the focus on judges at the Hearing distracted the TRC's inquiry from more important issues.

However, I believe such a focus to be both inevitable and productive. Robert Cover, an American Professor of Law, showed why this is the case in his pioneering work on a group of judges in antebellum America who, despite their commitment to the abolitionist cause, almost relentlessly interpreted laws enforcing slavery in such a way as to shore up the institution of slavery.[63]

Cover pointed out that studies of the relationship between law and justice—a relationship highlighted when one studies the role of law in implementing and sustaining injustice—for the most part accepted "the perspective of the established order".[64] For such studies took the drama of the "disobedient" as exemplary of the problem—the stories of those who appeal to a "juster justice" beyond the law to justify disobedience.[65]

The disobedients, and any study which makes them exemplary of the relationship between law and justice, take the perspective of the established order because they assume that the law is what the

[63] Robert Cover, *Justice Accused: Antislavery and the Judicial Process* (New Haven, Conn.: Yale University Press, 1975).

[64] Ibid., p. 1. [65] Ibid.

powerful in that order suppose it to be. Disobedients make their moral stand on the basis of the utter injustice of the law, an injustice created by the arbitrary will of a powerful and unjust ruler. And they therefore exclude the possibility that the law is more than the static embodiment of some ruler's will, determinable (as the plain fact approach suggests) as a matter of fact.

It is important, Cover thought, that a study of law and justice canvass that excluded possibility by asking whether the law provides opportunities to do justice which rulers, no matter how powerful they are, cannot completely control. Only that possibility allows that the relationship between law and justice might be an intrinsic one, one which creates tensions within the law when the powerful use the law as an instrument of oppression.

We have already seen that the central figure in the South African legal order, President of the Constitutional Court Arthur Chaskalson, and the central figure in the TRC, Archbishop Tutu, hold the view that the relationship between law and justice is to some extent intrinsic. And, as Cover argues, it is adjudication by judges which best manifests the tensions which arise out of that intrinsic relationship when law is put in the service of injustice. For judges everywhere claim that their duty is not simply to administer the law, but to administer justice. Indeed, the oath of office which South African judges swore during apartheid stated that they would "administer justice to all persons alike without without fear, favour or prejudice, and, as the circumstances of any particular case may require, in accordance with the law and customs of the Republic of South Africa".[66]

As I pointed out in my submission to the TRC, one can adopt the view that the justice of the law mentioned in the oath is simply the conception of justice which, as a matter of fact, the powerful have used the law to implement.[67] Alternatively, one can read some significance into the word justice, for example, by noting that the oath would look rather odd if one substituted for "justice" the phrase "ideology of the powerful".

Encapsulated in these two ways of viewing the relationship between law and justice is the age-old debate in the philosophy of law between legal positivists and natural law theory. Positivists argue that the relationship between law and "juster justice" or true justice is

[66] Supreme Court Act 1959, s. 10(2)(a).
[67] Dyzenhaus Submission, p. 1.

purely contingent on political circumstance, while the natural lawyers argue that there is some intrinsic relationship. The complexity of that debate, especially in its more technical aspects, goes well beyond the confines of this book.[68]

But an important, and I would argue the principal, aspect of that debate is illuminated by a focus on the role of judges at the TRC, even though their role was confined to some written submissions. For if we are concerned with the relationship between law and justice, then, as Cover says, we cannot study that relationship without maintaining the possibility that it is an intrinsic one. The relationship has to be instrinsic if law is to provide a place where those subject to it can contest it when it is used as an instrument of brute and arbitrary power. Only if the relationship is intrinsic can law provide the basis for judges to be more than the ants whom young Andrew Zondo encountered in the trial which culminated in his judicially-ordered death.

It is not that I think that the question of the relationship between justice and the law can be settled by three days of hearings before the TRC. But just as we hope to catch intimations of the answer to that question in the predicament of abolitionist judges in northern states in antebellum America, who sent escaped slaves back to slavery under the Fugitive Slave Laws, in the trial of judges at Nuremberg, or as people around the world struggle with the idea of how to do justice during periods of transition from one political order to another, so the TRC's Legal Hearing should echo beyond South Africa's borders. The three days in October 1997 when an entire legal order was in effect put on trial in Johannesburg provide a rare opportunity to reexamine the relationship between law and justice.[69]

[68] I deal with the technical aspects of the debate more fully in *Hard Cases in Wicked Legal Systems: South African Law in the Perspective of Legal Philosophy*, n. 29 above.

[69] The Hearing took place on 27, 28, and 29 October 1997.

4. Judging the Legal Hearing

"Treason is a crime in a very special category. Where the ideas and political aspirations of those charged are part of the issue in this very strange and complex society of ours as set out at the beginning of this judgment—and given the spectrum of politics of our citizens from Black to white and from far left to far right—with their grievances and aspirations—in most cases legitimate, and the often intemperate and exaggerated language and liberally spiced with political cliches, most of these citizens just striving for a better South Africa—a charge of treason should be very carefully considered and reconsidered before it is brought before the court".

Judge Piet J. van der Walt, in the course of his judgment aquitting the "Alexandra five" of the charge of treason, Johannesburg, 1985.[96]

In the passage just quoted, the judge recognises that the crime of treason is special; it should not be used to characterise the activity of legal subjects when what they are doing is basically organising local communities on the basis of a legitimate aspiration, the aspiration to give people living in those communities some control over their lives. He also recognises that the complexity and strangeness of South African society will lead to that aspiration being expressed in the florid language of the resistance to apartheid—the language of revolution. Finally, and most important, he takes the resisters before him to be part of a larger political community, one united by a desire for a "better South Africa" even if divided on every detail about how to achieve that desire.

It has been convincingly demonstrated that the South African judges who presided over political trials in the 1970s rejected outright the last assumption, which led them in turn to reject the first two.[97] Their own main assumption was that black South Africans were not part of the same political community as white South Africans, and so it was legitimate to close off to blacks legal channels of political opposition to the South African state. From that assumption it followed that any attempt by blacks to organise political resistance to the state inherently threatened an illegal and violent

[96] Quoted in Abel, *Politics By Other Means: Law in the Struggle Against Apartheid, 1980–1994*, n. 73 above, p. 369.

[97] Lobban, *White Man's Justice: South African Political Trials in the Black Consciousness Era*, n. 55 above.

overthrow of the state, in short treason. With this assumption in place, the aspiration by blacks to achieve political control over their lives in areas of white political control is by definition illegitimate. Talking about achieving such control, or any conduct that seems directed to this end, is always but a hair's breadth away from incitement to revolutionary overthrow of the state. So Van Der Walt's views represent the beginnings of a sea change in the South African judiciary's understanding of opposition to the apartheid legal order. The idea on which he implicitly relies is that it is a perversion of justice to use the law to punish individuals who are attempting to sustain a value—the value of political community—when that value is one which the law itself is supposed to sustain.

The virtue of the Legal Hearing is that it both brought that idea to the surface and, through its own legal process, showed how law can play a role in building political community. My claim is not that the Hearing was anything close to an ideal inquiry. But it had the merit of participating in establishing an archive, as Professor Pamela Reynolds observed in her inaugural lecture at the University of Cape Town, "Truth and Youth—An Anthropologist Observes the Truth and Reconciliation Commission".[98] The presence of the archive, she says, means that the country's "raw pain" is exposed—"no-one can now deny the cruel nature of much of the past".

Reynold's lecture is a lament for the way in which the pain of the youth of South Africa—pain suffered because of both the ordinary and the extraordinary violence of apartheid—did not, perhaps could not, get fully articulated at the TRC. As she shows, that criticism of the TRC should not obscure that the archive which a TRC Hearing establishes is more than an obstacle in the way of forgetting the past. The archive is an invitation to do better; indeed, in understanding the flaws of any particular hearing, one gets a sense of how to continue the work of elaborating the archive. One can opt to treat the trauma of the past, and the problems in retelling it, as a promise.[99]

Reynold's comments are about the Victim Hearings, but they are pertinent also to the Legal Hearing. The snapshots of that Hearing which have been given here—the absence of the judges, the hubris of the advocates, the dismal record of the attorneys, the amnesia of the academics, and the display of rectitude by the Attorneys-General—

[98] I am grateful to Professor Reynolds for her permission to quote from the draft of her lecture.

[99] I owe this phrase to Scott Veitch.

are now part of an archive, and an archive has an independence and potential which escapes the control of any contributor to it. We have already seen this demonstrated in the facts of the record which the advocates presented, facts which are sometimes at odds with their own account of that record, raising questions about their role which they did not fully answer.

Particularly important is the public nature of the event, part and parcel of the TRC's commitment to transparency. The paradoxes of the apartheid legal order have been explored in several comprehensive monographs. But, in the nature of things, their audience is the legal academy, their focus is limited to particular institutions or to a particular period, and they were written at a time when the future was too uncertain for their authors to attempt to link exploration of the past to future illumination.

In contrast, the Hearing was public both in its media coverage and in the sense that it addressed all South Africans. It also raised questions about the role of all important legal actors in a way designed to link the past to the future. The fact that the range of defences enlisted by many of those who appeared, or who declined to appear, got in the way of discussion cannot detract from the fact that at the same time they initiated a discussion. Indeed, the very fact that these defences were raised should prompt and then aid a discussion of what sort of institutional change is required in a process of reconstructive justice, one which seeks to establish democracy in South Africa.

There is little doubt in my mind that without the Hearing such issues would not have been so firmly placed on the public political agenda. In *Divided Memory: The Nazi Past in the Two Germanys*,[100] Jeffrey Herf shows how conservative forces in post-war West Germany deliberately weakened memory of the Holocaust and delayed bringing Nazis to justice (thus eventually letting them escape justice) because of the perception that too much memory and justice might produce a right-wing revolt that would destroy a "still fragile democracy".[101] In contrast, in East Germany, memory of the Holocaust was suppressed in order to portray the past as a simple battle between good and evil in which the good—communism—had triumphed over the bad—capitalism/fascism. Indeed, this suppres-

[100] Jeffrey Herf, *Divided Memory: The Nazi Past in the Two Germanys* (Cambridge, Mass.: Harvard University Press, 1997).

[101] Ibid., pp. 6–7.

sion of memory allowed the East German government to make the small Jewish community that survived in East Germany a convenient scapegoat for the sins of cosmopolitan international capitalism.

Herf points out that in order to suppress memory or to attempt to create a weak public memory, those who seek to control memory must themselves remember.[102] Much of Herf's book is devoted to exploring the attempts by individuals and groups within West and East Germany to resist official suppression of memory. In the East, the attempts backfired, resulting in the silencing of those who wanted to remember or even in increased anti-semitism. In the West, the attempts eventually gained ground, largely through the efforts of the Social Democratic Party. Of great significance here is Chancellor Willy Brandt's gesture in the late 1960s, when he knelt at the memorial for Jews killed in the Warsaw Ghetto uprising to symbolise public acknowledgment of and repentance for German war crimes.[103]

Herf argues that the restoration of memory in West Germany was not a threat to a fragile democracy in the process of making a democratic state. Indeed, his conclusion seems to be that the delay in restoration of memory in the West together with the suppression of memory in the East is what renders the attempt to democratise the East after reunification so problematic.[104]

Similarly, in a work which focuses on the role of law in creating collective, public memory, Mark Osiel argues that public memory of past wrongdoing has to be established for a transition to democracy to be successful.[105] However, in his examination of several important attempts to use the law in such a way, the Nuremberg Trials, the Tokyo Trials, the Eichmann prosecution and more recent trials in France and Argentina, he suggests that the main mechanism of the criminal law, the trial, is probably not best suited to this task.[106] The

[102] Here he quotes (ibid., p. 10) from Theodor Adorno's classic essay, "What does coming to terms with the past mean?"; for the relevant passage, see the opening quote to Chapter 3.

[103] One can contrast here former President P.W. Botha's refusal to appear before the TRC on the ground that an Afrikaner kneels only before God. A particularly repugnant attempt to justify Botha's stance can be found in Rian Malan, "Crises Show Up the Demise of the Rainbow Nation", *Business Day*, 21 April 1998, and see also the critique by Max du Preez, "'Boers' Tired of Reactionism in their Name", *Business Day*, 24 April 1998.

[104] Herf, *Divided Memory: The Nazi Past in the Two Germanys*, n. 100 above, p. 394.

[105] Mark Osiel, *Mass Atrocity, Collective Memory, and the Law* (New Brunswick, New Jersey: Transaction Publishers, 1997).

[106] See on the same issue, Jennifer J. Llewellyn and Robert Howse, "Institutions for Restorative Justice: The South African Truth and Reconciliation Commission as a model for dealing with conflicts of the past", unpublished paper.

risk he finds is that "legal concepts and doctrines" often lose "their normal connection to the underlying moral and political issues at stake". His solution is to "widen the spatial and temporal frame of courtroom storytelling in ways that allow litigants to flesh out their competing interpretations of recent history, and to argue these before an attentive public. Only in this way can the debate within the courtroom be made to resonate with the public debate beyond the courtroom walls".[107]

I suggested in Chapter 1 that at the Legal Hearing the apartheid legal order was put on trial—law found itself before a tribunal. But the legal order was put on trial in order to assist in the transition from apartheid to democracy, in order to help root and nurture a fragile plant. Moreover, the legal order was put on trial before a democratically constituted body, which sought to engage the most important legal actors in both the old and the new orders in a constructive debate, one which would resonate outside of the Hearing in the way Osiel suggests.

The public archive which the Legal Hearing established is in place and this book aspires to be part of its work—the work of, as the General Council of the Bar put it, the struggle against forgetting. In particular, the Hearing showed that we should not forget that questions about the relationship between law and justice are inherently political but at the same time morally loaded. As Richard Abel has argued, the story of law and apartheid tells us that law is "politics by other means" but those means do make a difference.[108] Government under the rule of law amounts to politics under the constraints of legal order, constraints which impose conditions of publicity, obligations to justify official decisions, and a general obligation on judges to find a role for themselves as the enforcers of legality, not just of positive law. Hence, Abel warns against the false conclusion that law "either makes all the difference or no difference at all".[109]

Law, we have seen, can make a difference, even under the very unpromising conditions of apartheid South Africa, and this goes a long way to show that legal order or legality places constraints on the powerful which at bottom are political and moral constraints—the

[107] Osiel, *Mass Atrocity, Collective Memory, and the Law*, n. 105 above, p. 296.

[108] Abel, *Politics by Other Means: Law in the Struggle Against Apartheid, 1980–1994*, n. 73 above.

[109] Ibid., p. 549.

constraints of commitment to a community of free and equal citizens. Of course, there will be many ways of understanding that commitment and legal actors will have to take seriously the idea that they have an obligation of fidelity to law before the commitment has effects on legal practice. But at least one should rule out any legal theory or ideology which attempts to reduce our understanding of law to what a plain fact approach determines to be the content of the commands of the powerful.[110] For law is better understood as the expression of a relationship of reciprocity between ruler and ruled,[111] one in which the rulers commit themselves not only to being accountable to law, but to making law before which all subjects are equal. That in turn suggests that the rule of law is best understood as the institutional expression of democracy.

And here, or so I have argued, we have the explanation of why some judges and some lawyers were able, despite apartheid, to provide the basis for a new democratic legal order.

[110] And thus to the extent that various versions of legal positivism either require this understanding of law, or invite it, or even fail to supply a good reason for rejecting it, we have reason to opt for an anti-positivist theory of law. Similar conclusions about legal positivism are suggested by Mark Osiel, *Mass Atrocity, Collective Memory, and the Law*, n. 105 above, pp. 299–300, and by Carlos Santiago Nino, *Radical Evil on Trial* (New Haven, Conn.: Yale University Press, 1996), pp. 149–56.

[111] See Lon L. Fuller, *The Morality of Law* (New Haven, Conn.: Yale University Press, rev. edn. 1969).

[19]

Are There Systemic Ethics Issues in Dispute System Design? And What We Should [Not] Do About It: Lessons from International and Domestic Fronts

Carrie Menkel-Meadow*

I. Introduction: Is Dispute System Design ("DSD") a Professional Field Ready for a Code of Ethics?

The process by which new fields of knowledge and practice are defined, developed, and demarcated from other fields has long been described by sociologists of the professions.[1] As new competencies are created and studied, the progression from initial theorization, to the development of practice protocols, training and education, attempts at credentialing, and "monopolization of expertise," to the development of "best practices" and ethics codes, marches on to the eventual state of exclusionary practices, such as degree requirements, licensing, and formal professional discipline. All the basic professions (medicine, law and clergy) have gone through this process and many other professions exist in different stages of this inexorable march toward "professionalization"—e.g. nursing, social work, psychological counseling, building contracting, hairstyling, and paraprofessionals in medicine and law. Recent work by an interdisciplinary team of scholars, including Howard Gardner (education and cognitive psychology), Mihaly Csizkszentmihalyi (social psychology) and William Damon (developmental psychology and education) has explored how

---

* A.B. Chettle Jr. Professor of Law, Dispute Resolution and Civil Procedure, Georgetown University Law Center. Thanks to the Harvard Negotiation Law Review for hosting this stimulating symposium and to Robert Bordone, Howard Gadlin, Christopher Honeyman, and Peter Reilly for helpful comments and suggestions.

1. *See, e.g.*, Andrew D. Abbott, The System of Professions: An Essay on the Division of Expert Labor (1988); Eliot Friedson, Professional Powers: A Study of the Institutionalization of Formal Knowledge (1986); Margali S. Larson, The Rise of Professionalism: A Sociological Analysis (1979).

professions attempt to constitute "cultures" of professional excellence, using both internal and external social and ethical commitments.[2] Whether a field or discipline requires ethical standards to be considered a profession remains an issue of some debate due to its tendency to "exclude" some professions or to mark them as separate from important lay expertise and service.

The field of conflict resolution, broadly defined, is currently at what I would describe as a "mid-point" in this quest for formal recognition as a profession. There are competing theories of practice in each of the constituent fields. Mediators advocate evaluative, facilitative,[3] transformative,[4] understanding,[5] narrative,[6] and eclectic models of mediation.[7] Negotiators contrast different models or approaches to negotiation, pitting adversarial-competitive models "against" collaborative and problem-solving models, with still others suggesting negotiation is more often "mixed" in its conceptual goals and behaviors (creating and claiming value).[8] Another set of dispute resolution professionals offer yet a different set of practices for arbitration,[9] where there are already some relatively established practice protocols. The larger, more inclusive, field of conflict resolution has

2. *See also* HOWARD GARDNER ET AL., GOOD WORK: WHEN EXCELLENCE AND ETHICS MEET (2001) (exploring and contrasting the internal ethics and integrity of the profession of geneticist-scientist with the more externally directed profession of journalism).

3. *See* Leonard Riskin, *The New Old Grid and the New New Grid System*, 79 NOTRE DAME L. REV. 1, 3 (2003).

4. *See generally* ROBERT A. BARUCH BUSH & JOSEPH P. FOLGER, THE PROMISE OF MEDIATION: RESPONDING TO CONFLICT THROUGH EMPOWERMENT AND RECOGNITION (2nd Ed. 2006).

5. *See generally* GARY FRIEDMAN & JACK HIMMELSTEIN, CHALLENGING CONFLICT: MEDIATION THROUGH UNDERSTANDING (2008).

6. *See generally* JOHN WINSLADE, GERALD D. MONK & GERALD MONK, NARRATIVE MEDIATION: A NEW APPROACH TO CONFLICT RESOLUTION (2000).

7. *See generally* CARRIE MENKEL-MEADOW ET AL., MEDIATION: PRACTICE, POLICY AND ETHICS (2006) (summarizing presentations of different models of mediation); Carrie Menkel-Meadow, *The Many Ways of Mediation: The Transformation of Traditions, Ideologies, Paradigms and Practices*, 11 NEGOT. J. 217 (1995); DEBORAH KOLB ET AL., WHEN TALK WORKS-PROFILES OF MEDIATORS (1994).

8. *See* Carrie Menkel-Meadow, *Toward Another View of Legal Negotiation: The Structure of Problem Solving*, 31 UCLA L. REV. 754 (1984); Carrie Menkel-Meadow, *Why Hasn't the World Gotten to Yes?*, 22 NEGOT. J. 485 (2006).

9. *See, e.g.*, Carrie Menkel-Meadow, *Are Cross-Cultural Ethics Standards Possible or Desirable in International Arbitration?*, *in* MÉLANGES EN L-HONNEUR DE PIERRE TERCIER (P. Gauch, F. Werro & P. Pichonnaz, ed. 2008).

developed more or less agreed-to knowledge bases,[10] and a robust effort to develop codes, standards of practices and ethical rules.[11]

A few states have begun processes to require specific numbers of training hours and some form of certification, especially with respect to mediation within the courts.[12] Recently, the American Bar Association's Section on Dispute Resolution published a report from its Task Force on Improving the Quality of Mediation[13] that addressed questions of quality, ethics, subject matter expertise, and other issues related to the choice and use of mediators. In a similar vein, a new international group called the International Mediation Institute, based in The Hague, The Netherlands, is also engaged in a project to develop standards of Competency in International Mediation,

10. As evidenced by the growing number of both school and degree programs, and professionally based courses and texts in all fields of dispute resolution – arbitration, mediation, negotiation, facilitation and consensus building, as well as dispute system design, *see, e.g.*, CATHY A. COSTANTINO & CHRISTINA S. MERCHANT, DESIGNING CONFLICT MANAGEMENT SYSTEMS: A GUIDE TO CREATING HEALTHY AND PRODUCTIVE ORGANIZATIONS (1995); WILLIAM L. URY ET AL., GETTING DISPUTES RESOLVED: DESIGNING SYSTEMS TO CUT THE COSTS OF CONFLICT (1988); LAWRENCE SUSSKIND ET AL., THE CONSENSUS BUILDING HANDBOOK (1999); LAWRENCE SUSSKIND & DAVID CRUICKSHANK, BREAKING ROBERT'S RULES (2006); MICHAEL L. MOFFITT & ROBERT C. BORDONE, eds., THE HANDBOOK OF DISPUTE RESOLUTION (2005); MENKEL-MEADOW ET AL., DISPUTE RESOLUTION: BEYOND THE ADVERSARY MODEL (2005); ANDREA SCHNEIDER & CHRISTOPHER HONEYMAN eds., THE NEGOTIATOR'S FIELDBOOK (2006).

11. *See, e.g.*, ABA LITIGATION SECTION, STANDARDS FOR NEGOTIATION OF SETTLEMENTS (2005); AAA ETHICS RULES FOR COMMERCIAL ARBITRATORS (2006); AAA-ABA-ACR STANDARDS FOR MEDIATORS (2005); GEORGETOWN-CPR PROPOSED MODEL RULE FOR LAWYERS AS THIRD PARTY NEUTRALS AND GEORGETOWN-CPR PRINCIPLES FOR ADR PROVIDER ORGANIZATIONS (2001), *available at* http://www.cpradr.org/Portals/0/final-Provider.pdf (last visited May 20, 2009). SPIDR GUIDELINES FOR THE DESIGN OF INTEGRATED CONFLICT MANAGEMENT SYSTEMS WITHIN ORGANIZATIONS (2001). For related efforts, *see also* Peter Adler, A Credo for Facilitators, mediate.com, July 24, 2008 and Directive 2008/52/EC on certain aspects of mediation in civil and commercial matters, May 21, 2008.

12. *See, e.g.*, FLORIDA, MASSACHUSETTS, CALIFORNIA, DEVELOPMENT OF QUALIFICATION STANDARDS FOR MEDIATORS SERVING IN COURT-CONNECTED MEDIATION PROGRAMS FOR CIVIL CASES (California Judicial Council, Notice for Public Comment by July 7, 2008).

13. ABA SECTION OF DISPUTE RESOLUTION, TASK FORCE ON IMPROVING THE QUALITY OF MEDIATION (April 2006-March 2007) Final Report (convened to consider a national credential in mediation, concluding that market conditions made it not feasible and suggesting other indicators of mediator quality to be further studied).

including a specialized Inter-Cultural Mediator Competency Certification.[14] Similar optional and private, *i.e.* not state sanctioned, certification programs exist for arbitrators.[15]

Even the relatively newest forms of dispute resolution practice have begun developing professional associations and discussion of appropriate standards, practice protocols and ethics, such as IAP2[16] (the International Association of Public Participation, which includes mediators, public policy facilitators, and consensus builders) and the Deliberative Democracy Network.[17]

As an ethicist, scholar, and practitioner, I have participated in a variety of efforts to specify the professional content of work and ethics standards for many of these dispute resolution professions. As Chair of the Georgetown-CPR Commission on Ethics and Standards of Alternative Dispute Resolution ("ADR"), I helped convene a diverse commission of practitioners and consumers to draft suggested ethical standards for lawyers acting as third party neutrals in a variety of roles, and worked with a committee to specify standards and principles for organizations providing ADR services.[18]

As a member of the self-appointed "Senior Mediators Group," I participated in an effort to develop a "credo" for mediators, suggesting, among other values, that mediators, particularly in public policy disputes should:

1. Do no harm;
2. Involve a broad array of interested and affected stakeholders;
3. Facilitate maximum opportunities for participation and voice of participants;

---

14. *See* Draft Competency Certification Scheme, www.IMImediation.org (last visited Mar. 12, 2009).

15. *See* The Chartered Institute of Arbitrators, www.arbitrators.org (offering courses and credentials, including degrees, etc. in arbitration and other dispute resolution services, "seeking to set global standards for professional education in dispute resolution") (last visisted Mar. 12, 2009).

16. See the homepage for the International Association for Public Participation, http://www.iap2.org (last visited Mar. 14, 2009) for organization's goals, training programs and information about facilitated public policy mediation, deliberation and decision making.

17. *See, e.g.*, The Deliberative Democracy Consortium, http://www.deliberative-democracy.net (last visited Mar. 14, 2009); The Collaborative Policy Center, http://www.csus.edu/ccp (last visited Mar. 14, 2009); The Policy Consensus Initiative, http://www.policyconsensus.org (last visited Mar. 14, 2009).

18. *See generally* CPR PRINCIPLES FOR ADR PROVIDER ORGANIZATIONS, *supra* note 11.

4. Encourage participants to develop their own agreements on process and ground rules;
5. Encourage participants to develop (and understand the significance of) decision rules and voting procedures;
6. Encourage participant recognition of opportunities for joint, and not only, individual, gain;
7. Require that parties express and explain their reasons and justifications for views, arguments, proposals and needs;
8. Provide an atmosphere of fair hearing and respect for all participants;
9. Seek to explore creative and tailored decisions and solutions to problems, issues and disputes;
10. Be impartial, unbiased and "clean" (with adequate disclosures) with respect to their relationships to parties;
11. Facilitate open dialogue, discussion and deliberation between and among parties;
12. Encourage and educate for enhanced capacity of parties to participate in decision making that affects them;
13. Probe the practical implementation issues and consequences of all agreements reached;
14. Monitor the parties' process and decision rules, consistent with whatever law, rules or other governing materials are applicable to the context;
15. Ensure an atmosphere of respectful awareness and sensitivities to differences, whether substantive, institutional, social and cultural;
16. Avoid presiding over any outcomes which would be "unfair" or "unjust" to participants or those affected by decision making of the parties.[19]

And now, as one of the newest strands of this new profession, Dispute System Design, begins to consolidate definitions, skills, techniques, knowledge, and practices, the question is raised: Should there be a separate set of ethics standards or guidelines for those who design "systems" of dispute resolution for institutions or other parties with recurring disputes and internal processes for their resolution?

19. *See* Carrie Menkel-Meadow, *The Lawyer as Consensus Builder: Ethics for a New Practice*, 70 Tenn. L. Rev. 63, 105-10 (2002). This "credo" was never formally endorsed by any group, including the self-appointed Senior Mediators Group at which it was first discussed.

In this essay I explore some of the issues implicated in the question of whether DSD should develop its own Code or Credo of Ethics, specifying good and bad practices of those professionals who design systems of dispute resolution in recurring or aggregated conflict situations. Defining what an ethics code is or should be is problematic enough. Should an ethics code serve the consumers of services or the providers of services (they will be constructed differently depending on who the audience is)? At what level of aspiration or code should rules be designed? For many years the American Bar Association Code of Professional Responsibility for Lawyers ("the CPR") contained three levels: Canons (aspirational statements of good practices), Disciplinary Rules (specific rules for which lawyers could be sanctioned and disciplined by appropriate ethics bodies), and Ethical Considerations (fuller textual commentary designed to explicate the meaning of rules and good practices with no disciplinary bite). When the CPR was changed to the Model Rules of Professional Conduct in 1983, the form changed to "simple" blackletter rules with accompanying Comments to explicate the rules (in part because many thought the aspirational canons and ethical considerations were hardly observed).

Does drafting ethical "rules" cut with too blunt a knife — opposing what is prohibited or permitted in simplistic and binary terms for discipline that is contrary to the more nuanced form of judgment that most professionals must exercise to behave well or with due consideration of situations that do not fall into easy black and white categories? Should ethics codes aim high for encouragement ("best practices"), the mean or "norm" of practice ("good practices"), or for the bottom or bad practices that should be prohibited, condemned and disciplined ("worst practices")? When is ethical practice the same as effective practice? When does practice become so poor it raises issues of ethics? Is malpractice an ethics matter?

Those who perform dispute system design services come from several different constituent professions, including law, city and urban planning,[20] social work, psychology, political science, journalism,[21] and those who are newly educated in formal degree programs

20. *See, e.g.*, JOHN FORESTER, THE DELIBERATIVE PRACTITIONER: ENCOURAGING PARTICIPATORY PLANNING PROCESSES (2001).

21. Some of the eclectic founders of this field come from a wide variety of backgrounds including John Marks of Search for Common Ground who began in the State Department, was a journalist and now designs peace seeking programs through media and other interventions and Patrick Phear who became a mediator after a career as a dentist (is resolving conflicts better/easier than pulling teeth?).

in conflict resolution[22] or self-educated facilitators. So, one important preliminary issue is what self-constituted group could effectively and legitimately develop the content of such ethical standards? And, perhaps even more problematically, what enforcement of such standards could there be without an underlying professional organization or structure? Each of the above mentioned fields and professions has its own set of professional standards, or as some would say, the values of craft or calling that might be compromised or diluted by a more eclectically formed field. What are the "core values" of a dispute system designer?

Furthermore, given the wide range of activities that could be included in any definition of system design (developing procedures and processes for resolving or handling internal organizational conflicts, settling and paying claims in adversarial mass legal actions (e.g. consumer, employment, or torts[23]), mass human rights violations,[24] governmental and citizen disputes (e.g. negotiated rule-making or reg-neg,)[25] peace seeking or peacekeeping in on-going or post-conflict situations among nations, ethnic, religious or other cultural groups, or facilitating competing groups in seeking good political outcomes, such as in the field now denominated "deliberative democracy"),[26] is it possible to develop a general enough set of standards of good practices that will provide guidance in a field characterized by many different contexts and locations of use?

Finally, as the work we have discussed includes both domestic, and multi-national and international forms of dispute system design,

---

22. *See* George Mason University Institute for Conflict Analysis and Resolution, http://icar.gmu.edu/ (last visited Mar. 14, 2009) which offers both masters and PhD degree programs; Other universities also offer degree programs in conflict management and related fields, both as separate degree programs and as elements, specialization or certificates within other programs. *See, e.g.*, American Association of Law Schools, Section of Alternative Dispute Resolution, Programs in Conflict Resolution; Association of Conflict Resolution, Programs in Conflict Resolution.

23. Francis McGovern, *Dispute System Design: The United Nations Compensation Commission*, 14 HARV. NEGOT. L. REV. 171 (2009); KENNETH FEINBERG, WHAT IS LIFE WORTH? (Public Affairs 2006).

24. See Andrea Schneider, *The Intersection of Dispute Systems Design and Transitional Justice*, 14 HARV. NEGOT. L. REV. 289 (2009).

25. Philip Harter, *Negotiating Regulations: A Cure for the Malaise*, 71 Geo. L. J 1 (1982); Susskind, et.al, *supra* note 10; Jody Freeman, *Collaborative Governance in the Administrative State*, 45 UCLA L. Rev. 1 (1997).

26. JAMES BOHMAN, PUBLIC DELIBERATION: PLURALISM, COMPLEXITY AND DEMOCRACY (MIT Press 1996); DELIBERATIVE DEMOCRACY (Jon Elster, ed., 1998); Carrie Menkel-Meadow, *The Lawyer's Role(s) in Deliberative Democracy*, 5 Nev. L.J. 347 (2004-2005); Amy J. Cohen, *Negotiation Meet New Governance: Interests, Skills and Selves*, 33 Law & Soc. Inquiry 503 (2008).

an important question is whether ethics or standards can be described and enforced across cultural and political boundaries and jurisdictions (what ethicists have labeled the universality vs. particularity problem). As I will more fully explore below, recent work on "ethics" in good works in international economic and humanitarian aid is raising similar questions about how transborder, transdisciplinary, well-intentioned work can be monitored and scrutinized for ensuring best possible outcomes and disciplining of bad acts and bad effects.[27]

I will state my views at the outset and then explore, with examples, and my own analysis, why even though we clearly have ethical *issues* to consider and deal with in this nascent field, at this point in time I still think it is premature to draft a separate *ethics code* for our field. Since I have long advocated for separate ethics codes for mediators and arbitrators[28] (including in international settings[29]), I will have to explain why dispute system design is different or, in my view, "not quite ready for prime-time" in terms of ethics regulation.

On the other hand, just because I do not think the field of DSD is ready for a formal ethics code, does not mean that I do not see some very important ethics issues in the field. I hope this essay will contribute to an on-going discussion of those issues so that in time, after deliberation on some of the more controversial issues, we might be able to begin to specify our core ethical principles.[30]

---

27. *See, e.g.*, Ethics and International Affairs: Extent & Limits (Jean-Marc Coicaud & Daniel Warner eds., 2001) (exploring international ethics issues from a traditional (statist), analytic (universality-cosmopolitan vs. particularity) and critical perspective, with a focus on both principles and institutions needed for international ethics in diplomacy, war, foreign aid, etc.)

28. *See e.g.*, Carrie Menkel-Meadow, *The Silences of the Restatement of the Law Governing Lawyers: Lawyering as Only Adversary Practice*, 10 Geo. J. Legal Ethics 631 (1996-1997); Carrie Menkel-Meadow, *Ethics in Alternative Dispute Resolution: New Issues, No Answers From the Adversary Conception of Lawyers' Responsibilities*, 38 S. Tex. L. Rev. 407 (1997); Carrie Menkel-Meadow, *Ethics and Professionalism in Non-Adversarial Lawyering*, 27 Fla. St. U. L. Rev. 153 (1999-2000); Carrie Menkel-Meadow, *The Limits of Adversarial Ethics*, in Ethics in Practice (Deborah L. Rhode ed., 2000).

29. Menkel-Meadow, *supra* note 9, at 18-22.

30. I can't resist at this point describing my own naiveté when I set about some 15 years ago to delineate what I thought were "core" and uncontroversial ethical issues in mediation, including conflicts of interests, fees, etc. *See* Menkel-Meadow, *Professional Responsibility for Third Party Neutrals*, 11 (9) Alternatives (Sept. 1993); *see also* Menkel-Meadow, *Ethics in ADR: The Many "Cs" of Professional Responsibility and Dispute Resolution*, 28 Fordham Urb. L.J. 979 (2000-2001). What turned up instead was a maelstrom of controversy and disagreement about downstream/upstream conflicts of interests in law practice and mediation and arbitration, and whether fees

First, we must identify the method by which we should develop ethical reasoning in DSD: either *inductively,* what the ethical problems are or might be (reasoning from examples and cases presented with ethical dilemmas) or *deductively* determine what core principles our field should be expressing, which should then be applied to particular cases. Then we will have to specify rules, standards, principles, and the organizational or institutional apparatus for enforcement of those standards. Pending clear enforcement mechanisms, we must also consider what should happen in this "interim" period of discussion and debate, before codes and rules are framed, but while problematic activities are still occurring. Are "DSDers" subject to the professional codes of their professions of origin for their acts as DSDers?[31]

II. The Inductive Method of Ethics: Some Examples of Questionable Practices and Issues in DSD

The inquiry of whether ethics rules or standards should be promulgated for the new field of DSD stems from its use and problems that have already been exposed. In this section, I will consider and illustrate some examples of core ethical dilemmas and issues that arise in the use of a professional to design a system of

could be contingent, paid by one party only, or a third party, or waived for some parties, but not all. *See e.g.*, Carrie Menkel-Meadow, *When Dispute Resolution Begets Disputes of Its Own: Conflicts Among Dispute Resolution Professionals*, 44 UCLA L. Rev. 1871 (1997); Carrie Menkel-Meadow, *Ethics in ADR Representation: A Roadmap of Critical Issues*, 4(2) Disp. Res. Mag. 3 (1997). As ADR practice has both matured and ventured into new forms and locations, the "ethics" of particular practices continues to evolve, so my basic point is that a new field, like DSD, derived from ADR, needs some "habitus" or common routines and enough experience (Pierre Bourdieu, Outline of a Theory of Practice, 1977) of practice, before we can "codify" anything. This does not mean, of course, that we can't "know it when we see it" (bad conduct, worthy of some condemnation, apologies to Justice Stewart, concurring opinion in Jacobellis v. Ohio, 378 U.S. 184, (1964)).

31. For many years, in the absence of special ethical rules and codes for mediators and arbitrators, this question has been asked about lawyers serving in those capacities. There are now such ethical codes for mediators and arbitrators but relatively little enforcement. Lawyers can be disciplined for any act which would constitute professional misconduct, regardless of whether the act is formally performed as a lawyer. *See* Model Rules of Prof'l Conduct R. 8.4 (2009). (Thus, real estate, sports, entertainment or other agents who have law degrees and licenses can lose their legal license for deceptions or lies committed while serving as agents. Recall that both Presidents Nixon and Clinton were disbarred for acts of deception while they were President of the United States.).

dispute resolution for a wide variety of different clients, organizations and causes.[32]

A. *For What Purpose Are We Designing a Dispute Resolution System?*

Is DSD a "neutral" activity? Consider the following: A major cultural institution seeks a DSD professional to design a new internal grievance system for its employees. Some of the employees are unionized (security guards and other low wage employees) and others (mid-wage and more professional workers are not). After several information gathering sessions with institutional managers, it becomes clear that one of the intended purposes of designing an internal employment conflict system is to marginalize and make unpopular the union's contractual grievance system (usually utilizing some form of arbitration) and to structure an environment in which union support is eroded.

Is this a purpose a DSD professional should facilitate with her expertise? What, if like me, the DSD professional was a former labor and employment lawyer particularly concerned about employee choice, rights of collective bargaining and due process? When, in this case, I asked that union stewards and employee representatives become part of an internal planning committee for the internal grievance system design process, it became clear that management was not interested in encouraging multilevel participation and preferred, instead, a top-down designed system.

What should a DSD professional do? I withdrew from this particular work, suggesting a few other names of professionals whom the institution could consult, and some reading materials. I suspect—but do not know—that many of the people I offered in referral would have reactions similar to mine. Consider how many mediators, facilitators and other ADR professionals of the first generation also have employment, labor, civil rights and anti-discrimination backgrounds. I imagine that at some point another DSD professional who would do the work would be found.[33]

---

32. A disclaimer – all examples are taken from my own practice (with names of clients changed or concealed to protect both confidentiality and the "guilty"). Some examples are in the public domain.

33. One reader of this paper suggested that the initial commitments and professions of origin of the first generation of dispute system designers might be particularly important in situations like this. For example, the former labor and discrimination lawyer, former divorce lawyer, former social worker or city planner might have commitments to social justice that a "deracinated" or specifically trained dispute system designer might not. On the question of whether dispute resolution

In another example, discussed more fully below, I report on an internal dispute resolution system for employees that was clearly designed to discourage employees from filing any formal employment litigation claims or charges (a common and more or less legitimate purpose) but one which can be used to have an "*in terroram*" effect on employees with potentially legitimate claims. In one matter with which I am familiar, a multi-national corporation used its domestically created employment dispute system to give workers outside of the United States the perception that they had grievance and conflict resolution rights, which appeared generous because domestic employment laws do not necessarily apply abroad.[34] But, in fact, the employer used the system to deflect employment disputes and litigation, and failed to enforce its own procedures and outcomes.

Who is ethically responsible for such design? The original designers of the domestic employee grievance system? Or, only those who implement and transfer its use from one arena to another?

When DSD professionals, lawyers, or other professionals[35] do not feel ethically comfortable with the uses to which their services will be put, they can usually withdraw or reject a particular assignment.[36]

---

professionals in general should be neutral, see BERNARD MAYER, BEYOND NEUTRALITY: CONFRONTING THE CRISIS IN CONFLICT RESOLUTION (2004).

34. In EEOC v. Arabian American Oil Co., 499 U.S. 244 (1991), the United States Supreme Court held that Title VII prohibiting discrimination in employment did not apply outside of the United States. This decision was subsequently reversed by Congressional action. Civil Rights Act of 1991, Pub. L. No. 102-166, § 109, 105 Stat. 1071 (1991). However, in my experience as a mediator of such cases, many employees do not think that they have any American legal rights for work performed outside of the United States. In general, courts will look to Congressional intent for the decision about whether a particular statutory scheme is intended to have extraterritorial effect, and many domestic labor and employment protections have been held not to apply abroad. *Cf.* O'Mahony v. Accenture Ltd., 2008 WL 344710 (S.D.N.Y. 2008).

35. As I write this, an ethics issue in the field of court language translation and interpretation has erupted. A certified U.S. federal court translator of twenty-three years broke confidentiality to denounce the U.S. Customs and Immigration Service raids on a meat-packing plant in Iowa which, in his view, violated basic human rights. In a powerful essay and a series of interviews, Dr. Erik Camayd-Freixas has defended his decision to break neutrality and go public when he felt a "conflict of interest" because his translating services were being used to wrongfully convict undocumented workers of identity theft. *See* Julia Preston, *An Interpreter Speaking Up for Migrants*, N.Y. TIMES, July 7, 2008, at 1; Erik Camayd-Freixas, Interpreting after the Largest ICE Raid in US History (June 13, 2008) (unpublished manuscript, on file with the author). I also defended Professor Camayd's actions. *See Aqui y Ahora* (Univision television broadcast, July 22, 2008).

36. This is in contrast, for example, to the British "cab rank" rule which does not entitle British barristers to turn down a "brief," but which they do manage to control and manipulate through other means. *See* Peter Tague, Criminal Defense in the U.K. (unpublished manuscript, on file with the author).

Refusing to work, withdrawing on principle or ethical objections, and referring others to do the work are somewhat analogous to the "noisy withdrawal" problem faced by lawyers who learn that clients are engaged in unlawful or unethical behavior and seek to withdraw without violating client confidences.[37]

B. *Selection of the DSD Professional: Serving Few or Many?*

As the above examples illustrate, the DSD professional usually serves an institutional client. When should a DSD professional engage in due diligence to determine who seeks the dispute system design and for what purpose, particularly, where, as above, there is some evidence of conflicting interests within the organization? Consider this next example: I am often engaged, as a member of the Association of American Law School Resource Corps,[38] to facilitate and organize strategic planning events for law schools. Usually the Dean of the school is the contact person, but our protocol is that Resource Corps facilitators communicate privately with virtually all faculty members, senior administrative staff, and occasionally, some students before convening meetings and planning the work. Sometimes the request for facilitation may come from a faculty planning committee or the request might be initiated by a particular interest group on the faculty. What should a DSD professional do when it becomes clear, either before, or during the facilitation, planning, or structuring of the process, that a particular interest group is using the process for its own ends?[39]

37. *See, e.g.*, Geoffrey Hazard, *The Duty or Option of Silence*, 23 LAW & SOC. INQUIRY 339 (1998); William H. Simon, *The Kaye Scholer Affair: The Lawyer's Duty of Candor and the Bar's Temptation of Evasion and Apology*, 23 LAW & SOC. INQUIRY 243 (1998).

38. The AALS Resource Corps consists of a group of about twenty legal educators who have been specifically trained to conduct strategic planning and other organizational retreats and conflict resolution programs for "developing the capacity for collegial deliberation and decision-making" in law schools. We perform our work without fees. *See* AALS Resource Corps Resources Page, http://www.aals.org/resources_resourcecorps.php (last visited Mar. 10, 2009). Some of us (and others not part of this group) are also engaged, for fees, to perform similar functions for law schools or universities who seek particular expertise outside of the Resource Corps. *See, e.g.*, Report of Center for Collaborative Governance, California State University at Sacramento (2008) (on file with author).

39. In several cases in which some of us have worked, it has become clear that one faculty group organized such planning events in order to expose decanal mismanagement or other negative internal and private events in order to provoke a crisis or effectuate a change of leadership. I am familiar with at least one case in which this strategy was successful. The facilitator became the unknowing "tool" of a well organized and legitimated (through faculty committee structure) faculty faction.

Once again, although the goal of this work may be to act "neutrally" or to serve "the organization's best interest," such overarching principles may be difficult to observe when choices must be made (specific interventions, exposure of secret or private meetings or plans, advice for leaders or managers, withdrawals of service), particularly in cases where the DSD professional may be *manipulated*, either by management, or the representatives of the organization who have selected him. Obviously, good practice and due diligence suggest that any DSD professional should undertake preliminary inquiries about the organization, its constituents, and the reasons DSD is being sought, but in some cases, such issues may not emerge until the consultation has begun or, where selection as a DSD professional is competitive, candidates may not fully scrutinize or investigate those who are hiring them.

C. *Professional Responsibilities of the DSD Professional*

There are a host of issues and ethical dilemmas that confront the DSD professional before, during, and after engagement in dispute system design. For example, should the DSD professional have particular subject matter, as well as process, expertise when undertaking a matter? Increasingly, large corporations, universities, hospitals, research facilities, and government departments are utilizing Ombuds or Ethics Officers to develop internal complaint, grievance and justice systems of various sorts. In situations where the organization's mission (*e.g.* science, technology, religion) is highly specialized, should the DSD professional self-select away from that which he does not know? Or is the DSD professional, like many lawyers, a generalist who can prepare and learn about new fields and new organizational schemes?[40]

As organizations become more multi-national and multi-cultural, should dispute system designers, like managers, mediators, and other dispute resolution professionals have inter-cultural competencies (see more below)? The newly formed International Mediation Institute thinks so and has drafted standards and a protocol for certification of mediators with intercultural competency,[41] applying specific standards, measures and client feedback.

---

40. *See, e.g.*, Model Rules of Prof'l Conduct R. 1.1 cmt. (2009).

41. International Mediation Institute Independent Standards Commission, http://www.imimediation.org/isc_list.html (last visited Mar. 10, 2009). *See also* Judith Meyer, *Mediators' Alert: Now, Certification Goes Global*, 26 Alternatives to the High Cost of Litig. 57 (2008).

Should a DSD professional ever advise a potential client that a new design or any design of a dispute system is not necessary? Like most professionals with particular expertise, when would a DSD professional recommend against the use of her services on efficiency, judgment, fairness, or other grounds, especially if she stands to earn a fee?

Consider this example from my own experience: Virtually all of the international bodies created by the Bretton Woods agreement (the World Bank, the International Monetary Fund and now, the World Trade Organization) and the United Nations, as well as many other non-governmental, and governmental international and multinational organizations, have created internal systems of conflict and dispute resolution, particularly for their own employees. Indeed, some have also created quite effective systems for external conflict resolution. Companies selling goods offer online or other forms of speedy and systematic complaint handling.[42] The World Bank has not only an internal and "integrated" conflict resolution system for its own employees,[43] but it offers a separate body to deal with complaints of those affected by World Bank Projects,[44] and a formal arbitration system for private investor-state disputes (the International Center for Settlement of Investment Disputes, ICSID). Many organizations must craft internal (and external) dispute and complaint systems for a wide variety of constituents—customers, different classes of employees, patients, doctors, students, union members, part-time workers, vendors, suppliers, etc. and so the need for multiple or ever-changing dispute systems may be great. What should a DSD professional do when confronted (as I have been) with organizations that repeatedly engage consultants and dispute designers to design, and then consult and evaluate dispute or conflict resolution programs repeatedly at a potential cost to the organization and adding confusion about the stability of any one system?

Similarly (and related to section A above), what should a DSD professional do when a particular consultation is designed to increase

42. *See, e.g.*, E-bay Online Dispute Resolution, http://pages.ebay.com/help/buy/disputes.html (last visited Mar. 10, 2009).

43. World Bank Integrated Conflict Management System, http://www.worldbank.org/crs (last visited Mar. 10, 2009).

44. World Bank Inspection Panel, http://www.worldbank.org/inspectionpanel (last visited Mar. 10, 2009).

services and funding for dispute systems in institutional or organizational environments in competition for funds with perhaps more deserving needs?[45]

As noted above, the DSD professional has a particularly tricky ethical dilemma or conflict of interest in the organizational setting. Most often hired by management or the "top" of an organization to design a conflict system for workers, customers, or others who constitute the "bottom" or lateral tiers of an organization, to whom does a DSD professional owe his or her professional duty? I was not a designer of the dispute resolution system created for arbitration of claims in the Dalkon Shield mass tort case,[46] but I was a dispute resolver (arbitrator) in the system, and I felt the ethical dilemmas of presiding over a process I thought was sometimes ill-suited to its purpose. I would have preferred a more mediational, rather than "arbitrary"/arbitration process. And, since I was a neutral "judge," I could feel the instrumental use of the arbitration process to efficiently allocate limited funds (located within a bankruptcy proceeding) which failed, in my view, to fully compensate or deliver justice to the users ("victims" of the tort) of the system. Designers and managers of that process were well qualified dispute resolution experts (some of whom appeared at this Symposium – Francis McGovern and Kenneth Feinberg, along with Georgine Vairo), but they were responsible to the bankruptcy judge and proceedings (and later to a Board managing the limited Dalkon Shield Trust), not directly to the claimants.

Thus, in formal terms, DSD professionals also suffer from agent-principal and moral hazard dilemmas and conflicts when users or those affected by professional work are not the same as those directing or controlling the work, who may seek implementation of other values (efficiency, for example, over "justice" or even due process).

Finally, what responsibility does a DSDer have for the implementation, evaluation, and enforcement mechanisms of any systems

45. From my own experience, I know that I have been asked to evaluate and redesign a well financed international dispute resolution system and help make the case for more internal funding. Is it ethical or appropriate for me to recommend a "top of the line," multi-tiered and expensive program when there are competing and perhaps better uses of the scarce resources inside the organization? Is it enough to say that that decision belongs to the managers and not to the system designer? (I say this as someone who was once queried by a member of the board of a major institution about whether I would advise spending limited funds on an "integrated, multi-tier dispute resolution system" or higher wages for the employees.).

46. Carrie Menkel-Meadow, *Taking the Mass Out of Mass Torts: Reflections of a Dalkon Shield Arbitrator on Alternative Dispute Resolution, Judging, Neutrality, Gender and Process*, 31 Loy. L.A. L. Rev. 513 (1998).

he helps effectuate? Like the growing controversy in mediation practice about how much responsibility a mediator should have for implementation and enforcement of contracts, promises and outcomes,[47] is the DSDer's job complete when the design is described or does responsibility extend to its appropriate development, implementation and enforcement?

Consider another example: In a matter I alluded to above, I served as a mediator in a multi-tiered, well designed, and much acclaimed multi-national corporation employee grievance system, in a case involving employment outside of the United States. Both parties (a discharged employee), and a representative from Human Resources, appeared without counsel and participated willingly and effectively in a mediation which resulted in a signed agreement, pursuant to all the standards, rules and policies of a written dispute resolution program published by the corporation and distributed to all employees. Many months later I was contacted by the employee who indicated that the company had not fulfilled any of the conditions of the mediation agreement and no lawyer would take his case because in their view there were no legally enforceable employment rights for an international worker and because, by the time of the "breach," the company had moved completely offshore.[48] So why do I think the application of the dispute systems program developed domestically was merely window-dressing in the international context? Does anyone, such as designers (internal and law firm lawyers), implementers (managers), and participants (Human Resources)) have ethical responsibility for this (participation in a dispute resolution proceeding with probably no intention of adhering to its outcomes)?

If ethics or best practice standards have no possibility of enforcement, what does that do to the legitimacy of the whole enterprise?

47. *See, e.g.*, Lawrence Susskind, *Expanding the Ethical Obligations of the Mediator: Mediator Accountability to Parties Not at the Table*, *in* WHAT'S FAIR: ETHICS FOR NEGOTIATORS 513-18 (Carrie Menkel-Meadow & Michael Wheeler eds., 2004) (suggesting that mediators have responsibility for parties not at the table and should 1) consider the precedent effects of any agreement reached, 2) use their leadership roles to do all they can to maximize joint gain for all relevant stakeholders, and 3) consider the reputation and educative function of the highest quality of the field of mediation).

48. This situation would not preclude an effective lawsuit. Although corporate headquarters are elsewhere, personal and subject matter jurisdiction requirements for a lawsuit in the United States are met by sufficient minimum contacts and by the fact that a contract was effectively formed under American law inside the United States. More likely, the monetary stakes were not high enough and the likelihood of enforcing the company's non-monetary promises by injunction was very small.

D. *Outcomes/Consequences/Purposes of the Dispute System*

As the final example above indicates, once a dispute system has been designed and implemented, the question of what effects it has on its intended beneficiaries and constituencies is another important ethical question to be considered. Recently, at the First National Congress on Mediation in Brazil, I learned about a very effective new informal dispute resolution system. In the teeming "favellas" (shantytowns) of Rio de Janeiro, where drug lords and other gangs and community leaders essentially control the community, there are very effective systems of dispute resolution for handling internal community conflicts (so as to avoid contact with the police, courts and formal authority). Systems I have come to call A5 (Alternative Alternative) Dispute Resolution can be quite effective (as were the old dispute resolution systems of political ward leaders, or the "warlords" currently operating in many countries), operating outside of any formal justice system and providing peace and conflict solutions (often backed up by threats of force), in a sort of "wise elder" arbitration system. Should these gang leaders be credited as being effective dispute resolution designers, even if the effects of their programming is to establish systems outside of any formal institutions and are often backed by violence, intimidation, and fear, not to mention the patronage, bias, bribery and corruption that generally characterize such "outsider" dispute resolution systems?

But if conflict is reduced, "peace" is achieved, and the parties are satisfied, is that enough to characterize a dispute system design as effective and ethical? If not, whose principles are we using to judge these systems? The participants or some external measure of justice and ethics?

III. Deductive Ethics in DSD: Are There Core Ethical Principles in the Field?

The examples I present above are only a few of the kinds of ethical dilemmas that a dispute system designer might face:

1. Who is the client? To whom is the DSDer accountable?
2. What is the purpose of the DSD? Are there any that are illegitimate?
3. When should a DSDer withdraw or refuse to design or consult about a particular process or system?
4. How does the DSDer make decisions or choose among alternatives and how are those choices/decisions justified?

5. How much responsibility does the dispute designer have for implementation, enforcement, consequences and effects of the system he designs?
6. What responsibility does the DSDer bear for most efficient and fair use of organizational/institutional/governmental resources? (How should DSD be weighed against competing organizational and individual needs and resources?)
7. How much independence does the DSDer have from the client? (When is the DSDesigner being used for illegitimate ends?)
8. When does a DSDer have a conflict of interest (because of different or competing needs within the client organization or because of other work for other clients or other professional commitments)?
9. What are the sources of "values," norms, ethics or good practices in DSD?

These general questions, then, suggest some general principles for developing a set of "best practices" or ethics for the field of DSD centered around responsibility, accountability, fairness, independence, judgment, participation (of affected parties) and pursuit of legitimate goals. These "general" principles could be used to derive, deductively, some general norms for the profession of DSD.

Nevertheless, I suggest that the tension of universality or generality and particularity or cultural differences may make agreement on ethics principles difficult in DSD. I will make my arguments from both domestic and international forms of dispute resolution—mass torts and so-called "restorative or transitional justice."[49]

If modern ADR theory and practice has taught us anything, it is that modern process is plural.[50] Claimants, victims, parties, defendants, law reformers, judicial officers and other decision makers, and policy analysts all may desire different things from a legal or dispute resolution system. Some want vindication, others want apologies and forgiveness; some want clear legal rules, others want more subtle terms for ongoing relationships. Some desire punishment and retribution.

49. *See, e.g.*, Ruti G. Teitel, Transitional Justice (2000); Carrie Menkel-Meadow, *Restorative Justice: What Is It and Does it Work?*, 3 Ann. Rev. L. & Soc. Sci. 161 (2007).

50. *See* Carrie Menkel-Meadow, *Peace and Justice: Notes on the Evolution and Purposes of Legal Processes*, 94 Geo. L.J. 553 (2006); Paul Schiff Berman, *Global Legal Pluralism*, 80 S. Cal. L. Rev. 1155 (2007).

As Lon Fuller so clearly described and anticipated in his many articles on legal process,[51] DSD is based on the idea that different processes are necessary for different kinds of contexts and party needs. So mediation is appropriate in ongoing relationships for its flexibility, ability to tailor solutions to the particular needs of parties, and opportunity for open-ended narratives and human interaction. Arbitration is most appropriate when decisions and final settlements are required, but choice of law (contract provisions), decision makers (chosen by parties), privacy and flexibility on rules of procedure or evidence are consensually desired by the parties. Some processes are private (most forms of mediation and arbitration); other legal processes are intended to be public (courts, international tribunals, truth and reconciliation commissions) and parties may have different needs and desires with respect to the transparency and privacy of the legal harms they have suffered. Consider the case of discrimination claimants, some of whom desire to "go public" and make big statements on their cases and others who prefer some privacy (AIDS victims, gays or transsexual claimants, some rape and war crimes victims).

Thus, in a modern world characterized by "process pluralism," is it possible to develop generalized, universal and robust ethics principles across process differences? Is the act of "designing" processes sufficiently coherent and uniform to allow general principles, even if the processes designed are themselves different or pluralistic?

A. *Domestic Cases: Mass Torts and Organizational Design*

Consider what we have heard at this Symposium from Kenneth Feinberg, designer of the September 11 Victim's Compensation Fund.[52] Designed to swiftly and fairly allocate a relatively open-ended and significant amount of money provided by the government to victims, survivors and family members of the World Trade Center

51. *See, e.g.*, Lon L. Fuller, *The Forms and Limits of Adjudication*, 92 HARV. L. REV. 353 (1978); Lon L. Fuller, *Collective Bargaining and the Arbitrator*, *in* COLLECTIVE BARGAINING AND THE ARBITRATOR'S ROLE: PROCEEDINGS OF THE FIFTEENTH ANNUAL MEETING, NATIONAL ACADEMY OF ARBITRATORS (Mark L. Kahn ed. 1962); Lon L. Fuller, *Mediation—Its Forms and Functions*, 44 S. CAL. L. REV. 305 (1971); LON L. FULLER, THE PRINCIPLES OF SOCIAL ORDER: SELECTED ESSAYS OF LON L. FULLER (Kenneth I. Winston ed., rev. ed. 2001).

52. *See generally* September 11th Victim Compensation Fund of 2001, 28 C.F.R. § 104.1-6, .21-.22, .31-.35, .41-.47, .51-.52, .61-.63, .71 (2003) (outlining claim process for the fund); KENNETH FEINBERG, WHAT IS LIFE WORTH? THE UNPRECEDENTED EFFORT TO COMPENSATE THE VICTIMS OF 9/11 (2006) (describing the difficulty in compensating families of 9/11 victims).

terrorist attack, the Victims' Compensation Fund used an arbitral process. But, as Special Master Feinberg has indicated on more than one occasion, what many of the family members wanted was an opportunity to tell their story, to narrate the value of their loved one's life—perhaps suggesting a more mediative or "narrative" dispute resolution process, in a situation that was not very adversarial.

In contrast, with a similar desire to narrate (but in private) their injuries, the claimants I saw in the Dalkon Shield mass tort claims facility (also in an arbitral, but more adversarial context, with extremely limited funds to be allocated) also would have preferred a more mediative, less adversarial process. While some victims, survivors and family members of mass tort injuries, through single events (building collapses, natural disasters, man-made disasters) or more gradual processes (defective products, chemicals or environmental degradation) desire public hearings, others desire privacy.

In a creative attempt to design a particularly innovative process, Judge Sam Pointer, who presided over the Multi-District Litigation in the Silicon Breast Implant Litigation,[53] sought mediator-like consultants and counselors to advise claimants of their legal rights under a proposed settlement in private and group settings,[54] varied by client desires for privacy or group solidarity.

In other cases of mass injury some claimants have desired more public fora—victims or family members of injuries due to some medical products (heart valves, diet plans), or environmental disasters (Love Canal, Buffalo Creek dam disaster,[55] Woburn, Massachusetts water pollution[56]) have preferred high profile lawsuits or well publicized settlements.[57] Some have wanted to resist the now common design device of establishing "grids" of settlement that achieve fairness

53. *In re* Dow Corning Corp., 244 B.R. 705 (Bkrtcy. E.D. Mich. 1997) (paying claims after bankruptcy in class action settlement).

54. I was one of these consultants. The innovative design for this mass tort was derailed by both the expert's report on scientific causation and bankruptcy proceedings for Dow Corning. *See, e.g.*, Eric Green, *What Will We Do When Adjudication Ends? We'll Settle in Bunches: Bringing Rule 23 into the Twenty-First Century*, 44 UCLA L. Rev. 1773 (1997); Deborah Hensler, *A Glass Half Full, A Glass Half Empty: The Use of Alternative Dispute Resolution in Mass Personal Injury Litigation*, 73 Tex. L. Rev. 1587 (1995); Francis McGovern, *Settlement of Mass Torts in a Federal System*, 36 Wake Forest L. Rev. 871 (2001); Carrie Menkel-Meadow, *Ethics and the Settlements of Mass Torts: When the Rules Meet the Road*, 80 Cornell L. Rev. 1159 (1995).

55. *See generally* Gerald Stern, The Buffalo Creek Disaster: How the Survivors of One of the Worst Disasters in Coal-Mining History Brought Suit Against the Coal Company—and Won (1974).

56. *See generally* Jonathan Harr, A Civil Action (1996).

57. Many of these mass injuries and the subsequent litigation have spawned a variety of books and commentaries. Sometimes the critics and authors (who are either

by quantifying injuries and regularizing payments (as in worker's compensation schemes).[58] Critics of the use of ADR in the mass tort arena or of settlement generally continue to insist that every case of wrongful injury be exposed to public process and trial.[59]

Thus, in the context of aggregate injury claims (as contrasted to the slightly simpler aggregate consumer, stock, and antitrust claims which are perhaps easier to monetize and quantify) there are likely to be variations in the desires of claimants for types of processes (public vs. private; fast and final (arbitration) vs. more narrative and cathartic (mediation or some hybrid thereof); as well as type of relief (compensation, accountability, apologies, storytelling, changed practices)). When coupled with the great variety of contexts of mass claims (natural and man-made single disasters, more gradual degradation,[60] product design defects, etc.) and variations in the pool from which relief may be granted (limited funds, bankrupts, market share, insurance funded, government funded, less limited resources), the possible kinds of DSD are enormous if not infinite.

In the early years of mass torts, DSDers (including symposium participants Francis McGovern and Kenneth Feinberg and others working with ENDISPUTE[61] and JAMS[62]) tended to replicate a few simple plans (grids of payments for "mature" torts, hearing processes of arbitration to establish some claims, aggregate settlements with

---

lawyers or journalists) make clear their own preferences for more public litigation, without necessarily polling or questioning the claimants. *See, e.g.*, RICHARD SOBOL, BENDING THE LAW: THE STORY OF THE DALKON SHIELD BANKRUPTCY (1991).

58. Efforts to establish a national claims fund for the hundreds of thousands of victims of asbestos lung disease have failed in almost every Congress for the last twenty years. This legal claim, perhaps the largest mass tort ever, continues to fill courthouses (in hundreds of thousands of cases) at both federal and state levels and to result in delayed individual and collective settlements, in my view because of the inflexibility of the American legal system (and Rule 23 class action law in particular) to adapt to such mass claims. *See* Menkel-Meadow, *supra* note 54. *See also* American Law Institute, Principles of the Law of Aggregate Litigation (Samuel Issacharoff, Richard Nagareda, Robert H. Klonoff and Charles Silver, Reporters, 2009)

59. *See, e.g.*, Hensler, *supra* note 54; Owen Fiss, *Against Settlement*, 93 YALE L.J. 1073 (1984); David Luban, *Settlements and the Erosion of the Public Realm*, 83 GEO. L.J. 2619 (1995); *cf.* Carrie Menkel-Meadow, *Whose Dispute Is It Anyway? A Philosophical and Democratic Defense of Settlement (in some cases)*, 83 GEO. L.J. 2663 (1995) (discussing the difficulties in choosing between settlement and adjudication of disputes).

60. *See* Carrie Menkel-Meadow, *Getting to Let's Talk: Comments on Collaborative Environmental Dispute Resolution Processes*, 8 NEV. L.J. 835, 844 (2008).

61. ENDISPUTE was one of the first private organizations to offer dispute system design. Formed by a group of lawyers, including Professor Eric Green (currently at Boston University Law School), this private firm provided the design ideas for "mini-trials" and other process innovations for large scale, usually corporate disputes.

class lawyers with the responsibility for payment allocation), with varying degrees of court monitoring and intervention.[63] More modern designs for mass claims (torts, consumer, anti-trust, securities) have been a bit more creative and varied, including auctions for class lawyers, in-kind, non-cash settlements or discounts on future goods or services (airline tickets, products, etc.), which suggests that process (and outcome) pluralism has come to the field of aggregate litigation and mass claims settlements.

Given the increasing diversity of designs for both process and outcomes, I wonder whether it is possible or desirable to craft ethical rules for this line of work. In my view, as both an ethicist and a proceduralist, I wonder whether, at least in the case of mass claims that could be or are litigated, some of these issues would better be dealt with by procedural rules for accountability, transparency, and due process, as are currently being drafted by the Reporters for the ALI Project on Aggregate Litigation (both restating the law and offering suggestions and solutions to legal issues in class litigation, including proposed revisions to Rule 23, attorney selection and fees, judicial approval of settlements and relief to be granted).[64] At least in this context there is the possibility of some court review of such issues as:

ENDISPUTE and lawyers in private firms, as well as government agencies also provided advice on the development of internal grievance and organizational dispute resolution systems as a way to structure "preventative dispute resolution" and reduce litigation expenses for their clients.

62. Judicial Arbitration and Mediation Services (JAMS) was founded in Orange County, California by retired state court judge Warren Knight in the 1980s and ultimately grew from an organization primarily offering arbitration services by retired judges in California, to a national organization with offices in many major cities, offering mediation, arbitration, training, and dispute system design services by mediators, arbitrators, former judges, and other dispute resolution professionals. See www.JAMSADR.com (last visited May 20, 2009). JAMS merged with ENDISPUTE (and several other ADR provider organizations in the late 1990s and early 2000's) to become one of the largest private providers of ADR services in the United States. There are many other provider organizations including the National Academy of Arbitrators (primarily labor arbitrators), the Center for Public Resources, the American Arbitration Association, and many others.

63. Indeed, although it is somewhat beyond the scope of this essay, serious ethical questions could be (and have been) raised about the selection and accountability of those who designed mass tort systems for the courts, (often serving as Special Masters under Rule 53, Fed. R. Civ. Proc.). *See, e.g.*, Vicki C. Jackson, ***Empiricism, Gender, and Legal Pedagogy: An Experiment in a Federal Courts Seminar at Georgetown University Law Center***, 83 GEO. L.J. 461 (1994) (reporting on the under-representation of women as special masters).

64. American Law Institute, Principles of the Law of Aggregate Litigation (Samuel Issacharoff, Richard Nagareda, Robert H. Klonoff and Charles Silver, Reporters, 2009)

1. Selection of the DSDer (or Special Master under Rule 53);
2. Monitoring of attorney/representative behavior;
3. Class certification hearings for determinations of representativeness of parties, lawyers, party preferences;
4. Hearings on proposed processes and settlements and finally;
5. Some monitoring of the fairness of actual processes and settlements (Rule 23 (e).[65]

At least in this context, there is some possibility of public hearings and court monitoring. Increasingly, some state court systems are promulgating standards and requirements for their court mediators.[66] I recognize that this does not fully account for those mass claims settlement processes that are privately bargained for or fully negotiated in the shadow, not the light, of the courthouse[67] and that is why some urge that dispute designers develop ethics standards.[68]

In addition to domestic mass dispute litigation matters, dispute designers work for public and private organizations, corporations, government entities, and educational institutions and also design dispute processes for both ongoing and *ad hoc* matters, especially those involving multiple parties, such as in environmental disputes. Some who do this work, such as Ombuds who handle, manage, and

65. See requirements of Amchem Prods., Inc. v. Windsor, 521 U.S. 591, 613 (1997); Ortiz v. Fibreboard Corp., 527 U.S. 815, 827-28 (1999).

66. *See e.g.*, Memorandum from Heather Anderson & Alan Wiener, Staff Counsel, Alternative Dispute Resolution Subcommittee, Civil and Small Claims Advisory Committee, Judicial Council of California, to members of the Administrative Office of the Courts, Judicial Council of California (May 6, 2008) (on file with the author).

67. Nancy Morawetz, *Bargaining, Class Representation and Fairness*, 54 Ohio St. L. J. 1 (1993).

68. Some of the major private providers of dispute and dispute design services have promulgated internal ethics codes for their members. *See e.g.* CPR Commission on Ethics and Standards for the Third Party Neutral and CPR Provider Principles, *supra* note 11; JAMS Ethics Guidelines for Mediators and Arbitrators; http://www.jamsadr.com (last visited May 20, 2009); American Arbitration Association, Ethics for Commercial Arbitration, Ethics for Mediators, and Guidelines for Arbitrators Concerning Exchanges of Information in International Commercial Arbitration, www.adr.org/icdr (including such matters as informing parties about process, voluntary participation of parties, competency of third party neutral, confidentiality, impartiality, refraining from giving legal advice, situations indicating withdrawals and avoidance of misleading marketing). There are also ethics standards that have been jointly promulgated by several organizations, such as AAA, ABA, CPR Ethics Rules for Commercial Arbitration; AAA, ABA, ACR, CPR, Standards of Conduct for Mediators. To my knowledge there is no currently existing set of standards or rules for dispute system design, even for those organizations that specialize in dispute design and multi-party facilitation, *see e.g.*, http://www.policyconsensus.org (last visited May 20, 2009).

design conflict resolution systems have established some very basic ethical guidelines or standards[69] including such matters as:

1. Maintaining confidentiality;
2. Maintaining impartiality and neutrality;
3. Maintaining independence (from management); and
4. Remaining an informal process (no participation in formal adjudicative matters).[70]

Other groups or organizations who design dispute systems in situations like environmental disputes (among competing groups) have suggested some basic rules and principles including:

1. Determine what process is appropriate for the situation;
2. Ensure appropriate parties participate in the process (or process design);
3. Engage an appropriate third party to facilitate or guide (or design) the process;
4. Ensure that parties have full capacity to participate;
5. Ensure that process/third party adds value in the situation;
6. Ensure that relevant information is incorporated into the process;
7. Ensure that participants can effectively communicate and collaborate and hear each other's views and perspectives in order to improve understanding of each other and any problem situation; and
8. Ensure any agreement achieved be long-lasting, implementable and of high quality;
9. Measure and assess impact;
10. Enhance participants and parties ability to resolve conflicts;
11. Ensure processes used are efficient and effective when compared to most likely alternatives;
12. Ensure benefits of a process (or design) outweigh the costs; and
13. Ensure party satisfaction and public benefits to the processes used.[71]

69. See e.g. www.ombudsassociation.org/standards.

70. These basic guidelines are supplemented by a fuller set of standards of practice and a list of "best practices." *See* http://www.ombudsassociation.org (last visited May 20, 2009).

71. *See* Patricia Orr, Kirk Emerson & Dale Keyes, ***Environmental Conflict Resolution Practice and Performance: An Evaluation Framework***, 25 (3) Conflict. Res. Q. 283 (2008).

Such general standards could be adapted for DSDers but are not likely to help deal with or resolve some of the more difficult issues described above, such as possible conflicts of interests between managers who hire a dispute system professional and those who will be the end users, such as employees or customers (efficiency and cost savings versus full hearings, documentation, and compensation). In many organizational settings, managers seek to establish dispute systems to develop fair, but cost-efficient processes in situations where employees, unions or others might want to pursue or preserve external dispute resolution rights.[72] These issues present complex questions of judgment, experience, and both personal and political values.

B. *International DSD*

All of the issues reviewed above are compounded when one turns to implementation of DSD in transnational or international settings. Several other panels at the Symposium have focused specifically on institutional design and legitimacy in international disputing and constitution drafting,[73] whether focused on very formal systems for dispute resolution like constitutional allocations of governmental power at both the international and national level (courts, international tribunals) or the less formal processes used in inter-state conflicts (diplomacy, mediation, arbitration, appeals panels) or intra-state conflicts (truth and reconciliation commissions, consociative governments and power sharing[74] etc.).

I am skeptical of any efforts to generate sufficiently helpful normative standards for international DSD at this point in the development of the field because of the wide variety of contexts, situations, and cultures, which are involved at the international level.

I begin with an observation that I am not alone in making: without a strong and enforceable international legal order, backed up

---

72. *See* Lauren Edelman, Howard Erlanger, John Lande, *Internal Dispute Resolution: The Transformation of Civil Rights in the Workplace*, 27 Law & Society Rev. 497 (1993) (work critical of "I(nternal) Dispute Resolution"); Laura Nader, *Controlling Processes in the Practice of Law: Hierarchy and Pacification in the Movement to Reform Dispute Ideology*, 9 Ohio St. J. of Disp. Res. 1 (1993) (criticizing "harmony culture" and its proliferation through legal and dispute resolution process reform).

73. Panel Discussion at the Harvard Negotiation Law Review Symposium: Dispute System Design on a Global Scale (March 7, 2008); Panel Discussion at the Harvard Negotiation Law Review Symposium: A Constitutional Issue: DSD at the Birth of a Nation (March 7, 2008).

74. *See, e.g.*, Robert Mnookin, *Ethnic Conflict: Flemings and Wallloons, Palestinians and Israeli* 136 Daedalus 103 (2007); Arend Liphart, Power Sharing in South Africa (1985).

with effective courts or peace enforcing mechanisms and "the rule of law," international dispute design does not have the backbone of default enforcement of courts and legitimate institutions on which domestic dispute design depends (if only as a shadowy "threat" of an alternative command process).[75] Despite the increasing caseloads of a number of international tribunals (particularly those dealing with human rights) and the effective development of new international institutions, like the World Trade Organization Appellate Body,[76] there are few effective enforcement mechanisms for trans-national or international disputes (though they are getting better, both courts and informal sanctions, at enforcing some notions of "rule of law"). Some would argue that without strong and effective formal institutions the design of voluntary, informal, and multiple systems for dispute resolution should flourish, offering "alternatives" where there may be none in formal settings. Nevertheless, enforcement of any set of standards or guidelines of behavior for informal dispute processes are not likely to be formally enforceable, if there are no formal institutions to enforce substantive agreements.[77]

There is, of course, the most effective form of regulation of ethical conduct: reputation, which is self-enforcing or market driven.[78] But in a field as new and dispersed as international DSD, information about activities generating an "ethical" reputation may be hard to come by.

More importantly, in international contexts we may not have agreement on some of the most basic, core values: peace at any cost, punishment of wrong doers, forgiveness, precedent setting, standard articulation, private vs. public proceedings, formal vs. informal mechanisms and institutions, local (indigenous) vs. national, regional or

75. Carrie Menkel-Meadow, *Correspondences and Contradictions In International and Domestic Conflict Resolution: Lessons From General Theory and Varied Contexts*, J. OF DISP. L. RES. 319 (2003) at 348-349; Schneider, *supra* note 24; Andrea Schneider, *Not Quite a World Without Trials: Why International Dispute Resolution is Increasingly Judicialized*, 2006 J. DISP. RESOL. 119 (2006); JANE STROMSETH, DAVID WIPPMAN, ROSA EHRENREICH BROOKS, CAN MIGHT MAKE RIGHTS?: BUILDING THE RULE OF LAW AFTER MILITARY INTERVENTION (2006); Tom Ginsburg & Richard McAdams, *Adjudicating in Anarchy: An Expressive Theory of International Dispute Resolution*, 45 WM. & MARY L. REV. 1229 (2004).

76. JOHN JACKSON, SOVEREIGNTY, THE WORLD TRADE ORGANIZATION AND THE CHANGING FUNDAMENTALS OF INTERNATIONAL LAW (2006); Andrea Schneider, *Getting Along: The Evolution of Dispute Resolution Regimes in the International Trade Organizations*, 20 MICH. J. INT'L L. 697 (1999).

77. *See* Menkel-Meadow, *supra* note 9.

78. *See generally* Eleanor Holmes Norton, *Bargaining and the Ethics of Process*, 64 NYU L. REV. 494 (1989).

international locuses of dispute resolution fora, compensation, apologies, rights of past (right of return) vs. present (compensation) vs. future (affirmative action, land rights, social welfare, etc.).

In recent years I have been researching and teaching in several countries that have experienced either serious internal conflict (through violent conflicts or military dictatorships), or transitions to democracy and the development of new legal systems. While my work so far is preliminary,[79] it has persuaded me that there is so much variation in what individuals, collectivities at all levels, sub-groups, and nation-states hope to accomplish with dispute resolution that any effort to suggest ethical guidelines, by us in an academic-practitioner community in the United States, for other cultures, nations and groups, is presumptuous and premature. If I had only several "canons of ethics" to suggest they would be:

1) be truly sensitive to local conditions and "thick descriptions of cultures"[80] in all their variety;

2) Do no harm; and

3) Make no assumptions about what people want.

I will illustrate very briefly with some very complex examples. While Desmond Tutu and South Africa get most of the credit for implementing a mostly successful Truth and Reconciliation Commission in post-apartheid South Africa,[81] the first Truth and Reconciliation Commissions actually were formed in South America, first in Bolivia, then Chile and Argentina, followed by Guatemala and El Salvador.[82]

---

79. The larger project is called "Cultural Variations in Restorative Justice".

80. *See generally* CLIFFORD GEERTZ, THE INTERPRETATION OF CULTURES (1977).

81. Actually both the academic and practical debate about how successful this TRC actually was is growing larger. *See* DAVID DYZENHAUS, JUDGING THE JUDGES: JUDGING OURSELVES: TRUTH RECONCILIATION AND THE APARTHEID LEGAL ORDER (2003); James Gibson, OVERCOMING APARTHEID; CAN TRUTH RECONCILE A DIVIDED NATION? (2004); PENNY ANDREWS & STEPHEN ELLMAN, THE POST-APARTHEID CONSTITUTION: PERSPECTIVES ON SOUTH AFRICA'S BASIC LAW (2002); DESMOND TUTU, NO FUTURE WITHOUT FORGIVENESS (1999). Some of the criticism suggests that important perpetrators did not participate; that too much amnesty was granted, that a Christian and African tribal culture of "forgiveness" was used as social control to prevent more anger and greater demands for accountability, and that social and economic justice remain very far from being realized. *See* Kevin Avruch and B. Vejarano, *Truth and Reconciliation Commissions: A Review Essay and Annotated Bibliography*, 2 (1-2) SOC. JUSTICE, ANTHROPOLOGY. PEACE AND HUMAN RTS. 47 (2001).

82. *See generally* PRISCILLA HAYNER, UNSPEAKABLE TRUTHS: CONFRONTING STATE TERROR AND ATROCITIES (2001); ERIN DALY, JEREMY SARKIN, RECONCILIATION IN DIVIDED SOCIETIES: FINDING COMMON GROUND (2007); MARTHA MINOW, BETWEEN VENGEANCE AND FORGIVENESS: FACING HISTORY AFTER GENOCIDE AND MASS VIOLENCE (1998).

These Truth and Reconciliation Commissions operated in very different ways. With the transition to democracy in Chile, many of the former military dictatorship members remained in power. Military dictator Augustin Pinochet called an election to test his own legitimacy in office. He was in office from the 1973 *coup d'etat* against socialist leader Salvador Allende until the election in 1986 (surprisingly for him) defeated his request for electoral legitimacy. Pinochet, unlike most military dictators, left office relatively peacefully, while much of the military, including Pinochet, remained in power (he as a Life Senator) and amnesty laws were passed to ease the transition with the new democratic regime. As dramatized in Ariel Dorfman's famous play, *Death and the Maiden*,[83] the Chilean TRC focused only on deaths and very serious torture and did not deal with many of the other thousands of serious detentions, beatings and other human rights violations. The Chilean process consisted of semi-private hearings of those who came forward to testify and a well documented set of files kept during the military dictatorship by the Jesuit Order and currently housed in a Human Rights Library at Alberto Hurtado Universidad in Santiago, Chile. The published report of the Commissions findings may be found,[84] with some effort, in a few libraries but is not readily available. In recent years, Chile, like Argentina, has begun to rescind some of the amnesty laws (through court, as well as legislative action) and some military officers (and priests who assisted the regime) are coming to trial. As is well known, Pinochet was indicted in Spain and incarcerated in the United Kingdom,[85] where he was eventually deported back to Chile (on humanitarian grounds for illness,[86]) and died without being tried for his human rights violations. Chile is now heralded as one of the most successful transitions to democracy with a coalition government of the center-left party, *Concertacion*, currently headed by President Michele Bachelet, herself a victim of human rights violations (imprisonment and some torture) during the Pinochet regime (and during which her military

83. *See* ARIEL DORFMAN, DEATH AND THE MAIDEN 9 (1991); movie version DEATH AND THE MAIDEN (Roman Polanski, director, 1994). *See also* David Luban, *On Dorfman's Death and the Maiden*, 10 YALE J.L. & HUMAN. 115, 117-18 (1998).

84. CHILEAN NATIONAL COMMISSION ON TRUTH AND RECONCILIATION, REPORT OF THE CHILEAN NATIONAL COMMISSION ON TRUTH AND RECONCILIATION (Phillip E. Berryman trans., University of Notre Dame Press 1993) (1991).

85. ARIEL DORFMAN, EXORCISING TERROR: THE INCREDIBLE UNENDING TRIAL OF GENERAL AUGUSTO PINOCHET 40 (2002).

86. In a great "thumb nose" to the human rights community, Pinochet, though he argued he was too ill to stand trial, proudly walked from the plane, unassisted, when he arrived in Chile to great cheers by his still remaining supporters, *see id.* at 128-29, 131.

officer father was murdered). Pinochet's family is being pursued in the courts for tax crimes. Nevertheless, it was common from those I interviewed (except a few of my most left or progressive friends and informants, including many who had grown up in exile in Europe, the United States or ironically, Argentina because their fathers were in the deposed Allende government[87]) that the Pinochet regime had led to economic success with the reforms of the "Chicago boys" and free market economics.[88] Pinochet's daughter talked of running for office in the Senate to replace her deceased father and many in Chile working on human rights complained of "collective amnesia" in the desire to move forward, through economic success, and "forget the past." Members of the military dictatorship government continued to serve in the government for some years. While transition to democracy has been quite successful in Chile, there has been less abrupt a departure of the old regime in Chile than in many other nations making transitions to new regimes, such as in neighboring Argentina where the military leadership was totally removed from power following the unsuccessful "War of the Malvinas (Falkland Islands)" in 1983. And, it should be pointed out, as horrible as he was,[89] Pinochet left office voluntarily after an election.

In contrast, the shorter lived military dictatorship in Argentina (known as "the Dirty War" which lasted from 1976-1983, ending with the loss of the Falklands-Malvinas War) has produced a "longer memory" in Argentina. Newly elected president Raul Alfonsin asked legal scholar and jurisprudence expert Carlos Santiago Nino[90] to assist in the transition to democracy. The Truth and Reconciliation process in Argentina was designed to be more public and had greater scope than that of Chile's. The Report of the Commission of the Disappeared Persons (CONADEP), *Nunca Mas!* has had over 25 printings, with at

87. *See, e.g.*, ARIEL DORFMAN, HEADING SOUTH, LOOKING NORTH: A BILINGUAL JOURNEY (1998); MATILDE URRUTIA, MY LIFE WITH PABLO NERUDA (Alexandria Giardino trans., Stanford General Books, 2004) (1986); MARC COOPER, PINOCHET AND ME: A CHILEAN ANTI-MEMOIR (2001).

88. YVES DEZALAY, BRYANT GARTH, THE INTERNATIONALIZATION OF PALACE WARS: LAWYERS, ECONOMISTS AND THE CONTEST TO TRANSFORM LATIN AMERICAN STATES 141-42 (2002).

89. It is estimated that 3,000 died at the hands of the Pinochet military government and thousands more were detained and tortured, SAMUEL TOTTEN ET AL., DICTIONARY OF GENOCIDE 331 (2008).

90. Who spent part of the Dirty War years teaching at Yale Law School and was (he is now deceased) still writing significant works of jurisprudence, *see, e.g.*, CARLOS SANTIAGO NINO, THE CONSTITUTION OF DELIBERATIVE DEMOCRACY (1996); CARLOS SANTIAGO NINO, RADICAL EVIL ON TRIAL (1996); Carlos Santiago Nino, *The Duty to Punish Past Abuses of Human Rights Put Into Context: The Case of Argentina*, 100 YALE L.J. 2619 (1991).

least 300,000 copies sold as of the time of this writing. It is available in any bookstore and in most street-side news kiosks in Buenos Aires. Like Ariel Dorfman's powerful play, *Death and the Maiden* (which is not set in Chile but in a nameless South American country that could be Chile, Argentina, Brazil, Paraguay, or Uruguay, all of which had military dictatorships in the 1970s), powerful memoirs,[91] films,[92] literature,[93] and continuing political action by a group of human rights NGOs that developed to fight the human rights abuses, serve to keep the memory more or less fresh in Argentina so that, it will not happen again. Most distinctively, in Argentina, the *Madres de Plaza de Mayo* (mostly grandmothers of the disappeared) began a march to protest their children and grandchildren's forced disappearances during the dictatorship, and they continue to march to the present time (every Thursday in the Plaza de Mayo). They have founded a human rights organization that supports various activities to commemorate and protest human rights violations.[94] In Argentina, a movement and legal action to learn the truth of the birth of about 500 children (now in their 30's or more) who were stolen from their detained and murdered mothers and given to military families is currently active.[95] Argentina has repealed many of its amnesty laws, and prosecutions in about 15 cases are currently ongoing with both public and private prosecutors. (In many civil law systems, including Argentina, victims have their own representatives who assist in the prosecution). Wherever I go in Argentina (I have taught there regularly and once in Chile) the military dictatorship comes up in conversation very quickly. Argentineans do not have "collective amnesia." Although certainly there are many conservatives who approved of the military regimes (at the time when many supported military regimes' promises of order against the perceived violence of communist revolutions),[96]

91. *See e.g.*, Jacobo Timerman, Prisoner Without a Name, Cell Without a Number (Toby Talbot trans., University of Wisconsin Press, 2002) (1980).

92. *See e.g.*, The Official Story (Luis Puenzo, director, 1986).

93. *See, e.g.*, the powerful novel based on real events, Nathan Englander, The Ministry of Special Cases (2007).

94. *See* Jo Fisher, Mothers of the Disappeared xi, xiii, 95 (1989).

95. See among other sources the films, *The Official Story, supra* note 92 and *Our Disappeared* (Juan Mandelbaum, 2008) dramatizing this situation, and the public service film *Identidad Perdida (2007)* (illustrating the process of rediscovering one's real parents).

96. Che Guevara is now a world wide symbol of liberation and socialist revolution. His face is everywhere in Argentina. But it is important to remember that even though he was many people's hero (including mine, in my more activist youth), he believed in violence to overthrow capitalist governments and many, especially those with land and money, feared violent and confiscatory political movements. Commentators suggest that most of South America has now found a "third way" with coalition

the break with military government was much sharper in Argentina than Chile.

There is much more detail to both of these important stories which I have simplified and very briefly recounted here. My point is that Chile and Argentina, speaking the same language, separated by a mountain range, have widely different cultures. Argentina, like the United States, is a nation constituted by European immigration. It is stunningly white, with small metizo populations, and still looks to the past to its glory days of having the ninth largest economy in the world (1920s) and to European notions of justice and law. Though both share a civil law system and a Spanish and Catholic colonial history, these nations have approached their somewhat similar political experience of military dictatorships differently.

To generalize, one culture continues to mine their memory and to seek justice;[97] the other seeks to move forward with economic growth and plans for the future. I do not sit in judgment of these different approaches. As a student of restorative justice (from my own history as a child of Holocaust refugees) I know there are many ways to process the past.[98] Some are obsessed by it; some draw a dark curtain and choose to forget. Some seek punishment, incarceration, and permanent memorials; others "turn the other cheek," grant forgiveness, and move to create a new political system, culture or society. Some demand reparations and "rights of return" for lives, land and other losses. Others emigrate and seek to build new lives in new places. In a stunning and, similarly overly simplistic cultural sweep, travel journalist Colin Thubron recently wrote the following after traveling through China and Russia:

> The Gulag commissars had retired long ago, with medals and pensions. Not one had been arraigned. Russia had turned its

governments and mixes of socialist, capitalist, and hybrid political regimes (consider the wide berth of Peronism). *See generally* MICHAEL REID, THE FORGOTTEN CONTINENT: THE BATTLE FOR LATIN AMERICA'S SOUL 264-92 (2007) (discussing Latin American countries as "flawed democracies" influenced by a variety of political systems).

97. There are many forms of justice, of course. I refer here to the argument that justice can only be served by formal court proceedings, prosecutions and punishments, *see, e.g.*, Diane Orentlicher, *Settling Accounts: The Duty to Prosecute Human Rights Violations of a Prior Regime*, 100 YALE L.J. 2537, 2542-44 (1991) (in dialogue with Nino, *supra* note 90),

98. *See generally* AVISHAI MARGALIT, THE ETHICS OF MEMORY (2002); EVA HOFFMAN, AFTER SUCH KNOWLEDGE, MEMORY, HISTORY, AND THE LEGACY OF THE HOLOCAUST (2004); Carrie Menkel-Meadow, *Remembrance of Things Past? The Relationship of Past to Future in Pursuing Justice in Mediation*, 5 CARDOZO J. CONFLICT RESOL. 97 (2004).

back on the past. And I, how could I understand? Since the Holocaust, my world had made a *duty* of remembrance. Russia, like China, had chosen forgetfulness. That, said the writer Shalamov, was how people survived. A nation was not built on truth.[99]

In time we may learn that the greatest human rights violations of the twentieth century were not those of the Nazis in Europe, or the Pol Pot regime in Cambodia, or Stalin's purges, or the South American dictatorships. It is just possible that we may learn that tens of millions perished during the Great Leap Forward and the Cultural Revolution[100] without the bureaucratic efficiency and accountability of names and numbers of the Germans or South American dictators. Yet, so far, China appears to be following a strategy closer to Chile's –some individual rehabilitations when the need for educated comrades returned[101]—but mostly a focus on economic growth, westernization and modernization, where economic success is supposed to make up for or dull the senses to human rights violations.[102]

Many of the political regimes that created the worst atrocities in the twentieth century have created some of the best new processes in the twenty first. While I was in Chile, I observed native Mapuche land claims (disputes within Mapuche communities) mediated by a government agency (CONADI[103]) in the field, on the land, that sensitively and with full community participation negotiated land and disputed family claims.[104] In Argentina, I observed one of the most progressive forms of prisoner rehabilitation—contained at a maximum security prison within the city limits of Buenos Aires, a fully

99. Colin Thubron, The Shadow of the Silk Road 204-05 (2007).

100. Evidence to support this claim exists, see the memoir of Mao's doctor, Li Zhi-Sui, The Private Life of Chairman Mao (1994) and Jung Chang & Jon Halliday, Mao: The Unknown Story (2006).

101. *See, e.g.*, Jung Chang, Wild Swans: Three Daughters of China (1991).

102. Philip Pan, Out of Mao's Shadow: The Struggle for the Soul of a New China (2008).

103. Corporación Nacional de Desarrollo Indígena.

104. This will be the subject of a separate article, but I should mention that this excellent mediation program, run by government lawyers committed to indigenous people is necessitated by Pinochet's land policies. Unlike U.S. treatment of indigenous populations with land removal to reservations, Pinochet "privatized" Mapuche land, granting many Mapuche families a limited number of hectares of land for them to "produce" with economic individualism (not joint ownership). Now in their third generation, heirs of the original beneficiaries have disputes about their shares of land. The government-run mediation program settles land claims with consent, and actually goes further in "deep, facilitative" mediation to help the parties mediate their internal family issues. That, however, is a story for another day. The hero of that story is Lohengrin Ascensio, a lawyer-mediator with CONADI who has mediated thousands of these cases.

operational branch of the prestigious Universidad de Buenos Aires grants five degrees to self-governing prisoners—in law,[105] economics, sociology, psychology and humanities, all taught in the prison by regular UBA professors. Can you imagine such programs in the United States?

In South Africa, unlike most of the Central and South American Truth and Reconciliation Commissions, testimony and proceedings were publicly televised. Political scientist James Gibson's work documents that those who watched the programming developed a heightened sense of "human rights consciousness" and a belief that citizens were entitled to justice, even though reactions to the "justness" of the South African TRC in particular were still largely correlated with race, color and class.[106]

These progressive and varied processes of dispute resolution or restorative justice each present specific ethical issues of their own. Can a well designed and executed mediation program be considered just when it is operated by a successor government to the government that created great injustice (by allocating land unfairly to begin with)? How does a progressive rehabilitative prison program allocate its limited places which promise a possibly successful new life? Should a TRC promise amnesty for confession? What should be done when perpetrators do not participate?

There is an ever expanding set of possible conflicts and disputes in the international arena; some internal to a wide variety of countries, others crossing boundaries, whether intentionally or unintentionally (as when refugee situations are created by those fleeing genocides or other abuses). Some of these I have personally witnessed, others are more remote, but equally challenging – all are different. I have recently spent time teaching conflict resolution in Israel and working on and thinking about the next process stages for a "new" peace process among, for and with Israelis and Palestinians and other Arabs.[107] In the United States, we have many major past

105. Lawyers are qualified to practice after receiving a degree and performing an internship. There is no bar exam or morals committee. So successful graduates have undertaken their internships on day release from the prison and can become fully qualified attorneys. As of this writing, the program has produced about 60 law graduates. In the sociology department (within the prison) pictures of Mao, Che, Durkheim and Marx were hung in the self-governing classroom office. I was given a newsletter, written by prison students, on Foucaldian cultural analysis, worthy of any graduate student in a prestigious sociology department in Europe or the United States.

106. GIBSON, *supra* note 81.

107. *See* Carrie Menkel-Meadow & Irena Nutenko, *The Next Generation: A New Peace Process in the Middle East by Those Who Live There* (forthcoming NEG. J., October, 2009).

disputes to reconcile – reparations for slavery, and "conquest" of indigenous peoples, internment of Japanese-Americans in WW II,[108] and more recently, unlawful detention and torture of terror war detainees, not to mention more mass torts and aggregate injuries of various sorts.

Countries like Sierra Leone, Liberia, Uganda, Rwanda, Kosovo, Bosnia, Serbia, East Timor and Cambodia are struggling with transitions to new, and hopefully more democratic and better regimes for their peoples. Some have opted for prosecutions (some of which are international as with the International Criminal Tribunal for the Former Yugoslavia,[109] others of which are both national and local, such as in Rwanda and Cambodia, and others of which are mixed jurisdictionally, such as in East Timor),[110] while others have chosen Truth and Reconciliation processes or local healing processes, like Rwanda's *inkiko-gacaca.*[111]

IV. Conclusion?

What emerges, for me, from these great variations in human wrongdoing and right-seeking, is that clearly one size or one process does not and cannot fit all. As dispute resolution process professionals, we know a lot about dispute processing and we have structured a variety of forms and processes such as "multi-door courthouses," hybrids like med-arb or arb-med, negotiated rule-making, reg-neg and multi-party consensus building fora. If we have learned anything it is that modern process is plural and varied. The "appropriateness" of the process depends on the numbers of parties, whether they are in continuing or one-shot or ending relationships, whether they are disputing scarce or divisible or sharable resources, whether they want to resolve their disputes privately among themselves or to educate the public, change the rules or begin a new relationship or society. Some disputes are private; others involve the government or important public policy issues. Some disputes are very serious and affect life

108. One of the few groups to actually receive reparations so far, by act of Congress.

109. *See e.g.*, John Hagan, Justice in the Balkans: Prosecuting War Crimes in the Hague Tribunal (2003).

110. *See* Jane Stromseth et al., *supra* note 75.

111. Catherine Honeyman et al., *Establishing Collective Norms: Potentials for Participatory Justice in Rwanda*, 10 Peace & Conflict: J. of the Amer. Psychological Ass'n. 1, 13 (2004); Jessica Raper, *The Gacaca Experiment: Rwanda's Restorative Justice Dispute Resolution Response to the 1994 Genocide*, 5 Pepp. Disp. Resol. L.J. 1 (2005); Maya Goldstein-Bolocan, *Rwandan Gacaca: An Experiment in Transitional Justice*, J. Disp. Resol. 355, 364 (2004).

and death; others are purely monetary or may seem more "minor." These variations in process have been formed, matured, and varied in the last 30 years and we are still creating new forms of process as new disputes and conflicts present themselves.

Within each conflict or dispute setting, will be victims, survivors, or other injured who may differ among themselves about what they want. Any choice of any one process may advantage or disadvantage both particular collectivities and certainly, particular individuals. Not to make any choice at all advantages the guilty or those who have committed some wrong. Ethical issues in international DSD are legion, at both macro and micro levels.

Ethics standards, guidelines, and even rules for professional discipline and sanction have now been promulgated for mediators, arbitrators, and even negotiators by private professional associations, courts and international organizations.[112] I suspect that it would be possible to adapt some of these standards for the deliverers of these services for those who design systems of dispute resolution, but as an ethicist and as a practitioner in this field, I think it is simply too early to inductively collect our cases, with the vividness of the few examples we have of ethical difficulties, as illustrated here. And, in my view, our contexts, locations, and types of dispute design are, in my opinion, too varied to permit the generation of usable specific deductive ethical principles. If I had to craft a few general rules of thumb for the well-meaning process designer, they would be simply:

1. Do no harm—do not make the parties worse off than they were before you were hired. Don't make waste (Cost and expenses without benefits).
2. Do not become a "tool" of a client or organization or government that wants to use process design to achieve inappropriate or illegitimate ends (deterring rightful complaints, manipulating workers or customers, "cooling" out or ignoring claims).
3. Be sure that the end users of any dispute system have had input into the design. (This suggests full participation and bottom-up sensitivity, rather than control by "top-down" officials of organizations, institutions and governments).

---

112. Not only the International Mediation Institute which seeks to credential international mediators, but the International Bar Association has developed a very sophisticated set of Guidelines for Conflicts of Interests in International Commercial Arbitration. *See* http://www.ibanet.org/Document/Default.aspx?DocumentUid=e2fe5e72-eb14-4bba-b10d-d33dafee8918 (last visited May 20, 2009).

4. Attempt to ensure that any process you design can actually accomplish what it was designed to do. Take some responsibility for implementation and evaluation.
5. Know what participants' legal rights are (and what they might be giving up or waiving to participate in a particular system).
6. Be sure, as much as you can, that a system of dispute resolution does not systematically discriminate against or harm particular individuals.
7. Be prepared and be competent. Learn about particular organizations, cultures, groups, and histories before embarking on a design project.
8. Consider whether processes should include multiple choices, menus, gateways or tiers. One size does not fit all, even within the same organization, nation-state, and culture. Individuals will have different preferences even within affinity or other groups.
9. Ensure that any process designed can be adequately explained to and understood by its users.
10. Suggest that any system designed should be evaluated and revised as conditions change.

And that's about it for my 10 commandments of DSD. Pre-publication readers have suggested that these canons are either too vague or too aspirational and impossible to achieve and enforce. There is concern that overly vague and platitudinous ethical canons which cannot be enforced will undermine the entire enterprise of designing good processes with clear standards of practice and evaluative criteria. Yet, I think the elaboration of very specific guidelines or ethical standards is unlikely to be much better. Casuistic reasoners will be able to distinguish their specific contexts and situations and argue (as do lawyers and politicians) that particular rules just don't apply in this or that particular setting.

In my view, the limits of good or best practices and ethics (and these may be different things) in this new field are still being framed and developing. I leave to the next generation of DSDers to flesh these out and add others as our experiences grow and we are able to learn from each other. What we do or advise others to do now in the liminal or transitional state we are in now is a difficult question.[113] However, we went many years with no clear standards for mediation

113. I thank Bob Bordone for raising it.

as that field developed, short of a few general ideas about what constituted fairness (such as my overly broad and vague standards above).

Make no mistake, however, I do think there are ethical issues, dilemmas and limits in this new professional field, as there are in any profession. We can only learn to be better at what we do when we design processes for our own deliberation and learn about what those ethical limits are or should be. I hope new examples and cases will help us induce or deduce some clearer ethical standards, hopefully with little or no harm to those we serve with our designs.

[20]

REMEMBRANCE OF THINGS PAST? THE RELATIONSHIP OF PAST TO FUTURE IN PURSUING JUSTICE IN MEDIATION

Carrie J. Menkel-Meadow *

> *The process [the Truth and Reconciliation Commission in South Africa] was backward-looking in the sense of being expected to document and deal with the gross human rights violations of the past, but it was forward-looking in trying to prevent future tyranny.*
>
> —James L. Gibson, *Truth, Reconciliation, and the Creation of a Human Rights Culture in South Africa*[1]

> *Justice, after all, is the principle of mediation between people who are not necessarily conjoined by bonds of mutual affinity or shared histories, but who yet need to coexist together in the same society, or to negotiate their interests across national borders.*
>
> —Eva Hoffman, AFTER SUCH KNOWLEDGE: MEMORY HISTORY AND THE LEGACY OF THE HOLOCAUST[2]

What must be remembered and acknowledged before we can move forward to create a future together, whether individually or collectively? Or, as Avishai Margalit has recently put it, is there an ethics of memory[3] – must some things be remembered; what can be forgiven or forgotten in a moral sense? I have long been worried about the emphasis in mediation to focus on the future, to seek "solutions" to problems in which the parties are guided to "move

---

* Professor of Law and Director, Georgetown-Hewlett Program in Conflict Resolution and Legal Problem Solving, Georgetown University Law Center. This essay is inspired by the memory of the work of Trina Grillo in mediation and the experiences of my parents and relatives in the Holocaust, as well as the claim for reparations by former American slaves and the development of new forms of mediative processes in Truth and Reconciliation Commissions in national political experiences and restorative justice in individual criminal cases. Thanks to Jonathan Hyman for his suggestions and to Benjamin N. Cardozo Law School of Law for inspiring this article.

1 38 LAW & SOC'Y REV. 5 (2004).

2 *See generally* EVA HOFFMAN, AFTER SUCH KNOWLEDGE: WHERE MEMORY OF THE HOLOCAUST ENDS AND HISTORY BEGINS [hereinafter "AFTER SUCH KNOWLEDGE"] (2004).

3 *See generally* AVISHAI MARGALIT, THE ETHICS OF MEMORY (2002).

forward," even while "reorienting the parties to each other,"[4] in crafting a more productive relationship. With the growing use and adaptation of meditative-like processes in collective, political, and nation-state conflicts, as well as individualized conflicts in divorce, commercial, employment and criminal matters, this worry has grown into a larger concern about the role of the past in achieving justice in such settings. In this Article I seek to explore, not resolve, some of the issues and tensions in the role of temporality in achieving justice through mediative processes and to suggest some correctives at the practice level, as well as encourage some deeper thinking at the theoretical level. I focus here on issues of expression of temporality ("the past") in the "justice and mediation" question, not on issues of how the past should be judged – by the rule of law, culture, or universal human rights principles, or even how it can be "managed" when understandings of the past conflict or cannot be "resolved." I leave those bigger questions for another day or another writer.

There are many descriptions and purposes claimed for the mediation process.[5] Whether mediation is used to solve problems, transform parties, while acknowledging and recognizing their issues with each other, settle lawsuits, facilitate legal rule-making, or create new entities, a large part of the ideology of mediation that informs its *raison d'etre* or sensibility is to focus on the future and to "make the world anew." Mediation is offered in contrast to more traditional legal processes, particularly adjudication, but also arbitration, precisely because it can craft future relationships and does not have to find facts, assign fault and blame, or issue judgments or awards about the past. Structurally and functionally, this is one of mediation's defining characteristics—*mediation is not required to deal with the past; it asks the parties to look to their futures and remake their duties and responsibilities toward each other.*[6]

In contrast to mediation, adjudication, and to a lesser extent arbitration, require the participants to bring evidence of what happened in the past so that a third party decision-maker can assign

---

4 Lon Fuller, *Mediation – Its Form and Its Functions*, 44 S. CAL. L. REV. 305, 327 (1971).

5 *See generally* MEDIATION: THEORY, POLICY AND PRACTICE (Carrie Menkel-Meadow ed., 2001).

6 Of course, this is not the only salient characteristic of mediation. Mediation also promises confidentiality, privacy, creativity, direct communication, no rigid rules of evidence, and facilitative, not authoritative, third party participation and leadership. And relevant to this Article, mediation does not require the application or use of law or any other laid-down principles.

blame and fault, and assess damages and order remediation, in forms of cash payments, punishments, or sometimes injunctions about future behavior (usually, but not always, negative), typically using legal or other laid-down principles such as a collective bargaining agreement. For a long time adjudication has been the process thought to provide "justice."[7] This is not to say that justice itself is not a much contested concept, as its various forms are endlessly debated by philosophers and jurisprudes – should justice be distributive, restorative, retributive, equitable, or equal?[8] Nevertheless, lawyers in particular, and some political theorists and philosophers, see justice as located in the home of courts. As we here well know, over the years, those who have been disturbed by the growing use of "settlement" processes to decide cases have lamented, most recently "the Vanishing Trial,"[9] "managerial judges,"[10] and the "compromised" or privatized justice[11] that is said to occur outside of courtrooms, where justice is meted out by an authoritative decision-maker, whether judge or jury. Even some within the mediation community have suggested that whether mediation delivers justice or not should be assessed by how closely mediative outcomes track those which would be ordered by courts.[12] I have not been among those, arguing instead that legal justice (as ordered by a court) is not co-extensive with "human" justice, and mediation can often offer a more tailored, particularized, and more "just" outcome (as well as process) for

---

7 In the sense of application of generally agreed to principles to the specific acts of human wrongdoing for the purpose of reallocation of rights, whether civil, personal or propertied.

8 *See, e.g.*, John Rawls, A Theory of Justice (rev. ed. 1999); Ronald Dworkin, Law's Empire (1986); Jurgen Habermas, Between Facts and Norms, (William Rehg, trans., MIT Press 1996).

9 Marc Galanter, *The Vanishing Trial: An Examination of Trials and Related Matters in Federal and State Court,* 2003 A.B.A. Sec. Litig. Symp., *available at* http://www.abanet.org/media/dec03/120803.html. (Dec. 8, 2003); Patrick Higginbotham, *Judge Robert A. Ainsworth, Jr. Memorial Lecture, Loyola University School of Law: So Why Do We Call Them Trial Courts?* 55 SMU L. Rev. 1405 (2002).

10 Judith Resnik, *Managerial Judges*, 96 Harv. L. Rev. 376 (1982).

11 *See* Owen M. Fiss, *Against Settlement*, 93 Yale L. J. 1073 (1984).

12 *See* Jacqueline Nolan-Haley, *Court Mediation and the Search for Justice Through Law*, 74 Wash. U. L.Q. 47 (1996); David Luban; *Settlements and the Erosion of the Public Realm*, 83 Geo. L.J. 2619 (1995); Nancy A. Welsh, *Making Deals in Court-Connected Mediation: What's Justice Got to Do With It?*, 79 Wash. U. L.Q. 787 (2001); Robert J. Condlin, *"Cases on Both Sides": Patterns of Argument in Legal Dispute-Negotiation*, 44 Md. L. Rev. 65 (1985); Judith Maute, *Public Values and Private Justice: A Case For Mediator Accountability*, 4 Geo. J. Legal Ethics 503 (1991).

parties that choose to use it.[13] As I have argued extensively elsewhere, mediated solutions are not always compromises; but even if they sometimes are, compromises are often more fair and just than "winner take all" outcomes. Mediation offers the opportunity for participating parties to have more authentic dialogues and make decisions about what is fair and just to them than when an outsider applies rules that have been enacted by a legislature for some generalized mean, rather than for particularized human individuals.[14]

Mediative processes[15] have now affected a growing number of legal and political processes beyond the simple dyadic dispute between two parties. Increasingly, in criminal law (victim-offender and restorative justice),[16] in post-conflict intra-national and civil wars and even in international disputes, processes deploying mediative approaches are being used with the hope of creating different forms of "justice" for the parties, including reconciliation, forgiveness,[17] amnesty, some restitution and acknowledgment of wrongdoing and in some cases, the creation of documented "truth" or records, often in more hybridized forms of mediation when used in mass, not individualized settings. In general, I regard this as a positive development, having recently argued that conventional forms of institutionalized searches for justice, in the form of courts and trial, are diminishing in use for a reason. They are suffering from evolutionary demise because they are failing to satisfy modern requirements for voice, justice, and conflict resolution.[18]

Nevertheless, despite my generally appreciative and productive participation in the mediation movement, both in theory development and in practice, I want to express some concerns in the hopes we might "reorient" our own process to seek more sophisticated and nuanced ways to achieve justice in mediative processes.

---

[13] *See* Carrie Menkel-Meadow, *Whose Dispute Is It Anyway? A Philosophical and Democratic Defense of Settlement (in Some Cases)*, 83 GEO. L.J. 2663 (1995).

[14] *See generally* DISPUTE PROCESSING AND CONFLICT RESOLUTION: THEORY, PRACTICE AND POLICY (Carrie Menkel-Meadow et al. eds., 2003).

[15] By which I mean, the use of direct party narratives of complaints, grievances, conflicts, disputes or wrongdoing to negotiate for recognition, remediation, restitution, recompense, or some other result, with the assistance or facilitation by some third party "neutral" person or body.

[16] *See, e.g.*, MARK S. UMBREIT, THE HANDBOOK OF VICTIM OFFENDER MEDIATION (2000); Susan M. Olson & Albert W. Dzur, *Revisiting Informal Justice: Restorative Justice and Democratic Professionalism*, 38 LAW & SOC'Y REV. 139 (2004).

[17] *See, e.g.*, MARTHA MINOW, BETWEEN VENGEANCE AND FORGIVENESS: FACING HISTORY AFTER GENOCIDE AND MASS VIOLENCE (1998); ACCOUNTABILITY FOR ATROCITIES: NATIONAL AND INTERNATIONAL RESPONSES (Jane E. Stromseth ed., 2003).

[18] *See, e.g.*, STUART HAMPSHIRE, JUSTICE IS CONFLICT (2000).

I beg the question of whether justice ought to be a concern for mediation, as others have articulated other values, some potentially inconsistent with justice[19] in the uses and practice of mediation. In short, peace and resolution may sometimes be more animating or important to the parties than total or complete justice or recounting of past and painful histories.[20]

The Future Orientation in Mediation Theory and Practice

Consider the critique of mediation made so movingly by Trina Grillo in *The Mediation Alternative: Process Dangers for Women,*[21] where she outlines one of mediation's animating principles – prospectivity. Citing some of the early training materials and writings about mediation, Grillo points out that mediators often "police" the acceptability of particular narratives by reminding the parties that "[i]n mediation the past history of the participants is only important in relation to the present or as a basis for predicting future needs, intentions, abilities, and reactions to decisions."[22] Early ground rules, especially in divorce mediation, suggested that the focus should be on future needs (particularly of children) and not to "fighting and arguing about the past,"[23] which was regarded as unproductive, preventing agreement, and not useful for the parties. For Grillo, writing from her own experiences as a mediator and then as a divorcing parent herself, too much focus on the future and elimination of discourse about the past eliminated the context in which a particular issue, conflict, or dispute was located. Assumptions in mediation of prospectivity, equality of participation and responsibility, "controlling of emotions," espoused values of self-determinism and contextualism in the face of differential experiences and unequal power[24] all enable, in her view, a process

19 Such rationales have included: simple case settlement, docket reduction, termination of harmful relationships, "cooling out" disgruntled customers, employees, and establishing rules and terms for ongoing relationships as in families, employment settings, etc.

20 *See, e.g.*, Hephzibah Levine, *From a War of Olives and Pines to Agreements About a Park: Consensus-Based Land Use Planning in a Multi-Cultural Setting- Nahal Tzalmon, Israel* (2004) (unpublished case study, on file with author).

21 100 Yale L. J. 1545 (1991).

22 Jay Folberg & Alison Taylor, Mediation: A Comprehensive Guide to Conflict Resolution 14 (1984).

23 *See, e.g.*, Donald T. Saposnek, Mediating Child Custody Disputes (1983).

24 Whether social, economic, political, identity-based or role-based.

intended to do good and empower parties, but that instead does great harm by cutting off experiences of past wrongs and banishing rights-based consciousness of legitimate entitlements.

Grillo's work greatly influenced my own practice of mediation[25] in critically observing how the social control and policing (in Foucaldian terms)[26] of mediation language and practice pushes parties to "put aside the past" and generate "new solutions or relationships" for the future. Even the Bush and Folger model of mediation, focused as it is on mutual understanding and recognition, and not, on its terms, on case settlement, encourages parties to look at how they can achieve "personal growth" and achieve personal and moral "transformation." Although Bush and Folger insist on "transformative" mediation's eschewing of the need to finally resolve or settle a matter, even their form of mediation focuses on the choices and decisions that parties will make in a mediation to empower the self, while still recognizing "the Other."[27] Mediation is still a process in which two parties (or more) in conflict or dispute, relate their stories, complaints or grievances and seek to *do* something about them – create a new family constitution, set up some informal guidelines for the workplace, or develop some new understandings about communication patterns.

Recent treatments of mediation purposes, skills, techniques and processes focus more on party satisfaction while meeting underlying needs and interests, wherever those needs and interests might come from, and also acknowledge the importance of party expressions of emotions as part of the mix of what is "permitted" in the stylized discourse of mediation. I still worry, however, that mediation as a process is too associated with an instrumental need to "move forward," whether it be in the more material aspects of case settlements, agreements, contracts and payments made, or in the more psychological realm of acknowledgment and recognition of the existential reality and intersubjective experience of others. Mediation remains an instrumental tool of propulsion into a better state in the future. I have no real quibble with this as an aspiration, as long as we take full account of and time for what else we might be losing in the process, if for no other reason, than to make room

---

25 *See* Carrie Menkel-Meadow, *What Trina Taught Me: Reflections on Mediation, Inequality, Teaching and Life*, 81 MINN. L. REV. 1413 (1997).

26 *See generally* MICHEL FOUCAULT, POWER/KNOWLEDGE: SELECTED INTERVIEWS AND OTHER WRITINGS, 1972-1977 (Colin Gordon ed. & trans., 1980).

27 *See generally* ROBERT A. BARUCH BUSH & JOSEPH P. FOLGER, THE PROMISE OF MEDIATION: RESPONDING TO CONFLICT THROUGH EMPOWERMENT AND RECOGNITION (1994).

for other things at the mediation table, such as some appreciation of the importance of the past.

If we want to adapt mediation's methods of: direct narrative; guided communication; facilitated and mutual bargaining; empathy training; understanding; and mutually beneficial, tailored and creative solutions to settings as diverse as family breakdowns and national post-conflict reconciliation, we have a great opportunity to consider what is helpful in traditional mediation methods and what might be altered for different purposes.

Justice in Mediation? The Past or the Future?

This is where justice comes in. Among the critiques of mediation processes in the last two decades have been the obvious ones of power imbalances,[28] ethnocentric and culturally specific protocols (mediation is after all a "talking cure"),[29] lawless or "rightsless" outcomes, manipulation of lay disputants by professionalized third parties, conflicts of interests and the absence of true neutrality, diminishment if not elimination of true self-empowerment[30] and the privatization of justice[31] or its opposite – the increase of state control over private disputes.[32] Those outside of the practice of the field have been most critical of how mediation might do right by the parties inside the process, but still harm the rest of us outside of a particular mediation by excluding us from participation in matters that effect the public[33] through failing to elucidate principles or rules for the rest of us to follow or to let us see exactly what is going on inside the black and mysterious box of private conflict resolution. Add to this the use of mediation-like processes in such public matters as mass torts, negotiated rule-making, environmental citings and pollution control and remediation, resource

28 *See generally* Grillo, *supra* note 21; *see also* Richard Delgado et al., *Fairness and Formality: Minimizing the Risk of Prejudice in Alternative Dispute Resolution*, 1985 Wis. L. Rev. 1359 (1985).

29 *See* Carrie Menkel-Meadow, *The Many Ways of Mediation: The Transformation of Traditions, Ideologies, Paradigms and Practices*, 11 Negot. J. 217 (1995).

30 *See* Nancy A. Welsh, *The Thinning Vision of Self-Determination in Court-Connected Mediation: The Inevitable Price of Institutionalization?*, 6 Harv. Negot. L. Rev. 1 (2001).

31 *See, e.g.*, Fiss, *supra* note 11.

32 *See, e.g.*, Richard Abel, *The Contradictions of Informal Justice, in* Politics of Informal Justice: Comparative Studies (Richard Abel ed., 1981).

33 *See generally* Luban, *supra* note 12.

allocation, municipal finance[34] and those concerned about mediation raise issues at both the process and outcome level. Justice may demand public processes and substantively "just" or fair outcomes. These are all important issues, and I have weighed in on them in other places.[35]

Given the new uses of mediative-like techniques and approaches in new processes and institutions (which I generally applaud as evidence of our evolutionary development in legal and conflict processes),[36] I want to reflect on how these new processes, like Truth and Reconciliation Commissions, with their documentation of the past "truth," teach us new lessons in the quest for justice in mediation.

First, *the past is an essential part of justice.*

Second, *how the past is treated is an essential part of the justice of any dispute resolution process, including both mediation and the newer forms of "mediation-like" processes.*

Third, *the past is no more knowable or stable than the future, so there are likely to be many "pasts" and "mediation-like" processes have both a special ability and a special disability to deal with this. Mediation permits several realities to "co-exist." Mediation cannot adjudicate or judge the past or "find a truth." It can enable relevant parties to "mediate" their own stories and realities of the past.*

Fourth, *the past must be acknowledged and responsibility taken in meditative-like processes if they are to be considered legitimate and "just" processes. The past cannot be banished or proscribed from mediation. Different kinds of outcomes in such processes must be clearly understood – ranging from amnesty, forgiveness, restitution, restoration, recompense, and punishment.*

Fifth, *mediation and various kinds of the "mediation-like" processes must be made more variable and accountable for their different purposes and to their different constituencies, including both those inside and outside of the processes.*

---

34 *See, e.g.*, LAWRENCE SUSSKIND, THE CONSENSUS BUILDING HANDBOOK (Jennifer Thomas-Larmer et al. eds., 1999).

35 *See, e.g.*, WHAT'S FAIR: ETHICS FOR NEGOTIATORS, INTRODUCTION (Carrie Menkel-Meadow et al. eds., 2004).

36 *See generally* Menkel-Meadow, *supra* note 13.

Consider this thought experiment. *Imagine* if you can, that you are not a mediator, but a person who feels grievously wronged – a terminated employee, an abandoned spouse, a victim of an urban American police beating, a victim of economic, if not physical, discrimination in apartheid South Africa, a released political prisoner from an opposition party in Guatemala, El Salvador, Chile or Argentina, a family member of a murdered Tutsi in Rwanda, a property owner in a formerly Communist regime in Eastern or Central Europe, a displaced resident of East Timor or Kosovo, an aged Korean comfort woman or a survivor of the German Holocaust. In any or all of these cases, whether by virtue of an overwhelming caseload (Rwanda, East Timor, South Africa) or because of an innovative design for forging new governments and new processes (South Africa, American employment or civil rights dispute panels, Rwanda) or because documentation of claims may be stale or unavailable (Eastern and Central Europe and Holocaust victims, comfort women), you are asked to participate in a community dispute and grievance panel, an organizational mediation or dispute resolution program, a Truth and Reconciliation Commission hearing or a traditionally adapted community justice process, like Gacaca in Rwanda.[37] How would you decide if you had been treated justly? All of these processes, recently designed, do things differently than courts. For example, most cannot punish, though some can order remuneration or compensation of some kind. Some offer nothing more than an opportunity to "testify" about wrongs done – what kind of process creates justice?

Assessments of justice invariably involve judgments themselves – about process, about outcomes, and about who gets to make the assessments. In some of the aforementioned cases, justice is an individual matter (within a marriage); in other cases, it is a communal matter in which collective or group issues are implicated (mass and group-based atrocities, formal unjust legal and political systems, competing property claims). In some cases the harm is "over" in the physical sense (relatives have died, property has been confiscated) even if psychic harm remains. In some cases harm is continuing and competition or violence may continue between conflicting groups (whites and blacks and others in South Africa, Serbs and Muslims in Kosovo, political regime differences). Do completed acts call for different processes or outcomes than those that might continue to be engaged or fester? What is the

[37] *See, e.g.*, Jason Strain & Elizabeth Keyes, *Accountability in the Aftermath of Rwanda's Genocide*, *in* ACCOUNTABILITY FOR ATROCITIES, *supra* note 17.

obligation of a process to educate and preserve the knowledge and legacy of wrongdoing for those both inside and outside of the process?

I approach these important questions from inside my own experience as a justice-seeking mediator with her own one-step removed experience of these issues – a second-generation daughter of Holocaust survivors.[38] Some of you may have equivalent experiential bases (experiences of racial or religious discrimination of very profound kinds, loss of marriages, property, crime victims, diasporas of modern history or similar wrongs). To be a "moral witness" in Avishai Margalit's terms you must actually have experienced some wrong (and not just heard about it or observed it as I have) to get inside this question I have put before you. To consider what is just, or in Margalit's terms, what can be termed an "ethical memory," you must be directly affected by what has gone wrong. Grillo, in these terms, was a "moral witness" about the mediation process because she was not only a mediator, but she was a divorcing party in a mediation. I think it crucial in evaluating the "justice" of mediation, that we stand as much "inside" the process as we can, and not explain, justify or defend it from our stances as mediators, law professors, theorists, writers, or trainers in the field.

I suggest that anyone inside any of these grievous wrongs would not be totally comfortable with a process that asked them only to "think of the children" or to "move forward" in the spirit of national peace and reconciliation or world peace. Whether testimony, stories, and narratives to create a "record" of remembering is enough will likely vary from person to person and group to group, and some social science evidence suggests that it is not only degree of injury that affects such judgments. Even among the most scarred by the Holocaust, some were able to lead what others call "productive" lives, expressing what one writer has called a "*carpe diem* energy,"[39] while others become totally disabled by painful memories of experiences.[40] Some will want retribution, some

38 *See generally* EVA HOFFMAN, LOST IN TRANSLATION: A LIFE IN A NEW LANGUAGE (1989); *see also, e.g.*, HOFFMAN, *supra* note 2; HELEN EPSTEIN, CHILDREN OF THE HOLOCAUST: CONVERSATIONS WITH SONS AND DAUGHTERS OF SURVIVORS (1979).

39 HOFFMAN, *supra* note 2, at 7.

40 Such ranges of human behavior exist in all aspects of life. Why are some poor people still so happy and cheerful and some wealthy people constantly depressed? Why do some cancer patients continue to thrive and work during painful and disabling treatments while others collapse, not perfectly correlated with the level of disease? *See, e.g.*, JEROME GROOPMAN, THE ANATOMY OF HOPE: HOW PEOPLE PREVAIL IN THE FACE OF ILLNESS (2003).

"payment," some "righting" of wrongs to mark the losses suffered, both for individual relief and for human legacies to be left. In Margalit's words again, "[m]ust some things be remembered?"; and if so, what does mediation do to erase or preserve such "ethical memories?"

From a victim's (or party's) perspective what is likely most wanted is some sense of restoration (of self, of the moral order, of the *status quo ante* to the extent that is possible) and acknowledgment by someone outside of the self (the "perpetrator" of wrongdoing, a third party neutral, a witness) that injury has been suffered, that wrong has been committed. Consider the abandoning, but truthful, spouse who says, "I admit I did wrong, I had an affair, but I love another person." This is painful and causes harm to the spouse (and perhaps to children), but it is sadly honest and acknowledges wrongdoing.[41] What should flow from that acknowledgment remains complicated and problematic (especially after the elimination of fault divorce). Acknowledgment may be far easier in such settings of individual harm than in the larger mass or group harms that constitute my other examples. Traditional mediation can be adapted to deal with the past "injustices" of failed familial, commercial, or employment relationships. Mediators and parties can "stay with" the past longer, recounting, restating, and understanding both facts (establishing the "facticity" of wrongs is crucial to any justice process) and the more interpretive and hermeneutic and personal meanings of those facts. Indeed, mediation may be especially appropriate for allowing non-evidence based narratives to be told, heard, repeated, clarified, and understood, if not "agreed to" or formally adjudicated. For many, just being "heard and understood" or having "voice" may be enough. In Margalit's interesting categorical distinctions between "ethicality" (what we owe those with whom we have "thick" relationships) and "morality" (what we owe more generalized others with whom we have "thin" relationships),[42] ethical discourse and ethical memory keeping in a mediation will probably work better (if more deeply and thickly) than in more public or traditional settings.

The point here is that mediators need to reorient their practices to allow, tolerate, and perhaps "structure" stories of what happened and the meanings of the past, rather than hurrying the

---

41 I reference here the small movement to return to fault-based divorce, not only for financial equity grounds but for a legal acknowledgment for wrongdoing in the legal promise of marriage.

42 *See* MARGALIT, *supra* note 3, at 7-8.

parties on to "future-oriented" creative problem-solving when it is too premature. We must not be fearful of the past, even if some conflicts, disagreements and arguments arise from its retelling. I fear that too often conflict-aversive mediators suggest the parties move on; "talk about the future," "talk about your plans. . . .," and, "what would you like to see happen" are often used as a way of managing what they fear will be contests about the past. With skillful communication and facilitation, mediation may be just the most appropriate place for telling narratives about the past meanings and hurts. Further, mediation, at least in such "thick" settings, usually, though not always, permits negotiation of restorative, restitutionary, or compensatory, if not "punitive" outcomes.

The social, political, and juridical experiments that have developed to deal with modernity's horrific mass atrocities, such as using some of the learning from mediation and criminal victim-offender processes, provide us with special opportunities for learning about different forms and varieties of justice. As structured to require acknowledgment of wrongdoing and guilt (and thus avoiding lengthy and sometimes inconclusive trials for fact-finding purposes) as a condition for either full amnesty or lesser punishments or restitution, the modern Truth and Reconciliation Commissions, first in South Africa and now used in various forms in Central and South America, are exploring a more public form of "mediated" justice. How successful they have been in fulfilling their promise is beginning to be a highly contested matter,[43] with some suggesting that with all the "truth," not enough justice has been served (punishments and exemptions). More recent efforts at creating such alternative institutions have seen them as working parallel to more traditional prosecutorial processes with classifications and stratifications, based on severity of cases.[44]

Some recently reported empirical data suggests that the processes of Truth and Reconciliation Commissions have important public functions, as well as private ones. Political scientist James Gibson found that attitudes toward the rule of law and fairness of governmental institutions retain a strong racialized element. Blacks and coloreds (primarily ethnic Asian Indians in

---

43 *See, e.g.*, TRUTH VS. JUSTICE: THE MORALITY OF THE TRUTH COMMISSIONS (Robert I. Rotberg et al. eds., 2000); Ruti Teitel, TRANSITIONAL JUSTICE (2000); Minow, *supra* note 17.

44 *See, e.g.*, Laura Dickinson, *The Dance of Complementarity: Relationships Among Domestic, International and Transnational Accountability Mechanisms in East Timor and Indonesia*, *in* ACCOUNTABILITY FOR ATROCITIES, *supra* note 17.

South Africa) have less of a commitment to the rule of law than whites, but that *participation in the Truth and Reconciliation Commission, participation in the creation of the country's new collective memory, had a positive effect on the positions that individuals held about both the rule of law and the creation of a "human rights" culture in South Africa.*[45] Gibson's findings, soon to be elaborated in a book, *Overcoming Apartheid: Can Truth Reconcile a Divided Nation?*[46] suggest that exposure of the past abuses of human rights and law under the apartheid regime and the application of a seemingly "universal" application of human rights principles, if not law, to these past abuses in a somewhat public setting fostered some attitude change to occur among those who participated in the process. All elements of the process are important: exposure of past acts and wrongs, acknowledgment of wrongdoing, public settings, and participation in the process. Thus, while even some worry that many "offenders" did not participate[47] and that many were inadequately punished, the very act of publicly, individually, and collectively acknowledging guilt had a salutary effect on how citizens conceived of their new political order. Even if the kind of individualized and bargained for agreements in mediation or rule-based court convictions do not occur, airing of and confrontation of the past can have some positive effects on the creation of a future order.

In Truth and Reconciliation Commissions, individual agreements are not "mediated" as in conventional mediations. Further, neither are claims adjudicated, but recitation of victims' stories of the past harms and injuries they suffered are documented, told and the national "truth" recorded. In some of the South and Central American Truth and Reconciliation processes families who do not know what happened to their "disappeared" relatives learn both individualized and more collective truths about the political regimes that tortured and killed their family members. Repair may be impossible but some responsibility and "closure" may be possible and "facts" that would not emerge in a court of law may be exposed. Thus, more public and collectivized modifications of mediative processes may indeed assist in the development of new national and political cultures. Many have suggested that mediated

---

[45] *See* Gibson, *supra* note 1, at 21-25.

[46] JAMES L. GIBSON, OVERCOMING APARTHEID: CAN TRUTH RECONCILE A DIVIDED NATION (2004).

[47] Such as judges of the apartheid regime. *See, e.g.*, DAVID DYZENHAUS, JUDGING THE JUDGES, JUDGING OURSELVES: TRUTH, RECONCILIATION AND THE APARTHEID LEGAL ORDERS (2003).

dialogues about the past, such as facilitated meetings of second generation Germans and Jews[48] (with no issues between them except the past, as so many of the children of survivors have been repatriated through the diaspora of the World War II), will be essential for any possibility of peaceful co-existence in the Middle East.[49] Without a full airing of our past sufferings, we cannot move on. To suffer is human – so is to share and seek acknowledgment of our pain so we *can* move on. The pessimistic story of humankind is that we will destroy each other; the more optimistic story is the one that recognizes our resiliency and lets some, if not all of us, build again.[50] If we have learned anything from the mass violence

---

[48] *See* HOFFMAN, *supra* note 2, at 268.

[49] *See* PROMISES (Cowboy Booking International 2001) (demonstrating the powerful effort to create such a "mediated" dialogue and relationship in a documentary film). The film raises the same issues for filmmakers as mediators – when do we actively "intervene" to help shape the reality we are facilitating or filming? When is "neutrality" not morally appropriate in our roles or justifiably violated? *See id.*

[50] In the words of Nobel Poet Laureate, Wislawa Szymborsk:

> After every war
> Someone has to clean up.
> Things won't
> Straighten themselves up, after all.
> Someone has to push the rubble
> To the side of the road,
> So the corpse-filled wagons
> Can pass.
>
> Someone has to get mired
> In scum and ashes,
> Sofa springs,
> Splintered glass,
> And bloody rags.
>
> Someone has to drag in a girder
> To prop up the wall,
> Someone has to glaze a window,
> Rehang the door.
>
> Photogenic it's not,
> And takes years.
> All the cameras have left
> For another war.
>
> We'll need the bridges back,
> And new railway stations.
> Sleeves will go ragged
> From rolling them up.
>
> Someone, broom in hand,
> Still recalls the way it was.
> Someone else listens
> And nods with unsevered head.

of the twentieth century it is that we must find new ways to seek understanding across differences. Mediation is one such way, but as a process, it cannot abjure the past. Even the most conventional mediation process must focus more on the experience of the past, as suffered by the parties, if they are to go forward and find new relationships or agreements.

Lessons for Mediation: Recognizing the Past, Taking and Making Responsibility and Changing our Practices

These new justice institutions raise important issues with respect to both individual and collective harms and injuries– issues that philosophers have grappled with for years, but which I think need revisiting in light of all kinds of mediative efforts at conflict management, resolution, prevention and yes, containment. What is the relationship of acknowledgment and responsibility for harms caused to forgiving and forgetting? While philosophers and theologians discuss the differences between "forgiving and forgetting" and "remembering and forgiving" or as Margalit puts it, the differences between "covering up" and "blotting out,"[51] we, who participate in mediation, both as parties and as mediators, need to be

---

But already there are those nearby
Starting to mill about
Who will find it dull.

From out of the bushes
Sometimes someone still unearths
Rusted out arguments
And carries them to the garbage pile.

Those who knew
What was going on here
Must make way for
Those who know little.
And less than little.
And finally as little as nothing.

In the grass that has overgrown
Causes and effects,
Someone must be stretched out
Blade of grass in his mouth
Gazing at the clouds.

Wislawa Szymborsk, *The End and the Beginning, in* WISLAWA SZYMBORSK, MIRACLE FAIR: SELECTED POEMS OF WISLAWA SZYMBORSK (Joanna Trzeciak trans., 2001).

[51] MARGALIT, *supra* note 3, at 191-92. "There are four different pictures of forgiveness in the Bible: as carrying a burden, as covering up, as blotting out, and canceling a debt. . . Forgiveness means overcoming anger and vengefulness." *Id.*

more mindful of what we ask parties and ourselves to do and say. To say such things as "we don't need to decide who is right or wrong to move on to a solution," or "this is not a court to assign blame," or "you don't have to admit anything to participate in this process" may contribute to the widespread perception that mediative processes are ones which do not provide justice, but only traded preferences or instrumental bargaining. To expand on what I think the more controversial obligations of mediation could be, recognition and responsibility are not just about apprehending the intersubjective reality of another person in interpersonal terms, but recognition and taking responsibility for harms caused or injuries delivered, whether intentionally or not.[52]

When mediation is conducted in the same spirit as Truth and Reconciliation Commissions—seeking "truth" as well as reconciliation, we can learn to forgive without forgetting; for the hurts, harms, and injuries we bring to mediation are real and often are constitutive of who we are, both as individuals and in our affiliations, chosen or given, in particular identities or groups. Mediators' desires to remain neutral, never to assess blame or to call into account the responsibility of parties (which can of course be both or more than one)[53] preserve several elements of classic mediation – its detached, neutral and facilitative forms. But, if the mediator is too passive, if the mediator excludes "past" testimony, if the mediator encourages the parties to "just get over it" and tries to resolve the problem without proper respect for their relative histories, then I fear mediation will continue to have a mixed reputation, as well as fail to perform some of its most valuable functions of encouraging authentic encounters of human beings who seek to make better what has gone wrong.

---

52 Without getting into it at great length here, it is useful to point out that people often do not want to take responsibility for harms they have "inflicted" on others. "I didn't intend to hurt you and I am sorry you feel hurt" is a common refrain. Unlike formal court proceedings, mediation actually allows exploration of non-intentional hurts and harms and lets the injurer know how the injury felt to the person injured. A skillful mediator can often help the injurer see his "responsibility" or the mutual responsibility for pain incurred (especially of the non-compensable psychological kind).

53 I do not mean to suggest here all harm, blame, or responsibility rests on one side only of any dispute. The South African Truth and Reconciliation Commission explored the human rights violations committed by the ANC in the years leading up to the abolition of apartheid, and some Holocaust scholars and historians are exploring some of the acts Jews perpetrated on other camp victims. Obviously, in familial, commercial, and employment mediation settings, wrongful, problematic, or conflicting acts as well as breaches of contract, relationships, and expectations can easily happen on "both" or "all" sides.

Sometimes "righting a wrong" means it cannot go unacknowledged or dealt with by impunity or compromise. Whether the state or some other public entity has to be the sole judge of wrongdoing, or whether those injured should have a right to determine what would make them whole, is precisely the question raised by such dispute innovations as victim-offender mediation and truth and reconciliation commissions. Whether communities, and other stakeholders, need to be invited into some mediations (children in divorce?) to participate in or bear witness to particular agreements, is a question we should be exploring in particular contexts as the mediation model is employed in increasingly diverse and complicated settings. Whether a "record" of some mediations (contrary to our basic values of confidentiality) might be necessary to preserve certain stories and to create important legacies for the prevention of future harms is another question we should explore. Adaptations of the mediation process to such fora as consensus-building meetings and negotiated rulemaking have already borrowed from mediation methods, adapted for use in public settings for transparency, accountability, and publicity in both the process used and the outputs produced. Confidentiality has been modified, for example, when mediation-like processes are used in public settings (consensus-building fora) requiring transparency and the use of joint fact-finding and substantive experts has sometimes modified conceptions of neutrality or truth-finding in "mediative-like" processes. In short, the processes themselves must be adapted for particular purposes. We can no more say "never the past" than we should say "never evaluate."

If patterns of retribution, revenge, and vengefulness have any hope of being averted, there will likely have to be some public shaming, as well as public forgiving. Reparations, recompense, apology, and acknowledgment, all sometimes part of private justice, may have to be public in some cases for purposes of deterrence, prevention of future harms, and for individual accountability. Consider the tensions in promising confidentiality to sexual harassers in mediation sessions and victims' desires to have perpetrators publicly labeled simply to give notice to other possible victims in the workplace.

The search for justice in some mediation settings may seem misplaced. Mediation is about confidential, usually individualized, bargained for solutions to interpersonal, contractual, or relational conflicts. Mediation, until recently was conceived of as primarily a "civil," not criminal process, with no power to punish or order. Yet the power of direct dialogue between those engaged in conflicts of all kinds, from individual to dyadic to now even mass atrocities, seeking to find points of reconciliation, ways to create new relationships, as well as new governments and states, has encouraged the use of "mediation-like" processes in many different settings. As traditional mediation has served as a model for some of these new forms of conflict resolution, we should now look at what these new forms might teach us about how we should or could reconceive the mediation process to meet some of the basic needs of parties to feel they have been justly, as well as fairly, treated. In the international arena, where justice must often be defined as broadly and non-specifically as possible, justice is often described as requiring the development of accurate factual records, acknowledgment that basic human (or legal) standards have been violated, individual and governmental accountability, granting of appropriate compensation, restoration of rights and property and the giving of apologies or creation of reconcilative acts or rituals to "repair" as much of the harm as possible.[54] Not all mediations implicate the grave issues of human harm and injury that inspired the Truth and Reconciliation Commissions or the Nuremberg Trials, but the recent engagement of the human rights movement with the conflict resolution movement offers much food for thought and adaptation of our practices at all levels.

In my career, I have most often defended mediation against attacks made by the litigation romanticists who tend to see conventional adjudicative processes and the "rule of law" as the only measure of justice. Mediation offers an often better process, by providing direct party engagement, open dialogue unrestricted by rigid rules of evidence and the possibilities that parties can craft their own solutions. To the extent that this process has all too often restricted discussion of the past in its promise to "move forward constructively," I now think it is time for us to reconsider some of our dogmas and doctrines to see whether mediation is as adaptive and fair as we have claimed. My hope in suggesting that we look at constructive ways to bring the past and future together in mediation, both in ideology and conception and in our practices, is that we might then create a truly sacred place[55] in mediation for

---

[54] *See* Jane Stromseth, *Introduction: Goals and Challenges in the Pursuit of Accountability*, *in* ACCOUNTABILITY FOR ATROCITIES, *supra* note 17.

[55] *See* Sara Cobb, *Creating Sacred Space: Toward a Second Generation Dispute Resolution Practice*, 28 FORDHAM URB. L.J. 1017 (2001)(suggesting that mediators should take an active role in shaping and crafting moral dialogues and responsibility in mediation, with reference to community values, as well as the values the parties bring to the mediation);

truth, human understanding, and justice to co-exist. As they say, without peace there will be no justice, but with no justice, there will be no peace.

Carrie Menkel-Meadow, *And Now a Word About Secular Humanism, Spirituality and the Practice of Justice and Conflict Resolution*, 28 FORDHAM URB. L.J. 1073 (2001); Carrie Menkel-Meadow, *Practicing "In the Interests of Justice" in the Twenty-First Century: Pursuing Peace as Justice*, 70 FORDHAM L. REV. 1761 (2002).

[21]

IS ALTERNATIVE DISPUTE RESOLUTION CONSISTENT WITH THE RULE OF LAW? LESSONS FROM ABROAD

*Jean R. Sternlight**

Introduction

What is the relationship between alternative dispute resolution (ADR) and the rule of law? In the United States, critics often argue that the informal, private nature of ADR[1] is hostile to the rule of law—and ultimately to justice itself. Yet over the last ten years, a broad, international array of groups has advocated including ADR in projects designed to foster the rule of law in other countries. This Article explores the paradox. Have we erred in condemning ADR domestically or in promoting it internationally? Or does the desirability of ADR depend upon the nature of the system in which it is being utilized? By studying this paradox, we can enrich our understanding of the ultimate purposes of both ADR and the rule of law, and thus assist our search for justice.

II. The Domestic Critique of ADR as Hostile to the Rule of Law

Although disputes have been resolved through means other than litigation for thousands of years, it is well established that an ADR

* Michael and Sonja Saltman Professor of Law and Director of the Saltman Center for Conflict Resolution, University of Nevada, Las Vegas. I thank Raquel Aldana, Amy Cohen, Richard Reuben, Leticia Saucedo, and participants in the Twelfth Annual Clifford Symposium for comments on an earlier draft. I thank Stephan Landsman both for inviting me to participate in the Symposium and for commenting on the draft. And I thank students Matthew Engle, Michael Hammer, Charles Rainey, and Hetty Wong for their assistance on this project.

1. Although I use the term ADR in this Article extensively, I have previously expressed, and continue to hold, many reservations about the value of the term. Jean R. Sternlight, *Is Binding Arbitration a Form of ADR?: An Argument That the Term "ADR" Has Begun to Outlive Its Usefulness*, 2000 J. Disp. Resol. 97. As I argued in that article, arbitration and mediation are extremely different from one another, and arbitration is more similar to litigation than it is to mediation or negotiation. I generally prefer the phrase "*appropriate* dispute resolution" because it more accurately captures the notion that litigation, arbitration, mediation, and negotiation are alternatives to one another. *Id.* at 97 n.1. Nonetheless, in this Article I will use the common definition of ADR.

boom took place in the United States beginning in the 1970s.[2] Inspired by concerns about efficiency, access, and justice, ADR advocates urged that disputes be resolved, not only in public trials, but also through negotiation, mediation, and arbitration.[3] The growth of ADR also sparked a series of significant critiques by people concerned with the privatization and informalization of dispute resolution. They argue that the privatization of dispute resolution is problematic because the elaboration of law achieved in public trials and published decisions is necessary to protect and enhance individual rights.[4] Similarly, some critics urge that treating disputes as matters of individual, rather than public, concern eliminates important public accountability.[5] Others argue that dispute resolution fails to serve an important educational function when it is privatized.[6] Another common criticism is that the establishment of dispute resolution processes weakens the position of less powerful members of society.[7] For example, when pri-

2. Harvard Law Professor Frank Sander's speech at the 1976 Pound Conference is often used to mark the date of the resurgence of ADR. Frank E.A. Sander, *Varieties of Dispute Processing*, 70 F.R.D. 79 (1976); *e.g.*, Jeffrey W. Stempel, *Reflections on Judicial ADR and the Multi-door Courthouse at Twenty: Fait Accompli, Failed Overture, or Fledgling Adulthood?*, 11 OHIO ST. J. ON DISP. RESOL. 297, 309 (1996).

3. *See, e.g.*, Deborah R. Hensler, *Our Courts, Ourselves: How the Alternative Dispute Resolution Movement Is Re-shaping Our Legal System*, 108 PENN ST. L. REV. 165, 170–85 (2003) (discussing the community justice, court administration, and business interest strands of the ADR movement); Carrie Menkel-Meadow, *Pursuing Settlement in an Adversary Culture: A Tale of Innovation Co-opted or "the Law of ADR,"* 19 FLA. ST. U. L. REV. 1, 6 (1991) ("In what has become a commonly recognized division in the literature and advocacy about ADR, we see two basically different justifications for processes that resolve cases short of trial—what I call quantitative-efficiency claims versus qualitative-justice claims.").

4. *See, e.g.*, Harry T. Edwards, Commentary, *Alternative Dispute Resolution: Panacea or Anathema?*, 99 HARV. L. REV. 668, 675–82 (1986) (cautioning that a virtue of adjudication is its ability to ensure the proper resolution and application of public values, and that public officials, not private individuals, must interpret the values of the Constitution and statutes); Owen M. Fiss, Commentary, *Against Settlement*, 93 YALE L.J. 1073, 1075 (1984) (urging that by resolving disputes through settlements rather than through adjudication, justice is sacrificed for peace); David Luban, *Settlements and the Erosion of the Public Realm*, 83 GEO. L.J. 2619, 2622–23 (1995) (noting that private adjudications fail to produce rules or binding precedents).

5. *See* Carrie Menkel-Meadow, *Whose Dispute Is It Anyway?: A Philosophical and Democratic Defense of Settlement (In Some Cases)*, 83 GEO. L.J. 2663 (1995) [hereinafter Menkel-Meadow, *Whose Dispute Is It Anyway*] (providing a balanced discussion of this critique and raising the question of whether it is best to approach disputes as an individual or group concern).

6. *See, e.g.*, Jean R. Sternlight, *Creeping Mandatory Arbitration: Is It Just?*, 57 STAN. L. REV. 1631, 1661–65 (2005) (discussing the public education function of dispute resolution systems).

7. *See, e.g.*, Hensler, *supra* note 3, at 196 ("In a democracy where many people are shut out of legislative power . . . collective litigation . . . provides an alternative strategy for group action."); Laura Nader, *Controlling Processes in the Practice of Law: Hierarchy and Pacification in the Movement to Re-form Dispute Ideology*, 9 OHIO ST. J. ON DISP. RESOL. 1, 14 (1993) (arguing that the unwritten, informal law of mediation avoids "[d]iscussion of blame or rights," and is "replaced by the rhetoric of compromise and relationship," which "thereby obscur[es] issues of unequal social power"); Judith Resnik, *Procedure's Projects*, 23 CIV. JUST. Q. 273, 276 (2004)

vate companies use form contracts to require their customers or employees to resolve disputes outside the courtroom, companies have an incentive to skew the processes in their favor.[8] In addition, some have criticized the informalization of dispute resolution on the ground that prejudices are more likely to manifest themselves in informal settings.[9] Similarly, some have argued that women—traditionally less powerful members of society—may be worse off in mediation or other ADR processes than they are in litigation, especially in family law matters.[10]

Together, these critiques can be seen as attacking alternative modes of dispute resolution for undermining the rule of law. Certainly, the private and informal resolution of disputes does not allow for the formal explication of rules envisioned by Lon Fuller and other rule of law advocates.[11] While supporters of ADR have responded to these critiques,[12] few commentators have defended ADR on the ground

(stating that while adjudication is far from perfect due to lack of access, it is relatively attractive as compared to ADR "because it is self-limited, self-conscious, and relatively transparent, whereas the alternative forms of process attend too little to their own power as well as to the effects of disputants' power and position on strategic interaction, opportunities, knowledge, and the legitimacy of outcomes").

8. *See, e.g.*, Jean R. Sternlight, *Panacea or Corporate Tool?: Debunking the Supreme Court's Preference for Binding Arbitration*, 74 WASH. U. L.Q. 637, 674–97 (1996).

9. *See, e.g.*, Richard Delgado et al., *Fairness and Formality: Minimizing the Risk of Prejudice in Alternative Dispute Resolution*, 1985 WIS. L. REV. 1359, 1375–91 (explaining that traditional adjudicatory settings with defined rules and a formal structure provide rational control, whereas informal settings encourage prejudicial behavior because majority group members are allowed a wider scope for emotional and behavioral idiosyncrasies); *see also* Richard Delgado, *Alternative Dispute Resolution Conflict as Pathology: An Essay for Trina Grillo*, 81 MINN. L. REV. 1391, 1398 (1997) (reiterating concerns that without a formal court proceeding to remind participants of the American values of equality and fairness, majority group members are less hesitant to express and act upon their prejudices).

10. *See, e.g.*, Trina Grillo, *The Mediation Alternative: Process Dangers for Women*, 100 YALE L.J. 1545 (1991).

11. LON L. FULLER, THE MORALITY OF LAW 38–39 (1964) (explaining that compliance with the rule of law demands that laws must actually be established, that such laws must be adequately publicized, that rules should apply only prospectively, that rules must be understandable, that rules shall not be contradictory, that it must be possible to conform to the rules, and that the rules must be administered in the intended manner in which they are announced); Antonin Scalia, *The Rule of Law as a Law of Rules*, 56 U. CHI. L. REV. 1175 (1989) (advocating that judges rely, to the extent possible, on general rules, rather than on totality of the circumstances analyses).

12. *See, e.g.*, Robert C. Bordone et al., *The Next Thirty Years: Directions and Challenges in Dispute Resolution*, *in* THE HANDBOOK OF DISPUTE RESOLUTION 507, 510 (Michael L. Moffitt & Robert C. Bordone eds., 2005) (suggesting that while concerns about ADR may be valid, critics often overstate their arguments and depict an oversimplified understanding of dispute resolution); Menkel-Meadow, *Whose Dispute Is It Anyway*, *supra* note 5, at 2669–70 (responding to criticisms voiced by Professor Owen Fiss and others, and urging that settlement promotes such values as "consent, participation, empowerment, dignity, respect, empathy and emotional catharsis, privacy, efficiency, quality solutions, equity, access, and yes, even justice").

that it enhances the rule of law. The strength and appeal of the rule of law critique should not be underestimated. In the United States, even many of ADR's staunchest advocates recognize that there are circumstances in which disputes are better resolved publicly, through litigation, rather than through negotiation, mediation, arbitration, or some other private means.[13]

III. The International Export of ADR in Rule of Law Projects

The relationship between ADR and the rule of law is seen quite differently in the context of international law reform efforts. Internationally, the rule of law has been converted from a philosophical construct into a series of aid projects involving significant funding. One commentator notes that since 1990 the World Bank alone has sponsored 330 rule of law projects totaling $2.9 billion.[14]

Traditional rule of law programs have been designed to train judges, build courthouses, publicize judicial decisions, and computerize and organize court files. But beginning in the mid-1990s, international aid organizations began to urge foreign countries to adopt ADR as a means to modernize their legal systems and instill greater respect for the rule of law. Recent international ADR projects often include efforts to train mediators and arbitrators, revise laws to make them more supportive of mediation and arbitration, inform judges about the benefits of ADR, and provide technical support and training materials.

The United States Agency for International Development (USAID) has been one of the leading organizations sponsoring the use of ADR as part of rule of law projects. In March 1998, USAID's Center for Democracy and Governance published an extensive manual entitled *Alternative Dispute Resolution Practitioners' Guide* (*ADR Practitioners' Guide*), which explained the nature and benefits of ADR and provided numerous examples of ADR throughout the

13. *See, e.g.*, Menkel-Meadow, *Whose Dispute Is It Anyway*, *supra* note 5, at 2695 (recognizing that certain settlements, such as mass tort actions, have such a significant impact on our justice system that "public exposure of such cases may be a necessary part of our democratic process" (internal quotation marks omitted)).

14. David M. Trubek, *The "Rule of Law" in Development Assistance: Past, Present, and Future*, *in* The New Law and Economic Development: A Critical Appraisal 74, 74 (David M. Trubek & Alvaro Santos eds., 2006).

world.[15] The introduction to the *ADR Practitioners' Guide* explains the purported link between ADR and the rule of law:

> USAID's work in promoting the rule of law in developing and transitional societies over the last decade has led to an interest in the use of . . . "ADR." Several reasons underlie this interest. ADR is touted as more efficient and effective than the courts in providing justice, especially in countries in which the judiciary has lost the trust and respect of the citizens. Moreover, ADR is seen as a means to increase access to justice for populations that cannot or will not use the court system, to address conflicts in culturally appropriate ways, and to maintain social peace.[16]

While recognizing that ADR programs "cannot be a substitute for a formal judicial system," the *ADR Practitioners' Guide* urges that ADR can decrease the cost and length of dispute resolution, increase access to justice for disempowered groups, and "increase disputants' satisfaction with outcomes."[17] Nonetheless, it explains that ADR is not always appropriate; programs must be properly designed to suit the unique circumstances of the particular country.[18]

USAID backs its philosophy that ADR is an important component of the rule of law by funding ADR projects in various countries. For example, in El Salvador, where USAID seeks to increase access to justice, transparency, and accountability, the agency plans to strengthen and expand mediation centers throughout the country.[19] In Guyana, USAID has created a mediation center to resolve civil disputes and reduce case backlogs.[20] In Honduras, it has sponsored the development of ADR systems as a means of improving "access to

15. CTR. FOR DEMOCRACY & GOVERNANCE, ALTERNATIVE DISPUTE RESOLUTION PRACTITIONERS' GUIDE (1998), *available at* http://www.usaid.gov/our_work/democracy_and_governance/publications/pdfs/pnacb895.pdf [hereinafter ADR PRACTITIONERS' GUIDE].

16. *Id.* at 1. The *ADR Practitioners' Guide* also spells out how ADR can serve rule of law objectives in more detail. *See id.* at 7–17. It urges that "ADR programs can support not only rule of law objectives, but also other development objectives, such as economic development, development of a civil society, and support for disadvantaged groups, by facilitating the resolution of disputes that are impeding progress toward these objectives." *Id.* at 3.

17. *Id.* (emphasis omitted).

18. *See id.* In its appendix, the *ADR Practitioners' Guide* provides case studies of ADR programs used in Bangladesh, Bolivia, South Africa, Sri Lanka, and the Ukraine as a means to examine when ADR is and is not effective in developing and transitioning countries. ADR PRACTITIONERS' GUIDE, *supra* note 15, app. B.

19. USAID, Budget: El Salvador (2006), http://www.usaid.gov/policy/budget/cbj2006/lac/sv.html; USAID, Data Sheet: El Salvador (2005), *available at* http://www.usaid.gov/policy/budget/cbj2005/lac/pdf/519-002.pdf.

20. USAID, Budget: Guyana (2006), http://www.usaid.gov/policy/budget/cbj2006/lac/gy.html; USAID, Data Sheet: Guyana (2005), *available at* http://www.usaid.gov/policy/budget/cbj2005/lac/pdf/504-006.pdf.

justice for marginalized groups, including women and the poor."[21] On the other side of the world, USAID is supporting Nepalese community mediation as a way to resolve disputes locally and promote community solidarity.[22] In Africa, it has supported the Rwandan Gacaca, an indigenous mediation program promoting truth and reconciliation.[23] Finally, in Yemen, USAID has sought to formalize conflict resolution solutions initiated by local council members and integrate traditional means of conflict resolution into more modern techniques.[24]

The American Bar Association (ABA) has been another leader in the movement to encourage greater reliance on ADR as part of its international rule of law projects. The most active arm of the ABA has been its Central European and Eurasian Law Institute (CEELI).[25] The organization's website explains that "CEELI is a public service project of the American Bar Association that advances the rule of law in the world by supporting the legal reform process in Central and Eastern Europe, Eurasia and the Middle East."[26] Since the mid-1990s, CEELI has engaged in projects including training mediators in Armenia,[27] fostering the development of small businesses in Azerbaijan by providing ADR assistance,[28] promoting ADR in Bosnia,[29] assisting in the drafting of a new Bulgarian Mediation Act, providing mediation training to Bulgaria's judges, attorneys, and citizens,[30] and producing a mediation bench book for Serbian trial judges and a training video to inform the general public about the potential advantages of mediation.[31]

21. USAID, Data Sheet: Honduras (2005), *available at* http://www.usaid.gov/policy/budget/cbj2005/lac/pdf/522-021.pdf.

22. USAID, Data Sheet: Nepal (2005), *available at* http://www.usaid.gov/policy/budget/cbj2005/ane/pdf/367-007.pdf.

23. Erin Daly, *Between Punitive and Reconstructive Justice: The Gacaca Courts in Rwanda*, 34 N.Y.U. J. INT'L L. & POL. 355, 357 n.6 (2002).

24. USAID, Data Sheet: Yemen (2005), *available at* http://www.usaid.gov/policy/budget/cbj2005/ane/pdf/279-zzz.pdf.

25. For general background on CEELI, see Central European and Eurasian Law Initiative, http://www.abanet.org/ceeli (last visited Jan. 17, 2007).

26. *Id.*

27. CEELI: Armenia, http://www.abanet.org/ceeli/countries/armenia/program.html (last visited Jan. 17, 2007).

28. CEELI: Azerbaijan, http://www.abanet.org/ceeli/countries/azerbaijan/program.html (last visited Jan. 17, 2007).

29. CEELI: Bosnia & Herzegovina, http://www.abanet.org/ceeli/countries/bosnia/program.html (last visited Jan. 17, 2007).

30. CEELI Programs: Bulgaria, http://www.abanet.org/ceeli/countries/bulgaria/program.html (last visited Jan. 17, 2007).

31. CEELI Programs: Serbia, http://www.abanet.org/ceeli/countries/serbia/program.html (last visited Jan. 17, 2007).

In addition, ABA law reform groups around the world have advocated the use of ADR as part of rule of law projects. For example, the ABA Latin American Legal Initiatives Council has been operating a mediation project in Mexico that promotes "court-annexed mediation in twenty-two states" and has now trained over 200 mediators.[32] Similarly, the ABA Africa Law Initiative Council has done extensive training of Rwandan community mediators,[33] and the ABA Asia Law Initiative has sought to ensure that the Emergency Loya Jirga, essentially an indigenous Afghan ADR system, operates fairly and transparently.[34]

Other international aid organizations are also sponsoring ADR projects to foster the rule of law. For example, the World Bank is promoting ADR in Bangladesh, Peru, and Sri Lanka to improve access to justice, as well as efficiency, transparency, and responsiveness.[35] Similarly, the High Level Commission on Legal Empowerment of the Poor (HLCLEP) sponsored a conference in May 2006 to consider whether and how ADR might be used to "expand access to legal protection and the rule of law" and to "contribute most effectively to poverty reduction."[36]

In the international context, ADR is said to foster the rule of law in several ways: (1) it may increase access to justice by making it easier for people who are poor, illiterate, or geographically dispersed to bring or respond to a claim;[37] (2) it may reduce the amount of money and time needed to resolve disputes;[38] (3) it may provide an alterna-

32. ABA-LALIC: Mediation Project in Mexico, http://www.abanet.org/lalic/mediationproject mexico.html (last visited Jan. 17, 2007).

33. ABA Africa Law Initiative: Access to Justice, http://www.abanet.org/aba-africa/projects/ accessjustice.shtml (last visited Jan. 17, 2007).

34. INT'L RES. GROUP ET AL., FILLING THE VACUUM: PREREQUISITES TO SECURITY IN AFGHANISTAN 1, 10, 31–33 (2002), *available at* http://www.ifes.org/publication/0f5d46d1bd36b7b79c 03116bc523cc72/CRAFT.pdf.

35. *See* The World Bank, Legal and Judicial Capacity Building Project: Bangladesh (2001), http://web.worldbank.org/external/projects/main?pagePK=64312881&piPK=64302848&theSiteP K=40941&&Projectid=P044810; The World Bank, Judicial Reform Project: Peru (1997), http:// web.worldbank.org/external/projects/main?pagePK=64312881&piPK=64302848&theSitePK=40 941&Projectid=P040107; The World Bank, Legal and Judicial Reforms Project: Sri Lanka (2000), http://web.worldbank.org/external/projects/main?pagePK=64283627&piPK=73230&the SitePK=40941&menuPK=228424&Projectid=P044809.

36. HLCLEP, UK DFID/UNECE Regional Conference on Alternative Dispute Resolution, Mediation and Third Party Arbitration (TPAC) (May 23–24, 2006) (on file with author).

37. ADR PRACTITIONERS' GUIDE, *supra* note 15, at 13; Robert Kossick, *The Rule of Law and Development in Mexico*, 21 ARIZ. J. INT'L & COMP. L. 715, 786 (2004).

38. ADR PRACTITIONERS' GUIDE, *supra* note 15, at 16; Maria Dakolias, *A Strategy for Judicial Reform: The Experience in Latin America*, 36 VA. J. INT'L L. 167, 201 n.144 (1995).

tive to corrupt or biased court systems;[39] (4) it may promote foreign investment opportunities;[40] (5) it may provide justice to groups, such as women and minorities, whose interests are not well served by the formal legal system;[41] (6) it may bring community members together and establish greater social harmony;[42] (7) it may bring about political reform;[43] and (8) it may help community members work together to better protect their individual rights.[44]

Some doubt whether ADR actually serves these admirable purposes.[45] Furthermore, some argue that the exportation of ADR may be imperialistic.[46] However, rather than focus on the practical ques-

39. ADR PRACTITIONERS' GUIDE, *supra* note 15, at 10; Dakolias, *supra* note 38, at 200; Thomas J. Moyer & Emily Stewart Haynes, *Mediation as a Catalyst for Judicial Reform in Latin America*, 18 OHIO ST. J. ON DISP. RESOL. 619, 621 (2003).

40. Anthony Wanis-St. John, *Implementing ADR in Transitioning States: Lessons Learned from Practice*, 5 HARV. NEGOT. L. REV. 339, 345 (2000); *see also* ADR PRACTITIONERS' GUIDE, *supra* note 15, at 17.

41. ADR PRACTITIONERS' GUIDE, *supra* note 15, at 10; Amy J. Cohen, *Debating the Globalization of U.S. Mediation: Politics, Power, and Practice in Nepal*, 11 HARV. NEGOT. L. REV. 295, 299 (2006). *See generally* Christopher Gibson & Michael Woolcock, *Empowerment and Local Level Conflict Mediation in Indonesia: A Comparative Analysis of Concepts, Measures, and Project Efficacy* (World Bank Policy Research Working Paper 3713, Sept. 2005), *available at* http://ssrn.com/abstract=806225 (arguing that deploying mediation in Indonesian communities can empower local populations and ultimately promote equality).

42. ADR PRACTITIONERS' GUIDE, *supra* note 15, at 11, 19; Moyer & Haynes, *supra* note 39, at 654 ("[M]ediation can act as a unifying process by bringing disparate groups together to work collectively to establish peace in war torn societies."); Okechukwu Oko, *The Problems and Challenges of Lawyering in Developing Societies*, 35 RUTGERS L.J. 569, 641 (2004) (urging that ADR can play an important role in reestablishing social harmony, and focusing specifically on the example of Nigeria).

43. ADR PRACTITIONERS' GUIDE, *supra* note 15, at 7, 18 (asserting that ADR programs can increase civic engagement and improve the skills and abilities of local political leaders); Moyer & Haynes, *supra* note 39, at 667 (arguing that mediation promotes participation in government by engendering trust in governmental institutions).

44. ADR PRACTITIONERS' GUIDE, *supra* note 15, at 14 (stating that Bangladeshi women who participate in ADR "believe that they receive better protection and more compensation . . . than from the formal court system"); Cohen, *supra* note 41, at 337–40 (exploring the use of "rights-based" mediation in Nepal); *see also* C.J. Larkin & Pamela A. DeVoe, *Community Mediation in the Shadow of Revolution: The Nepal Experience*, ACRESOLUTION, Summer 2006, at 20 (describing the use of rights-based community mediation in Nepal).

45. *See, e.g.*, Cynthia Alkon, *The Cookie Cutter Syndrome: Legal Reform Assistance Under Post-communist Democratization Programs*, 2002 J. DISP. RESOL. 327, 346–47, 365 (cautioning that ADR is "no magic pill" that can solve every country's legal system ills); Douglas H. Yarn, *Transnational Conflict Resolution Practice: A Brief Introduction to the Context, Issues, and Search for Best Practice in Exporting Conflict Resolution*, 19 CONFLICT RESOL. Q. 303, 304 (2002) (suggesting that external mediators may sometimes, particularly in Africa, impede the progress toward peace).

46. *See, e.g.*, Laura Nader & Elisabetta Grande, *Current Illusions and Delusions About Conflict Management—In Africa and Elsewhere*, 27 LAW & SOC. INQUIRY 573, 591 (2002) ("U.S.-style alternative dispute resolution is being imposed on many unwilling recipients in foreign countries as a requirement for development aid . . . ."); Matthew C. Stephenson, *A Trojan Horse Behind Chinese Walls? Problems and Prospects of U.S.-Sponsored "Rule of Law" Reform*

tion of whether or when ADR actually fulfills its espoused goals, this Article examines the more theoretical question of whether ADR is consistent with the rule of law in the international context. Many commentators have questioned whether ADR can actually achieve its goals, but few, if any, have challenged this fundamental premise.

IV. Reconciling the Domestic and International Perspectives on the Relationship Between ADR and the Rule of Law

If ADR is seen as an important component of international rule of law efforts, why do critics in the United States think it is inconsistent with the rule of law? I see three ways to resolve this apparent conflict. First, one of the perspectives may simply be wrong. Perhaps either the domestic critics of ADR or the international advocates of ADR have missed the boat and need to learn more from the writings or experiences of the other side. Many who criticize ADR domestically would also criticize ADR internationally, and many who defend ADR domestically would also defend it internationally. Second, perhaps the domestic and international contexts are distinguishable, so that ADR might be hostile to the rule of law domestically and yet supportive of it internationally. This explanation has some attractive aspects. However, after exploring these two theories, I offer a third, which I believe is more useful and enriches our full understanding of the relationship between ADR and the rule of law, and how both relate to justice. Specifically, I urge that those who advocate the use of ADR as part of international rule of law projects have instinctively and intuitively recognized that both ADR, and more traditional litigation-based rule of law projects, can be useful under certain circumstances. Yet more work needs to be done to determine how litigation and ADR properly relate to one another.

A. *Is One Side or the Other Flat Wrong?*

While some would argue that one group or the other is just wrong, this explanation does not seem to be the most likely or desirable way to resolve the paradox. As I have noted, although some may view the domestic ADR critics or the international ADR advocates as extremists, few commentators would go so far as to say there is no tension

---

Projects in the People's Republic of China, 18 UCLA Pac. Basin L.J. 64, 89 (2000) (suggesting that rule of law projects being undertaken in China are eroding native ADR techniques, thereby adversely affecting access to dispute resolution for the poor); Wanis-St. John, *supra* note 40, at 345–46 (questioning the efficacy of ADR programs and noting that problems of asymmetry may arise when mediation is used to resolve disputes between parties of disparate power).

between ADR and the rule of law domestically. At least in some situations, such as the oft-cited *Brown v. Board of Education*,[47] virtually all ADR advocates admit that litigation serves important public purposes that should be protected and preserved.[48]

Similarly, while the international export of ADR has been criticized in particular situations, and while the specific content of the export can be problematic, it is hard to deny that some forms of ADR can, on occasion, serve laudable rule of law purposes. For example, USAID and the Inter-American Development Bank are sponsoring mediation training in Nicaragua to provide disputants with greater access to justice.[49] Interestingly, the Nicaraguan model permits the mediation of domestic violence claims, even though mediating these claims is typically frowned upon in the United States.[50] Although program observers Raquel Aldana and Leticia Saucedo criticize the way mediation is being implemented in Mulukukú, they find it preferable to retain a mediation program and to continue to apply it to certain domestic violence cases, rather than rely purely on a litigation model.[51] They conclude that, in some cases, mediation could be more successful than litigation in addressing the root causes of domestic violence, and that mediation has the advantage of "relatively easy access to justice and

47. 347 U.S. 483 (1954).

48. *See, e.g.*, Bordone et al., *supra* note 12, at 510 (rejecting the idea that all disputes should be resolved consensually, rather than through litigation); Lela P. Love, *Images of Justice*, 1 PEPP. DISP. RESOL. L.J. 29, 29–30 (2000) (emphasizing the public's interest in litigation given its openness, impartiality, and opportunity for appellate review); Menkel-Meadow, *Whose Dispute Is It Anyway*, *supra* note 5, at 2670 (advocating the value of settlement in dispute resolution, but acknowledging that the public's interest in litigation may sometimes outweigh that value).

49. Raquel Aldana & Leticia Saucedo, *The Illusion of Transformative Conflict Resolution: Mediating Domestic Violence in Nicaragua* (undated manuscript) (draft on file with author) (describing a project known as Caminos, which includes work with six pilot communities).

50. The Maria Luisa Ortiz Center, a feminist cooperative, "convinced the Nicaraguan Supreme Court to establish a mediation center in Mulukukú," and urged that domestic violence claims should be mediated. *Id.* at 1, 21–22. Yet feminists and others in the United States are often staunchly opposed to the mediation of domestic violence claims. *See, e.g.*, Karla Fischer et al., *The Culture of Battering and the Role of Mediation in Domestic Violence Cases*, 46 SMU L. REV. 2117 (1993); Scott H. Hughes, *Elizabeth's Story: Exploring Power Imbalances in Divorce Mediation*, 8 GEO. J. LEGAL ETHICS 553, 569–70 (1995).

51. In particular, they are skeptical that mediation can truly transform disputants, particularly where the mode of mediation being used is not that proposed by the advocates of "transformative" mediation. Aldana & Saucedo, *supra* note 49, at 2. They are also concerned that the emphasis on harmony and procedural informality may aggravate victimization caused by domestic violence, and that by emphasizing individual over collective approaches, mediation may undercut group political efforts. *Id.* Aldana and Saucedo rely substantially on the work of anthropologist Sally Engle Merry in structuring their critiques. *See generally* SALLY ENGLE MERRY, HUMAN RIGHTS AND GENDER VIOLENCE: TRANSLATING INTERNATIONAL LAW INTO JUSTICE (2006); Sally Engle Merry, *Rights, Religion, and Community: Approaches to Violence Against Women in the Context of Globalization*, 35 LAW & SOC'Y REV. 39 (2001).

its relative avoidance of re-victimization issues in the domestic violence context."[52] By contrast, they concluded that the litigation approach is severely impeded by a lack of access to justice—particularly in rural areas where roads are virtually nonexistent—as well as by the criminal justice system's inability to fundamentally address the root causes of domestic violence.[53] Thus, they propose retaining and refining the mediation program so that it becomes an adjunct to litigation, rather than its replacement.[54] They further propose that the mediation model should be adjusted in order to "be able to reclaim the 'political' in the personal, and . . . incorporate and capitalize on the local strengths of Mulukukú, including their own cultural notions of conflict resolution."[55]

Similarly, Professor Amy Cohen describes a mediation project in rural Nepal and finds that "mediation," at least as defined and implemented there,[56] is being used to enforce and support human rights.[57] In particular, Cohen describes a donor-sponsored "mediation" training session:

> The facilitator in Nepal . . . began his training . . . by lighting three candles: the first dedicated to the "martyrs of democracy," the second to "fighters for human rights," and the third to "victims of [state] torture." Voice rising, he continued to describe the desperate state of human rights in Nepal: "When will this end? We don't know. Even the government does not obey the Constitution. We must protect the human rights guaranteed in our Constitution, especially women's rights. . . . *This* is what this training is for." And by *this* he meant using the dialogic practices of mediation to work towards the non-violent resolution of disputes—a classic ADR aspiration—yet, in so doing, deploying a range of interventionist

52. Aldana & Saucedo, *supra* note 49, at 25.

53. *Id.* at 2–3, 6–7. Aldana and Saucedo note, for example, that most government services are administered in Siuna, the region's governmental seat, which is approximately seventy kilometers away from Mulukukú. *Id.* at 7. While that might not seem terribly far on a highway, traveling seventy kilometers on a washed out road can take hours and hours. Even phone service is minimal in rural areas like Mulukukú. Additionally, the Nicaraguan legal system requires women who file private claims against their batterers "to bear the costs of the investigation, an attorney, and the prosecution of the claim." *Id.* at 27.

54. *Id.* at 3.

55. *Id.*

56. I put "mediation" in quotes because some would disagree that the dispute resolution tool that Professor Cohen described was appropriately labeled "mediation." She explained that the Nepalese process "is often public and coercive," and purposely enunciates the political demands of members of the society. Cohen, *supra* note 41, at 298.

57. *Id.* at 297; *see also* Larkin & DeVoe, *supra* note 44 (explaining that Nepalese mediation is special because mediators use their powers to protect human rights, the mediation is a substitute for, rather than an alternative to, litigation, and mediation programs seek to remedy power imbalances by affording legal counsel to less powerful disputants).

> strategies to push forward a substantive—and classically non-ADR—human rights project.[58]

The reports on the uses of ADR in Nicaragua, Nepal, and elsewhere cast doubt on the idea that ADR cannot be supportive of law and rights.

B. *Distinguishing the Domestic and International Contexts*

One way to reconcile the two alternative perspectives on ADR is to view ADR as a second-best means of achieving justice. Specifically, one could argue that while an efficient, fair, independent, and accessible judicial system is essential to the rule of law, ADR can be superior from a rule of law perspective when a litigation system is inefficient, corrupt, biased, or inaccessible. This argument has significant appeal, and is consistent with our ADR export practices. The organizations that have urged the export of ADR have focused on developing and transitioning countries that have problematic litigation systems. Efforts to encourage countries with better respected litigation systems to adopt ADR have not occurred with the same frequency.

However, this notion that ADR is a second-best rule of law fails to explain all of the justifications for sponsoring ADR in developing countries. The organizations that have urged adoption of ADR as part of rule of law efforts have not done so merely to promote access to justice where courthouses are too costly, distant, or corrupt, but also to build communities and promote conciliation.[59]

Thinking of ADR as a second-best rule of law is not intellectually satisfying because it fails to take into account the significant differences between litigious and nonlitigious modes of dispute resolution. Specifically, where litigation is based on an attempt to follow publicly enunciated statutes and rules, ADR often resolves disputes without referencing such rules.[60]

Finally, if ADR is needed as a rule of law supplement to litigation to promote access to justice in other countries, surely that rationale has some appeal in our country as well. While we may not have significant access problems due to lack of roads or even illiteracy, economic barriers prevent many, if not most, disputants in the United States from obtaining meaningful access to courts.[61] Thus, if lack of access

---

58. Cohen, *supra* note 41, at 297 (third alteration in original).

59. *See* ADR PRACTITIONERS' GUIDE, *supra* note 15.

60. This is particularly true of mediation, and less true of arbitration.

61. *See, e.g.*, DEBORAH L. RHODE, ACCESS TO JUSTICE 3 (2004) (explaining that while we boast of our support of access to justice, in reality, millions of Americans are denied real access); Robert Rubinson, *A Theory of Access to Justice*, 29 J. LEGAL PROF. 89, 100–02 (2005) (urging

justifies the use of ADR as part of the rule of law abroad, that same rationale should apply domestically as well.

C. The Third Way: Rethinking the Relationship Between ADR and the Rule of Law

Can ADR be supportive of the rule of law for reasons beyond the inadequacy of litigation? Or can ADR be supportive of justice, if not the rule of law, for reasons beyond the inadequacy of litigation? How do societies' laws and ADR procedures relate to societal norms? Although exporters of ADR have not put a great deal of theoretical thought into the question of whether or why ADR might be consistent with the rule of law, their projects offer some useful insights for exploring these concepts.

1. The Relationship Between ADR and Litigation Systems

Domestically, there has been a tendency to view ADR and litigation as mutually exclusive terms. Many assume that either a dispute will be resolved formally and openly through litigation, or it will be resolved informally and privately through ADR. Though experienced practitioners typically avoid this fallacy, students—and even academics—often presume that disputes will be resolved exclusively through one means or the other.

Yet by exporting ADR as part of rule of law projects that also emphasize litigation, the exporters have made clear that ADR and litigation approaches often go hand in hand. For example, court-connected mediation, arbitration, or other programs can be adjuncts to the existing litigation system, and judges can order disputes in litigation to be transferred to those regimes. It seems that ADR and litigation approaches are closely related domestically as well, as I have discussed in greater depth in other works.[62] Whether the ADR process originates from court orders, administrative rules, or contractual agreements, a given dispute tends to shift back and forth between the two systems over time. For example, in the United States, negotiations and mediations are conducted in the shadow of possible litigation; arbitration agreements, awards, and settlements are enforced in court, and cases that have been litigated for years may ultimately be

that, for the most part, the only persons or groups able to obtain access to the U.S. litigation system are commercial organizations, affluent individuals, and persons engaged in "values conflicts" of significant interest to attract pro bono or reduced-fee representation).

62. Jean R. Sternlight, *Separate and Not Equal: Integrating Civil Procedure and ADR in Legal Academia*, 80 Notre Dame L. Rev. 681, 690–700 (2005).

resolved through ADR.[63] While this relationship can be explored outside the international context, the inclusion of ADR as part of international rule of law projects may help make the connections more obvious to commentators and policymakers at home.

I believe that the relationship between ADR and litigation, both domestically and internationally, may be reflective of a more general tension between formal and informal approaches to justice. Formal and informal approaches each have their virtues and vices.[64] Whereas formal rule-based systems can potentially offer more certainty and transparency, such systems are frequently slower and more costly, and they often fail to distinguish individual circumstances.[65] Thus, throughout history and throughout the world, we have seen oscillations and tensions between formal and informal approaches.[66] For example, a recent book describing dispute resolution in rural China shows that these tensions exist in societies quite different from our own.[67]

2. *Relating ADR and Litigation to Norms*

An extensive and rich domestic literature has explored the link between law and norms. While scholars' perspectives differ somewhat,

63. *See id.*

64. *See, e.g.*, Jean R. Sternlight, *ADR Is Here: Preliminary Reflections on Where It Fits in a System of Justice*, 3 NEV. L.J. 289 (2002–2003) (urging that a proper system of justice should resolve societal as well as individual interests, seek societal harmony, and that both litigation and ADR can serve such goals); Jean R. Sternlight, *In Search of the Best Procedure for Enforcing Employment Discrimination Laws: A Comparative Analysis*, 78 TUL. L. REV. 1401 (2004) (examining tensions between using formal and informal systems to resolve employment discrimination complaints in the United States, Great Britain, and Australia).

65. *See* Roscoe Pound, *The Causes of Popular Dissatisfaction with the Administration of Justice*, 40 AM. L. REV. 729, 731 (1906) ("The most important and most constant cause of dissatisfaction with all law at all times is to be found in the necessarily mechanical operation of legal rules. . . . Legal history shows an oscillation between wide judicial discretion on the one hand and strict confinement of the magistrate by minute and detailed rules upon the other hand.").

66. *See, e.g.*, Thomas O. Main, *ADR: The New Equity*, 74 U. CIN. L. REV. 329, 329–30 (2005) (urging that just as the British system of equity sought to relieve problems and tensions created by the strict common-law approach, ADR today is a release for pressures created by our formal litigation system); Jacqueline M. Nolan-Haley, *The Merger of Law and Mediation: Lessons from Equity Jurisprudence and Roscoe Pound*, 6 CARDOZO J. CONFLICT RESOL. 57, 58–59 (2004) ("Both equity and mediation offer a form of 'individualized justice' unavailable in the official legal system, and each allow room for mercy in an otherwise rigid, rule-bound justice system.").

67. *See* Frank K. Upham, *Who Will Find the Defendant if He Stays with His Sheep? Justice in Rural China*, 114 YALE L.J. 1675, 1714 (2005) (reviewing ZHU SULI, SENDING LAW TO THE COUNTRYSIDE: RESEARCH ON CHINA'S BASIC-LEVEL JUDICIAL SYSTEM (2000), describing justice in rural China and urging that "[t]he solution [to the tension], therefore, may be to institutionalize the dialectic that Zhu describes between formal and informal, modern and customary, center and periphery in a manner designed to make the norms created more accessible to the public while also being respectful of local practices").

virtually all agree that law and norms are distinct. The causal relationship between law and norms, however, is less clear. Some suggest that norms influence laws;[68] others think that law influences norms.[69] Still others believe that judges can find ways to influence norms using means other than the mere issuance of final decisions on the merits.[70] Another popular belief is that the norms can be at least as important as law in structuring social behavior.[71] Indeed, some have argued that the imposition of law can be counterproductive to social order, in that it can undermine norms that are already operating effectively.[72] In addition, some claim that norms are more predictable than law.[73]

By studying ADR in other countries, we may learn more about the relationship between ADR and norms. Domestically, it is often suggested that one of the advantages of mediation is that it allows parties to resolve disputes according to their own preferences[74] or according

---

68. *See, e.g.*, Robert D. Cooter, *Decentralized Law for a Complex Economy: The Structural Approach to Adjudicating the New Law Merchant*, 144 U. PA. L. REV. 1643, 1694–95 (1996).

69. *See, e.g.*, Cass R. Sunstein, *On the Expressive Function of Law*, 144 U. PA. L. REV. 2021, 2025–29 (1996).

70. Susan Sturm, *Law's Role in Addressing Complex Discrimination*, *in* HANDBOOK OF EMPLOYMENT DISCRIMINATION RESEARCH: RIGHTS AND REALITIES 35, 50 (Laura Beth Nielsen & Robert L. Nelson eds., 2005). Professor Sturm explained that judges can affect norms in three ways:

> 1. Structuring occasions for collective norm development and problem solving in the penumbra of formal judicial process;
> 2. Increasing non-legal actors' capacity to conduct conflict resolution and problem solving that generates and institutionalizes efficient, fair, and workable norms; and
> 3. Developing the capacity of mediating actors, such as experts and administrative agencies, to connect the domains of formal and informal norms.

Id.

71. *See, e.g.*, ROBERT C. ELLICKSON, ORDER WITHOUT LAW: HOW NEIGHBORS SETTLE DISPUTES (1991) (showing that a close-knit group of Shasta County cattlemen structured their fencing and other behavior based on norms rather than law); Eric A. Posner, *The Regulation of Groups: The Influence of Legal and Nonlegal Sanctions on Collective Action*, 63 U. CHI. L. REV. 133, 155 (1996) ("The importance of maintaining a good reputation and of avoiding ostracism deters improper behavior."); Robert E. Scott, *The Limits of Behavioral Theories of Law and Social Norms*, 86 VA. L. REV. 1603, 1603–04 (2000) (showing the impact of informal sanctions such as shaming); Cass R. Sunstein, *Social Norms and Social Roles*, 96 COLUM. L. REV. 903 (1996) (showing the significant influence of extralegal norms on smoking, littering, and other human behaviors).

72. *See, e.g.*, Richard H. Pildes, *The Destruction of Social Capital Through Law*, 144 U. PA. L. REV. 2055, 2057 (1996).

73. *See, e.g.*, Haini Guo & Bradley Klein, *Bargaining in the Shadow of the Community: Neighborly Dispute Resolution in Beijing Hutongs*, 20 OHIO ST. J. ON DISP. RESOL. 825, 885–86 (2005) (stating that in China, formal law is "muddy" and more unpredictable than social norms).

74. In mediation lingo, disputants are encouraged to engage in self-determination. *See* MODEL STANDARDS OF CONDUCT FOR MEDIATORS (Am. Arbitration Ass'n., Am. Bar Ass'n & Ass'n for Conflict Resolution 2005), *available at* http://www.abanet.org/dispute/news/ModelStandardsofConductforMediatorsfinal05.pdf ("A mediator shall conduct a mediation based on the principle of party self-determination. Self-determination is the act of coming to a voluntary,

to relevant social norms, rather than strictly according to law.[75] Thus, in societies such as ours where law plays a central role, mediation offers disputants an opportunity to resolve their disputes in a manner different than the law might require. In societies in which formal law does not play a central role, mediation or conciliation is conducted in accordance with societal traditions or norms.[76] While many American ADR advocates think a mediator should be a completely neutral party, other societies believe that a mediator may help to infuse social norms into the resolution of the dispute.[77] Similarly, arbitration is often praised because it permits disputants to use their own selected norms, which may be different from those chosen by the society at large.[78]

Just as litigation and ADR can go hand in hand, a society can blend reliance on norms and reliance on law. While we tend to assume that law must be applied through formal government structures and that norms can be applied only through informal nongovernment struc-

uncoerced decision in which each party makes free and informed choices as to process and outcome."); *see also* Wayne D. Brazil, *Should Court-Sponsored ADR Survive?*, 21 OHIO ST. J. ON DISP. RESOL. 241, 270 (2006) ("If there is one mantra that dominates mediation theory, it is party self-determination."). *But see* James R. Coben, *Gollum, Meet Sméagol: A Schizophrenic Rumination on Mediator Values Beyond Self-Determination and Neutrality*, 5 CARDOZO J. CONFLICT RESOL. 65, 70–72 (2004) (arguing that while self-determination is said to be mediation's "prime directive," it is appropriate to question "the underlying legitimacy of a disputing process committed to self-determination and neutrality of intervention in a society plagued by asymmetric distribution of power"); Nancy A. Welsh, *Making Deals in Court-Connected Mediation: What's Justice Got to Do with It?*, 79 WASH. U. L.Q. 787 (2001) (contrasting the aspiration of party self-determination with the realities of court-connected mediation, and expressing concern that many court mediation programs do not serve disputants' interests in procedural justice).

75. *See generally* Clark Freshman, *Privatizing Same-Sex "Marriage" Through Alternative Dispute Resolution: Community-Enhancing Versus Community-Enabling Mediation*, 44 UCLA L. REV. 1687 (1997) (suggesting that mediation can be a means for disputants to enforce the community's norms that they deem most relevant); Clark Freshman, *The Promise and Perils of "Our" Justice: Psychological, Critical and Economic Perspectives on Communities and Prejudices in Mediation*, 6 CARDOZO J. CONFLICT RESOL. 1 (2004) (examining the extent to which mediation may promote justice by permitting social subgroups to base decisions on their own norms).

76. *See, e.g.*, James A. Wall, Jr. & Ronda Roberts Callister, *Ho'oponopono: Some Lessons from Hawaiian Mediation*, 11 NEGOTIATION J. 45 (1995) (describing the traditional Hawaiian and Polynesian dispute resolution method, Ho'oponopono); Robert Yazzie, *"Life Comes from It": Navajo Justice Concepts*, 24 N.M. L. REV. 175, 180–87 (1994) (describing the Navajo peacemaking process).

77. Yazzie, *supra* note 76, at 181–82; *see also* Donna Coker, *Enhancing Autonomy for Battered Women: Lessons from Navajo Peacemaking*, 47 UCLA L. REV. 1, 35 (1999) (describing the role played by tribal "peacemakers" in Navajo peacemaking procedures and noting "[t]he peacemaker, usually chosen by his or her chapter, is a respected person with a demonstrated knowledge of traditional Navajo stories" (citation omitted)).

78. Lisa Bernstein, *Opting out of the Legal System: Extralegal Contractual Relations in the Diamond Industry*, 21 J. LEGAL STUD. 115, 135–43 (1992) (discussing the shortcomings of the American legal system as it relates to the diamond industry and how the industry has adapted to enforce extralegal agreements).

tures, a fascinating recent study of dispute resolution in rural China shows that this assumption can be wrong. It demonstrates that residents of Beijing neighborhoods called "hutongs" relied primarily on informal social norms to resolve their disputes,[79] although these norms were applied with the assistance of committees of local residents and the neighborhood police.[80] Similarly, Professor Susan Sturm has recently urged that we rethink our core assumptions about ADR. She argues that nonlitigation dispute resolution need not always be private, and that conciliatory approaches can enforce disputants' legal rights and inculcate social norms.[81]

3. *What Can We Realistically Expect from ADR or Litigation Alone?*

Given the links between ADR and litigation, and the important role played by societal norms, advocates of both ADR and litigation have a tendency to be unrealistically optimistic regarding the possible benefits of either approach. By examining the international blending of ADR and rule of law efforts, we can better understand the cultural, economic, and social limits that potentially constrain progress when either approach is used alone. We may also begin to understand how blending ADR and the rule of law yields a more just dispute resolution system than either single approach can.

a. Limits to the Traditional Rule of Law Approach

As has been thoroughly discussed in the academic rule of law literature, there seem to be limits on the extent to which traditional rule of law projects, particularly those imported from other countries, can fundamentally change a country's approach to law.[82] Whether the goal is to eliminate corruption, increase access to justice, promote transparency, or protect individual rights, it is clear that providing judicial training and modernizing courthouses may not be sufficient to change a legal culture. For example, it is well recognized that the ex-

79. Guo & Klein, *supra* note 73, at 827 (commenting that more formal channels were typically "viewed as too costly, socially disruptive, and unpredictable to be an efficient option in all but the most serious disputes").

80. *Id.* at 827–28.

81. Sturm, *supra* note 70, at 54–56 (explaining that although current critiques that ADR is private, unaccountable, and does not generate norms are often well founded, we must consider the possibility that judicial involvement can be used to ensure ADR is "norm generating, transparent, and accountable, at least at the systemic level").

82. To some extent rule of law and other development projects can be counterproductive. *See* David Kennedy, The Dark Sides of Virtue: Reassessing International Humanitarianism 3–35 (2004) (detailing numerous problems with using a human rights-based approach to assist other countries' development).

tensive, traditional Latin American rule of law projects in the 1970s made few fundamental advances.[83] Professor Rosa Ehrenreich Brooks and others have analyzed how entrenched legal norms impede rule of law efforts.[84] A number of scholars have emphasized that the rule of law is an inherently Western construct and that persons in countries with different cultures and histories, such as China, may not share the perspective that increasing the role of formal law is the best way to create a just society.[85] Further, countries may be unable to provide effective access to litigation due to their limited resources. The well-developed domestic literature on problems of access to justice shows that, even in a rich country like the United States, we have grave problems assuring that the average person can obtain justice.[86] Moreover, Professor Marc Galanter's work shows that even an ostensibly fair litigation system can prove ineffective in eliminating economic and social inequalities.[87]

b. Limits to the ADR-Only Approach

The limitations of ADR, at least in the international context, have not been as thoroughly analyzed. Yet it seems that the proponents of ADR in international rule of law projects may be unduly optimistic in

83. Such projects were called democratization, but their content was similar to what we now call rule of law projects. *See, e.g.*, JAMES A. GARDNER, LEGAL IMPERIALISM: AMERICAN LAWYERS AND FOREIGN AID IN LATIN AMERICA (1980) (voicing regrets of a former Ford Foundation official regarding 1970s rule of law projects in Latin America); David M. Trubek & Marc Galanter, *Scholars in Self-Estrangement: Some Reflections on the Crisis in Law and Development Studies in the United States*, 1974 WIS. L. REV. 1062 (critiquing development approaches used in the early 1970s); *see also* THOMAS CAROTHERS, AIDING DEMOCRACY ABROAD: THE LEARNING CURVE (1999) (setting out mixed views of democratization projects from the 1960s through the 1990s); PROMOTING THE RULE OF LAW ABROAD: IN SEARCH OF KNOWLEDGE (Thomas Carothers ed., 2006) (collecting essays on democratization efforts).

84. Rosa Ehrenreich Brooks, *The New Imperialism: Violence, Norms, and the "Rule of Law,"* 101 MICH. L. REV. 2275, 2283–89 (2003).

85. *See, e.g.*, Lan Cao, *Introduction* to Symposium, *The "Rule of Law" in China*, 11 WM. & MARY BILL RTS. J. 539, 542 (2003) (noting that the Chinese may have a very different attitude toward the rule of law than Americans do, and that "rule of law" translates into Chinese as "rule *by* law," which implies a more authoritarian approach); Pat K. Chew, *The Rule of Law: China's Skepticism and the Rule of People*, 20 OHIO ST. J. ON DISP. RESOL. 43, 48–54 (2005) (discussing China's ongoing tension between the Western rule of law approach and the traditional Chinese preference for rule of people); Stephenson, *supra* note 46, at 76 (discussing the Chinese government's resistance to the phrase "rule of law"); Benedict Sheehy, *Fundamentally Conflicting Views of the Rule of Law in China and the West and Implications for Commercial Disputes*, 26 NW. J. INT'L L. & BUS. 225 (2006). *But see* RANDALL PEERENBOOM, CHINA'S LONG MARCH TOWARD RULE OF LAW (2002) (presenting a more optimistic view on Chinese enthusiasm for the rule of law).

86. *See* Rubinson, *supra* note 61, at 100–02. *See generally* RHODE, *supra* note 61.

87. Marc Galanter, *Why the "Haves" Come out Ahead: Speculations on the Limits of Legal Change*, 9 LAW & SOC'Y REV. 95, 119–22 (1974).

their belief that ADR can solve problems of corruption, access to justice, and social inequality.

First, while advocates suggest that replacing or supplementing litigation with ADR could reduce corruption, it is not obvious why this would be so. To the extent that a culture of corruption exists, mediators and arbitrators could fall prey to the same temptations as judges. Even though mediation does not result in resolution unless all of the disputants come to an agreement, a corrupt or biased mediator could still have a significant impact on that resolution. The private setting of ADR may also enhance existing corruption problems. Proponents urge that transparency and public access are important ways to fight corruption and bias, yet ADR is typically conducted privately.

Second, although it is often true that ADR is less expensive than litigation, this does not necessarily mean that providing ADR solves problems of access to justice. Depending on the type of ADR and the quality of the results, ADR may not provide access to justice. If the ADR process is biased and unfair, there may be no justice at all.

Third, to the extent that rule of law projects establish significant ADR programs in the absence of effective accessible litigation, whether such programs can truly provide justice is unclear. In the United States, ADR typically works because it operates in the shadow of an effective litigation system.[88] Disputes are often resolved in negotiation or mediation because parties know that if they do not resolve the disputes informally, they will have to resort to litigation. Similarly, parties contract to take disputes to arbitration because they know that courts exist to ensure that the arbitration clause and arbitral award are enforced. It is also unclear whether ADR can work without the threat of litigation. This issue is critically important to contemplating the effectiveness of ADR in some of the countries to which it is currently being exported.

There is no doubt that societies can effectively resolve disputes independently of the litigation system. Comparative and historical legal research shows that many societies, including our own, have used means other than litigation to resolve disputes.[89] Absent court en-

88. *See* Raymond Shonholtz, *The Mediating Future*, 552 ANNALS AM. ACAD. POL. & SOC. SCI., July 1997, at 139, 141 (recognizing that the Western conception of mediation depends on the existence of a background formal legal structure).

89. *See* SIMON ROBERTS, ORDER AND DISPUTE: AN INTRODUCTION TO LEGAL ANTHROPOLOGY 26–27 (1979) ("[E]ven where judicial institutions are found they do not always enjoy the unchallenged pre-eminence in the business of dispute settlement which our courts claim and manage to exercise. Fighting and other forms of self-help, resort to supernatural agencies, the use of shaming and ridicule, or the unilateral withdrawal of essential forms of cooperation may all constitute equally approved and effective means of handling conflict."). *See generally* JER-

forcement, arbitration can work to the extent that the society's respect for the status of the arbitrator and the process of arbitration is sufficient to ensure compliance with arbitral agreements or awards. Similarly, conciliatory forms of dispute resolution, such as negotiation and mediation, can be effective, absent litigation, to the degree that social norms and bonds pressure parties into resolving their disputes and abiding by their agreements. In short, what we might call peer pressure can take the place of an effective litigation system, and allow ADR mechanisms to function without a backdrop of litigation.[90]

However, to the extent that the effectiveness of ADR relies on the existence of such social norms and pressures, it is unclear whether ADR alone can ensure justice or resolve social inequalities. ADR programs have been implemented abroad for many reasons. Some of these programs use ADR to empower the powerless or wrest control from the elite. For example, recall the Nepalese "mediation" program described by Cohen, which was geared toward protecting human rights,[91] and the Nicaraguan mediation program designed to protect women from domestic violence.[92] To the extent that ADR programs like these are not linked to a functioning litigation system, established social interests may have little incentive to relinquish any of their power in mediation. Idealists might believe that once the powerful elite are eye to eye with the powerless, they will decide to share their

OLD S. AUERBACH, JUSTICE WITHOUT LAW? (1983) (examining informal and nonadversarial forms of justice throughout American history); Laura Nader, *Harmony Models and the Construction of Law*, *in* CONFLICT RESOLUTION: CROSS-CULTURAL PERSPECTIVES 41 (Kevin Avruch et al. eds., 1991) (considering cultural aspects of alternative dispute resolution models and discussing modern anthropologists' frequent biases in favor of harmony models).

90. Nepalese mediation apparently relies on community pressure. Professors C.J. Larkin and Pamela DeVoe explain that mediation sessions include villagers as well as disputants and mediators, and that the villagers are "both audience and participants." Larkin & DeVoe, *supra* note 44, at 23. They also report that failure to reach an agreement "appears to be rare," and that at least one study showed "a decline in the level of violence and prejudice against women in areas where there were women's community mediation groups." *Id.*; *cf.* Richard L. Abel, *Introduction*, *in* 2 THE POLITICS OF INFORMAL JUSTICE 1 (Richard L. Abel ed., 1982). Professor Abel explains that the informal justice that works well in precapitalist societies "cannot be recreated under Western capitalism":

> Precapitalist legal informalism is embedded in and contingent upon a social structure in which: relationships are multiplex and continuous, the supporters of one disputant are bound to the other by crosscutting ties, there is little residential mobility, and reputation in the face-to-face community is highly valued and easily lost in the absence of privacy. Western capitalism not only lacks these qualities but also actively rejects them. . . . It is not surprising, therefore, that when informal legal institutions are introduced into Western capitalist societies they do not help to preserve relationships . . . but rather serve to celebrate their termination.

Id. at 2–3.

91. Cohen, *supra* note 41.

92. Aldana & Saucedo, *supra* note 49.

power and wealth.[93] This may occur. But it seems more likely that such mechanisms will be successful in redistributing power only to the extent that the weaker members of the society can use political, physical, or economic influence to demand such redistribution.[94]

Empirical investigations may teach us how to blend formal and informal justice systems. While a full study is beyond the scope of this Article, India and Japan offer intriguing possibilities. In India, substantial efforts have been made to informalize the justice system to provide greater access to justice. A number of analysts have criticized these attempts, urging that they ultimately do not serve the purposes for which they were designed.[95] But at least one analyst suggests that Japan's concerted effort to rely more extensively on conciliation and other informal means of dispute resolution has been effective. Professor Frank Upham explains that, although it is widely assumed that Japan has always been an antilitigious country, Japan's preference for conciliatory approaches has been instilled deliberately by political forces.[96] Upham notes that while in the early 1970s litigation was common in Japan, thereafter the government, courts, bar associations, and others reduced the number of lawyers and lawsuits, and replaced them with an array of administrative and ADR processes.[97] Given the great economic success of the Japanese while using a substantially conciliatory system, Upham urges that developing countries may not necessarily want to adopt a formal rule of law system.[98]

93. *See, e.g.*, ROBERT A. BARUCH BUSH & JOSEPH P. FOLGER, THE PROMISE OF MEDIATION: RESPONDING TO CONFLICT THROUGH EMPOWERMENT AND RECOGNITION 261–84 (1994) (arguing that when disputants come face to face in mediation, there is at least the potential that they will develop a better understanding of, and empathy for, their fellow disputants' perspectives, and become empowered to resolve the disputes in ways that are mutually beneficial).

94. Aldana and Saucedo have reached a similar conclusion, and thus, urge that mediation must be linked to rather than replace litigation. Aldana & Saucedo, *supra* note 49, at 3.

95. *See, e.g.*, Marc Galanter & Jayanth K. Krishnan, *Debased Informalism:* Lok Adalats *and Legal Rights in Modern India*, *in* BEYOND COMMON KNOWLEDGE: EMPIRICAL APPROACHES TO THE RULE OF LAW 96, 126 (Erik G. Jensen & Thomas C. Heller eds., 2003) (urging that lok adalats, established in the 1980s, "hold little promise for delivering effective legal services to those most in need"); *see also* Sarah Leah Whitson, *"Neither Fish, nor Flesh, nor Good Red Herring"* Lok Adalats*: An Experiment in Informal Dispute Resolution in India*, 15 HASTINGS INT'L & COMP. L. REV. 391, 392 (1992) (claiming that the lok adalats have become yet another "moribund institution" that subverts the rights of the poor).

96. Frank Upham, *Mythmaking in the Rule-of-Law Orthodoxy*, *in* PROMOTING THE RULE OF LAW ABROAD, *supra* note 83, at 75, 91–98; *see also* John Owen Haley, *The Politics of Informal Justice: The Japanese Experience, 1922–1942*, *in* 2 THE POLITICS OF INFORMAL JUSTICE, *supra* note 90, at 125 (providing another account of the Japanese attempt to replace litigation with conciliation).

97. Upham, *supra* note 96, at 91, 97.

98. *Id.* at 98–101.

V. Is the Rule of Law an End in Itself or a Means to an End?

The relationship between ADR and the rule of law and how countries might structure their legal systems is now clearer. As Professor Carrie Menkel-Meadow has explained, one of the real virtues of the American export of ADR is that it offers the United States the opportunity to *import* additional knowledge about ADR.[99] The comparison of the domestic and international discussions of the relationship between ADR and the rule of law offers several key insights.

First, attempting to build dispute resolution systems that are either exclusively formal or exclusively informal can be problematic. Exclusively formal systems are often expensive, inaccessible, and unable to serve all of the conciliatory interests that can be served by an informal system. Purely informal systems can also be problematic, unless the community is small enough that the informal mechanism will be sufficiently transparent and enforceable. We must also consider norms, as well as formally adopted laws, in determining how societies' disputes are and ought to be resolved.

Second, the question of whether ADR and the rule of law are consistent is semantic. If the rule of law is narrowly defined only to include litigation-oriented approaches, then most ADR processes are inconsistent with the rule of law. If, on the other hand, the rule of law is more broadly defined, as it sometimes has been in the international context, then rule of law projects may include ADR elements. To the extent the discussion remains on this purely semantic level, it is not particularly interesting.

Third, a far more interesting and substantive question is whether we should favor the rule of law as an end in and of itself, or whether we should treat the rule of law as a means to an end. In my view, comparing the domestic and international treatments of ADR and the rule of law shows that we ought to consider how the rule of law is or can be part of a larger vision of justice.[100] Interestingly, this fundamental issue is not typically explored in any depth. While commentators often examine the virtues of the rule of law (transparency, fairness, equality, etc.), they rarely consider whether a rule of law approach is essential to protect those values, or whether other systems of dispute resolution might be as good as, or even better than, the rule of law. Whereas

99. Carrie Menkel-Meadow, *Exporting and Importing ADR: "I've Looked at Life from Both Sides Now,"* Disp. Resol. Mag., Spring 2006, at 5.

100. *Cf. id.* (explaining that ADR's legitimacy can be established by values other than the rule of law, such as treaties, consent, and economic and trade values).

Westerners typically place great value on the rule of law for fostering individual rights and protecting the individual from the state, not all societies share this vision. Some Chinese, for example, see the rule of law as a tool of state oppression, and favor reliance on informal norms and personal relationships over reliance on formal law.[101] Similarly, ADR may operate differently in societies, such as China, that are more communitarian and less individualistic than our own. The goal of mediation in many societies is to preserve or create harmonious social relationships, and not merely to maximize individual self-interest. For example, mediation in China focuses more on preserving relationships, status, and social ties, and less on protecting individual rights.[102]

Fourth, examining the links between ADR, the rule of law, and justice requires us to rethink the meaning of these terms. Creating a harmonious society is not part of the traditional definition of the rule of law, and yet some would say that learning to live together harmoniously, as a community, is a critical aspect of justice. For example, Aristotle's and Plato's definitions of justice emphasized the importance of all components of the society joining together to do a job well.[103] A variety of non-Western societies also rely on their systems of justice to provide harmony, balance, or reconciliation.[104] At the same time, some might advocate using dispute resolution processes to effectuate social change and eliminate inequalities. But while American commentators who adopt this belief tend to assume that rights-based litigation is the best dispute resolution technique for achieving social change, perhaps it is not. For example, Professors Amy Cohen and Ellen Deason write that "[c]ommunity mediation boards in Nepal and Bangladesh combine individual dispute settlement with attention to remedying some of the cultural and class inequalities affecting women and other marginalized groups."[105]

In short, the efforts to include ADR as part of the rule of law projects intuitively recognize the importance of harmony, reconciliation, balance, and equality as parts of a fundamental vision of jus-

101. *See* Chew, *supra* note 85, at 51–52.

102. *See* GOH BEE CHEN, LAW WITHOUT LAWYERS, JUSTICE WITHOUT COURTS: ON TRADITIONAL CHINESE MEDIATION 15–18 (2002).

103. Sternlight, *supra* note 64, at 302.

104. *Id.* at 301; *see also* MERRY, *supra* note 51, at 113–33 (discussing the traditional Fijian process of "bulubulu," during which "a person apologizes for an offense and offers a whale's tooth (*tabua*) and a gift and asks forgiveness," and also describing this process as a traditional means for achieving reconciliation within the society, but one which sometimes creates problems, particularly in modern settings, like rape crime proceedings).

105. Amy J. Cohen & Ellen E. Deason, *Comparative Considerations: Toward the Global Transfer of Ideas About Dispute System Design*, DISP. RESOL. MAG., Spring 2006, at 23.

tice.[106] By labeling ADR projects as rule of law projects and using them to achieve or work toward peace, perhaps we are beginning to recognize that our definition of justice ought to be broadened to include harmony and social equality as well as individual rights.[107] As Roscoe Pound explained a century ago, while law may serve justice, justice is broader than law.[108]

Those who have included ADR as part of rule of law projects may not have consciously focused on the meaning of justice or where ADR and the rule of law might fit into a definition of justice. Nonetheless, the intuition that led to the expansion of rule of law projects may help us to broaden our inquiries into the nature of justice—both here and abroad.

---

106. *See* Richard L. Abel, *The Contradictions of Informal Justice*, *in* 1 THE POLITICS OF INFORMAL JUSTICE 267 (Richard L. Abel ed., 1982). Abel approaches some of the issues discussed in this Article from a somewhat different perspective, focusing on the contradictions of informal justice. He concludes that informal processes can both ameliorate and aggravate existing inequalities, and can stimulate and prevent popular participation. *See id.* While clearly recognizing flaws of informal justice, he also sees potential virtues:

> Yet, if the goals of informal justice are contradictory, and if it is incapable of realizing them because of contradictions inherent in advanced capitalism, informalism should not simplistically be repudiated as merely an evil to be resisted, or be dismissed as a marginal phenomenon that can safely be ignored. It is advocated by reformers and embraced by disputants precisely because it expresses values that deservedly elicit broad allegiance: the preference for harmony over conflict, for mechanisms that offer equal access to the many rather than unequal privilege to the few, that operate quickly and cheaply, that permit all citizens to participate in decision making rather than limiting authority to "professionals," that are familiar rather than esoteric, and that strive for and achieve substantive justice rather than frustrating it in the name of form. Those ideals must, and will, continue to inspire the struggle to create the institutions—and the society—that can realize them.

Id. at 310.

107. *See* Robert M. Ackerman, *Disputing Together: Conflict Resolution and the Search for Community*, 18 OHIO ST. J. ON DISP. RESOL. 27, 91 (2002) ("The ultimate promise for dispute resolution is that it can harness and nurture the *will* to play together so that society is more than the sum total of disparate notes, but rather a cohesive—albeit sometimes discordant—tune."); Stanley Lubman, *Bird in a Cage: Chinese Law Reform After Twenty Years*, 20 NW. J. INT'L L. & BUS. 383, 388 (2000) (observing that much of China's pro-mediation philosophy stems from Mao's insistence that unlike litigation, mediation will serve to bring the community together rather than push it apart). *See generally* Oko, *supra* note 42 (asserting that for some countries, development of the rule of law may not be the ultimate end, and that, instead, the ultimate end sought ought to be peaceful resolution of disputes); Shonholtz, *supra* note 88.

108. Pound, *supra* note 65, at 732–33 ("Justice, which is the end of law, is the ideal compromise between the activities of each and the activities of all in a crowded world. The law seeks to harmonize these activities and to adjust the relations of every man with his fellows so as to accord with the moral sense of the community. When the community is at one in its ideas of justice, this is possible. When the community is divided and diversified, and groups and classes and interests, understanding each other none too well, have conflicting ideas of justice, the task is extremely difficult. It is impossible that legal and ethical ideas should be in entire accord in such a society.").

Part IV
Coda

Coda

As the essays in this volume illustrate, international conflict resolution is a growth industry, as well as field of study, not only because human conflicts continue to proliferate in our increasingly globalizing and increasingly complex world, but also because we continue to invent more processes for attempting to resolve, or at least manage, those conflicts.

All of the basic and foundational processes of conflict resolution – negotiation, mediation, arbitration, adjudication, fact-finding, conciliation, enquiries, complex multi-party consensus-building (whether facilitated or not), and public policy formation and negotiation (for example, in treaty negotiations and peace conferences) have been and are being utilized in transnational dispute resolution. Many of these processes are now initiated in private (commercial), public (formal adjudication) and hybrid (investor–state) settings. In addition, conflict resolution in the transnational, national and subnational (for example, civil war) spheres have spawned a variety of new processes, such as truth and reconciliation commissions, and adaptations of older, indigenous processes, such as *gacaca*, further elaborating on and modifying older processes with cultural, political and economic variations, now called 'bespoke transitional justice' (Ramji-Nogales, 2010).

The expansion of conceptions of what constitutes 'international' or 'transnational' conflict resolution, including the ability of individuals to sue or make claims in new venues such as the regional courts for human rights violations (Schneider, 2009) and the growing role of non-governmental organizations as parties and advocates in disputes – for example, the 'anti-globalization' efforts against the WTO (Held and McGrew, 2007) – demonstrate how conflict creation and conflict resolution are ever changing and responding to new conditions. It would seem unlikely, then, that conflict resolution in a transnational context will ever become any single or stable system. As new conflicts and situations arise, new forms of process seem to be continuously evolving to offer new and different approaches to new conditions, new parties and new configurations of political and other organizational life. As many scholars in the field of international law and relations have argued, new 'governance' in international relations is often international, transnational and subnational, all at the same time (Twining, 2000; Shaffer, 2010), meaning that policy, law-making, and dispute resolution are all conducted in a variety of different sites, including formal bodies, but also including informal networks and other locations of action (Slaughter, 2004).

As these three volumes have illustrated, the field of conflict resolution has developed a wide range of theory about human behaviour, in both formal and informal settings, and has developed its own canons, concepts and claims about how people in conflict do (descriptive) and should (prescriptive) behave. Adding consideration of 'foreign' (to Western- and Northern-dominated theory development – see Ramraj, 2011; Sen, 2009; Sornarajah, 2010), 'transnational' and 'comparative' perspectives on conflict resolution, as offered by many of the essays in this volume, suggests that many of those principles, concepts and ideas not only might be culturally specific or variable, but also might require both more conceptualization and empirical study as we look more broadly at different forms of conflict resolution in increasingly diverse and complex settings.

Consider some examples of conflict resolution theory and practice challenged by international or multicultural settings:

- How do we know when parties have reached an *agreement?* (What different expressions of *consent* are there in multicultural and multi-party settings?)
- Who has *authority* in transnational settings? Government/formal representatives only? Others? How many different *tracks* of engagement are possible in international conflicts? State to state? Private parties? Mixed – for example, trade and economic issues, terrorism policy?
- Who makes *decisions* in state conflict resolution? Are there *democracy deficits*? Does that matter for all issues? Whose democracy? Is *deliberation* and democracy essential for good conflict resolution? (See Volume II.)
- How can consensual agreements in transnational settings be *enforced* without command institutions (courts) or effective 'rule of law' (Ginsburg and Shaffer, 2010)? What *alternative incentives* are there for compliance with international conflict resolution agreements and other international undertakings (Koh, 1997)?
- How do *processes or organizations of conflict resolution* and *transitional justice* (Teitel, 2000; Stromseth, Wippman and Brooks, 2006) affect the development of more permanent dispute resolution mechanisms, legitimacy and/or democratization of regimes? Is *legalization* or *judicialization* inevitable? A good thing?
- Should we continue to encourage some *informalism* and *experimentation* in dispute system design in multicultural or post-conflict settings –consider the hybrid processes in East Timor, among others (Stromseth, Wippman and Brooks, Chapter 13, this volume)?
- What is the role of, and how effective are, *formal international organizations* (for example, the UN, World Bank, International Red Cross and the International Crisis Group) in sponsoring dispute resolution?
- How does conflict at *group or nation-state* levels differ from *individual conflict*?
- How do *state-sponsored* dispute resolution efforts compare to the efforts of *private organizations* (both *formal* – for example, the International Chamber of Commerce – and *informal* as in the variety of peace-seeking NGOs)?
- If parties' needs, interests, objectives and goals are multiple and complex in any one society or social or legal setting, how are *needs, goals and objectives* to be assessed in more multicultural settings?
- What is the relationship of the resolution of *individual disputes* in the multinational arena to *state and international* policy (Dunoff, Ratner and Wippman, 2010; Schneider, 1998; see, for example, the Iran Claims Tribunal) and to *legitimacy* of process and justice for whole regimes (consider the amnesty processes in many truth and reconciliation processes).
- Is *neutrality* ever possible or desirable in multicultural, international settings?
- How can transnational agreements be achieved across great *value divides*?
- What is the proper relation of truth-finding and punishment for *past* wrongs to *reconciliation* and healing for the *future* (Nino, 1991)?

- What *remedies* are available in international dispute processes? Which are implementable or enforceable?
- What is the relationship of *truth, justice and peace* in international (or any) dispute resolution process (Menkel-Meadow, Chapter 20, this volume)?
- How do *basic dispute resolution concepts* – BATNAs (best alternatives to negotiated agreements), ZOPAs (zones of possible agreements), resource- or pie-expanding outcomes, 'principled' or 'objective' solutions – have to be adapted or changed in the *international or multicultural* arenas?
- What *concepts* ('ripeness', 'hurting stalemates', 'two- or multiple-track' negotiations), initially developed in *international relations*, might have some explanatory purchase in more general dispute resolution theory?
- How much flexibility or 'plastic' process development is optimal in international dispute resolution? When is a court no longer a court? When is mediation no longer mediation? Does or should each dispute resolution process have its own 'process' integrity, ethics and logic (Fuller's (2001) 'process integrity' principles)?

The essays in this volume, as only a small representation of all the centuries of experience and more modern theory development, demonstrate that conflict resolution in the international and multicultural sphere will continue to develop more 'memes' or ideas as new parties participate, more and more 'cultures' and people interact with each other, and new ideas and forms of process are created. It is hoped that readers of these volumes will themselves become the new 'process architects', seeking new ways for people to continue to flourish and to achieve peace and justice simultaneously wherever possible. It is clear that both more study and much more practice is necessary in this field of complex international dispute resolution.

References

Dunoff, Jeffrey, Ratner, Steven R. and Wippman, David (2010), *International Law, Norms, Actors, Process: A Problem-oriented Approach* (3rd edn), New York: Aspen Publishers.

Fuller, Lon (2001), *The Principles of Social Order: Essays of Lon Fuller* (rev. edn), ed. Kenneth Winston, Oxford: Hart Publishing.

Ginsburg, Tom and Shaffer, Gregory (2010), 'Does International Law Work?', in Peter Cane and Herbert M. Kritzer (eds), *The Oxford Handbook of Empirical Legal Research*, Oxford: Oxford University Press.

Held, David and McGrew, Anthony (2007), *Globalization/Anti-Globalization: Beyond the Great Divide* (2nd edn), Cambridge: Polity Press.

Koh, Harold Hongju (1997), 'Why Do Nations Obey International Law?', *Yale Law Journal*, **106**, pp. 2559–659.

Nino, Carlos (1991), 'The Duty to Punish Past Abuses of Human Rights Put Into Context: The Case of Argentina', *Yale Law Journal*, **100**, pp. 2619–40.

Ramji-Nogales, Jaya (2010), 'Designing Bespoke Transitional Justice: A Pluralist Process Approach', *Michigan Journal of International Law*, **32**, pp. 1–72.

Ramraj, Victor (2011), 'Asymmetric Transnationalism: The Multiple Roles of Law in a Complex World', in Carrie Menkel-Meadow, Victor Ramraj and Franz Werro (eds), *Transnational Law and Legal Education* (forthcoming).

Schneider, Andrea Kupfer (2009), 'The Intersection of Dispute Systems Design and Transitional Justice', *Harvard Negotiation Law Journal*, **14**, pp. 289–315.

Schneider, Andrea Kupfer (1998), 'Democracy and Dispute Resolution: Individual Rights in International Trade Organizations, *University of Pennsylvania Journal of International Economic Law*, **19**, pp. 587–638.

Sen, Amartya (2009), *The Idea of Justice*, Cambridge, MA: Belknap Press of Harvard University Press.

Shaffer, Gregory (2010), 'Transnational Legal Process and State Change: Opportunities and Constraints'. Available at: http://papers.ssrn.com/sol3/papers.cfm?abstract_id=1901952.

Slaughter, Anne-Marie (2004), *The New World Order*, Princeton, NJ: Princeton University Press.

Sornarajah, M. (2010), 'Why "No" to Transnational Legal Studies', in David Cole *et al.* (eds), *Why Transnational Legal Education?*, London and Washington, DC:, Center for Transnational Legal Studies.

Stromseth, Jane, Wippman, David and Brooks, Rosa (2006), *Can Might Make Rights? Building the Rule of Law after Military Intervention*, Cambridge: Cambridge University Press.

Teitel, Ruti (2000), *Transitional Justice*, New York and Oxford: Oxford University Press.

Twining, William (2000), *Globalization and Legal Theory*, Cambridge: Cambridge University Press.

Name Index

For Product Safety Concerns and Information please contact our EU representative GPSR@taylorandfrancis.com
Taylor & Francis Verlag GmbH, Kaufingerstraße 24, 80331 München, Germany

www.ingramcontent.com/pod-product-compliance
Lightning Source LLC
LaVergne TN
LVHW080758011026
849160LV00015B/1487

* 9 7 8 1 1 3 8 3 7 8 5 1 3 *